The Issue of War

Ideology and Power

Chartism

The Approach of War, 1938–1939

The Limits of Foreign Policy: the West, the League and the
Far Eastern Crisis of 1931–1933

Allies of a Kind: The United States, Britain and the War
Against Japan, 1941–1945

Racial Aspects of the Far Eastern War of 1941–1945

CHRISTOPHER THORNE

The Issue of War

States, Societies,
and the Far Eastern Conflict
of 1941–1945

HAMISH HAMILTON
LONDON

First published in Great Britain 1985
by Hamish Hamilton Ltd
Garden House 57–59 Long Acre London WC2E 9JZ

Copyright © 1985 by Christopher Thorne

British Library Cataloguing in Publication Data

Thorne, Christopher
    The issue of war: states, societies, and
    the Far Eastern conflict of 1941–1945.
    1. World War, 1939–1945 – Campaigns – East Asia
    I. Title
    940.54′25   D767
    ISBN 0-241-10239-1

Typeset by Computape (Pickering) Ltd
Printed in Great Britain by
St Edmundsbury Press, Bury St Edmunds, Suffolk

To friends in some of the countries involved in the
war who have helped and encouraged
over the years:

Dorothy Borg and Lloyd Gardner; Albert Kersten
and Marinus Meijer; Ogata Sadako and
Ikeda Kiyoshi

'Captains and soldiers are smeared on the bushes and grass;
The General schemed in vain.
Know therefore that the sword is a cursed thing
Which the wise man uses only if he must.'

From a work by the Chinese poet,
Li Po (8th century, A.D.)

'War is human, it is something that is lived like a
love or a hatred... It might better be described as a
pathological condition...'

Marcel Proust, *A la Recherche du Temps
Perdu* (trans. C. K. Scott Moncrieff,
1969 edition, Vol. 12, 382)

Contents

A map of East Asia, Southeast Asia, Australasia and the Pacific
(drawn by Patrick Leeson) appears on pages 98–9.

Preface

This book, while intended to be complete in itself, is in effect a complement to my previous study of the Far Eastern war of 1941–1945, *Allies of a Kind*, which concentrated upon Western policies in that context, and, in particular, Anglo-American relations. Whilst exploring that earlier subject, I became increasingly aware of how little I knew and understood about those Asian states and societies that were caught up in the conflict, and also curious as to the ways in which the war had affected, and been affected by, the extraordinarily wide variety of peoples and polities that were involved together. After completing *Allies*, therefore, I sought to learn more in these two respects (though the outcome, of course, has as usual been a rather better appreciation of how little one knows), and to see if it were possible to write something in the nature of the book that follows.

Two matters need further explaining immediately, however. The first is why I have chosen to label the conflict that took place between Japan and her enemies between December 1941 and the summer of 1945 'the Far Eastern war'. To American and Japanese readers, in particular, this is likely to appear an unusual designation, for in both their countries the struggle is generally known as 'the Pacific war'. This description is readily understandable, but it appears to me to do much less than geographical and geo-political justice to the conflict, especially in regard to its wider repercussions. The alternative designation, 'the Far Eastern war', is itself, I realise, open to serious objection, in that it derives from a Eurocentric view of the world and its affairs. Indeed, it was on these very grounds that the Japanese Government decreed immediately after Pearl Harbor that the term 'the Far East' (*kyokuto*), an 'obnoxious' reflection of the notion 'that England was the centre of the world', was not to be used, and that the war was to be known instead as that of 'Great East Asia' (*Daitoa*). Nevertheless, it seems to me that, while still less than satisfactory, the 'Far Eastern' label is preferable to the other one, especially in relation to the purposes of this study that are set out below – always provided that such a study at least seeks to avoid adopting a single set of perspectives and assumptions that are themselves Eurocentric. As for the actual geographical connotation of the term 'Far East' as I have employed it, it embraces a number of areas which are separately designated where necessary: East Asia, Southeast Asia, the Western Pacific, and Australasia. In that India, too, was deeply involved in the war in a number of ways, South Asia, also, though not falling within the Far East, is included in the scope of the book.

At this point, however, I should explain why I have chosen to extend that scope further still, to take in not simply states but societies – Dutch, French, British and American – which were far removed, geographically speaking, from the military conflict itself, and for the first three of which the European struggle was the one which was, literally, vital, with Germany, not Japan, the main enemy. Why place these societies alongside those others – for the most part seemingly so different – on which the Far Eastern war had a much more direct, sustained and pervading impact?

There have been three reasons for doing so, and for accepting in consequence a greater degree of difficulty (in several respects the task is, I think, impossible) when it comes to separating out the impact of the Far Eastern conflict from that of the Second World War as a whole. The first is that, for a long while before Japan's attack in December 1941, these Western states and societies had been involved in a network of relationships with many of the peoples in Asia who now found themselves caught up in the war; involved of course through formal or informal empires above all. The second (and equally obvious) reason is that, during their war with Japan, these Western countries despatched forces to fight in those Far Eastern parts of the world, or at least continued to regard them as being of considerable importance in relation to their own, post-war futures. (Although Russia/the Soviet Union had made its own, expansionist presence felt in China since the seventeenth century, and joined in the fighting at the very last moment, I have not included its society in the study, any more than I have Germany's. On the other hand, Moscow's position and policies in regard to the Far Eastern war, not least as seen by others, have obviously been taken into account.)

But there was a third and wider reason for bringing together on a comparative basis those Western and Asian societies, and not merely states, that were involved in some way in this particular aspect of the Second World War. To do so would, I thought, afford an opportunity for trying 'to abrogate the boundaries between Western and non-Western history'. The very fact that I can borrow this description of intent from the Preface of Eric Wolf's *Europe and the People Without History** is an indication, if one were needed, that such an aspiration is in no way new. And reference to that particular and remarkable study, many of the arguments of which, if not its Marxist premises, seem to me persuasive, serves also as a reminder that most of us are unlikely ever to match the learning of various scholars who over the years have chosen to follow such a path. In this connection, my own reliance upon the work of others, particularly as regards the social and

* E. R. Wolf, *Europe and the People Without History* (Berkeley, 1982).

political history of countries in Asia, will be apparent throughout this book. Equally, I must at the outset acknowledge my position as tyro in another respect, for (again, with Dr Wolf) I have also ventured in what follows 'to cross the lines of demarcation' – or at any rate, some of them – 'that separate the various human disciplines'. It has increasingly seemed to me well-nigh unavoidable that international historians should pursue their enquiries into areas which are usually thought of as the domain of the sociologist or social-psychologist, say, or of the economic or intellectual historian. But it is of course impossible to be carried far in such directions without becoming aware of how limited are one's qualifications when it comes to applying initial concepts or reaching some kind of judgement. Therefore, while I have retained the temerity to act in such a fashion, it is right that I should also underline my amateur status in the fields in question.

This brings me to a wider issue still, concerning the nature of this or any other work of historical analysis as I see it. Here again, explanations are made easier in that what I have to say has already been expressed by others. Like Theodore Zeldin, for example,* I believe that 'historical study is a personal experience', and that 'the subjective elements in it deserve to be valued'; that 'the extremely varied way in which history is studied is the very source of its strength and will be of its continued popularity'. My own aproach to the subject of this book, for example, has obviously been influenced by, *inter alia*, the times through which I myself have lived (which have helped direct my attention towards such themes as race relations and the position of women in society), and has been shaped in part by my inability to read Japanese or Chinese sources in the original, as well as by great variations in the quantity and quality of historical material available to me in other respects.

Of course, I put forward throughout the book what I see as having been relationships of a causal kind. All historians do so, though often it is by implication only, and without an acknowledgement that the element of theory is inevitably present on such occasions.† I also suggest various ways of conceptualising about the subject which seem to me helpful when one is trying to reach a better understanding of these particular aspects of our recent past, and I indicate certain patterns which to my mind can be discerned in the history of the states and societies which were caught up in the Far Eastern war. Whether or not such suggestions carry conviction will depend to a considerable extent on the nature of the evidence I have been able to advance in their support, as well as, no doubt, on the individual reader's own predisposition in these respects. What I wish to emphasise at the outset, however, is that I regard such concepts and patterns as repre-

* T. Zeldin, *France, 1848–1945* (Oxford, 1973–77).
† See below, 13, note.

senting no more than possible ways among many of looking at the subject.
They are ways which at the time of writing seem to me helpful, interesting,
and susceptible of reasoned justification; but I do not regard them as
diminishing what Margaret Mead, for example, has seen as 'the special
value' that historians and anthropologists alike 'place on the unique event in
all its uniqueness'.* And while endeavouring to profit from a number of
broad hypotheses advanced by social scientists, and to indicate ways in
which certain features of the pre-war and war-time years could be related to
such propositions, I have not made it part of my task to try fully to test the
hypotheses in question, or to conclude the book by putting forward alternatives of my own. A historical undertaking like the present one is, I believe,
not only quite enough to cope with from the point of view of size and
complexity, but also sufficient in itself in terms of its own central discipline –
as some social scientists themselves are indeed ready to acknowledge.†

As far as the scope and structure of the book as it stands are concerned, I
have not set out to write fully on the origins of war. But it is impossible to
appreciate the ways and extent to which the conflict, when it came, affected,
and was affected by the states and societies involved without observing not
simply the situation as it existed, internationally and domestically, on the
eve of Japan's attack on the West, but various trends and issues that had
been developing over a lengthy period beforehand. I have therefore provided an opening section which surveys such developments within a variety
of time-spans, and which does so, where domestic societies are concerned,
on a thematic and comparative, rather than on a country-by-country, basis.
A comparative approach of this kind is obviously beset with dangers,
especially when dealing with societies as different from one another as those
of America and India, for example. There is little or no value to be gained
from juxtaposing such entities in terms of certain specific features and issues
to be found within each unless at the same time their often vastly differing
mores and circumstances as a whole are borne in mind. (To cite Margaret
Mead again: 'Every culture must be seen as a whole, with its value system as
an inextricable component'.)‡ I have therefore thought it right to provide an
occasional reminder of the need to apply such cultural relativity when
considering whether there existed any broad similarities across societal

* M. Mead, 'Anthropologist and Historian: Their Common Problems', in *Anthropology: A Human Science* (Princeton, 1964).
† E.g. Barrington Moore, in the Preface to his *Injustice: The Social Bases of Obedience and Revolt* (London, 1978): 'Historical facts have a certain patterned relationship to each other, ... [and] forcing them through a conceptual sieve in order to "test" hypotheses ... would obliterate and destroy [it.] ... Furthermore, it is a provincial and philistine notion of "relevance" which requires all worthwhile knowledge to be relevant to either political action or scientific theory or both. Historical inquiry can have other purposes without falling into mere antiquarianism'.
‡ 'The Comparative Study of Cultures', in *Anthropology: A Human Science.*

boundaries; and indeed, in an area where it is for the most part the differences that stand out, I would argue that it is only when such relativity has been allowed for that certain likenesses do sometimes begin to emerge.

I have not attempted to pursue the overall question of the impact of the war beyond 1945. Such an exercise would be extremely interesting, though difficult, and would need to include among other topics the complex issues surrounding the war-crimes trials* and the various ways in which the conflict as a whole came to be seen and explained as it receded into the past. But to be treated adequately on both the international and domestic planes the subject would need a book to itself – one entitled, perhaps, 'The Consequences of the Far Eastern War'. I have therefore contented myself here with simply a few glances ahead, beyond the Japanese surrender, in order to note, for example, that not all the developments and changes brought about by and during the conflict were to prove lasting in the event, and that within twenty years or so the war's international repercussions could be viewed in ways that would have appeared extraordinary to most contemporaries in 1945.

Where the war years themselves are concerned, I have begun with a survey of the military, strategic and political confrontation between Japan and her enemies, in order to orientate the reader who is not already familiar with the shape and major events of the conflict. The pattern adopted thereafter requires only brief comment, I think, although again questions arise that go beyond matters of order and convenience alone. The immediate problem has been that it is impossible to bring together at one and the same time the entire range of contexts and perspectives surrounding a single event or development, which has in turn given rise to the need to provide signposts of the 'as-will-be-seen-below' variety without becoming tedious in that regard, and to return to a single spot on a number of occasions. The underlying problem, however, once more concerns the matter of causality. I have chosen, for the reason stated, to place chapters whose main focus is upon the international dimensions of the conflict before those which look particularly at domestic features of the period; but it could well have been the other way around. The fact that in the event every section represents an admixture of the international and the domestic will I hope ensure that the reader does not infer that the flow of influence and effect was moving solely from outside societies to within them, any more than the reverse direction on its own would have been implied had the order of chapters been inverted. A two-way process was

---

* See e.g. R. H. Minear, *Victor's Justice: the Tokyo War Crimes Trial* (Princeton, 1971), and L. Taylor, *A Trial of Generals: Homma, Yamashita, MacArthur* (South Bend, Indiana, 1981).

involved overall, though varying greatly in the strength and direction of its flows from one moment and issue and set of circumstances to another.*

As already indicated, I have tried to ensure that the contents of the book stand on their own, and do not require a prior reading of either *Allies of a Kind* or the study of the Far East in the 1930s that preceded it, *The Limits of Foreign Policy*. That has meant, of course, especially in regard to Anglo-American relations in the context of the Far Eastern war, that it has been impossible to avoid referring to topics and evidence that I have considered on a previous occasion. Where this occurs, however, I have kept the treatment of the subject in question as brief as possible, supplying references to the earlier work while at the same time seeking to bring fresh evidence and considerations into the reckoning. Similarly, and again in the interests of making the present book complete in itself, I have not excluded from the list of sources items which appear in the similar section of *Allies of a Kind*, although I have simplified archival details as far as possible. The documentary and secondary material which went into the making of that previous volume has played a large part in the shaping of this one, also; but it has been interwoven with a great deal that I have gathered only subsequently, as well as being placed within a new framework of reference altogether.

Finally, I have preferred not to give the book's 'conclusions' a chapter to themselves, as is usually the practice, since in this instance such an arrangement seemed less than satisfactory from an organic point of view. Instead, issues and reflections which are raised at the end of the section devoted to the pre-war years (where they are related to various fears and uncertainties which had become widespread by 1941) are taken up again in the final stages of chapter nine, where they are placed alongside some of the ways in which contemporaries were looking at the war in wider perspectives by the time Japan surrendered.

*

It follows from the foregoing comments on the sources of the present work that I have continued to be indebted, when writing it, to those participants in the events in question who were good enough to allow me to probe their recollections of the war years when I was preparing *Allies of a Kind*. At the same time, I must add my thanks to four men in particular who have kindly responded to my questions since 1978: Dr J. H. van Roijen, who was the

* It will be apparent that I find it difficult to take very seriously arguments over whether, as a social-scientific 'rule', domestic or external factors are decisive (*Innenpolitik* or *Ausenpolitik*, in other words). For reflections on such 'theological' quests, see e.g. the relevant essays in Pieter Geyl, *Encounters in History* (London, 1963), and my own essay, 'International Relations and the Promptings of History', *Review of International Studies*, 9 (1983).

senior permanent official in the Netherlands Foreign Ministry at the begin-
ning of the war, and was later his country's Foreign Minister; Colonel Hugh
Toye, whose war-time knowledge and understanding of the Indian National
Army was later embodied in his fine study, *The Springing Tiger*;* Dr Hank
Bethe, who was a member of the Dutch Resistance; and Dr Anak Agung
Gde Agung, who became Prince of Bali during the war and was sub-
sequently Foreign Minister of the Indonesian Republic.

My conversations with Dr Anak Agung on the subject of the East Indies
under both Dutch and Japanese rule, like those with Dr Bethe, took place
when the three of us were Fellows of the Netherlands Institute for Advanced
Study, and I am most grateful to that foundation for providing me with an
ideal environment in which to read, think, and draft some early sections of
the book – this last exercise being undertaken with the patient assistance of
Pilar van Breda, who unravelled my alien handwriting with much skill and
good humour. I wish to thank, also, other bodies which have helped in
various ways: the International Relations Department in the Research
School of Pacific Studies at the Australian National University, and particularly Professor Bruce Miller, who once more made me welcome as a Visiting
Fellow; the Japan Foundation, which made it possible for me to visit and
travel in that country for the first time, and the Yoshida Foundation, which
facilitated the research I undertook there. My major debt in this field,
however, is owed to the Economic and Social Research Council (as it has
become), without whose support over many years my international archival
work would not have been possible.

I should also like to mention three other institutions which have provided temporary bases for me during the past six years: the International
House of Japan in Tokyo; its counterpart in New Delhi; and the Netaji
Bureau in Calcutta, particularly its Director, Dr Sisir Bose. Among the
many librarians and archivists who have assisted me I should like to thank
especially Dr D. N. Panigrahi for his guidance in the Nehru Memorial
Library, and above all David Kennelly, who, nearer to home, has helped
me obtain newly-published secondary material with the minimum of fuss
and delay.

My warm thanks are also due to a number of scholars who have helped me
over this period in various ways: those from Japan and Britain who
participated in a conference on the Second World War that was held in
London in July 1979, particularly Professor Hosoya Chihiro; Dr Roger Bell,
who prompted various ideas about aspects of Australian policy; William
L. Holland, former Research Secretary of the Institute of Pacific Relations,
who kindly lent me his collection of the relevant pamphlets produced under
the auspices of the American Council of the Institute during the war; and the

* H. Toye, *The Springing Tiger: A Study of a Revolution* (London, 1959).

late Stephen Roskill, whose encouragement and companionship I greatly miss, as do many others who were privileged to count him as a friend. I am also most grateful to the British Academy for inviting me to deliver its sixty-second Raleigh Lecture on History, thus enabling me to put forward for consideration those ideas which were subsequently published by the Academy under the title of *Racial Aspects of the Far Eastern War*.

There remain three groups of people to whom I am especially beholden. The first consists of those friends to whom the book is dedicated, each of whom contributed in some way to its gestation. Marinus Meijer, scholar and diplomat, has responded to numerous questions over the years regarding both his experiences as an internee of the Japanese in the East Indies and his understanding of Indonesian, Chinese and Japanese societies. Professor Albert Kersten has continued to be an indispensable partner in Dutch archival work, and has provided the lengthier translations from that language which appear in what follows. Professor Ogata Sadako helped make it possible for me to visit Japan and to meet various scholars there, while among the latter, Professor Ikeda Kiyoshi has helped by talking around the subject of the war both as he experienced it in the Imperial Japanese Navy and as he has come to see it as a historian. As for Dr Dorothy Borg, every student of twentieth-century international relations in the Far East will be aware of her special position in that field, and I am simply one of many who have benefited from the knowledge and advice which she dispenses from Columbia University's East Asia Institute.

I leave Professor Lloyd Gardner till last among the dedicatees because, as well as providing encouragement over many years, he has also been kind enough to read and comment on the manuscript of the present work. Professors James Joll and Ronald Dore have also very generously undertaken this same labour, and while I must emphasise that I alone am ultimately responsible for everything that appears between these covers, it has meant a great deal to be able to obtain the reactions and advice of these three scholars. (I have set down as footnotes one or two of Professor Dore's stimulating sociological reflections for all to share, as well as seeking to convey indirectly the benefit of others.)

Finally, there are those who have been more directly involved on those occasions – known to other authors before me – when it seemed that the fates were set upon preventing the book being written. In those circumstances, the patience and understanding displayed by my two publishers, Christopher Sinclair-Stevenson in London and Sheldon Meyer in New York, have been invaluable, and one reason for being happy over the completion of the project is that it enables me to pay warm tribute to both of them. Above all, however, it has been the unfailing support of my wife and daughters that has enabled me to overcome a series of rather trying setbacks. To my wife, Beryl, I owe additional gratitude for finding the time, alongside her own work in other fields, to type the final version of the text. But it is in more profound and less definable ways that she, Alison and Stephanie have made the book possible.

Christopher Thorne
Wassenaar and Brighton, 1978–1984

Notes on Abbreviations, etc.

Abbreviations

A.B.D.A.	American, British, Dutch and Australian Command.
A.F.L.	American Federation of Labor.
A.F.P.F.L.	Anti-Fascist People's Freedom League (Burma).
A.I.C.C.	All-India Congress Committee.
A.I.F.	Australian Imperial Force.
ANZUS Pact	Australia, New Zealand, U.S. Pact (1951).
B.A.A.G.	British Army Aid Group (in China).
B.D.A.	Burma Defence Army.
B.I.A.	Burma Independence Army.
B.N.A.	Burma National Army.
C. in C.	Commander in Chief.
C.B.I.	China-Burma-India Command (U.S. Army).
C.C.S.	Combined Chiefs of Staff (U.S.–G.B.).
C.I.O.	Congress of Industrial Organization.
C.O.S.	Chiefs of Staff Committee (G.B.)
G.I.	American non-commissioned soldier.
G.N.P.	Gross National Product.
I.I.L.	Indian Independence League.
I.M.T.F.E.	International Military Tribunal for the Far East.
I.N.A.	Indian National Army.
I.P.R.	Institute of Pacific Relations
I.W.M.	Imperial War Museum (London).
J.C.S.	Joint Chiefs of Staff (U.S.)
M.P.A.J.A.	Malayan People's Anti-Japanese Army.
M.P.A.J.U.	Malaya People's Anti-Japanese Union.
N.A.A.C.P.	National Association for the Advancement of Colored Peoples.
O.S.S.	Office of Strategic Services (U.S.).
O.W.I.	Office of War Information (U.S.).
R. and A.	Research and Analysis Branch of the O.S.S.
R.A.F.	Royal Air Force.
R.I.I.A.	Royal Institute of International Affairs.
R.N.	Royal Navy
S.E.A.C.	South East Asia Command.
S.O.E.	Special Operations Executive (G.B.).
S.W.N.C.C.	State-War-Navy Coordinating Committee (U.S.).
S.W.P.A.	South West Pacific Area.
U.A.P.	United Australia Party.

W.R.A.   War Relocation Authority (U.S.).

Further notes

Unless otherwise stated, numbers in references are to pages. Japanese names are set down in their native version, that is, with the surname before the given name; on the other hand, Japanese accents are omitted. *The Times* refers to the London paper, the *New York Times* being named in full. The term 'Siam' is generally used, rather than 'Thailand', for reasons that are explained in the text. Since central Chinese figures in this period, such as Chiang Kai-shek and Mao Tse-tung, were referred to in this form at the time, the modern, Pinyin system of romanisation has not been adopted.

PART ONE

The Approach of War

First Reactions

The Far Eastern war began, as it was to end, in a fashion so dramatic as to compel the attention of contemporaries. In the space of those few days early in December 1941, American sea-power in the Pacific and British sea-power east of Suez were shattered; the territorial presence of all Western states in Southeast Asia was threatened with destruction; Western possessions further afield, in Australasia, in India – even, some believed, on the west coast of the United States itself – were rendered newly vulnerable. At the same time, the existing struggle between the Chinese and the Japanese was given a new context, and the European war of 1939, too, became merged within a conflict of world-wide proportions. Japan's attack on the Western powers, followed as it was by declarations of war on the United States by Germany and Italy, had brought about a set of international circumstances that dwarfed those of the so-called Great War of 1914–18.

Not everyone, of course, was taken by surprise. For those men who had been planning the Japanese assault, for example, this was a time of tension and elation as confident expectations were more than fulfilled.[1] Among those involved in the actual attacks, the great majority had come to believe by one process or another that the very existence of their country was at stake. Some also held that, in the later words of a senior officer of the 25th Army in Malaya, 'Japan's fate was the fate of East Asia'.[2] And though his assertion that this was the case with all officers and men is certainly erroneous, such an intertwining of fortunes was fundamental to that small contingent of Burmese, for example, who, as the Burma Independence Army, stood ready in Thailand to move back into their country alongside the Japanese.[3]

Meanwhile, however, there were also those among the Japanese themselves who, despite having had foreknowledge of the blows now being struck, and despite the remarkable degree of success achieved, were filled with apprehension rather than elation. The very architect of the Pearl Harbor attack, Admiral Yamamoto Isoruku, was one such person; the Marquis Kido Koichi, elder statesman and adviser to the Emperor, another. In less exalted positions, too, there were those whose gloom set them apart from their rejoicing fellow-countrymen.[4]

As an initial response, however, foreboding was more widespread in the ranks of Japan's enemies, particularly among those peoples who appeared to stand in the path of the onslaught. In Australia, for example, the *Sydney Morning Herald* pronounced it to be 'the gravest hour in [the country's] history' – although it went on to predict that the outcome would be such that the Japanese could be seen as committing 'hara kiri on a national scale'.[5] 'We must be ready for anything,' warned the New Zealand Labour Party's newspaper, *The Standard*. 'Japan in China has displayed a ruthlessness that has no parallel. She will not be beaten easily . . . No longer can we hope to enjoy the comparatively easy life we have been accustomed to.'[6] In some quarters, reactions went beyond apprehension. Thus, for instance, the American Minister to Australia was to describe in a private letter in January 1942 what he termed the 'period of blue funk' that many Australians had been going through. 'It has at times looked,' he added, 'as though they were just ready to give up everything.' His junior colleague, the U.S. Consul in Adelaide, likewise recorded that the general public of that city had been 'the closest to actual panic that I have ever seen', with 'staid businessmen, who only the day before were complacent about the menace of the "yellow dwarf", [being] reduced almost to wringing their hands.'[7]

Panic was even to be found in the United States itself, for all its greater distance from Japan and its vast potential might. As Raymond Clapper, an outstanding member of the Washington press corps, left the gallery of the Senate on December 9, after listening to details of the Pearl Harbor disaster,

> 'Reports flew through the Capitol', he noted privately, 'that enemy planes were an hour from New York. Several Senators said they heard it – an elevator man said he heard planes were only 150 miles from Washington. He was frantic . . . All over [the] country signs of panic coming up . . .'[8]

Those nearer to the enemy, on the West Coast, who for a while lost their composure included the military commander of that area, Lt. General John L. De Witt, who asserted that Japanese planes had been over San Francisco on the night of December 7.[9] Meanwhile, in India, too, not yet directly under attack but clearly, after the initial Japanese triumphs, a potential target and even battleground, the shock of events was apparent. 'The outbreak of war in Malaya and the news of air raids in Burma,' concluded a sub-committee of the All India Congress Committee, 'appear to have intensified fears of air attacks . . . and caused a wave of panic among the people of the country.'[10]

In the new war zones themselves, men and women faced the Japanese advance with a range of attitudes and behaviour far too wide to make any generalization feasible. In Hong Kong, doomed to fall from the outset, there was resolution and panic; confusion, incompetence and bravery. (The colony enclosed, of course, in the words of a major study of the subject, 'an artificial society', including large numbers of recent refugees from mainland

China. And few of the Chinese in general entertained feelings of loyalty to the state that ruled them.)[11] Similar extreme differences of behaviour were manifested among both the military and civilian ranks of Americans in the Philippines. And while determination was on display at the Manila head-quarters of General Douglas MacArthur, so, too, was a muddle and lack of balance that was at least partly responsible for the exposure of U.S. Army Air Force planes to easy and avoidable destruction by the enemy.[12] In the East Indies, also, where Dutch expatriates knew that their turn to face the triumphant Japanese forces must soon come, there were to be marked contrasts in performance among various units of the Netherlands armed forces when the moment of confrontation arrived.[13]

The reactions of some prominent individuals and political organisations to the outbreak of war were deliberately concealed. It was not known, for example, that both the British and American Ambassadors to Japan, Sir Robert Craigie and Joseph Grew, believed that the conflict could have been postponed, at least, if not avoided altogether, had Washington chosen to play its cards differently in the preceding negotiations with Tokyo. (Both men were to incur much displeasure from their seniors when, on their repatriation to their respective countries, they each drew up a report in which such an opinion was advanced.)[14] Others chose to avoid public comment for different reasons. The Soviet Union in particular, fighting for its life against the invading Germans, was obviously thankful for that quiescence on its eastern borders that had been guaranteed not many months before, on paper at least, by a Non-Aggression Pact with Japan, and was not going to jeopardise that state of affairs by openly criticising Tokyo. Communist parties and newspapers elsewhere – in occupied France, for example – duly maintained their own near-silence.[15]

For those other Frenchmen whose territory in Indochina had already been occupied by the Japanese themselves, the situation was clearly more delicate still, and their press reflected the desperate hope that somehow neutrality and safety alike could be preserved in these new circumstances.[16] Indeed, both in Indochina and in metropolitan France, supporters of the Vichy regime (which had sought in vain to obtain American help to resist Japanese pressures on Indochina) could not but display a certain *Schadenfreude* at the sight of perfidious Albion and moralising America suffering in their turn – and this time violently – at the hands of an expanding Japan. Still more was this the case where French fascists were concerned, especially in the light of the support given by the two Western powers since June 1941 to that centre of corruption, the Soviet Union.[17]

As for Hitler, informed shortly beforehand of Tokyo's decision to launch its assault, he rejoiced at his ally's successes, and paused only a few days before committing Germany in its turn to the fight against the United States.

The Japanese attack, he confessed privately a few weeks later, had come as 'an immense relief' to him – although he could not refrain from expressing a degree of regret over what he saw as 'a turning point in history', which would entail 'the loss of a whole continent . . . [with] the white race [as] the loser'.[18] Another in Berlin who delighted at the news was Subhas Chandra Bose, former president of the Congress party in India, who had escaped from house arrest by the British in Calcutta early in 1941, and from Germany had been prophesying that Japan would achieve a dramatic victory over the Western, imperialist powers when the time came for her to strike.[19] For Bose, the new war was doubly welcome in that it enabled him to view in a fresh and more comfortable light the existing conflict between the Japanese and their fellow Asians, the Chinese. The Chungking regime could now be seen as misguided dupes of the Western imperialists, who refused to acknowledge that Japan ('not the Japan of 1937,' Bose was to write in 1944) had taken upon herself the cause of Asia as a whole.[20]

Bose at the time could speak only for that handful of Indians, recruited from Axis prisoner-of-war camps, who had enrolled in his Indian Legion.[21] In the East Indies, however, the nationalist leader, Soetan Sjahrir (who had urged in vain that the Dutch authorities should modify their policies in order that rulers and ruled in the colony could cooperate against Tokyo's militarism), had to acknowledge privately and to his keen regret that it was apparently a majority of his fellow-countrymen who 'rejoiced over the Japanese victories'.[22] Such sentiments, of course, were well-nigh universal in Japan itself. In Tokyo, for example, following a stunned pause, even the initial news that the war had been launched had been greeted on the streets by crowds whose every face displayed (according to a French journalist who was present) 'an air of relaxation and of intense satisfaction'. Their Emperor, the radio told them, had committed their country to the fight in order to achieve stability in Asia and to help usher in an era of peace throughout the world.[23]

For the Japanese, joy was mingled with relief: relief from the tension of the preceding months that had been spent under the threat of Western economic sanctions. 'There had been a mood of oppression and gloom clamped in our minds,' one writer was to recall later, 'like dark clouds. Then, with the promulgation of the Imperial Rescript on December 8, the clouds scattered, the fog disappeared.' Now, too, the seemingly fruitless and never-ending war in China could be seen in a more acceptable light: as part of the decisive struggle against those forces of Western imperialism and greed that had been propping up Chiang Kai-shek only in order to keep East Asians divided amongst themselves and thus more easily exploited. 'I remember,' recorded another writer later, 'the feeling of relief bubbling up inside me. There was the joy of having been given a direction clearly . . .';

and another: 'Never in my life [had I experienced] such a wonderful, such a happy, such an auspicious day.'[24] Nor, as our French observer noted, were reactions of this kind confined to Japan's intellectuals alone. 'The excitement created by the initial victories swept over the whole nation,' concludes Dr Shillony, 'including editors and writers who, like most of their compatriots, believed in the justice of Japan's cause and in her ultimate victory.' And he adds that 'the concept of a mission on behalf of Asia as a whole fired the imagination of both traditionalists and progressives, and was a goal that left and right could support'.[25]

What is particularly striking in retrospect, however, is the extent to which the sense of relief evident in Japan on the outbreak of the war was also experienced, not simply by Hitler, Bose and others who looked to Tokyo for help, but by many on the opposite side. In India, for example, the strongly nationalist *Bombay Chronicle* (which as recently as December 6 had been forecasting the imminent outbreak of a conflict that was 'inevitable' since no compromise was possible 'between the expansionist, jingoistic plans of the [Japanese] militarists and the interests of the democracies') declared on the morrow of Pearl Harbor:

'Expectancy of danger is worse than danger, and a crisis poised perilously over several months is such a strain on human nerves that when finally it is precipitated it almost comes as a relief. That is the general reaction to the war in the Pacific . . .'[26]

For the *Chronicle*, these sentiments were accompanied by the conviction that swift and total defeat would now be the price exacted from Japan for its aggression. 'It is one thing,' the paper observed, 'to harass an impoverished, ill-equipped and defenceless China, or to make surprise air-raids, and quite a different matter to challenge the might of Britain, the U.S.A. and Russia [sic].' A similar blend of relief and confidence was entertained by those Filipinos who had been concerned over the threat that might arise from Japan after they had achieved their independence from the United States, due to be granted in 1946. Indeed, President Manuel Quezon had even gone so far as to suggest, shortly before the Japanese attack actually materialised, that such an eventuality would have the advantage of allowing the Philippine people to fulfil their debt of gratitude to America, and of enabling the youth of the country, so long protected, to learn 'how to suffer, how to die', a lesson without which 'no nation is worth anything'.[27]

For the leaders of Nationalist China, Japan's new embroilment brought special relief. Not only did the defeat of the enemy who had beset them since 1937 and earlier at last appear certain: the possibility, which had been hovering around in the autumn of 1941, that Washington would arrive at some compromise understanding with Tokyo was now removed. Moreover, within the wider international context that had been created by Japan's move, China could hope to achieve enhanced status as a leading member of the coalition pledged to defeat the German, Italian and Japanese signatories of the Tripartite Pact of 1940. The world from now on, declared Sun Fo, a senior Kuomintang official, on the day of Pearl Harbor, would be 'a world of America, Britain, China and Russia'.[28]

From Yenan, too, the Chinese Communist leaders, their charges that Roosevelt was trying to involve America in 'the imperialist war' of 1939 no longer being voiced since Hitler's attack on the Soviet Union, now emphasised, rather, the importance of a new, Western contribution to the fight against the imperialism of Japan.[29] Even in India, where nationalist, anti-British ferment was mounting, the Communist Party, no longer outlawed, urged the workers of the country to maximise production in the overriding cause of defeating fascism. Although the evils of alien, British rule and capitalist exploitation could not be overlooked, the attacks of Germany on the Soviet Union and of Japan on the United States had, as the (Communist) All India Students' Federation put it in a policy statement,

'completely transformed the character of the war ... [which] had no longer the significance of an Imperialist War. It was now a just war, a peoples' war, waged in defence of the land of Socialism for the purpose of crushing Hitler-Fascism ... It was a war waged for India's freedom by the most powerful allies ... that India had ever had ... The aims and intentions of the British and American Governments did not matter one jot. What did matter, what was decisive, was the big *fact* that these Governments had lined up with the U.S.S.R. to conduct a joint war against the aggressor ... What mattered now to the workers and peoples of Britain and America who have no imperialist aims ... and for the Soviet peoples ... was a single aim: ... the final destruction of Fascism.'[30]

The wider international scene, and in particular the existing war inaugurated by Hitler, was also an overriding consideration for most Australian and New Zealand commentators who analysed Japan's new course. Thus the *Sydney Morning Herald*, for example, was referring on December 9 to the 'folly' of Tokyo's decision, which had been brought about, not by the pursuit of its own interests, but by 'Germany's sore need for help'. Likewise, the same newspaper depicted the Japanese in the ensuing weeks as 'Hitler's Oriental imitators' and 'Hitler's new and venomous ally', whose methods were 'modelled on those of the Nazi savages at Guernica and Mussolini's blackguards in Abyssinia'.[31] In occupied France, too, it was, not surprisingly, the context of the existing European conflict that tended to predominate in comments on what was happening in the Far East. The Gaullist Resistance paper, *Combat*, for example, pointed to the conclusion to be drawn by those Frenchmen who had been misguided enough to compromise with the invading Germans: that, with the Americans now fully engaged in the fight against the Axis, collaboration had become not only treasonable but utterly stupid.[32]

Meanwhile, among those Americans themselves, and especially during the interim period before the details of Japan's success at Pearl Harbor became generally known, there was considerable rejoicing, as well as the panic referred to earlier, over the coming of war. The staff in the New York office of *Time* magazine, recalls the journalist, Theodore White (who had himself only recently returned from China), 'were gleeful, I most of all . . . It was the right war, a good war, and it had to be fought and won.' White's employer, too, Henry Luce, son of a former missionary to China who died on the day following the attack, was to find consolation for his bereavement in the fact that his father had 'lived long enough to know that now China and America are on the same side'.[33] The prominent banker, Thomas W. Lamont, was another who drew satisfaction from the task now facing his country. Japan's actions had come as something of a shock to him (as late as the middle of November he had been asserting privately that there was no danger of her launching an assault), but at least they had committed the United States fully to what he had for some time seen as 'the cause', alongside Britain and against the dictators.[34]

Britain's struggle to survive against Germany had also long formed the overriding concern for Roosevelt and several of his senior colleagues in the Washington administration. For them, however, unlike Lamont, the Japanese attack was not unexpected. The nature and results of the actual blow delivered at Pearl Harbor were themselves a great shock.[35] Thanks above all to the successful breaking of certain Japanese codes and ciphers, however,[36] a select few in Washington had been well aware that something of the kind was coming. The Secretary of War, Henry Stimson, for example, had recorded in his diary for November 25 that the President had on that day 'brought up the event that we were likely to be attacked, perhaps next Monday, for the Japanese are notorious for making an attack without warning . . . The question was how we should manoeuvre them into the position of firing the first shot without allowing too much danger to ourselves'. On December 2, Stimpson had advised T.V. Soong, a senior representative of the Nationalist regime in Chungking, who was in Washington at the time, to tell Chiang Kai-shek 'to have just a little more patience and then I think all things will be well'. And, when the news of the attack did eventually come through, Stimson confided in his diary that his 'first feeling' had been one 'of relief that the indecision was over and that a crisis had come in a way that would unite all our people'.[37]

For Roosevelt himself, also, it seems that relief was the predominant emotion. For months he had sought to aid Britain against Germany and – in that same cause above all – to check Japan's expansion southwards towards the vital raw materials of Southeast Asia. But at the same time he had confined himself within what he saw as the limits of national consensus, which had meant a refusal, even in the face of German provocation in the Atlantic, to take the initiative in declaring war. Now Tokyo, and shortly afterwards Berlin and Rome, had enabled him to reconcile the two considerations and goals, foreign and domestic. It is thus not surprising to find Eleanor Roosevelt recalling subsequently that, on the day of Pearl Harbor, 'Franklin was in a way more serene than he had appeared in a long time'.[38]

Meanwhile, in London, Churchill's reaction was essentially the same. Until the very last moment, when he had been alerted by the President, the Prime Minister had been strongly discounting, even within the innermost councils of his Government, the idea that Japan would be so foolish as to attack the Western powers.[39] (Nor had he been alone in thus mistaking entirely the direction and character of Tokyo's thinking. 'We're all astounded over Japan,' noted the Foreign Secretary's Principal Private Secretary when the news of the onslaught came in. 'We never thought she would attack us and America at once. She must have gone mad.')[40] Yet now that the decision had been taken out of the hands of the Western powers altogether, nothing, for the Prime Minister, could match the vast implications for Britain of the American entry into the war as a whole. Hence his subsequent summary of the thought that was uppermost in his mind when he retired to bed on the day of Pearl Harbor: 'So we had won after all!' And in 1943 he was to note privately regarding Japan's attack: 'Greater good fortune has rarely happened to the British Empire.'[41]

Seen in the retrospective light of what the Far Eastern war was to mean for that Empire east of Suez, such a contemporary comment, not least coming from Churchill himself, is not without its irony. One returns, however, to the remarkable degree to which relief and positive expectation, as well as shock and foreboding, were aroused in those early days of the conflict. As a final example of this phenomenon, let us take the edition of the Dutch newspaper, *Vrij Nederland*, that was being published at the time by exiles in Britain. Looking at the consequences of developments for the East Indies, it argued that now that the Indonesian people were facing up to the Japanese, they would bestow far greater trust upon the Dutch, whose own struggle against the Germans would be viewed as a matching experience. Indeed, the paper not only saw in this expected *rapprochement* in the Indies grounds for welcoming the new war, but went on to draw a wider conclusion still, the nature of which, however surprising it may seem in retrospect, was far from atypical in December 1941. On the 13th of that month, it felt able to declare: 'We live in great times.'[42]

Notes

1 See, e.g. A.J. Marder, *Old Friends, New Enemies: The Royal Navy and the Imperial Japanese Navy* (Oxford, 1981), 294. Prange makes an appropriate comparison between the Japanese and American planning processes leading up to Pearl Harbor: 'In theory the American plans could scarcely have been improved . . . But . . . they lacked the psychological impetus which only a genuine belief can impart . . . In contrast, the Japanese plan appeared fantastic . . . almost suicidal . . . Yet the task force carried it out because [Admiral Yamamoto and many others] breathed life into it by their dynamic faith'. G.W. Prange, *At Dawn We Slept: the Untold Story of Pearl Harbor* (London, 1982), 188.

2 M. Tsuji, *Singapore: the Japanese Version* (London, 1962), 71.

3 See, e.g., Maung Maung, *Aung San of Burma* (The Hague, 1962).

4 See, e.g., S. Ienaga, *Japan's Last War* (Oxford, 1979), 141; *Proceedings of the British Association for Japanese Studies, vol. 2*, (1977), 134–5; H. Agawa, *The Reluctant Admiral: Yamamoto and the Imperial Navy* (trs. J. Bester, Tokyo, 1979), 232–3.

5 *Sydney Morning Herald*, e.g. 7 Oct., 29 Nov., 6 and 9 Dec. 1941.

6 *The Standard* (Wellington), e.g. 4 and 11 Dec. 1941.

7 Johnson to Hornbeck, 20 Jan. 1942, Hornbeck Papers, box 262; Hutchinson to State Dpt., 12 Jan. 1942, ibid, box 22.

8 Clapper journal, 9 Dec. 1941, Clapper Papers, box 9.

9 A. Girdner and A. Loftus, *The Great Betrayal: the Evacuation of the Japanese Americans During World War II* (Toronto, 1969), 6.

10 War Conditions Sub-Cttee. rpt., 28 Dec. 1941, AICC Papers, file No. 1, part 1.

11 G.B. Endacott and A. Birch, *Hong Kong Eclipse* (Hong Kong, 1978), 27. On the European defenders, see the descriptions contained in O. Lindsay, *The Lasting Honour* (London, 1978); but also the contempt for the behaviour of various regimental officers recorded in the diary of Regimental Sergeant Major (subsequently Major) E.C. Ford: document AL 5294, Imperial War Museum archive, London. See also E. Ride, *British Army Aid Group: Hong Kong Resistance 1942–1945* (Hong Kong, 1981).

12 E. Morris, *Corregidor: the Nightmare in the Philippines* (London, 1982); W. Manchester, *American Caesar: Douglas MacArthur, 1880–1964* (London 1979), cap. 5; L.H. Brereton, *The Brereton Diaries* (New York, 1976), entries from 4 Dec. 1941 onwards.

13 Interviews with M.J. Meijer and Anak Agung Gde Agung; M. Aziz, *Japan's Colonialism and Indonisia* (The Hague, 1955), 143.

14 See Thorne, *Allies of a Kind* (hereafter *Allies*), 74–5, and J.K. Emmerson, *The Japanese Thread* (New York, 1978), 123. And e.g. Grew to English (a daughter), 30 Oct. 1941; Grew to Moffat (a daughter), 16 Feb. 1941; Grew to Castle, 7 Jan. 1941, Grew Papers, vol. 111.

15 See e.g. *L'Humanité*, 20 April and 12 Dec. 1941. In retrospect, the paper's reluctance even to report items of news from the Far East at this time is remarkable.

16 E.g. *L'Indépendence Tonkinoise* (Hanoi), 20 Dec. 1941; *L'Union* (Saigon), 21 Dec. 1941.

17 E.g. *Le Temps*, 31 July, 9 Dec. 1941, 23 Jan. 1942; *L'Union*, 14 Dec. 1941, 11 Jan. 1942; *L'Action Française*, 15 June, 31 July, 20 and 29 Dec. 1941. And see R.O. Paxton, *Vichy France: Old Guard and New Order, 1940–1944* (New York, 1972), 41 ff.

18 B. Martin, *Deutschland und Japan im Zweiten Weltkrieg* (Göttingen, 1969), 34 ff.; J.M. Meskill, *Hitler and Japan: the Hollow Alliance* (New York, 1966), 41 ff.; H. Trevor-Roper (ed.), *Hitler's Table Talk* (London, 1953), entries for 18 Dec. 1941 and 5 Jan. 1942.

19 See e.g. S.C. Bose, *Crossroads* (Bombay, 1962), 291; Bose, *Testament* (New Delhi, 1946), v; N.G. Jog, *In Freedom's Quest* (New Delhi, 1969), 202.

20 For Bose's earlier criticism of Japan's attack on China, see e.g. his *Testament*, v–vi; on his later attitude, see ibid, 219; 225, and typescript essay, 'If I Were Chinese', 5 Dec. 1944, Bose Papers; also *Azad Hind* (Berlin), No. 3/4 of 1942 and No. 9/10 of 1944.

21 See M. Hauner, *India in Axis Strategy: Germany, Japan and Indian Nationalists in the Second World War* (Stuttgart, 1981), 237 ff., 357 ff., 576 ff. By early 1943, the Indian Legion in Europe numbered only just over 3,000.

22 S. Sjahrir, *Out of Exile* (New York, 1949), e.g. 209, 219, 231–2.

23 R. Guillain, *La Guerre au Japon* (Paris, 1979), 23–5.

24 See *Proceedings of the British Association for Japanese Studies*, vol. 2, (1977), 92, 133–5; A. Iriye, *Power and Culture* (Cambridge, Mass., 1981), 36ff.
25 B.A. Shillony, *Politics and Culture in Wartime Japan* (Oxford, 1981), 97, 175.
26 *Bombay Chronicle*, 9 Dec. 1941.
27 D.J. Steinberg, *Philippine Collaboration in World War Two* (Ann Arbor, 1967), 27–9.
28 A. Iriye, *Across the Pacific* (New York, 1967), 232.
29 S. Schram, *Mao Tse-tung* (London, 1967), 224.
30 *Draft Statement of the All-India Students' Federation on the Anti-Fascist Peoples' War* (n.d.).
31 *Sydney Morning Herald*, 9, 10, 30 Dec. 1941; 2 Jan. 1942. See also Prange, op. cit., 558.
32 *Combat*, No. 1, Dec. 1941; see also e.g. *L'Université Libre*, 9 Dec. 1941.
33 T. White, *In Search of History* (New York, 1978), 130.
34 Lamont to Lippmann, 13 Nov. 1941, Lamont Papers, box 105/3; Lamont to Halifax, 17 Nov. 1941, ibid, box 84/23. And see W.I. Cohen, *The Chinese Connection* (New York, 1978).
35 On the renewed 'conspiracy thesis', that Roosevelt actually had foreknowledge of, and permitted, the Pearl Harbor attack, Prange's comment is apposite: it squares with neither the evidence nor common sense. (Op. cit., xi). See also R. Lewin, *The Other Ultra* (London, 1982), cap. 3, and R.H. Spector, *Eagle Against the Sun: the American War With Japan* (New York, 1984), cap. 5.
36 Lewin, caps. 2 and 3; Prange, passim; Spector, cap. 20.
37 Stimpson diary, 25 Nov., 2, 7 Dec. 1941.
38 R. Dallek, *Franklin D. Roosevelt and American Foreign Policy, 1932–1945* (New York, 1979), 310–11.
39 See Thorne, *Allies*, 3–4; 56. On the extent to which secret intelligence regarding the Far East had been shared by Britain and the U.S.A. before Pearl Harbor, see Lewin, op. cit., and F.H. Hinsley et al., *British Intelligence in the Second World War*, vol. 1 (London, 1979), 454.
40 J. Harvey (ed.), *The War Diaries of Oliver Harvey, 1941–1945* (London, 1978), entry for 8 Dec. 1941.
41 W.S. Churchill, *The Second World War, vol. III* (London, 1950), 539; Thorne, *Allies*, 75.
42 *Vrij Nederland* (London edition), 13 Dec. 1941.

CHAPTER TWO

International Contexts

Initial reactions to the events of December 1941, whatever their nature, can be understood only in the context of earlier developments and perceptions. The need for a perspective reaching back in some respects many years before Pearl Harbor will also arise when we come to consider the various interpretations and purposes that were subsequently to be attached by contemporaries to the struggle as it unfolded between the end of 1941 and Japan's surrender in the summer of 1945. Moreover, judgements that we make now, some forty years after the war, concerning its impact upon both domestic societies and international relations must also depend in part on the view one takes of issues and trends before 1941. Domestic contexts, as they stood in the years leading up to the war, will form the subject of chapter three. Here, the intention is to consider, not the detailed origins of the conflict, but those preceding developments of an international nature, together with a number of related perceptions on the part of contemporaries, that are relevant to our overall purpose.

*

Assertions regarding the 'origins' of a war frequently appear to rest upon criteria and theories that remain unstated – sometimes, perhaps, unrecognized even by the writer in question. A point of departure is confidently and precisely identified, but the assumptions underlying the choice have to be inferred by the reader.* In the case of the Far Eastern war, the two dates commonly offered as the moment of origination – the Manchurian crisis of 1931 and Japan's attack upon China in 1937 – have often been endowed with greater significance still, as the commencement of the Second World War as a whole.[1] Alternatively, at the International Military Tribunal set up by the Allies after the war the first count of the indictment identified as the moment

---

* Thus Professor Marder asserts that 'the origins of the [Far Eastern] war were cumulative and date back to the Manchurian and China Incidents [of 1931 and 1937 respectively]' Yet, at the outset of the same book, he emphasises that he brings to bear 'no theories of history', being concerned only 'to tell a story and tell it well'. (He adds, in immediate contradiction to his disclaimer regarding theories, that he has supplied 'a liberal infusion of the personal, the human component', as that represents the essence of historical developments.) *Old Friends, New Enemies*, xi, 254.

of origin the year 1928, when officers of Japan's Kwantung Army murdered the ruler of Manchuria, Chang Tso-lin.[2]

In what follows, no single date or event will be put forward in this way. The underlying premise is, rather, that in order to seek an understanding of the impact of the war – as would also be the case if one were studying its origins in detail – it is necessary to cast back along a variety of lines or themes, each of which has its own point of departure: some in the years immediately preceding the Japanese attack; others much further in the past. Such an approach, of course, does not invalidate questions of degree, and it would be legitimate to ask in a study of the war's origins whether there was a moment when such a conflict became well-nigh inevitable, for all that historians rightly tend to shy away from using such a term. Here, it is sufficient to note that it was during the two years before Pearl Harbor that a number of developments greatly increased the likelihood of an eventual armed clash between Japan and the Western powers, both as seen in retrospect and through the eyes of a growing number of contemporaries.

In the broadest terms, what were taking place between the end of 1939 and December 1941 were far-reaching changes in the very structure of international relations. The military triumphs of Nazi Germany had brought her to a position of massive predominance in Europe. (By the end of 1940, for example, the annual steel-producing capacity of German-occupied areas amounted to 212 million ingot tons. That of the British Commonwealth at the time was 18.5 million, and of the United States, 50 million.)[3] The complete unbalancing by Germany of the European system, in the making since at least the 1870s, was now accomplished.[4] France, seemingly during the inter-war years a major power still, was swept aside, its empire in the Far East now exposed, like that of the Dutch, as lacking all protection by its metropolitan owners.

Where Indochina was concerned, indeed, the French authorities were left with no more than nominal control after the Japanese had demanded and obtained entry into the northern part of the territory for their forces in September 1940,[5] and into the southern part as well in July 1941.[6] This second move, especially, greatly altered the strategic situation in Southeast Asia. Both the Netherlands Indies (where Japan had been vainly demanding privileged access to greatly increased supplies of oil and other vital strategic raw materials)[7] and the Malay Peninsula now lay under the shadow of a possible direct attack. Meanwhile other, political developments had already made such a move by Tokyo seem more likely to some observers. Japan's decision to sign the Tripartite Pact of September 1940 with Germany and Italy, whereby she recognized their leadership in the creation of a 'new order' in Europe in return for their backing for her equivalent role in the East, appeared to align her completely with Nazi and Fascist aggression.

Her securing of a Non-Aggression Pact with Moscow in April 1941,[8] and, even more, the German attack on the Soviet Union in the following June, clearly reduced the possibility of danger from the north should she resort to military action against the Western powers. And if in China, meanwhile, her forces had been unable to follow up their seizure of the north-eastern and coastal regions by destroying the centres of continuing resistance in Nationalist Chungking and Communist Yenan, a decisive Chinese resurgence seemed far distant, with the renewal of internecine strife between those two contenders for power in the country, and with the establishment in March 1940 of a pro-Japanese puppet regime in Nanking under a former leading member of the Kuomintang, Wang Ching-wei.

In fact, as already noted, the continuing burdens of the war in China were imposing considerable strains on Japan. (By 1940, the conflict there was absorbing over 40 per cent of the national budget, while 1.1 million men were abroad on military duty in that year.)[9] At the same time, the sense of being faced with a crisis of, literally, vital proportions was heightened by the embargo placed on supplies of oil to Japan by the Western powers following the former's move into southern Indochina.[10] Within this context, significant shifts were taking place in the balance of power inside those circles where Japan's policies were being shaped. At the beginning of 1940, it was still not certain that a solution to the country's problems would be sought by fresh military action, nor that such action, if it were indeed taken, would be directed against the Western powers rather than the Soviet Union. (The latter course was urged by Berlin for some while.) Nor, again, was it axiomatic that an attack on the European colonial powers, if decided upon, would extend also to one against the United States. By the summer of 1941, however, the upper hand in Tokyo had been gained by those who were determined to pursue the alignment with Nazi Germany. Above all, the predominant attitude was ceasing to be one whereby Japan's chances of achieving success by military means had to be weighed with care. Rather, it was that the only option left was to strike – and to do so against the Western powers as a whole.[11]

The final negotiations that then took place in the late summer and autumn of 1941 were, of course, between Japan and the United States, just as those two countries were to figure as the main contestants in the war – 'the Pacific War', as the revealing phrase has it – that ensued. Yet in its origins, that conflict was in essence as much, if not more, Anglo-Japanese in nature. 'In terms of actual American interests in China,' writes Professor Hosoya, 'there was hardly any need for a military clash with Japan; it was only that America's global interests would not permit her to sit by idly while the British Empire in Asia collapsed. In any case, Japan's foreign policy for a "new order in east Asia" made war between Japan and Britain inevitable

and that, in turn, made inescapable the war between Japan and both Britain
and the United States.'[12] As the German Naval Attaché in Tokyo had
expressed it in his diary in 1936 (at a time when he found senior Japanese
naval officers agreed that Britain was the forthcoming enemy): 'Every future
expansion, whether economic or territorial, on the part of Japan must
necessarily affect the position of England and consequently provoke English
resistance.'[13] In the mid 1930s, a book written by a retired Japanese naval
officer, *The Certainty of an Anglo-Japanese War*, sold in his own country
over one million copies.

A full-scale break-out by Japan would, indeed, put British interests at risk
on a massive scale: the colonies of Southeast Asia and their dollar-earning
raw materials; perhaps a restless India, as well as Australia and New
Zealand; Hong Kong and its investments and *entrepôt* trade. Moreover,
major and long-term issues were involved, besides immediate and tangible
matters such as trade and territory. In terms of the entire nature and
development of relationships within the Commonwealth, for example,
Britain's handling of Far Eastern affairs, and particularly her ability to
assure Australia and New Zealand of her understanding and protection,
were of great importance.[14] The Japanese blockade of the British concession at Tientsin in 1938–39 and, even more, the temporary closure of the
Burma Road into China in 1940 at Tokyo's bidding, underlined how
vulnerable Britain's Far Eastern presence had become, above all in the
context of another, mortal threat nearer home. By the summer of 1940,
indeed, those responsible for policy in London were faced with a situation
that Vansittart, as Permanent Under Secretary at the Foreign Office, had
foreseen as long before as 1932: that unless the United States stood by her,
Britain 'must eventually be done for in the Far East'.[15] 'We must rely on the
United States to safeguard our interests in the Far East,' noted the Chiefs of
Staff in May 1940.[16] As Vansittart's successor, Cadogan, acknowledged in
October 1940, the country had for a long while been maintaining its
international position on the basis of what was essentially a series of bluffs;
now that 'all bluffs have been called', everything must depend 'on the
willingness and the ability of the U.S. to share our burden'.[17]

This summary applied to more than the Far East alone. It described what
had become Britain's only realistic hope of seeing Germany beaten. 'The
active belligerency of the United States,' admitted a section of the Joint
Planning Staff in London in June 1941, 'has become essential for the
successful prosecution and conclusion of the war.'[18] Yet the American
position continued to stop agonisingly short of a full commitment to the
struggle against Germany. Roosevelt told Churchill at Placentia Bay in
August 1941, when they met to draw up the Atlantic Charter, that he 'would
wage war but not declare it, and ... would become more and more

provocative . . . look[ing] for an incident that would justify him in opening hostilities'.[19] There is good reason to believe, nevertheless, that even at this stage the President remained intent on maintaining the United States in the role of 'the arsenal of democracy' rather than that of a belligerent.[20]

Moreover, although in the late summer of 1941 Washington in effect, and with Churchill's blessing, virtually took over negotiations with Tokyo on behalf of London, as well as itself (in the event it did not choose to keep its partner fully informed, even so),[21] Britain still could not be sure that if the Japanese chose to attack her alone in the Far East the United States would enter the fray. Only on December 1 did Roosevelt give an assurance in this long-awaited sense. By then, in any case, the crucial decisions had been taken elsewhere. On July 2, an Imperial Conference in Tokyo had resolved that 'to obtain its objectives the Empire will not hesitate to engage in war with the United States and Britain'; and on November 5, that same body concluded that, unless Washington accepted Japan's terms for regulating international affairs in the Far East, war would be launched early in December.[22]

*

Despite the mounting tension in the Far East during the two years immediately preceding the war, however, the belief that such an outcome between Japan and the Western powers was likely or even inevitable was by no means universal. In many instances, of course, especially in the West, a relative lack of concern sprang from ignorance or indifference where that part of the world was involved. Understandably, in France and the Netherlands, as in Britain and Germany, the conflict within Europe itself helped ensure that Far Eastern developments received little attention.[23] But in the United States, too, lobbyists who were striving to secure aid for China found to their cost that concern over international affairs was focused almost exclusively upon Europe; and though Japan's decision to sign the Tripartite Pact with the Axis dictators did much to bring together in American minds the sufferings of China and those of the European democracies, it was still the latter that took precedence.[24]* Even those Americans living beside the Pacific in California, according to a survey conducted during the first three months of 1940, viewed the war in Europe 'as one which may not only touch [them] personally in the long run, but which also involves the civilization of which [they are] a part, in a way which no Asiatic conflict has yet seemed to do'.[25]

* In a poll taken by the American Institute of Public Opinion in September 1937, 55 per cent of those questioned had declared themselves to be 'neutral' as between China and Japan. In a further poll, taken in February 1938, 64 per cent were opposed to shipping arms to China. Dpt. of State files, Far Eastern Division memo. of 21 Sept. 1942, 694.119/360½.

There were others in the West and in Western territories in the East who, although their lives in one way or another were more plainly bound up with developments east of Suez, discounted even so the idea that Japan would pursue her ambitions to the point of conflict with the white man. For some – in Singapore, for example – 'the cry of wolf' had been heard often enough for its impact to be lost.[26] In Hong Kong, too, there were many who shrugged off as by then routine the crises surrounding that part of the world. ('Outwardly,' the Commander of its Field Ambulance Unit was to write, 'Hong Kong fell because its garrison was outfought. Actually it fell weeks, months before, psychologically defeated.')[27] Among the Dutch in the East Indies, again there were those who felt secure in the thought that Japanese demands for privileged access to the territory's oil had been successfully resisted;[28] among Americans in the Philippines, those who dismissed the very idea that Japan would be so foolish as to confront the manifestly greater power of the United States.[29]

Nor was it simply those without responsibility for protecting Western interests or without access to official appraisals of the situation who believed that a major conflict in the Far East could be avoided. The Prime Minister of Australia, Robert Menzies, wrote privately in 1940 that, given the 'marked inferiority complex' of the Japanese, 'a real gesture of friendship with some real assistance in the settlement of the Chinese question . . . [and] a proper recognition of Japanese trading ambitions' might 'very easily produce peace in the Far East . . . '[30] Even during the final weeks before Japan launched her attack, Stanley Hornbeck in Washington, Adviser on Far Eastern relations to the Secretary of State, for all his conviction that Tokyo's aims were fundamentally opposed to America's interests, was dismissing Japanese bellicose behaviour as mere bluff.[31] Churchill, too, was arguing to his Defence Committee only four days before Pearl Harbor that a Japanese attack was 'a remote contingency'.[32]

Such beliefs, together with the often-accompanying one that if war did come Japan would meet with swift defeat, were frequently based, in part at least, on a belittling of the Japanese people on racial grounds. 'Americans,' writes Professor Prange in his history of the Pearl Harbor attack, 'held the average Japanese in utter contempt.'[33] The British Commander-in-Chief in the Far East, after visiting mainland Hong Kong in 1940 and viewing at close range across the frontier 'various sub-human specimens dressed in dirty grey uniform, which I was informed were Japanese soldiers', dismissed the idea that 'they would form an intelligent fighting force'. One of the local commanders in Malaya likewise expressed the hope that the defences of the peninsula would not be so strengthened that the Japanese would be deterred from attempting a landing – and thus deny his British troops a signal victory.[34] Churchill, for his part, believed that a small force of modern ships of the Royal Navy would be sufficient to provide 'a decisive deterrent' to any such move on Japan's part, a conviction that led him to despatch the *Prince of Wales* and *Repulse* to their well-nigh certain destruction.[35] The time to deal with the Japanese, believed Queen Wilhelmina of the Netherlands, would come once Germany had been defeated: the West should then 'drown them like rats'.[36]

Racist assumptions, whether explicit or implicit, did not of course provide the only bases upon which the conclusion was drawn that war was by no means inevitable. There were those, for example, who continued to believe that differences between Japan and the Western powers were capable of being patched up, if not finally resolved. The British and American Ambassadors in Tokyo, Sir Robert Craigie and Joseph Grew, have already been mentioned in this respect, as has the banker, Thomas Lamont; others – more naïve – included those members of the American Maryknoll Catholic Foreign Mission who during 1941 interfered in and confused the diplomatic exchanges between Tokyo and Washington.[37]

As for assumptions of a racist kind, there is a further, and ironic, qualification to be made. For if, where many Westerners were concerned, such convictions tended to point against the likelihood of war, the opposite was the case for those Japanese 'double patriots' who had long urged that a conflict with the West must and should come, and who emphasized in their reasoning the common belief that their country had unique and divine origins, its people, in Professor Reischauer's phrase, 'almost a different species of animal from the rest of humanity'.[38] (The creation of a Greater East Asia Coprosperity Sphere, declared the Imperial Rule Assistance Association in March 1941, 'by no means ignores the fact that Japan was created by the Gods or posits an automatic equality', a philosophy that was entirely in line with the basis of the country's rule over Koreans during the preceding four decades.)[39] Moreover, for all such blatant racism among the people of Nippon, there were also by 1940–41 those Chinese ('Chinks', to most Japanese, despite their often ambivalent attitudes towards China generally)[40]* who rallied to Tokyo's call for a greater Asian league, based on Japan, China and Manchukuo, that would remove Western influence from that part of the world. To this end, Miao Pin and other former Kuomintang officials had already joined the society – the Hsin-min Hui – that served as the main vehicle for Sino-Japanese collaboration (5,000 Chinese were to hold office in the organisation by 1943),[41] while the ideas put out by the Wang Ching-wei puppet regime in Nanking pointed in a similar and

---

* Commenting on Tokyo's failure to induce Chiang Kai-shek to accept a settlement of the conflict in 1940 – on terms that would have been harsh and humiliating – Dr David Lu concludes: 'In the end it was Tokyo's contempt for China that caused the failure of both its war and peace efforts.' Morley (ed.), *The China Quagmire*, 303.

anti-Western direction.[42] (Obviously, the motives of the individuals concerned varied greatly, and it may be useful in this respect to borrow a distinction that has been made in relation to French attitudes towards Germany after 1940: between the 'collaborator' who acts primarily from considerations of personal advancement or material gain, and the 'collaborationist' who genuinely espouses the political cause involved.)[43] .

Again, even when considering an area where Japanese expansion was already in progress, the ignorance and indifference of many people regarding the broader trends of international politics has to be borne in mind. Despite an initial surge of anti-Japanese sentiment in 1937 and the extensive and hideous atrocities committed against the Chinese people by the invading forces thereafter, it appears that, in the words of a leading student of the subject, 'many Chinese – especially . . . the peasantry – were by no means hostile to them', and that a lack of nationalist concern over the outcome of the war 'was everywhere apparent'.[44]* In Korea, too, despite a strong sense of national identity based on centuries of independence; despite, also, a tenacious guerrilla resistance to Japanese rule, native landlords and other elite groups collaborated with their imperial masters through such bodies as the Central Advisory Council and the Japan-Korea Harmony Society (*Naisen kyowakai*), while Korean police and para-military units hunted their resisting fellow-countrymen with a will.[45]

At the same time, it must be noted in relation to other territories in the Far East that during this pre-Pearl Harbor period attitudes were not always as unambiguous as subsequent versions tended to have it. In the East Indies, for example, there were those Dutch who were ready to seek some accommodation with the 'new order' being created by Germany back in Europe. Indeed, the Dutch Government in exile in London was far from wholeheartedly determined at this stage of the war to throw in its lot with Britain. What one Dutch historian has described as 'violent and painful' discussions were held on the issue of whether to 'come to terms with reality' and to seek a separate peace with Germany. And even when such hopes faded, there

---

* During the battle of Central Honan in 1944, 'Chinese peasants armed with farm tools and crude weapons attacked T'ang En-po's Chinese soldiers as they retreated before the Japanese. They disarmed an estimated 50,000 of those soldiers and even murdered some of them.' Lloyd Eastman, *Seeds of Destruction: Nationalist China in War and Revolution, 1937–1949* (Stanford, 1984), 141. Ambivalence, at the very least, also marked the attitudes of those who were engaged in the flourishing trade across the line separating the invader from Kuomintang forces. During 1941, the average monthly tonnage of goods entering Nationalist China from Hong Kong, Macao and Kwangchowan alone through the Japanese positions amounted to approximately twice that arriving via the Burma Road. In return, the Japanese received not only foodstuffs but strategically important commodities such as tungsten, and medical supplies obtained by the Kuomintang from the Red Cross. During the war, also, between half a million and a million Chinese troops served under the Japanese, many of them having defected from the Nationalist army. Eastman, 'Facets of an Ambivalent Relationship', in Iriye (ed.), *Chinese and Japanese*.

remained the intention to maintain a strictly neutral position in any conflict between Britain and Japan. In the East Indies themselves, the attitude of the authorities towards the Japanese was marked by considerable flexibility – even to the point of contemplating for a time accepting the term 'coprosperity' favoured by Tokyo. Only in February 1941 were Japan's demands that the colony should be brought within such a 'sphere' rejected.[46]

In some cases, not surprisingly, the attitudes expressed could vary greatly according to the audience being addressed. Jawaharlal Nehru, leader of India's Congress party, provides a clear example of this – not for the last time during the Second World War, as will be seen below. Thus, when addressing Western politicians and readers – for instance in the revised edition of his book, *Toward Freedom*, that was to be published in New York in 1942 – he emphasised his conviction that, from the Spanish Civil War onwards, he had viewed international developments as constituting a single, world-wide struggle involving fundamental political issues, a struggle in which the Nazi and Fascist dictatorships were the embodiment of evil.[47] Yet in private, in both January and February 1940, he expressed in letters to Gandhi his strong aversion to 'seeing India entangled' in the conflict, not simply because Britain had yet to grant the country her freedom, but because it was in any event no more than an 'imperialist war' and an 'imperialist adventure'.[48]

As for those who, between the onset of war in Europe and December 1941, did judge an additional great-power conflict in the Far East to be likely, in many instances it was the local and practical rather than the global and philosophical context that was uppermost in the mind. Thus, while a growing number of Indonesians – often citing local legend to support the prediction* – looked forward to an anti-Western drive by Japan, they thought in terms, as the nationalist leader Sjahrir put it, 'not [of] a world conflict between two great forces' but of 'a struggle in which the Dutch colonial rulers finally would be punished by Providence for the evil, the arrogance, and the oppression they had brought to Indonesia'.[49] Likewise, for nationalists in Indochina what mattered most was the weakening of the French position at the hands of Japan – though in their case the Japanese, too, were seen as an imperialist enemy.[50] Meanwhile, despite the signing of the Tripartite Pact and the crucial conclusions drawn in Tokyo from Germany's dramatic victories in Europe, what dominated the thoughts of those struggling to shape Japan's policies was neither a world-wide ideological confrontation nor the need to lead an Asian crusade against the West,

---

* That is, the *Djojobojo* legend, according to which, after the overthrow of white rule, a yellow people, coming from the north, would rule the Indies for 'a hundred days'.

but how to ensure that their country would 'survive' and how to win 'a sphere for the self-defence and self-preservation of our Empire'.[51]

Regardless of perspective, however, an increasing number of people in East and West were coming to expect a major conflict in the Far East. By January 1941, for example, Stanley Bruce, the Australian High Commissioner in London and a former Prime Minister, who had previously hoped that a comprehensive agreement with Japan might be achieved, was 'quite sure that . . . she would cause trouble if things went badly for us in Europe'.[52] Many of his country's military and political leaders were deeply disturbed by the same prospect, even to the point of envisaging a Japanese invasion.[53] 'North or South?', asked *The Standard* in New Zealand. 'Which will Japan choose as she threatens the Pacific with a clash of arms?'[54] A similar belief that Tokyo's policies were leading to war existed in the minds of a substantial number of Americans by that autumn of 1941.[55] 'There can be doubt,' declared a leading French paper in Indochina in May of that year,

'that in order to achieve its aims the United States will be obliged to invervene directly in the conflict [in Europe]. And one must also expect that the conflagration will spread to the Pacific. It seems only a matter of time before Japan intervenes, assured against attack on her Russian flank as she now is. It is general war, a truly world war, that is taking shape, and no people can be sure of being spared.'[56]

Such a perspective: that what had emerged was essentially a single international crisis, was in the forefront of Roosevelt's mind, for example, not least in strategic terms. 'There is a very close connection,' he wrote privately at the end of 1940 to the U.S. High Commissioner for the Philippines,

'between the hostilities which have been going on for three and a half years in the Far East and those which have been going on for sixteen months in . . . Europe . . . For practical purposes, there is going on a world conflict, in which there are aligned on one side Japan, Germany and Italy, and on the other side China, Great Britain and the United States. If Japan, moving further southward, should gain possession of the region of the Netherlands East Indies and the Malay Peninsula, would not the chances of Germany's defeating Great Britain be increased . . . thereby?'[57]

Others in Washington – Henry Morgenthau (Secretary of the Treasury) and Harold Ickes (Secretary of the Interior) among them – not only shared this viewpoint in ideological terms, but regretted that Roosevelt himself did not act more decisively to commit the United States to the fray.[58]

A more unusual concern among Americans in this period, however, was the one voiced privately by the diplomat, John Carter Vincent: that the U.S.A. was heading for a conflict with the destructive forces represented by Japan and Germany without itself having long-term and creative ideas for social and international reform to put before the world at the same time.[59]* Less surprisingly, this was a line of thought that had been pursued in public since the outbreak of Hitler's war by the *Bombay Chronicle*, a paper that (like Sjahrir in the Indies), while strongly nationalist, was from the outset unequivocally hostile to Nazi Germany and the militarists in Japan. Potentially, it argued in September 1939, 'more than two-thirds of the world', including 'millions in Asia and Africa', were recruits for the struggle against such evil powers. But there remained to be answered 'the crucial question':

> 'Is the present war imperialistic? Or, more accurately, is Britain's policy in it imperialistic? ... She has yet to establish her *bona fides*, and the [Congress] Working Committee rightly contends that "if Great Britain fights for the maintenance and extension of Democracy, then she must necessarily end Imperialism in her own possessions, and establish full Democracy in India, and the Indian People must have the right to Self-Determination ... and must guide their own policy ..." ... The destruction of Hitlerism can have only one meaning. It must mean the end of the domination of one nation over another.'[60]

This conviction: that the existing European war – and the Far Eastern one that was likely to follow – had major implications for imperialism as a feature of the international scene, was shared by Bose, for example, and by the Indonesian nationalist leader, Ahmed Soekarno, though in their eyes Japan had a benificent, rather than a destructive, role to play in the process.[61] In France and the Netherlands, in contrast, such an issue had as yet scarcely made an appearance. (One exception was provided by the organ of the French Communist Party, *L'Humanité*, which – before the involvement of the Soviet Union turned the war into a sacred struggle – devoted a special number to the cause of 'the right of colonial peoples freely to determine their own future'.)[62] In Britain, too, still fighting for her very existence, long-term issues of this kind were seldom being raised among the public at large. (Harold Laski, for the Labour Party, did pose the question in pamphlet form: *Is This An Imperialist War?*, and was able to answer himself in the negative, while the Party's National Executive called for 'colonial peoples everywhere [to] move forward as speedily as possible towards self-govern-ment'.)[63] Still less were such matters being pondered at length in those official circles that were not only hard-pressed, but were under the

---

* See below, 295 ff., on the ways in which Vincent's fears proved justified in the event.

control of a Churchill who was resolutely opposed to the consideration of any subject but the road to victory.[64]

What was appreciated, on the other hand, by a wide variety of commentators around the world during this period, was that the mounting crisis in the Far East, coupled with developments in Europe, pointed towards a vastly enhanced role for the United States in international affairs generally. (Such expectations were far more common at the time than parallel views of the Soviet Union, especially where the future of the Far East was concerned.)[65] Private acknowledgements of this kind among British policymakers have already been noted, and of course the need to keep in step with Washington was a cardinal consideration for Churchill himself – for all the frustrations and indignities that London was already having to accept as the price of such a vital relationship.[66] It is interesting to find Stafford Cripps, too, the left-wing Labour politician who by 1942 would be giving vent to strong resentment over what he saw as American high-handedness, envisaging in June 1940 a world in which Britain, in order to survive, would have to become 'merely the European outpost of an Anglo-Saxon group largely controlled in the West'.[67] Another Englishman of left-wing convictions, the Cambridge scientist Dr Joseph Needham, soon to be absorbed in a cultural mission to China, and later to be a fierce critic of American economic and military activities overseas, wrote in March 1941 to the *New York Times* to suggest that

> 'the Nazi-Fascist-Japanese pact offered two alternatives to the United States, and only two – either to sink to the status of a third-rate power trembling within her own frontiers and hoping not to be disturbed, or to rise to the occasion of this crisis in the world's history, and to join with England, the original home of her culture, and play perhaps the greatest part in moulding the future of humanity, not only in Europe, but necessarily throughout the whole world.'[68]

Similar ironies (when viewed in the light of post-1945 developments) are to be found elsewhere. 'The Americans are going to be the principal eventual winners,' predicted the Gaullist clandestine paper, *Vérité*, in September 1941, when surveying the Far Eastern scene. 'The role of the United States is hourly becoming more significant. It is they who will be dictating the terms of peace to the *Boche*.'[69] In Australia, meanwhile, the British-orientated Menzies had been envisaging in 1940 that 'in the long run, the United Kingdom might be defeated in the war', and that consequently 'a regrouping of the English-speaking peoples might arise'. Like a growing number of politicians and diplomats in his country, therefore, he was concerned to foster American awareness of, sympathy for, and, ultimately, commitment to Australia.[70] Similar notions were being voiced in Dutch diplomatic and political circles after the Netherlands had been overrun by Germany, and in 1941 a Netherlands Information Bureau was established in New York in consequence.[71]

Not surprisingly, there were also those Americans themselves who were beginning to see developments in international affairs, including the likelihood of a confrontation between their country and Japan, as pointing in the direction of what Henry Luce publicly hailed in February 1941 as 'the American Century'. 'It seems to me,' wrote Raymond Clapper in January of that year, 'that everything is shaping up so that we must either seize the [leading] role ourselves, or be content to accept a good deal of domination from others.'[72] On the morrow of Pearl Harbor, the Secretary of the American Asiatic Association wrote privately to his friend Stanley Hornbeck in the State Department: 'It will be a long, hard war, but after it is over Uncle Sam will do the talking in this world.'[73]

*

International developments during the two years before December 1941 had to some extent sharpened and simplified attitudes and opinions regarding Far Eastern issues. The same thing had tended to happen in earlier crises:* during the Japanese seizure of Manchuria in 1931–33, for example, and at the outbreak of the Sino-Japanese war in 1937. Yet even during such periods of heightened tension, and even if one focuses upon a single set of policy-makers, a wide variety of underlying assumptions and interpretations is often to be found. The same is true concerning longer-term issues having major implications for international relations in the Far East. Three examples from British official circles will suffice to illustrate the point: the protracted battles during the inter-war period over the building of the Singapore naval base (without which, the country's entire credibility as a major power in that part of the world would be lost);[74] the fierce disagreement in the mid-1920s between the Admiralty on the one hand and Churchill as Chancellor of the Exchequer on the other over whether Japan need be considered a potential, long-term threat to Britain's interests in the Far East (Churchill denied the proposition);[75] and the contrast, within the British Embassy in Tokyo in the late 1930s, between the relatively sanguine views of the Ambassador, Craigie, and the conviction of his Commercial Counsellor, Sir George Sansom, that 'all Japanese want a "new order" in Asia, and a

---

* The term 'crisis' is a convenient, portmanteau one. Strictly speaking, during the 1931–33 Far Eastern turmoil, for example, not every one of the Governments directly or indirectly involved saw matters in 'crisis' terms throughout the period, if we adopt the useful criteria suggested by Hermann: i.e., that decisions have to be made without prior planning, in circumstances allowing only a short time for response, and with high values at stake. See H. C. Kelman, *International Behavior* (New York, 1966), 442 ff.

"new order" involves the ultimate displacement of Great Britain in the Far East'.[76] Similar differences are to be found on the American side, and elsewhere.[77]

There can be no question, then, of doing justice here to the complex and shifting ideas that existed among officials and others during a lengthy period before the 1939–41 crisis regarding the future of international relations in the Far East. What can be done, however, as for the period immediately preceding the 1941 war, is to indicate something of the variety of perspectives that were involved, particularly with regard to those who, at one time or another, anticipated an eventual conflict between Japan and the Western powers.

Since the later years of the nineteenth century there had been those, for example, both in the West and in the Far East itself, for whom it was the economic dimension that was crucial. Thus there were some in America and in Japan before the First World War who, viewing relations between their two countries in terms of such matters as emigration and trade, believed that a violent collision was likely or even 'fated'.[78] (The reasoning behind such a conclusion could vary, of course. It might derive from the notions of Malthus – who was widely read in Japan in the late nineteenth century – or from beliefs about the inescapable dynamics of international economics and the requirements of self-interest in that regard. The nation could not survive, urged some Japanese writers, unless it bent its skills to that 'economic warfare' which had become the crucial feature of international affairs.)[79] An emphasis upon economic factors as a potential source of international conflict was again to be heard in some quarters during the depression of the late 1920s and early 1930s. Sir Victor Wellesley of the British Foreign Office, for example, believed that if China were to cut off trade with Japan, then the latter 'would be forced to fight for her very existence'.[80] In Japan itself, a major strand among policy considerations during the 1930s was the quest for an area of economic self-sufficiency, while those who argued that the West would never treat the country as an equal in this and other respects could point to the tariff and quota barriers that were being raised against Japanese goods at the time. (Some made use of the 'geopolitical' concepts of the German writer, Karl Haushofer, when developing the idea of a regional 'Co-Prosperity Sphere' as the solution to the country's problems.)[81] Marxist observers, too, of course, especially since Lenin's analysis of the dynamics of imperialism, had their own economically-orientated interpretation of the rivalries that promised to embroil Japan and the Western powers in a region where both strove for captive markets, a guaranteed supply of raw materials, and cheap labour.[82]

It must not be thought that such arguments and conclusions went unchallenged at the time. In the early years of the century, for example, for all the economic problems facing Japan, many writers in that country rejected the notion that competing interests would lead to a clash with the United States,[83] while in London in the 1930s Wellesley's belief that the economic aspects of international relations were fundamental was less typical than Neville Chamberlain's assumption, as Chancellor of the Exchequer, that they could be divorced from the 'high politics' of political and strategic agreements, not least where Anglo-Japanese relations were concerned.[84] Even so, ideas pointing towards lasting economic rivalry rather than cooperation did tend to figure also within other intellectual frameworks that emphasised, for example, the inescapable (even desirable, in Social Darwinist terms) role of war in the rise and fall of states, and the geopolitical aspect of such struggles.[85] They also contributed (together with beliefs of a religious or spiritual nature, for example) to arguments regarding a particular territory, and its vital role in the 'destiny' of one's own society – China being depicted in these terms within both Japan and the United States.[86]

The economic dimension also featured at times within wider sets of assertions regarding the essential nature of particular states and societies that were involved in Far Eastern affairs. Thus for Soekarno, the Indonesian struggle against Dutch rule could be understood and brought to a successful conclusion only as part of a conflict involving the entire region. 'European nationalism,' he wrote in 1928, 'has an aggressive character, is a nationalism that is concerned only with its own needs, a commercial nationalism that can lead to profit or loss but that in the end must perish or be destroyed.'[87] In similar vein (though in these instances without the economic emphasis), observers like Soekarno's compatriot, Sjahrir, and America's Secretary of State during the 1931–33 crisis, Stimson, believed that it was the fundamental nature of Japanese society, especially as now led, that made conflict on an international scale well-nigh inevitable. It was 'almost impossible', as Stimson saw it in 1932, that 'two such different civilizations' as Japan and the United States could avoid clashing head-on, especially over the fate of China.[88]

Stimson's reference to 'contrasting civilizations', like Soekarno's assertions concerning 'Europeans', indicates a further perspective within which Far Eastern developments were viewed: a perspective which set up in opposition to one another not simply individual states or societies but entire portions of mankind that were given a number of labels – often jumbled and meaningless in strict anthropological terms:[89] 'coloured' or 'yellow' vis-à-vis 'white'; 'Europe' or 'the West' vis-à-vis 'Asia' or 'the East'. When, in this vein, Sir Frederick Maze, the British Inspector General of China's Maritime Customs, saw the Tientsin crisis of 1939 as constituting a confrontation, not merely between Japan and Britain, but of 'the Orient against the Occident – the Yellow Race against the White Race',[90] he was adopting a perspective that can be traced back to the Roman Empire and the Greek city states. Among Europeans, the assumption that Asians and their societies were inherently inferior – were 'backward' and 'uncivilized' – had become particularly marked in the nineteenth century. The West, invigorated by the Renaissance, triumphantly striding down that road of perpetual progress that had commenced with the seventeenth-century scientific revolution, embodied both dynamism and spiritual enlightenment. The East – as Marx among others emphasised – bred despotism, obscurantism and stagnation. If it could be coaxed or bludgeoned into progress at all, such a change was to be measured by the degree to which Western ideas and constitutions were adopted. 'Better fifty years of Europe than a cycle of Cathay.'[91]

Attitudes of this kind remained widespread among Europeans and Americans alike during the years leading up to the final Far Eastern crisis of 1940–41. ('"Race",' wrote Ashley Montagu, 'is the witchcraft of our time. The means by which we exorcise demons. It is the contemporary myth. Man's most dangerous myth.')[92] Before Britain could surrender her extra-territorial privileges in China, insisted the Government in London in 1929, 'Western legal principles should be understood and be found acceptable by the [Chinese] people at large not less than by their rulers'.[93] (The codification and development of law in China, of course, had preceded by centuries such achievements in the West.)[94] 'What is wrong with China,' pronounced the British Ambassador to that country, Sir Alexander Cadogan, in the mid-1930s, 'is that there is something wrong with the Chinese – something at least that does not conform to Western standards.'[95] The notion of an inherent and racially-based Western superiority had long helped underpin the rule of British, French and Dutch alike in Southeast Asia, as elsewhere.[96] Many white Americans, too – whose belief in their own racial superiority had a far more powerful domestic impulsion than did that of their European kin – shared the assumptions lying behind President McKinley's avowal that the country's task in the Philippines was to 'uplift, civilise and Christianise' the people of those islands.[97] Among Americans in official circles in the 1920s and '30s, the notion of sustaining the white presence and of bearing a share of 'the white man's burden' in the East was not uncommon, [98] while similar assumptions required that the immigration of Asians into the United States, as into Australia, should continue to be banned.

By the inter-war period, however, such an apportioning of mankind into Westerners and Asians had come to be surrounded by arguments and predictions that adulterated the confidence and arrogance that had predominated among the former for much of the nineteenth century. Even before the shattering European civil war of 1914–18, some voices within the continent – Paul Valéry's was one[99] – were suggesting that in its uncritical faith in reason and science European civilization had fallen into error. The apparently futile blood-letting of the Great War not only gave much wider currency to such conclusions (the previous century had witnessed the death of God, argued Malraux in his *La Tentation de l'Occident*; now, optimistic, perfectible European man had died as well); it encouraged some contemporaries like Romain Rolland to look to Asia for the inspiration and example by which Europe's *malaise* could be cured.[100] Here was a line of thought that was to be given prominence during the 1941–45 war itself by Pearl Buck and her fellow Sinophiles in particular,* and that was to lead some thereafter to question radically the significance of modern European civilisation in the context of the entire history of mankind.†

It was not, however, admiration of the East that did most in the pre-war years to qualify Western confidence. Rather, it was a growing fear that from those Eastern parts of the world there was arising a major challenge to the entire position of the white man and to the civilisation that he had developed. 'A hundred years hence,' Charles Pearson – late-Victorian academic and man of affairs – had prophesied,

> 'when these ... Chinese, Hindu and negro ... races, which are now as two to one to the higher [white race], shall be as three to one; when they have borrowed the science of Europe, and developed their still virgin worlds, the pressure of their competition on the white man will be irresistible. He will be driven from every neutral market and forced to confine himself within his own ...'[101]

By the turn of the century, indeed, some had been anticipating an even earlier culmination of that overriding conflict between the civilisations of East and West that Rear Admiral Alfred Mahan in America, among others, was depicting.[102] Men as politically diverse as Kaiser Wilhelm II in Germany (stressing the well-known 'yellow-peril' theme), Viscount Esher in Britain, and the socialist leader, Jean Jaurès, in France had shared the belief that the peoples of the East were likely to rise up as one.[103]

In some quarters, this prospect was given added edge and immediacy by events in Russia in 1917. The Revolution, asserted Henri Massis and others, signified that that country, after two centuries of enforced Europeanisation, had reverted to its primitive, Asiatic origins, and was setting out to lead a violent assault by all Asiatics against a newly-hesitant and troubled West. [104] Lenin himself was indeed emphasising the immense revolutionary potential of 'the entire East, with its hundreds of millions of exploited working people'.[105] For his part, the British Marxist, H. M. Hyndman (founder of the Social Democratic Federation), writing during the First World War, set

* See below, 181 ff.
† See below, 316.

out in detail the argument that the world stood in need of 'the genius of the East and the genius of the West combined in one noble effort'. In his *The Awakening of Asia*, Hyndman coupled his conclusion that 'the influence of the white man on the Far East . . . had been almost wholly harmful' with the warning that the West must give immediate and practical recognition to the principle: 'Asia for the Asiatics.' And he went on to be more precise in his forecast. A 'warlike Japan', though bent upon exploiting China, was creating for itself a position as 'the champion of Asia against Europe'; and however much many Asians might dislike the Japanese *per se*, large numbers of them could well support the latter in a war of hatred and revenge against the West.[106]

By the time that Anthony Eden, as British Foreign Secretary in 1938, was privately urging the need to 'effectively assert white-race authority in the Far East',[107] Hyndman's warning had accumulated a great deal more weight. If those aggressive features of Japanese society and policies that had troubled the Indian poet and mystic, Rabindranath Tagore, earlier in the century had become more pronounced, so, too, in some eyes, had the possibility increased that Japan, as Tagore had also proclaimed, would play a special role in the renaissance of Asia vis-à-vis the West.[108] Both Soekarno and Bose, for example, were insisting during the 1930s that Japan was already, as the latter put it, 'shattering the white man's prestige in the Far East and putting all the Western powers on the defensive', and would soon bring to a head what the former described as 'the greatest . . . problem: Asia against Europe'.[109] 'As far as I can make out,' wrote Sjahrir regretfully in 1937, 'the whole Islamic population of our country is now pro-Japanese . . . [and is] firmly convinced of the power of the Japanese.'[110]

Such expectations on the part of people in various Asian societies had been facilitated by the spectacle of the major European powers mutilating one another between 1914 and 1918 – a decisive illustration, as Tagore saw it at the time, of the ultimately self-destructive nature of Western materialism.[111] Even before this, however, in 1904–5, Japan's defeat of a white power, Russia, had been hailed by nationalists in India, China and Vietnam as proof that the apparently supreme West was not after all invincible and that 'the regeneration of the yellow race' could now be expected.[112]* Some Chinese nationalists, indeed, including Sun Yat-sen, had for a while looked to Japan herself for assistance and advice.[113]

---

* Fear remained, however. In the introduction to his book, *On Greater East Asianism* (*Dai Ajia Shugi ron*) in 1916, Odera Kenkichi, for example, wrote: 'Is it not strange that in the Europe which has come to control or overwhelm Asia the talk of the yellow peril is boisterously heard, . . . when the yellow peril is no more than an illusion while the white peril is real . . .' Quoted in K. Miwa, 'Japanese Policies and Concepts for a Regional Order in Asia, 1938–1940', Institute of International Relations research paper, Sophia University, Tokyo, 1983.

Not – obviously – that faith in Japan was a prerequisite for a belief in the need for 'Asia' to assert itself against 'the West'. Whether adherents of the Kuomintang or of the Communist Party, those Chinese for whom the urgent national task came to be the struggle against the same neighbouring predator could nevertheless continue to view world politics in terms of 'yellow' or 'coloured' versus 'white'. Among Chinese Marxists, for example (the growth of whose party contributed to the pressures directed against Stalinist Eurocentrism within the Comintern),[114] Li Ta-chao, for one, explicitly argued that in global terms the class struggle had taken on the form of a racial conflict.[115] Generalissimo Chiang Kai-shek and his wife, also, in their correspondence with Indian nationalist leaders, emphasised the common characteristics of their two Asian peoples and the great role they should together play in the world,[116] while Nehru, for his part, was writing privately in 1939 that what he had seen of 'the East beyond India' made him 'feel strongly how our cultures intermingle and how much there is in common between us'.[117] And for Marcus Garvey, the black Jamaican whose outspoken views were made known to a wide audience from within the United States in the 1920s, the recovery of racial pride by non-whites was an essential aspect of the process whereby freedom would be won by all colonial and oppressed peoples.[118]

Meanwhile, among the Japanese themselves, the subject of their country's identity, location and role in world affairs had been surrounded with ambiguity and fierce debate since the abrupt arrival of a newly strong and insistent West in the form of Commodore Perry's American 'black ships' in the 1850s and the Meiji restoration of 1868.[119] Was it a part of Asia, or was it in essence a Westernized outsider merely located on the edge of that continent? 'What we have to do,' argued one of the country's Foreign Ministers in the 1880s, 'is to transform our empire and our people and make the empire like the countries of Europe and our people like the people of Europe.'[120] Yet, from the outset, it was opposing beliefs that commanded wider support. Doubtless it was a small minority who, like Yamagata Aritomo in the 1890s, pondered on 'a world-wide racial struggle between the white and coloured races'. All the nationalists of the Meiji period, however, had, in the words of one scholar, 'again and again preached the same ideal' of Japan's 'mission' to lead all of Asia against white dominance.[121] During the 1920s and – in a more favourable climate – the 1930s, 'double patriots' continued to proclaim that a confrontation between East and West was inevitable, a vision linked by certain publicists to the idea of some kind of 'coprosperity sphere' which would be developed in the East under Japan's leadership.[122]

To single out such assumptions and predictions does not mean, of course, that they were at all times decisive in the shaping of policy. Between the attack in Manchuria in 1931 and the confrontation with the West in 1940–41, the belief that Japan had a mission to create a new order in East Asia and beyond did not provide a touchstone for every discussion in Tokyo, any more than Indonesians in general were motivated in their day-to-day political attitudes by the kind of vision of world politics articulated by Soekarno. The origins of the war of 1941–45 were not solely racial in nature, any more than they were solely economic. We shall observe below, however, how, when that war was being waged, the beliefs, hopes and fears of contemporaries, and the explanations that were handed out to them by those in authority, frequently echoed arguments employed long before 1941 – not least those of a racial kind.

*

So far in this chapter, then, we have noted some of the assumptions, opinions and expectations surrounding international relations in the Far East, both during the period immediately preceding the outbreak of the war and within a much wider time-frame.[123] But what of the same set of Far Eastern developments as they appear now, over forty years after Japan's attack on the Western powers? Again, it needs to be emphasised that, given the focus of the present study, there is no intention of attempting even a summary of events from, say, 1931 or 1902 onwards. Still less is it possible to explore those relevant themes – the shaping of American political culture and attitudes regarding international affairs, for example, or the same for Japan – that would require us to look back well beyond the encounter between Japan and the West in the 1850s. All that will be done is to single out certain features and trends, first in terms of individual states and then in relation to the international setting as a whole.

Where Japan was concerned, one can point in this respect to a persistent inclination to regard neighbouring islands and areas of the Asian mainland as territories to be secured for defensive purposes, at least, and to be exploited and dominated if not annexed outright.* (In the case of China, there existed also, in some minds, the notion of a special 'mission' to save that country from herself.) At the same time, one clear thread running through the complex tangle of attitudes regarding the Western powers from the 1850s onwards was epitomised by the slogan, *sonno joi*: 'honour the Emperor and expel the barbarian.' We can observe, also, a marked pre-dilection for the use of armed force to achieve Japan's ends, together with

* 'In the Japanese perspective, each new imperial possession required the control of a buffer territory adjacent to it. Ever subject to expanding redefinition of national interest, the perimeters of the empire thus came to involve Japan in a successive series of strategic problems which tortured Japan's domestic politics and imperilled its foreign relations.' Myers and Peattie, *The Japanese Colonial Empire*, 9.

the conviction that the country's interests and actions were to be judged solely by its own, unique set of values and its special status as the land of the chosen. Certain prominent features of Japan's political culture helped ensure that, in Professor Maruyama's words, 'international problems were reduced to a single alternative: "conquer or be conquered" '; that, in the absence of any higher norms that stood outside the long-isolated country itself, 'power politics [was] bound to be the rule, and yesterday's timid defensiveness [became] today's unrestrained expansionism'.[124]

To conclude a summary of Japan's attitudes and behaviour at this point, however – as her opponents during the 1941–45 war were commonly to do – would amount to a distortion of history. The 1894–95 war against China (a 'bigoted and ignorant colossus of conservatism', in the opinion of the Japanese Foreign Minister of the time);[125] the pressure exerted on that country during the First World War and the assaults on her in the 1930s; the subduing of Korea: these and other episodes must indeed figure prominently in any survey of the antecedents of the Far Eastern conflict. At the same time, however, it is necessary to recall that Japan was obliged, in effect, at the point of a gun, to abandon over two centuries of 'self-imposed seclu-sion';[126] that, as she began thereafter to prosper in terms of the expansionist, imperialist *Machtpolitik* practised by the major powers at the time, she was presented at the end of the First World War with a drastic change in the international 'rules of the game' – a change based on Western precepts and insisted upon by those powers who continued to dominate the international economic order and who, as Britain's First Sea Lord was to acknowledge privately in 1934, had 'got most of the world already, or the best parts of it', and sought to 'prevent others taking it away'.[127]

Moreover, the Japanese were correct in concluding that the new inter-national morality did little to reduce racial discrimination and an implicit sense of superiority on the part of white powers (Japan was unable, for example, to get the principle of racial equality embodied in the Covenant of the League of Nations); that Western insistence upon an 'open door' for their own exports in the Far East did not preclude measures to close doors to Japanese exports elsewhere; and that the continued existence of areas such as the Panama and Suez Canals that were deemed in Washington and London to be vital to the national interest and dominated accordingly did not mean that Tokyo's right to similar perceptions and policies (above all, regarding Manchuria) would be acknowledged. Japan had ostensibly been granted the status of a 'civilized' country by the West, in terms of inter-national agreements, at the turn of the century. And Japanese themselves were ready to declare in their turn, for example when justifying the annexa-tion of Korea: 'The world can enjoy peace only when all countries reach the same level of civilization. It cannot permit such a thing as countries with low civilization.' But they, as well as Koreans, were to discover thereafter that in a white-ordered world, 'like Sysyphus, the less "civilized" were doomed to work toward an equality which an elastic standard of "civilization" put forever beyond their reach'.[128]

The new international order that was proclaimed after the Great War was symbolised, where the Far East was concerned, by the Washington Conference of 1921–22, which put an end to the alliance Japan had maintained with Britain since 1902. Here again, however, it soon became apparent that the principle of cooperation among the powers over China, which had lain at the heart of the Conference, would be ignored by American administrations in particular if their interests appeared to be better served by dealing with the Chinese on a bilateral basis. Japan's own direct action over China subsequently stood out for its aggressive and military features, but she was by no means alone in undermining any hope of an ordered framework of international relations in the area.[129] 'What united the military, the nationalist groups and the bulk of the intellectuals,' writes Professor Iriye concerning Japan in the 1930s, 'was the shared perception of the 1920s as a decade of futile attempts at peaceful expansion through international cooperation.'[130]

Even had the Washington Conference been followed by international collaboration over China, this would not have embraced the Soviet Union, despite the latter's potential significance as an East Asian power. But above all, it would not have entailed the treatment of China itself as a sovereign state of equal standing – as the Conference made clear by failing to put an end to the extraterritorial privileges enjoyed by foreigners in that country. The overthrow of the Manchu dynasty in 1911 had not led to the establishment of a strong and efficient central government, and even after the installation of Chiang Kai-shek's regime in Nanking in the late 1920s, large areas remained under the control of warlords, the Communists, and, indeed, a rival faction of the Kuomintang itself. It was thus not difficult for the assumption still to be made during the inter-war years that China's fate would be decided by others in the last resort; that she was a country more acted upon than acting in terms of international politics.

From a Chinese point of view (involving, in particular, those elements whose growing nationalism had been symbolised by the Fourth of May movement in 1919), the argument could be, and frequently was, stated the other way round: that is, that the absence of an effective central authority in the country, far from justifying the continued intervention of others, was itself fostered by outsiders who had a selfish interest in perpetuating the fragmentation of China's political structure. The Chinese were also correct in perceiving, alongside the territorial imperialism of the foreigner, his cultural imperialism to match, whether in the form of, say, the British demand, noted above, that all Chinese should imbibe the principles of

Western law, or the 'missions' proclaimed by Americans and Japanese to 'lead' China into a new age (whilst deriving profit from her in the process).[131]

Yet for all the hopes of, for example, Christian missionaries, the outsiders, despite their power, had in fact made little impression upon the lives of the vast majority of the Chinese people during the century before the Far Eastern war. Moreover, even where – in the ports above all – the foreigner was of major significance, he was often being obliged during the inter-war period to react to Chinese initiatives, not least to the boycotting of his goods. Even the triumphant Japanese army, extending its dominance from Manchuria into Northern China between 1933 and 1937, found the resistance of the people to its political schemes such that, before the Marco Polo Bridge incident provided the excuse for full-scale, punitive war, it was thinking of withdrawing from the area. In short, in so far as the 1941–45 conflict was to be, in one of its dimensions, a Japanese-American struggle over the control of China's destiny, it was to be a war of illusions. China's destiny lay in the hands of the Chinese people themselves. And if one of the contexts within which that war was to be fought was that of Japan's rise, since the 1860s, to the position of a major power on the international scene, then another, evident in retrospect at least, was the rapid transformation of China's standing, too, as was to be demonstrated in 1950, for example, by the decisive intervention of the People's Republic in the Korean war.

A further, and in terms of the 1941–45 war even more significant, international development was the emergence of the United States as a power of enormous magnitude, deeply involved in all aspects of international relations. As we have seen, even before Pearl Harbor this major change in the configuration of world politics had already been perceived by a good many contemporaries. The role of the United States during the First World War; her position as a major creditor state thereafter; the size, potential and reverberations of her economy; the significance of her naval power in relation to the pursuit of arms-limitation in the 1920s and '30s: these and other features had, for thirty years or more, been pointing in such a direction. Even the attitudes and policies associated with 'isolationism' between the wars often served to underline the potentially decisive role America could play if she had a mind to do so.

And yet in the Far East itself, the antecedents of the war of 1941 by no means provided a clear indication of increased involvement and expansion on the part of the United States in that area of the world. Despite the acquisition of the Philippines in 1898, and for all the aspirations expressed by missionaries and the small number of businessmen who saw in China, especially, a potential market of vast proportions, in reality both the American stake in the Far East and American concern over those regions remained very limited. Though politicians could surround with rhetoric the subject of the welfare of China in particular, there was no readiness to see the United States make sacrifices and become involved on the mainland of Asia in order to give substance to such professed sympathies. Even after Japan's barbaric attack on Chinese cities in 1937 had aroused great pity for the victims among the American public at large, American firms continued to supply Japan with essential sinews of war. American business in general had demonstrated little inclination to underwrite China's future, and, by comparison with its British, Dutch and Japanese counterparts, had little invested in the Far East as a whole. Even the Philippines, it was decided in 1934, would be given their independence only twelve years later.[132]

The United States was not an East Asian power, and, for all that an evangelist like Henry Stimson could declare the Far East to be 'our part of the world', roughly 7,000 nautical miles separated San Francisco from the U.S. Navy's advanced base in the Philippines. One of the consequences of this simple geographical fact was that in the strategic situation brought about by the Washington Conference, which in effect gave the Japanese predominance in the Western Pacific, the Navy's contingency plans for a war with Japan (based on a blockade of that country conducted from the Philippines) were unrealistic.[133] Equally unrealistic – and arguably more dangerous in its consequences – was the belief among Americans in general that their country's presence and policies in the Far East (and above all in China) were such as to set the Great Republic apart from other Western states in that context. Indeed, it was to take the Vietnam war to bring about any significant weakening of this assumption that the motives of the United States were so disinterested and its actions so enlightened that Asian nationalists who were stirring against the Europeans would nevertheless accept an American presence and gratefully look across the Pacific for guidance and inspiration. Such beliefs, derived as they were, of course, from nineteenth-century American convictions concerning the contrast between the nature of their own society and that of the corrupt communities of Europe, were facilitated by what Professor Fairbank has termed 'an accident of history: that we Americans could enjoy the East Asia treaty privileges, the fruits of European aggression, without the moral burden of ourselves committing aggression. It gave us a holier-than-thou attitude . . . that was built on self-deception and has lasted into our own day . . .'[134]

The United States did possess in the inter-war years the potential to become the dominant power in the Pacific Ocean. It could become an East Asian power, however, only by proxy: it would need an agent, a protégé in that part of the world; one that would not simply further American material interests there, but that by its acceptance of 'the American way of life' as its lodestar would bolster the convictions of Americans regarding the supreme and universally-applicable nature of their own societal values and organisation. China was cast for this role for the time being. When the Far Eastern war had been concluded, Japan would to some degree provide a replacement.

The United States was not an East Asian power, but Russia/the Soviet Union was, by virtue of its eastwards advance to the Pacific between the seventeenth and nineteenth centuries, culminating in 'unequal treaties' forced upon China that matched those being insisted upon by Western states. Neither defeat at Japan's hands in the 1904–5 war nor the accords with Japan that followed meant that the quest for further expansion in the East had been abandoned, especially as regards the acquisition of a warm-water port to the south of the partially ice-bound Vladivostok. Nor did Tsarist designs on both Outer Mongolia and Manchuria disappear once the Bolsheviks had come to power in 1917, notwithstanding the new regime's proclaimed sympathy for the cause of Chinese nationalism and its collaboration with the Kuomintang until 1927.[135] Thus, when the Chinese attempted to take over the Soviet-controlled Chinese Eastern Railway in 1929, they were put in their place by force of arms. And although, faced with Japan's drive into Manchuria in the early 1930s, Moscow sold the railway to Tokyo's puppet regime of Manchukuo, clashes between the Red Army and the Japanese on the borders of Manchuria, Korea, and the Maritime Provinces in 1938 and 1939 (battles in which the Soviet troops came off the better) underlined the lasting potential of the U.S.S.R. in the region. The importance that some factions in Tokyo attached to the Neutrality Pact of April 1941 between the two countries acknowledged as much.[136]

From that summer of 1941, however, Moscow's ability to exercise its influence in the Far East was obviously severely limited for the time being by the German onslaught from the west. In this indirect fashion, Germany itself was playing a significant part in Far Eastern international politics immediately before Pearl Harbor. Even earlier, however, and despite having been deprived of its colonies in the region after the First World War, Germany had been involved, commercially, militarily and, eventually, politically in East Asia. In particular, the decision in Berlin in 1937–38 (after a long struggle among rival factions there) to direct Nazi policies towards Japan, and away from China,[137] gave encouragement to those groups in Japanese military and political circles whose desire to align their country with Germany and against the democracies came to fruition in the Tripartite Pact of 1940. Thereafter, Tokyo maintained its freedom of manoeuvre (resisting, above all, Nazi promptings that Japan should attack the Soviet Union); nevertheless, Germany's victories of 1939–41 played a major part in bringing Japanese policy-makers to the conclusion that the time was propitious for launching a blow against the West.[138]

Those victories, as already noted, had rendered additionally vulnerable the colonial territories of France and the Netherlands in the Far East. In retrospect, indeed, and in the light of major developments within the European state system, it can be suggested that even before the Second World War such distant colonies had come to constitute liabilities for the metropolitan powers concerned.[139] A proposal that France should divest herself of Indochina had in fact been voiced in Paris in the early 1930s. (The thought of defending the colony against Japan, declared Admiral Raoul Castex, was 'a total illusion'.) Any such idea, however, was doomed to failure in the face of the constitutional creed that indissoluble links joined France to her overseas territories, and of a deeply-rooted lack of realism concerning the international position of the country, its large military establishment and glorious traditions merely a veneer on a body politic that was on the verge of disintegration.[140]

For the Netherlands, it is true, the great economic potential of the East Indies provided a more tangible reason for an overwhelming rejection of those few voices who over the years had argued that the colony should be given its freedom. (As the popular saying had it: 'Indië is de kurk waarop Nederland drijft': the Indies are the cork which keeps the Netherlands afloat.) Here again, however, one encounters a considerable lack of realism. The possession of the Indies, and of other, lesser colonies, was widely and erroneously believed to elevate the Netherlands well above the status of the small European state that she essentially was. At the same time, and in contrast to France, the very stability of Dutch society, together with some of its particular religious and political features, helped foster a sense of aloofness from the mêlée of international power politics. The country's escape from the 1914–18 war contributed to this same outlook. Even after the shock of the German invasion in 1940, Dutch policy-makers in exile were not simply having to adjust to the loss of their homeland, but were (slowly in some cases) having to adapt to an international environment that they had felt able almost to despise.[141]

Well before the crisis in the Far East reached its final stages, it had in any event become apparent that the position of both France and the Netherlands in the region depended to a large degree on that of Britain. Yet as a world power, Britain herself had been in decline since the last third of the nineteenth century, to the point where, as we have seen, her position had come to rest essentially on a series of bluffs. Between the outbreak of the war in Europe in 1939 and Japan's attack, it is true, the basis had been laid of a remarkable and saving partnership with the United States. But from the first that relationship was characterised by what David Reynolds has aptly termed 'competitive cooperation', and its competitive aspect found Britain already at a huge (though not total) disadvantage. In order to survive, in other words, she was being obliged to travel down a road towards a position that was to be acknowledged by a senior Foreign Office official during the final stages of the war: a position of such dependence on American aid that 'in order to preserve the good relations required we may well find ourselves forced to follow the United States in a line of policy with which we do not fundamentally agree'.[142]

Nowhere was the vulnerability of the British Empire and Commonwealth more acute by the 1930s than in the Far East. But earlier still, in 1902, the perceived need to conclude an alliance with Japan – an alliance subsequently revised to envisage even Japanese assistance in the defence of India – had in effect constituted an acknowledgement of the inadequacy of Britain's own strength in that part of the world. The revolutionary strategic implications for Britain of Japan's own expanding naval power – a potential enemy situated, for the first time, beyond Europe, and therefore not exposed to interdiction by the Royal Navy in waters nearer home – was not fundamentally altered by the slow construction of the Singapore naval base during the inter-war years.[143] Like the U.S. Navy's War Plan 'Orange' for trans-Pacific operations, the idea that the Royal Navy could rapidly despatch to Singapore a force of capital ships (even leaving aside the fragility of that particular weapon in the light of developments in naval aviation, to which Japan had devoted considerable attention)[144] sufficient to ensure the safety of Australia and New Zealand, let alone Malaya itself, had become a hollow one as the German and Italian threats mounted in the second half of the 1930s.

Only a few in Britain, even within official circles, were aware of the extent of the country's frailty east of Suez. ('The point that we are a much greater Asiatic Power than Japan,' pontificated a member of the Foreign Office in 1937, 'is one that might well be made to the Japanese when they become over-insistent on their claim to a leading role in Asiatic affairs.')[145] Yet in the field of commerce, too, the decline in the British performance in the Far East since the First World War had been so drastic* that a mission sent out from Whitehall to report on the subject in the early '30s forecast 'bankruptcy and disaster at home' were it to continue.[146] And there was a further respect, if a less measurable one, in which Britain's position was already shifting before the Far Eastern conflict: that is, in terms of her relations with Australia. For within that Dominion there was developing a greater sense of independence as a political entity and an inclination to pursue a national interest that by no means always coincided with that of the mother country.

* For example, whereas China's total volume of imports rose by 23 per cent between 1913 and 1931, Britain's contribution to this trade fell by one third in the same period. British exports to India fell from 1,175 million rupees in 1914 to 480 million in 1937, in which year the balance of trade between the two countries became favourable to India. Japan's share of all piece goods imported into British India rose from 18.4 to 47.3 per cent between 1928–9 and 1932–3, and in 1934 she displaced Britain as Australia's largest supplier of textiles.

Indeed, the very nature of Commonwealth relationships had become an issue of substance in Australia by the beginning of the Second World War, even though most British ministers and officials loftily failed to recognise that this was so. ('Mr Churchill has no conception of the British Dominions as separate entities,' reported Australia's Prime Minister, Menzies, to his Advisory War Council after returning from London in May 1941, '[and] the more the distance from the heart of the Empire, the less he thinks of it.') Strategic and command issues involving Australian forces in North Africa and Greece in 1940–41 were to exacerbate matters. And the suspicion that British protection against Japan (despite glib assurances to the contrary) might not be adequate was also troubling the Australian and New Zealand governments – though this did not mean that within Australia, particularly, there was a lessening of isolationist attitudes or a greater readiness to pay for the country's own defences.[147]

Britain's severely over-extended situation also had major implications for her imperial territories east of Suez. In that they were not at the time independent actors on the international scene, consideration of them can be left to the following chapter, in terms of the various societies involved. In passing, however, it is worth underlining the international issue that, as we have seen with reference to Subhas Chandra Bose, was already facing nationalists in dependent territories before the Far Eastern war broke out: that is, whether to further one's own quest for freedom by siding with the enemies of the imperial power. In India, for example, as already noted, the respective responses of Bose and the *Bombay Chronicle* were diametrically opposed to each other, with that of Nehru remaining more ambiguous than either. In Burma, Aung San and his companions had already decided to throw in their lot with Japan, whereas in Malaya it was certain that the Chinese population would be overwhelmingly hostile to the invader of their native land. In other colonial territories, too, inclinations already pointed in differing directions. In the East Indies, a Soekarno could welcome the Japanese, a Sjahrir had to reject them as militarist aggressors. In the Philippines, for all Quezon's rhetoric, there were those whose own close ties with fascist Spain made it unlikely they would resist Japan on grounds of political principle, and whose privileged position in society had traditionally been preserved by accommodation with the dominant power in the islands.[148]

There was also a further issue of an international kind for some, at least, in these dependent territories. The course of international politics during and since the First World War could be seen as raising questions of a general nature regarding both practical and moral precepts for one's own later behaviour. For example, both Nehru in India and Quezon in the Philippines, having seen Czechoslovakia swallowed up by Germany in 1938–39, drew the conclusion that for a small or even medium-sized state to build up its armed forces was merely to invite the painful attention of greater powers. As Nehru put it: 'Unless you arm to the same strength [as them], then your arms will be of no avail.' 'What is the use of an expensive and highly-trained army,' asked Quezon privately – devaluing as he did so all that General MacArthur had done in the 1930s to develop the forces of the Philippines – 'if a Great Power decides to conquer a small one?'[149] Meanwhile, Gandhi, of course, had long enunciated his own doctrine of non-violence, and in 1940 was applying it in his advice to the British as they faced the prospect of a German invasion. ('Assuming that God had endowed me with full powers,' he wrote, '. . . I would at once ask the English to lay down their arms, free all their vassals, take pride in being called "little Englanders", and defy all the totalitarians of the world to do their worst. Englishmen will die unresistingly and go down as heroes of non-violence . . . in this godly martyrdom.')[150] These notions, too, could be tested nearer home if the Japanese brought about a genuinely world-wide conflict.

*

During the seventy years or so before the war of 1941–45, the Far Eastern international scene witnessed considerable changes in the position and fortunes of individual powers. Viewed in retrospect, the relative decline of the European imperial states (above all Britain), and the swift growth of Japan's economic and military potential as a modern state; the underlying resilience of a China that was on the verge of major social and political change, and the lasting potential significance in the region of a Soviet Union whose super-power capabilities were soon to become apparent; those features of a growingly interdependent world that were pulling the United States towards a fuller involvement in international politics: all these were significant contexts within which the war was engendered and fought. At the same time, that increase in interdependence that was making impossible a genuinely isolationist position on the part of America was also heightening the tension surrounding those other aspects of international relations that cut across the policies and fortunes of individual states: population growth and the movement of peoples, for example, and the quest for markets and for raw materials. Even a state as extensive as the U.S.A. could feel threatened by relatively small numbers of immigrants from an 'alien' cultural background. Nor had the vast supply of industrial resources from within its own territory prevented that country from becoming dependent on Southeast Asia for its tin and crude rubber. (Indeed, stocks of rubber from that source were seen by the State Department's Economic Adviser as 'an index of American security'.)[151]

During the inter-war years, in particular, a considerable degree of disharmony and dislocation is evident in retrospect in several aspects of Far Eastern international affairs. There was a tendency, for example, for politicians and policy-makers to deal with the region in isolation, at a time when many of the issues involved were increasingly bound up with developments on a wider scale. There was a tendency, also, to treat economic aspects of international affairs as belonging to a separate and subordinate sphere, while in these economic terms there was no congruence between the political and territorial framework of activity on the one hand and the dynamics of Japan's rise, in particular, on the other. Britain's resources did not match her commitments in the region; American rhetoric about China, especially, did not match the limited nature of the country's tangible interests in the Far East, its reluctance to pay the kind of costs that would accompany any attempt to exert a major influence on developments there, or its distant geographical position. Misperceptions abounded,[152] in London, Paris and The Hague, as well as in Washington. The same was true in Tokyo, both as regards China and, ultimately, Japan's ability to secure from the Western powers by means of war a compromise peace that would give her autarky and security. (Total victory was not anticipated, and America's 'impregnable position, superior industrial power and abundant resources' were openly acknowledged during the decision-making process in Tokyo. The belief was, however, that, faced with war in Europe, and held back by a society unable to sustain hardship and sacrifice, Washington would come to terms with a Japan ready to fight to the death for the area it had seized.)[153]

A lack of alignment is also apparent when we turn to other aspects of Far Eastern affairs. Despite the fact that Japan had joined the Western powers at the end of the 1914–18 war in subscribing to those values and norms of international behaviour that were enshrined in the League of Nations Covenant, by the 1930s it was the sharp contrast between her political culture and those of the other major actors in the region that stood out, and that constituted a formidable obstacle to dialogue and agreement. There existed also a set of conflicting assumptions and perceptions among the states involved regarding the phenomenon that was known as 'imperialism'. To most Japanese, for example, there was a clear distinction between the predatory imperial presence of the Western powers in the region and their own country's essentially defensive acquisition of certain neighbouring Asian territories.[154]* Likewise, to most Americans imperialism was essentially an activity of the Europeans, in no way to be placed in the same

* Japan's colonialism did clearly differ (in all but Micronesia) from that of the West in several respects: for example, in the contiguity of metropolitan and colonial territories; in the element of the direct defence of the former; and in the racial and cultural similarities between ruler and ruled. Financial (as distinct from other economic) motives were not prominent; on the other hand the fostering of industrialisation in Korea, especially, was not matched in any

category as the expansion of the United States across the North American continent or into Hawaii and the Philippines.

Meanwhile the pre-eminent powers at the Washington Conference of 1921–22, the United States and Britain, both of which aspired to prevent any violent or radical change in the existing Far Eastern international order, had nevertheless accepted a set of agreements that gave Japan, desirous and potentially capable of overturning the *status quo*, an overwhelming strategic advantage in the region.* Yet another lack of alignment is evident in this connection. In retrospect (for all that the one was a waning, the other a burgeoning, power), Britain and the United States possessed during the inter-war years an underlying community of interests where Far Eastern affairs were concerned, and especially vis-à-vis Japan. Yet their cooperation was minimal, disapproval and suspicion (and in some quarters a sense of rivalry) on the American side being matched by exasperation and distrust in the other direction.†

Western colonial territory. Until the 1920s, some Japanese colonial administrators (like Goto Shimpei in Taiwan and then the Kwantung Peninsula) sought to emulate Western, and particularly British, imperial models; yet as Marius Jansen sees it, in Japan itself imperialism 'probably . . . never became a very important part of the national consciousness. There were no Japanese Kiplings, there was little mystique about Japanese overlordship, and relatively little national self-congratulation.' Ironically, however, it was in the 1930s, when new emphasis was placed on the contrast between predatory Western imperialism and Japan's defensively-inspired rule over fellow-Asians, that racist notions of Japanese superiority over Chinese and Koreans also became more pronounced still, as did the drive to weld the empire into a single economic unit.

Under Japanese rule (which was administered by a vast number of officials in comparison to Western colonial regimes), elementary education was extended and the standard of health much improved in Korea, Taiwan and Karafuto (South Sakhalin). But the educational effort was aimed at the production of subordinates only, and the idea of developing the capacity for eventual self-government was absent. In Taiwan, the Chinese population, after an initial resistance, became essentially compliant subjects. In Korea, on the other hand, the spread of education only served to foster an already-strong sense of national identity and resentment against Japanese control. When this resentment burst into the open in 1919 especially, it was brutally punished by the Japanese Army, which played a prominent imperial role generally. See Myers and Peattie (ed.), *The Japanese Colonial Empire*; also Cumings, *The Origins of the Korean War*, 12.

* The world-wide nature of Britain's naval commitments, and the two-ocean requirements of the U.S. Navy contributed to this situation, of course, as did the aversion of the British and American publics to expenditure on armaments. In terms of the Washington agreement, Japan's advantage sprang from the freezing of the fortification of certain potential or existing naval bases, as well as the extent of the capital-ship tonnage she was allotted. In 1935–6, Japan's withdrawal from the London Naval Conference, coming as it did in a period that witnessed the Abyssinian and Rhineland crises, was of grim significance for Britain especially.

† For a recent survey of the relevant patterns in Anglo-American relations since the end of the nineteenth century, see D. C. Watt, *Succeeding John Bull: America in Britain's Place, 1900–1975* (Cambridge, 1984). For a foreshadowing during the First World War of one line of American thinking that was to be prominent during the Second, see e.g. Woodrow Wilson to Colonel House in July 1917: 'England and France have not the same view with regard to peace that we have by any means. When the war is over we can force them to our way of thinking, because by that time they will, among other things, be financially in our hands.' Quoted in ibid, 32.

The particular grounds for this strained aspect of transatlantic relations have already been partially touched upon in connection with American attitudes towards European empires and American self-images regarding the Far East. In the inter-war period, however, Anglo-American difficulties tended to be exacerbated – during the Far Eastern crisis of 1931–33, for example[155] – by the perceived need, in an age of League Covenants and Kellogg Pacts, to present one's policies to one's own public, especially, as being in accord with certain enlightened standards of international behaviour. The pragmatic dictates of self-interest that are embedded in the very nature of international politics, and that British and American governments alike responded to over Far Eastern affairs, made communication and comprehension between the two doubly difficult at a time when a failure to be seen to be behaving in a more normative manner could incur both international and domestic criticism.

That is not to say, however, that all politicians and officials in Washington and London were themselves privately dismissive of the requirements of some kind of internationally-recognised standards of behaviour, or were confident in following simply the dictates of immediate self-interest. There were, it is true, those who thought and argued in such a fashion. What stands out in retrospect, however, is the degree of uncertainty and confusion surrounding the conduct of international relations at the time. Behind the forceful pronouncements of the American Secretary of State, Henry Stimson, during the 1931–33 crisis, for example, there lay, as he confided to his diary, 'tumultuous changes in my mind and attitude':

> 'Had the theory of offensive defense gone by the board?' he had asked his officials. 'Did the Kellogg Briand pact [to outlaw war] so change human nature that only the defense of one's actual territory was essential?' . . . He 'had had to unlearn a great deal of what was axiomatic in [his] youth, and did not have very clear-cut convictions as to the new order.'[156]

Or one could cite, from the same period, Stanley Baldwin, former Conservative Prime Minister in Britain and subsequently a leading member of its National Government: inclined towards a policy of disarmament; aware, nonetheless, of the possibility of armed conflict breaking out if, over Manchuria, one took action against Japan under the Covenant of the League of Nations; yet ready to acknowledge in private that the 'old diplomacy' of alliances and armaments had brought about the 1914–18 war. It was, he observed to a friend, 'a terrible dilemma'.[157] Even those like Lord Cecil, whose support for the new international morality as embodied in the League was apparently unqualified, could find themselves obliged to prevaricate or make exceptions when brought to the point where only war itself seemed capable of halting the slide into international anarchy.[158]

Many of the underlying questions of the time, then, concerned the causes of armed conflict among states and, in consequence, both the essential nature of man and the characteristics of various kinds of social and political organisation.[159] Some, making their appearance especially in the aftermath of the financial and commercial crash of 1929–31, focused upon the international economic scene. Should and could the international community legislate against economic, as well as armed, aggression, for example? (In 1931, the United States declined a League invitation to join a committee to study the issue.)[160] Was there, as some in Whitehall and Washington were concluding in 1940–41, a need to find an entirely new basis for the international economic order altogether?[161]

Aspirations, issues and dilemmas of this kind concerning the capacity of mankind to achieve a harmonious existence on an international scale were particularly prominent in the Western – and especially Anglo-Saxon – democracies. The shock of the 1914–18 war and the vital need to avoid a repetition preocupied people in the West above all, whilst the assumptions and principles that appeared to point the way to salvation were those of Western liberalism.[162] The uncertainties and arguments involved, however, were not exclusive to politicians and publics in Europe and the United States. The conflicting beliefs and precepts surrounding, for example, French decisions over the quest for security in the early 1930s[163] were paralleled in Tokyo over the question of whether or not to accept the London Naval Agreement of 1930, and over the country's entire diplomatic stance in the preceding decade.[164] When the Kwantung Army provided its own, unambiguous answer to the problems of achieving Japan's well-being by resorting to force in Manchuria, the well-nigh universal acclaim that arose from the public would seem to have contained an element of relief similar to that which was to be present in December 1941: at last, a clear and familiar path ahead had been indicated.

In other ways, too, as we have seen above, notions of a potentially confusing kind were coming to surround the international system (not that such a term was current at this time), its nature and its dynamics. Might not races rather than states, for example, constitute the essential units involved? How 'civilised' did a newcomer to the West's international order have to become before being accorded genuine, and not simply formal, equality of status? If the seizure of colonial territories and the exercise of *force majeure* generally was now declared by the dominant Western powers to be a transgression against international society, why did those powers continue to preserve and profit by the acquisitions of their misguided past? (This last question was to be pressed after the

1941–45 conflict had been concluded by the Indian judge at the Tokyo War Crimes trial.)[165]

The degree to which beliefs involving the fundamental properties and precepts of international relations were in a volatile state in the post-1918 period generally becomes all the clearer if one looks ahead to the years after the Second World War: when, for example, a British Labour Government, far from proclaiming again that armaments merely engendered war, was to embrace the theory of deterrence and preside over the country's acquisition of nuclear weapons; when the United States, rather than shunning alliances as entanglements of a kind that had brought about the disaster of 1914–18, was eagerly to construct a chain of such undertakings around the world; when the Nehru who (as we have seen) had concluded that the possession of a military capability on the part of small or medium powers was futile and potentially disastrous was to direct the use of free India's army against Pakistan, Goa, and eventually China; and when large numbers of Japanese, incidentally, were to accept the proposition that their country should eschew such a capacity for the employment of armed force.

An analysis of the impact of the war of 1941–45, then, must take account of the preceding confusion surrounding international relations as a whole. It must also set the war in the context of what constituted a major cause of such confusion: that is, the speed and extent of the changes that were engulfing the international system itself. For students in the 1980s, it should not be difficult to appreciate such a context or the accompanying uncertainties, living as they do in a period when the apparently settled configurations, dynamics and 'rules of the game' that emerged in the 1950s[166] have been overtaken by an infinitely more complex and confusing set of circumstances.[167] In the comparatively short period between the emergence of Japan, Russia and the United States onto the Far Eastern international scene in the latter part of the nineteenth century and the coming of the 1941 war, the old European balance of power, as we have seen, had been destroyed by the rise of Germany, and the European state system itself was in the process of being absorbed into one of world-wide proportions, dominated (as was to begin to be apparent around 1943) by two 'super-powers', the Soviet Union and the United States.

As James Joll has put it, 'whichever way you looked at international relations before 1914' – as a system to be managed diplomatically; as a society requiring the application of liberal principles to bring it to peace and perfection; or as the corrupted product of capitalism, awaiting the socialist revolution – 'the First World War and its consequences forced a radical change of view and made it increasingly hard to apply old categories, both practically and theoretically, however much people went on trying to adapt their old ideas to new experiences'.[168] 'I have lived seventy-eight years without hearing of bloody places like Cambodia.' Churchill's outburst in 1953 was to reflect how exasperating the continuing need for adjustment could be.[169] Economically as well as strategically, states were being bound closer together in a complex network of inter-relationships that (as a result of the seemingly inexorable swoops of the trade cycle) helped heighten the demands of citizens for their government to protect their well-being, and at the same time greatly reduced the ability of most governments to comply. Rapid developments in the fields of science and technology were tending to exacerbate this dilemma, while also, through their application to the instruments of war, making it harder for those same governments to afford their peoples a high level of protection of a military kind. ('The bomber will always get through,' warned Baldwin.) In short, when contemporaries sought to establish, in the shape of the League of Nations, a set of rules for international behaviour, they were in effect erecting a tall and stately edifice on ground that was rapidly shifting beneath themselves and their construction alike as a consequence of what Robert Gilpin has termed 'systems change' – 'a major change in the character of the international system itself'. In such conditions, the need for normative behaviour on the part of the entire international community could be seen as all the more pressing; but the adoption by individual states of pragmatic actions, rather – a series of *ad hoc* adjustments in an attempt to stay upright as the fissures opened up on every side – was all the more likely.

Meanwhile, stimulated partly by the liberal principles of the West itself, partly by the repercussions of the Russian Revolution, nationalist and socialist movements added their own challenges to the old order beyond Europe: as France's Colonial Minister saw it in 1932, 'the restless surf in the sea of progress, the counter-offensive of native energy, stirred up by European dynamism, a peril ... to be feared'.[170] In retrospect, it is clear that the war of 1941–45 fell within a period of extraordinarily rapid change in this respect also. The dull roar that Albert Sarrault was hearing in the inter-war years (in 1927, for example, a Congress of Oppressed Nationalities in Brussels set up a League Against Imperialism) was to become within thirty years a flood of new states: states which not only became members of the United Nations Organisation, but profoundly changed the preoccupations and tenor of that body's proceedings. In the late 1920s, Asiatic and other non-European delegates to the League of Nations were warning their colleagues of the dangers of the Eurocentrism that predominated at Geneva.[171] In 1960, it was to be the U.N. Declaration on the Granting of Independence to Colonial Peoples that reflected the spirit of the times.[172]

By the 1970s, the rejection of many of those Western values and norms on which the U.N., like the League, had been based had become sufficiently widespread and emphatic to give a new urgency to a problem that had also been embedded in Japanese-Western relations before Pearl Harbor: the problem of finding a basis for coexistence among interdependent states in a multicultural world.[173]

Notes

1 See e.g. H. L. Stimson and M. Bundy, *On Active Service in Peace and War* (New York, 1948), 221. Also C. Thorne, 'Viscount Cecil, the Government and the Far Eastern Crisis of 1931', *Historical Journal*, vol. 14 No. 4, 1971, and C. Thorne, *The Limits of Foreign Policy: the West, the League and the Far Eastern Crisis of 1931–1933* (London and New York, 1972; hereafter *Limits*), cap. 12.
2 A copy of the full proceedings and records of the IMTFE is kept in the Imperial War Museum, London. For an edited version, see F. J. and S. Z. Pritchard, *The Tokyo War Crimes Trial* (New York, 1981).
3 H. D. Hall, *North American Supply* (London, 1955), 206.
4 See in general A. W. DePorte, *Europe between the Superpowers* (New Haven, 1979).
5 This episode provides a good example of the complexities and inter-factional wranglings lying behind a phrase such as 'Japan demanded' in this period. See I. Hata, 'The Army's Move into Northern Indochina', in J. W. Morley (ed.), *The Fateful Choice: Japan's Advance into Southeast Asia, 1939–1941* (New York, 1980).
6 See S. Nagaoka, 'The Drive into Southern Indochina and Thailand', in ibid.
7 S. Nagaoka, 'Economic Demands on the Dutch East Indies', in ibid.
8 See C. Hosoya, 'The Japanese-Soviet Neutrality Pact', in ibid.
9 See T. Nakamura, 'Japan's Economic Thrust into North China, 1933–1938', in A. Iriye (ed.), *The Chinese and the Japanese* (Princeton, 1980); T. R. Havens, *Valley of Darkness: The Japanese People and World War Two* (New York, 1978), 34ff., 135; J. Morley (ed.), *The China Quagmire: Japan's Expansion on the Asian Continent, 1933–1941* (New York, 1983), passim; C. A. Johnson, *Peasant Nationalism and Communist Power* (Stanford, 1963), e.g. 39.
10 See Iriye, *Power and Culture*, 28. Roosevelt himself had not intended that so drastic a measure be taken, but was presented with a fait accompli by the actions of certain Washington officials. See Dallek, op, cit., 274–5.
11 See Morley, op, cit.: R. J. Butow, *Tojo and the Coming of War* (Princeton, 1961); D. Borg and S. Okamoto, *Pearl Harbor as History* (New York, 1973); N. Ike (ed.), *Japan's Decision for War* (Stanford, 1967); Martin, op. cit.
12 C. Hosoya, 'Britain and the United States in Japan's View of the International System', in I. Nish (ed.), *Anglo-Japanese Alienation, 1919–1952* (Cambridge, 1982).
13 J. W. Chapman, *The Price of Admiralty: the War Diary of the German Naval Attaché in Japan, 1939–1943, Vol. 1* (Ripe, 1982), xii.
14 See in general R. F. Holland, *Britain and the Commonwealth Alliance, 1918–1939* (London, 1981); also e.g. D. M. Horner, *High Command: Australia and Allied Strategy, 1939–1945* (Sydney, 1982), caps. 1 and 2. For a contemporary comment on the shifting relationships between Britain and increasingly assertive Dominions, see *Asia*, July 1940.
15 Thorne, *Limits*, 247
16 Thorne, *Allies*, 71.
17 Quoted in D. Reynolds, *The Creation of the Anglo-American Alliance, 1937–41* (London, 1981), 264.

18 See Thorne, *Allies*, 110–11.
19 See Dallek, op. cit., cap. 11.
20 See Reynolds, op. cit., 217–20.
21 Ibid, 230ff.
22 Ike, op, cit., 77ff.; 208ff.
23 On Britain, see e.g. I. McLaine, *Ministry of Morale: Home Front Morale and the Ministry of Information in World War II* (London, 1979), 158.
24 See Cohen, 'The Role of Interest Groups', in Borg and Okamoto, op. cit., 447–9.
25 Alexander report, April 1940, Hornbeck Papers, box 22.
26 C. Brown, *Suez to Singapore* (New York, 1943), e.g. 126, 157.
27 Ride, op. cit., 2.
28 Eggleston Papers, MS. 27, series 9/395.
29 Morris, op. cit., 10.
30 C. Haselhurst, *Menzies Observed* (Sydney, 1979), 181; and e.g. Horner, *High Command*, 31ff.
31 See Thorne, *Allies*, 82–3; and J. Thompson in Borg and Okamoto, op. cit., 102.
32 Thorne, *Allies*, 4.
33 Prange, op. cit., 35 and passim. And see Manchester, op. cit., 185–6.
34 L. Allen, *Singapore, 1941–1942* (London, 1977), 63–4.
35 See S. W. Roskill, *The War at Sea, Vol. 1* (London, 1954); Marder, op. cit., cap. VIII; P. Haggie, *Britannia at Bay* (Oxford, 1981), cap. VIII.
36 A. E. Kersten (ed.), *Het Dagbook van dr. G.C.H. Hart* (The Hague, 1976), entry for 21 Feb. 1941.
37 R. J. Butow, *John Doe Associates: Backdoor Diplomacy for Peace, 1941* (Stanford, 1974).
38 E. O. Reischauer, *The Japanese* (Cambridge, Mass., 1978), 411. And see, e.g. G. R. Storry, *The Double Patriots* (London, 1957).
39 S. Ienaga, *Japan's Last War* (Oxford, 1979), 57, 154, 156ff.; R. H. Myers and M. R. Peattie (ed.), *The Japanese Colonial Empire, 1895–1945* (Princeton, 1984), 119ff. and passim.
40 See e.g. Ienaga, 57; Havens, 104; Iriye (ed.), *Chinese and Japanese*.
41 See Iriye, 'The Hsin-min Hui', in Iriye (ed.), *Chinese and Japanese*.
42 See J. H. Boyle, *The Sino-Japanese War, 1937–1945* (Stanford, 1972); S. H. Marsh, 'Chou Fo-hai' in Iriye, *Chinese and Japanese*; Johnson, *Peasant Nationalism*, 41 ff.
43 See B. M. Gordon, *Collaboration in France in the Second World War* (Ithica, 1980), 18–19, and e.g. E. Weber, *Action Française* (Stanford, 1962).
44 Lloyd Eastman, 'Facets of an Ambivalent Relationship', in Iriye, *Chinese and Japanese*, 298–303. And see e.g. W. Hinton, *Fanshen. A Documentary of Revolution in a Chinese Village* (New York, 1968), 73ff.
45 B. Cumings, *The Origins of the Korean War: Liberation and the Emergence of Separate Regimes, 1945–1947* (Princeton, 1981), 9, 22, 28, 30ff., and Cumings, 'The Legacy of Colonialism in Korea', in Myers and Peattie, op. cit.
46 A. F. Manning, 'The Position of the Dutch Government in London up to 1942', *Journal of Contemporary History*, vol. 13 (1978); Sjahrir, op. cit., 217; J. M. van der Kroef, *The Dialectic of Colonial Indonesian History* (Amsterdam, 1963), 31–3. For details of Dutch policy in 1940–41, see A. F. Manning and A. E. Kerston (ed.), *Documenten Betreffende de Buitenlandse Politiek van Nederland, 1919–1945, periode C, 1940–1945, Vols. I–III* (The Hague, 1976–80).
47 J. Nehru, *Toward Freedom* (New York, 1942), 345ff., 359, 369.
48 Nehru to Gandhi, 24 Jan. and 4 Feb., 1940, Nehru Papers, vol. 26.
49 Sjahrir, 219. Also interviews with Dr Anak Agung Gde Agung.
50 W. J. Duiker, *The Rise of Nationalism in Vietnam, 1900–1941* (Ithaca, 1976), 257ff., 275.
51 See, e.g. Ike, op. cit., 139ff., 208ff., and Iriye, *Power and Culture*, cap. 1.
52 E.g., Bruce, Monthly War Files, entries for 18 July 1940 and 28 Jan. 1941, Bruce Papers.
53 See D. M. Horner, *Crisis of Command: Australian Generalship and the Japanese Threat, 1941–1943* (Canberra, 1978), 17ff., and Horner, *High Command*, caps. 1 and 2.
54 *The Standard* (Wellington), 4 Dec. 1941.
55 See e.g. Cohen, *The Chinese Connection*, 242; Dallek, op. cit., 301ff.

56 *L'Union*, 3 May 1941.
57 Roosevelt to Sayre, 31 Dec. 1941, Sayre Papers, box 7.
58 E.g. Ickes diary, 26 April, 10 May, 22 June, 30 Nov. 1941; J.M. Blum, *Roosevelt and Morgenthau* (Boston, 1970), 391ff., 418. It seems that although Morgenthau endorsed the plan put forward by one of his subordinates, Harry Dexter White, whereby a *modus vivendi* between Japan and the U.S. could be attained, he had not thought through its wider implications.
59 G. May, *China Scapegoat: the Diplomatic Ordeal of John Carter Vincent* (Washington D.C., 1979), 62.
60 *Bombay Chronicle*, 2 and 16 Sept. 1939; also 4 and 6 Dec. 1941.
61 See B. Dahm, *Soekarno and the Struggle for Indonesian Independence* (Ithica, 1969), 122–4, 212–16. On Bose, see the works cited above, and H. Toye, *The Springing Tiger: a Study of a Revolution* (London, 1959).
62 *L'Humanité Clandestine, 1939–1944* (Paris, 1975): edition of December 1940.
63 See Thorne, *Allies*, 58–9; M. Perham, *Colonial Sequence, 1930–1949* (London, 1967), 189; P. S. Gupta, *Imperialism and the British Labour Movement, 1914–1964* (London, 1975); J. M. Lee and M. Petter, *The Colonial Office, War and Development Policy* (London, 1982).
64 See e.g. McLaine, op. cit., 105; *International Affairs*, articles in issues of e.g. June 1940 and Sept. 1941; Bruce to Halifax, 21 July 1940, Monthly War Files, Bruce Papers.
65 For one example of emphasis in this period on the U.S.S.R.'s significance for the Far East, see F. Steinberg, 'Russia and Asia's Future', in *Asia*, February 1940. On the insignificant part played by such considerations in the shaping of British Far Eastern policy, see P. Lowe, 'The Soviet Union in Britain's Far Eastern Policy, 1941', *International Studies* (London School of Economics), 1981, 1.
66 See Thorne, *Allies*, and Reynolds, op. cit., passim.
67 Thorne, *Allies*, 104.
68 *New York Times*, 20 April 1941; Needham Papers, section 14.
69 *Vérité*, 5 Sept. 1941. And see, e.g. *Le Temps*, 15 June 1940.
70 Thorne, *Allies*, 71–2; and e.g. Clunies Ross paper, 'Australia and the United States: the Problems of Establishing Closer Relations', 22 Jan. 1940, Australian-American Relations file, Bruce Papers.
71 A. E. Kersten, 'The Dutch and the American Anti-Colonialist Tide, 1942–1945', in R. Jeffreys-Jones (ed.), *Eagle Against Empire: American Opposition to European Imperialism, 1914–1982* (Aix-en-Provence, 1983).
72 Clapper to Taylor, 14 Jan. 1941, Clapper Papers, box 9. And see Reynolds, op. cit., 252–4.
73 Chevalier to Hornbeck, 8 Dec. 1941, Hornbeck Papers, box 6.
74 See J. Neidpath, *The Singapore Naval Base and the Defence of Britain's Eastern Empire, 1919–1941* (Oxford, 1981).
75 See e.g. S. W. Roskill, *Naval Policy Between the Wars, Vol. 1* (London, 1968), and S. W. Roskill, *Hankey, Man of Secrets, Vol. III* (London, 1974).
76 Thorne, *Allies*, 37; K. Sansom, *Sir George Sansom and Japan: A Memoir* (Tallahassee, 1972), 116; C. Hosoya, 'George Sansom: Diplomat and Historian', *Hitotsubashi Journal of Law and Politics*, vol. 8, March, 1979.
77 See e.g. on the differences between President Hoover and his Secretary of State, Stimson, during the 1931–33 crisis, Thorne, *Limits*, and on the complex and contending currents regarding Germany's Far Eastern policies in the 1930s, J. P. Fox, *Germany and the Far Eastern Crisis of 1931–1938* (Oxford, 1982).
78 See A. Iriye, *Pacific Estrangement* (Cambridge, Mass., 1972).
79 Ibid, 18ff.; Peattie, 'The Nan'yo: Japan in the South Pacific, 1885–1945', in Myers and Peattie, op. cit.; and e.g. A. K. Weinberg, *Manifest Destiny* (Chicago, 1963), 275.
80 Thorne, *Limits*, 237.
81 See J. Crowley, *Japan's Quest for Autonomy* (Princeton, 1966); Thorne, *Limits* cap. 11; K. Miwa, 'Japanese Policies and Concepts for a Regional Order in Asia, 1938–1940', Institute of International Relations research paper, Sophia University, Tokyo, 1983.

82 See H. Carrère d'Encausse and S. Schram, *Le Marxism et l'Asie, 1853–1964* (Paris, 1965), passim.
83 See e.g. Iriye, *Pacific Estrangement*, 148.
84 See Thorne, *Limits*, 399–402.
85 See e.g. Iriye, *Pacific Estrangement*, caps. VI and VIII; Weinberg, op. cit., 234ff., 259–60.
86 See e.g. Iriye, *Pacific Estrangement*, cap. VII; M. Hunt, *Frontier Defense and the Open Door* (New Haven, 1973); B. Hashikawa, 'Japanese Perspectives on Asia', in Iriye (ed.), *Chinese and Japanese*.
87 Dahm, op. cit., 68.
88 Sjahrir, op cit., 186, 209; Thorne, *Limits*, 268.
89 See e.g. the comments on the notion of 'Asiatic society' of Dr R. Iyer in his editor's introduction to *The Glass Curtain Between Asia and Europe* (London, 1965). Also on this subject in general, e.g. M. Banton, *The Idea of Race* (London, 1977); and, in the context of Western-Chinese relations, R. Dawson, *The Chinese Chameleon* (London, 1967), 90ff.
90 Maze to Little, 12 July 1939, Maze Papers, Private Correspondence.
91 On this vast subject, see e.g. J. Ch'en, *China and the West* (London, 1979); R. Murphy, *The Outsiders: the Western Experience in India and China* (Ann Arbor, 1977); d'Encausse and Schram, op. cit.; P. A. Cohen, *Discovering History in China* (New York, 1984); D. W. Treadgold, *The West in Russia and China, Vols. 1 and 2* (Cambridge, 1973); E. W. Blyden, *Christianity, Islam and the Negro Race* (first published 1887; Edinburgh 1967); E. W. Said, *Orientalism* (London, 1978) (though cf. B. Lewis 'The Question of Orientalism', *New York Review of Books*, 24 June 1982); A. B. Bozeman, *Politics and Culture in International History* (Princeton, 1960). J. Needham, *Within the Four Seas* (London, 1969); V. G. Kiernon, *The Lords of Human Kind* (London, 1969); O. Mannoni, *Prospero and Caliban: the Psychology of Colonization* (New York, 1964); G. W. Gong, *The Standard of 'Civilization' in International Society* (Oxford, 1984).
92 M. F. A. Montagu, *Man's Most Dangerous Myth: the Fallacy of Race* (New York, 1974), 3; first published 1942.
93 *Documents on British Foreign Policy, 1919–1939, Second Series, Vol. VIII* (London, 1960), No. 12.
94 See e.g. C. A. Ronan, *The Shorter Science and Civilization in China, Vol. 1* (Cambridge, 1978).
95 W. R. Louis, *British Strategy in the Far East, 1919–1939* (Oxford, 1971), 233–4.
96 See e.g. M. Howard, 'Empire, Race and War in Pre-1914 Britain', in H. Lloyd Jones et al. (ed.), *History and Imagination* (London, 1981); van der Kroef, op. cit.; E. J. M. Schmutzer, *Dutch Colonial Policy and the Search for Identity in Indonesia, 1920–1931* (Leiden, 1977).
97 See e.g. R. F. Weston, *Racism in U.S. Imperialism* (Columbia, South Carolina, 1972), and R. Drinnon, *Facing West: the Metaphysics of Indian-Hating and Empire-Building* (New York, 1980).
98 See e.g. Thorne, *Limits*, 44–7, 55–7. Of course, there were a good many Americans who had little interest in, or actively opposed, the country's possession of the Philippines, just as the anti-colonial movement in Britain had been making itself felt for some time. See e.g. A. P. Thornton, *The Imperial Idea and Its Enemies* (London, 1966).
99 P. Valéry, 'Le Yalou', as discussed in J. Cruickshank, *Variations on Catastrophe: Some French Responses to the Great War* (Oxford, 1982).
100 See e.g. R. Rolland, *Inde Journal, 1915–1943* (Paris, 1960). And, on the European situation in general, e.g. O. Spengler, *The Decline of the West: Form and Actuality* (trans. C. Atkinson; London, 1926); L. Mumford, *Technics and Civilization* (London, 1946); S. Giner, *Mass Society* (London, 1976); S. N. Hay, *Asian Ideas of East and West: Tagore and His Critics in Japan, China, and India* (Cambridge, Mass., 1970), cap. 4.
101 C. H. Pearson, *National Life and Character* (London, 1894), 137.
102 J. Crowley (ed.), *Modern East Asia: Essays in Interpretation* (New York, 1970), 133.
103 See C. Thorne, *Racial Aspects of the Far Eastern War of 1941–1945* (London, 1982), 339.
104 H. Massis, *Défence de l'Occident* (Paris, 1927), e.g. 14–15, 69.
105 V. I. Lenin, 'Better Fewer, But Better' (1923), *Collected Works, Vol. 33* (Moscow 1965).

106 H.M. Hyndman, *The Awakening of Asia* (London, 1919), vii–viii, 107, 143, 155, 197–8, 278, 282–3.
107 Quoted in B. A. Lee, *Britain and the Sino-Japanese War, 1937–1939* (Stanford, 1973), 94.
108 R. Tagore, *Nationalism* (London, 1917); Hay, *Asian Ideas*, cap. 2 and 319 ff.
109 Dahm, op. cit., 62–3, 69; Bose, *Testament*, v–vi.
110 Sjahrir, entry for 19 Aug. 1937; also entries for, e.g. 28 June and 16 Nov. 1936, 28 Oct. 1937.
111 See, e.g. Ch'en, op. cit., 70, 89, 278ff; Hay, *Asian Ideas*, cap. 1.
112 See Iriye, *Pacific Estrangement*, 98; B. N. Pandey, *The Break-Up of British India* (London, 1969), 68; K. M. Panikkar, *Asia and Western Dominance* (London, 1953); K. C. Chen, *Vietnam and China, 1938–1945* (Princeton, 1969), 15.
113 See M. B. Jansen, *The Japanese and Sun-Yat-sen* (Cambridge, Mass., 1954). On a similar phase among Vietnamese nationalists, see Duiker, op. cit., 38ff.
114 See d'Encausse and Schram, op. cit., 41ff.
115 Ibid, 83
116 E.g., Chiang Kai-shek to Gandhi, 21 Nov. 1939; Mme Chiang to Nehru, 10 Sept. 1940 and 28 Aug. 1941, Nehru Papers, vol. 13.
117 Nehru to Tagore, 19 Aug. 1939, ibid, vol. 90.
118 See P. J. Garvey (ed.), *Philosophy and Opinions of Marcus Garvey* (New York, 1967), and E. O. Cronon, *Black Moses: the Story of Marcus Garvey and the Universal Negro Improvement Association* (Madison, 1969).
119 See, e.g. Reischauer, op. cit.; R. Storry, 'Changing Japanese Attitudes to the West', in Iyer, op. cit.; M. B. Jansen (ed.), *Changing Japanese Attitudes Toward Modernization* (Princeton, 1965); W. G. Beasley, 'Japan and the West in the Mid-Nineteenth Century', *Proceedings of the British Academy, Vol. LV* (London, 1971).
120 Quoted in Crowley, *Modern East Asia*, 114.
121 Jansen, *Changing Japanese Attitudes*, 243ff., 441.
122 See, e.g. Storry, *Double Patriots*; J. C. Lebra (ed.), *Japan's Greater East Asia Coprosperity Sphere in World War II: Selected Readings and Documents* (Kuala Lumpur, 1975; hereafter, Lebra, *JGEACS*), x–xi; J. Crowley, 'A New Deal for Japan and Asia: One Road to Pearl Harbor', in Crowley, *Modern East Asia*.
123 For further exploration of the American-Japanese-Chinese aspects of the subject, see Iriye, *Across The Pacific*.
124 M. Maruyama, *Thought and Behaviour in Modern Japanese Politics* (London, 1963), 138–40.
125 G. M. Berger (ed. and trans.), *Kenkenroku: A Diplomatic Record of the Sino-Japanese War, 1894–95* (Tokyo, 1982), 28.
126 Reischauer, 68.
127 Thorne, *Limits*, 419 and 48.
128 Gong, *The Standard of 'Civilisation'*, 63; Myers and Peattie, op. cit., 77. For personal recollections of Japanese resentment over such matters, see G. C. Allen, *Appointment in Japan* (London, 1983), 55–6, 180.
129 See A. Iriye, *After Imperialism: The Search for a New Order in the Far East, 1921–1931* (Cambridge, Mass., 1965), 87, 300–3 and passim.
130 J. W. Morley (ed.), *Dilemmas of Growth in Inter-War Japan* (Princeton, 1972), 107.
131 See Gong, op. cit., 146ff.
132 See in general, e.g. the relevant essays in W.I. Cohen (ed.), *New Frontiers in American-East Asian Relations* (New York, 1983); on the U.S. and China in general, W. I. Cohen, *America's Response to China* (New York, 1971), and on the 1930s in particular, D. Borg, *The United States and the Far Eastern Crisis of 1933–1938* (Cambridge, Mass., 1964). Also D. Borg, *Historians and American Far Eastern Policy* (New York, 1966).
133 See Thorne, *Limits*, 72–5, 390.
134 J. K,. Fairbank, ' "American China Policy" to 1898: a Misconception', *Pacific Historical Review*, November 1970.
135 See P. S. Tang, *Russian and Soviet Policy in Manchuria and Outer Mongolia, 1911–1931* (Durham, N.C., 1959).

136 See Hosoya, 'The Japanese-Soviet Neutrality Pact', in Morley, *Fateful Choice*.
137 See Fox, op. cit.
138 See Ike, op. cit., e.g. 157–9.
139 For contrasting views on European colonial empires in general at this time, see, e.g. D. K. Fieldhouse, *The Colonial Empires: a Comparative Survey from the Eighteenth Century* (2nd edn., London, 1982), and V. G. Kiernon, *European Empires from Conquest to Collapse, 1815–1960* (London, 1982).
140 See, e.g. H. Tint, *The Decline of French Patriotism, 1870–1940* (London, 1964); J. B. Duroselle, *La Décadence, 1932–1939* (Paris, 1979), 267, 435.
141 See Manning, op. cit.; H. Daalder, 'The Netherlands and the World, 1940–1945', in J. H. Leurdijk (ed.), *The Foreign Policy of the Netherlands* (Alphen, 1978); A. E. Kersten, *Buitenlandse Zaken in ballingschap* (Alphen, 1981); H. Baudet, 'Nederlands en de rang van Denemarken', in C. Fasseur (ed.), *Geld en geweten Vol. 2* (The Hague, 1980).
142 See Reynolds, op. cit.; Thorne, *Allies*; C. Barnett, *The Collapse of British Power* (London, 1972).
143 See Neidpath, op. cit.; Haggie, op. cit.; and the relevant essays in P. Kennedy, *Strategy and Diplomacy, 1870–1945* (London, 1983).
144 On the two navies in these and other respects, see Marder, op cit.; also S. W. Roskill, *Naval Policy Between the Wars, Vol. II* (London, 1976).
145 Quoted in Lee, op. cit., 46–7.
146 Thorne, *Limits*, 42.
147 See e.g. P. Hasluck, *The Government and the People, Vol. I, 1939–41* (Canberra, 1952); A. Watt, *The Evolution of Australian Foreign Policy, 1938–1965* (Cambridge, 1967); Holland, op. cit.; Horner, *High Command*, caps. 4, 5, 6; Thorne, *Allies*, 62–4; P. G. Edwards, *Prime Ministers and Diplomats: the Making of Australian Foreign Policy, 1901–1949* (Melbourne, 1983).
148 See Steinberg, op. cit.; T. Friend, *Between Two Empires* (New Haven, 1965).
149 Clapper cable (n.d., 1942) on talks with Nehru, Clapper Papers, box 36; Sayre memo. of talk with Quezon, 8 Jan. 1940, Sayre Papers, box 7.
150 *Asia*, Jan. 1940.
151 See Thorne, *Limits*, 58, and *Allies*, 52, 54, 101, 208–9.
152 On this subject in general, see R. Jervis, *Perception and Misperception in International Politics* (Princeton, 1976).
153 Ike, e.g. 139, 207.
154 See M. Mayo, 'Attitudes Toward Asia and the Beginnings of the Japanese Empire', in G. K. Goodman (ed.), *Imperial Japan and Asia: A Reassessment* (New York, 1967); Iriye, 'Imperialism in East Asia', in Crowley, *Modern East Asia*; Miwa, 'Japanese Policies and Concepts for a Regional Order in Asia, 1938–1940', loc. cit.
155 Thorne, *Limits*, caps. 7 and 12.
156 Ibid, 246.
157 Ibid, 409; T. Jones, *A Diary with Letters* (London, 1954), 93.
158 See C. Thorne, 'Viscount Cecil, the Government and the Far Eastern Crisis of 1931', *Historical Journal*, vol. 14, no. 4, 1971, and *Limits*, 380–4.
159 See, on the subject in general, K. N. Waltz, *Man, the State and War* (New York, 1959).
160 Thorne, *Limits*, 117. And on the significance of the League's Economic Conference of 1927, see the essay by J. Halperin, in *The League of Nations in Retrospect* (Berlin, 1983).
161 Reynolds, op. cit., 281; R. N. Gardner, *Sterling Dollar Diplomacy* (Oxford, 1956), passim.
162 See M. Howard, *War and the Liberal Conscience* (London, 1978).
163 See Thorne, *Limits*, 308–9, and e.g. *Documents Diplomatiques Français, 1932–1939, 1ʳᵉ série, Tome 1* (Paris, 1964), Nos. 250, 268, 272, 273, 286.
164 See e.g. Thorne, *Limits*, 22, 37–8; S. N. Ogata, *Defiance in Manchuria* (Berkeley, 1964); Morley, *Dilemmas of Growth*.
165 See Thorne, *Limits*, 418–9.
166 See e.g. the predictions of two leading students of the subject at the time concerning the lasting nature of the new, bi-polar international system: M. Wight, 'The Balance of

Power', in H. Butterfield and M. Wight (eds.), *Diplomatic Investigations* (London, 1966), and F. H. Hinsley, *Power and the Pursuit of Peace* (Cambridge, 1967), 349.
167 See e.g. J. Joll, 'The Ideal and the Real: Changing Concepts of the International System, 1815–1982', *International Affairs*, Spring 1982.
168 Ibid. See also H. Bull and A. Watson (ed.), *The Expansion of International Society* (Oxford, 1984), and for a theoretical discussion of such developments, R. Gilpin, *War and Change in World Politics* (Cambridge, 1981), esp. caps. 2 and 5.
169 Lord Moran, *Winston Churchill: the Struggle for Survival, 1940–1965* (London, 1966), 405.
170 Thorne, *Limits*, 40–1.
171 E.g. *League of Nations Official Journal, Special Supplement No. 93*, 49–50.
172 See e.g. R. Emerson, 'Colonialism and the U.N.', in *International Organisation*, 1965.
173 See A. B. Bozeman, *The Future of Law in a Multicultural world* (Princeton, 1971); and for a counter-argument, R. P. Dore, 'Unity and Diversity in World Culture', in Bull and Watson, op. cit.; also Mead, 'World Culture', in *Anthropology: A Human Science*.

CHAPTER THREE

Domestic Contexts

The foregoing account of international relations in the Far East before the war of 1941–45 has of necessity included references to some of the ways in which they were affected by developments of a domestic kind: by a state's underlying political culture, for example, or the condition of its economy, or the outcome of its political rivalries. The present chapter will seek to survey in broad, comparative terms a number of such features to be encountered in the societies that were in their turn to be affected by a single international event: the war itself.

There is, however, an underlying and all-embracing issue that needs to be acknowledged at the outset. For if we are to include in one work developments of both an international and a domestic kind, and if we are to compare the internal developments concerned across a number of societies, the question arises: were there connections involved that went deeper, and extended over a far longer period, than simply the particular domestic sources of a foreign policy, say, or the existence of a particular colonial relationship, or the repercussions of a particular international conflict?

There were, of course, contemporaries who discerned such underlying connections of one kind and another. Kita Ikki, for example, one of Japan's 'double patriots', argued in 1924:

'The socialists of the West contradict themselves when they admit the right of class struggle to the proletariat at home and at the same time condemn war, waged by a proletariat among nations, as militarism and aggression ... If it is permissible for the working class to unite to overthrow unjust authority by bloodshed, then unconditional approval should be given to Japan to perfect her army and navy and make war for the rectification of unjust international frontiers.'[1]

The intention here, however, is to provide a reminder that various theses have been advanced regarding connections of this kind by students of such disciplines as anthropology, economics and political philosophy: theses that focus on, for example, attitudes towards both overseas empire and the social structure at home;[2] or even, as essayed by Eric Wolf in the work that was cited in the Preface, on the interrelationships involved in the development of 'the social system of the modern world' and of all societies within it.[3]

At the conclusion of the present chapter, a general proposition will be put

forward regarding the question of continuity and change[4] in the period
under scrutiny, and the perceptions of contemporaries in that context. For
the moment, however, it may be helpful to turn aside briefly in order to
illustrate the issue of underlying connections in terms of one of the areas
where the present study observes specific historical developments: that of
the relationships between the Western colonial powers and their Far
Eastern subject territories. On the question of whether or not certain
economic dynamics – and, if so, of what kind – have lain at the heart of such
imperial relationships, Lenin, Hobson, and others have of course offered
contending theories.* But when, as in the previous chapter and this one, we
note two associated features of the pre-1941 period: nationalist movements
and debates over the issue of 'modernization' (neither, of course, confined
to colonial territories), it should be borne in mind that there, too, various
propositions have been advanced regarding sets of underlying and long-term
causal connections. For Ernest Gellner,[5] for example, both of these
phenomena, and not simply the latter, derive from 'the distinctive structural
requirements of industrial society'. In other words, the widespread movement in modern times whereby what he terms 'low' or spontaneously-
reproducing cultures are swallowed up in the extension of those 'high'
cultures that depend upon education and specialist institutions is, for
Gellner, the mainspring of modern nationalism also. As mankind has
become 'irreversibly committed to industrial society, and therefore to a
society whose productive system is based on cumulative science and technology', so nationalism is merely the reflection and corollary of the establishment of 'an anonymous, impersonal society, with mutually substitutable,
atomized individuals, held together above all by a shared [high] culture'.
Thus, in Gellner's view, the conflicts surrounding European imperial rule in
our period are to be seen in terms not of the 'awakening' of some latent force
and self-awareness on the part of various colonial peoples, but of uneven
economic and social development, of the diffusion of industrialism and new
forms of social organization, of 'low cultures aspiring to high cultures', and
to their own, matching political units.

* It does not lie within the scope of the present book, nor does the author possess the necessary
expertise, to enquire into the general dynamics of imperialism. For a brief survey of
contending economic theories in this area, see A. Hodgart, *The Economics of European
Imperialism* (London, 1977), and for a discussion of the notion, for example, of 'the
development of underdevelopment', see R. von Albertini, *European Colonial Rule,
1880–1940: the Impact of the West on India, Southeast Asia, and Africa* (trans. J.G.
Williamson, Westport, Conn., 1982). On scientific and technological aspects of the subject,
see D.R. Headrick, *The Tools of Empire: Technology and European Imperialism in the
Nineteenth Century* (Oxford, 1981), and R.F. Betts, *Uncertain Dimensions: Overseas
Empires in the Twentieth Century* (forthcoming). For a comparison between the dynamics of
Western and Japanese imperialism, see the relevant essays in Myers and Peattie (ed.), *The
Japanese Colonial Empire*; and, for reflections on the psychological processes involved,
Mannoni, *Prospero and Caliban: the Psychology of Colonization*.

Obviously, this is simply one among many differing perceptions and analyses of the connections in question.* Gellner does acknowledge that the ethnic dimension may well come to the fore when the political, economic and educational inequalities resulting from the uneven spread of industrialism coincide with inequalities in that sphere as well.[6] Or again, his emphasis on the educational requirements and processes bound up with the extension of 'high' cultures from the few to the many can be seen as chiming to some degree with the view advanced by Benedict Anderson,[7] that what the latter calls a 'print language' has been central to the establishment of the 'imagined community' that becomes the focus of nationalism, and that 'schooled youth' played a crucial part in the development of such nationalisms in, for example, Southeast Asia. Nevertheless, the pattern of causality set out by Gellner is very different from the underlying processes discerned by students of nationalism whose attention has been directed towards, say, the historic *volk*, or the intellectual arousal of national self-awareness, or the political processes involved in nationalist movements.[8] And, if we were to pursue the underlying issues involved, we would need to examine, for example, whether there were differences of kind among the nationalisms encountered in our period;[9] whether, say, the plural nature of some of the societies involved (a topic that will be considered below) can be aligned with the thesis that there is a major distinction to be made between what have been termed 'Western' nationalisms, based on an existing 'high' culture, and 'Eastern' ones which entail a process of social engineering in order to create a single people from diverse groups and to 're-equip [such a people] culturally' in such a way as to enable them 'to assert themselves as equals in a civilisation not of their own making'.[10]

The present work, however, is not directed towards establishing a typology of nationalisms, nor towards the larger goal of testing general theories regarding the connections among all the societies that come within its

* It will be sufficient simply to indicate a few neighbouring lines of enquiry. For a complementary emphasis on the multi-faceted nature of a single culture, and on the possibility that one part may change more slowly than others, see W.F. Ogburn, 'Cultural Lag as Theory', in his *On Cultural and Social Change* (Chicago, 1964). For a not wholly dissimilar view of the way in which 'the dynamics of interdependencies . . . keep men moving and press towards changes in their institutions and indeed in the overall structure of their figurations', see N. Elias, *The Civilizing Process, Vol. 2: State Formation and Civilization* (trs. E. Jephcott, Oxford, 1982), 232, 320 and passim. For an attempt to distinguish between, not 'high' and 'low' cultures, but 'ideational' and 'sensate' ones (the former emphasising values, universal principles and the group; the latter more individualistic, grasping and worldly), and ensuing conclusions regarding the nature of conflict, see P.A. Sorokin, *Social and Cultural Dynamics: Vol. 3: Fluctuations of Social Relationships, War and Revolution* (New York, 1937), 132–3, 373. For an alternative, though in parts overlapping, approach to the issues of colonialism and nationalism, see P. Mason, *Patterns of Dominance* (Oxford, 1979), and for a recent survey of the more frequently emphasised ethnic dimensions of such conflicts, see A.D. Smith, *The Ethnic Revival* (Cambridge, 1981).

purview. The purpose of these preliminary observations is, rather, to acknowledge that to bring together a number of states and societies on the grounds that they were involved in the Far Eastern war; to observe that they were all, in one way or another, being affected by the spread and vicissitudes of industrialism, and to draw out certain characteristics or problems that transcended the state and societal boundaries of the time: that to do this involves making choices that are open to question at a fundamental level. The purpose is also to encourage those readers so inclined to pursue such issues further for themselves, and to express the hope that the arguments and historical evidence they will find in this study may provide additional grist to their mills.

*

Dividing the societies of the world into broad categories was a task that attracted specialists and the common man alike in the years preceding the 1941 war. As we have seen, one of the distinctions frequently made was that between the peoples of 'Asia' or 'the East' on the one hand and those of 'Europe' or 'the West' on the other. Weber, for example, had argued before the First World War that 'the Occident' was set apart from the rest of mankind by what he termed 'the specific and particular rationalism of [its] culture'.[11] 'One of the notorious differences between the Orient and the Occident,' asserted Chicago University's Robert Park in 1931, 'concerns the attitude prevalent in those two grand divisions of culture in the world in respect to change. Most of the ideas, beliefs and practices peculiarly characteristic of the Occident are associated with the fact of change.' And earlier, in 1926: 'The conflict between the Orient and the Occident which presents itself in one of its aspects as external and international, assumes, in another aspect, the character of an internal and moral conflict.'[12]*

Among those who employed this basic categorisation, in the West and in Asia alike, were both admirers and denigrators of what they saw as societies so different from their own: a Soekarno and a Sjahrir ('only by a utilization of the dynamism of the West,' concluded the latter, 'can the East be released from its ... subjugation');[13] a Massis and a Rolland. Yet, whatever the particular judgement that was involved, the underlying assumption that

---

* Distinctions of this kind also appeared in the form of metaphor or simile. Thus, Bertrand Russell, for example, summarised his main impression of Lenin in terms of the latter's 'bigotry and Mongolian cruelty', while Rosa Luxemburg referred to the 'Tartar-Mongolian savagery' of the Bolsheviks. More recently, Lord Kinross, in his biography of Atatürk, describes certain (negative) aspects of his subject's character as 'Oriental', despite his having been born in Europe and desiring to 'Europeanise' Turkey. *Atatürk: The Rebirth of a Nation* (London, 1964), e.g. 392, 423. See also e.g. Henri Troyat, *Tolstoy* (London, 1979), passim, and Hay, *Asian Ideas of East and West*.

there existed an entity that could be defined as 'Asian man' or 'Asian society' was, as already emphasised, entirely without anthropological validity. The geographical area termed 'Asia' contained in the 1930s both nomadic tribes and the citizens of Yokohama, and indeed, in the words of a distinguished Japanese sociologist, 'Japan never was a typically Asian society'.[14] 'What is there of the East,' asked Sjahrir himself, 'in Hong Kong or Shanghai or Tokyo?',* and he acknowledged that 'Western influence' had penetrated even into the rural areas of the Indies: 'into the masses, into people's customs, into the group imagination.'[15] Likewise, 'Europe' – a concept, in societal terms, that itself had emerged only in the later Middle Ages[16] – was home to the bourgeois of Amsterdam and the peasant of Calabria alike.

Moreover, the 'East/West' dichotomy was inadequate in terms of perceptions, as well as anthropologically-speaking. When we advance beyond the purely geographical dimension, the question arises of whether or not individuals or groups felt themselves to be essentially 'Asian', say. And here, during the seventy years or so preceding the Far Eastern war, we encounter considerable confusion and contradictions. Where 'the West' is concerned, it is sufficient to recall, for example, those perceptions, opposed as they were to any notion of homogeneity, of fundamental distinctions between Britain and the remainder of Europe; between, say, Northern Italy and the Mezzogiorno; between the 'new society' of the United States and those of a corrupt Europe (so that for one of Pearl Buck's disciples, for example, writing in 1941, 'the Chinese, in general attitude and thought, [were] a good deal more like an American than a good many Europeans').[17]

Variations of this kind, possibly more extensive and profound, are likewise to be found within the geographical limits of Asia in this period. Two particular areas will suffice as illustration: the mutual perceptions of Japanese and Chinese, and reactions to the presence of the West in China and India respectively. Thus, while for some Japanese China, for all its deplorable features, remained the home of that Confucian civilization that formed a central element in Japan's own heritage and present culture, to Mutsu Munemitsu, Foreign Minister during the war with China in the 1890s, that conflict represented 'a collision between the new civilization of the West and the old civilization of East Asia'.[18]† Conversely, where Sun Yat-sen, for one, among the Chinese had seen Japan as a natural, fellow-Asian ally

* The same point was made – in anger – by Japanese ultra-nationalists who deplored the eclipse of the country's agrarian and provincial life. 'According to a common expression,' wrote Tachibana Kosaburo, 'Tokyo is the hub of the world. But in my eyes it appears unhappily to be nothing but a branch shop of London. At all events, it is undeniable that the villages are being destroyed in direct proportion to the expansion of Tokyo.' Quoted in Maruyama, *Thought and Behaviour in Modern Japanese Politics*, 42.

† Maruyama suggests that one reason why Japan's intelligentsia did not subscribe to what he calls the 'radical fascism' of the 1930s was bcause it was 'essentially European in culture'. Op. cit., 59.

against Western imperialism, others regarded her as a totally alien power with its own, equally menacing brand of aggression and expansion.[19] As for the reactions of India and China to a Western presence, the dissimilarities involved arose in part (of course, the nature of that alien presence was itself far from the same in the two cases) because, as a recent study of the subject concludes, 'the indigenous contexts were fundamentally different', a contrast that, on the Chinese side, involved a far greater 'cultural identity, national pride, coherence and sense of self-sufficiency', as well as more tangible factors.[20]

An alternative distinction that was employed by many contemporaries during the 1930s especially, as we have seen, was between societies that were 'free' or 'democratic' on the one hand, and those that were 'fascist' or 'totalitarian' or 'militarist' on the other. As with the 'Asia/West' dichotomy, it cannot be dismissed as lacking any foundation whatever. In the context of the time, the values, goals and characteristics of Japan, Germany and Italy were such as to make their Pact of 1940 more than a merely arbitrary grouping.[21] It is equally apparent, nevertheless, that in terms of many important features of social history the dividing line is unwarranted in several respects. Moreover, even if attention is confined to the area of political philosophy, organisation and practice, there are still a number of ways in which it remains unacceptable. For example, it was and continues to be misleading to some extent to link the European dictatorships to the Japan of the 1930s by employing the term 'fascist' to describe the latter. (There was no 'leader' figure in Japan whose position was equivalent to that of Hitler or Mussolini, for example, nor had the regime been instituted by a mass movement from below.)[22] Civil liberty, democracy and individualism as known in the West were alien to the essential spirit of post-Meiji Japan, and above all to the militarism that came to dominance in the 1930s. But the regime that controlled Japan between 1941 and 1945 was to be, in the words of one student of the subject, 'not an "ism" but a temporary adaptation of the pre-war political structure to the extraordinary circumstances of total war'.[23]

Further objections can be raised on the political level to the simple dichotomy that would place the aggressor-states of 1937 and 1939–41 in one all-embracing category and their victims in another. The nature of the Soviet regime raises one obvious question; so, too, does the existence in the Far East of colonial administrations like that of France in Indochina. And indeed, if the term 'fascist' is to be employed in a non-European context for the 1930s, to no regime is it more appropriate to attach it than that of the Kuomintang in China. 'Fascism,' declared Chiang Kai-shek to a gathering of his Blue Shirts in 1935, 'is a stimulant for a declining society . . . Can fascism save China? We answer: yes.' Even before the Japanese attacked in 1937, the Generalissimo and the various cliques which sustained him had, as Professor Eastman has demonstrated, failed to meet both demands for wider political participation and the need for urgent social and economic reform. That liberal democracy which Americans in particular were wont to assume was a creed shared by China's leaders was in fact in their eyes a poison to be expelled from the country's body politic. (In this connection, the comparison sometimes made by observers – a British Ambassador, for one – between Tai Li, head of the Kuomintang's 'Special Services', and Himmler was not without foundation.)[24]

It is unnecessary to pursue further the inadequacies of the simple categories that were often employed at the time to distinguish among societies that were soon to be caught up in the Far Eastern war. So various were the cultures, political cultures, and social and economic bases involved, and so great the forces working for change, that any distinctions of this kind are bound to raise serious objections. Instead, an attempt will be made to bring out some of the major challenges and issues that were facing the peoples concerned before the war. It must again be emphasised that the existence of a certain similarity among societies along one dimension does not mean that other things were equal. The contrasts that existed among the relevant groups of mankind are so obvious and have been described so often that for the most part they will be taken as read in what follows. What will be suggested, rather, is that, within the geographical and political boundaries set for this study by the 1941–45 war, it is possible to discern certain patterns which cut across the dividing lines already mentioned and across the line that was about to separate the combatants in the forthcoming conflict.

*

In the 1890s, as we have seen, one of Japan's foreign ministers viewed his own society as a standard-bearer of 'the new civilization' that had originated in the West. China was antiquated and obscurantist; Japan was enlightened and 'modern'. The concept of 'modernization' is inescapable in our present context, not simply because, as we have seen, it was to become central to various retrospective analyses of the processes that were taking place in this period, but because it was employed by many of those we are studying when they defined what they saw as a crucial issue for their society. It is important to add at once, however, that the term is not being used here as some kind of historical measuring-stick, shaped by the assumption that reached its apogee during our period:* that to 'modernize' is a requirement of 'progress';[25]

---

* The assumption may well have reached its peak in America later, however, after that society's victories and enrichment during the war itself, thus helping to distance it from others less fortunate and more sceptical.

that, in the words of a recent survey, 'all social change is progressive, organic, linear'.[26] Likewise, the remarks already made about the inadequacy of crude categorisation would certainly apply to any attempt to label some societies as 'modern' and the remainder as 'traditional'; and if the dimensions of the present study entail an emphasis upon the repercussions of a Western presence and Western ideas within various Asian societies, this must not be taken as implying that all social and political issues, or all change, within those societies were related solely to matters foreign.

For these reasons, the term 'modernization' will often appear in what follows within inverted commas, as one that was widely employed by people at the time. When they did so, one of the phenomena that was in the forefront of their minds was the development of an industrialized economy. Even this phrase conceals numerous variations, and a full analysis of the subject would obviously require the process to be broken down in order to explore, say, education and means of communication, urbanisation (not new with the coming of the West, of course), patterns of employment (and unemployment), ownership of the means of production, and – not least – the organisation of state, bureaucracy and society.[27] If, however, we take simply the phenomenon in its broadest terms: the development of industrial production resting on applied science and technology, together with accompanying patterns of international trade that increasingly tied in non-industrialised societies and economies as providers of primary products and/or markets for manufactured goods, then, as Gellner, for one, argues, it was by then affecting virtually all the societies involved in the 1941–45 war. In other words, the making of 'a world market economy', as Gilpin terms it, was already well advanced.*

The immediate industrial process itself, for example, had made inroads into many of the Asian territories concerned by the 1930s, usually centred upon towns where the Western presence was a strong one.[28] In Vietnam, for instance, an urban proletariat (increasing in size from about 100,000 to

---

* Indeed, A.J. Latham, for example, argues that Asia in general, and especially China and India, had become crucial to the international economy during the fifty years before the First World War. (*The International Economy and the Underdeveloped World, 1865–1914*, London, 1978, cap. 2.) The impact of Western economic developments on the lives of large numbers of Asians in this period can be illustrated by reference to, for example, the 42,000 Chinese miners who were at work in the gold-fields of Australia by 1859, and the 200,000 Chinese labourers who were despatched to California between 1852 and 1875. (Wolf, *Europe and the People Without History*, 377–8.) Earlier consequences of Western economic activity in Asia are well known: for example, those undergone by tens of thousands of Chinese who pandered to British greed by purchasing opium. At the same time, however, it is also possible to emphasise, as does Dr Latham (op. cit., 162, 165), that 'the market-widening effect of [European enterprise] liberated the energies of Asians and Africans', who 'seized the new economic opportunities which opened up to them after 1865 ...' See also P. O'Brien, 'Europe in the World Economy', in Bull and Watson, *The Expansion of International Society*.

220,000 between 1919 and 1929) and a more prosperous commercial class already existed, a development that facilitated nationalist agitation but at the same time fostered, especially among the commercial elite, 'modernist' and often pro-Western inclinations that were far removed from the outlook and interests of the mass of the population.[29] In the Netherlands East Indies, the number of workers in factories trebled between 1935 and 1940, with a big increase in the number of large weaving mills and the establishment of plants by General Motors and Goodyear Tyres among others. Ownership, investment and control, however, remained in Western hands, and the depression brought extensive unemployment and other forms of hardship among the local population.[30] India, meanwhile, presented a somewhat different picture, for there a growing number of native entrepreneurs were joining a hitherto overwhelmingly European private business sector (by 1938, over 28 per cent of the capital invested in business was of native origin, with a further 32 per cent being mixed, Indian-European). Moreover, industrialisation was developing in the field of consumer goods for the domestic market, as distinct from the export goods that had predominated before the 1914–18 war, while the diminishing significance to each of the two parties of trade between Britain and India during the inter-war years, together with the international economic dislocation of the time, offered at least potential stimulants to the further growth and diversification of Indian industry. Yet despite these apparent advantages and signs of socio-economic change, the political ties and sterling indebtedness that still bound India to Britain, together with the essentially negative attitude of the British authorities towards native entrepreneurs and the low rate of European investment, helped ensure that in the event India had not achieved a broad and solid industrial base by the time war came.[31]

By contrast, another imperial territory, Korea, was being thrust far more swiftly through the modernising process – at a speed and in a manner, indeed, that were at odds with the nature of the country's social structure. The expansion of heavy industry there was such that by 1936 it accounted for 28 per cent of industrial production as a whole, while the number of workers employed in that industrial sector nearly doubled between 1932 and 1940, to over 700,000. Many of the larger towns almost trebled their population in the same period. Even so, it was Japanese state enterprises, banks and large private combines that dominated this drastic economic shift, rather than a well-established commercial class among the Koreans themselves. And as the country's agriculture and industry alike were drawn along a network of new railways 'not only into market relations with the Japanese metropole but into the world market system', as Bruce Cumings describes the process, the fissures within its society were rapidly being deepened.[32]

Of all societies in Asia, however, independent or otherwise, it was that of

Japan itself that stood out for the degree to which it had industrialised by the 1930s. (The contrast with China, for example, was particularly marked: in the mid-1930s, only around 13 per cent of that country's production emerged from the 'modern' sector of the economy.)[33] Capitalising on certain features of the preceding Tokugawa period, spurred on by a keen sense of comparison with the West and the conviction that China's vulnerability sprang from her resistance to change, Japan after the Meiji restoration had pursued industrialisation as indispensable to the fulfilment of the slogan, *fukoku kyohei*: 'enrich the nation; strengthen its arms.'[34] The military victories of 1895 and 1905, together with the boom enjoyed during the First World War, appeared fully to vindicate such a course. And although the country entered into recession in 1920; although, too, the industrial proletariat remained a smaller proportion of the population than was the case in Western Europe, ensuing attempts to find a way forward resulted in the beginnings of policy and planning concepts that were to be crucial to subsequent and remarkable growth.[35] Even between 1931 and 1934, when the shock-waves of the 1929–31 depression in the West hit Japan, her industrial output increased by 81.5 per cent, while in the decade from 1930 mining and manufacturing production more than doubled. Urbanisation, too, moved rapidly ahead, 38 per cent of the population living in towns by 1940 where less than 25 per cent had done so ten years earlier.[36] The same period also saw the installation of that bureaucratic 'general staff' who were to realise the country's full economic potential after 1945, while technical and university education were already making their mark on industry far more than was the case in Britain.[37]

Even so, as things stood in the 1930s the development of Japan's economy was set about with problems and unpleasant consequences for her society. Despite the impetus imparted to exports by the reduced value of the yen, rapid increases in military expenditure had helped create a balance of payments and inflation crisis even before the 1937 conflict with China.[38] Real wages fell by 17 per cent between 1937 and 1940 as heavy industry and inflation both grew further still under the stimulus of that war.[39] Well before this, depression in 1931 had brought widespread hardship to rural areas, highlighting strains in the very structure of society that had been in the making since the preceding century.[40]

At one level, these strains derived, not simply from the rapidly shifting relationship of town to country consequent upon a crash programme of industrialisation, but from the swiftly changing life-styles of many of the population. (Although, as we have seen, 38 per cent lived in towns by 1940, 80 per cent of the population had been born and brought up in a village.)[41] Removed from their familiar community, 'their lives shaped by the cold logic of a monetary economy', the new blue- or grey-collar workers faced challenges to their entire set of values and social assumptions.[42] Yet, on another level, the tension within Japanese society sprang from the very resilience of an outlook shaped by the village and, even more, by the feudalism of the family unit (the *ie*) as the ever-extending, all-encompassing determinant of status. Even in urban areas, this traditional focus of exist-ence remained strong, while the 'familistic' basis of social relations extended into the worlds of business, politics, and the bureaucracy. At the same time there was a lack of natural, resilient bonds of a nation-wide, horizontal kind that could complement these family-like vertical ties. The concept of the Empire itself as a family under its divinely-appointed head did not provide a sufficient nexus between the local community and society as a whole. Indeed, by reinforcing the powerful inhibitions placed by the system of the *ie* upon 'the capacity to act according to one's own judgement and carry through principles one personally believed in', it ruled out what Professor Fukutake calls 'the autonomous cohesion of the modern citizen'. 'From the beginning of the century onwards,' he writes, 'there was a conscious fear of the development of critical attitudes and active attempts to suppress them.'

As a consequence, the lives of the Japanese people were dominated by 'supremacy of custom' and 'submission to authority'; by 'an avoidance of responsibility' that was rationalized by reference to the force of 'surrounding circumstances'.[43] Thus, although a 'modernized' state in economic terms, Japan, for all its fierce nationalism, was socially brittle. 'National conscious-ness,' in Maruyama's words, 'did not result from the conquest of traditional social consciousness, but was implanted by a systematic mobilization of traditional values. Consequently, Japan did not produce *citoyens* able to bear the burden of political responsibility in a modern nation-state. In their stead came qualities of loyal but servile lackeys.'[44] 'The tragedy of the Pacific War,' concludes Fukutake, 'was [to be] the final reckoning of these accumulated contradictions.'[45]

Meanwhile, quite apart from short-term periods of recession, the direct or indirect intrusion of industrialisation and its associated international economy had also brought dislocation and hardship to other parts of Asia. Thus, for example, whilst the massive poverty of rural India was not new, the harnessing of the country's economy to the requirements of that of Britain had intensified the 'essentially parasitic nature' of the relationship of the urban to the rural areas.[46] The basically self-interested direction of the economy of the Indies by the Dutch had likewise contributed to the extensive rural poverty in Java, the area most affected by these external pressures.[47] In southern Vietnam, beneath the veneer of modern civilization introduced by an intensely exploitative French regime, rural indebtedness increased fourfold between 1900 and 1930. With the establishment of a money economy, writes one student of the subject, local institutions had declined, thus 'fostering the accumulation of wealth in the hands of a few while the great majority sank into deeper poverty. In an agrarian economy, the land itself became the domain of a small elite who commanded all the avenues to power and who exploited an impoverished peasantry totally subject to their will'.[48]

A broadly similar situation obtained in the Philippines, where the degree of economic dependence on the metropolitan power was greater than in any other Southeast Asian colony. Here, American policies designed to improve the lot of tenants and the landless were rendered largely inoperative, and the 'modernization' of the economy again meant that 'peasants remained impoverished while the elites prospered' in a country where nearly two-thirds of those aged twenty in 1939 had had no schooling.[49] For the majority of Burmese, too, the main problem had become one of indebtedness, with over half the cultivated land in lower Burma belonging to non-agricultural landlords by 1937, and a further quarter to *chettyars* (Indian money-lenders).[50]

In Nationalist China, severe and extensive hardship in the countryside owed much to natural disasters, but also to what Professor Eastman has termed 'an exploitative sociopolitical system' and a refusal by the regime to contemplate land redistribution. Misery was also increased after 1931 (by 1934 farm prices were under half what they had been eight years earlier) by developments on the international economic level, not least the self-interested policies of the United States over silver, which formed the basis of the Chinese currency.[51] Upheaval was likewise rapidly spreading across the Korean countryside, especially in the south, as large numbers of peasants were dispossessed by a consolidation of properties that benefited the collaborationist landed elite, and were driven to seek a living in the growing industries either of Korea itself or of Manchuria, or were shipped off to work in Japan's home islands.[52]

Among administrators and settlers in the European colonial territories, policies and attitudes regarding the problems created by economic change varied greatly. In Hong Kong, where conditions had deteriorated as a result of the flood of refugees from Republican China after 1937, and where over half the Chinese population, according to the *North China Herald*, were living 'in a state of semi-starvation', the indifference of the European element to the welfare of those who helped create their wealth could shock a newcomer like F.C. Gimson, who arrived to become Colonial Secretary in 1941.[53] On the other hand, sustained attempts by the British administration in Malaya to protect the rural Malay communities from the disruptive effects of the urban economy helped widen the gap between the former, 'backward' section of the population and the often-prospering Chinese in the towns. (Not entirely dissimilar problems existed in Fiji, where the strains attendant upon the advance of a money economy were exacerbated by the growing predominance of the Indian community in the agricultural sector, especially the growing of sugar cane.)[54] Likewise, Colonial Office officials in London in the late 1930s were, according to a recent study, 'acutely conscious, on the one hand, of the poor standard of life enjoyed by many colonies during the depression of trade, and, on the other hand, of the major disruptions in the customs of native peoples which almost any kind of industrial investment seemed to bring'.[55]

Despite such problems and penalties surrounding the shift from a purely agricultural economy, a significant number of articulate people in Asia considered the 'modernization' of their society to be essential. We have already heard Sjahrir, for example, on this subject, and Inouye Kaoru, who wished to see the Japanese people become 'like the people of Europe' – thus coming close to echoing Karl Marx, who had defined Britain's task in India as being 'the annihilation of the Asiatic society and the laying of the material foundations of Western society in Asia'.[56] Many of those who opposed Western colonial rule shared this attitude. Phan Boi Chau, for example, leader of the anti-colonial movement in Vietnam in the early part of the twentieth century, looked forward to 'a modern, prosperous state built on the Western model'.[57] Nehru, like Sun Yat-sen, welcomed 'the gift of science' that the West had brought to Asia, and was to reflect that 'perhaps only a succession of violent shocks', of the kind that were involved in the collision of the two civilisations, 'could shake us out of our torpor'.[58] Even a Subhas Chandra Bose, though in some ways one of the most Indian of the nationalist leaders of that country – he was far less Westernised than Nehru, for example – had nevertheless imbibed Western concepts of nationalism, sought (in contrast to Gandhi) a synthesis of East and West, and looked ahead to an India that would be 'modernized' economically and would base its political culture on another blend: 'of what modern Europe calls socialism and fascism'.[59] (Marcus Garvey, too, saw modernisation as a vital means to the achievement of freedom and dignity by black peoples in Africa and the United States alike.)[60]

Meanwhile, in the West itself, the more efficient and extensive industrialisation of economies continued to form the basis of most prescriptions, whether capitalist or socialist, for the improvement of society.[61] Yet the very urgency of such programmes testified in part to the extent to which, before the Far Eastern war, industrialised societies in the West had themselves been experiencing prolonged disruption and widespread hardship. Indeed, there had been those who, like Arnold Toynbee in 1931 (a year when eight million Americans were unemployed, for example), were 'seriously contemplating the possibility that the Western system of society might . . . cease to work . . . [as a result of] a spontaneous disruption . . . from within'.[62]

A questioning of the very essence of modern Western civilisation was not new in the 1930s, of course. Before the end of the nineteenth century, for example, Tennyson, who earlier had hymned a Europe that was triumphantly spinning down 'the ringing grooves of change', was asking, rather:

'Is it well that while we range with Science, glorying in the Time,
City children soak and blacken soul and sense in city slime?'[63]

Well before the First World War, fears had begun to be expressed regarding the possible destructive consequences of science and technology, their dehumanising and alienating effects and their relationship to the phenomenon of war.[64] Some went further, and pronounced against the very nature of the 'mass societies'* that had developed on the basis of industrialisation.[65] As indicated in the previous chapter, however, it was the apparently futile carnage of total war in Europe between 1914 and 1918 that, more than any other event, gave rise to the questioning or outright condemnation of industrial civilisation. To some, the war itself came to epitomise that wider phenomenon. 'Instead of escaping the soul-killing mechanism of modern, technological society,' wrote the German, Ernst Toller, '[those who fought] learned that the tyranny of technology ruled even more omnipotently in war than in peace-time.'[66] For Valéry, as expressed in his famous essay, *La Crise de l'Esprit*, the war merely reflected that pursuit of materialism for its own sake that he had condemned at the end of the preceding century: 'purposeless materialism [and] superfluous power,' Lewis Mumford was to term it shortly afterwards.[67] The accompanying conflict of opinion regarding the lessons to be learned from Asia or, alternatively, the heightened threat confronting the West from that part of the world has already been indicated.†

There is an obvious irony in the coincidence of fundamental criticism of industrial society in the West and the desire of reformers in Asia to 'modernise' on Western lines. ('The Europeans,' observed a Chinese intellectual during a visit to the West in 1919, 'have dreamed a vast dream of the omnipotence of science; now they decry its bankruptcy. This is a major turning point in current world thought.')[68] It was far from being a case, however, of a complete reversal of goals and values. Just as in the industrialised West many, probably the majority, accepted (and regarded as superior) the existing bases of their societies, so in other parts of the world, not least in the Far East, there remained substantial numbers of people who sought to resist the encroachment of various features of that 'modern' world centred on Western Europe and North America. In broad terms, this last

---

* As distinct from the 'mass' nature of Asian societies as often perceived by Westerners, associated with the 'hordes' of Genghis Khan and of the 'yellow peril' generally.
† See above, 28–9.

response was similar to that of the Slavophils in nineteenth-century Russia, and of those before them who had opposed the 'Westernising' endeavours of Peter the Great.[69] In post-1918 Turkey, too, there were those who were demanding of Kemal Atatürk: 'What does this word "modern" mean?', rejecting his vision of their country's destiny as being 'always to walk from the East in the direction of the West'.[70] And, in Spain, the championing of wider 'European' *mores* by Ortega y Gasset and others was under attack by those who held to the country's unique values and culture and warned against an insidious process they termed 'japanization'.[71]

For some in the Far East – in late nineteenth-century Japan, for example – the central question was the one put to Atatürk: 'What does this word "modern" mean?' Was 'to modernise' synonymous with 'to Westernise'?[72] (Was it, for example, incompatible with Islam, as Atatürk himself believed?) Could one draw a distinction, as one student of the subject was seeking to do at the time, between a 'culture', which was unique and marked 'a group that could act collectively', and a 'civilisation', in the sense of 'an aggregate of people who use the same artefacts and who have no solidarity at all'?[73] Could such a distinction form the basis of a social and political programme, as it did for the Japanese commentator who, on the eve of Pearl Harbor, defined his country's task as being to 'Asianise the Europeanisation of Asia'?[74] Or did Toynbee have the truth of it when he asserted in 1931 that since the nineteenth century 'the whole of mankind was . . . being enrolled in Western societies through a vast process of "Westernization"'?[75]*

For the great majority living in the area to be directly affected by the Far Eastern war, of course, the processes and reactions involved were far removed from the debates among the clerisy. It is clear, however, that over extensive areas Toynbee's 'Westernization' had made little headway by 1941. In China, for example, as we noted in the previous chapter, 'the staying power of the traditional system of production and its management' had presented an effective obstacle to its progress, while in general in Asia, in the opinion of one student of the subject, 'however effective and compelling the Western model and Western power became, and however much it was able to manipulate and provoke responses from the Asian

---

* See also e.g. Thomas Masaryk's confident assertions (*The New Europe: The Slav Viewpoint*; Washington D.C., 1918) regarding the world-wide emergence of 'the new man, *homo Europoeus*'. Gong (*The Standard of 'Civilization' in International Society*, 82–3) cites Oppenheim's *International Law* (1905) as providing 'a classic example of the difficulty of delineating and differentiating the "modern", the "Western", and the "civilized"'. Oppenheim wrote: 'Persia, Siam, China, Korea, Abyssinia and the like are civilised, but their civilisation has not yet reached a point to enable them to carry out the rules of international law.' Nevertheless, he added, 'all of them make efforts to educate their populations, to introduce modern institutions, and to raise thereby their civilisation to the level of the Western'. See also the relevant essays in Bull and Watson, *The Expansion of International Society*.

systems, it was never completely able to move or to prevail against the mass
... and [its] weight of deep-rooted and highly developed traditional
culture'.[76]

Moreover, even the extensive adoption of artefacts and processes developed originally in the West, together with an involvement in a Western-
dominated economic system, does not necessarily entail the abandonment
of a distinctive set of beliefs, customs and loyalties. On Southeast Asia, for
example, Victor Purcell was to comment in the 1960s:

'The view generally held in the West is that [the region] is undergoing
"Westernization" and that its countries differ from those of Europe or
America only in being more "backward" or "under-developed". But this
is an oversimplification. In spite of an awakened interest in science,
technology and improved living standards, the [peoples of Southeast
Asia] . . . retain all their distinguishing characteristics . . . and these indeed
seem more important to them than aeroplanes, hygiene, or even political
ideology.'[77]

Similarly, Professor Reischauer was to write of post-1945 Japan:

'[She] has not been Westernized, as is commonly asserted . . . What the
Japanese have taken over are the modern aspects of Western culture;*
which for the most part the West too has only recently developed in
response to modern technology . . . In this sense Japan has more significantly become modernized, not Westernized, and the process . . . has
taken place on the base of Japan's own traditional culture, just as
happened in the West, with the same sort of resulting contrasts and
strains.'[78]

Yet even so, as Reischauer himself acknowledges, those Japanese and
other Asians who, on encountering the superior technology of the West,
took comfort in the belief that they could adopt 'Western science' but adhere
to 'Eastern ethics' 'soon learned that there was no clear dividing line
between techniques, institutions and values. They tended to be all of a
piece'.[79] Small wonder, then, that during the century between Britain's
seizure of Hong Kong and Japan's assault on the Western powers it seemed
to many in Asia that the very soul of their societies was under threat.
'Machinery,' declared Gandhi, 'is the chief symbol of modern civilisation,
and it represents a great sin;' and in 1910 he depicted India as 'being ground
down, not under the English heel, but under that of modern civilisation',
which for 'the nations of Europe', too, meant 'degradation and ruin day by
day'.[80] Similarly, the machine-like state, fed by the lust of modern, Western

* The difference between the use of the term 'culture' here and that advocated by Park, cited
   earlier, illustrates the semantic difficulties surrounding the topic as a whole.

nationalism, was attacked by Tagore as a corrupting and evil phenomenon.[81]* Small wonder, either, that the entire subject created confusion and uncertainty. As one scholar puts it in relation to the final years of the Tokugawa shogunate: 'Where did Japan stand in the world now that the world itself had begun to change before the eyes of the Japanese? The issue was one of national identity more than of shogunal policy.'[82] 'A search for definition' is the term used by another historian to describe the fierce debates in the Japan of the 1880s and '90s that accompanied the quest for what one journalist termed at the time 'the true nature of our country, our national character'.[83] And of the 1930s, another student has recently observed that 'concern with "national essences" typified Japanese thinking', with attempts being made to assert 'the primacy of culture' (and Japan's uniqueness) as against 'the primacy of economics' (which threatened to submerge the country in the general run of industrialised societies).[84]

If such self-examination was particularly Japanese, the underlying issues were nevertheless seen as urgent within other Far Eastern communities as well.[85] In Vietnam, where in the early years of the century many pillars of traditional society (Confucianism and village leadership, for example) were weakening, moderate reformers like Pham Quynh argued for a blend of what the West and traditional values had to offer, only to find that the task of defining what exactly was to be blended was beyond them and that they were being undermined repeatedly by the strength of social, economic and political realities.[86] Those who ruled the still-independent country of Siam 'both admired and feared the West', wanting to be 'both Thai and modern', while in Malaya, a complex social battle was waged between those '*Kuam Muda*' who rejected tradition and eagerly took up the new, and the '*Kuam Tua*' who clung fiercely to familiar ways.[87] In China, fundamental social issues, above all relating to the rural areas, 'kept on exploding in the faces of the [Nationalist] leadership' in the complex political environment that developed after the Fourth of May movement in 1919.[88] At the same time, the question of the possible relevance of Western ways engendered much intellectual contortion and ambivalence, with events such as the 1895 defeat at the hands of Japan and the 1914–18 spectacle of internecine destruction within Europe helping to sway the debate now one way, now another. The very intellectuals who were 'the vehicle of Westernization' also constituted,

---

* Tagore was nevertheless unable to accept Gandhi's political programme of *satyagraha*, while he declined to join his friend in rejecting every aspect of modern Western civilization. Indeed, in 1924 he advised students in China: 'Since the West is aggressive towards us, we should also be aggressive. I have only one piece of advice for China: "Learn science quickly." What the East lacks and badly needs is science.' Hay, *Asian Ideas of East and West*, 235, 276 ff.

it has been suggested, 'the field of struggle for the interplay of many disparate influences'.[89]

As in Vietnam, those in China who sought a middle ground between Confucianism and Western learning faced the problem that the former could appear to represent no more than a token acknowledgement of the past, while those who found in Tagore reinforcement for a belief in the uniquely spiritual character of 'Asian civilisation' as a whole were mocked by radicals more concerned with the country's immediate weakness.[90] Connections between domestic reform, domestic politics and the country's position internationally further complicated the issue, for 'if everyone should be educated, not just in Confucian homilies but in nationalism and the tools for the defence of the motherland, then by implication the population was invited to participate in the nation's politics'.[91] In more specific terms, one can point, for example, to the attempt in the 1920s and '30s to develop cooperative movements. Where these involved the provision of credit, the interests of the elite rapidly prevailed at the expense of the ordinary peasant,[92] while those industrial cooperatives that were established in certain rural areas[93] were regarded by Chiang Kai-shek (whose own 'New Life' movement offered the masses discipline, rather, and hearty Confucianism) as left-wing and subversive institutions.[94]

'The nub of the problem,' writes Eastman, 'was that China's political culture was well suited to a relatively slowly changing agrarian society but was ill-suited to the needs of modernisation.'[95] The dilemma involved, as seen by Joseph Needham, was underlined by him in a document which in strictly chronological terms belongs to a later section of the present study, for it was written in 1945, when the Far Eastern war was over. In it, Needham, whose war-time mission in China marked the beginning of his remarkable studies of that country's civilisation,[96] reported to Chiang Kai-shek on 'The Position and Prospects of Science and Technology in China' as he saw them – and in terms that amounted to a condemnation of the basis of the Kuomintang's rule. It was entirely wrong, he argued, to believe, as did many of the Nationalist regime's officials, 'that science can be accepted by China, not as the supreme transformer of man's whole world-outlook, but as the mythology accompanying a useful set of techniques'. A repressive political regime and a backward-looking philosophy were alike inimical to the growth of science; so, too, were corruption, exploitation and resistance to mass-education.

> 'This will be a hard transition', he continued, 'but it is absolutely essential for the welfare of China ... The Government, therefore, should have a programme for the fostering of science and technology based on a broad recognition of the human needs of the people and the safety of the nation,

and should be prepared to exert some pressure on the wealth-owning groups to induce them to participate in the programme . . .'[97]*

*

The nature and depth of the problems that were posed for a society and body politic like China's once it chose to follow the industrialised path to greater wealth were in some ways, of course, far removed from those facing the already-industrialised states on the eve of the war. Yet if we go to the other end of the spectrum, and to the United States, we find that there, in a society that was still 'predominantly rural and small-town' in nature, between nine and eleven million people were unemployed in 1938–40.[98] In other words, acute pressures and problems, linked to the process of industrialisation and to the essentially anarchic nature of what was increasingly becoming a single international economy, were being experienced there as well. And if, as a consequence of the continuing application of science and technology and of shifts in the political and economic settings, further major changes were to take place in the nature and extent of American industrial production, then more upheavals also lay in store for that mainly 'rural and small-town' society as a whole.

In fact, as we shall see, for many of the societies involved the coming war was to have repercussions in this broad area encompassing both the structure of the economy and attitudes concerning its current and future nature. Meanwhile, some of the international and domestic economic forces that had helped to create the shifting and critical situations existing by the 1930s had also played their part in shaping another issue that was facing a good number of the societies which were to feel the impact of the war: that is, their plural nature. And here, too, the approaching conflict was in many cases to have a significant effect on attitudes and developments.

Again, it is merely in the broadest of fashions that this feature of domestic settings as they existed before the war is treated here. The term 'plural society' is most commonly used to describe one which contains groups differing in their racial and/or ethnic nature. Here, it will be taken wider still, with reference also to divisions of other kinds: religious, social, and sexual. The focus, in other words, is upon societies in which sections of a substantial size were in some way 'apart', and in which major problems surrounded the achievement of integration and harmony at the fundamental level involving shared values and loyalties, and a coherent political culture.

Once more, huge variations are obviously entailed in the extent and

---

* Maruyama comments on what he discerns as 'the sterility of political science' in Japan: 'It is unreasonable to expect any genuine social science to thrive where there is no undergirding of civil liberty.' *Thought and Behaviour in Modern Japanese Politics*, 227.

nature of the groups concerned, as is evident if we examine, say, divisions of a religious kind, where the 'great gulf in culture' and outlook between the Christian and non-Christian peoples in the Philippines, for example,[99] did not at the time pose a threat of the magnitude created by the communal divide between Hindus and Moslems in India. (One must add that Islam did not provide the decisive criterion of political identity for all its followers within India, as the subsequent disintegration of Pakistan was to underline.)[100] Likewise, questions concerning the position of the 80,000 or so Maoris in New Zealand (less than 5 per cent of the total population) were not attended by potential repercussions of the size involved in the case of the nearly 13 million blacks in the United States.[101] Nor, again, was the position of those blacks in America – they were *American** – exactly the same in its nature as that of the Indian population in Burma, for example (where there was rioting between communities in 1938);[102] nor (blacks were *poor* Americans) was it the same as that of the commercially powerful Chinese in Malaya and the Philippines.[103] Nevertheless, in all of these instances, it was the problems rather than the benefits of a plural society that stood out.

In several of the Asian territories that were to become involved in the war, this plurality, of course, derived in part from the presence of a small, white section of the population, coming mainly from the imperial power in question and – as in the Philippines and Hong Kong, for example – living a privileged existence remote from the lives and concerns of the indigenous majority.[104] Something of the complex social dynamics that could arise from the existence of such a white minority can be illustrated from the case of Malaya.[105] For although during the inter-war years many Europeans there liked to emphasise the apparent absence of racially-based tension, their own attitudes towards the country tended to remain ambivalent. It was not felt to be 'home' (such a positive identification was far more common among the Dutch living in the Indies); yet it was where they could obtain not only a higher standard of living but a higher social status than the one open to them back in the metropolitan country – their true 'home', yet now the scene of what was for many of them unwelcome social and political change. Change was also occurring in Malaya itself, however, fostered by events both in the wider world (not least, the nature of the 1914–18 war) and closer at hand (the influx of the Europeans into the colony after that war, for example). Meanwhile, an emphasis on racially-based distinctions was growing, partly and ironically as a consequence of the diminishing cultural gap between whites and Asians:

---

* The failure of Garveyism, and the opposition to it of the N.A.A.C.P. and other black leaders, underlined the fact that most American blacks saw their future in terms of that country – albeit changed as regards its racial discrimination.

'On the one hand,' concludes the main study of the subject, 'Europeans wished to inculcate Asians with their values and to introduce them to their institutions and pastimes, but on the other, as the gap narrowed they could not feel certain of their distinctiveness, and, by implication, their superiority ... [Thus] the colour bar [of 1904, concerning the civil service], however it was justified, was the only remaining means Europeans had of maintaining their superiority over Asians within the sphere of governmental activity.'[106]

Such a white, imperial presence could also create or exacerbate divisions of another kind within the society in question: those between the mass of the population and native elites. Thus, for those Malays who were eventually trained at Kuala Kangsar College for the country's Administrative Service, 'social distinctions were made an integral part' of the experience.[107] In the Philippines, a powerful landowning class had become an indispensable instrument of American policy, the political and social views of some of its members, as already mentioned, being akin to those of the Falangists in Spain (Japanese authoritarianism was also attractive to them), its interests and attitudes completely at odds with those of a landless and impoverished peasantry whose protest was already gathering strength in Central Luzon where it was to merge with the *Hukbalahap* movement in 1942.[108] A huge gap also separated what Attlee was to term the 'brown oligarchy' of major commercial entrepreneurs in India from the mass of the population, although in this case the former did identify themselves with the political struggle against the imperial power. ('For hard-shelled, profit-hunting individualism regardless [of the] general consequences,' a visiting American journalist, highly sympathetic to the nationalist cause, was to note in his diary in 1942, 'native industrialists [would] be hard to beat ... [They] see in Congress party [the] opportunity [to further] their own business expansion as against British interests ...')[109]

Deep divisions, like elements of change, could also exist, of course, quite independently of a foreign, imperial presence. The caste system, and above all the position of the 'Untouchables' in India, is an obvious case in point, as was the not dissimilar position of the *burakumin* in Japan, where they commonly experienced segregation and ill-treatment as inferiors.[110] In China, the ineffectual, corrupt and repressive nature of Kuomintang rule sprang from its factional and class basis, as well as from the country's traditional political culture – a situation that was not changed, it should be added, by the extent to which American-educated Chinese had achieved positions of responsibility in the government by 1941. H.H. Kung (Oberlin and Yale), T.V. Soong (Harvard), Wellington Koo (Columbia) and their like were as far-removed from the Chinese people as a whole – farther, perhaps – as was the Generalissimo himself.[111]

Indeed, the extreme nature of the domestic cleavages involved in the Chinese case, with a fundamental shift of power and priorities likely to come about only through revolutionary violence, would seem to place it in an entirely different category from the divisions and antagonisms that existed within, say, the societies of the colonial powers of north-west Europe. Yet if the necessary allowance is made for the very different political cultures that were involved, it could be argued that, *mutatis mutandis*, the fissures within French society were scarcely less profound than those within China's.* The extent to which those fissures were manifesting themselves by the 1930s and in the events of 1940 do not need rehearsing here. It is worth noting in the present context, however, that one interpretation of France's internal conflicts emphasises 'the attitude different areas have towards innovations and to capitalism'.[112]

Again, it could be maintained that France itself was an exceptional case, as epitomised by the depth and bitterness of the antagonisms that stood revealed by the end of 1941. Although major differences of degree were indeed clearly involved, however, it should not be forgotten that Britain, too (again, in the context of its own, distinct political culture), was experiencing considerable domestic tension in the period leading up to the Second World War. For some of those who faced, as well as long-term unemployment, the harsh social and political philosophy of a Neville Chamberlain, the prime foe, as Aneurin Bevan put it, was not fascism in Germany and Italy but 'the enemy within'.[113] Similar convictions on the left of Australian politics at the time were no less bitter or profound. 'In defeating the enemy from outside,' declared the Labour Party's leader, John Curtin, in October 1939, 'we must not give strength to the anti-social enemy within.' And to the Bishop of Newcastle, who had urged that Labour should join a war-time national government, he wrote in July 1940:

> 'The people and the Labour Movement would then have no representative institution to speak for it. Dissatisfaction, faction and political chaos would result ... The Labour movement in Australia is the spiritual force in Australian politics ... It is the one thing that stands between Australia and the acquisitiveness of powerful interests which seek exploitation and advantage ... I am willing to do all that I can for Australia ... but I

---

* In certain respects, one could also argue that the question summarised by Gellner (*Nations and Nationalism*, 128) in relation to the transformation to a modern industrial society: 'whether the rulers are willing and able to run a mobile society, one in which rulers and ruled can merge and form a cultural continuum', still hung over some Western societies, as well as, more obviously, over less developed ones in the Far East.

refuse to desert the great body of labour to prop up the political parties of reaction and capitalism.'[114]

*

We have already passed from societies that were manifestly 'plural' in ethnic and/or racial terms[115] to ones which were plural in the sense of Disraeli's 'two-nation' description of Britain in the nineteenth century. The same line of thought points to another aspect of 'plurality' and to another issue that spanned societies differing enormously among themselves in many other respects: the position of women.* For the most part it was an issue that was latent rather than in the forefront of the contemporary scene. And, once again, a pattern embracing numerous societies that were to be affected by the Far Eastern war will appear hopelessly strained unless due allowance is made for the particular social context in each case, and relativity applied accordingly. If it can be said, however, that in, say, the United States and Western Europe what was at stake was not simply employment prospects for women but their entire status in those societies ('My position,' recalls Simone de Beauvoir of her life in France in the 1930s, was that of 'any women in a society where the sexes are two embattled castes'; and in Margaret Mead's words, Ruth Benedict and other women in inter-war America were 'struggling to break the bonds of their traditional identification'),[116] then the issue in those parts of the world can be placed alongside questions concerning the roles of women in certain Asian societies that were being subjected to change.

The traditionally inferior position of women in societies such as those of India, China, and Japan needs no underlining. Between the late nineteenth century and the end of the 1930s, however, the processes of modernisation and urbanisation were helping in some areas to foster discontent and even defiance in a small minority, at least, regarding the condition of their sex. Ideas derived from Europe and the United States also played a significant part in shaping the demands that were beginning to be heard: for an end to foot-binding in China, for example, and an opening up of educational opportunities in Japan; for new laws in China, in India, and in Japan, even, regarding marriage, divorce, and property; from some quarters, for the introduction of birth control, and for political emancipation. Even fifty years before, the existence of bodies such as the All India Women's Conference (founded in 1927) or the New Women's Association in Japan (1920–22), or

* The suggestion that there are certain common elements surrounding racial, class, and sexual pluralities and prejudices has of course become familiar as a result of recent feminist writings. It will also be found, however, in, for example, Philip Mason's essays on attitudes about empire and class, *Prospero's Magic*, and in Ashley Montagu's essay, 'Antifeminism and Race Prejudice: A Parallel', in his *Man's Most Dangerous Myth: the Fallacy of Race*, 186ff.

the holding of the first Congress of Indonesian Women in 1928, would have been unthinkable. So, too, would the emphasis that was now being placed on the general issue of the position of women in society by established (male) political figures such as Gandhi and Bose in India. Of the situation that had developed in his Pacific islands, a Fijian administrator wrote in 1926: 'The freedom now enjoyed by women and‐girls appals the older generation.'[117]

Of course, in each of the Asian countries mentioned, the movements concerned, and, even more so, their achievements, were extremely limited. It was a small, educated elite among women that was seeking in each case to lead the way, and in every instance they signally failed to win anything approaching a mass following. In the authoritarian and frenziedly nation- alistic atmosphere of the 1930s, the movement in Japan actually faded in the years immediately preceding the Far Eastern war. Even elsewhere, the calls of those within the existing, male-dominated political order who believed that in certain respects the status of women should be enhanced were usually ambivalent or restricted in some way or other. In India, for example, where, as Dr Everett has emphasised, the very notion of equal rights for women came up against 'the hierarchical world view of Hinduism', and where the women's movement was divided between those who sought such equal rights and those who set their sights on the lesser goal of 'uplift', merely, Gandhi's emphasis on equality in human terms was not acccompanied by a wish to see women participate to the full in public life. ('Equality of the sexes,' he observed, 'does not mean equality of occupations.') Meanwhile in Nationalist China, although the Kuomintang in the 1930s was supporting the idea of increased educational and economic opportunities for women, it was woman's domestic role, surrounded by 'the feminine mystique', that contin- ued to lie at the heart of the party's concepts in this sphere; and while the position of women in the countryside if anything worsened amidst the upheavals and disasters of the time, a Madame Chiang Kai-shek was still likely to find herself being strongly criticised by her husband's advisers for being unduly outspoken – one of those 'modern women' who were 'a dangerous threat to social stability and domestic tranquility'. Even in the areas controlled by the Chinese Communists, the relationship between the women's movement and the party has been summarised by Elisabeth Croll as 'uneasy, complex, and, at certain junctures, antagonistic'.[118]

Nevertheless, the degree to which accepted social patterns and values had come to be questioned and challenged in this field was such – even in Japan; though to a much lesser extent there than in China or India – that, as we will see in a later chapter, the upheavals of total war were to bring about developments of lasting significance within a short space of time. Above all, in the East Indies, China and India, the women's movement was already becoming politicised, in ways which linked the domestic, social and sexual cause to that of the nation vis-à-vis external oppressors. Thus in India, for example, Gandhi's ideology and, not least, his non-violent techniques, 'inspired women', in Dr Everett's words, 'to participate in public activities and broke down opposition to their entry into social service and nationalist associations'. And in China, as Professor Spence has summarised the process, 'the growing number of girls' schools, . . . the influence of Western missionary teachers and of Chinese reformists, the founding of hostels for women and of clubs to promote the marriage of those with unbound feet, the return of the first Chinese women college graduates from overseas, the publication of magazines and newspapers focusing on women's issues, the translation of books and pamphlets about Western feminist leaders – all contibuted to the radical nationalism of the day.'[119]

In broad terms, 'radical nationalism' was, of course, a feature of the politics of the pre-war period that was to be found in Europe as well as in Asia. Here, too, in other words, it is possible to discern certain patterns that cut across some of the categories frequently employed at the time: patterns which go beyond, say, the obvious linking of a Curtin in Australia with a Bevan in Britain. It would be misleading (and Anglocentric) to label one of these patterns 'the decline of liberal democracy', for that could be read as implying that that political creed had previously attained widespread adherence. Nevertheless, it is possible, even within the broad context of those numerous and varied societies that were to be caught up in the 1941 war, to see as a significant development in the preceding years the increasing attacks that were launched against liberal democracy, and its being found wanting by a good many of those who had invested belief and hope in its tenets. In the case of European societies, this trend scarcely requires enlarging upon. The nineteenth-century alternatives to liberalism represented by étatist and Marxist philosophies; the challenges to it arising from the hardships experienced within mass, industrialised societies; the immense blow struck against it by the events of 1914–18: these are well known. As James Wilkinson has written, 'For the generation just reaching maturity before 1930, Europe's vitality seemed at an end'; and the 'despair of Western values' that carried some towards Communism, others to the conservative or radical right, and yet others into an insidious '*trahison des clercs*',* grew at the expense, above all, of beliefs that emphasised the value of the individual and that looked for social improvement through the power of reason and along the path of peaceful change.[120]

Such beliefs had never established a firm hold in, or were entirely alien to, many of the Asian societies that were to be involved in the war. Yet here,

* That is, a betrayal of fundamental liberal principles by the learned. The phrase derives from the title of Julien Benda's justly celebrated book on the subject. See below, 297.

too, there had been individuals or groups who at one time had found in Western liberal, democratic principles an inspiration and a possible way forward for their own people. And here, too, by the 1930s, disillusionment had led to a turning elsewhere. For the Western-educated Sun Yat-sen in China, for example, sharing with fellow-countrymen a growing disenchantment with the West, first Japanese radicalism and then Soviet Communism had appeared to offer alternative sources of sympathy and support.[121] In Japan itself, for all the adoption of Western forms of political structure after the Meiji restoration (though significantly, it was the German model on which several important constitutional features were based), democracy, in Reischauer's words, 'did not have a firm institutional framework ... and lacked wide emotional and intellectual support'.[122] Meanwhile, in Southeast Asia the direction being taken by Sun Yat-sen and Chinese nationalism, as well as the spectacle of the European civil war of 1914–18, made a considerable impression.[123] In the East Indies in the 1930s, as we have seen, there existed among the Indonesians an increasing enthusiasm for Japan's militarist successes, while extreme right-wing tendencies were manifesting themselves in some sections of the white community.* In the Philippines, for all the American proclamations to the contrary, democracy's roots were shallow, and as indicated above both Spanish-style fascism and a revolutionary agrarian challenge lay in wait for the future.[124]

We have already encountered some of those alternative political philosophies that were being propounded in Asia – Bose's recipe for India, of a synthesis of socialism and fascism, being one. And in respect of these anti-liberal doctrines, too, further broad patterns that encompass both Asian and European societies can be discerned. One, obviously, is the growing prominence of Marxist analyses and prescriptions: within French politics between the wars, for example; as an ingredient in that decisive blend of socialism, nationalism and Islam that was being shaped by Soekarno in the Indies;[125] in what was to prove the major challenge to French rule in Indochina;[126] within the Thakin Party in Burma;[127] and in the formulation of what was to amount to a new political culture in China.[128] (Indeed, not only had Asiatic societies, thanks to Lenin above all, been brought within the Marxist programme of fundamental change, but already there existed the makings of what has been termed an 'Asiocentric communism'.)[129]

A further development that is embodied in the foregoing examples is also clear in retrospect: that is, the extent to which Marxist movements shared, too, in the nationalism that was another outstanding feature of the politics of

* See above, 20–21.

the period, both in Europe and in Asia.[130]* At the same time, nationalism formed a major element in another anti-liberal political phenomenon: one which combined a common fear and rejection of the Marxist alternative as hurled forth in 1917 with other ingredients that were of their very essence local and particularist. The traditionalist and conservative right within various societies were at one in condemning both socialism in any form and what they saw as the corrupting materialism and individualism that had developed as the bases of European societies from the sixteenth century onwards. Beyond this, of course, they emphasised what at another level divided them: that is, what they proclaimed to be the deeply-rooted, distinct and vital qualities of their own national genius.

Here is a further pattern in the years leading up to the war, in other words, which takes in, for example, those elements in French politics that in 1940 adhered to the Vichy regime and looked to a revival of certain pre-Revolutionary, even pre-Renaissance, features of French society: who romanticised the past, proclaimed order and duty as the watchwords for the present, and envisaged for the future a truly harmonious existence based on discipline, spiritual values and social solidarity. The goal, Pétain proclaimed, was 'a new order that would be other than a mere servile imitation of things foreign, and would be quintessentially French'.[131] Chiang Kai-shek was laying down similar aims and means for the people of China: a 'resurrection of the nation' through the 'New Life' way of 'propriety, justice, honesty and self-respect', with the Three People's Principles Youth Corps leading the way.[132] In Japan, Mori Kaku, Okawa Shumei and others had been urging that the corruption of the nation's soul and welfare internally and the weakness of its position internationally should alike be remedied by a return to its own unique values and disciplines: 'a national reformation through a national movement', in Okawa's words.[133] And in the very different political and social context of the United States, powerful forces existed in the 1930s that denounced Roosevelt's New Deal as a corrupting betrayal of the values and virtues which had made the Great Republic into the finest society the world had ever seen: forces that, in Richard Hofstadter's words, were 'determined to try to repossess America and to prevent the final act of destruction';[134] forces that were causing a New Dealer like Harold Ickes, Secretary of the Interior, to be 'haunted by the spector [sic] of an American Fascist state'.[135]

For those who felt and argued along political lines such as these, the state's external foes were again, in a sense, less dangerous in the long run than the more insidious 'enemy within'. It could follow, as we have already observed,

---

* There was, of course, a latent tension between nationalist analyses and prescriptions on the one hand and those – observed above – of a racial or racist nature on the other. On this, see Anderson, *Imagined Communities*, 135–6.

that attitudes towards even an invader from outside could be ambivalent at the least. This was all the more so in that, despite major differences between them, the cause of the conservative right tended to overlap with that of more radical right-wing zealots whose nationalist fervour did not preclude an admiration for foreign movements of a like kind. Thus, before the Far Eastern war broke out, some of the factions gathered around Vichy had identified themselves with the triumphant Germans;[136] former Kuomintang officials in China had done the same with the Japanese, and although Chiang Kai-shek himself had not yet reached an accommodation with Tokyo, the possibility that he might do so was a real one, as his forces in January 1941 renewed the fight against their fellow-Chinese Communists.[137]

Even though there were those – and it has been suggested above that they were many – who had little or no inclination to formulate responses of a political kind to the arrival of an invader in their midst, war had already, before December 1941, made its mark upon individuals and families, as well as entire societies. It would perhaps be misleading to think of such developments solely in negative terms. (It could be argued, for example, that British society had, *in extremis*, found in 1940 a sense of identity, pride and purpose after years of dislocation and division.) But the costs of international conflict were in several cases already high – even for the Japanese, who had been fighting on another's territory. The glorification of war as an institution (it was, an army pamphlet had declared in 1934, 'the father of creation and the mother of culture')[138] was at odds with the perception of a good many Japanese by 1940–41, where a curiously relaxed censorship policy allowed audiences to watch films in which the horrors of combat were realistically portrayed.[139] The economic costs to Japan of the struggle to subdue China have already been indicated.*

Among the Chinese themselves, meanwhile, notwithstanding the indifference or suppleness with which some regarded the national cause, Japan's aggression since 1937 had brought great suffering. Thousands had been the victims of hideous cruelties on the part of the invader.[140] It has been estimated that, over the entire period of the war, some forty million were to be rendered homeless, and already the removal of vast numbers of people, of institutions and of industries from the Japanese path had constituted a social upheaval of remarkable proportions.[141] Among the peasantry of Korea, too, Japan's expansion was bringing hardship, as Tokyo began to import rice from the newly-occupied French Indochina rather than from its own colony.[142] In Western Europe, meanwhile, the full harshness of German rule and its accompanying material deprivation had yet to be felt by the peoples of France and the Netherlands as a whole.[143] Yet even so, there, too, the circumstances of many individuals' lives had already been drasti-

* See above, 15, 64.

cally changed, as was the case in a Britain mobilised to the full and under sustained attack from the air[144] – or, indeed, if less dramatically, in a far-off New Zealand which was to send a substantial proportion of its men overseas during the conflict.[145]

One of the spheres in which, even before Pearl Harbor, war was helping to bring about social change in both Asia and the West was that of relations between governments and the governed. At one, obvious level this involved the actual forms and degree of governmental control. In both Britain and Japan, for example, there had already been major developments in this respect under the pressures of a national emergency. Thus, legislation such as the Emergency Powers (Defence) Act of 1939 and the Emergency Powers Act of 1940 enabled the Government in London, through its rapidly expanding administrative organs, to acquire an almost unlimited ability to mobilise both people and resources. ('Almost' unlimited, because in the last resort that same Government remained dependent on Parliamentary support.)[146] In Japan, under an order issued in September 1940, the Government set about establishing a network of community and neighbourhood councils, which were not only to organise the life of the people (including all its economic aspects) but also to facilitate their 'moral training and spiritual unity': in short, to bring about what one historian describes as 'a gigantic piece of social engineering to prepare everybody for a concentrated war build-up'.[147] Other legislation, such as the National Defence Security Law of May 1941, together with Japan's underlying political culture, helped ensure that there was little freedom for the individual citizen. Despite these new developments, however, and despite the earlier consequences of the 1938 National General Mobilization Law, the qualification made earlier remains valid. Even under Tojo, the Government did not possess the powers of an absolute dictatorship, and in the economic sphere, for example, the continued existence of powerful and varied interest groups meant that centralised control was far from being achieved.[148]

The pattern of increased governmental intervention on a statutory basis could be traced elsewhere – in Vichy France, for example. Equally significant for the future, however, could be less easily measured changes involving the relationships between government on the one hand and various sections of society on the other. Although the United States was not yet at war, for example, the mounting international crisis in the Far East was itself sufficient to involve a company like Standard-Vacuum Oil more closely with Washington's foreign-policy decisions.[149] On the domestic scene – where the New Deal had already enhanced the role of the administration, of course, and where Roosevelt was making his contribution to the long-term creation of an 'imperial presidency'[150] – the gradual gearing-up for war, even if only as the supplier of other democracies,* was also restoring the prestige and opportunities of corporate business, and bringing individuals from its ranks into the Washington apparatus.[151] In turn, as the New Deal coalition that Roosevelt had put together began to split apart, leaders of the labour unions argued among themselves over the likely consequences for programmes of social reform of this move towards a war economy. And here, too, the line of policy that was adopted led to an increased involvement with – and, in this case, dependence on – the power and processes of Washington.[152]

War was also affecting attitudes towards the people as a whole, and towards the purposes and priorities of administration, among governmental and bureaucratic elites. Officials within Britain's Ministry of Information, for example, who initially placed considerable emphasis upon 'class feeling' as a potential threat to morale, had before the end of 1941 come to concede with relief that the public had after all proved stalwart and essentially united in the face of adversity.[153] As for the attitudes of officials involved at the London end in administering Britain's colonial territories, even before September 1939 the economic depression had fostered in the Colonial Office greatly increased concern over matters of social welfare – though it was a concern that obviously sprang in part from the fear that hardship would fuel political unrest. The view that had come to predominate by 1941 – summarised in a recent study as the belief that 'capitalism could not be left to proceed [in the colonies] without the moderating restraints of an administration equipped with a knowledge of social welfare' – found expression in the Colonial Development and Welfare Act of 1940.[154] In that same year, too, the leasing of West Indian bases to the U.S.A. was already giving a new, international dimension to such issues. (Churchill himself was anxious to ensure that welfare provisions in the islands should not seem less advanced than those in the American-administered areas, just as Washington was concerned lest unrest among West Indian blacks fuel racial unrest within the U.S.)[155] Meanwhile, the need to mobilise fully the resources of the Empire in the face of Germany's attack was producing a web of new controls and instructions where the colonies were concerned. 'The colonial system became more regularised and colonial societies more regulated.'[156]

Involvement in war was also raising issues within a number of societies regarding the basis on which the government of the day was to be established. In Japan, for example, the perception of a sustained national crisis had contributed to that eclipse of the party system and predominance of the military that had developed during and after the Manchurian episode in 1931–33. In contrast, the widespread belief in Britain that the conflict against Germany was 'a people's war' was reflected in the multi-party nature

* U.S. munitions production increased by 285 per cent in 1941.

of the National Government and the crucial role within it of Ernest Bevin as Minister of Labour. In both Australia and New Zealand, even so, war-time governments continued to rest upon a single-party basis. As we have seen, the Australian Labour Party remained profoundly hostile towards those sections of society – 'interests who hope to make large profits out of the war,' H.V. Evatt called them in September 1940 – which they identified with Robert Menzies and his U.A.P.–Country Party administration; in return, Menzies viewed Curtin and his Labour colleagues, who themselves formed a Government in October 1941, as 'scum – positive scum'.[157] Strong currents of antipathy and suspicion, essentially political in nature, also swirled around relations between Curtin's new administration and the country's senior military figures.[158] As for the Netherlands, where both the Head of State and Government were out of the country, we have already noted the varied and uncertain reactions to the German conquest. (D.J. de Geer, for example, who was the first Prime Minister in exile, resigned in September 1940 and, having made his way from London back to the Netherlands, sought to explain his actions in a thoroughly defeatist sense.)[159] In addition, however, there were those others who were moved to question the very basis upon which the country's political life had been organised: a basis (*verzuiling*, or separate pillars upholding the state) involving the segmentation of both political culture and social activities, above all along religious lines; a basis which, some now felt, should be replaced by one which promoted political and labour organisations of a less sectional kind.[160]

But what was the existing war *for*? What should follow such a cataclysm? What positive, long-term goals could and should accompany the suffering and the sacrifice? In East Asia from 1937 and in Europe after 1939 such questions were already being formulated, or at least were latent in the situation. As we have seen in the preceding chapter, they were addressed in part to issues of an international nature, including those concerning the future of empires. A frequent argument, however, was that a just and stable post-war international order could be created only if the appropriate conditions were achieved within individual societies. 'The collapse of nation after nation before a doctrine of ethical nihilism,' declared the historian, Alfred Cobban, in 1941, 'is proof of the inadequacies of the principles on which Western civilisation rests today.'[161] 'It is around the concept of security, both international and social,' argued the *Sydney Morning Herald*, 'that our concepts of post-war reconstruction must revolve ... There is a very real sense in which it is true to say this terrible tragedy ... is the result of unemployment.'[162] 'Democracy can only survive,' wrote E.H. Carr in 1940, 'by ceasing to be a competitive institution, primarily concerned in the distribution of rewards, and by becoming a cooperative institution for producing a more abundant and cheap output ...'[163]

In besieged Britain, then, as in occupied France[164] and in some quarters, at least, in China[165] and the Netherlands,[166] the experience of total war, while on the one hand it was giving added urgency to a preoccupation with the present, was also fostering a desire to establish the bases of long-term and radical social change. Nor were such attitudes to be encountered solely on the left of the political spectrum. To take a single example, among those in London who believed in 1940 that Churchill's Government was failing in its duty in not proclaiming such war aims for both domestic and international societies was the Australian High Commissioner, Bruce. And his own draft for such a statement included, in addition to items on the prevention of war, 'the effective utilisation of our powers of production for human welfare, and the provision of social justice'. What was required, he privately urged prominent politicians, was 'a national revolution' in Britain that would inspire others in Europe and the Dominions: a revolution that would 'actively realise the partnership of all citizens in the productive capacities of the nation', provide 'a new definition of a minimum standard of living', and acknowledge 'the obligation of the State to give all its citizens adequate training and a full opportunity for useful work'.[167]

Some believed that fundamental social and political change was in fact already under way, whether governments chose to see it or not. 'The masses are on the move,' was how Harold Laski was soon to describe the situation to Roosevelt.[168] 'Behind the smokescreen of battles,' wrote the American diplomat, John Carter Vincent, privately in 1940, 'great social forces are at work.' As he saw it, the development amounted to 'a dynamic revolt against anti-social national sovereignties and anti-social free capitalism', a revolt 'of the subordinate majority [against] the static, dominant minority'. Hence his fear, already noted in chapter two, lest the United States should find itself directly involved in the war without having established beforehand within its own body politic 'social reform and social objectives' that would not then be submerged in the military struggle that would ensue.[169]

*

If, looking back on the pre-war years, we bear in mind the extent and depth of the changes that were indeed in the making within domestic contexts, as well as internationally, it is scarcely surprising, as we have remarked before, that many contemporaries felt that they were standing on uncertain ground. 'Our generation,' wrote Sjahrir in the East Indies,

> 'is more or less undergoing a change at this time. We have a concept of life, we have conviction, but it is not yet mature within us . . . This period of history . . . is one of confusion, wandering and spiritual suffering . . . We belong to a generation of transition . . .'[170]

Against such a background, it is possible that even the loud confidence in their own society's qualities and mission* being expressed by 'double patriots' of various nationalities was sometimes the manifestation of an underlying and unacknowledged sense of insecurity. Beneath the xenophobic outcry in Japan, suggests one student, there was much 'pessimism and passivity', arising in part because 'so many of the actors saw themselves removed from stage to balcony, being more and more part of a mass society ...'[171] Certainly, one of the features that stands out in retrospect as embracing many of the societies that were to be involved in the 1941 war is a pronounced degree of not merely questioning but self-criticism and lack of confidence. Among Indian nationalists, for example, were those who saw in the caste system what the *Bombay Chronicle* termed 'an unmitigated disgrace to Indian culture and nationhood'.[172] Phrases such as 'age-long torpor' were also employed by Congress politicians to describe the attitude of the Indian people towards both the struggle for independence and the social evils in their midst.[173] 'Even the most militant part of our Indonesian people,' reflected Sjahrir, '... remain still a part of this passive East,' while he attributed their enthusiasm for Japan's successes in the 1930s to their underlying 'inferiority feelings' vis-à-vis the white man.[174]† In the 1900s and the inter-war years, Vietnamese nationalists argued that independence could be achieved only if there took place 'a transformation and revitalization of the national character', a 'spiritual rebirth'.[175] In Malaya, meanwhile, the fiercely Islamic periodical, *Al-Imam*, founded in the early years of the century, indulged in what has been termed 'an orgy of self-condemnation', while of young Malays in the 1920s, such as those who were training to be teachers, it has been written that they possessed 'the underlying conviction ... that as people they were politically incapable, economically inept, and culturally inferior to others ...'[176]‡

There were, clearly, particular conditions that were conducive to such attitudes among those living under colonial rule. Among the Chinese, too, however – so long assured of their identity and superior culture within 'the Middle Kingdom'[177] – there were a good many, according to Eastman, who now felt that 'there was something basically and radically wrong with the Chinese people', so that the 1930s witnessed in consequence 'a period of painful, remorseless, national self-flagellation' that amounted in some cases

* Beside Japanese and American voices being raised in this sense, Bose, for example, drawing parallels with seventeenth-century England, eighteenth-century France, nineteenth-century Germany and twentieth-century Russia, foresaw for India 'an important role in world history in the near future'. M. Bose, *The Lost Hero*, 105.

† For a discussion of the related psychological process, see Mannoni, *Prospero and Caliban*, passim.

‡ In this context, it is also worth looking ahead to the post-war criticisms that were to be levelled against the character and qualities of his fellow-Burmese by the leading nationalist politician of the day, Aung San. See Maung Maung, *Aung San*, 141.

to a 'cultural despair'.[178] As the iconoclasts, in the words of another scholar, 'paid their bitter respects to the old China' with their anti-Confucianism, Marxism became all the more attractive as a means of finding confidence in the face of the Western challenge.[179]

The strong element of self-criticism that existed at the same time in European societies has already been indicated. In this respect, at least, André Gide was not a-typical when, in 1934, he saw around him 'nothing but distress' and 'monstrous blindness' – reflections far removed from his certainty in May 1914 'that our Occidental (I was about to say French) civilization is not only the most beautiful; I believe that it is the *only one* ...'.[180] Faced with the might of the Germans and the betrayal of the Vichyites, France by December 1941, declared the Resistance paper, *Combat*, was in danger of losing 'at one and the same time her body and her soul'.[181] The only way to achieve salvation, another clandestine publication was to argue, in a phrase that many in Britain and elsewhere would have echoed, was to fight 'in order to achieve a complete break with the past'.[182]

A Frenchman or a Chinese who thought and spoke in such terms did so in the context of a long and proud national tradition. For some in Australia, on the other hand, the fear was that a truly organic society, possessing its own distinct identity and capable of generating a unifying sense of purpose, had yet to be created. Conclusions of this kind, which, as we shall see, were to be loudly voiced during the Far Eastern conflict, were already being prompted before December 1941 by such phenomena as strikes for higher pay that were taking place despite the fact that the country was at war. Thus, in July of that year, the *Sydney Morning Herald* found it

> 'saddening and perplexing to contemplate, as events are moving to a climax in the Far East, the industrial and political discord which is today an outstanding feature of the Australian scene. The disunity which is holding the country back from a full and concentrated war effort must obviously spring from a deficient sense of realism and responsibility in some quarters, and from a failure to understand the true nature of our present danger.'[183]

'Unfortunately,' the same newspaper had argued at the end of 1940, 'we have not, in Australia, begun to tread the path of national regeneration on which the British people are moving.' And it had added a reflection (all the more interesting when coming from what was an essentially conservative organ, politically speaking) that points us back to both the social and the international consequences of the struggle Japan was soon to launch in the Far East:

'The war,' it asserted, 'will certainly leave the material basis of our civilisation so shaken and changed that the old habits of thought and the old social and political prejudices will be outmoded and dangerous.'[184]

*

We have seen in the preceding chapter how 'old habits of thought' were proving inadequate in relation to international society: how it had become 'increasingly hard', in James Joll's words, 'to apply old categories, both practically and theoretically', to a rapidly changing system. It is evident in retrospect that acute problems of conceptualising were also present or rapidly approaching within many of the individual societies that were to be caught up in the 1941–45 war. And this leads us to a further way – in addition, that is, to the various patterns of connections that were illustrated at the beginning of the chapter – in which it is possible to bring together and view both the domestic and the international contexts of the Far Eastern conflict.

It is a truism to observe that in the years leading up to that struggle the pace as well as the extent of change was increasing in numerous respects. Indeed, if we accept the division of historical time proposed by Fernand Braudel:[185] that is, into the rapidly-moving 'individual' (or political) time; the slower rhythms of 'social' time; and, slowest of all, 'geographical' time (described by Braudel as the 'almost changeless history of man in relation to his surroundings'), then we can see that in this period not only was the social metronome beginning to beat a pace closer to that to which individuals and political events were moving, but that even its geographical counterpart was starting to race, as scientific discovery and technological innovation diminished space and natural obstacles alike.

Within such a context, with its domestic and international dimensions, the challenges to the assumptions and perceptions of contemporaries may to some extent be likened to the situation depicted by Kuhn in relation to the gestation of revolutions in scientific thought.[186] In such periods, Kuhn argues, existing paradigms* are increasingly unable to cope with the phenomena and problems being encountered (the eventual outcome being 'changes of world view'; 'significant shifts in the criteria determining the legitimacy of both problems and of proposed solutions'). The suggestion being advanced here, in other words, is that Einstein's description, for example, of the confusion that arose from the inadequacy of existing

---

* Kuhn employs the term paradigm to denote shared values and a shared commitment to certain fundamental beliefs in particular models (*The Structure of Scientific Revolutions*, 180 ff.). He himself emphasises that the central theses of the work were derived from non-scientific fields; it is thus the less surprising if it appears appropriate to 'borrow them back', so to speak.

scientific paradigms on the eve of the revolution associated with his own work in particular – 'It was as if the ground had been pulled from under one, with no firm foundation to be seen anywhere, upon which one could have built' – broadly speaking matches some of those we have seen being employed, after 1918 especially, by observers of both the international scene and individual societies.

Obviously, the analogue must not be pushed too far. The composition of entire societies or bodies politic, for example, and the concerns and thought processes to be encountered within them, are far removed from those of the scientific community. (In other words, the basic concepts of social and political thought will never be radically transformed by the universal acceptance of a paradigm that can be encapsulated in the proposition, say, that $E = mc^2$.)* But in terms of domestic and international structures, the ground was indeed in the process of being pulled from under the feet of a large proportion, if not all, of those who were to be involved in the coming war. 'Mankind has come to a crisis where none of the old formulae work,' wrote the British author, Naomi Mitchison, at the end of 1938: 'everything is on too big a scale. Physics has done in psychology.'[187] And if it was from among the clerisies that there emerged, on the one hand, the desperate reiteration of old values and prescriptions, and, on the other, calls for 'new habits of thought' and new foundations, the sense of uncertainty and even of crisis went much wider.† The origins of the Far Eastern conflict need to be

---

* And as J.G. Pocock has emphasised in his *Politics, Language and Time* (London, 1972), in the political arena paradigms simultaneously perform a variety of functions on a variety of levels and within a variety of contexts. Pocock himself, however, points to a societal process that is not entirely dissimilar to the one Kuhn has explored in terms of the world of the scientist: 'When a change in a society's self-awareness has become at all widely disseminated, that society's style of thinking and acting have been irreversibly altered. There may still be much in its traditions of behaviour which has not emerged into consciousness and perhaps never will; what has changed, however, is its mode of being and becoming conscious of itself and its existence in time, and once that has happened a society is no longer what it was.' (Op. cit., 15ff., 239.) It is also worth recalling that the 'scientific revolution' of the seventeenth century, for example, was 'as much a social and cultural phenomenon as a revolution in scientific method and cosmology'. (*New Cambridge Modern History, Vol. XIII*, 250.) For those who, like the present writer, still need help with $E = mc^2$, see e.g. J.A. Coleman, *Relativity for the Layman* (New York, 1954).

† See e.g. D.G. Marr's description of the situation in Vietnam from the 1920s onwards: 'Most of the world had undergone momentous change by [then]. First in ripples, then in waves, the impact would be felt in Vietnam . . . [which] was [now] a part of world history as never before imagined . . . The critical, sustained challenge to the Vietnamese identity that had affected the elite of the previous generation had at last become the apocalyptic nightmare of the millions. Economic crisis intensified the fears and torments of almost every segment of the population . . .' (*Vietnamese Anti-Colonialism, 1885–1925*, 253, 276.) The situation was broadly similar in Korea, for example. And in Europe in the 1930s, Norbert Elias was writing: 'It is clear in what turmoils and dangers we live . . . It is [structural] forces, . . . it is tensions and entanglements of this kind, which at present constantly expose the individual to fear and anxiety. The tensions between states . . . impose upon individuals a mounting work-pressure and also a profound insecurity which never ceases . . . The same holds true of

seen, in part, as stemming from these circumstances. The process of the conflict was to contribute to their development.

Notes

1 Quoted in Storry, *The Double Patriots*, 38. And see the comments of Maruyama on the support of the lower middle class or 'pseudo intellectuals' in Japan for the China and the 1941–5 wars. Op. cit., 64–5.
2 E.g. P. Mason, *Prospero's Magic: Some Thoughts on Class and Race* (London, 1962). And see below, 77.
3 Wolf, *Europe and the People Without History*.
4 On this question in general, see e.g. F. Braudel, *On History* (trs. S. Matthews, London, 1980), and P. Burke, 'Concepts of Continuity and Change in History', *New Cambridge Modern History, vol. XIII* (Cambridge, 1979).
5 E. Gellner, *Nations and Nationalism* (Oxford, 1983); *Thought and Change* (London, 1964). The contribution offered in this field by D. Bell in his *The Cultural Contradictions of Capitalism* (New York, 1976) is impaired by a number of facile historical assertions.
6 *Nations and Nationalism*, 111.
7 B. Anderson, *Imagined Communities: Reflections on the Origins and Spread of Nationalism* (London, 1983).
8 See e.g. E. Kedourie, *Nationalism* (London, 1960); H. Kohn, *The Idea of Nationalism* (New York, 1946); J. Breuilly, *Nationalism and the State* (Manchester, 1982).
9 See e.g. Breuilly's comparison of Japan and China in this respect: op. cit., 215ff.
10 See J. Plamenatz, 'Two Types of Nationalism', in E. Kamenka (ed.), *Nationalism: the Nature and Evolution of an Idea* (London, 1976).
11 M. Weber, *The Protestant Ethic and the Spirit of Capitalism* (trs. T. Parsons, New York, 1958), 26.
12 R.E. Park, *Race and Culture* (New York, 1950), 9, 249.
13 Sjahrir, op. cit., 144.
14 T. Fukutake, *The Japanese Social Structure: its Evolution in the Modern Century* (trs. R.P. Dore, Tokyo, 1982), 4.
15 Ibid, 124, 159.
16 See e.g. D. Hay, *Europe: the Emergence of an Idea* (Edinburgh, 1968).
17 J. Marquand, in *Asia*, July 1941.
18 Berger (ed.), *Kenkenroku*, 55.
19 See Jansen, *The Japanese and Sun Yat-sen*, and Iriye (ed.), *The Chinese and the Japanese*.
20 Murphy, *The Outsiders*, 7, 9, 72–4; Cohen, *Discovering History in China*; cf. Jansen, *Changing Japanese Attitudes Toward Modernization*, 277ff., and J.R. Levenson, *Confucian China and its Modern State*, 3 vols. (London, 1958, 1964, 1965).
21 On Japan in this light, see e.g., Maruyama, *Thought and Behaviour in Modern Japanese Politics*, 34 ff.
22 See K. Hayashi, 'Japan and Germany in the Interwar Period', in Morley, *Dilemmas of*

the tensions within each of the different state societies ... The case is no different with economic struggles.' (*The Civilizing Process: State Formation and Civilization*, 329–32.) Cf. Margaret Mead's comments in 1941 on the need for 'a critical re-evaluation of our culture in the light of the changes resulting from the extraordinary advances in technology which have introduced so many discordances into our way of life and our value system' (*Anthropology: A Human Science*, 97), and the subsequent work done by her and others on the consequences of such changes in the realm of mental health (Mead, ed., *Cultural Patterns and Technical Change*, New York, 1955).

Growth in Pre-War Japan. Cf., however, Maruyama's essay, 'The Ideology and Dynamics of Japanese Fascism', op. cit.

23 B.A. Shillony, *Politics and Culture in Wartime Japan* (Oxford, 1981), 11, 175.

24 L.E. Eastman, *The Abortive Revolution: China Under Nationalist Rule, 1927–1937* (Cambridge, Mass., 1974).

25 See Nisbet, *History of the Idea of Progress*, and I.F. Clarke, *The Pattern of Expectation* (London, 1979).

26 M.H. Hunt, in W.I. Cohen (ed.), *New Frontiers in American-East Asian Relations* (New York, 1983), 19. And see Cohen, *Discovering History*, cap. 2 and passim.

27 See, e.g. the relevant essays in *New Cambridge Modern History, vol. XIII*; and on the development of a 'world market economy'. Gilpin, op. cit., 127ff.

28 See, e.g. Murphy, op. cit., 24.

29 Duiker, op. cit., 103ff., 134ff., 190ff.

30 P.H.W. Sitsen, *Industrial Development of the Netherlands Indies* (New York, 1944); W.F. Wertheim, *Indonesian Society in Transition* (The Hague, 1964), 101ff.; J.M. van der Kroef, *The Communist Party of Indonesia* (Vancouver, 1965), 19.

31 R.C. Ray, *Industrialization in India: Growth and Conflict in the Private Corporate Sector, 1914–1947* (Delhi, 1979), 1ff., 45, 52, 251, 354ff.; B.R. Tomlinson, *The Political Economy of the Raj, 1914–1947* (London, 1979), 1–56; R. von Albertini, *European Colonial Rule. 1880–1940: the Impact of the West on India, Southeast Asia, and Africa* (trans. J.G. Williamson; Westport, Conn., 1982), 58ff., 504.

32 Cumings, *The Origins of the Korean War*, xxii, 13ff., 26, 54; S. Pao-San Ho, 'Colonialism and Development: Korea, Taiwan and Kwantung', in Myers and Peattie, op. cit.

33 See P.K. Sih (ed.), *Nationalist China During the Sino-Japanese War, 1937–1945* (Hicksville, N.Y., 1977), 205.

34 See Jansen, *Changing Japanese Attitudes Toward Modernization*, passim.

35 Maruyama, op. cit., 78; C. Johnson, *MITI and the Japanese Miracle* (Stanford, 1982), 96ff., 113.

36 Fukutake, *The Japanese Social Structure*, 21.

37 Johnson, *MITI*, 6, 155–7; Allen, *Appointment in Japan*, 73–4, 160.

38 Johnson, *MITI*, 119ff.

39 Havens, *Valley of Darkness*, 35.

40 See e.g. Morley, *Dilemmas of Growth*, and Ogata, *Defiance in Manchuria*.

41 Fukutake, *Japanese Social Structure*, 33.

42 Ibid, 71.

43 Ibid, 14–15, 25ff, 42ff., 52ff. This section rests essentially on Professor Fukutake's analysis. On the related weakness of ostensibly democratic politics in Japan, see R. Scalapino, *Democracy and the Party Movement in Prewar Japan* (Berkeley, 1962).

44 Maruyama, op. cit., 146.

45 Fukutake, 16.

46 Ray, 339ff.

47 See e.g. Tate, *The Making of Modern South East Asia, vol. 2* (Kuala Lumpur, 1979), 34, 94–5; and, on the related debate among the Dutch themselves, van der Kroef, op. cit. and Schmultzer, op. cit.

48 Tate, 345ff.

49 L.E. Bouzon, *Philippine Agrarian Reform. 1880–1965: the Revolution that Never Was* (Singapore, 1975); Tate, op. cit., 438, 474ff.; C. Porter, *Philippine Emergency* (New York, 1941), 31; B.J. Kerkvliet, *The Huk Rebellion: a Study of Peasant Revolt in the Philippines* (Berkeley, 1977), 22 ff. and cap. 2.

50 von Albertini, op. cit., 121.

51 Eastman, *Abortive Revolution*, 181ff.

52 Cumings, op. cit., 27–8, 42ff. For assessments of the social consequences of Japanese imperial rule overall, see Myers and Peattie, 35ff., 43ff., 380ff.

53 Endacott and Birch, *Hong Kong Eclipse*, 11, 329, 361.

54 W.R. Roff, *The Origins of Malay Nationalism* (New Haven, 1967), 124; Tate, op. cit., 241;

D. Scarr (ed.), *Fiji: The Three-legged Stool: The Selected Writings of Ratu Sir Lala Sukuna* (London, 1984), e.g. 1ff., 74ff., 131, 212ff.
55 J.M. Lee and M. Petter, *The Colonial Office, War, and Development Policy* (London, 1982), 25.
56 D'Encausse and Schram, op. cit., 13ff.
57 Duiker, op. cit., 45.
58 Nehru, *Toward Freedom*, 278.
59 See e.g. M. Bose, *The Lost Hero* (London, 1982), 30, 76, and above all the issues of Bose's own journal, *Forward Bloc*, founded after his defeat by Gandhi within Congress.
60 See Garvey, op. cit., e.g. on 'World Materialism', and Cronon, op. cit., on e.g. Garvey's ill-fated Negro Factories Corporation and Black Star shipping line.
61 John Curtin, for example, leader of the Australian Labour Party and war-time Prime Minister, stressed that this was the only means by which the country could carry through socialist policies. Statements by Curtin, 19 Aug. 1942 and 24 April 1944, Prime Minister's Papers (A 1608), D/41/1/5 and A21/1/2, Australian National Archives.
62 A. Toynbee, introduction to his *Survey of International Affairs, 1931* (Oxford, 1932).
63 Tennyson, 'Locksley Hall' and 'Locksley Hall Sixty Years After' respectively.
64 See, e.g. Clarke, op. cit.; Cruickshank, op. cit.; J.U. Nef, *War and Human Progress* (London, 1950); R. Caillois, *Bellone, ou la pente de la guerre* (Brussels, 1963).
65 See Giner, op. cit., and M.D. Biddiss, *The Age of the Masses: Ideas and Society in Europe since 1870* (Hassocks, 1977).
66 Quoted in Cruickshank, 31; and see, e.g. 89, 125. Also, R. Wohl, *The Generation of 1914* (London, 1980); E.J. Leed, *No Man's Land: Combat and Identity in World War One* (Cambridge, 1979); P. Fussell, *The Great War in Modern Memory* (London, 1975); M. Eksteins, 'When Death Was Young', in R. J. Bullen et al. (ed.). *Ideas Into Politics* (London, 1984).
67 L. Mumford, *Technics and Civilization* (London, 1946), 273.
68 Liang Qichao, quoted in J.D. Spence, *The Gate of Heavenly Peace: the Chinese and their Revolution, 1895–1980* (London, 1982), 206.
69 See, e.g. Treadgold, vol. 1, 85ff., 166ff., and Gong, op. cit., 99ff.
70 Lord Kinross, *Atatürk: the Rebirth of a Nation* (London, 1964), 377ff.
71 R. Carr, *Spain, 1808–1939* (Oxford, 1966), 530–1.
72 See, e.g. Ch'en, op. cit., 33; Murphey, op. cit., 28 ff.; Jansen, *Changing Japanese Attitudes*, 205ff., 311ff.
73 Park, 'Culture and Civilization', in *Race and Culture*.
74 Quoted in Iriye, *Power and Culture*, 34. And see G.M. Wilson, 'Reflections on Japanese Imperialist Ideology', in Goodman (ed.), *Imperial Japan and Asia*, 48–9.
75 Toynbee, loc. cit. Cf. Margaret Mead's essay, 'World Culture', in *Anthropology: A Human Science*.
76 Murphey, 2ff., 27.
77 Purcell, *The Revolution in Southeast Asia*, 11.
78 Reischauer, op. cit., 228.
79 Ibid, 128.
80 M. Gandhi, 'Hind Swaraj', in his *Collected Works, vol. X* (Delhi, 1963), 18–24.
81 Tagore, *Nationalism*.
82 Crowley, *Modern East Asia*, 90.
83 Ibid, 118–9. And see Jansen, *Changing Japanese Attitudes*, passim.
84 A. Iriye, 'The Ideological Background of Japan's War Against Asia and the West', *International Studies*, 1982, II.
85 On this issue in general, see Smith, *The Ethnic Revival*, 96ff.
86 Duiker, 104ff., 177ff., and D.G. Marr, *Vietnamese Anti-Colonialism, 1885–1925* (Berkeley, 1971).
87 Wyatt, *The Politics of Reform in Thailand*, quoted in Gong, op, cit., 244; Roff, 87.
88 Crowley, *Modern East Asia*, 176, 214.
89 S. Schram, in *Times Literary Supplement*, 19 Aug. 1983. And see e.g. Ch'en, 173, 204, 428, 432, 437–8, and Spence, op. cit., passim.

90 See Levenson, *Confucian China*, vol. I, 59ff., 95ff.; Spence, 213–16; Hay, *Asian Ideas*, caps. 2 and 6.
91 Crowley, *Modern East Asia*, 158.
92 Eastman, *Abortive Revolution*, 214. Johnson (*Peasant Nationalism*, 69 and passim) over-states the extent to which 'prior to 1937 the peasants were a passive element in politics' and understates the domestic causes of their politicisation.
93 See e.g. the article by Rewi Alley (a New Zealander who did much to assist the industrial cooperative movement) in *Asia*, Jan. 1940; Thorne, *Allies*, 68, 193.
94 E.g,. Mme Chiang to Nehru, 22 April 1942, Nehru Papers, Correspondence, vol. 13.
95 Eastman, *Abortive Revolution*, 310.
96 See J. Needham, *Chinese Science* (London, 1945), and *Science Outpost* (London, 1948).
97 Needham Papers, section 15; and see e.g. S.H. Frankel, quoted in Gilpin, op. cit., 64.
98 R. Polenberg, *One Nation Divisible: Class, Race and Ethnicity in the United States Since 1938* (London, 1980), 17.
99 Tate, 464.
100 See Breuilly, *Nationalism and the State*, 229.
101 On the position of blacks in America at the time, see e.g. G. Myrdal, *An American Dilemma* (2 vols.; New York, 1944); Polenberg, *One Nation Divisible*; Smith, *The Ethnic Revival*, 160ff.
102 R. Hunt and J. Harrison, *The District Officer in India, 1930–1947* (London, 1980), 161; Tate, 130–1.
103 See Tate, 235, 463; Roff, passim; and V. Purcell, *The Chinese in Southeast Asia* (Oxford, 1965).
104 See e.g. Morris, *Corregidor*, 3, 189, and Endicott and Birch, passim. Also, in general terms, Smith, *The Ethnic Revival*, 141ff.
105 The following passage is based upon J.G. Butcher, *The British in Malaya, 1860–1941* (Kuala Lumpur, 1979).
106 Ibid, 122, For an exploration of similar topics in nineteenth century India, see K. Ball-hatchet, *Race, Sex and Class under the Raj* (London, 1980), and on the psychological aspects of such situations, Mannoni, *Prospero and Caliban*.
107 Roff, 101.
108 E.g. Tate, 476; Steinberg, 23; Kerkvliet, cap. 2. On MacArthur's relations with this oligarchy, see the Ickes diary (Library of Congress), passim. On the Hukbalahap move-ment, see below, 153.
109 Clapper report, 1942, Clapper Papers, box 36.
110 M. Hane, *Peasants, Rebels and Outcastes: the Underside of Modern Japan* (New York, 1982), 139ff. On the development of the Indian caste system in the context of religious and philosophical beliefs, see D. P. Singhal, *A History of the Indian People* (London, 1983).
111 Eastman, *Abortive Revolution*, 239ff., 284ff. and e.g. May, *China Scapegoat*, 72; White, *In Search of History*, 72.
112 T. Zeldin, *France, 1848–1945, Vol. 1* (Oxford, 1974), section 3.
113 M. Foot, *Aneurin Bevan, Vol. 1, 1897–1942* (London, 1975), 148ff.
114 Curtin statement of 19 Oct. 1939, and letter to Bishop of Newcastle, 12 July 1940, Tonkin Papers, box 28.
115 On the distinction, as it existed within the U.S.A. at the time, see Polenberg, *One Nation Divisible*, 24ff.
116 S. de Beauvoir, *The Prime of Life* (London, 1981), 367; M. Mead, *Ruth Benedict* (New York, 1974), 17.
117 See E. Croll, *Feminism and Socialism in China* (London, 1978), caps. 2–4; B. Siu, *Women of China: Imperialism and Woman's Resistance, 1900–1949* (London, 1982), cap. 4 and 128ff.; J.M. Everett, *Women and Social Change in India* (New Delhi, 1981), caps. IV–VI; Bose, op. cit., 66; D. Robins-Mowry, *The Hidden Sun: Women of Modern Japan* (Boulder, Colorado, 1983), caps. 2–3; Hane, op. cit., 79ff.; Fukutake, op. cit., 31; S.A. Chipp and J.T. Green (ed.), *Asian Women in Transition* (Pennsylvania, 1980), passim; Scarr, *Fiji*, 105.

118 Robins-Mowry, 80; Everett, 76ff., 110; Croll, 5, and cap. 6. And see e.g. V. Mehta, *Daddyji. Mamaji* (London, 1984).
119 Chipp and Green, 159ff.; Everett, 80–1; Spence, op. cit., 84; Ch'en, op. cit., 380ff.
120 J.D. Wilkinson, *The Intellectual Resistance in Europe* (Cambridge, Mass., 1981), 7; R.H.S. Crossman (ed.), *The God That Failed* (New York, 1954), 4.
121 Ch'en, 70, 82, 90; Jansen, *The Japanese and Sun Yat-sen*; Tang, op. cit.; Cowley, *Modern East Asia*, 215ff.
122 Reischauer, 97; and see Maruyama, op. cit.; Scalapino, op. cit.; Crowley, *Modern East Asia*, 180ff.
123 Purcell, *Revolution*, 55–6.
124 See above, 75; Kerkvliet, op. cit.; and, for the post-war reflections of an American Ambassador to the Philippines, C.E. Bohlen, *Witness to History* (London, 1973), 452.
125 See Dahm, 43, 68–9, 107–8.
126 See Duiker, passim, and Chen, *Vietnam and China*, 15ff.
127 On the Thakin Party and other features of the Burmese political scene, see the Introduction to H. Tinker (ed.), *Burma: the Struggle for Independence. 1944–1946, Vol. 1* (London, 1983).
128 See e.g. S. Schram, *Mao Tse-tung* (London, 1967).
129 D.Encausse and Schram, section III.
130 See e.g. Royal Institute of International Affairs, *Nationalism* (Oxford, 1939) for a contemporary survey of the phenomenon, and above, 56–8. On the attractions of Marxism for Asian nationalists, see Wang Gungwu, 'Nationalism in Asia', in Kamenka (ed.), *Nationalism: the Nature and Evolution of an Idea*, 90.
131 *Le Temps*, 23 Feb. 1941. And see in general, Paxton, op. cit.
132 Eastman, *Abortive Revolution*, 41, 66ff.; Eastman, *Seeds of Destruction*, cap. 4.
133 See e.g. Ogata, op. cit.; Storry, op. cit. Also, e.g. International Military Tribunal for the Far East, document no. 1908 B.
134 R. Hoftstadter, *The Paranoid Style in American Politics* (New York, 1967), 23.
135 Ickes diary, 30 Nov. 1941.
136 See Gordon, op. cit.
137 See L. van Slyke (ed.), *The Chinese Communist Movement: a Report of the U.S. War Department, July 1945* (Stanford, 1968), 82, 105; Boyle, op. cit., 209, 222, 289ff.; Cowley, *Modern East Asia*, 277ff.; Johnson, *Peasant Nationalism*, 136–40.
138 D. Wilson, *When Tigers Fight: the Story of the Sino-Japanese War, 1937–1945* (London, 1982), 8.
139 R. Manvell, *Films and the Second World War* (London, 1974), 45ff.
140 See, e.g. Wilson, op. cit., 111.
141 Ibid, 1, and e.g. F.Schurmann and O.Schell, *China Readings: Republican China* (London, 1968), 252ff.; Spence, 315; Sih, *Nationalist China*, 98ff.
142 Korean exports of rice to Japan fell from 1.7 million metric tons in 1938 to 66,000 tons in 1940, when supplies from Indochina soared to 1.3 million tons. Cumings, op. cit., 51.
143 See, e.g. W. Warmbrunn, *The Dutch Under German Occupation, 1940–1945* (Stanford, 1963); J.C.H. Blom, 'The Second World War and Dutch Society: Continuity and Change', in A.S. Duke and C.A. Tamse (eds.), *Britain and the Netherlands, vol. VI* (The Hague, 1977).
144 On British society and the coming of war, see e.g. A. Calder, *The People's War: Britain, 1939–1945* (London, 1969); A. Marwick, *Britain in the Century of Total War* (London, 1968); McLean, op. cit.
145 'New Zealand War Effort', New Zealand Ministry of External Affairs files, 81/1/14, part 2.
146 See, e.g. W.K. Hancock and M.M. Gowing, *British War Economy* (London, 1949), 83ff.
147 Havens, 75ff.
148 Johnson, *MITI*, 139; Shillony, 9ff.; R. Rice, 'Economic Mobilisation in Wartime Japan: Business, Bureaucracy and Military in Conflict', *Journal of Asian Studies*, Aug. 1979.
149 See I.H. Anderson, *The Standard-Vacuum Oil Company and United States East Asian Policy, 1933–1941* (Princeton, 1975).

150 See A.M. Schlesinger, *The Imperial Presidency* (London, 1974), although it is a work that understates Roosevelt's contribution to the developments in question.
151 See, e.g. R. Polenberg, *War and Society. The United States, 1941–1945* (Philadelphia, 1972), 89ff.; J.M. Blum, *V Was for Victory: Politics and American Culture During World War II* (New York, 1976), 105ff.
152 N. Lichtenstein, *Labor's War at Home: the C10 in World War II* (Cambridge, 1982), 26ff., 33f.
153 McLean, 63ff., 93ff., 136; A. Marwick, *Class: Image and Reality in Britain, France and the U.S.A. Since 1930* (London, 1980), 220.
154 Lee and Petter, op. cit., 31–2.
155 Ibid, 80, 101ff., 113.
156 Ibid, 75.
157 Tonkin Papers, box 28, passim; Haslehurst, op. cit., 190–4, 257; Hasluck, op. cit., 159ff., 254ff., 272ff. On the relevant policy-making and advisory bodies, see Edwards, *Prime Ministers and Diplomats*, 130ff.
158 Horner, op. cit., 23 and passim; Wilkinson diary (Churchill College, Cambridge), passim; Gavin Long Papers (Australian War Memorial Library), passim.
159 See, e.g. Warmbrunn, op. cit., 131–2, and above, 21–21.
160 J. Bank, *Opkomst en Ondergang van de Nederlandse Volks Beweging* (Deventer, 1978); Blom, op. cit.; A.G. Vromans, 'Les Pays-Bas Dans la Seconde Guerre Mondiale', *Histoire de la Deuxième Guerre Mondiale*, April 1963.
161 A. Cobban, *The Crisis of Civilisation* (London, 1941), quoted in *International Affairs*, Sept. 1941.
162 *Sydney Morning Herald*, 15 March 1941.
163 Review of L. Dennis, *The Dynamics of War and Revolution*, in *International Affairs*, Dec. 1940-March 1941.
164 See H. Michel and B. Mirkine Guezévitch (eds.) *Les idées politiques et sociales de la Résistance* (Paris, 1954).
165 See, e.g. S. Schram, *The Political Thought of Mao Tse-tung* (1969), and Spence, op. cit.
166 See, e.g. A.H. van Namen (ed.), *Het Ondergroondse Vrij Nederland* (Baarn, 1970); Wabrunn, op. cit.; Blom, op. cit.
167 Bruce to Halifax et al., 21 July 1940, Bruce Papers, Monthly War Files. Cf. e.g. Foot, op. cit., 332; McLean, 59; Thorne, *Allies*, 97.
168 Thorne, *Allies*, 144.
169 May, 59–62.
170 Sjahrir, entry for 14 Aug. 1936.
171 Jansen, *Changing Japanese Attitudes*, 85–9; cf. Reischauer, 409, 414.
172 *Bombay Chronicle*, 7 Jan. 1942; and see, e.g. M. Bose, op. cit., 59, 61.
173 E.g. policy draft of 23 April 1942, AICC Papers, FN – 31B.
174 Sjahrir, entries for 24 Nov. 1935 and 28 Oct. 1938.
175 Duiker, 36, 140.
176 Roff, 57, 150.
177 See, e.g. C.P. Fitzgerald, *The Chinese View of Their Place in the World* (London, 1964).
178 Eastman, *Abortive Revolution*, 158–9; Spence, e.g. 142, 217, 303. And see Eastman, *Seeds of Destruction*, 90.
179 Levenson, vol. 1, 717 ff.
180 A. Gide, *Journals, 1889–1949* (London, 1967), 201, 576.
181 *Combat*, No. 1, Dec. 1941.
182 *Résistance*, 8 Dec. 1942.
183 *Sydney Morning Herald*, 19 July 1941.
184 Ibid, 30 Nov. 1940. And see, e.g. the issue for 9 Nov. 1940.
185 F. Braudel, *The Mediterranean and the Mediterranean World in the Age of Philip II* (trs. S. Reynolds, 2 vols., New York, 1972–74), Preface and passim.
186 T.S. Kuhn, *The Structure of Scientific Revolutions* (Chicago, 1970), 15ff., 109ff., and passim.

187 'Aldous Huxley on war and intellectual survival', *Times Literary Supplement*, 11 June 1982. Huxley, to whom Mitchison had addressed the remarks quoted, replied by pointing to 'the termite labours of psychologists, novelists, logisticians and so forth gnawing away the axioms on which nineteenth century life was founded'.

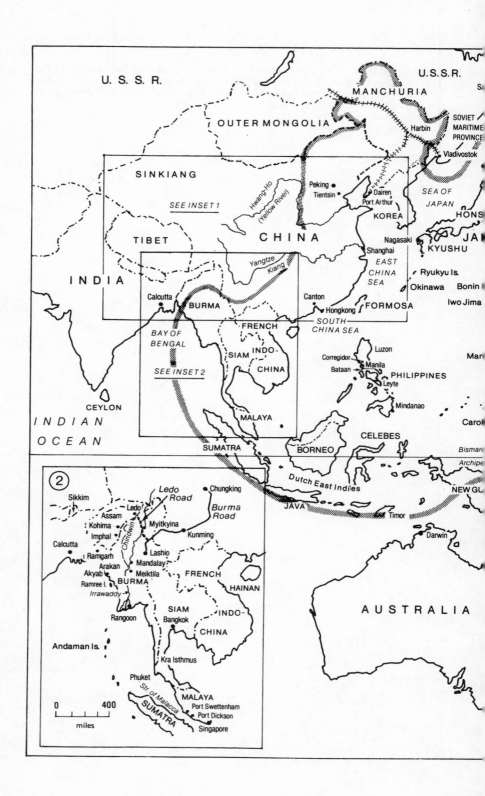

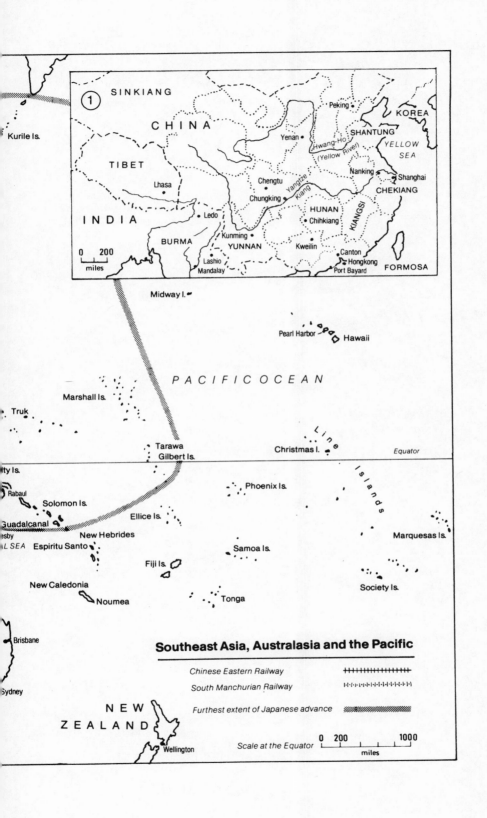

SINKIANG

CHINA

KOREA

Peking

Yenan

SHANTUNG

Hwang-Ho

(Yellow River)

YELLOW
SEA

TIBET

Lhasa

Chengtu

Nanking

Shanghai

Yangtze

Kiang

Chungking

CHEKIANG

INDIA

Ledo

HUNAN

KIANGSI

Chihkiang

Kunming

BURMA

YUNNAN

Kweilin

Canton

Lashio

Hongkong

Port Bayard

FORMOSA

Mandalay

0   200

miles

Midway I.

Pearl Harbor

Hawaii

PACIFIC OCEAN

Marshall Is.

Truk

Christmas I.

Line

Equator

Tarawa

Gilbert Is.

Islands

ty Is.

Rabaul

Phoenix Is.

Solomon Is.

Ellice Is.

Guadalcanal

Marquesas Is.

esby

New Hebrides

L SEA   Espiritu Santo

Samoa Is.

Fiji Is.

Society Is.

New Caledonia

Noumea

Tonga

Brisbane

Southeast Asia, Australasia and the Pacific

Sydney

Chinese Eastern Railway	+++++++++++++++++
South Manchurian Railway	·|·|·|·|·|·|·|·|·|·|
Furthest extent of Japanese advance	▨▨▨▨▨

NEW

ZEALAND

Wellington

Scale at the Equator

0   200   1000

miles

PART TWO

The Experience of War

'There were no fires, but there was an earthquake,
No one was sick, but there was war,
Life was lived at intervals.
The country grew bigger and bigger,
But the path of life grew steeper,
Then roses ceased to bloom.'

> From *Rekishi* ('History') by Horiguchi Daigaku
> Quoted in B-A. Shillony, 'Japanese Intellectuals
> During the Pacific War', *Proceedings of the British
> Association for Japanese Studies, Vol. 2* (1977)

'Battle is an organization of thousands of men and
machines, who dart with governing habits across a field,
sweat like a radiator in the sun, shiver and become still
like a piece of metal in the rain. We are not so discrete
from the machine any longer.'

> Norman Mailer, *The Naked and the Dead*
> (London, 1964, 479)

CHAPTER FOUR

Facing the Enemy

The Far Eastern war formed only a part of a conflict that was virtually world-wide. A summary of military and strategic developments in the area lying between India and California must therefore be prefaced with a reminder of some of the ways in which they were affected by the progress of the war between the Axis powers and the Allies elsewhere. For Washington and London, for example, there was the fear in 1942 that the Germans, driving along the North African shore and down through the Caucasus, would seek to effect a junction in the crucial area of Western Asia with a Japanese advance across India. For the Japanese themselves, the weight of the Western – and, ultimately, Soviet – military resources that were turned in their direction depended to a considerable extent on the fortunes of Germany, and, to a lesser extent, Italy. (This could involve a small but crucial item such as the availability of landing craft.) For others, too – not least China – the outcome of Germany's war with the Soviet Union was heavy with consequences in terms of Moscow's potential involvement in Far Eastern affairs.

The long-drawn-out war against Germany was also of great significance for the European colonial powers in relation to developments in Southeast Asia. Only when their metropolitan territories had been freed could the French and the Dutch hope to begin to play a substantial part in the ousting of the Japanese from their imperial lands in that part of the world. As for Britain, whose war-resources were at their peak in the latter part of 1943, the longer the fight against Germany continued (and it was extended by, for example, the failure to secure a Rhine bridgehead at Arnhem), the greater became her dependence on United States aid if she wished to play a substantial role in the final stages of the struggle against Japan. Other facets of the interrelationship between the wars in the two hemispheres will also emerge in the following chapters: in terms of men and matériel, for example, the consequences for Australia and New Zealand of making a major contribution in the Mediterranean theatre when their own territories and interests were directly involved in the Far Eastern conflict; in less tangible respects, the repercussions for Britain's military morale and standing generally of defeats in both the Mediterranean and the Southeast Asian theatres during the first half of 1942.

The wider context of the Second World War as a whole also has to be

borne in mind when considering the strategic planning involved in the Far
Eastern conflict. Here, the contrast between the Allies and their enemies
was considerable. Where Japan and Germany were concerned, cooperation
and coordination were minimal.[1] Despite a series of agreements to consult
each other and to furnish mutual assistance in the form of vital raw
materials, in the event no common, global strategy was established, even
within the promising circumstances that developed in 1942. Essentially,
each partner in the alliance went its own way. On the Allied side, on the
other hand, for all the suspicions and disputes that will be noted below, the
war as a whole was waged at the level of grand strategy, including the
management of economic resources, on a coordinated basis the like of which
had never before been seen between two major powers.[2]* At the same time,
the opponents of Germany and Japan enjoyed a further major advantage
(even allowing for the successes achieved by Berlin in the same field) in the
form of the strategic intelligence acquired through the breaking of certain of
their enemies' codes and ciphers.[3]

The ways in which machinery for directing the war functioned within each
of the combatant states have been examined in several other studies,
including the present author's *Allies of a Kind*, and will therefore not be
explored in detail here.[4] One further aspect of the conduct of the war as a
whole on the Allied side does require brief attention, however, since it
formed the subject of widespread assumptions on the American side that in
turn helped colour attitudes towards the Far Eastern conflict in particular.
The issue in question concerns the relationship between the shaping of
strategy in the strictly military sense and the pursuit of wider political aims.
And in this regard, it was commonly believed in the United States, both
within and outside official circles, that whereas the Republic itself was being
guided in its strategic decisions solely by the desire to defeat the enemy in the
shortest possible time, Britain was conducting an essentially 'political' war,
according immediate military requirements a lower priority than longer-
term, and selfish, *desiderata*. As General Joseph Stilwell's political adviser
put it:

'Most American military men think of the war as a soldier's job to be done
. . . as soon as possible with a minimum of fuss over international political
and economic issues . . . To our allies, the conduct of the war is a function
of overall political and economic policy. Military logic is therefore always

---

* Two powers rather than more because relations between the Western democracies and the
U.S.S.R. remained essentially distant, while Nationalist China, above all as a result of an
American veto, failed to gain admittance to the main Allied planning machinery. (See
Thorne, *Allies*, 183, 319.) As for the smaller members of the Allied coalition, such as
Australia and the Netherlands, their inability to exercise significant influence on such
planning will be demonstrated below.

subordinated to and sometimes violated in favor of political and economic considerations.'[5]

American assumptions of this kind* were focused in particular on what was seen as Britain's concern for the 'balance of power' in Europe, on the Mediterranean (where the British were believed by Henry Stimson, for one, to be 'straining every nerve to lay a foundation . . . for their own empire after the war'),[6] and, not least, on the Far East itself.[7] They were not entirely without substance. Numerous instances could be cited when Churchill, or the Foreign Office, or others in London approached a strategic issue bearing in mind the possible political outcomes that surrounded it: the desire to see Britain's colonial territories in Southeast Asia wrested back from Japan by her own military efforts, rather than as a consequence of American victories in the Pacific, is simply one particularly pertinent example.[8] Conversely, Cordell Hull's insistence to his subordinates in the State Department that once war had come their main task was to support the U.S. Army and Navy did reflect a compartmentalised approach to grand strategy in Washington – as did Hull's own subsequent exclusion from much high-level policy-making.[9] Just as Eisenhower's strategic decisions in the latter phases of the campaign in Europe lacked a broader political perspective, so, in the Far East, a wide gap opened up in 1944 and '45 between on the one hand Washington's desire to enhance the status of China for post-war political purposes and on the other its strategic planning, which relegated the Chinese theatre to a sideshow.

Yet in retrospect it is evident that to depict the contrast in these terms was simplistic and misleading. In reality, long-term political considerations represented simply one factor that made itself felt, now to a greater, now to a lesser degree in strategic decision-making processes on both sides of the Atlantic. Where Britain was concerned, it was by no means always decisive. Over the Mediterranean theatre, for example, the Chiefs of Staff in London approached strategic issues in a 'coldly professional' manner and with an overriding concern to defeat the enemy.[10] As for the Far Eastern war, one finds the Foreign Office, for example, advising the military planners that decisions on such matters as supplying aid to China or accepting the despatch of Chinese troops for training in India should be taken, not on political grounds, but according to whether or not such moves would be 'in the interests of strategy' and would hasten the end of the war.[11] Moreover, even if she had wished to do so, Britain simply did not possess the resources that would enable her to juggle with political calculations when it came to

* In that various post-war British histories of the 1939–45 conflict, including Churchill's own volumes, joined American cold-war zealots in criticising Washington's failure to forestall the Soviet Union in large areas of Central Europe in 1945, they, too, contributed to the persistence of these assumptions.

fighting the Japanese in particular. Thus, discussions in Whitehall in 1944 about where to concentrate the country's effort in this respect time and again came up against the reality that the means were lacking to make any such dispositions independently of the United States.[12] Even within Mountbatten's South East Asia Command, his Chief of Staff was moved to write privately: 'The hard fact is that the Americans have got us by the short hairs ... We can't do anything in this theatre ... without material support from them ... So if they don't approve they don't provide, and that brings the whole project automatically to an end.'[13]

On the American side, meanwhile, the intrusion of political considerations into the shaping of strategy was by no means unknown. MacArthur's successful arguments in 1944, against those of the U.S. Navy, for including the Philippines in the line of advance towards Japan's home islands were essentially political in nature, just as he resisted the transfer to a British commander of a portion of his South West Pacific Area on the grounds that such a move would lead to the 'deterioration ... of American prestige and commercial prospects throughout the Far East'.[14] Washington's determination to pursue a campaign in northern Burma in order to reopen a land route to China also owed much to political, rather than strictly military, assessments regarding the importance of Chiang Kai-shek's friendship for both the war-time and the post-war years.[15]

The foregoing is sufficient indication that inter-Allied stategic planning during the Far Eastern war was attended by a good measure of suspicion and discord. At the same time, Japan's own planning process, even in the early and, for her, triumphant stages of the conflict, was marked by struggles among various sections and factions within her armed forces. (Was Australia to be invaded, for example? Or India? How far should the thrust across the Pacific be carried, and should resources be husbanded for an eventual strike north-westwards, against the Soviet Union?)[16] Nevertheless, during the first half of 1942 the contending submissions were presented within a general climate of excitement and self-congratulation, as forces whose skill and resolve had been widely underestimated in the West took advantage of that strategic situation favourable to Japan that had been in the making since the 1920s, if not earlier.[17]

If the swift fall of Hong Kong had been foreseen by those responsible for British and American policies, the sinking of the Royal Navy's *Prince of Wales* and *Repulse* by Japanese planes only three days after the outbreak of war, though entirely predictable in retrospect, came as a shock to many, not least Churchill. A greater blow still to Britain's position and prestige followed when, after sweeping down the Malay Peninsula and at a cost of only around 15,000 casualties, the Japanese forced the surrender of Singapore on February 15, 1942, taking 130,000 prisoners in the process. At the same time, the Japanese Navy and Army were on their way to a victory in and around the East Indies which was complete by the end of April, with 98,000 members of the Dutch forces surrendering. In Burma, also, the British (together with those Chinese units that had entered the country to participate in its defence) had been swept aside by the summer, the sole remaining overland route for supplying Nationalist China, the Burma Road, being severed as a result. And, although Japanese troops encountered more stubborn resistance in the Philippines, there too, for all MacArthur's confident predictions earlier, the American and native forces had been obliged to surrender by the first week in May. Moreover, while in fact Tokyo's plans at the time did not aim at an invasion of either Australia or India, the threat to those two countries began to appear acute as the Japanese landed in New Guinea and the Solomon Islands and despatched heavy units of their fleet on a sortie into the Indian Ocean.

In the face of their well-nigh complete defeat in the field in the Far East, the British and American Governments nevertheless reaffirmed a decision regarding overall strategic priorities that had been arrived at (it is important to note) before Pearl Harbor by the American commanders on their own, without any prompting from London: that is, that the Allied war effort must be directed primarily against Germany, on the grounds that, once Nazi power had been destroyed, 'the collapse of Italy and the defeat of Japan must follow'.[18] It was one thing to set down this principle, however, and another altogether for those responsible for the direction of American strategy to abide by it as the shock of Pearl Harbor and of defeat in the Philippines was compounded by the knowledge that the Japanese, notably after securing the Bataan peninsula, had been treating many of their American captives with wanton savagery. A majority of the American public, also, regarded Japan, rather than Germany, as 'enemy number one'.[19] So too did Admiral Ernest King, Chief of Naval Operations, along with MacArthur and others in official positions, both military and civil. Small wonder, then, that, as the British provided their own stimulus to a development they deplored by insisting on a delay before a direct, cross-Channel assault was mounted against Germany, a growing proportion of American military resources was directed towards the Pacific.[20]*

The Pacific theatre itself, including the southern regions of that ocean and New Zealand, became an American responsibility in terms of command and local strategic planning, as did a South West Pacific Area under MacArthur (who had been ordered out of the Philippines before they fell) which embraced both Australia and the bulk of the Netherlands East Indies. (An

---

* By the end of 1943, 1,878,152 members of the U.S. forces were being deployed against Japan, slightly more than were engaged in the fight against Germany. The figures for combat naval vessels were 713 and 515 respectively; for aircraft, 7,857 as against 8,807.

American-British-Dutch-Australian command that had been established in the region early in 1942 fell victim, within weeks, to the rapid Japanese advance.) Liaison and supply matters between the Western Allies and China also came under Washington's control. In short, London was obliged to forego responsibility for the two Dominions now threatened by Japan and to acknowledge that Britain's pre-eminent position among the Western powers in China had come to an end once Japan had launched her attack. Even in the remaining strategic area of the Far Eastern war, stretching from India to Singapore, where control was vested in British hands, Churchill was speedily obliged to admit to Roosevelt that in terms of resources the burden was 'more than we can bear'.[21]

For all the tremendous efforts and – eventually – achievements* in that part of the world that were to follow on the part of Australian, British, Indian, New Zealand and other Imperial and Commonwealth forces, it was indeed the case that for the Allies the war against Japan rapidly became a predominantly American one. And it was American naval-air units that inflicted on the Japanese a defeat at the battle of Midway in June 1942 (following an indecisive encounter in the Coral Sea in the previous month) that in effect put an end to the latter's headlong drive for long-term mastery of the central and western Pacific. The Japanese public did not realise it at the time (elaborate measures being taken by the authorities to enable the engagement to be presented as yet another victory),† but they were already treading the road to defeat.

This did not mean that the Allies were to achieve unbroken success from then onwards. In Burma, for example, a series of campaigns in 1942–3, aimed at recapturing the initiative in that area, resulted in failure. Nor did it mean that the Japanese themselves were incapable of any further major advance: between April and December 1944, their 'Operation Ichi-go' in China was to constitute their largest land offensive of the war, resulting in the capture of Changsha, Lingling and Kweilin, and the opening up of a corridor through to their forces in Indochina.[22] Above all, their defeat at

---

* For example, those of Australian forces in New Guinea and of the British-Indian Fourteenth Army in Burma. The campaign in Burma was to cost the Japanese 128,000 lives.

† It was announced that the Imperial Navy, having lost only one aircraft-carrier to the Americans' two, had established 'supreme power in the Pacific'. In fact, four aircraft-carriers and a heavy cruiser, together with well over 200 aircraft, had been destroyed. The U.S. Navy lost the carrier *Yorktown*. (See, e.g. the Manila *Tribune*, 11 June 1942.) In its overseas propaganda, Japan's attempts to disguise subsequent defeats as victories became more remarkable still. Thus in broadcasts to Australia, for example, it was claimed that at Okinawa in the spring of 1945 *kamikaze* planes had sunk 13 American aircraft-carriers, 15 battleships and 48 cruisers. (L. D. Meo, *Japan's Radio War on Australia, 1941–1945*, Melbourne, 1968, 87.) On the Allied side, too, though to a much lesser degree, uncomfortable military losses were withheld from the public. See e.g. A. M. Winkler, *The Politics of Propaganda: the Office of War Information, 1942–1945*, (New Haven, 1978), 49–51, and Hilvert, *Blue-Pencil Warriors: Censorship and Propaganda in World War Two*.

Midway did nothing to diminish that self-sacrificial tenacity in defence that was to characterise the performance of the Japanese forces as the Allies advanced, and that made the likely costs of carrying the land war into Japan itself appear so dauntingly high.

Nevertheless, by the spring of 1943 the Japanese were struggling to defend the massive area they had seized, in the face of rapidly increasing Allied resources and initiatives. In the Solomons, after bitter fighting on land and sea, they were forced to abandon Guadalcanal in February of that year; in New Guinea, in campaigning conditions of an appalling nature, they had already by then lost Buna on the north coast, after failing earlier to take Port Moresby across the Owen Stanley mountains. In the Pacific, meanwhile, the Americans were building up a series of massive (yet bloody) assaults on the Gilbert Islands in November 1943 and the Marshalls early in 1944. Thus, two lines of advance: one from New Guinea towards the Philippines, the other along the island groups to the north, began to pose the main threat to Japan's home islands, and were endorsed as such by the Anglo-American Combined Chiefs of Staff at the Cairo Conference of November–December 1943.

This decision did not, however, put an end to the wrangling and uncertainty that tended to surround Allied strategic planning against Japan. Among the Americans themselves, rivalry between MacArthur and the Navy continued to colour such issues as the one mentioned above: of whether to retake the Philippines or, as the Navy argued, to by-pass them in favour of an attack on Formosa.[23] For the British, meanwhile, the dilemmas and frustrations of the Far Eastern war were greater still. In the hope of bringing vigour and success to the campaign in Burma, a new South East Asia Command under Lord Mountbatten had been established at the first Quebec Conference in August 1943. Even so, the mixed, Anglo-American nature of the forces involved, together with Washington's concern to see a land route reopened from Burma to China, had to be acknowledged by the appointment of an American Deputy Supreme Commander (General 'Vinegar Joe' Stilwell), and by the recognition that the Combined Chiefs of Staff, and not the British Chiefs of Staff alone, should exercise 'a general jurisdiction over strategy' in the area. A considerable degree of friction ensued between the two allies, notably over the desirability or otherwise of investing effort in a campaign in northern Burma and the construction of a new road from Ledo into China. The belief common among Americans, that Britain's only concern in the area was to ensure the re-establishment of her colonial rule and that of the other European imperial powers, also exacerbated disputes over whether Mountbatten had the right to operate into French Indochina and Siam without being subject to the veto of Chiang Kai-shek and the latter's American staff officers in China. During the final stage of the war, also, MacArthur ensured that suspicion was attached to the transfer to S.E.A.C. of Java and other islands in the Dutch East Indies (Indochina south of the 16⁰ line of latitude, too, was placed within S.E.A.C. at this time), even though the proposal had in fact emanated from Washington rather than from London.[24]

The overriding problem for the British in terms of strategic developments, however, was the likelihood of their being left on the periphery whilst the final, decisive attacks upon Japan were taking place. It was this situation that occasioned the extended debates in London in 1944, referred to above, on whether to concentrate on extending the existing S.E.A.C. campaigns from Burma into Malaya, or to shift the country's main effort against Japan to the South West Pacific.[25] Yet dependence on the United States remained unavoidable, regardless of the course adopted, and was to be all the more evident when it came to obtaining Washington's agreement for units of the Royal Navy to operate alongside the now-massive forces deployed in the Pacific by its American counterpart, for Pacific-island bases to be allocated to the R.A.F. (thus enabling it to join in the bombing of Japan), and for British, British Empire and Commonwealth troops to be included in the invasion of Japan's home islands that MacArthur was planning in 1945.[26]

The potential significance of the part that Britain could play in defeating Japan had declined – and had declined in American eyes – since the desperate, early stages of the war. The same was true of China in the period following the Cairo conference (at which, ironically, Chiang Kai-shek's international status had appeared to be greatly enhanced). In 1942, China's manpower and territory had seemed in Washington to hold out rich promise. In the event, however, despite Stilwell's efforts to create the nucleus of a modern army for the Generalissimo, those Nationalist divisions that were not engaged in sealing off the Communist area in the north-west were employed in a largely passive role against the Japanese forces that were ensconced in China, the invader being harried much more by the Communist units themselves. With the armies of provincial leaders being denied resources by Chiang for reasons of domestic politics; with widespread incompetence and corruption among the officer corps; with the morale of peasant soldiers undermined by brutality and neglect, Nationalist resistance came near to collapsing entirely in the face of Japan's 1944 Ichi-go offensive. And it was only with the greatest difficulty that Washington was able to push Chiang Kai-shek into a modest campaign of his own in the same year, directed from Yunnan into northern Burma.[27]

In the summer of 1944 also, the U.S. Army Air Force commenced the long-range bombing of Japan from bases in China; but even this development was eclipsed almost immediately as more advantageous bases became available in the newly-captured Mariana Islands. Moreover, as the strategic significance of China waned in the minds of American policy-makers, that of the Soviet Union was growing – a process that was fostered in part by a serious overestimation of the strength of the forces Japan had retained in Manchuria and northern China, and that culminated in Roosevelt's secretly agreeing at Yalta in February 1945 to the price Stalin was demanding for bringing his country into the Far Eastern war.[28]*

Meanwhile, for all that it had come to occupy a subordinate place within overall Allied strategy against Japan, the campaign in Burma had achieved considerable success. In the spring and early summer of 1944, and in fighting of a ferocity to match that taking place in the Pacific theatres, a Japanese attempt to break through into India was defeated at Imphal and Kohima. During the counter-offensive that followed, which resulted in the capture of Rangoon by General William Slim's Fourteenth Army in May 1945, those units of Bose's Indian National Army† that were accompanying the Japanese largely disintegrated. To the north, where Chindit columns had been operating in the jungle more successfully than in 1943, the capture of Mytkyina by American forces under Stilwell proved decisive in enabling the Ledo Road to be opened to traffic through to China in January 1945. (In his belief that such a road could be constructed, Stilwell had thus been vindicated; viewed in wider perspective, the achievement was nevertheless essentially futile, as the British had suspected would be the case, for by the time the route became available China's forces had little role to play, and were in any case soon in a position to be supplied by sea, as the Japanese began to relinquish their hold on the country's coastline.)

Within China itself, a project for the small British units operating escape and intelligence networks there to repossess Hong Kong before Chiang Kai-shek could lay hands on the colony was vetoed by the Ambassador in Chungking and the British General Officer Commanding, on the grounds that such an act would serve only to alienate Chinese and American opinion. (American commanders on the spot were in any case set upon thwarting any move of this kind.)[29] A more ambitious project of the Americans themselves, to supply and utilise the forces of the Chinese Communists in a coordinated campaign against the Japanese, likewise came to nothing in the face of opposition from both Chiang Kai-shek and the new American Ambassador to the country, even though a U.S. military mission, together with diplomatic observers, was established in Yenan.[30]

As already indicated, however, it was in the Pacific that the pressure on the Japanese was greatest. Finally driven from the Solomons and New Guinea by mid-summer 1944, they failed in October, after the largest naval engagement of the war, to prevent MacArthur's forces establishing them-

* See below, 228–9.
† See below, 148, 151.

selves on Leyte in the Philippines, an advance that moved on to the main island of Luzon in the following January. Meanwhile, as stages in the American thrust across the central Pacific, huge task forces had wrested the islands of Saipan, Tinian and Guam in the Marianas from the Japanese during the summer of 1944; and in the spring of the following year, despite the efforts of *kamikaze* suicide pilots against them, U.S. units moved closer still to Japan itself by taking the ferociously-defended islands of Iwo Jima and Okinawa. From the Marianas, B29 bombers were now pounding Japan from the air, switching in March 1945 to low-level attacks with incendiaries, which wiped out large areas of the enemy's cities through the creation of fire-storms. (Roughly sixteen square miles of the Sumida-river district of Tokyo were devastated in this fashion on the night of March 9–10, for example, with the death of somewhere between 80,000 and 100,000 people.)[31]

Subjected to this well-nigh unobstructed assault from the air, Japan by this time was also being deprived of the vital raw materials she needed in order to conduct modern warfare, as American submarines sent her merchant fleet to the bottom. (Almost ninety per cent of the shipping she had possessed at the outset of the war had been lost by March 1945.) Yet even now those in official circles who inclined towards surrender were not in a position to outweigh the determination of the High Command to continue the fight.[32] It took two developments more shattering even than the loss of Okinawa to change this situation. On August 6, following a decision that was in essence that of the United States alone,[33] an atomic bomb was dropped on Hiroshima. Three days later, a second bomb fell on Nagasaki. And in between, on the 8th, the Soviet Union declared war and sent its troops racing into Manchuria.

Japan surrendered on August 14. In a recorded broadcast to his people that went out over the radio the following morning, despite an attempt by a group of military fanatics to prevent this happening, the Emperor Hirohito explained that the country must accept the terms offered by its enemies, must 'endure the unendurable and suffer what is insufferable', because 'the war situation has developed not necessarily to Japan's advantage, while the general trends of the world have all turned against her interest'. (As Robert Butow has observed, 'the words "defeat", "surrender", and "capitulation" were taboo'.)[34] By choosing not to fight on, the Emperor continued, Japan would not only preserve herself as a nation; she would prevent 'the total extinction of human civilisation'. Similarly, the task now confronting the Japanese people was both to 'enhance the innate glory of the Imperial State' and to 'keep pace with the progress of the world'.

As for the conflict that had now come to an end, it, too, in this Imperial version, had been undertaken, not in the interests of Japan alone, but as part of a process of 'striving for the common prosperity and happiness of all nations':

> 'Indeed, We declared war on America and Britain out of Our sincere desire to ensure Japan's self-preservation and the stabilization of East Asia, it being far from Our thought either to infringe upon the sovereignty of other nations or to embark upon territorial aggrandisements.'

*

The establishment of stability in East Asia; the achievement of peace among all nations and universal prosperity: these had indeed been listed among Japan's aims in the Imperial Rescript that was issued on December 8, 1941 in order to explain why an 'inevitable' process had brought the war about.* Throughout the ensuing conflict, however, official statements from Tokyo regarding the purposes for which the country was fighting, together with the international arrangements she intended to make once victory had been secured, were remarkable above all for their vagueness. The Tripartite Pact of September 1940 had referred to the establishment under Japanese leadership of 'a new order' in 'Greater East Asia'.[35] And, in August of that year, the Foreign Minister, Matsuoka (moving beyond Prince Konoye's 1938 pronouncement on the subject of that 'new order', which had embraced only Japan, China and Manchukuo), had formally indicated that a 'Greater East Asia Coprosperity Sphere' would include 'Southern areas such as the Netherlands East Indies and French Indo-China'.[36]

What exactly the creation of such an entity would entail had remained unspecified, however. Matsuoka's speech had simply emphasised the basis provided by 'the great spirit of the Imperial Way', while subsequent explanations stressed the need for collaboration in the economic sphere. Japanese propaganda in occupied China had likewise been reiterating – through the Hsin-min Hui, for example, referred to in an earlier chapter – the need to create a new framework in East Asia for international and domestic societies alike. And indeed, the North China Army's 'outline of principles for ideological warfare' against the Western powers, that was adopted immediately following the Pearl Harbor attack, went further still, depicting the new conflict as 'a struggle between new order and old order, a sacred war for the liberation of Asia'. But still the question remained: what exactly did such high-flown phrases mean? Nor was uncertainty diminished

---

* Ienaga (*Japan's Last War*, 136–7) notes that, unlike the similar pronouncements issued at the outset of the wars of 1894 with China and 1904–5 with Russia, this Rescript deliberately contained no reference to the need to comply with the requirements of international law.

when the puppet regime of Wang Ching-wei in Nanking was not permitted to declare war on Britain and the United States in December 1941, as it wished to do – a step that would have enhanced its status, and possibly its resources, beyond what the Japanese military found convenient.[37]

During the early phase of the war, a few, more concrete, indications of Tokyo's intentions were forthcoming, when the Prime Minister, Tojo, spoke of Burma and the Philippines becoming independent if they agreed to cooperate in the establishment of the Coprosperity Sphere.[38] However, no such assurances were provided where India, say, or Korea were concerned, and in January 1942 Tojo's further pronouncement on the 'new order of coexistence and prosperity' that was to be created, by emphasising that Japan would constitute its 'core' and that other Asian peoples would 'be allowed to find their respective places in it', simply highlighted that hegemonic nature of the relationship that was already evident on the ground.[39]*

It was only when the war in the field began to move strongly in favour of the Allies that a somewhat more flexible attitude began to colour such Japanese statements. Thus in January 1943, when Wang Ching-wei was at last allowed to declare war on the Western powers, a pledge was delivered of respect for the principle of Chinese sovereignty and independence, whilst various Japanese extraterritorial privileges in the occupied areas, together with control over the International Settlement in Shanghai, were handed back to the Nanking regime. In theory, indeed (though matters were to turn out rather differently in practice), the administration of northern China as a whole was to be gradually transferred to Wang Ching-wei and his colleagues, while an outline was subsequently drawn up in Tokyo of the terms on which peace and a *modus vivendi* might be established with the Chungking Nationalist Government itself.[40] Tojo also indicated to Bose in June 1943 – the latter having been accepted by Tokyo after much hesitation, and transported by submarine from Germany[41] – that he intended to see India become independent. And when, in October of that year, Bose had established his *Azad Hind* provisional government in Singapore, he was formally given the Andaman and Nicobar Islands to administer – though, as in northern China, the reality proved otherwise.[42]

A major public event in this process whereby Japan sought to increase its support among Asian peoples took place in November 1943, when the Great East Asia Conference assembled in Tokyo. Representatives from Siam, Burma and the Philippines attended, as well as officials from the puppet regimes in Manchuria and China. (Bose was an observer.) Like the new treaty of alliance recently signed between Nanking and Tokyo, the gather-

---

* Australians, too, were invited in Japanese propaganda broadcasts to find their 'proper place', and to achieve happiness and prosperity, within the Sphere and New Order. Meo, *Japan's Radio War on Australia*, 57, 204ff.

ing, it was declared, would 'bring out in clearer light Japan's lofty aims in the moral war she is waging against the Anglo-Americans'.[43] And in his address to the Conference, Tojo poured scorn upon the hypocrisy of those Anglo-Americans in 'habitually stressing the need to uphold international justice and to guarantee world peace' while in reality pursuing 'the preservation of a world order of their own based upon divisions and conflict in Europe and upon the perpetuation of their colonial exploitation of Asia'. The alternative prospect that he held out to his audience was of a 'Greater East Asia' that would 'rest upon the spirit of justice' and on the 'autonomy and independence' of its member nations. Moreover, the repercussions of such an achievement, he declared, would be felt more widely still:

'A superior order of culture has existed in Greater East Asia from its very beginning. Especially the spiritual essense of [this] culture . . . is the most sublime in the world. It is my belief that in the wide diffusion throughout the world of this culture . . . [and] by its further cultivation and refinement lies the salvation of mankind from the curse of materialistic civilisation and our contribution to the welfare of all humanity.'[44]

This declared concern for 'the progress of the entire world' reappeared in the doctrines adopted by the Conference as a whole. So, too, did the intention to 'abolish systems of racial discrimination' and to 'plan the economic development' of the countries of Greater East Asia, whose relations among themselves would rest on the principles of 'coexistence and coprosperity'. The Conference thus gave voice to a line of thought that we observed in an earlier chapter in the context of pre-war developments in both the West and Asia: a disenchantment with that 'materialistic civilisation' that had emerged in Europe and the United States since the scientific and industrial revolutions. This was coupled with the growing sense of resentment against what were seen as racially-based injustices that were built into the existing, Western-dominated, international order. Yet at the same time the Conference's own emphasis on the need for planned economic development had a ring of the 'modern' and the Western about it. So, too, did the professed desire to further the 'progress' of mankind as a whole, a reference which did indeed reflect the intention of certain Japanese officials, notably the Foreign Minister, Shigemitsu Mamoru, to rally support for their country's cause by providing a statement of her war aims that would match the universal principles that had already been proclaimed by the Western allies.[45]*

* In April 1945, a meeting of ambassadors of the 'East Asian' states adopted a further declaration that expressed belief in such nineteenth-century and Wilsonian, liberal goals as economic reciprocity, arms reduction, and the use of peaceful means only when bringing about changes in the international system. The same meeting resolved that Indochina, like Indonesia, should become independent, and that a regional security organisation should be

Exactly what those Allies were fighting the war for, particularly in the Far East, was in fact by no means agreed among themselves or clear to all their citizens, as we shall see below. Nevertheless, by the time the Great East Asia Conference assembled in Tokyo, considerable significance – far more than had been intended by Churchill – had come to be attached to the Atlantic Charter that the Prime Minister and Roosevelt had drawn up in August 1941.[46] Earlier still, in January of that year, the American President had proclaimed the 'Four Freedoms' which should form the basis for creating a healthier society of nations: freedom of speech and expression; freedom of worship; and two which went beyond the classic liberal prescriptions of the eighteenth and nineteenth centuries: freedom from want, and freedom from fear. Now, in their joint declaration, the two leaders had set forth those 'common principles in the national policies of their respective countries' on which they rested their hopes 'for a better future for the world': their two states sought 'no aggrandisement, territorial or other', and desired to see 'no territorial changes that [did] not accord with the freely expressed wishes of the people concerned'; they respected 'the right of all peoples to choose the form of government under which they [lived]', and sought ('with due respect to existing obligations' – a concession, this, to British concern over Imperial tariff preferences) 'to further the enjoyment by all states . . . on equal terms to the trade and to the raw materials of the world which [were] needed for their economic prosperity'; they sought international collaboration in order to secure 'improved labour standards, economic advancement, and social security . . . for all'; and, in order that freedom from want and fear should be achieved, they proposed that the disarmament of aggressor states should serve merely as a prelude to 'the abandonment of the use of force' by all and 'the establishment of a wider and more permanent system of general security'.

Despite Churchill's subsequent insistence (private and public; direct and implied) to the contrary, it came to be widely assumed that the Charter's

established within the framework of some overall international machinery.

It perhaps needs emphasising, in the light of the remarkable theses advanced by Professor Iriye on the subject, that these apparently liberal and internationalist programmes, designed by a handful of bureaucrats in Tokyo, were divorced from the entire thrust of Japanese politics both before and during the war. It is a distortion of history to argue on the basis of such pronouncements that 'the two sides were conceptually close', that in the second half of the war 'shared Wilsonian internationalism of the 1920s' brought American and Japanese war-aims close together and that, had it not been for the use of atomic weapons, those two countries might have been able to 'resume their partnership in the world arena' within 'the familiar framework of international relations'. (*Power and Culture*, 120, 133, 265, and passim.) Quite apart from the differences between their war-aims, Japan and the U.S.A. had not 'shared' a 'Wilsonian internationalism' in the 1920s, had not been 'partners in the world arena', and were going to have to operate within a post-war international framework that, with or without the employment of the atomic bomb in 1945, would be greatly changed in many respects from that of the 1930s.

principles were, indeed, universally applicable, as Roosevelt himself suggested and as many British officials, too, including those in the Foreign Office, maintained.[47] In other words, even without the issuing of a parallel 'Pacific Charter' as some advocated, the Allies (as they became after Pearl Harbor) appeared to be committed to goals that not only militated against the continued existence of European empires in Asia, but also (if less obviously) required from the United States, too, a radically new approach to such issues as the welfare and security of others and the entire basis of international economic relations.

The Allies' intention to create 'a general international organisation . . . for the maintenance of peace and security' had also been underlined shortly before the 1943 Tokyo Conference in the Moscow Declaration that was issued in October of that year, and in which Britain and the U.S.A. were joined by the Soviet Union and – significantly – China. As for matters pertaining directly to the Far Eastern war itself, Churchill and Roosevelt had proclaimed at Casablanca in January 1943 that only the 'unconditional surrender' of their foes would suffice to bring the conflict to an end,* while at Cairo, in the company of Chiang Kai-shek, they went further, declaring that Japan would be stripped entirely of that overseas empire 'which she has taken by violence and greed'. Territories such as Manchuria, Formosa and the Pescadores, that had been plundered from China, would be returned to that country; Korea, 'in due course', would become independent.[48]

Japanese officials assumed, correctly, that this Cairo Declaration represented in part a sop offered by Washington in particular to the Chinese Nationalist regime (which was not to receive the strategic aid that it had hoped for). They also took comfort from the continued absence of the Soviet Union from these discussions on Far Eastern matters – not knowing that in October Molotov, the Soviet Foreign Minister, had promised that his country would join in the war against Japan once Germany had surrendered, or that Roosevelt already had in mind the possibility of transferring Sakhalin and the Kurile Islands from Japan to the U.S.S.R. Publicly, Tojo denounced the Cairo terms as demonstrating once more the essential selfishness and hypocrisy of enemy leaders who were bent upon extending their exploitation of Asia, Japan included, and whose high-sounding principles were not matched by any plans to divest the Western states themselves of their colonial possessions. In short, the contrast between the respective pronouncements of the Cairo and the Great East Asia Conferences amply demonstrated on which side of the war lay enlightened and constructive concern for all peoples.[49]

* On the British side, this pronouncement was designed in part to banish the suspicion that existed in some American quarters that once Germany had been defeated the U.S. would be left on its own to finish the war against Japan.

This theme of the inherent selfishness of the enemy was coupled in Japanese political warfare* with an emphaisis upon conflicts of interest among the Western Allies themselves. The United States, declared the collaborationist Manila newspaper, the *Tribune*, aimed to 'control the world' at the expense of Britain and Nationalist China among others.[50] The British, ran a propaganda summary, would find themselves stripped of their Empire for America's benefit and subjected to Washington's will, while Australians, too, were warned of a decadent America's imperialist designs on their country.[51] More persistently, Tokyo sought to develop the notion that both major Western powers ('the Anglo-Saxons') were simply exploiting their Chinese allies, and that the tragedy of the continuing Sino-Japanese war ('the people of Nippon consider the Chinese their brothers')[52] could be ended if Chiang Kai-shek would only negotiate on a reasonable basis.[53]

Japan's most urgent hopes and endeavours of this kind, however, came to be focused on the Soviet Union. Publicly, much emphasis was placed on the 'diametrically opposed' interests and aims of the Communist power on the one hand and 'the Anglo-Saxons' on the other. 'There can be no agreement which can satisfy both parties,' proclaimed the Singapore-based newspaper, *Syonan Shimbun*, as representatives of the coalition that had defeated Germany left Potsdam 'more suspicious of each other than ever before'.[54] And in private, as we shall see in a later chapter, considerable and naïve faith, especially after the Nazi surrender, was placed in diplomatic attempts to obtain the Soviet Union's good offices in negotiating an acceptable basis for ending the war, even though Moscow announced in April 1945 its intention to terminate the Neutrality Pact of 1941 between the two countries.[55]

Japan's attempts to discourage or divide her Western opponents (the American public in particular, it was suggested from Tokyo, were becoming disillusioned with the futility and sacrifices of the struggle)[56] proved as unrewarding as her overtures to the Soviet Union. Nor can it be said that the considerable efforts that were made by Western political-warfare organisations to weaken Japan's own will to fight were any more successful[57]† – this, despite the hope early in the war that the enemy's morale could be undermined (partly by 'harping on the fact' that they were 'hated by all' and 'could not make friends in any circumstances')[58] once they had experienced some heavy defeats; [59] that an effective appeal could be made to the

---

* That is, material directed against Japan's enemies. Japanese and Allied propaganda aimed essentially at third parties will be considered separately in the two following chapters.

† Although local psychological warfare efforts probably helped bring about the (highly unusual) surrender of over 10,000 Japanese soldiers and civilians during the campaign on Okinawa (Winkler, *The Politics of Propaganda*, 142), while Kase (*Eclipse of the Rising Sun*, 213) goes so far as to suggest that American broadcasts came to exercise 'a great influence on the minds of the Japanese people'.

Japanese people as a whole to liberate their Emperor from the clutches of the militarists;[60] or that in the last resort 'key Japanese statesmen and military leaders' would prove to be 'supreme realists' and surrender accordingly.[61]

In the event, the Allies' own demand that such a surrender must be 'unconditional' was no help in this respect, and the authorities in Washington (again, this had become an almost exclusively American matter) were correct in believing in the spring of 1945 that the peace-feelers that were put out then by a few Japanese officials were not representative of attitudes in Tokyo generally. Indeed, an Imperial Conference that was held in that city on June 8 took an explicit decision to fight on to the very end.[62] The failure of the Allied declaration on Japan that was issued at Potsdam on July 26 to include any reference to the future of the Emperor or the institution of the Throne – despite the belief of various ministers and officials in both Washington and London that a statement on this issue should be made – also handicapped those in Tokyo who had by now become convinced of the need to sue for peace.[63]

By the time each side had sufficiently shifted its position to make possible the ending of hostilities (in its response to a Japanese note of August 10, Washington employed a phrase that allowed for the retention of the Imperial institution), Nagasaki, as well as Hiroshima, had been devastated by nuclear bombardment. The predominant – but not the sole – American motive in resorting to this form of warfare had been the desire not to incur the huge casualties that were expected to attend an invasion of Japan's home islands.[64] The pressure which this consideration exerted on decision-makers in Washington is readily understandable, especially when viewed in the light of the nature of the land fighting up till then, and notwithstanding the effects of the submarine blockade of Japan and of the non-nuclear bombing of her cities. The use of a second atomic weapon so soon after the first, however, at a time when the political possibilities for achieving the enemy's surrender had been considerably enhanced, was an act thoroughly at odds with those high principles of international morality that had been proclaimed by the United States itself from Pearl Harbor onwards.*

*

When the world at large learned that a new and terrible weapon had been employed against Japan, reactions, even among the ranks of her enemies, varied considerably. In private, the Canadian Prime Minister, Mackenzie

---

* Ronald Spector (*Eagle Against the Sun*, cap. 21) has emphasised the degree to which both unrestricted submarine warfare and the indiscriminate bombing of civilian areas by the United States against Japan contradicted pre-war American pronouncements on these subjects.

King, for example, expressed his relief that the bomb had been dropped on Asiatic people, and not on 'white races' in Europe.[65] Among the American public (thirteen per cent of whom, according to a Gallup Poll taken at the end of 1944, were already of the opinion that all Japanese remaining alive at the end of the war should be exterminated),[66] a significant number – perhaps as many as one-fifth – believed that 'we should have quickly used more [such bombs] before Japan had a chance to surrender'.[67] Within the Foreign Office in London, on the other hand, the Far Eastern Department (which had no previous knowledge of the weapon's existence) drew up a strong protest against what had been done, deploring the harm that the act was likely to inflict upon the Allied cause and suggesting that it would have been preferable to proceed by giving Japan an ultimatum, together with details of the bomb's capacity, and then if necessary to have dropped it by way of demonstration on a city that had been evacuated by the enemy.[68]

Already, of course, in attempting to give an indication of some of the reactions to simply this one event in the Far Eastern war, we face the same difficulties that have already been encountered in earlier chapters in relation to perceptions that were entertained by contemporaries.[69] One person's interpretation of, say, the war in its entirety could shift according to the audience involved, as we have seen in the case of Nehru. Perceptions and emphases sometimes changed markedly between 1941 and 1945. The experiences and horizons of people living through those years varied greatly, as did their initial assumptions and inclinations. Often, the contrasts are obvious enough: for example (even if nationality and politics are left aside), as between on the one hand a Japanese housewife in the heavily-bombed port of Kobe and her counterpart in San Francisco.* Even within one small and otherwise homogeneous group in a single society, however, the differences involved could be considerable: so that in a London suburb, say, a family with a son serving in Singapore or with a daughter interned in a Japanese prison-camp might well approach the Far Eastern conflict in a way that was well removed from that of neighbours for whom Germany was the only enemy of any significance. Or again, for an Indonesian nationalist, say, the coming of the war could entail being forced to become a so-called 'economic soldier' (*prajurit ekonomi*) and to labour overseas for the Japanese in appalling conditions and virtual oblivion; or it could mean, by contrast, being able to remain at home in the Pioneer Corps (*Barisan Pelopor*) which the Japanese allowed Soekarno to form in 1944, and to help foster in the Indies that spirit of resistance that was to greet the returning Dutch in 1945.[70] Even among those Westerners imprisoned by the Japan-

---

* On such matters as the widely differing standards of living that were involved, see below, 257 ff.

ese, not only experiences but perceptions of the enemy could vary considerably. 'They really liked each other,' wrote one American woman of the relationship between guards and internees in the camp in the Philippines that became her home;[71] for other 'women beyond the wire', however, as we shall see below, it was the cruelty of their captors and the hatred that was felt in return that formed the essence of the exchanges between the two.

Given that selection and generalisation are unavoidable, then, together with the separation for analytical purposes of views that were often, in reality, jumbled up with one another, certain broad features of war-time ideas and perceptions are worth noting at the outset – some of them representing a continuation of what has already been observed in the years leading up to Pearl Harbor. In terms of entire societies, for example, the degree of attention that was paid to the Far Eastern conflict differed greatly. Thus, whereas for the majority of Americans, as we have seen, the fight against Japan formed the central element of the Second World War as a whole, for the British it was Germany that constituted 'the real enemy'. 'The Japanese war,' concludes Angus Calder, 'impinged remarkably little on the consciousness of the British people, except of course in those families who had members serving in the Far East. Save at the time of the fall of Singapore, the advances and reverses meant little in Britain. Only thirty thousand British servicemen died in the war against Japan, as compared to two hundred and thirty-five thousand in the war against Germany.'[72] 'In the U.K.,' wrote an officer after returning to S.E.A.C. from home leave, 'I travelled throughout the country by road and rail and I stayed for periods in London and other large cities. I found everywhere a dreadful ignorance about the Fourteenth Army and also generally about Burma.'[73]

Among British politicians and officials, too, little thought was given to Far Eastern matters. Churchill's gaze was fixed upon European and transatlantic issues, while Eden, as Foreign Secretary, was ready to admit privately that he knew little about the world east of India. 'No section of H[is] M[ajesty's] G[overnment],' wrote an Assistant Under Secretary at the Foreign Office in May 1942, 'is very much interested in, or very much linked up with, operations [against Japan],' and when the Chief of Staff of S.E.A.C. visited London in the following year he found that ' "they" . . . were absorbed . . . in European affairs to the almost total exclusion of Far Eastern problems'.[74] An even greater lack of interest in such distant matters existed, for obvious reasons, in occupied France and the Netherlands, and persisted in the former country even when it had been liberated from the Germans and when French forces in Indochina were attacked by the Japanese in March 1945.[75]

At the same time, an apparently widespread and sustained display of interest in the war among a people at large did not necessarily indicate the accompanying presence of knowledge or perspective in that regard. Five months after Pearl Harbor, when Chinese and Indian affairs were frequently the subject of headlines in the American press, sixty per cent of a sample polled in the U.S. were unable to locate either country on an outline map of the world.[76] Moreover, forty per cent of Americans questioned in a Gallup Poll in September 1942 (the results of which were kept confidential) professed not to know 'what this war is all about', while in the January of that year only twenty-three per cent of another sample of the population had heard of the Atlantic Charter, a mere one-third of those responding affirmatively being able to identify one of the points contained in that document.[77] Official reports concluded that there was 'very little idealism' among Americans in the armed forces, and subsequent studies have suggested that the magazine *Fortune* was indeed reflecting a widespread attitude when it described the war, not as a crusade, but as simply 'a painful necessity'. Idealists within the Office of War Information who sought to foster a wider and 'higher' view of the war among the American people quickly found that they 'lacked support at the top' in this regard. (The Government, commented the historian Bruce Catton soon afterwards, were 'wading hip-deep through a swamp toward a quite undefined goal, and making pretty heavy weather of it, too'.) Being thus unable to clear up 'the ambiguity over [the country's] basic aims in the war', the officials in question either resigned or fell back upon a more restricted interpretation of their task.[78]*

Nor, again, does it seem that Japanese troops in the field took an interest in any other theatres of the World War or in the parts being played there by Germany or Italy. Moreover, even where their own country's struggle was concerned the view generally expressed in diaries and letters found on killed or wounded Japanese soldiers in the South West Pacific Area in 1942 was simply that, 'since those in authority had declared war, it must be for the best'.[79] His subsequent interrogation of Japanese prisoners likewise suggested to the American diplomat, John Emmerson, that they were 'cynical' about the wider, 'holy' war aims proclaimed by their Government, while in Japan itself one diarist at least saw the civilian population there as being concerned predominantly with their own affairs rather than with their nation's cause.[80]

Yet if one must guard, therefore, against the assumption that the majority

* In Britain, too, a confidential report of March 1942 by the Home Intelligence Unit of the Ministry of Information concluded: 'The public has no clearly worked-out conception of the purpose of the war . . . We have only vague conceptions, fluctuating between ideas of holding what we have got and ideas of right and wrong.' (McLaine, *Ministry of Morale*, 149). Historical studies have also suggested that among the Dutch as well, for example, thinking about the war in a long-term way was limited and belated. E.g. Leurdijk, *The Foreign Policy of the Netherlands*, 76.

of those who found themselves caught up in the Far Eastern war viewed its events in broad or idealistic perspective, it is also important not to overlook the capacity of large numbers of 'ordinary' men and women, and not simply the clerisy, to combine a preoccupation with the immediate and practical exigencies of the conflict in terms of their everyday lives with reflections of a wider nature. A fine example of this capacity is to be found in the published diary of a Lancashire housewife and voluntary war-worker whose reactions to developments will sometimes be cited in what follows.[81] For Nella Last, the coming of war meant learning to live with German 'devil planes' overhead, to fire-watch all night, to create family meals out of a much-diminished supply of food; but it also meant being prompted to think about the nature and future of British society, the purposes of the fighting that was taking place, and the prospects for mankind as a whole. For Second Lieutenant Okuma of the Japanese Army, waiting on Bougainville in the Solomon Islands for the enemy to attack once more, it was a not dissimilar mixture of perspectives, *mutatis mutandis*, that was shaping his thoughts and the entries in his diary:

'13 September 1944. Our only worry is that the Japanese Empire, whose history has not been marred by a single blotch, is now pressed by its enemies. Something's got to be done! Tokyo is in danger! . . . I must live until the day when our offensive shifts and until the Rising Sun can be seen flying over these South Seas. The fluttering of the Rising Sun will turn this bitterness into happiness. I do wish I could see our aircraft as soon as possible!

14 September. Even in the Japanese Army old friendships dissolve when men are starving. Each man is always trying to satisfy his own hunger. It's much more frightening than meeting the enemy's assaults. There is a vicious war going on within our ranks. Can spiritual power degenerate to this only because battles are lost?'[82]

*

Whatever the extent to which populations in general might be uncertain 'what the war was about', the governments of the combatant states sought to provide their own citizens (as well as others) with a set of ready-made opinions on such matters, and zeal to match. Such official, or officially-sponsored, activities did not in every case involve the purveying of information and views that were crude and simplistic. The publications which the Institute of Pacific Relations was commissioned by the U.S. Government to provide for American soldiers and sailors departing to Far Eastern theatres, for example, while not always detached in their approach, did represent an attempt to convey knowledge and understanding on a wide range of historical and current topics.* In general, however, where the background to the war and the nature of the enemy were concerned, official propaganda sought to foster images that were crude, greatly distorted, or altogether false. And to some extent, of course, this represented a conscious attempt to inflame public attitudes. Churchill among others, for example, acknowledged privately that the 'creation of a hatred of the Japanese' by publicising the atrocities the enemy had committed against Allied prisoners – not that these had to be invented or exaggerated – would help stimulate the British people's efforts over the Far Eastern war, while in Japan, too, especially as the Allies began to advance, the need to 'rouse the spirit of enmity' against the foe was strongly emphasised.[83]

What the Japanese people learned about the war was strictly controlled by the authorities, as we have already seen in relation to the battle of Midway. Both the N.H.K. broadcasting corporation and the *Domei* press agency were in effect tools of the Government, while film-makers were required to make their own contribution to 'the total programme of our national consciousness'. Schoolchildren, especially, were subjected to an intensive campaign, continued from the years of the China war, to inculcate them with 'the moral principles of the Japanese Empire'. This involved lengthy sessions of military training, the frequent revision of text books to include justifications of the country's latest actions, and wholesale attacks on such Western evils as 'individualism, liberalism, utilitarianism, and materialism'.[84]

The enemy's lack of profound spiritual and moral qualities was not only reiterated in the official propaganda of both sides in the war but was widely believed. For the Japanese, American society in particular was repeatedly held up to scorn, as demonstrating that 'Western civilization' was 'a civilization in name only, [having] lost its spiritual values and [being] absorbed in a purely material outlook . . . [and] the worship of money and all that money can procure, completely suppressing the cultivation of all that is best in human nature'.[85]

'Money making is the one aim in life [of Americans]. The men make money to live luxuriously and over-educate their wives and daughters who are allowed to talk too much. Their lack of real culture is betrayed by their

---

* See below, 234. American IPR essays included: *Know Your Enemy: Japan*; *Our Far Eastern Record*; *China, America's Ally*, and *Meet The Anzacs*. The American Council of the Institute also prepared material on an extensive scale for use in schools across the U.S.A., together with radio programmes and a film about Japan that was hired out to labour groups especially. As seen and proclaimed by the Council at the time: 'The job of the Institute . . . is boundless – and the stakes are high.' *IPR in Wartime: Report of the American Council, 1941–1943* (New York, 1944), and *Windows on the Pacific: Report of the American Council, IPR, 1944–46* (New York, 1947).

love of jazz music . . . Americans are still untamed since the wild pioneer days. Hold-ups, assassinations, kidnapping, gangs, bribery, corruption and lynching of negroes are still practised. Graft in politics and commerce, labour and athletics is rampant. Sex relations have deteriorated with the development of motor cars; divorce is rife . . . America has its strong points, such as science, invention and other creative activities . . . [But while] outwardly civilized it is inwardly corrupt and decadent.'[86]

The scope and speed of Japan's early victories provided the opportunity to proclaim that it was this fundamental decadence of the West that was being manifested in the poor showing of its armed forces – a process of reasoning that, in the view of one foreign observer of the rejoicing in Tokyo, reflected in inverted form an underlying 'inferiority complex' on the part of the Japanese people themselves.[87] On the Western side, meanwhile, those same triumphs of Japan's were requiring a drastic and hasty revision of contemptuous pre-war notions about that country's fighting capabilities – a revision that indeed went so far in some cases as to produce an image of the enemy as a 'superman' when it came to jungle warfare, thus creating a major problem of morale for some of those commanding Allied forces in the field.[88]

At the same time, however, Japan's sudden assault was also prompting within Western official circles, especially in Washington, analyses of 'the Japanese character' so sweepingly negative in their judgements that to some extent they mirrored what was emanating from Tokyo. Thus, in an internal memorandum that was judged 'first rate' by the Chief of the Far Eastern Division, a State Department official sought to demonstrate the 'cultural inferiority' of the Japanese as a nation, the 'well-known sterility of the Japanese mind', and the 'Japanese character's . . . deficiency in the sense of abstract justice, its imperception of right and wrong [and] insensitivity to true ethics'. In short, the writer concluded, this was 'a pushing, vain, upstart' nation which, since it 'emerged from seclusion', had had 'no other guides but material gain, self-interest, and vanity'; a nation unequalled in the extent to which it was 'hated by its subject races and neighbours and generally mistrusted and disliked by the world at large'.[89] The Japanese people, it was frequently emphasised in political-warfare analyses, had 'a strongly developed herd instinct',[90] and 'European standards' were completely alien to them.[91]

Above all, the Japanese were seen and depicted in the West as profoundly militaristic and aggressive: 'a fanatic people', as the commentary of the American film, *Know Your Enemy: Japan*, put it; a people dedicated to the 'fanatical doctrine of Shintoism' and glorying in the *bushido* tradition that cultivated as an art 'double-dealing and treachery'.[92] Nor, again, was this simply the language of public exhortation. John Emmerson, for example, who was one of the State Department's experts on Japan (and whose memoirs, published long after the war, were to offer a somewhat different emphasis), stressed in a series of secret memoranda during the early months of 1942 that that country had 'throughout history glorified war and the man of arms'.

'The story of graft and corruption among the rulers,' he wrote, 'is a long and ugly one . . . [but] the Japanese public is singularly apathetic to reports of bribery and corruption in high places . . . The real rulers remain a small clique of ambitious militarists and military-minded civilians quietly manipulating the elaborate machinery which stands before the world as the "government" of Japan. *This government is supported by the people.* [Emphasis added] . . . Because of its picturesque vagueness, the Japanese language provides an excellent medium for the cloudy terms and hazy definitions by which the "Japanese Spirit" . . . is described . . . And in whatever terms of poetic imagery [it] is expressed, it can become easily an instrument of aggression directed by divine aim against declared enemies of the nation. Fanaticism grows out of the Japanese spirit, and reason and justice play little part in it . . . Japan has perverted the knowledge of things Western to fit the pattern of an extravagant and cruel imperialism. The materials, the inventions, the ideas, the sympathetic suggestions for the creation of a peaceful Pacific – all these have gone to Japan from America. With them in her possession, she has professed peace and treacherously planned for and waged war . . . Thus has Japan perverted all that she has received from us.'[93]

As well as seeing each other as 'uncivilised' and aggressive, both sides in the conflict also stressed the other's cruelty. This aspect of Japanese portrayals of the Western powers, while present from the outset – for example, in relation to Britain's treatment of India and the Indians[94] – became especially pronounced as the war began to turn in favour of the Allies.

'The history of the U.S.A.,' wrote Lt. Col. Takeda in 1943, 'is one of bloodshed. Their Pilgrim Fathers forgot their Puritan religion and massacred the Red Indians. Then followed the slavery of the Negroes . . . [who] are still ill-treated by such organisations as the K[u] K[lux] K[lan], and lynching is still common. The U.S. record in the Philippines is a continued story of cruelty . . . The success of Japanese immigration in Hawaii and the West Coast of the U.S.A. filled Americans with envy and provoked the restriction of immigration and other anti-Japanese propaganda . . . At the outbreak of the Great East Asia War Japanese residents were roughly rounded up, subjected to indignities and treated as criminals . . . Even on the battle fields gross cruelty was displayed against Japanese prisoners, who were crushed under a steam-roller. Against all international law ten Japanese hospital ships have been attacked and helpless fishing boats fired upon by enemy submarines. There is no effective way of stopping such cruelties except by a thorough extermination of Americans.'[95]

It was the American bombing campaign against Japan's cities, however, that brought to a climax denunciations of 'the Anglo-Saxon modern Vandals', with their 'utter disregard for the life and happiness, rights and interests of all peoples', their desecration of Japanese dead on the field of battle by sending home the latter's skulls as souvenirs. (This last accusation was levelled against the Americans by the Apostolic Delegate to the Philippines among others.)[96]*

Meanwhile, the innate cruelty of the Japanese, together with the fanaticism that made them hold life cheaply, had likewise figured in Western propaganda and popular depictions of the enemy from the outset; but here, too, additional emphasis and bitterness came to surround the subject as the war progressed. After some initial hesitation on the part of officials in Washington and New Delhi in particular – concerned lest Western prestige should be further lowered in the eyes of other Asians [97] – details of Japanese atrocities against prisoners of war† and civilian internees were released in 1942–43, and were reinforced as Allied units subsequently advanced into areas previously occupied by the enemy. The resulting outcry was particularly fierce in the United States (above all, over the Bataan death march), and in Australia and New Zealand.‡ The conclusions drawn by the *Sydney Morning Herald* early in 1944 were typical:

* The practice of sporting on their belts remains of enemy dead was indeed adopted by some American troops in the campaigns against Japan. The 'trophies' selected apparently included parts of the bodies of Japanese women who were killed on various Pacific islands. (See e.g. M. P. Motley, ed., *The Invisible Soldier: The Experience of the Black Soldier, World War II*, Detroit, 1975, 78, 103). The same practice was of course to signal the barbarism of certain units of the U.S. Army in Vietnam. For perspective on this, see Drinnon, *Facing West*, and for the shrewd reflections of a U.S. Marine veteran years later, Studs Terkel (ed.), *"The Good War": An Oral History of World War Two* (New York, 1984), 59 ff.

† Japanese contempt for Allied prisoners of war was in part the reflection of a code which marked surrender as the ultimate disgrace for the man-at-arms. In regulations promulgated by the Japanese War Ministry in January 1942, the death penalty was decreed for those Imperial troops who allowed themselves to be taken captive, while combat instructions issued to soldiers emphasised that if they should fall into enemy hands as a consequence of being wounded, then 'the moment consciousness is regained [you will] quickly commit suicide'. (See W. W. Mason, *Official History of New Zealand in the Second World War: Prisoners of War*, Wellington, 1954, 188.) For examples of the consequences in terms of individuals and the overall Japanese-Allied record, see below, 262–3, 276.

‡ It was not known in the West at the time – nor, thanks to collusion on the part of the U.S. authorities, was it to be revealed until long after the war had ended – that the Japanese were also using and destroying human guinea pigs in experiments for germ warfare. 'How Japan Planned to Unleash a Plague', *The Guardian*, (London), 2 April 1982.

'At last there can be seen, through these terrible disclosures, the true
nature of the race that aspires to the leadership of Asia. Brutal and
treacherous the Japanese had often showed themselves to be. The story of
their cruelties was written in characters of blood across the quivering body
of China before they leaped like crouching beasts upon their white
neighbours in the Pacific. But until now hope had lingered that, in respect
of helpless prisoners at least, Japan would be willing to follow the practice
of civilised Powers in whose ranks she had wished to be numbered . . .
Today the mask has been finally torn aside. Nothing remains of the suave,
smiling countenance that pre-war Nippon had turned to the outside
world. The cunning, ape-like visage that has replaced it appears to be
distorted into a hideous grin when Tokyo Radio mocks our soldiers for
surrendering – as if [this] entitled their captors to maltreat, torture and
murder them . . .'[98]*

It followed for many in the ranks of Japan's enemies that the fight could
only, and must, be pursued to the death: until, as the official organ of the
New Zealand Labour Party put it, 'a Maori, picking up a handful of dust, can
say: "That was Tokio"'; until, in Churchill's words to the United States
Congress, the 'necessary and desirable' process 'of laying the cities and other
munitions centres of Japan in ashes' had been completed.[99] Hence the
widespread judgement in the West in August 1945 – illustrated above in the
case of the American public – that, as one Australian newspaper phrased it,
'the use of atomic bombs against this atrocious race . . . [which] trained their
soldiers as thoroughly in lust as in arms . . . is fully justified . . . while it
refuses to accept defeat'.[100]† And when Japan had, indeed, surrendered,
the military observers and press correspondents of Australia and New
Zealand who arrived in that country with the Allied occupying forces were
to be all the more distrustful of the people they encountered there when they
set alongside the war-time record their current reception with a 'flood of

---

* Even so, a few, at least, of the prisoners involved came to pity their captors for 'the remote
and archaic nature of the forces which had invaded the Japanese spirit'. 'We found
ourselves,' recalls Laurens van der Post, ' . . . feeling deeply sorry for the Japanese, as if we
were the free men and they the prisoners – men held in some profound *oubliette* of their own
minds.' *The Night of the New Moon* (London, 1970), 36–7, 134.
† Note also, for example, the episode in the Errol Flynn film *Objective Burma* (released in the
U.S.A. in January 1945) when a (fictitious) American war correspondent, looking at the
mutilated body of a U.S. Army officer, bursts out: 'This was done by a people who claim to be
civilised. Civilised! They're desperate moral idiots! Stinking little savages! Wipe them out, I
say! Wipe them off the face of the earth!' Interestingly, U.S. Army studies found that while
'veteran enlisted men and officers in the Pacific were more vindictive toward the Japanese
than their counterparts in Europe toward the Germans', 'the men fighting the Japanese were
strikingly less vindictive toward the Japanese than were either soldiers training in the United
States or soldiers fighting the Germans in Europe.' Stouffer et al., *The American Soldier:
Combat And Its Aftermath*, 157.

subservient smiles, ultra-polite bows and acts of moral servitude in a saccharine desire to please'.[101]

On each side in the war, in short, the enemy came to be depicted as the embodiment of evil: 'the Powers of Darkness'; people driven by 'a perverted faith'.[102] On each side, too, the images that were widely employed in this context brought even further into the open, with a new harshness, those racist notions that we have observed in the years before 1941. The enemy, in other words, was widely labelled as belonging to a different, and inferior, species altogether.

It might be argued that in modern, total war the wholesale branding of the foe is a common occurrence, as is the distortion of truth in general.[103] But even the depiction during the First World War, for example, of the Germans as 'Huns' who had butchered Belgian civilians had not prevented a degree of fellow-feeling for the enemy troops from developing among British soldiers on the Western front. It had not created a situation akin to that in which Admiral William Halsey, one of the U.S. Navy's outstanding commanders in the Pacific in the 1941–45 conflict, could regularly urge his men to kill more of the 'low monkeys' facing them and to make more 'monkey meat' thereby.[104] During the Second World War itself, written propaganda, films and cartoons in the U.S.A. and Canada were directed in the main, where the struggle in Europe was concerned, against Hitler and Mussolini personally; but in the context of the Far Eastern struggle, they attacked the entire Japanese nation as evil animals. Americans and Canadians of German or Italian descent were for the most part not subjected to persecution; those of Japanese stock, on the other hand, as will be recounted in more detail in a subsequent chapter, were interned (and often well-nigh ruined in the process) on the basis of the conviction expressed by the commanding general of the western military zone in the United States when, in 1943, he was opposing their release: 'A Jap,' declared General De Witt on that occasion, 'is a Jap.'*

In Britain, also, whereas the Germans tended to be depicted publicly as a people who had been dragged down from a civilised condition by the evils of Nazism, the Japanese were commonly described, in the words of one study, 'in terms appropriate to a newly-discovered zoological species'.[105] And if British attitudes towards this 'species' sometimes inclined towards 'amused contempt',† they nevertheless embraced the frequent use of the analogue that Admiral Halsey was wont to employ and that was in virtually everyday

* See below, 273–4.
† It is interesting, for example, to encounter in the Ministry of Information film *War in the Pacific* (1943; Imperial War Museum film archive, No. CVN 212) the use of the term 'the Japanese' throughout, rather than the term 'Japs' that was well-nigh standard at the time in North America, Australia and New Zealand – and, indeed, was commonly employed in Britain itself.

use in America, Australia and New Zealand. It was to 'monkey men' that
Harold Nicolson, for example (former diplomat and writer; a man about as
far removed from Halsey in terms of personality as one could imagine),
referred in his diary when sadly reflecting on the early victories of the
Japanese.[106]

It seems evident, in other words, that, to a large proportion of the white
people involved, the war in the Far East was being waged against 'mur-
derous little ape-men'; 'little men with devil faces and devil minds'. And for
at least a substantial number, especially in Australia and the United States,
the slogan (proclaimed on posters in the former country): 'We have always
hated the Japanese', also appears to have reflected genuine sentiments, as
did the belief at the end of the war (voiced by the Sydney *Daily Telegraph*, for
example) that in order to render the enemy harmless one would have to 'lift
across 2,000 years of backwardness ... a mind which, below its surface
understanding of the technical knowledge our civilisation has produced, is as
barbaric as the savage who fights with a club and believes thunder is the voice
of his God'.[107]

'Defeating this [Japanese] nation is as necessary as shooting down a mad
dog in your neighbourhood.'[108] 'There is no effective way of stopping [U.S.]
cruelties except by a thorough extermination of Americans.'[109] The similarity of the propaganda imagery and prescriptions is evident, though one
must add that on the Japanese side one tends to encounter less of the
physically-orientated racism that led Roosevelt, for example (with the
encouragement of the Smithsonian Institution's Curator of Physical
Anthropology), to believe that Japanese 'nefariousness' derived from a
skull pattern that was less developed than that of the Caucasian.[110] More
common among Japanese propagandists, indeed, were manifestations of
what one of them acknowledged to be 'an inferiority complex ... [resulting
from Japan's being] suddenly dragged into Western culture'.*

Nevertheless, the inherently racist aspect of the Japanese belief in their
distinctive, divine status as a nation, noted in the context of the pre-war
years, was greatly in evidence between 1941 and 1945. It lay at the root of,
for example, the treatment accorded the large number of Koreans† who

---

* Takeda, *The Great East Asia War and Ideological Warfare*. 'In intellectual capacity,' Takeda
went on to reassure his fellow-countrymen, 'we are not inferior. Investigations show that
Japanese children in Honolulu, San Francisco and Los Angeles were rated highest in mental
tests ... Japanese children are shorter in height but are stockier and better developed
physically. In speed of work and ability to use machines Japanese stand first in the world. Our
lack of height is no handicap in practical life, especially in the Navy and factories.' Cf. an
American political-warfare draft of 1942: 'Except as swimmers and in a few specialities, the
Japanese are athletically inferior to Americans, and know it. Show that American sports-
manship has engendered an invincible will to win.' FO 371, F4684/200/61.
† 1.4 million Koreans were working in Japan by 1941, and a further half a million were sent to
join them between then and 1945. By the end of the war they constituted a substantial

were employed as 'virtual slaves' in the coal mines and factories of Japan, often being subjected to great brutality.[111] Vis-à-vis the white enemy, it manifested itself both in behaviour towards prisoners and in propaganda portrayals of cunning demons (this, for example, after the American bombing raid on Tokyo in 1942), of 'albino apes', of 'carnivorous beasts, devoid of all humanity, aiming at reaping a cruel, inhuman revenge on Japan'.[112]

*

Perceptions regarding the nature of the enemy were bound up, of course, with ideas concerning the nature and origins of the war itself. In this context it is interesting to note how change – usually unacknowledged – could take place once the fighting had actually begun. We have already seen, for example, that Joseph Grew, the American Ambassador in Tokyo, had believed until late in the day that, as he wrote to one of his daughters in October 1941, the United States could 'pull through' the crisis with Japan without war coming about. Yet by the end of 1943 he was explaining the conflict in a series of public addresses as having been launched by 'gangster elements' in control of Japanese policy: men who had 'for a long time wanted war', who had 'held it back . . . [only] because they were not ready', and who were still (in September 1943) 'proposing to invade' the United States as the crucial step in their 'mission of conquest'.[113] Likewise, the confidence before Pearl Harbor of the banker, Thomas Lamont, that the Japanese had no thought of attacking the U.S.A. had given place by September 1942 to the privately-expressed conviction that they had, in fact, entertained 'evil intent towards America for years'.[114] The same shift occurred in the mind of Father James Drought, whose unofficial and counter-productive involvement in Japanese-American diplomtic exchanges in 1941 had been based in part on a firm belief in Tokyo's reasonableness and good faith, but who was declaring in 1942 (the words were his, though they were spoken by another) that the total destruction of the United States had 'always been the aim' of an enemy who embodied 'the deep, planned malice of an evil soul'.[115]

This conviction that Japan had long prepared her assault against the West, and that fundamentally the war was one of survival, became widespread on the Allied side, both within official circles and among the publics at large. 'The reason why [Japan] began fighting this war was to conquer the countries which had [important raw materials] and to send her people there to settle,'

proportion of the entire labour force in that country. (Cumings, *Origins of the Korean War*, 28–9.) On the racist attitude of many Americans to Koreans when in that country after the war, see ibid, 390.

a senior Fijian civil servant* told his people. 'This was why we had to fight
. . ., for our very survival.' Also in the South Pacific, in Australia, the Prime
Minister John Curtin, like the press, was insisting as late as the summer of
1942 that the country stood in mortal danger.[116] 'The enemy's object,'
declared the *Sydney Morning Herald*, 'is our total destruction,' and when
Singapore, that 'buttress against the Asiatic tide', had fallen, it was generally
believed that 'the Battle of Australia' was about to commence; that 'Australia's hour is approaching'.[117] 'It is not a question of *whether* we will be
attacked, but *when*,' warned the organ of the New Zealand Nationalist
Party, while its socialist counterpart was likewise repeating as late as May
1942: 'The Japs *are* coming this way.'[118] And earlier, in February, the latter
newspaper had demonstrated to its readers by publishing extracts from the
'Tanaka Memorial' of 1927† that 'Japan's policy of expansion in the Pacific'
was 'no new thing', her 'master blow' having merely been delayed until the
moment was propitious.[119]

The same 'evidence' of the Tanaka Memorial figured prominently in a
film, *Prelude to War*, that was made by Frank Capra at the behest of the U.S.
Army's Chief of Staff, General George Marshall, as a means of explaining to
Americans 'why they are in uniform' and why the cause was 'worth fighting
and dying for'. Released in October 1942, this film, together with the series
of which it formed the first instalment, 'exposed tens of millions of theater-
goers', in Capra's words, 'probably for the first time, to what the war was all
about'.[120] And what it was about, where Japan was concerned, was her
intention – as revealed in the Tanaka document – to 'move eastwards and
crush the United States' after conquering Asia. Thus, the commentary to the
film continued, the process that had begun in Manchuria in 1931 would end,
unless Americans fought for their lives, in the District of Columbia itself:

> 'Yes. The conquering Japanese Army down Pennsylvania Avenue: that
> was the final goal . . . Imagine [in the light of what had recently occurred in
> Nanking, Hong Kong and Manila] the field-day they'd have if they
> marched through the streets of Washington.'

Within the State Department, too, although the scenarios envisaged were
somewhat less lurid, the fight against 'conquest-mad military dictators', as

---

* Ratu Sir Lala Sukuna (as he became) had fought with distinction in the French Foreign
  Legion on the Western Front in the First World War. During the Second World War he was
  appointed Recruiting Officer for the Fijian Military Forces, and in 1943 was made Advisor on
  (later Secretary of) Fijian Affairs. See Scarr, *Fiji: the Three-Legged Stool*, 286–8.
† This document purported to be a plan drawn up by Japan's Prime Minister at the time,
  General Tanaka Giichi, for the conquest of China, the United States, India, Central and
  Southeast Asia, 'and even Europe', and became widely cited as proof of Japan's world-wide
  aggressive intentions. It was almost certainly a forgery, fabricated probably by either a
  Chinese or a Japanese who was opposed to Tanaka. See J. Stephan, 'The Tanaka Memorial
  (1927): Authentic or Spurious?', *Modern Asian Studies, XII, No. 4*, 1973.

Emmerson termed Japan's rulers, was seen as having 'mortal implications'.[121] For the British, on the other hand, it was obviously Germany,
rather than Japan, that posed the threat to one's very existence. Not only
was an invasion by Tokyo's forces out of the question, but to the vast
majority neither the colonial empire in Southeast Asia nor India was so
integral a part of the country's territory that its retention was truly 'vital'.
Even so, however, the Japanese were depicted in Britain, too, as having
long dreamed of achieving 'world domination' by means of 'cold cunning
[and] sinister conquests'.[122] And throughout the war, polls indicated that
the public overwhelmingly supported the pledge given to the United States
by Churchill, that even after the Nazi menace had been removed Britain
would continue to fight to the very end to ensure that Japan, too, was utterly
defeated.[123]

For France and the Netherlands, also, the fate of the nation depended
totally on the outcome of the war in the West. Nevertheless, it was
frequently asserted in the Resistance press in each of these countries, as well
as by politicians in exile, that the recovery of imperial territories in Southeast Asia, too, was essential if the well-being and status of the nation were
to be restored. In this sense, at least, therefore, the Far Eastern war –
prepared for in detail by the Japanese and desired by them for twenty years
past, as *Combat* saw it[124] – could be regarded as involving one's long-term
survival. In de Gaulle's words:

> 'For us, the outcome of the war must be the restoration at one and the
> same time of the complete territorial integrity of the French Empire, of
> the heritage of France, and of the total sovereignty of the French
> nation.'[125]

The French Communist Party and the Vichy regime were also at one on
this issue: France must recover her imperial territories and her *'grandeur'*.
And despite Vichy's own agreements with Japan over the latter's occupation
of Indochina (agreements which, it was claimed, had helped safeguard the
Empire amidst the turbulent circumstances of the time); despite the
Schadenfreude with which Vichy's supporters tended to view the discomfi-
ture of the 'Anglo-Saxons' at Japanese hands during the early months of the
war; despite the admiration which publicists of the extreme right bestowed
upon Japan's *bushido* code and the vigour she was now deriving (as could
France) from a return to her own true spirit and genius ('son génie propre'):
despite all this, it was impossible to ignore the potential consequences for
France herself of the sharp decline in white prestige that Japan's triumphs
were bringing about in the minds of dependent peoples ('ces peuples dit
mineurs'), or, indeed, that country's intention to exclude all outside influence from Asia.[126]

In the Netherlands, meanwhile, however much the Communists and the Calvinists within the Resistance might differ in their attitude towards colonial peoples, they were agreed, in the words of the Communist underground paper, *Die Waarheid*, that 'the Netherlands and Indonesia must not be split from one another'. 'We know,' declared the Anti-Revolutionary Party's clandestine publication, *Trouw*, in the summer of 1944,

> 'the our country, if deprived of the Indies, would be a small and insignificant state which would be pushed about within the great turmoil of international relations. If we lose the Indies, we shall be able to perform no greater role than that of the "spearhead" of Britain [in Europe], and thereby be deprived of all potential significance. By contrast, with the possession of the Indies we are a great and strong empire which, with its population of 80 million, can take its place among the great empires [of the world].'[127]

If to some of the Dutch, at least, it was a sacred task to take part in liberating the Indies which were 'calling out' to them ('Indië roept ons'), to the Japanese the Far Eastern conflict represented in far more direct and immediate terms a struggle for survival. Once again, there are marked similarities between the interpretations that were advanced in Japan in this respect and those that were entertained by her enemies. In the Japanese version, the Anglo-Saxons had long intended to expand into and dominate all of East as well as Southeast Asia, such a move constituting for the United States in particular (thanks, not least, to the Jewish element in that country)* but one step towards 'world domination'.

As we have already seen, the need to ensure Japan's survival and freedom of action in the face of growing Western pressure had lain at the heart of the decision-making conferences that took place in Tokyo in the period leading up to the war. And if, with the military triumphs of the ensuing months, that emphasis tended for a time to become overshadowed by more 'bullish' sentiments, it nevertheless returned with growing intensity as the Allies began to press in towards the country's home islands, and as the Government found it increasingly difficult to suppress criticism and apprehension. ('Will it be Victory or will it be Defeat?', asked the newspaper *Mainichi* as early as February 1944.)[128] Japan, it was asserted, had been compelled to act in December 1941 'to defend her very life'. Now, her enemies were seeking, not merely to bring her to the point of unconditional

---

* Despite this anti-Semitic aspect of Japanese political warfare, however, some Jewish refugees from Europe were received in Japan with much less than total hostility and persecution. See M. Tokayer and M. Swartz, *The Fugu Plan* (London, 1979).

surrender, but 'by a cruelty hitherto unknown to the world . . . to wipe out everlastingly the memory of Japan from the face of the earth'. To achieve this evil end, they would

'destroy our peerless Constitution; burn our shrines and temples; occupy our six chief cities with [their] troops; deprive us of our freedom of education; fill their museums with our historical treasures; break up all our industrial plants; inflict a general massacre; trample on the chastity of our women; defile the purity of our blood [through miscegenation], and promote utterly immoral conditions.'[129]

*

Proposals for drastically punitive treatment to be meted out to the Japanese once they had been defeated were indeed, as we have noted, not lacking within the ranks of the Allies. While the idea of the wholesale extermination of that nation appears to have appealed to a significant proportion of the American public, a representative of the U.S. Navy who was a member of a State-War-Navy Coordinating Committee group in Washington that was making plans for post-war Japan likewise made clear his preference for 'the almost total elimination of the Japanese as a race'.[130] If Queen Wilhelmina had earlier talked of 'drowning them like rats', Admiral Halsey only a shade less drastically now emphasised the need 'to make them impotent for all time to wage another war'.[131] What Roosevelt, for his part, had in mind for a while at least was their enforced isolation within their home islands, in order that their congenital delinquency should not contaminate the process of bringing about more stable and peaceful conditions in the East through a programme of racial inter-breeding.[132]* Others, too, like the London *Daily Mail*, saw 'complete isolation from the rest of the world, as in a leper compound, unclean', as being the only suitable fate for what had been 'proved a sub-human race'.[133]

To the very end of the war, and beyond, loud demands were also uttered in the West, not simply for the rooting out of Japan's militarism, but for the exemplary punishment of Emperor Hirohito, who was for the Sydney *Daily Telegraph* among many others 'the symbol of a barbarism we fought to expunge' and 'the core of the social system which begot [Japan's] ambition

---

* The Resistance paper, *Défense de la France* (February 5, 1943), for one, also made particular reference to the need to put a stop to what it saw as Japan's politically-calculated policy of unbridled population growth. For a wide range of possible migration schemes that were studied for Roosevelt (whose amateurism and megalomanic tendencies are in retrospect particularly disturbing in this context), see H. Field, *'M' Project for F.D.R.* (Ann Arbor, 1962).

to rule the world and [her] assurance of racial superiority'. In the U.S.A., polls taken in July and August 1945 showed roughly one-third of those questioned opting for Hirohito's immediate execution, about one-fifth for his imprisonment or exile, and only three to four per cent for his employment by the Allies.[134]* In Australia and New Zealand especially, the predominant conviction continued to be that Japan 'must be dealt with ruthlessly', and much unease and anger was to be occasioned in those two countries by the manner in which MacArthur and his American advisers approached their task when the occupation of Japan had actually begun: by their 'bewildering disposition', as one paper saw it, 'to treat the surrendering enemy with a clemency wholly out of keeping with the retribution that [their] crimes demand'. 'A people who can commit the outrages that the Japanese in their thousands everywhere have been responsible for,' the Wellington *Standard* was to argue in September 1945 (echoing in public what was also being urged in diplomatic and political circles), 'cannot be "re-educated" with sugar-coated pills. They must be made to taste the tang of corrective medicine.'[135]

Yet even during the early days of the war there had been those in the West, especially in diplomatic circles and non-official 'foreign-policy communities', as they are sometimes termed, who had retained some hope in the post-war potential of what they saw as 'liberal' elements within Japanese politics, and/or believed that on grounds of *Realpolitik* Japan, while being disarmed, would have to be readmitted to the international community within a fairly short time of hostilities ending. John Emmerson, for example, had mentioned as a qualifying appendage to the main thrust of his State Department memoranda in January 1942

'those in Japan who do not subscribe to the philosophy of life which has in recent years led their nation down a path of aggression and destruction of the rights of peoples. The future hope of Japan,' he continued, 'will rest with new leaders and with a changed philosophy to arise when peace again prevails in the Pacific. And this can be accomplished through defeat of Japan's war effort and the inevitable repercussions in Japan and on the Japanese mind of such a defeat.'[136]

Other members of a small group of State Department officials who had experience of Japan – men such as Hugh Borton and Joseph Grew – were to contribute to this line of thought, in the face of much scepticism on the part

---

* General Tojo was also, of course, a target for Western anger. But so, too, before his death in 1943, was Admiral Yamamoto, who had planned the attack on Pearl Harbor, and who was described, far from accurately, in the American Council of the Institute of Pacific Relations volume, *Modern Japan* (written by W. H. Chamberlain and published in 1942), as having (p. 80) 'hated the West with the double hatred of a race-conscious Oriental and of a Japanese admiral', and having 'long looked forward to battle with the British and American fleets'.

of those Far Eastern Division colleagues whose expertise and primary concern were alike focused on China. And within the Office of War Information, Geoffrey Gorer, Ruth Benedict and others were to develop analyses of Japanese society that at least sought to move beyond facile stereotypes.[137] In British official circles, too, meanwhile – and with a more widespread concurrence within the Foreign Office – individuals like Sir George Sansom were arguing that, while Japan's record was 'certainly a discreditable one in many important respects', there was 'a better chance of her good behaviour if she [could] be invited to join the club and observe the rules instead of being blackballed';[138] that, now Japan's militants had 'had their fling' and had got the country into 'a disastrous mess', in due course an opportunity should arise 'for the liberal element (or as it would be more accurate to call them, the level-headed, worldly-wise element) to recover control'.[139]*

Indeed, by the final months of the war (and surely, in part at least, as a consequence of changed circumstances, preoccupations and requirements), the Japanese people as a whole were being described in some quarters in Washington in terms that suggested that they were an entirely different species from the nation whose deeply-ingrained propensity for militarism, dictatorship and xenophobia had been so carefully catalogued in 1942. Even the U.S. Navy Department was emphasising by July 1945 that 'numerous Japanese' would be 'disposed to accept and assist in the development of democratic principles' once their Government had surrendered. In this particular respect, the American officials concerned were virtually isolated in terms of the Allied governments and peoples as a whole, for even their British counterparts retained an underlying distrust – even dislike – of the Japanese as a nation, just as they looked with much scepticism at American plans to 're-educate' the defeated enemy.[140] (In many respects, this meant to Americanise them, just as China was to have been 'led into the twentieth century' and South Vietnam was to be the object of an exercise in 'nation-building'.)†

The details of the policy debates that took place within and among Allied authorities on these matters as the war approached its close have been set out elsewhere by the present writer and others, and will not be repeated

---

* During the war there were also those in Western states, both within and outside official circles, who protested at the more extreme forms of racist language employed against the Japanese by men like Halsey. See e.g. Merrill, *A Sailor's Admiral*, 53, 73–4; letter from the 'Good Companions of the Christian Social Order' (Australia) to Curtin, April 9, 1942, Curtin Papers, CP 156/1.

† It must be added, however, that Emmerson, for one, warned early in 1945: 'America cannot remake Japan. We shall incur only resentment and failure if we attempt forcibly to impose an American "way of life" on the Japanese.' (Memo. on 'Communism and the Future of Japan', February 16, 1945, St. Dpt. files, 894.00/2–1645.) And see e.g. Benedict, *The Chrysanthemum and the Sword*, 221–2.

here.[141] Should the Emperor, or at least the Throne, be retained? (Allied political warfare had taken care to steer around this particular topic.)[142] How great was the possibility of social and political revolution – of a Communist revolution, perhaps – taking place in Japan in the aftermath of defeat, possibly fostered by those Japanese Marxists who (like their counterparts in the Korean Volunteer Army which fought alongside Mao's troops) had found refuge with the Yenan regime in China?[143] Should the Allies occupy all of Japan, or only a few, key, strategic areas? Should a process of de-industrialisation, as well as of de-militarisation, be instituted, and how should the giant financial and manufacturing combines – the *zaibatsu* – be broken up? What role might the Soviet Union seek to play in the area? And so forth.

Discussions on such matters were often conducted with one eye on the need to avoid raising an outcry among one's own public by appearing unduly lenient towards a hated, or at the very least distrusted, foe. For British ministers and officials there was also the additional handicap created by their own somewhat tardy approach to such issues, together with problems that arose from the importance of not giving ammunition to those Americans in and around official quarters (not least, those who attended the international gatherings of the Institute of Pacific Relations) who were wont to accuse Britain of 'favouring a soft peace toward Japan'. Above all, however, London found itself coming up against the determination in Washington that it was going to be American plans and American administrators that would shape the new Japan and make the Pacific safe for democracy. Overwhelmingly (and, although incorrectly, not without reason), opinion in the United States saw the Great Republic as having won the Far Eastern war single-handedly. Now it would win the peace.

The winning of that peace, however, involved other major issues besides that of how to deal with the defeated enemy. Even in terms of Japan's confrontation with the Allies, we have already observed in our outline sketch of the war that both sides laid claim during the fighting to various aims and principles that went beyond that of preserving their own lives and territory. Moreover, the declarations and propaganda – even, to some extent, actions – that were involved set up reverberations across a web of interrelationships that was far more complex than the one implied in the simple distinction between Japan and her enemies.

In its wider and deeper aspects, the Far Eastern war did not resemble, say, a singles match at tennis. On either side of the net, to stretch the metaphor further, there were partners to consider. But even 'mixed doubles' (or, in the Allied camp especially, a higher multiplier) does not suffice as a descripton of what was taking place between 1941 and 1945. For there were others, still – spectators; those dragged into the game against their will – to consider and, if possible, to influence, convince, and win over to one's own side, not only for the rewards this could bring during the war years themselves, but for the advantages that could accrue in terms of the period beyond. It is to these further international dimensions of the conflict, therefore, that we must now turn.

Notes

1 See Martin, op. cit., passim, and Hauner, op. cit., 377ff.
2 See, e.g. the British official history's *Grand Strategy* series of volumes; Hall, *North American Supply*; M. Matloff and E. Snell, *Strategic Planning for Coalition Warfare, 1941–1942* (Washington, D.C., 1953), and M. Matloff, *Strategic Planning for Coalition Warfare, 1943–1944* (Washington, 1959).
3 See P. Calvocoressi, *Top Secret Ultra* (London, 1980); H. Hinsley et al., *British Intelligence in World War II* (London, 1979 et seq.); and, on the Far East in particular, Lewin, *The Other Ultra*; Horner, *High Command*, cap. 11; Spector, *Eagle Against the Sun*, cap. 20.
4 On, for example, 'the lack of direction and coordination in Australian defence and foreign policy', see Horner, *High Command*, 325 and 434ff, and on American internal conflicts, Spector, cap. 7 and passim.
5 Quoted in Thorne, *Allies*, 273.
6 Ibid, 274.
7 Ibid, passim.
8 E.g. ibid, 412.
9 Ibid, 113–4, 283, 395, 508–9.
10 See M. Howard, *The Mediterranean Strategy in World War Two* (London, 1968).
11 See Thorne, *Allies*, 190–2, 306, 316.
12 Ibid, 411ff.
13 B. Bond (ed.) *Chief of Staff: the Diaries of Lieutenant-General Sir Henry Pownall, Vol. II* (London, 1974), entry for 29 April 1944.
14 Thorne, *Allies*, 407, 485, 537.
15 Ibid, e.g. 171ff., 305ff.
16 See Ikeda Kiyoshi, 'Japanese Strategy and the Pacific War, 1941–5', and Nomura Minoru, 'Military Policy-Makers Behind Japanese Strategy Against Britain', in I. Nish (ed.), *Anglo-Japanese Alienation, 1919–1952* (Cambridge, 1982).
17 On the specific campaigns of the war see, e.g. the British official series: S. W. Kirby, *The War Against Japan* (four vols., London, 1957–65), and the relevant sections of Roskill, *The War At Sea*; on the American side, S. E. Morison, *The Two-Ocean War* (Boston, 1963) provides a sumary of his detailed, multi-volumed study of the subject, while Spector, *Eagle Against the Sun*, offers the best overall survey. J. Costello, *The Pacific War* (London, 1981) contains much colourful detail, but also inaccuracies.
18 See Thorne, *Allies*, 77–8, 134–5.
19 See ibid, 156.
20 See ibid, 136, 163, 165–6, 288–9, 295–6.
21 Ibid, 164.
22 See, e.g. Wilson, op. cit., cap. 15.
23 See Thorne, *Allies*, 407.
24 See ibid, 294–5, 298ff., 349, 409, 450ff., 522–3, 565.
25 See ibid, 411ff.
26 See ibid, 521ff.
27 See Wilson, 215; Eastman, *Seeds of Destruction*, cap. 6.

28 See Thorne, *Allies*, 296–7, 526ff.; J. Erickson, *Stalin's War With Germany: Vol. 2: the Road to Berlin* (London, 1983), 500–3.
29 Ibid, 557; Ride, op. cit., 264ff.
30 Thorne, *Allies*, 565ff.
31 See Havens, 176ff.
32 See R. J. Butow, *Japan's Decision to Surrender* (Stanford, 1954).
33 See Thorne, *Allies*, 532–3.
34 Butow, *Japan's Decision*, 3.
35 J. W. Morley (ed.), *Deterrent Diplomacy: Japan, Germany and the U.S.S.R., 1935–1940* (New York, 1976), appendix 7.
36 Lebra, *JGEACS*, 68ff.
37 Iriye, *Power and Culture*, 40ff.
38 Lebra, *JGEACS*, 78ff.
39 Iriye, *Power and Culture*, 117.
40 Ibid, 98ff.
41 See Hauner, 560.
42 See Toye, 77ff., 97.
43 Manila *Tribune*, 6 Nov. 1943.
44 Translation in the *Gaimusho* archives, Tokyo. See Lebra, *JGEACS*, 92.
45 Iriye, *Power and Culture*, 115ff.
46 See Thorne, *Allies*, 61, 78, 101–3; Reynolds, 213–4, 257–60.
47 See Thorne, *Allies*, e.g. 160–1.
48 On the various ideas regarding the future of Korea that existed within American official circles, see Cumings, op. cit., cap. 4.
49 Iriye, *Power and Culture*, 162–4.
50 *Tribune*, 19 Feb. 1944 and e.g. 16 March 1944.
51 Lt. Col. Takeda Koiso, *The Great East Asia War and Ideological Warfare* (Nov. 1943): translation and summary by Far Eastern Bureau, Ministry of Information, NZ External Affairs files, 84/6/1, part 3; Meo, *Japan's Radio War on Australia*, 106ff., and N. Ryo, 'Japanese Overseas Broadcasting: a Personal View', in K. Short (ed.), *Film and Radio Propaganda in World War II* (Knoxville, 1983).
52 *Syonan Shimbun*, 18 March 1943, and Takeda, op. cit.
53 On Japanese peace-feelers towards Chungking, see J. H. Boyle, *China and Japan at War, 1937–1945* (Stanford, 1972), 310ff., and Iriye, *Power and Culture*, 109ff.
54 *Syonan Shimbun*, 18 July 1945; and e.g. 8 Feb. and 1 May 1945; Manila *Tribune*, 11 July 1942 and 1 and 4 Feb. 1944.
55 See Iriye, *Power and Culture*, 180–1, 244ff., and T. Kase, *Eclipse of the Rising Sun* (London, 1951), 116, 154.
56 E.g. *Synonan Shimbun*, 1 Oct. 1942.
57 See e.g. C. Cruickshank, *SOE in the Far East* (Oxford, 1983), 236–7. For analyses, plans and efforts regarding political warfare against the Japanese, see e.g. the files of the Whitehall Cttee. on Political Warfare Against Japan (Foreign Office records, series 371, e.g. files 31760ff., 35878ff., 41700ff., 46313ff.), and the relevant Research and Analysis papers produced by the OSS in Washington (National Archives, Washington), e.g. no. 383.
58 'Guidance for Action on Aim 1 of the British and American Plan for Political Warfare Against Japan', 30 June 1942, Australian P.M.'s Dept. files, K 57/1/1.
59 Background Paper from Joint Intelligence Cttee., 28 Feb. 1942, for Political Wfre. Exec. (FO 371, F2121/289/61). This report described the Japanese as being 'fundamentally children' who were 'completely callous towards anyone not immediately connected with them, and totally unable to see any point of view but their own'. 'On the other hand,' it continued, 'their capacity for loyalty and devotion is deep, and they are always ready to sacrifice themselves for any thing or person they think worthwhile.'
60 E.g. FO 371, F3124/2000/61. G. F. Hudson ('Note on Principles of Propaganda to Japan', 31 March 1942, ibid, F2766/289/61) believed that 'a propaganda of violent social revolution would undoubtedly have a great effect in Japan', but that 'this kind of policital warfare is presumably not open to Britain . . .'

61 OSS Research and Analysis report no. 383 (October 1942). This report's main emphasis, however, was on the reasons why Japan was likely 'to fight to exhaustion, even beyond a point where other nations in her predicament would surrender'. On the nature and work of the R. and A. branch of the Office of Strategic Services, see B. F. Smith, *The Shadow Warriors: OSS and the Origins of the CIA* (London, 1983), 121, 174ff., 209ff., 360ff., and on OSS activities in the Far East generally, ibid, 193ff., 254ff., 307ff. On attempts to undermine Japanese morale in the field, and on related interviews with Japanese prisoners, see J. K, Emmerson, *The Japanese Thread* (New York, 1978), 166ff., 221ff.; also Winkler, *The Politics of Propaganda*, 137ff.

62 See Butow, *Japan's Decision to Surrender*, caps. 3–5, and on London's views, FO 371, files 41804 and 46453.

63 See Butow, 133ff., Thorne, *Allies*, 530–4, and Emmerson, 232ff.

64 See Thorne, *Allies*, 500; Emmerson, 239–40; M. J. Sherwin, *A World Destroyed: the Atomic Bomb and the Grand Alliance* (New York, 1975).

65 *The Times*, 3 Jan. 1976; and see S. Salaff, 'The Diary and the Cenotaph: Racial and Atomic Fever in the Canadian Record', *Bulletin of Concerned Asian Scholars*, vol. 10, no. 2, 1978.

66 FO 371, AN 4/4/45.

67 In a poll taken in Sept. 1945, 54 per cent of Americans approved the recent use of atomic weapons, with a further 23 per cent agreeing with the proposition quoted. J. E. Mueller, *War, Presidents and Public Opinion* (New York, 1973), 172–3. Cf. S. K. Johnson, *American Attitudes Toward Japan, 1941–1975* (Washington D.C., 1975), 33ff.

68 Thorne, *Allies*, 533–4.

69 See Jervis, op. cit., and Kelman, op. cit.

70 See Wertheim, 269–70; Dahm, 265ff.

71 *Time*, 24 March 1980, and N. Crouter, *Forbidden Diary* (New York, 1980). See also Johnson, *American Attitudes*, 24ff.

72 A. Calder, *The People's War: Britain, 1939–1945* (London, 1971), 563; and see McLaine, op. cit., 274.

73 M. Anglo, *Service Newspapers in the Second World War* (London, 1977), 117.

74 See C. Thorne, 'Wartime British Planning for the Postwar Far East', in Nish (ed.), *Anglo-Japanese Alienation*, 208–9.

75 See e.g. the columns of *Le Populaire* for March 1945, and of the entire clandestine press throughout the war. The judgement is also based in part on an interview with M. René Massigli, Commissioner for Foreign Affairs in the French Committee of Liberation.

76 H. Isaacs, *Scratches on Our Minds* (New York, 1958), 37.

77 Dallek, 350.

78 S. A. Stouffer et al., *The American Soldier: Adjustment During Army Life* (Princeton, 1949), cap. 9, and *The American Soldier: Combat And Its Aftermath* (Princeton, 1949), 151. Blum, *V Was for Victory*, 65ff., 89; Winkler, *The Politics of Propaganda*, 5–6, 40ff., 54; B. Catton, *The War Lords of Washington* (New York, 1948), 189.

79 'Beliefs of Average Japanese Soldiers in SWPA in 1942', 1 June 1943, NZ External Affairs files, 84/6/1, part 1.

80 Emmerson, 173; Havens, 6.

81 R. Broad and S. Fleming (ed.), *Nella Last's War: A Mother's Diary, 1939–1945* (London, 1981).

82 Australian Military Forces Weekly Intelligence Review no. 118, NZ External Affairs files, 84/6/1, part 3.

83 Bruce, Monthly War Files, entry for 24 Jan. 1944, and e.g. FO 371, file 35951; Calwell to Curtin, 3 Feb. 1944, Australian P.M.'s Dept. files, E/57/1/1, part 2; Thorne, *Allies*, 290; Takeda, op. cit.

84 Havens, 10ff., 61ff.

85 *Syonan Shimbun*, 3 Oct. 1942.

86 Takeda, op. cit.

87 Guillain, 73–4. For an example of this claim itself, see e.g. *Syonan Shimbun*, 23 Feb. 1942.

88 See e.g. Bond (ed.), *Chief of Staff*, passim; W. Slim, *Defeat Into Victory* (London, 1958), 137ff.

89 Langdon, 'Elements of Weakness in the Japanese People and in the Japanese Position', 30 April 1942, Dpt. of State files, 890.00/1174.

90 E.g. Joint Anglo-U.S. Plan for Psychological Warfare Against Japan, Annex A, 1944, NZ External Affairs files, 84/6/1, part 2.

91 E.g. Blamey to Forde, 8 April 1943, Australian P.M.'s Dpt. files, K/41/1/1.

92 Imperial War Museum, London, film collection: no. USA/004–01.

93 Emmerson, 'Japan's Philosophy of Life', 26 Jan. 1942, Dpt. of State files, 740.0011 PW/2037⅜; 'Japan's Government in Fact', 6 Feb. 1942, ibid, 740. 0011 PW/2037⅞; 'What the United States Has Done for Japan', 5 Feb. 1942, ibid, 740.0011 PW/2037%. (For a remarkable, 'hands-across-the-Pacific' rendering of this last memorandum, see Iriye, *Power and Culture* 58; also Philip Roth, *The Great American Novel*, London, 1981, 102). See also e.g. N. Peffer, 'Roots of the Pacific Conflict', *Asia*, Feb. 1942.

94 E.g. *Syonan Shimbun*, 22 Sept. and 25 Oct. 1942.

95 Takeda, op. cit.

96 E.g. Manila *Tribune*, 19 Feb., 4 and 17 March, 28 April, 10 Aug. 1944; *Syonan Shimbun*, 3 March 1945.

97 See e.g. Political Warfare (Japan) Cttee., 'Plan of Propaganda to India', Jan. 1942, NZ Ext. Affs. files, 84/6/1, part 1; material in Hornbeck Papers, box 21; Thorne, *Allies*, 156, 158; O. Lindsay, *At the Going Down of the Sun* (London, 1981), 148.

98 *Sydney Morning Herald*, 31 Jan. 1944; and e.g. 20 Nov. 1944.

99 *The Standard* (Wellington), 7 May 1942.

100 *Sydney Morning Herald*, 15 Aug. 1945.

101 Ibid, 1, 3, and 11 Sept. 1945; *Standard*, 20 Sept. 1945; *Dominion* (Wellington), 18 Aug. 1945; Col. R. W. Savage to Gavin Long, 8 Sept. 1945, Long Papers, Correspondence files. For a commentary on the Japanese behaviour in question, see R. Benedict, *The Chrysanthemum and the Sword* (London, 1967), 29 and 119.

102 E.g. *Sydney Morning Herald*, 3 April 1942; Walter Nash (NZ Minister to the U.S.) broadcast, 22 March 1942, NZ Ext. Affs. files, 64/3/3/1, part 1A.

103 See e.g. P. Knightly, *The First Casualty* (New York, 1975).

104 J. M. Merrill, *A Sailor's Admiral* (New York, 1976), 53, 85, 209.

105 McLaine, 158–9.

106 N. Nicolson (ed.), *Harold Nicolson, The War Years: Diaries and Letters, 1939–1945* (London, 1967), entry for 19 Dec. 1941.

107 Sydney *Daily Telegraph*, 3 Sept. 1945; and e.g. material in Curtin's correspondence, 1942, CP 156/1, Australian Commonwealth Archives; A. Rhodes, *Propaganda: the Art of Persuasion: World War II* (London, 1976), 163, 258ff.; films such as 'The Mask of Nippon' (Canada, 1942) and 'Know Your Enemy: Japan' (Frank Capra, U.S.A., 1945), IWM film archive, nos. AMY 517 and USA/004–01; *Standard* (Wellington), 26 March 1942.

108 Film: 'Know Your Enemy: Japan'.

109 See above, 127.

110 Thorne, *Allies*, 158–9, 167–8; Hrdlicka-Roosevelt correspondence, Hrdlicka Papers, Smithsonian Institution.

111 Hane, *Peasants, Rebels and Outcastes*, 237.

112 E.g. Rhodes, op. cit., 258–60; Takeda, op. cit.; Meo, op. cit., 89.

113 Grew, 'Truth About Japan', 9 Sept. 1943, Grew Papers, vol. 115. And see above, 5.

114 Lamont to Grew, 15 Sept. 1942, Lamont Papers, 96/19.

115 Butow, *John Doe Associates*, 34ff., 157ff., 340ff.

116 See P. Hasluck, *The Government and the People, 1942–1945* (Canberra, 1970), 39, 97ff., 156ff., and e.g. Sydney *Daily Mirror*, 16 Feb. 1942; Sydney *Daily Telegraph*, 27 Jan. 1942; Sydney *Century*, 23 Jan. 1942; *Sydney Morning Herald*, 24 Jan. 1942.

117 *Sydney Morning Herald*, 2 Jan., 10 and 20 Feb., 12 March 1942.

118 *Dominion*, 14 Feb. 1942; *Standard*, 7 May 1942.

119 *Standard*, 19 Feb. 1942.

120 IWM film archive, no. ADM/7; F. Capra, *The Name Above the Title* (New York, 1971), 327; D. Culbert, 'Why We Fight: Social Engineering For A Democratic Society At War', in Short, *Film and Radio Propaganda*.

121 Emmerson memo., 'Japan's Government in Fact', loc. cit.; Langdon memo., 28 March 1942, St. Dpt. files, 740.0011 PW/2677.
122 'Pacific Thrust' (Verity Films, for the Ministry of Information, Jan. 1945), IWM film archive, CVN 229–01/02.
123 Thorne, *Allies*, 155, 290.
124 *Combat*, May 1942.
125 Ibid, and e.g. *Les Petits Ailes de France*, 7 August 1941; *L'Aurore*, Oct. 1943.
126 E.g. *L'Humanité*, 3 Dec. 1943, 1 Jan. 1944, 11 Jan. 1945; *Le Populaire*, 8 Sept., 14 Nov. 1944; *Déstin*, May 1944; *L'Aurore*, Oct. 1943; *La France Libre*, 15 Feb. 1944; *Le Monde*, 12 Aug. 1945; *Le Temps* 23 Dec. 1940, 15 Feb., 7 April, 14 May, 3 Nov. 1942; *L'Action Française*, 24 Dec. 1940, 31 July 1941, 20 Feb., 28 April 1942, 4 March 1944.
127 E.g. *Die Waarheid*, 1 May 1943; *Trouw*, July, Dec. 1943, July 1944; *Vrij Nederland*, 30 July 1943; *Je Maintiendrai*, 10 May 1943; van Namen (ed.), *Het Ondergroondse Vrij Nederland*, 219.
128 Shillony, 103ff. And see e.g. Kase, 67ff.
129 Takeda, op. cit. And also e.g. Manila *Tribune*, 4 Oct. 1942 and *Syonan Shimbun*, 2 Sept. 1942.
130 Quoted in R. Buckley, *Occupation Diplomacy: Britain, the United States and Japan, 1945–1952* (Cambridge, 1982), 15.
131 Merrill, 209.
132 Thorne, *Allies*, 8–9, 167–8.
133 Quoted in Calder, op. cit., 563.
134 Thorne, *Allies*, 657.
135 E.g. Sydney *Daily Telegraph*, 13 Aug., 3 Sept. 1945; *Sydney Morning Herald*, 19 May, 12 Aug., 11, 12, 13, 15, 18, 19 and 26 Sept. 1945; *Standard* (Wellington), 20 Sept., 29 Nov. 1945; *Dominion* (Wellington), 18 Aug. 1945; 'New Zealand as a Pacific Country', notes received 3 Dec. 1945, NZ Dpt. of Ext. Affs., 56/1/1, part 2; Australian 'First List of Major Japanese War Criminals', 26 Oct. 1945, Washington Legation files, A3300, file 316; R. J. Bell, *Unequal Allies* (Melbourne, 1977), cap. 8; Buckley, op cit., passim; Thorne, *Allies*, 654ff.
136 Emmerson, 'Japan's Philosophy of Life', loc. cit.
137 See Mead, *Ruth Benedict*, 57ff., and Benedict, *The Chrysanthemum and the Sword*. For later assessments, see Johnson, *American Attitudes*, and the more critical R. H. Minear, 'Cross-Cultural Perception and World War II: American Japanists and Their Images of Japan', *International Studies Quarterly*, Dec. 1980.
138 Sansom to Ashley Clark, 29 Dec. 1942, FO 371, F186/186/61. And see e.g. material in ibid, file 35952; also the article by H. V. Redman, 'The Political Problem of Japan', in *International Affairs*, Jan. 1944.
139 Foulds memo. 11 Sept. 1944, FO 371, F4015/1/11.
140 See e.g. Buckley, 38, 67, 69–70, 196.
141 See e.g. Thorne, *Allies*, 371ff., 489ff., 654ff.; Thorne, 'Chatham House, Whitehall and Far Eastern Issues, 1941–1945', *International Affairs*, Jan. 1978; Thorne, 'Wartime British Planning', in Nish, *Anglo-Japanese Alienation*; Iriye, *Power and Culture*, passim; Emmerson, op. cit., cap. 9.
142 E.g. Allied Cttee. in Australia on Political Warfare Against Japan, June 1944 directive, NZ Ext. Affs. files, 84/6/1, part 2.
143 On various Japanese anti-war groups who established themselves in both Chungking and Yenan, see Emmerson, 180. On the Korean military group in Yenan, see Cumings, op. cit., 412, 423.

CHAPTER FIVE

Winning Friends and the Future: Japan and Asia

In March 1942, the Japanese Fourteenth Army, which was in the process of driving the Americans from the Philippines, made a special point of celebrating the anniversary of its country's victory over the Russians at the battle of Mukden thirty-seven years earlier. The struggle now being waged, proclaimed Army Headquarters in Manila, was but a continuation of the one Japan had launched so successfully in 1904: the struggle of the East to throw off the domination of the white man. 'History is repeating itself in the Philippines.'[1]

The claim that Japan's cause was that of Asia as a whole has already been noted in the context of the contending political statements of the two sides in the war. And in print, by radio, and on film, it was reiterated vigorously for the benefit of the peoples who now found themselves brought under Tokyo's rule.[2] The fall of Singapore, declared the Commander in Chief of the Fourteenth Army, heralded the securing of 'Asia for the Asians' by a Japan that had 'no intention of conquering any Asiatic people, nor ... any territorial desire on any Oriental nation'.[3] As General Yamashita Tomoyuki, the victor in Malaya, put it in a proclamation that was issued on the morrow of the surrender of the British in Singapore (now renamed Syonan):

'We hope that we sweep away the arrogance and uprighteous British elements and share pain and rejoicing with all coloured peoples in a spirit of "give and take", and also hope to promote the social development by establishing the East Asia Coprosperity Sphere in which the New Order of justice has to be maintained under "The Great Spirit of Cosmocracy", giving all content to the respective race and individual according to their talents and faculties.'[4]

Later in 1942, in a fuller statement of Japan's aims, it was explained to the people of 'New Malai' (as Malaya had become) that this 'New Order' would have nothing in common with Western imperialism so far as 'the peoples of Asia' were concerned:

'Nippon has no thought of establishing any regimented sphere of imperialism in East Asia. That would be contrary to her principles. Fundamentally, it is to be a union of neighbouring states, sharing to a

greater or lesser degree common racial and cultural origins and geographical propinquity, founded by their voluntary agreement for the
purpose of assuring their common safety and promoting their common
happiness and prosperity. The basic principle of association within the
New Order is to be *"Hakko Ichiu"*, which means "All nations in one
family, each enjoying its own proper place within it . . ." '[5]*

The 'principle of Asiatic Monroeism as against the aggressive Monroeism
of the United States'; the aim of assisting all Asians, not least the Chinese, to
hurl back the evil encroachments of the West upon their political, cultural
and spiritual freedom and self-expression; the need for all to dedicate
themselves to 'this sacred war that will signify racial resurrection in Greater
East Asia': these were the basic ingredients of the explanations and appeals
that acccompanied the triumphant march of Japan's forces in 1942.[6] Thus,
Decree No. 1 issued by the Sixteenth Army in Java proclaimed that
Japanese and Indonesians were members of one race, and that division and
privilege, as insisted upon by the Dutch, were now things of the past.[7]
Where a people's 'Asianness' was not in doubt, the message for them (as
conveyed in China, for example, by the Hsin-min Hui organisation that was
noted in an earlier chapter) was that 'Nippon was the logical nation to
provide . . . leadership [in the common struggle against the West] as it is her
strength which has succeeded in expelling . . . Anglo-American influence
from East Asia'. In addition, these peoples were reminded of the foundations for unity that lay in common cultural roots and opportunities:

'From a cultural standpoint, we have in the New Order the ancient culture
of China, which constitutes the basis of Asian civilization and to which all
of Asian peoples owe their origin or inspiration. Nippon culture is no
exception: the native civilization received the powerful influence of
Chinese culture at a very early stage and it was enormously enriched
thereby. Later, when India has secured her freedom and independence,
the ancient culture of India, the birthplace of the religion [sic] of the East,
will bring its influence to bear upon the New Order.

   Asian civilization is fundamentally ethical and aesthetic, but it has been
considerably weakened through the absence of the scientific element.
Nippon, however, blending Oriental and Occidental cultures, is creating a
new type of civilization, richer than any in existence. On this basis, the
New Order will erect an edifice . . . of such harmony which [will] include
the very best of human achievements.'[8]

---

* On the derivation of this concept from the place of the family unit within Japan's own society,
see above, 65.

This notion of blending the best of what each of the 'two civilisations', East and West, had to offer was also to be heard within the ranks of the Allies, as we shall see below. Meanwhile, it did not prevent the Japanese from urging those who had experienced long overlordship by the West to rediscover their true, Asian identity: 'to forsake the unnatural culture borrowed from a far-away country', as it was put to the people of the Philippines, 'the poisonous dung of material civilization'. 'You cannot alter the fact that you are Orientals,' insisted the Commander in Chief of the Fourteenth Army to his new charges in the islands,[9] and the doctrine was echoed by those native politicians who decided to throw in their lot with the invader. 'In essence and spirit we are Orientals,' insisted one of these collaborators, while others such as the pre-war government ministers José Laurel and Jorge Vargas hailed Japan's victories as 'vindicating the prestige of all Asiatic nations' in the face of 'Anglo-Saxon imperialism'. To a group of young Filipinos who were about to undertake an educational programme in Japan itself, Vargas explained that they were embarking upon 'a pilgrimage to the shrines of Orientalism', and that they would find that 'the Great East . . . is not and never has been a decadent world fit to be desecrated by Occidental adventurers and exploiters, but has in truth an ancient civilization built on unperishable institutions and immemorial traditions'.[10]

Chou Fo-hai and Miao Pin in China; Ba Maw and Aung San in Burma; Soekarno in the East Indies; above all, in terms of the standing he came to enjoy among the collaborating Asians, Bose: these and others like them also insisted that only the closest partnership with Japan could 'set Asiatic nations free' and lead to the creation (in Bose's words) of 'a great Asia that will be free, happy and prosperous'.[11] Some of these men, moreover, continued to speak and write in the same vein even when the conflict had begun to move in favour of the Allies. Soekarno, for example, from 1943 onwards, came 'more than ever to regard [Japan's] war as Indonesia's', reiterating the slogan: 'We will wipe out America and liquidate England.'[12] And Bose, for one, still expressed in public his confidence in a Japanese victory, even though there is good reason to believe that by the end of 1943 he had begun to realise in his own mind that all the Axis powers were going to be defeated.[13]

Japan herself increased her endeavours to win the cooperation of the peoples of her new empire as it came under mounting attack, as was noted earlier in connection with the Great East Asia Conference of November 1943 and the pronouncement there of what the Manila *Tribune* called 'Asia's lofty war aims'. Indeed, if one were to piece together the various items that, at one time and another, were placed by Tokyo on its agenda of reform, they might be seen as constituting a gleaming programme of widespread economic and social, as well as political, change. The Coprosperity Sphere, it was claimed, would incorporate a new system of regional economic cooperation.[14] Its 'new social order', in the words of the *Syonan Shimbun*, would be 'entirely different from the past'.[15] It would have as one of its fundamental goals 'the welfare of all' – 'the welfare of the common man', as José Laurel termed it, or, in Tojo's words, 'the common prosperity and well-being'.[16] Moreover, as we have seen, the principles and practices it was to enshrine were declared to provide the sole basis on which not simply the peoples in East Asia but all mankind could achieve lasting peace, social justice and spiritual enrichment. As Bose put it in a broadcast from Tokyo in November 1943: 'Light comes once again from the East . . . Upon its success depends . . . ultimately, the future of the whole world.'[17]

And yet during the latter part of the war, the image of itself that Japan projected upon the peoples of the conquered territories was that of protector and 'stabiliser', rather than that of architect of a radically new order. Indeed, the slogans that were employed not surprisingly took on an increasingly desperate tone as the Allies advanced: 'Live or die with Japan;' 'rise as one against the enemy;' 'from "liberation" liberate us;' '[resist the enemy's attempt to] found a new world – a Jewish and Anglo-Saxon world – through the destruction of all the Old World traditions.'[18] Events such as the levelling to the ground of the monastery at Monte Cassino and the bombing of German cities were now used by the Japanese to demonstrate to the peoples of Southeast Asia that it was the 'barbarian', 'the Anglo-Saxon brute', whose menace was reviving; that the war, more than ever, was between

'two types of civilization: the civilization of ideals, sentiment and human values which weaves an aura of culture about the gifts of the ages . . . and the other type of lower culture, which is characterized by an over-emphasis on material goods and their accumulation as the only source of power and human dignity'.[19]

In this connection, it was American society that figured most prominently in Japanese propaganda. But it was Britain's hold on India that was commonly used to illustrate the selfish cruelty of 'the Anglo-Saxons' in their dealings with Asian peoples, and the hypocrisy of the Atlantic Charter in this among other respects. The repressive measures employed by the Government in New Delhi in 1942 after the failure of the Cripps Mission and the ensuing 'Quit India' riots were contrasted with Tokyo's expressed intention to set the sub-continent free, and, of course, with the close ties between Japan and Bose's *Azad Hind* provisional government and Indian National Army. Further grist to the Japanese propaganda mill was provided by the Bengal famine of 1943, which was used to demonstrate that the only freedom Britain had granted to Indians was 'the freedom to die of hunger'.[20]

In their dealings with the peoples of South and Southeast Asia, the Japanese were assisted by the character and beliefs of some of their representatives on the spot. Individuals such as Major Fujiwara Iwaichi, for example (who sought to win the cooperation of Indian prisoners of war in Malaya) and Colonel Suzuki Keiji (who fostered the collaboration of Burmese nationalists) sincerely believed in their country's 'mission' to liberate fellow-Asians and in the need to work together with them on a basis of equality and for the common good.[21] At a more senior level, too, General Imamura Hitoshi, for one, commander of the Sixteenth Army in Java, was sympathetic to the cause of Indonesian independence, and believed that the people of the islands and the Japanese were indeed 'brothers'.[22] Even Tojo himself could make a favourable impression on visitors from the conquered territories: 'We found,' Ba Maw was to write after the war, 'that he really understood our problems.'[23]

Through the efforts of Fujiwara and others, the Japanese established various organisations in Southeast Asia that could be seen as providing firm evidence for the genuineness of their proclaimed goal of a 'New Order' and coprosperity. In Malaya, following the capture of around 45,000 troops of the Indian Army, something like 20,000 were recruited for an Indian National Army led by Captain Mohan Singh (Bose was still in Germany at the time), its political counterpart being an Indian Independence League that had been in existence beforehand.[24] In Burma, following the training of Aung San and his companions in Japan before the war, the Burma Independence Army (which had rapidly grown to around 200,000 men) was replaced in August 1942 by a more closely controlled Burma Defence Army of seven battalions.[25] A volunteer army, *Peta* (Army Defenders of the Homeland), was also established in Java and reached a strength of around 34,000 men, although in this case, unlike those of the I.N.A. and B.I.A., the move was prompted less by political considerations than by the perceived need in 1943 to reinforce Japan's own military resources as the Allies began to advance back towards the East Indies.

In the Indies, too, a number of institutions such as the 'School for Free Indonesia' and the 'Committee for the Study of Former Customs and Political Systems' helped foster nationalist sentiment, while larger organisations, notably the *Putera* movement and its successors, were employed to mobilise popular opinion in support of the pan-Asian struggle against the Anglo-Saxons, much as the Hsin-min Hui was seeking to do in occupied China.[26] Likewise in the Philippines, the *Kalibapi* movement, set up at the end of 1942 and in effect replacing all previous political parties, aimed 'to render service in the establishment of the Greater East Asia Coprosperity Sphere' and to support the Japanese forces in the islands. A Philippine Constabulary was also formed to enforce order, and in particular to combat the threat posed by guerrilla movements (especially the *Hukbalahaps*), while more overtly military bodies were hastily organised from among the native population when MacArthur's forces had landed in November 1944.[27] Where Indochina was concerned, the continued presence of a French regime created a context of a somewhat different kind, but even there the leaders of the Cao-Dai and Hoa-Hao sects in South Vietnam sometimes collaborated with the Japanese in order to strengthen their own positions vis-à-vis other native political groups.[28] In their own colonial islands of Micronesia, too, the Japanese were able to form a number of volunteer units on the outbreak of war thanks to 'the good will and loyalty of the native populations' there.[29]

When seeking to establish support for themselves and their professed cause in the occupied territories, the Japanese paid particular attention to the younger elements of the populations concerned, for whom special organisations were set up: the *Seineden* in Java, for example, the *Kesatuan Muda Melay* in Malaya, and the Junior *Kalibapi* in the Philippines. This feature of the period when control was exercised from Tokyo was to have considerable repercussions after the war had ended, and it has been argued that the young men concerned were 'the most revolutionary legacy that Japanese rule was to bequeath to the decolonisation process in many parts of Southeast Asia'.[30]

In some instances, there was also long-term significance in the use made of natives by the Japanese when it came to staffing the new administrations that had to be set up in the aftermath of victory on the battlefield. The case of Hong Kong is perhaps somewhat a-typical in this respect, in that it was declared by its conquerors to be an integral part of their own sovereign territory, and in that independence was not to be an option once the British had returned. Even here, however, the middle as well as the lower ranks of Japan's administration were staffed by Chinese, just as prominent members of the Chinese community (in some cases under threat; in some at the request of the departing British; but in others from a genuinely pro-Japanese inclination) declared their support for the New Order.[31] The role of Indonesians in the administration of Java, meanwhile, was creating a more significant impression, politically-speaking, on the minds of those involved, not least as a consequence of the incompetence they could perceive on the part of many of those Japanese themselves who had come to the region to take up bureaucratic posts.[32] The promotion of junior Malay administrators in that country, too, apparently tended to enhance the confidence of the Malay population generally, as well as gaining for the Japanese initially a reputation 'for being in earnest about their pan-Asianism'.[33]

As a further means of gathering support and of projecting the image of a spiritually-aware nation that had embarked on a sacred war for the benefit of others, Japan also paid particular attention to religion as a potentially powerful element on the international, as well as the domestic, scene. Even where Christianity was concerned, attempts were made to establish a special role for Nippon and its mission. The united Protestant churches within Japan itself, *Nippon Kirisutokyodan*, which were subject to strong government influence, urged all Christians throughout the East to reject the perverted Western versions of the faith, endorsing as they did imperialism and racism, and to look instead to the restored purity and idealism that were embodied in the Christianity that was to be found in Japan. (Christ himself having been an Oriental, Japanese theologians argued, it was the peoples of that part of the world who could best understand and interpret his doctrines.)[34] And a considerable degree of understanding and sympathy for Japan's crusade was indeed expresed by the Roman Catholic hierarchy in the Philippines in response to the overtures made to them by the invader.[35]

In Burma, on the other hand, the Japanese sought to make capital out of the existence in both countries of Buddhism.[36] Above all, however, the emphasis upon Japan's 'unsurpassed religious broadmindedness'[37] was linked to an appeal to the leaders and followers of Islam in Southeast Asia. Thus in Java, the Army's Department of Religious Affairs arranged for local Muslim leaders, the *Kiais* and *Ulamas*, courses that would 'improve their insight into the circumstances of the times, and create a cooperative spirit towards the military government'. Attempts were also made to establish a single organisation that would embrace and control such separate Islamic bodies as the progressive *Muhammadiyah* and the ultra-orthodox *Nahdat al-Ulama*, to make use of the force of Islam as a counterbalance to Indonesian nationalism, and to have the Great East Asia War officially proclaimed a 'holy' one for the faithful.[38]

The greatest single propaganda tool employed by Tokyo in Southeast Asia, however, was the one already noted in the context of Japan's political confrontation with the West: the promise or actual granting of 'independence' to the colonial territories of the region. Here, it was declared, lay overwhelming proof that Japan's military expansion and New Order were indeed utterly different from the imperialism of the white man; that, as Okawa Shumei and other zealots had long proclaimed and as Tojo himself emphasised at the Tokyo Conference in November 1943, the creation of a Coprosperity Sphere was a selfless task laid upon Nippon by destiny and the divine will.[39]

Parallel, therefore, to the proclamation in 1943 of a 'new policy' towards China (under which Japan would strive to ensure that country's 'sovereignty and independence' and would share with it as an ally 'joy and sorrow, life and death'),[40] Burma was declared 'independent' on August 1, 1943. This status, it was emphasised, was being 'resumed' after fifty years of illegal

British occupation. Members of the country's Thakin Party helped form an administration under Ba Maw, who had been imprisoned by the British in 1940 and who now enjoyed, according to his post-war testimony, 'close and warm' relations with the local Japanese C. in C. With Aung San taking office as Minister of Defence, the Burma Defence Army now became the Burma National Army, pledged to fight alongside the Japanese for final victory against the West.[41]

For the Philippines, it was October 14, 1943 that marked Independence Day: the day, proclaimed the country's main collaborationist newspaper, when 'Rizal's dream came true'.[42]* Under President José Laurel (who had been found by the Japanese to be more capable of enlisting wide support than Vargas), the new government of the islands promptly concluded a military alliance with Tokyo. Laurel did decline at first to complement the treaty with a declaration of war against the United States, but this final gesture of identification with Japan was taken in September 1944, after Manila had been bombed by the advancing Americans.[43]

Bose, for his part, was unable to commit India to membership of Japan's Coprosperity Sphere, since he was not in a position to form a government on his country's actual territory (beyond his token right to administer the Andaman and Nicobar Islands). He had, however, received from Tojo the assurance that Japan intended to grant India its independence once her forces had wrested control of the sub-continent from the British. And he in turn, as president of the I.I.L., commander of the reconstituted I.N.A.,† and head of the *Azad Hind* Provisional Government of Free India, left no doubt as to his commitment to Japan's cause, declaring war on Britain and the U.S.A. two days after his administration had been established in Singapore in October 1943.[44] Moreover, with the Japanese advance to Imphal in 1944, a campaign in which the I.N.A. were permitted to play a minor role, it seemed that 'the war of India's liberation' had truly begun and that the cry of '*Chalo Delhi*' ('on to Delhi!') might come to represent more than bravado. In the event, however, Bose was denied the opportunity to put to the test his belief that when he arrived in Bengal 'everyone would revolt', and as the Japanese forces fell back from Imphal and Kohima the I.N.A. units involved in the campaign were reduced to tatters – by desertion, as well as by disease and the bullet.[45]‡

* José Rizal (1861–1896) was a highly gifted proponent of Philippine nationalism who had been executed by the Spanish rulers of the colony.
† The first I.N.A. had been dissolved at the end of 1942. See below, 156.
‡ Toye (*Springing Tiger*, 119ff.) includes an estimate that of the 6,000 I.N.A. men sent to the front around 400 were killed in battle, around 800 surrendered, around 715 deserted, and around 1,500 died of disease and starvation. Japanese troops now began to express contempt for the I.N.A. (which at the end of 1944 still numbered over 20,000), as did the Indian Army on the other side of the lines.

The I.N.A. and I.I.L. had meanwhile become quite prominent features of the political landscape in Malaya, a territory for which the granting of 'independence' by Japan never became an issue, and whose Chinese population remained deeply hostile to the invader. (According to Victor Purcell, the Malayan People's Anti-Japanese Army and its political counterpart, while Communist-controlled, 'attracted the best of Chinese youth irrespective of their political convictions'.)[46] The Japanese did succeed to some extent, however, in fostering and making use of resentment on the part of Malays against those Chinese, and in stimulating anti-white, nationalist sentiment among the Malays as well.[47]

For administrative purposes, the Japanese for a time linked Malaya with Sumatra. And the idea of eventually bringing together in a single, independent state all peoples of Malay stock (even including the Filipinos, until their separate 'independence' ruled this out) was one that was entertained by Soekarno in Java. In the face of a Japanese refusal to accept this proposal, however, Soekarno had to settle for planning the independence of a country co-terminous with what had been the Netherlands East Indies. Even this project looked for a long time like being thwarted, given that Tokyo, and more particularly the Japanese Army, insisted on treating Java as a separate entity, and that General Yamamoto Moichiro, who replaced General Imamura as C. in C. there, was unsympathetic to the nationalist movement. In September 1944, however, Tojo's successor, General Koiso Kuniaki, promised that Indonesia, and not simply Java, would eventually become independent. And although it was not until the final months of the war that the Japanese set up the machinery to prepare for such a step, the nationalists were now able to use their newly-established Pioneer Corps as a means of mobilising support over a much wider area. Thus, despite the fact that Tokyo surrendered before the Indonesians could be granted their independence in formal terms as a gift from Japan, political developments in the territory had gone much too far for there to be any chance of a return to the situation that had existed in 1941. The proclamation of an Indonesian Republic on August 17, 1945 underlined the extent of the change that had taken place since Pearl Harbor.[48]*

*

'The Japanese,' concluded a French observer who had spent the years since 1941 in Batavia, 'though defeated in a general sense, have "won the war" in

---

* In Japan's own former colonies, a Korean People's Republic was to be proclaimed in the south of that country on September 6, 1945; but the body concerned was opposed by the right-wing Korean Democratic Party and by the self-styled Korean Provisional Government in Chungking. It also failed to win acceptance from the American Military Government, which rapidly came to rely heavily on natives who had collaborated with the Japanese.

this corner of Asia.'[49] And indeed, just as Japan had changed the context within which Communists and Kuomintang faced each other in China, so she had helped create in much of Southeast Asia a set of situations that were actually or nascently revolutionary in character, and that militated against any easy return of white rule.* Victor Purcell, who had been a member of the Malayan Civil Service before the war and had subsequently been engaged in conducting political warfare against the Japanese, was to summarise the change as follows:

'The Pacific War created an entirely new pattern in Southeast Asian politics – so much so that the observer who was fairly closely in touch with the situation in 1940 would, if he did not return to Southeast Asia until 1948 and had not kept himself up to date with a close study of reports, find himself unable to recognise what he saw.'[50]

This remarkable development had in part been brought about consciously and directly by Japan. But it was also one that had gone far beyond what she had intended, and that well before August 1945 had brought disadvantage to her as well as (in the longer term) to the white imperial powers. Certainly, the Japanese had failed to bring about that solidarity among all Asians that their propaganda had envisaged. Substantial numbers of people in the newly-conquered territories, in fact, quite apart from millions in China, had remained implacably opposed to their self-proclaimed deliverers: Sjahrir and those who joined him in defying the New Order in the East Indies; *Hukbalahaps* and other guerrillas in the Philippines;† the Chinese in

* The Japanese had not sought to make use of nationalist leaders and sentiment in Indochina against the French regime that remained there until March 1945. By drastically reducing the authority and prestige of the French, however, Japan had greatly improved the practical and psychological contexts within which the nationalists were to resume their struggle against the metropolitan power from the summer of 1945 onwards. (A Republic of Vietnam, with Ho Chi Minh at its head, was proclaimed in Hanoi at the beginning of September in that year.) See e.g. D. Lancaster, *The Emancipation of French Indo-China* (London, 1961), 96ff.; Chen, *Vietnam and China*, 99ff.

† The *Hukbalahap* movement (or 'People's Anti-Japanese Army') was formed in March 1942, and operated in Central Luzon. Its initial membership of under 300 had grown to somewhere between 10 and 12,000 in 1944, and according to some estimates it was responsible for the deaths of around 5,000 Japanese and over 15,000 Filipino collaborators. Individual members of the Philippines Communist Party (which was the major element in an anti-Japanese United Front that was established early in 1942) played important roles in the *Huk* movement, but appear not to have controlled it. Essentially, the movement grew out of the strong (though largely non-violent) peasant movement against landlords which had been growing for a decade or more before Pearl Harbor. (See above, 66.) As well as resisting the Japanese, it established its own form of local self-government. Its relations with less active, American-led guerrilla groups were poor, however, and when U.S. forces themselves returned to the islands most *Huk* units were forcibly disarmed. As the landed elite which had generally collaborated with the Japanese were restored to power, further drives were undertaken against the *Huks*, who, in turn, as 'The People's Liberation Army', broke into

Malaya, and some Malays, too, who remained loyal to the departed British; the Karen and Kachin hill tribes in Burma (where even some members of the Thakin Party went underground in opposition to the Japanese, and assisted British clandestine operations);[51] thousands of the inhabitants of East Timor, who paid dearly for the help given by fellow-countrymen to Australian commandos in resisting the Japanese advance;[52] those Indian prisoners of war who, despite both blandishments and in some cases extreme hardship, refused to abandon their sworn allegiance to the Raj by joining the I.N.A.[53] And beyond the reach of Japan's immediate power, the Indian Army itself, of course, though swollen in numbers, proved remarkably loyal to its white masters, as well as contributing many acts of gallantry to the fight against Germans and Japanese alike.*

Nevertheless, it is also evident that when the Japanese had first arrived in Western colonial territories they had been met by acquiescence or outright enthusiasm and collaboration on the part of a significant proportion of the native populaces. 'A large number of Malays', according to Purcell, initially welcomed the invader,[54] while in Burma a marked disinclination to assist the British in defending the country (a feature that was ruefully acknowledged by the Governor in private) was followed by open demonstrations of excitement when it became clear that the Japanese were winning the campaign.[55] Contemporary film and the testimony of eyewitnesses also reinforce Sjahrir's regretful conclusion, quoted in chapter one, that the great majority of his fellow-Indonesians in Java 'rejoiced over the Japanese victories' and remained 'strongly pro-Japanese' for a time after the Dutch had been driven out. Even before Japanese forces obtained complete control of the islands, many Dutch planters, in the words of a British officer on the spot, had had to 'flee for their lives from natives who had been their servants for 100 years or more', while in the three ensuing years very little help was forthcoming for Allied clandestine-warfare parties who tried to operate in the territory.[56]

It must be immediately be said (as it was earlier with reference to the situation in China between 1937 and 1941) that widely varying motives were present among (and often, no doubt, within) those who greeted the Japanese with apparent enthusiasm. Even if we take a single group – those Indian prisoners of war, say, who agreed to join the I.N.A. – this remains the case.[57] At the level of generalisation, however, an emphasis upon the anti-white, anti-imperial sentiments of those involved, rather than on a liking for the Japanese *per se*, frequently recurs. Purcell, for example, characterises the

---

open rebellion against the Philippines government in 1948. See Kerkvliet, *The Huk Rebellion.*

* Of the 27 Victoria Crosses awarded during the campaigns in Burma, for example, 20 were won by members of the Indian Army. P. Mason, *A Matter of Honour* (London, 1974), 472ff.

behaviour of the Malays in 1941–2 as 'the reaction of a proud people' to the 'intolerable attitude' of a colonial regime that had treated them 'like privileged children' in pursuit of the 'guiding fiction' that the country was still Malay in essence, whereas in reality they were being increasingly dispossessed.[58] Or again, Sjahrir attributed the pro-Japanese stance adopted by his fellow-Indonesians to their long-accumulated resentment against being treated as inferior by their Dutch masters, describing it as 'a projection of frustrated desire for freedom'.[59]

A similar emphasis is to be found in the individual testimony of, for example, two of the leading Indian Army officers who – for a time – threw in their lot with the Japanese after the Malayan campaign. For Captain Mohan Sing, the first leader of the I.N.A., there appeared to be a crucial contrast between Japan's proclaimed goal of Asian liberty and the fact that 'the British had not given even an empty promise to grant us complete freedom after the war. Their slogans, "Fight for the liberty of mankind", "Democracy in danger", etc. sounded quite hollow and meaningless.'

> 'The Japanese victory,' Mohan Singh wrote subsequently, 'greatly raised the morale of the Asians. With the change of bayonets from the British hands to the Japanese and Indian hands, wisdom was also transferred to us. The Asians in general, and the Japanese in particular, began to assume the air of being more civilised and more intelligent than the British and began to treat them as if they were an inferior race.'[60]

Mohan Singh was also influenced in his decision to cooperate with the Japanese by the character of Major Fujiwara and the assurances the latter provided. A fellow Sikh, the Sandhurst-trained Sardar Naranjan Singh Gill, emphasised for his part in his post-war reflections both the lack of understanding and sympathy for Indian political aspirations that he had encountered among British army officers before the war ('consciously or unconsciously,' he recalled, 'we [on the other hand] were affected by [Gandhi]'), and the shaking effects of the swift and totally unexpected collapse of British resistance to the Japanese attack on Malaya.[61] A civilian colleague who also for a time looked to Japan for sponsorship of the I.I.L.'s cause, S.C. Goho, president of the Indian Association in Singapore when the war came and appointed Agent of the Government of India there soon afterwards, likewise insisted subsequently that

> 'the running-away action of the Empire, both officials and non-officials, created a very deep impression in the minds of the people throughout Malaya. It brought great disgrace on the white race generally.'[62]

The two-pronged charge against the British and the Dutch – imperialists who could not even defend their acquisitions against a non-white assault* – clearly played a considerable part in shaping people's responses in the region in the immediate aftermath of the fighting.† Yet within months, the degree of good-will that had greeted the Japanese was beginning to be replaced by fear, dislike and hostility on the part of both Southeast Asian populations in general and those who had collaborated in some particular role. 'The Japanese,' wrote Goho, for example, 'behaved like animals whose language we could not understand. By comparison, the Englishman's sins were soon forgotten.' Mohan Singh and Gill, too, concluded (after Fujiwara had been replaced as their liaison officer) that their new allies were bent upon exploiting the Indian independence movement for their own ends. Gill was imprisoned by the Japanese when they realised that he was using I.N.A. intelligence agents to convey information to the British in India. As for Mohan Singh, after a series of tense exchanges with local Japanese officials he disbanded the I.N.A. in December 1942, and like Gill suffered considerable hardship at Japanese hands thereafter.[63] In Burma meanwhile (where Mohan Singh had noted the harshness of the conqueror's rule and an actual diminution of the degree of autonomy that had been enjoyed under the British), the racial 'polarity' between the Japanese and the native inhabitants, in Ba Maw's words, 'was complete'.[64] In Java, too (where no amount of talk about a common ancestry or religious tolerance could alter the status of the newcomers as 'unbelievers' in Muslim eyes), Indonesians began, in Sjahrir's words, 'to learn by bitter experience to hate and fear the Japanese secret police'.[65] In Micronesia, an initial good will 'soon evaporated with the great infusion of Japanese military and naval personnel, ignorant of native sensibilities and interested only in the [islanders] as a labor force for the construction of military facilities'.[66] And in the Philippines, the conviction that Tokyo's slogan, 'Asia for the Asiatics', meant in practice 'Asia for the Japanese' appears to have been widespread from the outset.[67]

As for the Japanese themselves, the fact was that, for all the talk over the years before 1941 of creating a Great East Asia Coprosperity Sphere, they

* In the East Indies, as in Malaya and Singapore, the nature of the defeat was startling. 55,000 Japanese troops took Java in ten days, General ter Poorten surrendering after only scant resistance had been offered by his forces. (See e.g. van der Post, *The Night of the New Moon*, 62, and above,107.) It should be added, however, that units of the Royal Netherlands Navy fought valiantly – albeit, inevitably, briefly – against greatly superior forces in defence of the colony. See e.g. D. Thomas, *The Battle of the Java Sea* (London, 1968).

† Beyond the reach of the Japanese, too, an Indian member of the Malayan Civil Service, for example, later acknowledged that 'though his reason utterly rebelled against it, his sympathies [had] instinctively ranged themselves with the Japanese in their fight against the Anglo-Saxons'. (Quoted in W.H. Elsbree, *Japan's Role in Southeast Asian Nationalist Movements, 1940–1945*, Cambridge, Mass., 1953, 163.) Even Nehru, according to Edgar Snow, talked privately to the latter of his 'emotional sympathy' for Japan's fight. E. Snow, *Journey to the Beginning* (London, 1959), 269.

had embarked upon their drive into Southeast Asia (as into China earlier) with only belatedly-prepared and superficial plans to guide them over the treatment of the territories they then proceeded to conquer. There remained neither agreed geographical limits to the envisaged Sphere and New Order nor a clear and commonly accepted version of the essential nature of the administrations to be established in the countries concerned. There was no existing basis of substantial trade relations with Southeast Asia (in contrast to the position Germany had established in Eastern Europe before the war), nor one of language (ironically, English often had to be used as the medium of communication with those whom the Japanese had come to rescue from the Anglo-Saxons). Just as responsibility on the ground for the control of those territories was fragmented (the Imperial Navy, for example, administered Borneo, Celebes, the Moluccas and other islands, the Sixteenth Army Java, and the Twenty-Fifty Army Sumatra), so, even within a single such zone, there was generally a lack of coordination among the various (often rival) bureaucratic organisations and factions within the military, and between the authorities on the spot and those in Tokyo. In Java, for example, where over 23,000 Japanese officials were at work by the end of the war, General Imamura's sympathy for Indonesian nationalists was met by disapproval and opposition among his younger staff officers and at Imperial General Headquarters in Tokyo. And in the capital itself, the decision to set up a Greater East Asian Ministry in November 1942 led to the resignation of the Foreign Minister, Togo Shigenori, while failing to put an end to the confusion that prevailed in the occupied area as a whole.[68]

There was no doubt, however, as to where the major emphasis of Japan's occupation policies lay. What stood out in a succession of documents drawn up in Tokyo from November 1941 onwards was the proclaimed task of 'acquiring and developing resources . . . from the Southern Areas . . . vital to national defence'. As for the native inhabitants of the region, they were to be 'guided to assume their proper place and cooperate in the establishment of the . . . Coprosperity Sphere under the leadership of the empire'.[69] As the C. in C. in the Philippines put it after assuring the people of the islands that territorial acquisition was far from Japan's thoughts, the alternatives were to cooperate or to be 'crushed with all our might and power'.[70] In the judgement of certain leading Japanese historians of the period,[71] the great majority of their country's civilian officials were cynical regarding the notion of a mission on behalf of fellow-Asians equal in standing to themselves, and we have already noted that a similar attitude was expressed by groups of Japanese prisoners when interviewed during the later stages of the war. 'True believers' like Fujiwara found themselves much criticised and were usually removed from their posts as liaison officers. The dominant attitude towards Malays, Burmese, Indonesians and others – as towards the

Chinese* – rested on a conviction of their inferior status. In their everyday life, such peoples were required to acknowledge the superiority of the Japanese and the divinity of Japan's Emperor. They were freely subjected to physical correction, and the savagery of the military police, the *Kempeitai*, could fall on them as well as on Europeans and expatriate Chinese. And at the level of overall control, the granting of 'independence' by Tokyo brought no weakening of the grip maintained by the Japanese armed forces as a whole.

Economically, as the directives drawn up in Tokyo had envisaged, the conquered territories were exploited for Japan's benefit, usually with grievous repercussions on the spot, despite the accompanying intention to try to make each region as self-sufficient as possible. The economic and social consequences of the war for the peoples involved will be examined more fully in a later chapter, but a few indications must be provided here of what Japan's economic policies and practices could entail in Southeast Asia. In the East Indies, for example, possibly as many as 300,000 men and women were forced to become 'economic soldiers' and labour for the Japanese both there and in Siam, Burma and elsewhere. (Only around 70,000 of those sent away in this manner were to return.)[72] At the same time, and against a background of rivalry among various Japanese official and business groups, certain products were fostered but others – rubber, remarkably, being among them – left to wither of neglect. (In Java, rubber production in 1943 reached only one-fifth of its 1941 level, and in Sumatra even less, while 170 out of the islands' 220 pre-war tea factories closed down.) Although the populace were encouraged to grow subsistence crops, the general decline of

---

* As noted earlier, however, there could exist an ambiguity of attitude where China as a country was concerned. And (a phenomenon, this, that reinforces the evidence indicating the strength of racial/coloured elements in the fierce perceptions of the enemy entertained on both the Japanese and the Western side) the degree of physical similarity involved between Japanese and Chinese could also, it seems, have an effect on the minds of some Japanese soldiers. One wrote in his diary: 'Whenever I see Chinese soldiers and civilians, their close resemblance to the Japanese gives me a strange feeling . . . I find it unpleasant that the enemy with whom we are locked in mortal combat should so resemble us as to feel like a neighbour.' (Quoted in Wilson, *When Tigers Fight*, 3–4). In this connection, Professor Ronald Dore has provided the author with the following comment on the differing 'conceptual maps' of Japanese and Westerners generally in the pre-war and war-time years: '"Asia" was a meaningful social category to Europeans, but not much to Japanese, although the latter did in the nineteenth century tend to define their options as "joining the West" or "staying with Asia". For Europeans and Americans, the broad division of the world was into white Caucasians and the rest. The Japanese, on the other hand, after they had got around the world a bit in the twentieth century, tended to work with a three-fold division: the Confucian-Mongolian world, into which the Japanese merged and where they felt no more alien than an Englishman in Sicily (and within which they believed they were destined to be masters); the white world, of which they wanted to be honorary members, but in which they never expected to feel at home; and the rest of the world's underclass, starting with alien Asia and extending to the more barbaric shores of Africa, which were seen as happy hunting grounds for anyone with the resources to hunt in them.' (Also see above, 31 ff.)

trade and its concentration in the hands of a few large Japanese concerns, together with a severe reduction in the amount of rice imported (both developments being hastened by the strangling of Japanese shipping by U.S. submarines), contributed to a situation of growing hardship, and then suffering, for large numbers of people.[73] In the Philippines, although in some rural areas the supply of food actually improved during the occupation as a result of good harvests and hoarding, the diminution in the amount of rice reaching the towns was such as to produce a crisis by the spring of 1944, and distress became widespread as the economy as a whole drifted into chaos: the pre-war sugar industry shrivelling away (Japan obtained her sugar from Taiwan); the cotton-growing that was meant to replace it proving a failure; inflation – as in the East Indies – rampant.[74]

In the cultural field, meanwhile, not only did the Japanese seek to wipe out all trace of Western influence and to humiliate the white man in Asian eyes, but the peoples of the conquered territories were themselves subjected to considerable pressure to learn from, and in various ways adopt, superior Japanese patterns of thought and behaviour. When groups of young people, as in the Philippines, were selected for special training, the fundamental requirement was that they should become 'thoroughly imbued with the *Kodo* [i.e., Imperial Way] spirit and a Japanese view of the world'.[75] Overall, the approach adopted rested on the notion that Japan, the divinely chosen of the nations, was 'the parent' and the peoples of the Coprosperity Sphere 'the children'. For the latter's benefit, therefore, frequent news-paper articles set forth the essence and greatness of the Japanese spirit, Japanese dynamism, Japanese ethics, and Japanese etiquette. Malays, Filipinos, Indonesians: all were urged to emulate the example now set before them of self-discipline and dedication to a higher cause. Lessons in basic Japanese language and customs appeared in the press, and the teaching of Japanese became compulsory in the schools of Java. There, too, dates were now reckoned according to the Japanese calendar, while at all public meetings proceedings had to begin with a collective bow in the direction of Tokyo and the Emperor.[76]

These endeavours on the part of the Japanese bore little fruit. Nor, despite the collaboration of men like Soekarno, Ba Maw, Laurel and Bose, were the conquerors able to establish local leaderships that could carry the mass of the people with them in any lasting commitment to the cause of Nippon. In the East Indies, for example, the strength of Soekarno's position derived from the nationalist movement which, like the territory's Islamic organisations, was moving as the war progressed in an anti-, not a pro-, Japanese direction, whilst other native leaders, notably Sjahrir and Moham-mad Hatta, no more shared Soekarno's personal leanings towards the invader than did members of the Communist underground like Amir

Sjarifudden. Those Indonesians who were employed in various bureaucratic capacities by the Japanese and fared reasonably well under their regime also tended to become divorced from the bulk of the population, a gap that was wider still in the Philippines, between the vast majority in the islands and those members of the established oligarchy who, as we have seen, chose to align themselves with the New Order.[77]

As a consequence of Japan's evidently selfish priorities, together with the arrogance and harshness of many of her representatives on the spot, a growing number of the people of Southeast Asia joined those Chinese and Koreans who had had longer experience of the same phenomena in regarding Tokyo's claim to be waging a sacred war on behalf of all Asians as a cynical deception. ('Nauseating hypocrisy' was what the strongly nationalist *Bombay Chronicle* had termed it at the very outset of the war.)[78] Some went further, embarking upon that course of armed resistance, noted above, that had been adopted from the first by, for example, guerrillas in the Philippines and the M.P.A.J.U. in Malaya.[79] At Blitar, in Java, a battalion of the volunteer native defence force, *Peta*, launched a brief attack on Japanese troops in February 1945 in the name of Indonesian independence.[80] More substantial and sustained defiance emerged in Burma, where the formation in September 1944 of what became the Anti-Fascist People's Freedom League was followed by guerrilla activity and the establishing of contact with members of the British Special Operations Executive's Force 136, who were operating within S.E.A.C. Finally, in March 1945, the bulk of the Burma National Army under Aung San broke into open revolt.

How much this last move was prompted by the fact that the Allies were now clearly going to win the war, and how much by disillusion and bitterness of an anti-Japanese kind, is difficult to say. But the second of these elements was undoubtedly present, and Mountbatten for his part was quick to encourage Burmese resistance, despite the political complications involved, as a complement to the drive towards Rangoon being made by Slim's Fourteenth Army.[81] Meanwhile, a strong desire to escape from Japanese tutelage was also being manifested in the ostensibly independent state of Siam,* which, under the guidance of its dictator, Luang Pibul, had joined Japan as an ally at the beginning of the war, and had benefited by being given territory taken from French Indochina and Malaya. Led by the country's Regent, Luang Pradit, a Free Siam Movement was in contact with both Britain and the U.S.A., and by the spring of 1945 Allied agents were able to move around fairly freely in Siam itself.[82] In a way, the six-foot-four figure of S.O.E.'s Brigadier Victor Jacques, being driven in full uniform through the

---

* The term 'Siam', rather than 'Thailand', is used here to avoid confusion arising from the existence of the self-styled Free Siam Movement. During the war years, the term 'Thailand' was associated with the government of Luang Pibul.

streets of Bangkok in the early summer of that year, epitomised how far Japan's achievements had by then fallen short of what had been promised during those heady days in 1941–2 when her forces had seemed invincible.

*

And yet, as suggested above, for all the hostility towards themselves that they had engendered, the Japanese could claim by the summer of 1945 that at least their aim of undermining the Western presence in the Far East had been substantially achieved. They had not created *de novo* the sentiments involved on the part of the peoples of the region, any more than the strains and problems surrounding the Western imperial presence there had suddenly appeared in 1941. But their remarkable victories in the first months of the war, together with their propaganda efforts thereafter, had greatly strengthened the readiness of colonial populations to assert themselves against the order of things that had obtained before Pearl Harbor. The standing of the white man, as Goho observed in the context of Malaya, had not recovered. Those Chinese guerrillas who fought on in the jungles of that country had, according to Spencer Chapman (who stayed to work with them), lost every shred of faith in the British,[83] and the same, broadly speaking, was true of the status of the Dutch in Indonesian eyes.[84] In the Philippines (though the event was of course hushed up by Washington), President Manuel Quezon had become so bitter in the first months of the war at the American failure to protect his people that, before being removed to the safety of the United States, he had asked Roosevelt to grant the islands their immediate independence, and thus enable him to treat with the advancing Japanese.[85]

Disillusion with the British likewise accompanied hatred for the Japanese among the Chinese of Hong Kong, whose consciousness of their own distinct cultural and national identity is said to have increased at the same time.[86] In India, meanwhile, the *Bombay Chronicle*, which, it will be recalled, had anticipated on the morrow of Pearl Harbor the swift punishment of Japan by the Western powers, was by March 1942 castigating the 'blunders and inefficiency' that had characterized the defence of Singapore, and was hailing, not the West, but China, as 'a heroic fighter against aggression and an embodiment of Asia's hopes for the future'.[87] 'God,' wrote a friend to Nehru soon afterwards about British officials generally, 'their *incompetence* is sickening,' while members of the Congress Committee, expressing their astonishment at the performance of the British Army in Malaya and Burma, drew the conclusion that the people of India must be prepared 'to rely upon and organise themselves' should the Japanese strike at them, too.[88] In May 1942, the Australian Minister to China concluded: 'The British Empire in the Far East depended on prestige. This prestige has been completely shattered.'[89]

As the Western democracies redeemed their early disasters and began to force back their enemies in Europe as well as in the Far East, their image did of course tend to improve somewhat in some Asian eyes. In particular, the might of the United States made a considerable impression upon those who were able to learn something of the true progress of the war, while Roosevelt, especially, was widely looked to as an important source of sympathy and assistance in bringing about a new, post-imperial order.[90] The arrival in office of a Labour Government in Britain in the summer of 1945 was also seen by some in Asia as heralding a more understanding attitude on London's part, and as a sign, as the *Bombay Chronicle* put it, that 'the world is going left, as it must. This movement is both clear and irresistible.'[91] The same victory of Attlee and his colleagues moved Aung San to declare in Burma: 'A new spirit is abroad in the world, and the peoples are coming into their own.'[92]

None of these developments or features within the West, however, could erase the impression left by the humiliation of the white man at the outset of the war.* As a British District Officer who returned to Burma in 1945 was to put it: 'The old unquestioning confidence had gone – on both sides. We had been driven out of Burma. The Burmans had seen this happen. In the trite phrase, things could never be the same again.'[93] And quite apart from those accusations of economic imperialism that had been directed against the United States by Bose and others who had sided with Japan, the fear had come to be quite widely voiced that the Americans, like the Europeans before them, might well now use their wealth and power to exploit a country such as India, whether intentionally or otherwise.[94]

The suspicion was also to be heard that even Roosevelt, who apparently had chosen not to push Churchill to the point of surrender over the issue of Indian independence in the summer of 1942,† might ultimately lean towards a peace that favoured the existing states of the West rather than the subjugated peoples of the East.[95] The Tehran and Cairo Conferences, for example, despite the welcome assurances that they produced regarding the restoration of China's pillaged territory, gave rise to alarm in this respect:

---

* The one essentially white power that avoided this loss of status in Asian eyes was the Soviet Union, whose fight against Germany evoked much admiration, and whose 'United Front' stance at the time helped enhance its appeal to socialists, as well as Communists, in colonial territories. See e.g. Thorne, *Allies*, 608; Jog, *In Freedom's Quest*, 204; Dahm, 197ff., *Bombay Chronicle*, 9 and 23 Jan., 28 July 1942; AICC Working Party statement on U.S.S.R. and China, 28 Dec. 1941, AICC Papers, file no. 2, part 1.

† See below, 218.

'"The Big Four" is a polite fiction,' argued the *Bombay Chronicle*, 'indeed a deliberate hypocrisy, calculated to hide the main design which is to divide the world of the new order into two parts; and to rule both. "The Big Three" will rule Europe direct and they will also rule Asia and Africa through European leadership [and] through their "interests" in Asia and Africa . . . We do not know whether Russia is a consenting party . . . to the outrage that is being contemplated . . . But the design is clear: two worlds are being constructed – one the world of white and Imperialist "Europe" – which includes America – and the other the world of its coloured "dependencies" of Asia and Africa, with a few countries like China accepted as independent but not allowed practical and working equality in world affairs. It will be a Trinity that will rule.'[96]

Suspicions and resentments of this kind were also present in the minds of Chinese politicians, notwithstanding the praise and hope lavished on Chiang Kai-shek and his people by the Americans and their Government. Just as American servicemen in India frequently displayed a racist disdain for the 'wogs' they found there, so many of them who actually served in China did not disguise their contempt for the 'slopeys' who inhabited that country.[97] Indeed, the behaviour of G.I.s was often such as to alienate even those Chinese students who were orientated towards American ideals. 'Seen in their off-duty hours in pursuit of booze, sex and other diversions,' writes John Israel of the situation in Kunming, 'G.I.s become the objects of increasing censure in proportion to their proliferating numbers and public visibility.'[98] Alienation of this kind was combined, for officials of the Nationalist Government, with resentment against Washington's refusal to allow Chungking any significant part in the direction of the war against Japan, and with unease over the extent to which American politicians and businessmen alike appeared to anticipate having a major say in the direction of the country's post-war economy. ('China is not yet an American colony,' her Minister of Economic Affairs remarked acidly in private, with reference to the pressure that was being exerted from Washington for various major projects to be directed towards U.S. firms.)[99] Above all, growing American criticism during the second half of the war of the corrupt and undemocratic nature of Chiang Kai-shek's regime* brought forth bitter reactions from Chungking. And the Generalissimo himself, as we shall see in a later chapter, made it plain in his (ghosted) book, *China's Destiny*,† that in his eyes Western political ideas, as well as Western materialism, represented a major threat to the health of Chinese society.[100]

As for the Communist regime in Yenan, it could enjoy the satisfaction of

* See below, 205.
† See below, 300, 302. The book was published in Chinese in 1943, but for obvious reasons its translation into English was forbidden at the time.

becoming admired – idealised, even – by various American diplomats and journalists who were allowed into the region by Chungking in 1944–45.[101] And Mao Tse-tung and Chou En-lai were clearly interested for a time in establishing links and an understanding with Washington, until, in the spring of 1945, various aspects of American foreign and domestic politics were seen as ruling out the chance of any worthwhile achievements in that direction. Yenan's attacks on American imperialism consequently began to increase thereafter. The question of how great an opportunity had in fact existed for a rapprochement and, in particular, of how flexible Mao Tse-tung and his colleagues were prepared to be at the time in relation to the promptings supplied by Marxist ideology remains a matter of scholarly dispute.[102] It seems evident, however, that, viewed from Yenan, the United States – and, of course, Britain and the other European imperial powers in the Far East – epitomised 'the cities' of the world, against which 'the countryside' must strive for ultimate, and inevitable, victory, just as China herself, a 'semi-colonised' state, must fight to win her complete independence.[103]

The exigencies of the conflict against Japan obviously had to be weighed in Chungking and Yenan alike when it came to dealing with the Western democracies. Nowhere did the war give rise to more ambivalance and confusion, however, than among Indian nationalists – excepting, that is, those who had joined Bose in adhering unequivocally to the cause of Britain's enemies, or who on the contrary put aside the issue of self-determination for the moment in order to fight unrestrainedly against those same fascist and militarist powers. As early as 1940, the Congress Working Committee had declined to follow Gandhi in his advocacy of an all-out (though non-violent) effort against the British while they were *in extremis* at home, and many Indians did not share the Mahatma's view, publicly expressed in May 1941, that 'in spite of all the will in the world' he had 'found no differences in kind' between the two sides in the European war.[104] Further disagreements arose during the first half of 1942, when it seemed that the Japanese might break into India itself. Gandhi at first continued to emphasise that he 'did not know why all this fighting is going on, for whose benefit, and with what end in view'; that he saw 'no difference between the fascist or Nazi powers and the Allies', all being 'exploiters resort[ing] to ruthlessness to the extent required to encompass their end'. India, he argued, was now at risk from Japan only because of the British presence on her soil, a presence that should be withdrawn immediately.

Yet Gandhi himself rejected in 1942 any suggestion that Japan should be seen as India's friend. If Tokyo's forces were to succeed in removing 'the British yoke', he argued, it would only be to 'put in [sic] their own instead', and he emphasised that if Bose were to arrive in India in order to set up a government under Japanese patronage 'he will be resisted by us'. But beyond this, Gandhi's stance regarding the war as a whole was also beginning to shift in this period. Blaming Britain for having failed to defend her Far Eastern possessions successfully, he was suggesting by June 1942 that an independent India would 'become the ally of the Allied powers out of gratefulness',* and that Indians could 'show our real grit and valour only when it becomes our fight'. 'I feel,' he declared to Muslim press correspondents in July, 'that now is the time for India to play an effective part in the fortunes of the war if she becomes free from British servitude.'[105]

Meanwhile, as Gandhi began to compromise his own principles – or so it would seem in retrospect – Nehru, too, was being thoroughly muddled and ambiguous in his attitude towards the Far Eastern war. Ready in April 1942 to dismiss as absurd the notion the Japan could be seen as a potential 'liberator' of India, and to assure Roosevelt that he and his fellow-countrymen were 'anxious and eager . . . to do our utmost for the defence of India and to associate ourselves with the larger causes of freedom and democracy . . . [with] our very great war potential and . . . vast man-power',[106] he nevertheless was able to set down less than a fortnight later the following instructions that Congress then issued to its supporters, regarding the behaviour to be adopted should Japanese forces actually penetrate deep into India:

'1. We may not bow the knee to the aggressor nor obey his orders.
2. We may not look to him for any favours, nor fall to his bribes. But we may not bear him any malice nor wish him ill.
3. If he wishes to take possession of our fields, we will refuse to give them up, even if we have to die in the effort to resist him.
4. If he is attacked by disease or is dying of thirst and seeks our aid, we may not refuse it.
5. In such places where the British and Japanese forces are fighting, our non-cooperation will be fruitless and unnecessary. At present our non-cooperation with the British is limited. Were we to offer them

---

* Asked how much such an alliance would square with the principles of non-violence, Gandhi responded: 'It is a good question. [But] the *whole* of India is not non-violent.' In 1944, following his release from imprisonment, he called for 'an immediate recognition of full independence for India as a whole, *subject to limitations for the duration of the war to meet the requirements of Allied operations*'. (Emphasis added.) He continued, however, to reject the notion, propagated by the Indian Communist Party, that World War Two had become 'a people's war'. 'Russia's limited alliance with the Allied Powers,' he wrote in July 1944, 'cannot by any stretch of the imagination convert what was before an imperialistic war against the Nazi combine into a people's war.' (Gandhi, *Collected Works, Vol. LXXVII*, Delhi, 1979, 387, 434.) His earlier advice on what to do should the Japanese succeed in invading India had been that they should be met with a 'non-violent resistance' based on 'the underlying belief . . . that the aggressor will, in time, be mentally and even physically tired of killing non-violent resisters and will probably desist from all further slaughter'. *Collected Works, Vol. LXXVI*, 7, 197.

complete non-cooperation when they are actually fighting, it would be tantamount to placing our country deliberately in Japanese hands. Therefore not to put any obstacles in the way of British forces will be the only way of demonstrating our non-cooperation with the Japanese. Neither may we assist the British in any active manner . . .'

To this was added a few days later, in a preamble to these 'simple principles of Non-Cooperation', the assertion:

'Japan's quarrel is not with India. She is warring against the British Empire . . . *If India were freed, her first step would probably be to negotiate with Japan*. [Emphasis added.] The Congress is of the opinion that if the British were to withdraw from India, India would be able to defend herself in the event of [the] Japanese or any other aggressor attacking India.'[107]

The contemporary comments of the pro-Congress *Bombay Chronicle* (its editor, Syed Abdullah Brelvi, was a nationalist Muslim and himself a member of the Congress) on these contortions on the part of Nehru and his Working Committee were very much to the point. These 'Simple Principles', it observed, amounted to a complete 'muddle'. And shortly afterwards, the same paper described the overall lead being given by the Congress to the Indian people at this critical juncture as consisting of

'a hundred men speak[ing] in a hundred voices, with the result that there is little definitive action against any of the dangers facing the people. Some Congress leaders are publicly criticising one another. Others are asking people to get ready for some sort of struggle that may have to be started one day. But what is the nature of the struggle? What exactly are its objectives? And how are the people to get ready for it? . . .'

And again, in July, as the Congress drew nearer to launching a major campaign of civil disobedience against the British, the newspaper, insisting that such a move would constitute 'a disaster of the first magnitude', addressed itself directly to what it saw as the confusion that existed in the mind of Nehru personally:

'Pandit Jawaharlal is aware that a campaign against Britain at this time may create grave complications and may temporarily give an advantage to Japan. But he satisfies himself with the thought that "in whatever we do our desire and our intention are clear: that we do not wish to injure the cause of China or the defence of India". But what avail our desire and intention if our actions gave advantage to the enemy of India, as well as of China? . . .'[108]

This last argument appeared to make an impression on Gandhi, who asked, early in August: 'If [the British] leave us, what will happen to us?', and supplied his own answer:

'In that case, Japan will come here. The coming of Japan will mean the end of China, and perhaps of Russia, too. I do not want to be the instrument of Russia's defeat, nor of China's. If that happened, I would hate myself. Britain has given India the greatest provocation, but in spite of all that we won't hit below the belt. We have too far progressed in real gentlemanly fashion, we will not stoop to any such thing.'

The Congress Working Committee, as well as Gandhi, now agreed, therefore, that British and American troops could remain in a free India in order to resist Japanese aggression and aid China in her struggle.[109] Nevertheless, the 'Quit India' campaign itself expanded into civil disobedience and disturbance in August 1942, Gandhi and the Congress leadership being promptly arrested by the British authorities. The ensuing strikes and rioting were condemned by the country's Communist Party as the action of 'struggle mad patriots' who 'destroy defence in the name of freedom'. Indeed, the Party strove to prevent the disruption of transport and industry during the upheavals, suggesting that Bose and his followers were secretly encouraging 'a treacherous fifth column' who were 'trying to spread panic ... in the interests of the Japanese invader'. The British, argued the Party, should release Gandhi and should establish a genuinely national government; but at the same time

'the worker [must be] roused to play his part in production [by being] made to realise the grim peril that fascism means for our country, [and must have] his patriotism roused to see that the fight for freedom and independence of the country now merges with the task of uniting the people to defend the motherland in alliance with the peoples of the Soviet Union, China, the U.S.A., and Britain'.[110]

Whether or not the 'Quit India' movement amounted to a national uprising has long been a matter for argument.[111] No political party other than the Congress supported it. The Sikhs, among other groups, condemned both the violence of the protesters and the counter-violence employed by the authorities. The Muslim League, now bent upon securing a separate, Pakistan state, stood aside. The spokesman for the Depressed Classes urged that there should be no revolt at a time 'when the barbarians are at our gates'. M.N. Roy's Radical Democratic Party (which claimed to have the support of 400,000 workers, as against the Communists' 200,000) decried both the unrest and the claims that the Congress was making even for the Indianisation of the existing Government ('five enlightened British anti-Fascists are better Councillors than five conservative Indian industrialists').

On the other hand, the extent of the initially-spontaneous outburst of resentment against British rule, following the failure of the Cripps mission,* became such as to justify the description of a mass movement. Spreading out into the countryside and incorporating a violence that Gandhi, as one historian puts it, 'had endorsed without advocating',[112]† it disrupted the preparation of the military campaign against Japan in Burma, and cast a further shadow over the position of the British in India. 'For the duration of the war and probably for some time after,' wrote the Military Secretary in the India Office in London privately in 1943, 'India must be considered as an occupied and hostile country,'[113] while the Chief Justice of India observed after the riots that 'so many Englishmen' in that country had 'ceased to believe in themselves or anything else'.[114] As Lord Wavell, for one, came to realise‡ – and the change in his attitude between 1942, when Commander in Chief, India, and 1943, when he became Viceroy, was marked – the will to independence had grown sufficiently powerful and widespread in the country to make not merely the reactionary bigotry of Churchill but also the caution or indifference of the British Cabinet as a whole thoroughly anachronistic.

As we have seen in the context of Japan's political war against its enemies, the demand that Western imperial rule should never return was gathering strength, too, in several of the occupied territories in Southeast Asia. Certain broad features of this movement, such as the combining of nationalism with socialist or Marxist principles, have also been noted already in terms of the pre-war scene, and will be further examined in a later chapter concerned with domestic developments between 1941 and 1945. What must be brought out here, again in very broad terms, are the international dimensions of what was taking place. For the essential nature of that 'entirely new pattern' of politics in Southeast Asia which Purcell was to describe after the war, and which was to have such major consequences for Europeans and Americans alike, was being shaped beneath the distracting, and in some ways superficial, military struggle between Japan and the Western powers: being shaped by Soekarno in the East Indies, as he blended

---

* See below, 192.

† Gandhi wrote in May 1942: 'We have to take the risk of violence to shake off the great calamity of slavery . . . I will prefer anarchy to the present system of administration because this ordered anarchy is worse than real anarchy . . . We will try our best to prevent violence. If in spite of that there is violence then it is His will.' (*Collected Works, Vol. LXXVI*, 160.) According to official statistics, 1,028 people were killed and 3,215 seriously injured in the riots. 60,229 were arrested. 318 railway stations were destroyed or severely damaged, and numerous railway and telegraph lines were cut. For the recollections of a British eyewitness, see I. Stephens, *Monsoon Morning* (London, 1966), 3ff.

‡ See below, 189

nationalism, Islam and socialism into a force that could, at the very least, prevent the reestablishment of a stable Dutch administration; by Ho Chi Minh in Indochina and across the border in southern China, developing the Vietnam Independence League (*Viet Nam Doc Lap Dong Minh*) into a nationalist movement much wider than its central Communist element;[115] by Aung San, negotiating with Mountbatten as a virtual equal over the conditions under which he and his forces would co-operate with the Allies against the Japanese, and the political implications for Burma of such a step.[116]

It is important to note that neither for Soekarno nor for Aung San did their collaboration with the Japanese (contrasting, as it did, with the stance adopted by Ho Chi Minh) constitute a handicap in terms of their position among their own people. Even in the Philippines, there was to be little inclination outside the ranks of the *Hukbalahaps* and other guerrilla groups to regard collaboration with the invader on the part of members of the oligarchy as having represented a betrayal of the nation, and it was this climate of opinion, as well as the support of MacArthur for his wealthy fascist friends in the islands, that enabled such men to continue to prosper, politically and financially, after 1945.[117] As for Bose (who was killed in an air crash as the war ended) and those who had followed him, the decision of the British authorities following Japan's surrender to put on trial in the Red Fort in Delhi selected members of the I.N.A. was to provoke a huge and irresistible surge of nationalist protest. 'India adores these men,' wrote Gandhi of the accused in October 1945, while Nehru, who in 1942 had deplored the I.N.A.'s alliance with Japan, now found it expedient to hail the war-time endeavours of that body as having been 'a brave adventure' that had sprung from 'a passionate desire to serve the cause of India's freedom'.[118]*

The cause of national freedom from imperial rule (in China, of a complete independence and sovereignty that had not been known since the 1840s; in Korea, of escape from over three decades of subjugation by Japan herself)† had thus come by 1945 to command the support of substantial proportions of those Asian peoples who, directly or indirectly, had become involved in Japan's violent surge. At the same time – and again this represented the strengthening of a feature of the pre-war years that we observed in an earlier chapter – the concept of 'Asia' in its entirety as a political, social and spiritual entity was receiving growing attention from others besides the Japanese and their collaborators. The gulf between a selfish West and an enslaved Asia, insisted Nehru's sister, Mrs V.L. Pandit, lay at the very heart of the Far

---

* Nevertheless, the authorities in independent India were to treat returned members of the I.N.A. thereafter in a manner (regarding pensions, etc.) which evoked much bitterness among them. See Mohan Singh, *Soldier's Contribution to Indian Independence*, cap. 28.
† See below, 293.

Eastern war,[119] and in India this concept became associated in particular with admiration for China* and her resistance to the Japanese. The greatly-exaggerated 'triumphs' of the Nationalist Army were given prominence in the Indian press, where, as we have seen, China was already being hailed in 1942 as 'an embodiment of Asia's hopes for the future' and as a country whose '"gallant Allies"' in the West had yet to prove worthy of her.[120] The Congress likewise applauded in the name of Asian brotherhood the nationalist movements in the East Indies and Indochina, and depicted India's forthcoming independence as 'a prelude to the freedom of all Asiatic nations under domination'. Even where the Japanese were concerned, the *Bombay Chronicle* was emphasising by 1945 that the people of that country, who had been led astray by 'a gang of militarists and ruling classes', should not be subjected to vengeful peace-terms by the West, and that India and China together must ensure that this did not happen.[121]*

Chiang Kai-shek for his part, much to the annoyance of the Government in New Delhi, made clear his sympathy for Indian demands for independence during a visit to that country in February 1942 (though in the following months his wife's reiteration, in letters to Nehru, of 'the strength of feeling and passion [that] India's suffering aroused' in the two of them, and of her intention to work on American opinion on India's behalf, was accompanied by messages from the Generalissimo to the effect that 'maximum forbearance' should be exercised vis-à-vis the British at a time when the threat from Japan had become so acute).[122] Chiang's colleague, T.V. Soong, also won Indian plaudits when he warned his audience at Yale in the summer of 1942 that 'Asia' was 'tired of being regarded only in terms of markets and concessions, or as a source of rubber, tin and oil, or as furnishing human chattels to work raw materials'.[123] For China's Communist Party, too, the experiences of the war years may well have reinforced those inclinations that were to lead after 1945 to the proclaiming of a Marxist analysis and prescription that had an 'Asian' focus, as Moscow continued to acknowledge and deal with Chiang Kai-shek as the ruler of China and exacted a high price at China's expense for the entry of the Soviet Union into the fight against Japan.[124]

It is not being suggested, of course, that large numbers of the populations inhabiting the regions lying between India and the Pacific were thinking of

* For most of the war, at least, the socialist Nehru and the Congress as a whole happily directed this admiration towards the essentially fascist Chiang Kai-shek ('the great leader', in Nehru's words, he and his wife being 'China's flaming and life-giving symbols'). By 1945, however, the *Bombay Chronicle*, for example, (issues of January 27 and August 28, 1945) was supporting Yenan's proposals for replacing Kuomintang rule by a coalition government, though it continued to see Chiang Kai-shek as the essential, central element in the process of unification.

† The same paper (August 13, 1945) also argued that the Throne should be retained in Japan as a vital social institution without which the democratic redemption of the people would be impossible.

themselves as 'Asians' on a day-to-day basis during the war. Notions of this kind doubtless remained for the most part the property of politicians, political commentators and the clerisies.* Nevertheless, many 'ordinary' Asians were, it seems, affected by the turmoil of the war, together with the pledges and propaganda emanating from the opposing states, when it came to thinking about race relations, and in particular those between 'white' and 'coloured' peoples. In other words, the repercussions of the war in this respect went wider than, for example, Gandhi's reminder to Roosevelt of the oppression suffered by blacks in the United States,[125] or Chinese and Indian requests for Washington to end its exclusion of immigrants from their countries.[126] Following the chaotic evacuation of Burma in 1942, for instance (when Europeans had made their way to safety but thousands of Indians had been unable to secure a passage by ship or plane, or even access to the better land-routes out of the country), widespread bitterness lay behind the condemnation by Gandhi and the Congress Working Committee of what they saw as the 'racial discrimination', the 'inhuman and insulting' behaviour that had been displayed 'at every step' by the British authorities on the spot.[127]†

When a young (and Christian) Indian stepped forward at a meeting called in Bihar Province at the end of 1941 in order to boost the war effort, and declared that military training was to be welcomed, not in relation to the Western-Japanese conflict, but for its value in terms of the inevitable further confrontation between whites and non-whites, his conviction, like his action, was perhaps a-typical.[128]‡ But the growing determination among

* To take one example of the limited horizons and perspectives that remained, it was found to be pointless for Allied clandestine-warfare parties to try to demonstrate the progress of Allied armies generally to the hill tribes of Burma, 'since the Karens and Kachins knew little of the world beyond their own district'. Cruickshank, *SOE in the Far East*, 233.

† The trek from Burma into India by land was carried out by at least 400,000 refugees. One estimate suggests that between 10,000 and 50,000 died *en route*. The behaviour of civil servants in Burma in this connection was in many cases totally inadequate, though there were those who acted in a very different manner. A member of the Indian Civil Service who was present has recalled, *à propos* the indiscipline and looting by Indian troops that also occurred during this retreat: 'With a few notable exceptions, British officers preferred to help no one but themselves, to ignore the men and make their own way out as quickly as they could. Civil officers, again with exceptions, were just as bad. It was altogether a shameful exhibition of rotten morale, and it was no wonder that the native soldiers – and for that matter most of the comparatively small number of British soldiers on the route – became increasingly aggressive and difficult to control.' (Hunt and Harrison, *The District Officer in India*, 168.) On the inability of the Governor of Singapore and High Commissioner of the Malay States, Sir Shenton Thomas, to prevent the Army giving similar priority to Europeans in the evacuation of Penang, together with his private comments on that Army's 'incompetence, muddle, and indiscipline', see B. Montgomery, *Shenton of Singapore: Governor and Prisoner of War* (London, 1984), 98–9, 133–4.

‡ It is worth citing, by way of contrast, the reflections of Captain Mohan Singh, the leader of the first INA, regarding the two British officers who, respectively, interrogated him and escorted him back to India after the Japanese surrender: 'I saw bright as a light the nobility of the race which I had bitterly hated as my rulers.' Mohan Singh, *Soldier's Contribution to Indian Independence*, 362.

Asians no longer to tolerate racist treatment at white hands was apparent, and was observed, for example, by the Chairman of the Netherlands Indies Commission in the U.S.A., G.H.C. Hart, who wrote privately to a government colleague in 1943:

'No point in the Queen's speech [i.e., Queen Wilhelmina's broadcast of December 1942 on the constitutional future of the Dutch Empire] has made more impression on the Indonesians in the Diaspora than the point [about the] abolition of racial discrimination ... The matter, even for the simple Indonesian crews [i.e., on Dutch ships, who were paid much less than European seamen] ... has become one of principle, a principle which they understand and about which they feel deeply now that they are running the same risks and are, more than ever, mixing with men of various nationalities.[129]

Partly in accordance with Japan's wishes, partly in defiance of her self-seeking arrogance, 'old habits of thought' were being given a shaking. But how far did the Western combatants in the Far Eastern war perceive that this was so? Would they respond to such a situation, as well as to the comparatively simple matter of Japanese territorial aggrandisement, and if so, in what ways? Would they recognise, as the *Sydney Morning Herald* had forecast in 1940 that they would need to do, that in this context, as in others, their own long-standing 'habits of thought and social and political prejudices' had become 'outmoded and dangerous'?

Notes

1 Manila *Tribune*, 10 March 1942.
2 On radio and film aspects of this campaign, see G. Daniels, 'Japanese Radio and Cinema Propaganda, 1937–1945: an Overview', in Short, op. cit.
3 Manila *Tribune*, 17 Feb. 1942.
4 *Syonan Shimbun*, 4 Sept. 1942.
5 Ibid, 4 Sept. 1942.
6 E.g. *Tribune*, 7 July, 8 Dec. 1942, and, for films, Japanese newsreels (with French commentary; for showing in Indochina), IWM collection, JYY 046–01 and 02; and 'Build New Philippines; Fight For Greater East Asia', ibid, JYY 046–03.
7 Aziz, 196.
8 *Syonan Shimbun*, 4 Sept. 1942.
9 *Tribune*, 3 Feb., 7 July 1942; Steinberg, 15ff., 49.
10 Steinberg, 36ff., 66, 77; *Tribune*, 8 Dec. 1942, 6 Nov. 1943; G.K. Goodman, *An Experiment in Wartime Intercultural Relations: Philippine Students in Japan, 1943–1945* (Ithica, 1962), 6.
11 See e.g. the relevant studies in Iriye (ed.), *Chinese and Japanese*; Maung Maung, op. cit.; Ba Maw, *Breakthrough in Burma*; Dahm, op. cit., 225ff.; Aziz, op. cit., 210.; Bose, *Testament*, passim.

12 Dahm, 249.
13 Dr Lakshmi Sahgal testimony, oral history collection, transcript no. 277, Nehru Library.
14 See e.g. Lebra, *JGEACPS*, 48ff.
15 *Syonan Shimbun*, 29 Oct. 1942.
16 Manila *Tribune*, 20 April, 6 May 1944; Tojo speech of Nov. 1943, loc. cit.
17 Bose, *Testament*, 214.
18 E.g. *Syonan Shimbun*, 10 May 1945; *Tribune*, 3 and 6 Nov. 1943, 4 May, 23 Aug., 12 Sept. 1944, 26 Jan. 1945; Aziz, 219.
19 *Tribune*, 8 Aug. 1944, and e.g. 7 Aug., 12 Sept. 1944; *Syonan Shimbun*, 6 April 1943.
20 E.g. *Tribune*, 4 April, 11 Aug., 25 Oct. 1942; 8 Aug., 22 Oct., 25 Nov. 1943; 1 April 1944;
    Syonan Shimbun, 2 April, 2 Oct., 24 Nov. 1942; 26 Feb. 1943; *Azad Hind*, nos. 1 and 2, 1944.
21 See e.g. Lebra, *JGEACS*, 122ff.; Lebra, *Japanese Trained Armies in Southeast Asia* (Hong Kong, 1977), 6–9; Fujiwara testimony, Imperial War Museum document collection, AL 827/9; Fujiwara, I., *F. Kikan* (trans. Akashi, Y.; Hong Kong, 1983). In his memoirs, Fujiwara acknowledges the atrocities committed by the Japanese Army in China and Southeast Asia, and the fact that the Japanese as a whole 'lacked understanding and sympathy for the aspirations of the local people' in Asia. Certain passages of the book, however, remain essentially propagandist in nature, and the figure given for the size of the I.N.A. is not to be relied upon.
22 Lebra, *Japanese Trained Armies*, 80; Dahm, 234.
23 Ba Maw typescript address; 'The Great Asian Dreamer' (1964), Netaji Bureau, Calcutta.
24 See Toye, op. cit.; Lebra, *Japanese Trained Armies*, 19ff.; Lebra, *Jungle Alliance: Japan and the Indian National Army* (Singapore, 1971); K.K. Ghosh, *The Indian National Army* (Meerut, 1969); Mohan Singh, *Soldier's Contribution to Indian Independence* (New Delhi, 1975).
25 See Maung Maung; Ba Maw, 138ff.; Lebra, *Japanese Trained Armies*, 39ff.
26 Lebra, *Japanese Trained Armies*, 91ff.; Lebra, *JGEACS*, 136ff.; Dahm, 239ff.; Aziz, 199ff.; I. Nish (ed.), *Indonesian Experience: the Role of Japan and Britain, 1943–1948* (London, 1979); H.J. Benda et al., *Japanese Military Administration in Indonesia: Selected Documents* (henceforth: *Documents*; New Haven, 1965).
27 Steinberg, 62; Lebra, *Japanese Trained Armies*, 140ff.
28 R.B. Smith, *An International History of the Vietnam War, Vol. 1* (London, 1983), 56.
29 Myers and Peattie, 208.
30 Goodman (ed.), *Imperial Japan and Asia*, 78.
31 Endacott and Birch, 124ff., 236ff.; Lindsay, *At The Going Down of the Sun*, 137.
32 Aziz, 198; Sjahrir, 248.
33 Lebra, *JGEACS*, 141ff.
34 Dept. of State files, 894.404/45 and 46; A.H. Ion, 'The Formation of the *Nippon Kirisuto-kyodan*', in *Proceedings of the British Association for Japanese Studies*, vol. 5, part 1, 1980.
35 See e.g. Manila *Tribune*, 14 and 20 Jan., 24 May 1942; 21 Feb. 1943; 10 Aug. 1944; Steinberg, 52.
36 Purcell, *Revolution*, 71.
37 *Syonan Shimbun*, 6, 27 Sept. 1942.
38 Cf. Dahm, 263, 285; Aziz, 200ff.; H.J. Benda, *The Crescent and the Rising Sun: Indonesian Islam under the Japanese Occupation, 1942–1945* (The Hague, 1958).
39 E.g. Okawa, 'The Establishment of the Greater East Asia Order' (1943), in Lebra, *JGEACS*, 36ff.
40 Takeda, op. cit.
41 See Ba Maw, 264 and passim; Thakin Nu, 38ff.; Maung Maung, 47ff.; Lebra, *Japanese Trained Armies*, 71ff.; Tinker, *Burma: the Struggle for Independence*, docs. no. 17, 18.
42 Manila *Tribune*, 14 Oct. 1943.
43 Ibid, 21 Oct. 1943; Steinberg, 70ff.

44 See Toye, 77ff.; Hauner, 215; Bose, *Testament*, 62ff.; *Azad Hind*, issues for 1943 and 1944, passim.
45 *Azad Hind*, no. 5/6, 1944; Lebra, *Jungle Alliance*, 124; Mohan Singh, 266, 275; Toye, 119ff.
46 V. Purcell, *The Memoirs of a Malayan Official* (London, 1965), 349.
47 See Purcell, *The Chinese in South East Asia*, 311, and Lebra, *JGEACS*, 141ff.
48 Lebra, *JGEACS*, 136ff.; Dahm, 246ff., 275ff.; Aziz, 233ff.; Nish, *Indonesian Experience*, 60; Goodman, *Imperial Japan and Asia*, 68ff.
49 FO 371, F11097/6390/61.
50 Purcell, *Chinese in South East Asia*, 551.
51 See Tinker, *Burma: the Struggle for Independence*, doc. 36, and Donnison narrative, p. 1000.
52 See J. Dunn, *Timor: A People Betrayed* (Milton, Queensland, 1983), 22ff.
53 See e.g. Toye, v, 9, and Cruickshank, op. cit., 69 and cap. 7.
54 Purcell, *Memoirs*, 300.
55 Thorne, *Allies*, 206; Thakin Nu, 3.
56 Nish, *Indonesian Experience*, 58; Aziz, 149; Sjahrir, 231, 240; Cruickshank, 80 and cap. 5.
57 See Toye, vi, 7ff.
58 Purcell, *Memoirs*, 299.
59 Sjahrir, 219.
60 Mohan Singh, 66, 111.
61 Gill interview, 1972, and oral history transcript no. 168, Nehru Library.
62 Goho report, 1945, K.P.K. Menon Papers, file 2.
63 Mohan Singh, op. cit.; Gill, op. cit.; K.P.K. Menon Papers, material in folders 7 and 8.
64 Ba Maw, 179ff.; Mohan Singh, 157; Tinker, *Burma: the Struggle for Independence*, doc. 367.
65 Sjahrir, 240; Aziz, 202.
66 Myers and Peattie, 208; see also ibid, 125.
67 Steinberg, 53; Kerkvliet, 66–8.
68 See Benda, *Documents*, passim; Lebra, *JGEACS*, xff.; Iriye, *Power and Culture*, 63ff.; Goodman, *Imperial Japan and Asia*, passim; Lebra, *Japanese-Trained Armies*, 80ff.; Miwa, 'Japanese Policies and Concepts for a Regional Order in Asia', and the same author's other Sophia University research paper: 'Japan in Asia, Past and Present' (1981).
69 See Benda, *Documents*, e.g. nos. 1 and 6.
70 Manila *Tribune*, 17 Feb. 1942, and e.g. Lebra, *JGEACS*, 78ff.
71 Interviews with Professors Hosoya Chihiro and Usui Katsumi, July 1979.
72 Wertheim, 269; Lebra, *Japanese-Trained Armies*, 147.
73 Aziz, 189, 191; Wertheim, 117ff.; Lebra, *JGEACS*, 136ff.
74 Steinberg, 86ff.; Kerkvliet, 75–7; Manila *Tribune*, e.g. 6 and 9 Jan., 24 Feb., 19 March, 16 May 1944.
75 Takeda, op. cit.; Goodman, *An Experiment in Wartime Intercultural Relations*, passim.
76 Aziz, 166ff.; and e.g. Shillony, 134ff., and Endacott and Birch, 138, 155; also e.g. *Syonan Shimbun*, 29 Sept., 21 Nov. 1942, 1 Jan. 1943; Manila *Tribune*, 15 Feb., 29 March, 14 June, 22 Aug. 1942.
77 See Dahm, 285ff.; Wertheim, 153ff.; Sjahrir, 242; Steinberg, 60; Kerkvliet, 65, 96; Goodman, *Imperial Japan and Asia*, 68ff.; van der Kroef, *The Communist Party of Indonesia*, 26ff.
78 *Bombay Chronicle*, 10 Dec. 1941.
79 See e.g. Butcher, *The British in Malaya*, 227; F.S. Chapman, *The Jungle is Neutral* (London, 1949), and the testimony of General Tasaka Senichi, IWM documents, 5009/8.
80 On this, and the BIA military revolt, see Lebra, *Japanese-Trained Armies*, 146ff.; also Dahm, 307ff.
81 See Thorne, *Allies*, 607ff.; Ba Maw, 357ff.; Thakin Nu, 98ff.; Maung Maung, 67ff.; B. Sweet-Escott, *Baker Street Irregular* (London, 1965), 243ff.; Cruickshank, *SOE in the Far East*, cap. 7; Tinker, *Burma: the Struggle for Independence*, docs. 42, 55, 181, and passim.
82 Thorne, *Allies*, 460–2, 614–6; A. Gilchrist, *Bangkok Top Secret* (London, 1970). In

neighbouring Laos, unlike in Vietnam, anti-Japanese resistance often had a pro-French flavour to it. See H. Toye, *Laos: Buffer State or Battleground* (London, 1971), cap. 3.

83 Chapman, 177.
84 E.g. Aziz, 143, 151; interviews with Anak Agung Gde Agung, July 1980.
85 See Thorne, *Allies*, 262.
86 Endacott and Birch, 136, 318.
87 *Bombay Chronicle*, 26 Feb. and 7 March 1942.
88 Mrs Rajkumari Amrit Kaur to Nehru, 22 May 1942, Nehru Papers, Corresp., vol. 2; draft paper, 'The Lesson of Rangoon and Lower Burma', 27 April 1942, AICC Papers, FN–31B. On the panic created in Calcutta by Japanese bombing at the end of 1942, see Stephens, *Monsoon Morning*, 80ff.
89 Eggleston to Evatt, 4 May 1942, Evatt Papers, Ext. Affs. Misc. Corresp.
90 See e.g. Thorne, *Allies*, 608; G.R. Hess, *American Encounters India, 1941–1947* (Baltimore, 1971), 63; R.H. Smith, *O.S.S.* (Berkeley, 1972), 321ff.
91 E.g. *Bombay Chronicle*, 27, 28 July, 2 Aug. 1945.
92 Maung Maung, op. cit.
93 Hunt and Harrison, 175.
94 E.g. *Bombay Chronicle*, 23 April, 11 June, 1942.
95 E.g. ibid, 18 Sept. 1944.
96 Ibid, 4 Dec. 1943.
97 E.g. Isaacs, *Scratches On Our Minds*, 176ff., 317, and *No Peace For Asia* (Cambridge, Mass., 1967), 10ff.; E. Taylor, *Richer By Asia* (London, 1948), 89ff.; White, *In Search of History*, 150ff.; Thorne, *Allies*, 566.
98 Sih, *Nationalist China*, 147.
99 Thorne, *Allies*, 421.
100 See ibid, e.g. 325, 426–7, 729.
101 See K.E. Shewmaker, *Americans and Chinese Communists, 1927–1945* (Ithica, 1971), and Thorne, *Allies*, 434ff., 566ff.
102 See e.g. J. Reardon-Anderson, *Yenan and the Great Powers: the Origins of Chinese Communist Foreign Policy, 1944–1946* (New York, 1980), and the relevant essays in D. Borg and W. Heinrichs (ed.), *Uncertain Years: Chinese-American Relations, 1947–1950* (New York, 1980).
103 See S. Schram, *The Political Thought of Mao Tse-tung* (London, 1969), 372ff.; D'Encausse and Schram, op. cit., 93ff.
104 Working Cttee., June 1940, AICC Papers, file 55; Gandhi statement, 4 May 1941, ibid, file no. 2.
105 Gandhi, *Collected Works, Vol. LXXVI* (Delhi, 1979), 2, 51, 109, 187, 197; AICC debates, April and 7–8 Aug. 1942, AICC Papers, G–22 part II; *Bombay Chronicle*, 18, 30 May, 23 June 1942.
106 Nehru press statement, 12 April 1942, AICC Papers, G–26 part 2; Nehru to Roosevelt, 12 April 1942, Nehru Papers, Corresp., vol. 89.
107 Working Cttee. drafts of 23 and 27 April 1942, AICC Papers, FN–31B.
108 *Bombay Chronicle*, 5, 18, 30 May, 4 June, 10 July 1942.
109 Working Cttee. resolution, 14 July 1942, and draft of 7 Aug. 1942, AICC Papers, FN–31B; Bombay AICC debate, 7–8 Aug. 1942, ibid, G–22, part II; Gandhi, *Collected Works, Vol. LXXVI*, 253.
110 N.K. Krishnan (ed.), *National Unity for the Defence of the Motherland* (Bombay, 1943); B.T. Ranadive, *Report to the First Congress of the Communist Party of India: the Working Class and National Defence* (Bombay, 1943).
111 Cf. e.g. R. Copeland, *Indian Politics, 1936–1942* (Oxford, 1944), 302, A. Prasad, *The Indian Revolt of 1942* (Delhi, 1958); F.G. Hutchins, *India's Revolution: Gandhi and The Quit India Movement* (Cambridge, Mass., 1973).
112 Hutchins, 199.
113 Hauner, op. cit., 542.
114 Hutchins, 273.

115 See e.g. E. Hammer, *The Struggle for Indochina* (Stanford, 1954), 102; Lancaster, op. cit., 112ff.

116 See Thorne, *Allies*, 611–12; N. Tarling, 'Lord Mountbatten and the Return of Civil Government to Burma', *Journal of Imperial and Commonwealth History*, vol. XI, no. 2, 1983.

117 Steinberg, 127ff.; and see Ickes diary, e.g. 5 and 12 Sept., 11 Dec. 1943, 9 Sept., 1 and 6 Oct. 1944.

118 Gandhi to Jenkins, 29 Oct. 1945, *Collected Works, Vol. LXXXI* (Delhi, 1980), 438; Nehru press statement, April 1942, AICC Papers, G–26, part 2; Nehru statement of 10 Oct. 1946, ibid, file 60/1946. See also Toye, 171ff.; Ghosh, 214ff.

119 V.L. Pandit, *The Scope of Happiness* (London, 1979), cap. 28; Dennett memo., n.d., Institute of Pacific Relations Papers, box 362.

120 E.g. *Bombay Chronicle*, 29 Dec. 1941, 14 Jan., 7 March, 21 May, 8 July 1942; Nehru to Mme Chiang Kai-shek, 21 Dec. 1942, Nehru Papers, Corresp., vol. 93; Nehru, 'India Can Learn From China', *Asia*, Jan. 1943.

121 Working Cttee. Resolutions of Aug. 1942, AICC Papers, G–22, part 2, and on 'Indonesia and Indo-China', 11 Dec. 1945, ibid, G–44 (1945); *Bombay Chronicle*, 9 Jan. 1945.

122 Mme. Chiang Kai-shek to Nehru, 22 Feb., 28 April, 2 May 1942, Nehru Papers, Corresp., vol. 13; Shen Shi-hua to Nehru, 8 July 1942 (Chiang message for Gandhi), ibid, vol. 93; Thorne, *Allies*, 237–8.

123 *Bombay Chronicle*, 12 June 1942.

124 D'Encausse and Schram, op. cit.; Reardon-Anderson, op. cit.

125 Thorne, *Allies*, 9.

126 Ibid, 183, 325, 360, 643.

127 Working Cttee., 'The Lesson of Rangoon and Lower Burma', 27 April 1942, AICC Papers, FN–31B; Gandhi observations, AICC debates, Aug. 1942, ibid, G–22, part 2. And see H. Tinker, 'A Forgotten Long March: the Indian Evacuation from Burma, 1942', *Journal of Southeast Asian Studies*, vol. VI, no. 1, 1975.

128 Hunt and Harrison, 212.

129 Hart to van Mook, 15 April 1943, van Mook Papers, folder 2.

CHAPTER SIX

Winning Friends and the Future: the West and Asia

George Hart's private observations, quoted at the end of the previous chapter, are themselves an indication that some Western observers were becoming aware during these years of the profound shifts of attitude and political forces that were taking place among Asians within the context of the Far Eastern war. Indeed, from the very early days of the fighting onwards, much concern was expressed among those in the West who gave a thought to the affairs of that part of the world, regarding the possible consequences of the conflict for the long-term position of the white man there. Even as the Japanese began to surge forward, for example, the Chief of the State Department's Far East Division was warning that if Singapore were to fall it would 'lower immeasurably . . . the prestige of the white race and particularly of the British Empire and the United States' in the eyes of the peoples of South and Southeast Asia.[1] And thereafter, numerous Allied officials privately acknowledged what Dr van Mook of the Netherlands (Minister for Colonial Affairs and then Lieutenant Governor General of the East Indies) termed 'the psychological appeal' of Japan's proclaimed goal of securing 'Asia for the Asiatics'.[2] 'The strength of this appeal,' concluded the Far Eastern sub-committee of the Political Warfare (Japan) Committee in August 1942, 'is twofold:

> first, all the peoples of East Asia [sic] have in greater or lesser degree experienced either the direct domination or the interference of the European powers; and all of them have come to resent it, and the superior racial attitude and the economic exploitation which went with it . . . Secondly, Japan was the first of the Asiatic nations to modernise herself and meet the European powers on their own terms . . . and thus has a strong claim in Asiatic eyes to lead the peoples of Asia in the revolt against the West. This claim is enhanced with every Japanese [military] success . . . which . . . appears to justify the Japanese contention that Asiatic peoples are at least the equals of the Western powers if only they have the will to stand up to them.'[3]

In terms of the future generally, disquiet of this kind tended to focus upon Japan herself and the possible 'resurgence of her influence' in later years, as Cordell Hull put it. Even when the enemy were being pressed back towards defeat, the Secretary of State expressed his fear that they were adopting 'a "scorched-earth" political course ... by identifying themselves as the champions of liberation who were thwarted ... by the Western imperial powers'.[4] And as late as February 1945, the New Zealand *Standard*, for example, was warmly endorsing the warning of the American Under-Secretary of the Navy, that 'if the Japanese ever get their hands on all the resources and people of eastern Asia, it will be the end of civilization as we have known it'.[5]

The underlying belief, however, was that, in the words of the Australian Minister in Chungking, 'Pan-Asianism' had 'an attraction to the Asiatic mind', and that, as Mountbatten's Political Adviser in S.E.A.C. argued, this pan-Asian sentiment had 'received a stimulus from the circumstances of war' rather than from the propaganda of the Japanese.[6]* In the privacy of Dutch, British and American official circles; among the officials and members of the 'foreign-policy communities' who attended the gatherings of the Institute of Pacific Relations; in journals like *Asia and the Americas*, numerous warnings were voiced of the kind sent to Roosevelt in 1943 by his long-time friend and now his Personal Representative in India, William Phillips:

> 'Color consciousness,' wrote Phillips, 'is ... appearing more and more under present conditions and is bound to develop. We have, therefore, a vast bloc of Oriental peoples who have many things in common, including a growing dislike and distrust of the Occidental.'[7]†

Some saw opening up before them not simply 'the chasm between Occident and Orient', as Stanley Hornbeck put it in a memorandum to Hull in 1943, but 'the chasm of color'.[8] Unease over pan-Asianism, in other words, could become entwined with the fear that America's own black population, for example, might come to align itself with non-whites beyond the borders of the Republic. (Within the State Department and the Department of the Interior, concern was expressed that Japanese propaganda was already winning sympathisers among blacks.[9] And away in South Africa, too, Jan Smuts noted privately: 'I have heard natives saying: "Why fight against Japan? We are oppressed by the whites and we shall not fare worse under the

---

* Esler Dening's immediate purpose in putting forward this analysis was to warn against imposing upon Japan peace terms so harsh that they would alienate Asian opinion generally.
† It was not simply politicians and journalists who generalised about 'Asia' and resorted to anthropomorphism in that regard. Dr J. F. Normano, for example, Director of Studies at the School of Asiatic Studies in the U.S.A., wrote in the June 1944 edition of *Asia and the Americas*: 'Asia is the centre of the world ... Asia resents a mechanical transplantation of western forms; she fights them; she wants to save her own Asiatic face while taking from the "barbarians" their technology ... She knows that in the West civilizations come and go ... [while] in Asia they are counted in thousands of years ... [The] dictum is still correct: "Asia is one. The Himalayas divide only to unite."'

Japanese." ")[10] A far greater danger, however, as seen from Washington, especially, in 1942–3, was that China might come to terms with Japan, and that India, for its part, would rise up against the British. If this were to happen, wrote the Chief of the State Department's Far Eastern Division in 1942, then 'psychologically Japan might well obtain such a secure place as the leader of the Asiatic races, if not the colored races, of the world, that [her] defeat by the United Nations might not be definitive'.[11]

Roosevelt and his senior advisers repeatedly returned to this theme, not least when addressing politicians and officials from Britain: only the presence of China and India in the ranks of the Allies was thwarting Japan's pan-Asian appeal and was preventing the war becoming racial in character. Even when victory was clearly approaching, the promptings remained the same, underlining 'the importance of turning the Chinese away from anti-white-race attitudes' (Roosevelt in January 1945); the need to accommodate the forces of nationalism and thus sustain 'the prestige of the white race in Asia' (Phillips in the following spring); the need to 'reckon with the future development of an "Asia for the Asiatics" movement' (Grew – now Under Secretary of State – in May of that year).[12]

Disquiet regarding the future of the West and its interests vis-à-vis Asia and the Asians was expressed in wider circles and ways than this, however. One finds Nella Last, for example, the Lancashire housewife referred to earlier, being prompted by the degree of devastation that was falling upon Europe at the time to pose the broadest of questions in her diary in 1943: 'Will the war see the end of the white people in power, and the slow uptrend of the coloured races? All this talk of what "WE" will do after this war – as if straws set the pace or the direction.'[13] More particularly, officials who had long observed the consequences of Chinese immigration for the societies of Southeast Asia, or had studied what Sir Olaf Caroe, head of the Government of India's External Affairs Department, described as 'the history of Chinese imperialism',[14] were concluding that, in van Mook's words, a drive for 'political penetration' from that quarter after the war would be a menace akin to, if not greater than, the one now posed by Japan.[15]

Others saw the future in terms of a 'tide' or 'mass' of Asians threatening to engulf their own existing and essentially white society, a vision that was frequently accompanied by assumptions and perceptions of a racist kind. Thus in Australia and New Zealand ('white men's countries', as Admiral Ernest King, Chief of Naval Operations in Washington, characterised them when they seemed to be in peril in March 1942),[16] officials and others were acutely aware of the possibility that growing pressures on living-space in the land-mass away to the north-west might lead to demands that their 'white-only' immigration policies be abrogated. (Japanese propaganda broadcasts to Australia were indeed suggesting that that country could absorb between one hundred and two hundred million Asians.)[17] Officials of the two Dominions agreed privately in 1944 that both Governments would pursue a policy of 'masterly evasion' over this immigration issue within Allied circles,[18] while in public the call was sounded in each country for a rapid increase in the size of its white population. It was 'folly', urged the *Sydney Morning Herald*, 'to think that we can hold this continent indefinitely with a handful of people'. In New Zealand, the Dominion Settlement Association adopted the slogan: 'Populate or Perish.'[19]

Nor was dislike of the prospect of having Asians as near-neighbours and social equals confined to these two countries on the Western side. In America's Philippine colony, as a survey by the Research and Analysis branch of the Office of Strategic Services acknowledged, 'socially the [white and coloured] races have been separated much as elsewhere throughout the Far East',[20] while within the United States itself, as we noted in an earlier chapter, those Asians who had managed to enter the country before such immigration was prohibited had frequently encountered discrimination and hostility, as expressed in legislative form as well as in everyday life. The underlying attitudes involved did not change during the war, despite the wave of propaganda and sentiment on behalf of China (and, to a much lesser extent, India). If Asians were now to be loved, it was at a distance, and those officials who explored the possibility of getting the ban on immigration lifted encountered strong opposition in Congressional and labour circles.[21] Even when the case for permitting the entry of Chinese in particular was argued, the reasoning employed could demonstrate a concern for American – and white – interests above all:

> 'China looms large as an oasis for post-war trade,' urged the Citizens Committee to Repeal Chinese Exclusion in 1943. 'Here is one of the last world frontiers to be industrialized ... A peaceful and friendly China, profiting by modern industrialization, will help to raise economic levels everywhere ... The Japanese know that we have not treated the Chinese with the ordinary consideration granted to people from any other country ... [and] one could not blame China if she should decide [in response to Tokyo's blandishments] ... that Japan, not America, can offer her better cooperation. Without China's good will, we shall incur the risk of another war in which *white supremacy may be openly challenged by the Oriental races.*'[22]

In its most extreme form, apprehension regarding the upheavals attendant upon the Far Eastern war was combined with racist convictions to produce a repeat of the 'yellow peril' cries of the early years of the century. If the United States were now to give a great deal of aid and encouragement to

China, warned Senator Elbert D. Thomas at a meeting of one of the State Department's advisory committees in March 1943, then just as 'Ghengis Khan got into Europe', so 'we can loose in Asia [today] forces so great that the world will be deluged'. And Representative Charles A. Eaton shared this apocalyptic vision. 'The desire is,' he declared, 'for the Oriental peoples to have independent and civilized nations, and eventually the United States [as well as the European imperialists] might be pushed off the map . . . ; there might be racial war between the yellow man and the white man in future, [and] we may be liquidated.'[23]

*

Quite apart from the frothings of these Congressional worthies, fear of the repercussions of Japanese propaganda among other Asians pointed towards the need to cater to the latter's susceptibilities. In addition, however, there existed, as some saw it, a number of more positive reasons why the Western powers should strive to establish an entirely new set of relationships with the peoples of that part of the world. To some extent, of course, such reasons were bound up with a larger set of requirements pertaining to the Second World War as a whole and to the circumstances that might (or should) obtain thereafter: the need to find ways of ensuring that the experience of total war itself would not be repeated; to provide assurances and hope for peoples now called upon to make sacrifices and endure suffering; to furnish a social and economic programme distinct from and superior to those of the European dictators – and of the 1917 revolution; to establish that there need not and would not be a return to the chaos and hardship of the 1930s.[24]

For some, however, both the nature of Asian societies and the history of their treatment at the hands of the West provided their own distinct and positive grounds for insisting upon the need for changes of attitude and policy on the Allied side. The circumstances created by the Far Eastern war, not least the partnership in arms between the United States and China, provided Pearl Buck and those associated with her in the United States* new reasons and new opportunities for propounding those convictions that were referred to earlier in the context of the period before 1941. (A measure of guilt among Americans over the country's failure to stand by China between

---

* Pearl Buck, author of, for example, the best-selling book (and film), *The Good Earth*, became president of the East and West Association, established 'to bring about, through these times of war, more mutual understanding between the ordinary people of Asia, Australasia and the Americas'. (The absence of Europeans from the list was not accidental.) Her husband, Richard J. Walsh, edited the magazine *Asia*, the name of which was changed at the end of 1942 to *Asia and the Americas*, and which became the official organ of the East and West Association. Its news-stand sales more than doubled in the year following Pearl Harbor.

1937 and Pearl Harbor may have contributed to the degree of acceptance now accorded the Sinophiles' message.) Western peoples, it was emphasised – and not least those Europeans who in 1939 had once more fallen into internecine conflict – had much to learn from their Asian brothers. The Chinese, insisted Pearl Buck, had 'progressed much further than we have in the science of human relations', adding that 'the concepts and practice of religion' of the people of India, too, were 'far above ours', and that Indians and Chinese alike 'understand the laws of the human mind and their relation to the body as we do not'.

> 'We of the West,' she concluded, 'need spiritual enrichment today as never before. In our preoccupation with the wonders of science applied to materials, we have forgotten the truth that man does not live by bread alone ... It is the people of the East who ... must teach us again [this] truth.'[25]

Standing alongside Miss Buck, so to speak, in the magazine *Asia and the Americas*, another writer foresaw 'a Chinese century' emerging from the war,[26] while American high-school pupils learned that Chiang Kai-shek was 'one of the greatest men of his time', who had 'thrown the fortunes of his country into the same scales as those of the democratic peoples of the world'.[27]* At the same time, deeply-rooted beliefs concerning the iniquitous nature of European empires in general and that of Britain in particular predisposed many Americans to see the colonial peoples of South and Southeast Asia, too, as united communities that were struggling to free themselves from tyranny as the thirteen colonies had done in the eighteenth century – a parallel which Roosevelt himself explicitly put forward in his exchanges with Churchill on the subject of India in 1942.[28] Fifty-six per cent

---

* American officials also helped cultivate such images. The film, *Battle of China*, released in the autumn of 1944 as part of the Frank Capra series, 'Why We Fight', made no mention of the Yenan regime and depicted China as a united, liberal society. (Imperial War Museum collection, ADM/18.) Over 3.75 million Americans had seen the film by July 1945, though during these months press reports on Kuomintang corruption and Chungking's confrontation with Yenan had been inceasing. (Short, *Film and Radio Propaganda*, 184.) Interestingly, in a poll conducted in Iowa in the spring of 1945, over 47 per cent answered in the negative when asked whether 'Chiang Kai-shek's government has been resisting the Japanese as fiercely as it could', and 40 per cent replied in the affirmative to the question: 'If the Chinese Communists should prove better able than the Chungking government to help us defeat Japan, would you be in favour of switching our military support to the Communists?' (*Asia and the Americas*, June 1945.) Meanwhile, the Chinese Nationalist regime had striven to project a suitable image of itself within the U.S.A. T.V. Soong informed a Carnegie Hall audience in October 1942 that 'the torch of democratic idealism and the revolutionary faith of the Chinese founding fathers was thrown to them from the fathers of your own Fourth of July'. Mme Chiang Kai-shek likewise assured the Washington press corps in 1943: 'We in China have always had social democracy through these thousands of years, and we are now depending on our press ... so that in time we shall really realise ... political democracy as well.' Material in Hornbeck Papers, boxes 49 and 79.

of Americans polled early in 1945 responded in the affirmative to the question: 'The English have often been called oppressors because of the unfair advantage some people think they have taken of their colonial possessions. Do you feel there is any truth in this charge?'[29] 'The American Revolution,' recalled one journalist in an article on 'The Dawn of the Pacific Era', 'involved two things: home rule and the question of who should rule at home. The first meant the revolt against colonial policy; the second the struggle for democracy. Today the same two issues are at stake in the East.'[30]

When contemplating the destiny of these 'exploited peoples' – what a book published by the American Council of the Institute of Pacific Relations termed 'Asia's Captive Colonies'[31] – many Americans, it is clear,* shared the concern voiced again by Pearl Buck:

'If we ally with the British Empire in any peculiar way,' she warned in November 1943, 'then in the eyes of the other [Asian and African] peoples we become part of the British Empire, and against that Empire all will begin desperately to arm themselves, and such militarisation can only be accomplished by the sort of ruthless process which Russia used after the First World War. If, on the other hand, we Americans follow our own genius in friendly relations with all and close alliance with no one above another, then the millions in Asia and Africa – yes, and I believe in Russia too – will breathe more freely and more slowly ... Our relations with postwar China, then, depend entirely on our relations to empire.'[32]†

The references here to the Russian Revolution and to the hope that 'the millions in Asia and Africa' would 'move more slowly' after the current war can be related to other manifestations of American concern over a possible

---

* Again, it was not merely journalists, officials and the clerisy who argued around these topics. For example, when a group of second-generation Japanese-Americans discussed among themselves in the summer of 1942 'what were we fighting for' (they had been placed in an internment camp as a potential threat to the security of the United States; but the 'we' reflected their complete identification with their country's cause), the key issue was seen as 'whether an Allied victory would be [a] solution to the whole [world] mess ... [and not that of] only the white races'. 'Will we,' asked one in his diary afterwards, 'be in a position to tackle the problem of India, China and the other "exploited" peoples? If not, our efforts will not have accomplished their purposes. The problem is so immense that it staggers the imagination.' J. Modell (ed.), *The Kikuchi Diary: Chronicle From an American Concentration Camp* (Urbana, Ill., 1973), entry for 8 May 1942.

† Note in the private realm of policy debate the similar observations in 1943 of General Stilwell's Political Adviser, for example, the American Foreign Service Officer, John P. Davies: 'Our policy is apparently based on the conviction that we need Britain as a first-class power; Britain cannot be a first-class power without its empire; we are accordingly committed to the support of the British Empire. [Yet] in the minds of most Americans a better world is identified with the abolition of imperialism, and there is a very real danger that the United States may again become isolationist after the war as a result of the feeling by the American people that they have been made dupes of British imperialism.' Thorne, *Allies*, 339.

Communist challenge, that will be noted later in this chapter. The conviction, as expressed by one American diplomat on the spot in 1944, that 'there are dynamic trends easily visible today which foreshadow the eventual dissolution of Western political domination in parts of South-eastern Asia and adjacent islands',[33] could be seen as having disquieting implications in terms of America's own geopolitical interests on a global scale. Or again, it could be set within a very different framework of aspirations, that would involve a fundamental set of changes within American society itself. For, following Japan's early triumphs over the Western powers, a significant proportion of that society's black population, as judged by Gunnar Myrdal among others, had begun to see the pattern of world events in terms of 'a colour scheme' of white versus the rest.[34] At the same time, the proclaiming, as Allied war aims, of freedom and opportunity for all peoples strengthened among America's blacks not only their profound sense of grievance with regard to the domestic order (a subject to which we will return in a later chapter), but their readiness to identify with oppressed non-whites throughout the world – as Marcus Garvey had called on them to do two decades earlier.

In their most radical form, the resulting perceptions were put into words by, for example, A. Philip Randolph, the militant organiser of the Brotherhood of Sleeping Car Porters, who asserted: 'This is not a war for freedom. It is a war to continue "white supremacy" and the . . . exploitation of people of color.'[35] More hopefully, Walter White, Executive Secretary of the National Association for the Advancement of Colored Peoples, strove both in public and in private to get Roosevelt to push Britain into granting Indian self-government in 1942. In addition, he called for an end to colonial empires in Southeast Asia once the Japanese had been driven from the region, drew attention to the racist behaviour of white American troops in China, and condemned Australia (where considerable difficulties had arisen over the arrival of black G.I.s)[36] for its whites-only immigration policy. If the war should end, he warned, 'with the continuing white overlordship over brown, yellow and black peoples of the world', there would 'inevitably be another war and continued misery for the colored peoples of the United States, the West Indies, South America, Africa and the Pacific'.[37]

Whether black or white, Americans who looked for the dawn of a new age in Asia in this way tended, as we have seen, to be strongly critical of the Europeans in this context. Yet there, too, on the other side of the Atlantic, there were a good many, both within and outside official circles, who were aware during the war that the old order in the Far East was on its way out, and who approached the issues surrounding such a change in an essentially positive manner. In some instances, this readiness to perceive and accept that a transformation was taking place can be accounted for in part by the location and role of those concerned – as when we find the Foreign Office in London, for example, being far readier than officials in New Delhi or in the India Office in Whitehall to accept that 'modern China has come to stay', emphasising (in private) the need to demonstrate the 'clean cut between the past and the future' in this respect by 'treating China as an independent sovereign state', and overriding the Government of India's objections to the training of Chinese troops within India as part of the war effort.[38] In other cases, the personality of an individual, as well as his experiences, clearly helped shape the attitudes in question. Thus, just as on the Japanese side the nature of Major Fujiwara, and not simply his assigned role as liaison officer with Indian prisoners, inclined him to seek to give effect to his country's proclaimed concern for its Asian brothers, so something in the make-up of Sir Reginald Dorman-Smith (former Conservative M.P. and Minister for Agriculture), and not merely his brief pre-war acquaintance, as Governor, with the Burmese political scene, led him to the conclusion (one to which he adhered in the face of fierce attacks from Churchill) that Britain must abide by the Atlantic Charter and must pledge that Burma would become self-governing soon after the war had been won.[39]*

The actual location of Western or Western-owned territories within the area encompassed by the Far Eastern war itself also helped foster one particular form of response to what was seen as a rapidly changing set of relations between 'Occident' and 'Orient': that is, the hope that certain peoples or societies could play a special 'bridging' role between those two sections of mankind. Some Dutch officials, for example, saw the East Indies as being naturally suited to such a task, and it was decided that Allied political-warfare campaigns in the region should emphasise the contribution to 'the new world order' that the people of the islands could make as 'natural mediators between the Orient and the Western world'.[40] French and Vietnamese journalists in Indochina, too, faced with the presence of Japanese armed forces, were wont to philosophise along similar lines (lines that, for the Vietnamese concerned, could be seen as

* Under extremely difficult circumstances, Dorman-Smith's post-war tenure of office in Burma came to be marked by vacillation on his part, and he was abruptly replaced as Governor in 1946. The notion, however – so sedulously and vindictively cultivated by Mountbatten – that Dorman-Smith had been simply 'stuffed-shirt' and reactionary in his attitude to Burmese affairs does not accord with the evidence. Some idea of Mountbatten's handiwork in this regard can be gained from document no. 644 in Tinker (ed.) *Burma: the Struggle for Independence*. Lord Mountbatten expounded the same view to the present writer in 1973; but in the summer of 1945 he was writing privately of the Governor's 'first-class ideas' about Burmese affairs. The dogmatic and egocentric manner in which Mountbatten himself pursued what he continually referred to as 'my policy' in Burma in 1945 is also manifested in the above volume of documents: e.g. nos. 139, 197, and 204.

offering a solution to those long-standing dilemmas surrounding the issue of 'modernisation' that were noted in an earlier chapter). 'Let us create a true synthesis of the two civilizations, Western and East Asian,' urged Nam Dong in the Hanoi daily newspaper, *L'Action*, 'blending the best of each in a manner that will ideally suit both the temperament of our race and the genius of our nation.' Others wrote of the possibility of reconciling Christianity and Confucianism, and, more delightfully, of the urgent need for a blending of Confucianism and Pétainism ('un rapprochement Confucius-Pétain'); of a 'Franco-Annamite' collaboration that already made the country a natural meeting place for the civilisations of East and West; of a drawing together of France and Japan that signalled the same joyous possibility of achieving a harmony between those two civilisations that would create inexpressible benefits for the whole of mankind.[41]

One can find even Australia being cast in this role – as 'the bridge between the great white West and the great yellow East, the catalyst of a new human family'.[42] And although this particular effusion – by the editor of the Sydney *Daily Telegraph* in 1944 – may have been shaped by the American audience that was being addressed at the time, it should be noted that neither in Australia nor in New Zealand did fears of pressure from the 'Asiatic millions' to the north-west preclude admiration for China's resistance to the Japanese or approval for the ending of Western extraterritorial privileges in that country (a move in keeping, wrote the *Sydney Morning Herald*, with that ' "New Order", vastly different and more attractive than that which the Axis has been advocating', that was being established throughout Asia).[43] Of the Chungking Government, the socialist *Standard* in New Zealand declared in December 1943: 'Democracy is not only a principle with China's leaders but a spirit and a passion.'[44] And if the stock of China as a fighting ally and of the Kuomintang regime in particular fell markedly in the two Dominions in 1944–5, as it did in the United States (by March 1945, *The Standard* was describing Chiang Kai-shek's rule as a highly effective dictatorship, with 'no freedom of speech, or of press . . . ; [with] secret police, concentration camps and firing squads for those who dare to speak . . . out of turn'),[45] there was still praise for the Yenan Communists – newly discovered, as it were – who tended to be seen (again, as in America) as 'agrarian reformers' rather than Marxists, and even as 'representing the fullest cross-section of the nation', as the *Sydney Morning Herald*'s correspondent in China put it.[46] Both the Australian and the New Zealand Governments also came out strongly in favour of an internationally-supervised trusteeship system for all colonies after the war, criticising Britain's insistence on continuing to administer her own colonial territories in a sovereign capacity as being out of keeping with the temper and needs of the time.[47]

Yet in Britain, too, the views of a substantial proportion of the population and of a good many officials were (as we have seen above in the case of the Foreign Office and China) far removed from those reactionary and imperialist attitudes that were embodied in Churchill, who was erroneously assumed by many Americans to speak for his fellow-countrymen on these matters, as he had voiced their defiance of Germany in 1940. Even the Conservative *Daily Telegraph*, for example, approvingly serialised the strongly anti-imperialist book, *One World*, written by the 1940 Republican candidate for the Presidency, Wendell Willkie,* and, together with the right-wing *Daily Express* as well as many other newspapers, called for increased aid to be sent to China. 'Full redress to her national self-respect' would have to be made to China for the humiliating treatment she had received at the hands of Western states in the past, argued *The Times*, which saw 'the establishment of her full independence and authority' as 'one of the principal aims of the allies', and which hailed the rendition in 1943 of British and American extraterritorial privileges in China as 'a guarantee that with victory she will take her part, as a Great Power, . . . in shaping the coming new order in Asia'.†

'The dawn of a new era in the Far East' was how Sir Frederick Maze, too, Inspector General of the Chinese Maritime Customs, viewed this last development, while in that same year, 1943, a discussion pamphlet issued to troops by the Army's Directorate of Education proclaimed that colonies were no longer to be considered as ' "a possession" ', and that relations with such territories were to be thought of in terms of 'a partnership'. 'Self-government is better than good government,' the soldiers read. And, in the same area of policy, *The Times* featured essays in which Margery Perham argued that an entirely new approach to colonial issues was called for: one that would be in harmony with the Allies' broad statements regarding freedom and self-government, and that would incorporate a recognition that the coming of the war in the Far East had 'produced a very practical revolution in race relationships'.‡ Nor, within the Cabinet, was it solely

---

* Willkie himself acknowledged in *One World* (p. 174): 'British public opinion on these matters [of decolonisation] is even ahead of opinion in the United States.'

† From China itself, the Australian Minister to that country, who could be highly critical of British policies and personnel, wrote privately in April 1943: 'I do not know anyone among . . . British officials and soldiers in Chungking . . . who is not genuinely friendly to China and anxious to be on the best of terms . . . So far as my observation goes, there is far greater personal hostility to the Chinese, and criticism of their inefficiency, among American diplomats and military officials and journalists . . . ' Thorne, *Allies*, 191.

‡ Sir Francis Younghusband, too, for example, wrote in the *Manchester Guardian* (issue of February 26, 1942): 'The utter collapse of European civilisation will only have strengthened the reverence both Indians and Chinese have for their own cultures, which both look upon as far superior to [that of] Europe . . . We may resent this hidden attitude towards us. But we must recognise it. And we must remember that both the Chinese and the Indians resent just as bitterly the attitude of superiority which Europeans have in the past adopted towards them.'

Labour Ministers such as Attlee, Bevin and Cripps who sometimes spoke in similar terms. It was the Tory, Duff Cooper, for example, who suggested to his colleagues that a major change was taking place in the Far East, not simply as a result of 'the revolution ... in the ease and speed of communications', but arising from 'the change in mental attitude of the oriental populations ..., vast populations of industrious, intelligent and brave Asiatics who are unwilling to acknowledge the superiority of Europeans or their rights to special privileges in Asia'. Even Leo Amery, the Secretary of State for India, could go so far as to acknowledge privately in 1942: 'It looks as if we were on the eve of very great changes in the relation of Asia to Europe.'[48]

Of course, where those in official or quasi-official positions were concerned, the requirements of secrecy, and of public respect for those limits to Government policy set by Churchill above all, meant that perceptions of this kind were often hidden from the outside world in general, and in particular from those crusaders like Pearl Buck who peddled in emotive stereotypes. Thus, for example, when American delegates to I.P.R. gatherings dismissively heard Sir John Pratt, late of the Consular Service and Foreign Office, follow the current Whitehall line regarding the future of Hong Kong, they had no idea that in London he had privately and fiercely been arguing that Britain should return that colony to China after the war.[49] Nor did American officials like John Paton Davies who encountered the Governor of Burma have any inkling of his confrontation with Churchill over the need to announce that territory's forthcoming independence, or his desire that British firms operating there after the war should be required to give the Burmese themselves some control over how much of the resulting profits could be taken out of the country.[50]

Among Dutch officials, too, those who approached colonial issues in a more radical and reformist fashion were seldom heard by a wider audience. The conviction of van Mook (who was regarded by his Prime Minister, Gerbrandy, and by Queen Wilhelmina herself with no little suspicion over such matters) that 'the abolition of all racial discrimination' in the East Indies after the war was essential[51] did at least find public expression in Wilhelmina's own broadcast at the end of 1942. But the general picture of European imperialists entertained by Americans and cultivated by the likes of Madame Chiang Kai-shek scarcely allowed for the contrasts to be found between, for example, on the one hand the Governor General of the Indies, van Starkenborgh Stachouwer, who had been interned by the Japanese and who continued to entertain a Churchillian conviction that Dutch resolve to restore imperial rule in the colony was the prime requirement of the situation in 1945, and on the other the

Minister for Overseas Territories in The Hague, Dr J. H. Logemann, who wrote to the former in the autumn of that year:

'The policy which your Excellency believes must be followed is simple in principle, being based on the assumption of an unshakeable Dutch authority standing above all groups and opinions, striving to achieve an objective fairness and justice. But in my sincere opinion it fails to take account of the relative strengths and interrelations of social forces at the present time . . . In my opinion, the basic difference between the situation in 1940 and in 1945 appears to be that forces in society that have been stimulated in the Indies as elsewhere render untenable a gradualist policy of the kind whereby the tempo was set by Dutch administrators and whereby they ultimately decided what was and what was not good for the Indies.

Nationalist, democratic and communist tendencies have become world-shaping forces. They have affected the Indies too, and for ever . . . I also think that less than ever before are we alone with our subjects in the Indies, for the whole world is concerned about what is happening and will continue to be so, from all kinds of motives and feelings . . . Under these circumstances, we cannot create a stable government [in the Indies] without the positive cooperation of a fundamentally important number of Indonesian nationalists.'[52]

*

Logemann's reading of the situation can be placed alongside that of Lord Wavell, for example, who became convinced after taking over from the reactionary Linlithgow as Viceroy of India in 1943 that it was a matter of urgency to seek a broad measure of agreement among and with the main sections of Indian society and politics regarding the country's constitutional future, and that Britain's 'prestige and prospects in Burma, Malaya, China, and the Far East generally' were 'entirely subject' to 'secur[ing] India as a friendly partner in the British Commonwealth'.[53] Yet in London Wavell felt obliged to conclude privately that the Cabinet as a whole, and not simply Churchill, 'was not honest in its expressed desire to make progress in India',[54] and when the war ended no advance had indeed been made in formal terms beyond the assurances that had been given in 1940 regarding that country's eventual achievement of Dominion status.* In The Hague, for all Logemann's perceptiveness, the decision was soon to be taken to

* See above, 164ff., and below, 192, 270–1.

launch Dutch forces in a bid to sweep aside the Indonesian Republic that had been proclaimed by Soekarno and his colleagues. In Washington, also, the anti-colonial fervour that had permeated official discussions in 1942–3 had by the spring of 1945 become so eclipsed by other considerations as to create bitterness and despair in those like Charles Taussig and Eleanor Roosevelt who remained convinced of the fundamental importance of that cause.[55] And at the United Nations' San Francisco Conference in May of that year, the United States and the European imperial powers were at one in insisting, against Chinese and Philippine, as well as Soviet, opposition, that the Organisation's new trusteeship scheme should apply to an existing colonial territory only if the metropolitan power concerned so wished,* and that those metropolitan powers as a whole should be called upon by the Organisation's Charter, not to move towards granting colonies their independence, but only to 'develop self-government ... according to the particular circumstances of each territory ... '[56]

Of course, the Western powers had by then taken some steps, or at least made certain pronouncements in addition to those contained in the Atlantic Charter and Cairo Declaration, indicating a willingness to acknowledge that long-term changes were occurring in Asia. For China, for example, there had been not only governmental and private aid from Britain and the United States but also, more significantly, the surrender of extraterritorial privileges by those two states in January 1943 that was referred to earlier.†And, at Roosevelt's insistence, China was also accorded great-power status in the plans that were being drawn up for a post-war international organisation and that were eventually hammered out at Dumbarton Oaks in August 1944 and then in San Francisco.[57] As for the colonial territories that had fallen into Japan's clutches, a number of statements of intent were forthcoming from the metropolitan powers. Legislation was passed in Washington in 1943 pledging independence for the Philippines 'as soon as feasible'. (The original Congressional resolution, drawn up in haste as a response to Japan's

---

* Apart from existing League of Nations mandated territories and those colonies taken from current enemy states. The desire of the U.S. Navy to secure unfettered control over certain Pacific islands was met by a provision in the Charter for designating some trusteeship areas as having special strategic significance, in which case the supervising power would be answerable to the Security Council and not to the General Assembly of the U.N. Among other schemes which American officials had considered during the war had been one for the creation of some kind of federation in Southeast Asia that would embrace the Philippines, the Malay Peninsula, the East Indies, and possibly Burma, Borneo and other territories also. See Thorne, *Allies*, 341, and e.g. Hamilton to Welles, July 30, 1942, St. Dpt. files, 890.01/7–3042.

† Other Western states followed suit, although in the cases of Australia and the Netherlands issues such as immigration created a long delay before the rendition of extraterritorial rights was formally agreed.

promises concerning the territory, would have granted independence there and then, which would have amounted to a recognition of the puppet government installed by the invader.)[58] In Britain, a White Paper on Burma, published in May 1945, envisaged a three-year period of direct rule after the war, followed by a return to the constitutional position as it had existed in 1941, with preparations to be made thereafter for the eventual institution of self-government, while greater autonomy was granted to Fiji in 1943–4.[59] For the Dutch, as we have seen, Queen Wilhelmina promised in December 1942 (the statement was directed towards American public opinion above all) that after the war a conference 'of the entire Kingdom' would be held in order to bring about 'a Commonwealth in which the Netherlands, Indonesia, Surinam and Curacao will participate, with complete self-reliance and freedom of conduct for each part regarding internal affairs . . . [and] no . . . discrimination according to race or nationality'.[60] For France, following a Gaullist conference on the country's African colonies in Brazzaville early in 1944, its Provisional Government declared in March 1945 that Indochina was 'called to a special place in the French Community'; that, under a federal government headed by a Governor General, the people of the territories concerned would enjoy citizenship both of that federation and of the French Union of which it would form a part; and that there would be the fullest development 'in every area: political, economic, social, cultural and moral . . .'[61]

But such gestures were entirely inadequate in terms of the currents of political awareness and expectation that were now flowing east of Suez. What stood out for those Asians who were informed on such matters, as it does to us in retrospect, is how limited were the actions or pledges involved (with the exception, perhaps, of the matter of Philippines independence – though even there much would depend on what conditions the United States attached to such an agreement). The Chinese were shut out from the central strategic and economic direction of the war by Washington and London, were granted by the U.S.A. far less than they demanded in the way of lend-lease and loans,[62] and only with difficulty obtained from the Americans the right to send a mere 105 people annually to live in their country.[63] (In 1946, the United States permitted one hundred Indians a year to enter as immigrants.)[64] Nationalists in Indochina and the East Indies could look forward to no more than the continuation of European rule within a somewhat amended framework. To their counterparts in Burma, as Dorman-Smith and other British officials realised, the 1945 White Paper was completely anachronistic in its gradualist approach. In India, neither the Cripps Mission in the spring of 1942 nor Wavell's convening of a conference of the leaders of various sections of the community and political parties three years later broke the deadlock among the Indians themselves or between them and London.*

Why, despite concern over the attractiveness of Japan's slogan of 'Asia for the Asians'; despite acknowledgements that the nature of relations between Asia and the West was being changed; despite the fervent desire of some that such a change should be both swift and radical, did the war-time performance of the Western powers remain so limited in this respect? Why did their actions and pronouncements not merely invite the inevitable scorn of Japanese propaganda, but stop so short that the strongly anti-Japanese *Bombay Chronicle*, for example, could conclude at the end of 1943, as we have seen, that 'two worlds were being created': one of 'white and Imperialist Europe – which includes America', the other of that group's 'coloured "dependencies" of Africa and Asia', which in essence would embrace even China?

One dimension of an answer to these questions lies, obviously, in the field of international relations among the Western powers themselves, which will be examined in the next chapter. Another emerges from a study of policy debates and conflicts within each of the states concerned, a subject that has already been explored in some detail elsewhere by the present author in his *Allies of a Kind*, and by Roger Louis in his *Imperialism at Bay*, and on which, therefore, merely a few, compressed illustrations will be provided here. A further dimension still should be indicated at the outset, however: one that involves the repetition of a general observation that was made in an earlier chapter in relation to the conflict between Japan and its enemies.† That is, that for all the perceptions and pronouncements of various kinds concerning Far Eastern affairs that are being assembled here from the war years, there existed among peoples in the West between 1941 and 1945 a considerable degree of ignorance and/or indifference in that regard. In the United States, as we shall see in chapters eight and nine, involvement in a global war did not preclude a turning inwards by society in general. In Britain, subjects like the future of India or Burma, as well as the fortunes of the Fourteenth Army, seemed to those who returned from such areas to arouse only a slight degree of interest,[65] while in official circles Churchill's predilection for the im-

---

* Sir Staffford Cripps brought from London proposals whereby the major parties in India could become associated with the shaping of policy and could look forward to the election of a constitution-making body once the war had ended. The Congress, however, rejected the offer because it excluded the immediate achievement of self-government, or at the very least Indian control over defence matters, and because in the longer term it left open the possibility that predominantly Muslim states could opt for partition and a 'Pakistan' solution of the communal problem. Wavell's Simla Conference of June 1945 also broke down over the communal issue. See N. Mansergh (ed.), *The Transfer of Power, 1942–7, Vol. 1, The Cripps Mission* (London, 1970); Pandey, *The Break-Up of British India*, 168–71; Thorne, *Allies*, 60–2, 235–6, 355ff., 474, 640-1; and below, 271.

† See above, 120–3.

mediate business of fighting the country's enemies, quite apart from his imperialist convictions, helped set fairly narrow limits to exercises in planning for the post-war era in the Far East or anywhere else. For the Dutch and the French, who for much of the war were virtually cut off from news and international currents of opinion regarding the Far East, there were far more vital and immediate matters to be concerned with when the fighting was over than what was to happen in Southeast Asia.[66] (In Vichy France, also, despite the trumpetings of the regime on the subject of empire, radio broadcasts and film newsreels reflected, in the opinion of a student of those media, 'a closed, introverted country which looked mainly at itself'.)[67]

As for the shaping of policies regarding the Far East within official bodies in the West, many of the contrasts in attitude and behaviour that were involved remained hidden from view, as we have seen above. Thus the failure of the British Government, for example, to develop a fresh and clear approach to colonial issues, as Margery Perham was urging, obscured the extent to which, within the Colonial Office itself, officials had become 'animated by the British reconstruction mood' of the war years, with its 'idealism, sense of urgency, and faith in planning'.[68] Indeed, if there was a contrast, especially in 1942 and 1943, between British caution and American radicalism at the level of broad policy over dependent territories, when it came to making specific plans for the rehabilitation and development of such areas once the Japanese had been expelled, the difference was one, rather, between care and effort in London on the one hand and on the other Washington's 'failure', as the Secretary of the Interior, Ickes, acknowledged privately, 'to formulate [any such] program' for the Philippines. (According to President Quezon, who spent most of the war years in the U.S.A., Roosevelt for one simply declined to turn his attention to such matters; nor did he seek to reverse what his High Commissioner in the colony had privately described to him in 1940 as 'the pronounced drift ... away from democracy and in the direction of dictatorship' that characterised Philippine politics.)[69]

Within a coalition administration such as the one in London (and in Washington, too, it was in effect a coalition of widely differing political groups that held office under the 'Democrat' label), disagreements over, say, colonial matters could be profound. (There was 'a real danger', as Gladwyn Jebb of the Foreign Office saw it at the end of 1942, that British policy over a possible joint declaration with the United States on dependent territories would be 'paralysed on the one hand by the attitude of Mr Amery [Secretary of State for India], whose tendency is to restore the status quo everywhere, and on the other by Mr Attlee, who seems to wish to internationalise the whole of our colonial Empire'.)[70] Such exchanges were also frequently influenced by what has been termed 'bureaucratic politics': by the differing priorities and perspectives of the Foreign, Colonial and India Offices in London, for example, or of the Far Eastern and European Divisions within the State Department. Among the Dutch, they were coloured at times by a division between those officials who identified strongly with the Indies and those whose standpoint was essentially metropolitan. Sometimes, as we noted above in relation to colonial issues alone, the personality and predilections of a single individual could make a considerable impression upon a state's entire policy-making process. Besides the obvious examples of Roosevelt and Churchill, this was so, for instance, in the case of Evatt as Minister for External Affairs in Canberra, whose strongly nationalistic impulses, together with his egocentricity, tended during the latter half of the war especially to distance him from his Prime Minister, Curtin, who set greater store by maintaining good relations with London, Washington, and, not least, General MacArthur. (The fissile nature of the Australian foreign-policy community was epitomised at the San Francisco Conference, where the country had in effect two rival delegations.)[71]

The degree of intensity with which a particular Far Eastern issue was debated within a single policy-making body could depend in part upon the extent to which it was believed that those concerned could in practice influence the outcome on the ground, so to speak. (This helps explain why, for example, the question of whether the Yenan regime in China was genuinely Marxist-inspired, and of whether it was likely to succeed in its challenge to the Kuomintang for control of the country as a whole, engendered much greater heat in Washington than in London during these years.)[72] As for the influence of public opinion, that of another country – the United States – frequently weighed more heavily with British and Dutch officials than did that of their own people: for the British, in regard to policy over China; for both, over colonial affairs.[73] Yet here again, strong differences of opinion could arise. Both the Colonial and India Offices in London, for example, believed that the Foreign Office was wont to pay far too much attention to Washington and the Americans in general over issues that, in their view, were matters for Britain alone. And during the later stages of the war an irreconcilable conflict of opinion arose between the armed Services, who wished to see Britain's post-war defences in the Far East designed to guard imperial territories against possible Soviet aggression, and the Foreign Office, which could perceive no such danger and regarded the scheme as gratuitously offensive to Moscow.[74] Members of the Dutch Government were similarly divided over whether the prospects for recovering the East Indies would best be served by cooperating closely with the British (bearing in mind the disturbing degree of American hostility towards colonial empires generally), or, on the other hand, by an alignment with MacArthur, whose South West Pacific Command embraced most of the colony, and who lost no opportunity to warn the Dutch privately against both British and (with more validity) Australian ambitions to extend their influence in that direction. (Gerbrandy and, according to him, Queen Wilhelmina herself inclined to the first of these options, van Mook and the Foreign Minister, van Kleffens, to the second, though van Mook remained uneasy over what he saw as 'a form of American imperialism' that could extend to an attempt to exercise control over the affairs of the Indies after the war.)[75]

The degree of similarity to be found between the Europeans on the one hand and Americans on the other when it came to contemplating the future position of their respective countries in the area encompassed by the Far Eastern war can be illustrated by brief reference to the particular issue of security in both its military and its economic sense. Little need be said regarding the assumptions and concerns on the European side in this regard. For the French and the Dutch, the need to recover and then defend their Southeast Asian colonies was, as we have already noted, virtually axiomatic, and for the latter, particularly, the economic resources provided by the Indies were widely believed to be vital. If that territory were lost, the popular saying was soon to run, disaster would follow. ('Indië verloren, rampspoed geboren.')[76] As for the British, for those who paid attention to Far Eastern affairs the need to rebuild the country's commercial and financial interests in that part of the world was a matter of much concern, despite the complication that, as one official put it in relation to China, 'to appear to compete with the Americans in either political or economic fields [there] would be . . . disastrous'.[77] Over military aspects of security, too, for all that British attitudes (especially with the removal of Churchill from office) were not such as to herald the kind of grim battles in which the French and Dutch were soon to become involved in Asia, the assumption in London was that even a self-governing India would continue to form a vital link in the chain of imperial and Commonwealth defence, and that a major British presence would remain east of Suez.[78]

In the United States, meanwhile, the need to ensure untrammelled American control over Pacific territories judged vital to the nation's safety was being loudly proclaimed in public, as well as by the Navy within official policy debates.* The principle of self-determination, asserted the *New York*

---

* Joseph Grew, writing to Hull in July 1944, observed that a review of Pacific island bases that had been written by Rear Admiral Richard Byrd rested on assumptions that did 'not seem to be in full accord with the views you and the President have expressed with regard to post-war organization', namely 'that reliance cannot be placed upon an international organization for the maintenance of peace; that there will be no general disarmament; that this country must maintain an overwhelmingly strong Army and Navy; that it should acquire a string of

Herald Tribune in common with a large section of the press, was irrelevant where 'the security of the United States and the stability of the Pacific world' were at stake.[79] Moreover, as suspicion and tension vis-à-vis the Soviet Union began to grow in Washington from the autumn of 1944 onwards, so, too, did the fear that the anti-white currents of feeling stirred up among Asians by Japan would mingle with bolshevism to form a major threat to American interests. When referring to Siam as 'the largest unexploited colonial region of the Far East' in 1944, the area head of the Office of Strategic Services' Research and Analysis branch added: 'The U.S. position in the next Pacific war will be greatly influenced by the present effectiveness of the O.S.S. in this theater,' while one of the State Department's advisers, speaking as a member of the U.S. delegation to the U.N. Conference at San Francisco in May 1945, asked his colleagues: 'When perhaps the inevitable struggle comes between Russia and ourselves . . . would we have the support of Great Britain if we had undermined her [imperial] position [in the Far East]?' Care must indeed be taken 'not to undermine the influence of the West' in that part of the world, argued the State Department itself in a major survey of June 1945, given that 'Soviet ideology will be a rising force throughout the Far East'. And two months before, the O.S.S. had reasoned in similar terms: given that the Soviet Union could 'become a menace more formidable to the United States than any yet known', the country

> 'should realize . . . its interest in the maintenance of the British, French and Dutch colonial empires. We should encourage liberalization of the colonial regimes in order better to maintain them and to check Soviet influence in the stimulation of colonial revolt.'

Over Korea, too, officials in Washington were already thinking of the military occupation of that country as a means of containing the U.S.S.R. in East Asia. As Representative Eaton, for one, saw it (and expressed it in the American delegation's private discussions at San Francisco), 'The basic problem was who was going to be master of the world.'[80]*

By no means all Americans, of course, had come by the end of the war to view international affairs in such Manichean terms (the outcry that was to greet Churchill's 'Iron Curtain' speech in 1946, for example, needs bearing

additional bases across the Pacific; that it should assume virtually sole responsibility for the peace of the Pacific'. See Thorne, *Allies*, 491.

* These lines of thought that were developing in Washington did not mean, as will be seen in the next chapter, that by the summer of 1945 the belief in an inevitable confrontation with the U.S.S.R. was universal among American officials; still less that hostility to European imperialism in Asia (and elsewhere) was being cast aside. Where the O.S.S. was concerned, for example, some of its agents on the spot were ready to cooperate with Vietnamese nationalists against the French, while at its senior levels the organisation was no more a solidly right-wing, anti-Soviet body than it was radical in an opposite direction. See Smith, *The Shadow Warriors*, 328, 355ff.

in mind), or to identify East or Southeast Asia as vital to their country's security, or to accept the need to preserve European empires in that part of the world, however reformed they might become. Some, indeed, warned against the implications surrounding the growing preoccupation with the acquisition of territories and bases deemed vital to American security. 'If we free the Philippines on the one hand,' insisted Ralph Bunche to his fellow U.S. delegates to an I.P.R. conference at Hot Springs in October 1944, 'and take over the [Japanese] mandated islands on the other hand, it won't prove much and could lead to the development of an American empire in the Pacific.'[81] As regards economic and commercial matters, too, Pearl Buck was one who urged the importance of avoiding the establishment after the war of an American 'empire of business domination' over Asian countries and peoples.[82]

In this last context, however, far more than was the case over military bases, the current of American opinion was by 1945 running in a very different direction. Here, too, of course, security considerations were involved, and a determination never again to be dependent on European-controlled supplies from Southeast Asia of strategic raw materials such as tin and rubber.[83] At the same time, acutely conscious of the vastly increased productive capacity and prosperity that the war had brought to their country,* fearful lest the return of peace should also herald the reappearance of the economic and social conditions of the 1930s, officials and others looked eagerly to Asia, among other areas, as a future source of demand that would help preserve what had been gained since 1941. (The target set in Washington was to ensure employment for 56 million Americans after the war, and obtain outlets for a gross national product of $150 billion annually.)[84] As one of Pearl Buck's own collaborators, Eliot Janeway, put it in *Asia and the Americas* in April 1944:

> 'America's postwar foreign policy ... will have to find customers for an unprecedented volume of export business; and it will have to arrange for these customers to accommodate American opinion ... by buying its surplus at a profit to American producers. And then ... those in charge of American foreign policy will have to see to it that the customers who buy America's surpluses will be reliable friends and potential allies.'

The same call was to be heard from radical, as well as conservative, sections of American opinion regarding the politics of Western-Asian relations. 'Americans must realise,' wrote Owen Lattimore in 1944, 'that Asiatic problems are not academic. They work out to a plus or minus in American exports, imports, jobs – or breadlines, because unless we do our share in developing markets in Asia for what we produce ... we shall not be able to

* See below, 211, 250ff.

employ all the men who should do the producing.'[85] The left-wing magazine *Amerasia* – soon, like Lattimore, to be the focus of allegations that it had acted to enhance the prospects of Communism in China – similarly argued that India in particular should be seen as 'the "new economic frontier" ' for the United States economy,[86] while Vice President Wallace – dropped from that post by Roosevelt in 1944 because of his strong adherence to New Deal policies – returned from China to emphasise the vast commercial possibilities awaiting Americans in the Far East.[87]

The message was also being proclaimed by members of Congress. 'A free Orient,' declared Representative Walter H. Judd, 'will become a huge market,' while another member who was serving in the Pacific wrote home to urge that millions of 'potential customers' in that part of the world could 'keep our tremendous shop open for business' after the war.[88] Business organisations were doing the same. 'New horizons for American trade and investments in China unfold,' submitted the China-America Council of Commerce and Industry in its 1944–5 report, ' . . . [and] it is important for us that the basis of China's industrialization be the free-enterprise system, with encouragement and protection of foreign investments'.[89]* Within official circles, Donald Nelson, sent by Roosevelt in 1944 to investigate China's post-war production facilities, emphasised in his report to the President that U.S. assistance in that sphere would help foster the 'market of enormous size' that after the war should 'progressively open up for American export industries' in that country.[90] State Department officials, too, repeatedly drew attention to the benefits awaiting the United States in Southeast Asia from the region's 'vast wealth of raw materials and large populations of varying degrees of economic and social advancement which constitute actual or potential markets of great value'.[91] 'After we have won the war in the Pacific,' submitted the former Consul General in Batavia in 1942, *'and we must win it alone*, . . . we shall be in a position to insist on the "open door" in matters of imports, exports, industries, the development of resources and the improvement of the condition of the native.'[92] Three years later, the commander of U.S. naval-intelligence operations in China was haranguing his staff in the same vein, on the vital need to 'protect the commercial field' in that country that the war had opened up to America's burgeoning industrial capacity.[93] And as we saw in an earlier chapter,† MacArthur's resistance to the transfer of a sector of his South West Pacific Area to a British commander was grounded in part on the argument that such

* The officers of this Council included representatives of Firestone, Goodyear, the U.S. Rubber Company, Standard Oil of California, the Aluminium Company of America, Thomas A. Edison Inc., Boeing, International Harvester, International General Electric, Remington Rand, Standard Vacuum Oil, the Chase Bank, Time Incorporated, Pan American Airways, International Business Machines, and Pepsi-Cola.

† See above, 106.

abnegation would seriously harm the 'commercial prospects', as well as the prestige, of the United States in the Far East.

We also noted in an earlier chapter that, for some Chinese and Indians, for example, concern over the long-term future of their respective countries was focused, not so much on European possessiveness, as on the resources and ambitions that were now flooding out of the New World.* Their apprehension did not lack foundation.

*

If we return at this point to the question of the underlying attitudes and assumptions that existed in the West during the war as regards the peoples and countries of Asia, we are bound, of course, to be reduced ultimately to judgements of both a very broad and an essentially impressionist kind. It is not difficult, however, to arrive at the conclusion that neither the effusive enthusiasm of a Pearl Buck for Asia and Asians on the one hand nor the fearful, 'yellow-peril' racism of a Senator Thomas on the other was typical. Indeed, where beliefs of a racist kind were concerned, they appear to have been more commonly linked to a profound confidence in the destiny, as well as the inherent superiority, of the white man and his society. American troops in India or China who, as noted earlier, saw before them 'wogs' and 'slopeys' did not quail at the prospect of the Great Republic being eclipsed by such peoples. When Churchill talked of the 'gross, dirty and corrupt baboos' of India or the 'Chinks', 'pig-tails' or 'little yellow men' of China ('Winston thinks only of the colour of their skins,' noted his doctor in 1943; 'it is when he talks of India or China that you remember he is a Victorian'), he did not doubt the continuing greatness of that 'Anglo-Saxon' partnership of British and Americans which was central to his thoughts on the future.[94]

Even this kind of strident, ignorant and contemptuous racism was probably not typical, however, as it might well have been fifty years earlier. An underlying belief in the superiority of Western civilisation and the peoples who had created it is more often to be encountered in less aggressive forms: in what was said or written in parenthesis, so to speak, or in what was merely implied. Yet here again, of course, considerable variations of approach and tone were involved. To take simply some American instances, a deeply-implanted tendency to judge others by Western standards and values is to be encountered, for example, in the 'bullish' admiration of the banker Thomas Lamont for the British Empire,[95] but also in the reluctant doubts which grew in the mind of Raymond Clapper, after his war-time visits to India, as to

---

* 'In the name of expanding production in India after the war,' observed the *Bombay Chronicle*, for example, on June 11, 1942, 'both Britain and America may, in effect, . . . exploit the resources of India in their own interests.'

whether the people of such dependent territories were ready to assume the responsibilities of self-government;[96] in the slighting references to non-white peoples Roosevelt himself chose to make in private from time to time;[97] in the frequent assertion by American officials that their country had led the people of the Philippines towards maturity,[98] and in the secret assessment of the Filipino by the Research and Analysis branch of the O.S.S. as being

> 'emotionally unstable ... [and unable to] stand up to opposition ... He cannot be trusted with Government funds or official positions as far as an Occidental ... [and] in military ability does not compare favorably with an Occidental soldier. A feeling [in him] of duty to city, state or nation ... tends to break down under stress.'[99]*

Satisfaction among Americans concerning their country's record and 'civilising mission' in the Philippines was matched by what often amounted to a strong pride among Europeans concerning the imperial record of their respective states. Dutch, French and British all tended to believe that they had worked long, hard and well to bring benefits to the peoples of their dependent territories.† Many socialists in all three countries, as well as those on the right of the political spectrum, shared these perceptions of the past, and criticism from outside only strengthened the process of self-approval. Thus when Britain's imperial performance, for example, came under attack at the international conferences of the Institute of Pacific Relations, an Arthur Creech Jones (who was to be the Labour Government's Colonial Secretary) would respond with justifications similar to those advanced by a

---

* American officials and other observers also frequently made distinctions between the Chinese and Indian peoples. To Hornbeck in the State Department, for example, while the former were 'industrious' and admirable, the latter were likely to prove 'more a liability than an asset' to any post-war grouping of states, and he dismissed any claim they might make to be allowed to send emigrants to the U.S.A. as not having been backed by effort in the war. (Hornbeck to Hull, 20 Sept. 1943, Hornbeck Papers, box 4; Hornbeck to Berle, 10 June 1943, ibid, box 81.) Americans on the spot, like the journalists Raymond Clapper and Eric Sevareid, and General Stilwell himself, also commented on what they saw as the contrast between the laughing, energetic Chinese and the apathetic inhabitants of India. (E.g. material in Clapper Papers, box 36; Sevareid broadcast, 11 Sept. 1943, Sevareid Papers, box D3; T. H. White, ed., *The Stilwell Papers*, New York, 1948, entry for 4 Jan. 1943.) The 'national characters' of the two countries, and the question of which of them would eventually become the leading Asian power, were also subjects considered at the meetings of a quasi-official British discussion group in New Delhi. See Thorne, *Allies*, 318, 559.
† Of course, there remained great differences among those Europeans in terms of underlying assumptions, as epitomised by the post-war comment of a French intellectual: 'The English would be shocked that a foreigner could have the idea of becoming British. The French are shocked when a foreigner does not have the idea of becoming French.' On this and other contrasts, see e.g. C. M. Andrew, 'France: Adjustment to Change', in Bull and Watson, *The Expansion of International Society*, and M. Kahler, *Decolonization in Britain and France: the Domestic Consequences of International Relations* (Princeton, 1984).

businessman like Sir Andrew McFadyean or distinguished students of colonial history like Lord Hailey and Professor W. K. Hancock.[100]

It is not being suggested here that all such justifications were entirely lacking in validity, or that all the judgements they contained derived from racial prejudice. But an underlying paternalism did continue to colour the attitudes of most Europeans regarding future relationships between the metropolitian country and its Asian dependencies, even when it was acknowledged that 'a change in a fundamentally democratic sense' should and would occur in those territories. In other words, a determination to recover the colonies Japan had taken, noted in chapter four in the context of international power-politics, was accompanied by a conviction that there remained a task to be fulfilled there on behalf of both the indigenous populations and mankind as a whole. Thus, the Communist Dutch under-. ground paper *Die Waarheid* might proclaim: 'No nation is free that suppresses another nation,' and call, with other organs of the clandestine press, for the radical reform of Netherlands-Indies relations; but, like Queen Wilhelmina or Gerbrandy or van Mook in their various ways, it refused to contemplate the tragedy of a complete separation between the two countries.[101] More conservative journals were naturally more patronising (as seen from an Indonesian point of view). The 'deification of the Asian in the form of the Japanese' that had been spread throughout the Indies since 1942 would be rooted out, declared the Calvinist paper *Trouw*, and the great spiritual mission of the Netherlands would be resumed. The task remained 'to foster the . . . political capacities' of a native people who were still in the condition of 'a child that wishes to grow into an adult'.[102]

Likewise in France, although the Communist *L'Humanité* declared its support for those Vietnamese who resisted the old-style imperialism directed from Paris; although other Resistance publications such as *Libération* and *Combat* called for a peace 'of free men', for an end to 'national imperialism', and for a recognition of the principle of 'the right of all peoples freely to decide their own destiny', all sections of the undergound press, including *L'Humanité*, nevertheless assumed, like the Vichy regime and the Gaullists and others in London, that France should and would recover all her overseas territories and resume there her beneficent task – a task, declared *Défense de la France* in 1943, that was reflected in the glory surrounding 'the very name of Western civilization'. Racism of the Nazi, anti-Semitic variety was widely condemned, but the white-versus-coloured variety was seen as alien to that 'civilising mission'. France, insisted *J'accuse*, had been 'the first to proclaim the equality of all races, to free her slaves, and to bestow civic rights on non-white peoples'.[103]

For Britain, meanwhile, the determination to retain sovereign responsibility for the country's colonial territories, together with the freedom to judge whether and when a dependency was ready for self-government, was made plain to the United States Government during a series of secret exchanges between 1942 and 1944 over a possible joint declaration on colonial policy.[104] In public, too, the same message was conveyed to meddling and ignorant cousins across the Atlantic with less than diplomatic finesse by the Labour M.P., Emmanuel Shinwell, among others. 'We have no intention,' he growled in the House of Commons, 'of throwing the British Commonwealth of Nations overboard in order to satisfy a section of the American press' – and he pronounced himself to be 'in hearty accord' with Churchill's own fierce rejection of any proposal to 'liquidate' the Empire.[105]

Many – perhaps most – Europeans tended to assume that, however many changes had been brought about by the war, their subject peoples in Asia would still welcome their return in place of the ruthless and exploiting Japanese. (It is worth repeating that, for the French and the Dutch, the years they had spent virtually cut off from information relating to those distant parts of the world obviously helped heighten the degree of misperception involved.) 'Far too many of the French,' noted Jean Sainteny after vainly attempting to warn officials in Paris in 1945 of the increased strength of Vietnamese nationalism, 'assume that the people of Indochina are impatiently awaiting our return and are preparing to greet us with open arms.'[106] As for the Dutch, even an official as sensitive to Indonesian opinion and interests as van Mook, waiting in the summer of 1945 to return to the East Indies as Lieutenant Governor General, could believe that 'an important part of the more educated people' in the colony appreciated 'the importance and necessity of Western leadership and help', and that the Indonesians as a whole, having suffered under the Japanese, 'longed for a return to the good old days' ('de bevolking als geheel . . . hartelijk terug verlangt naar den goeden ouden tijd').[107]

We have seen in an earlier chapter how the assumptions and attitudes that were being manifested here had developed over a very long period, being rooted in European experiences and beliefs that went back to the sixteenth and seventeenth centuries, if not further. It was scarcely likely, then, that even a series of events as cataclysmic as those which overtook Britain, France and the Netherlands, between 1939 and 1945 would result in the acceptance of a set of perceptions as radically different as changing circumstances – and, certainly, as the convictions and determination of many Asians – required.[108] And if, in certain respects, it seemed that in the United States, at least, there existed during the war years a more realistic appreciation that, as Roosevelt thought of writing to Churchill in 1942, 'the old relationship . . . between Europeans and Americans on the one side with the many varieties of races in eastern and southern Asia and the Indians on the other side' had 'ceased to exist ten or twenty years' before,[109] in retrospect it is apparent that there, too, *mutatis mutandis*, misperceptions of an essentially paternalist kind were widespread, quite apart from the racist arrogance already noted. Indeed, the war itself was greatly reinforcing a process whereby the confidence that had long lain at the heart of European attitudes towards the rest of the world was, rather, becoming far more powerful a feature of American society,* and was helping shape American assumptions regarding the outsider.

Those assumptions were not, of course, identical to the ones that predominated among the French, or Dutch, or British, though they contained elements – for example, a belief in the Christian evangelising mission† – which had been prominent in European approaches to Asia also. Essentially, as was suggested earlier in relation to pre-1941 American perceptions and policies regarding the Far East, they derived from a self-image that was fundamental to American political culture: from the conviction that American society was not only *sui generis* but was 'the greatest hope of mankind'; a model and a goal for all.‡ As Theodore White was later to write of General Stilwell's approach to Chinese problems at the time: 'He came of a tradition ... of Americans who felt so strongly that we were the good people that wherever they went they were convinced that they, as Americans, brought virtue. Nor could Stilwell conceive that what was good for America could possibly be bad, or wrong, for other peoples.'[110]

The very composition of American society: the historical experience whereby millions of people with the most diverse backgrounds had passed through the 'melting-pot' to become, not Poles or Chinese, but 'Americans', obviously encouraged such assumptions, together with a tendency to see the inhabitants of other parts of the globe, too, as in a sense nascent Americans, at least. There was also, perhaps, an element of insecurity in this process: a need to be reassured as to the virtues, significance and coherence of one's

* See below, 211, 321.
† In a memorandum of January 1942, for example, a State Department official asked rhetorically: 'Are Christianity and its great teachings and its charities and humane works to continue among the millions of Chinese and Koreans and other Asiatic peoples, or are they to be stopped ... by Japanese state action and by Japanese forms of idolatry?' (Langdon, 'Japanese Attitudes Toward Christianity', 17 Jan. 1942, Dpt. of State files, 740.0011 PW/2037⅛.) After the war, in Japan, MacArthur was to inform George Kennan that he had come to that country to satisfy the 'thirst' of its people 'for guidance and inspiration' with the gifts of 'democracy and Christianity'. And, in his own mind, the thousands of Bibles he had distributed created 'a spiritual revolution' which 'almost overnight tore asunder a theory and practice of life built on 2,000 years of history and tradition and legend'. Kennan, *Memoirs, Vol. 1*, 384; MacArthur, *Reminiscences*, 310–11.
‡ See, for example, Jefferson: 'The principles of society [in Europe] and here are radically different.' 'A just and solid republican government maintained here will be a standing monument and example for the aim and imitation of the people of other countries ... ' 'We feel we are acting under obligations not confined to the limits of our own society. It is impossible not to be sensible that we are acting for all mankind ... ' E. Dumbauld (ed.), *The Political Writings of Thomas Jefferson* (New York, 1955), 71ff.

own society; a need which, as was suggested in an earlier chapter in relation
to China in particular before 1941, manifested itself in part in a quest for
protégés among the 'emerging' peoples of the world.

The war provided a powerful thrust to attitudes and assumptions of this
kind. Once more, the inadequacies and corruptness of other societies and
states had brought conflict and wretchedness to the world; for a second time
the American people were having to descend into this sordid arena, *deus ex
machina*, in order to restore the peace. But on this occasion, unlike that of
1914–18, the turmoil had spread far beyond an unregenerate Europe; had
encompassed what Douglas MacArthur, for one, saw as 'Western civilization's last earth frontier': 'Asia and its island outposts';[111] had provided
Americans with a new opportunity and a new power to re-mould the lives of
a substantial portion of mankind and, indeed, the very nature and processes
of international society as a whole.

Small wonder, then, that in Washington confidential surveys prepared by
prominent academics who staffed the Research and Analysis branch of the
O.S.S. repeatedly emphasised how others were looking to the United States
for inspiration, guidance and protection. American policies in China and the
Philippines had 'aroused the admiration' of other Asians. 'The Annamese
people', 'politically enlightened Burmese', the Malays, the Indonesians and
others were 'enthusiastically pro-American'. 'American leadership would
be far more welcome in the area than would Britain's.'[112] The American
public, too, were time and again assured (and such statements by no means
lacked foundation) that their country had become, as an I.P.R. book put it,
'a symbol of hope to the peoples of this vast region'.[113] They were also
shielded from such uncomfortable and potentially myth-disturbing developments as the one mentioned in an earlier chapter: President Quezon's bitter
desire early in 1942, as the Japanese pressed on towards total victory in the
Philippines, for the islands to be given their independence in order that he
might come to terms with the invader. (Even worse, in the eyes of men like
Stimson, was the endorsement of the proposal provided by MacArthur
himself, who at that time, and possibly in contravention of the requirements
of his terms of service in the U.S. Army, was accepting a personal gift of
500,000 U.S. dollars from Quezon on behalf of a grateful Philippines, and
who thereafter had to perform further mental gymnastics in order to
preserve the myth of total Filipino loyalty to America – and to himself –
when he found that 'many of [his] friends in the Manila elite' had been very
ready to cooperate with the Japanese.)[114]

The bonds which it was believed the United States had forged with the
people of China were even more important in this connection than was the
'model' relationship between Americans and Filipinos. (The bitterness, as
well as shock, that was to be displayed in 1949 over the 'loss' of China to

Communism is obviously related to such previous assumptions.) The Chinese, moreover, were frequently depicted in the war years, not simply as liking Americans, but as *being* like them.* 'There is something very much like the American pioneers in these people,' broadcast Clapper from Chungking in 1942 over N.B.C., 'and many of their leaders were educated in America.'[115] 'China,' proclaimed the *Chicago Daily News* in a revealing phrase, 'is our "White hope" in the East,' while the *Christian Science Monitor*, too, emphasised the significance of Chiang Kai-shek's being 'a Christian and his wife American-educated'. 'The two peoples are nearer alike,' asserted Representative Walter Judd (a former medical missionary in China) '[and] we are nearer to the Chinese in our basic beliefs ... [and] personal habits of democracy than we are to most of the countries of Europe.'[116] And although images of the Nationalist regime became tarnished in the latter part of the war, American correspondents and diplomats who visited Yenan, as we noted in passing in the previous chapter, tended to describe the Communists they found there in terms that again encouraged the notion that these were people with essentially American characteristics – more so, indeed, with their informality, directness, and rejection of mysticism, than the Chinese of the older order.[117] 'Practically no Americans,' concludes one student of the subject, 'understood the immense cultural distance actually separating Chinese society from themselves.'[118]

There were, of course, exceptions: Americans who did not unwittingly indulge in this ignorant and patronising form of paternalism. And, when it came to fostering Sino-American understanding, the first Chief of the State Department's Division of Cultural Relations went out of his way to emphasise that 'there must be no imposition of one people's culture on another'.[119] Even the belief, as expressed by the distinguished scholar John K. Fairbank (who was one of those involved in the cultural programme on the spot), that China was 'a battleground where American values are in conflict with other values, and where we should seek to make our values prevail', did not necessarily preclude an awareness that it would be absurd and impossible, as Fairbank himself emphasised, to try 'to make China like the United States'.[120]

Nevertheless, in their hope of seeing a strong, democratic and united China emerge from the war – a China that would naturally align itself with the United States – even Americans who, like Fairbank, were deeply versed in Chinese history and culture could reach impatiently for concepts and

---

* For an earlier example of this conviction, see above, 59. Such a process of cultural projection was of course also to feature in American foreign relations after the war, as when Lyndon Johnson, for example, recalled his own experiences and priorities when drawing up plans for social engineering in Vietnam, where 'the Mekong [was to be turned] into a Tennessee Valley'. See D. Kearns, *Lyndon Johnson and the American Dream* (London, 1976), 265ff. On ethnocentric aspects of much post-war American historical writing on China, see Cohen, *Discovering History in China*.

remedies of a Western nature. 'China needs more of the Puritan spirit,' wrote the diplomat, John Paton Davies, who had been born of missionary parents in that country,[121] while the 'small but powerful arsenal of democratic thought and precedent' that one member of the Cultural Relations Division, supported by the Secretary of State's Political Adviser, wished to see placed in the hands of those 'enthusiastic allies' of America, Chinese who had been educated in the U.S.A., included a Chinese-language edition of *Reader's Digest*.[122]

In short, the underlying conviction for many Americans, including those whose admiration and concern for the Chinese people was great, was the one expressed by Pearl Buck herself: that it was essential for 'the American way of life to prevail in the world', and in Asia above all.[123] And in this cause, as has already become apparent in the context of colonial issues, the struggle had to be waged, so it was believed, against the Western allies of the United States no less than against the Japanese. The need was urgent; but the means were coming to hand as the country's might spread out over the Pacific and beyond. As one American official put it to a visitor from London: 'It is now our turn to bat in Asia.'[124]

Notes

1 Thorne, *Allies*, 207.
2 van Mook policy outline regarding occupied territories in S.E. Asia, 13 Nov. 1944, van Mook Papers, folder 14.
3 'Guidance for Action ... on Political Warfare Against Japan', 17 Aug. 1942, Australian P.M.'s Dpt. files, K/57/1/1.
4 Thorne, *Allies*, 207.
5 *Standard*, 8 Feb. 1945.
6 Thorne, *Allies*, 8, 539.
7 Ibid, e.g. 157, 158, 359; and e.g. Thorne, 'Chatham House, Whitehall and Far Eastern Issues', loc. cit.; Janeway, 'Fighting a White Man's War', *Asia and the Americas*, Jan. 1943; Bruce, Monthly War Files, entry for 14 Sept. 1942, Bruce Papers.
8 Hornbeck to Hull, 20 Sept. 1943, Hornbeck Papers, box 4.
9 E.g. State Dpt. Cttee. on Colonial Problems, 15 Oct. 1943, State Dpt. files, Notter files, box 120; Ickes diary, 24 May 1942; and, on Japanese propaganda directed towards American blacks, e.g. Walter White, report on Pacific tour, 13 July 1945, NAACP Papers, box 576; *New York Times*, 17 Sept. 1943.
10 Smuts to Gillett, 7 June 1942, in J. van der Poel (ed.), *Selections From the Smuts Papers, Vol. VI* (Cambridge, 1973).
11 Thorne, *Allies*, 8.
12 Ibid, 175, 291, 359, 539.
13 R. Broad and S. Fleming (ed.), *Nella Last's War: A Mother's Diary, 1939–45* (London, 1981), entry for 14 Feb. 1943.
14 Thorne, *Allies*, 310.
15 van Mook policy paper, 13 Nov. 1944, loc. cit.; and e.g. Lovink to van Mook, 10 July 1943,

van Mook Papers, folder 2; Bruce Monthly War Files, entries for 29 Dec. 1942 and 21 Nov. 1944, Bruce Papers; Thorne, *Allies*, 190, 559.
16 Thorne, *Allies*, 259.
17 Meo, op. cit., 217.
18 Records of Jan. 1944 Australia-NZ Conference, NZ Dpt. of Ext. Affs., file 153/19/4 part 1. And e.g. Australian Dpt. of Ext. Affs., files A989/44/655/25 and 37; A989/43/735/301 and 313; A989/43/150/5/1/2; Robinson to Evatt, 12 Nov. 1942, Evatt Papers, Robinson file.
19 *Sydney Morning Herald*, 29 May 1943, 22 Sept. 1944, 11 July 1945; Sydney *Daily Telegraph*, 15 Nov. 1944; *Standard* (Wellington), 20 Jan. 1944.
20 OSS R and A, No. 760, loc. cit.
21 Material in Breckenridge Long Papers, box 89.
22 *Our Chinese Wall* (1943), Hornbeck Papers, box 19, italics added.
23 Thorne, *Allies* 291.
24 See in general e.g. Addison, *The Road to 1945*; Wright, *The Ordeal of Total War*; Polenberg, *War and Society*; Michel and Guetzévitch, *Les idées politiques et sociales de la Résistance*.
25 *Oregonian*, 14 Feb. 1943 (article and related papers in Hornbeck Papers, box 40); 'People, East and West', *Asia and the Americas*, June 1943.
26 Hulder, 'A Chinese Century?', *Asia and the Americas*, July 1943.
27 G. E. Taylor, *Changing China* (I.P.R., New York, 1942), 85, 92–3.
28 Thorne, *Allies*, 242–3. And see Louis, *Imperialism At Bay*, passim, and D. C. Watt, 'American Anti-Colonial Policies and the End of European Colonial Empires', in A. N. den Hollander (ed.), *Contagious Conflict* (Leiden, 1973).
29 Thorne, *Allies*, 593.
30 Weiller, in *Asia and the Americas*, Feb. 1943.
31 P. E. Lilienthal and J. H. Oakie, *Asia's Captive Colonies* (IPR, New York, 1944). Also e.g. E. Janeway, 'The G.I. and Imperialism', *Asia and the Americas*, Nov. 1944; F. Sternberg, 'The Struggle for Asia's Future', ibid, March 1945.
32 Buck, 'Postwar China and the United States', *Asia and the Americas*, Nov. 1943. On the wider issue of American attitudes towards revolution and change in world affairs, see L. C. Gardner, *Covenant with Power* (New York, 1984), especially essay 1.
33 Bishop to State Dpt., 10 March 1944, State Dpt. files, 740.00119 PW/37.
34 G. Myrdal, *An American Dilemma, Vol. II* (New York, 1944), 1006.
35 See J. Anderson, *A. Philip Randolph* (New York, 1973).
36 E.g. Johnson to Hornbeck, 8 and 20 Jan. 1942. Hornbeck Papers, box 262; cable NR 41, 29 March 1942, MacArthur to Marshall, U.S. War Dpt. files, Exec. 10, item 7d; 'Civilian Morale in North Queensland', report of 1 Feb. 1943, Australian P.M.'s Dept. files, BA/29/1/2 (also B45/1/20); material in NAACP Papers, box 625.
37 Material in NAACP Papers, boxes 316, 519, 576, 583, 623.
38 See Thorne, *Allies*, 184ff., 237–8, 308ff., 318ff.
39 See ibid, 660, 221, 345, 459, 608ff.
40 E.g. Hart talk, 'The Future of the Netherlands Indies' (n.d.; 1943?), Gerbrandy Office papers, 338.13; Regional Political Warfare Directive, 1 June 1943, NZ Ext. Affs. file 84/6/1, part 1.
41 *L'Action* (Hanoi), 24 April, 20 May, 27 June, 14 Sept. 1942; *L'Union* (Hanoi and Saigon), 26 April 1942.
42 Penton, 'Those Ties of Empire', *Asia and the Americas*, Jan. 1944.
43 *Sydney Morning Herald*, 13 Oct. 1942.
44 *Standard*, 9 Dec. 1943, and e.g. *Dominion* (Wellington), 13 Jan. 1942.
45 *Standard*, 1 March 1945.
46 *Sydney Morning Herald*, 7 Sept. 1944, and e.g. Australian Army Directorate of Research report, Sept. 1944, Blamey Papers, file 8.3, China.
47 Documents and resolutions of the Australia-New Zealand conferences of January and October-November 1944, NZ Ext. Affs. files, 151/2/1 part 1, and 153/19/4 part 1; Thorne, *Allies*, 601–3.
48 M. Perham, *Colonial Sequence* (London, 1967), passim; Maze to Pouncey, 10 April 1943,

Maze papers, CLR, vol. 15; Directorate of Army Education, *The British Way and Purpose*, no. 3, Jan. 1943; Thorne, *Allies*, 61, 157, 193, 196, 211. For the sympathetic attitude towards Indian aspirations (though not the Quit India riots) adopted by the British editor of *The Statesman* in Calcutta, see Stephens, *Monsoon Morning*, passim; also his Appendix II for the similar views of 'a British Soldier'. On the seemingly less caring attitude of Duff Cooper himself towards Asians when he was on the spot in Singapore in 1941–42, see Montgomery, *Shenton of Singapore*, 98ff.

49 Thorne, *Allies*, 311, 547–8.
50 See ibid, 345 and 459; also 607ff.
51 van Mook paper on occupied territories in Southeast Asia, 13 Nov. 1944, loc. cit. And see e.g. *Het Parool*, 28 May 1943.
52 Logemann to van Starkenborgh, 9 Oct. 1945, Gerbrandy Office Papers, 353.83.003. And see e.g. *De Vrije Katheder*, 13 Sept. 1943.
53 P. Moon (ed.), Wavell: *The Viceroy's Journal* (London, 1973), entry for 24 Oct. 1944 and passim.
54 Ibid, entry for 8 Oct. 1943.
55 See Thorne, *Allies*, 597ff.; 630ff., 663ff.
56 See ibid, 456–7, 595–9.
57 See ibid, 178–9, 195–6, 307, 318, 421, 579.
58 Ibid, 368; Friend, *Between Two Empires*, 237; Ickes diary, 25 Sept. and 10 Oct. 1943; Stimson diary, 27 Sept., 1 Oct. 1943.
59 Thorne, *Allies*, 607–10; Scarr, op. cit., passim.
60 Ibid, 218–9; drafts and other material relating to the broadcast in van Mook Papers, file 4.
61 See D. B. Marshall, *The French Colonial Myth and Constitution-Making in the Fourth Republic* (New Haven, 1973), 102ff., 132ff.
62 See Thorne, *Allies*, 69–70, 173, 178, 188, 194, 311, 319, 325, 432–4, 443–4, 565.
63 Ibid, 325.
64 Ibid, 360, 643.
65 See e.g. *Wavell, The Viceroy's Diary*, entry for 1 July 1945; and in general, Thorne, 'Wartime British Planning for the Postwar Far East', loc. cit.
66 A study of the Resistance press in both countries makes this apparent. The point has also been made forcefully to the author in interviews with individuals who spent the war years under German occupation, and also M. René Massigli, who was Commissioner for Foreign Affairs on the French Committee of Liberation.
67 P. Sorlin, 'The Struggle for Control of French Minds', in Short (ed.), *Film and Radio Propaganda*.
68 Lee and Petter, *The Colonial Office, War and Development Policy*, 68, 85, 148 and passim.
69 Ickes to Truman, 17 July 1945, Office of Territories records, High Commissioner, Philippines, files, box 44; Lamont to Forbes, 13 Nov. 1945, Lamont Papers, file 94/14; Sayre-Roosevelt correspondence, Sayre Papers, box 7; Ickes diary, e.g. 17 May 1942, 5 Sept., 30 Oct. 1943, 1 and 10 Oct. 1944.
70 Thorne, *Allies*, 223.
71 See e.g. Horner, *High Command*, 138, and Edwards, *Prime Ministers and Diplomats*, cap. 5.
72 See Thorne, *Allies*, 174, 182–3, 320–2, 326, 434ff., 556ff., 562ff.
73 See e.g. ibid, 161, 189, 191, 222, 315; Kersten, 'The Dutch and the American Anti-Colonialist Tide, 1942–1945'.
74 Thorne, *Allies*, 489–90, 661–2.
75 See Thorne, *Allies*, 366, 481, 613; and e.g. van Mook to Warners, 25 Aug. 1944 and Warners to van Mook, 19 Sept. 1944, van Mook Papers, folder 2; van Mook to Logemann, 30 June 1945, ibid; van Aerssen to Loudon, 12 and 17 June 1944, ibid, folder 33; van Mook to Gerbrandy, 29 June 1944, Neths. Foreign Ministry files, Londens archief, Brandkast la 13; de la Valette report of conversation with van Mook, 5 March 1942, FO 371, file 31812.
76 See P. M. Maas, *Indië verloren rampspoed geboren* (The Hague, 1984); C. Fasseur, 'Nederland en het Indonesische nationalisme. De balans nog eens opgemaakt', *Bijdragen en Mededingen Betreffende de Geschiedenis der Nederlanden, Vol. 99*, 1984, 21–44; S. L.

van der Wal (ed.), *Officiële Bescheiden Betreffende de Nederlands Indonesische Betrekkingen, 1945–50, Vol. 1* (The Hague, 1970).

77 Thorne, *Allies*, 553; and see ibid, e.g. 185, 196, 311, 314, 318, 338, 421–2, 444, 548, 553.
78 Ibid, 661; and see P. Darby, *British Defence Policy East of Suez, 1947–1968* (London, 1974).
79 See Thorne, *Allies*, 490–1, 627–33, 664–7.
80 Ibid, 498–500, 598–600, 630–33; Smith, *The Shadow Warriors*, 322; Cumings, *The Origins of the Korean War*, cap. 4; O.S.S. memo., 'Problems and Objectives of U.S. Policy', 2 April 1945, Truman Papers, White House Central Files, O.S.S.
81 Thorne, *Allies*, 597.
82 *Asia and the Americas*, Nov. 1943.
83 See Thorne, *Allies*, 208–9.
84 On this topic in general see e.g. L. C. Gardner, *Economic Aspects of New Deal Diplomacy* (Madison, 1964), cap. 13.
85 O. Lattimore, *Solution in Asia* (London, 1945), 16.
86 *Amerasia*, 8 Sept. 1944.
87 *New York Herald Tribune*, 10 July 1944; H. Wallace, *Our Job in the Pacific* (New York, 1944).
88 Thorne, *Allies*, 293, 402.
89 Hornbeck Papers, box 56.
90 Thorne, *Allies*, 564.
91 E.g. Langdon memo., 'Post-war Status of Thailand', 10 Jan. 1945, Dpt. of State Files, 892.00, 1–1045; Division of Special Research, 'Statement of Major Post-war Problems in the Pacific Area', 20 Feb. 1942, ibid, Pasvolsky files, box 2; Grew-Dunn memo., quoted in Thorne, *Allies*, 160.
92 Thorne, *Allies*, 160.
93 Miles staff conference, 29 May 1945, Naval Group China files, U.S. Navy Operational Archives.
94 Thorne, *Allies*, 5–6, 730; Moran, *Churchill*, 131, 559.
95 E.g. Lamont-Halifax correspondence, Lamont Papers, files 84/24 and 85/1; correspondence on India in ibid, files 99/15 and 99/16.
96 E.g. Clapper cable from India, n.d. (1942), Clapper Papers, box 36.
97 See Thorne, *Allies*, 6.
98 See ibid, 103, 160, 214, 215, 231, 239, 247, 360, 368, 484, 592, 600, 714.
99 OSS R. and A. No. 760, 2nd edn., 1 Nov. 1943.
100 See Thorne, *Allies*, 212–14; Thorne, 'Chatham House, Whitehall and Far Eastern Issues, 1941–1945', *International Affairs*, Jan. 1978; Louis, *Imperialism At Bay*, passim; W. K. Hancock, *Argument of Empire* (London, 1943); Lord Hailey, *The Future of Colonial Peoples* (London, 1943).
101 *Die Waarheid*, 1 May 1943; also e.g. *Je Maintiendrai*, 10 May 1943; van Namen (ed.) *Het Ondergroondse Vrij Nederland*, 219.
102 *Trouw*, Dec. 1943; mid-July 1944.
103 *Défense de la France*, 20 Oct. 1943; and e.g. R. Aron, 'Pour l'Alliance de l'Occident', *La France Libre*, 15 Jan. 1944; *L'Humanité*, Dec. 1940, 1 Jan. 1944, 11 Jan. and 16 Sept. 1945; *Combat*, May 1942; *Libération* (zone Sud), 10 Jan. 1944; *Le Populaire*, 14 Nov. 1944; *Cahiers du témoignage Chrétien*, July 1944; *L'Aurore*, Oct. 1943; *J'accuse*, Feb. 1943; Michel and Guetzévitch, op. cit., 193ff. and 339ff.; J. Duclos, *Mémoires: Dans la Bataille Clandestine, Deuxième Partie, 1943–1945* (Paris, 1970); G. Madjarian, *La question coloniale et la politique du Parti communiste français, 1944–1947* (Paris, 1977).
104 See Thorne, *Allies*, 222–4, 341–2, 455–7; also J. E. Williams, 'The Joint Declaration on the Colonies', *British Journal of International Studies*, vol. 2, 1976.
105 See Thorne, *Allies*, 457; also P. S. Gupta, *Imperialism and the British Labour Movement, 1914–1964* (London, 1973), 260, 272–3; papers of the Labour Party's Advisory Cttee. on Imperial Questions, Leonard Woolf Papers, boxes 35, 40.
106 J. Sainteny, *Histoire d'une Paix Manquée* (Paris, 1953), 47.
107 van Mook to Logemann, 31 July 1945, and to van Starkenborgh, 3 Sept. 1945, van Mook Papers, file 2; interviews with Mr J. G. Kist, Secretary to the Government of the Indies in

Australia, Mr den Hollander, Naval Attaché to the Netherlands Senior Officer in Melbourne, and Dr J. E. van Hoogstraten, Chairman of the Netherlands Indies Commission in Australia.

108 On the stubbornness of long-held images in the face of contrary evidence, and on the conditions under which changes of perception tend to take place, see the relevant sections of Kelman, op. cit., and Jervis, op. cit.

109 Thorne, *Allies*, 242.

110 White, *In Search of History*, 178.

111 D. MacArthur, *Reminiscences* (London, 1964), 32.

112 E.g. 'Social Conditions, Attitudes and Propaganda in Indochina', 30 March 1942, OSS R. and A. No. 265; 'Suggestions for American Orientation Toward the Thai', 19 June 1942, ibid No. 301; 'Basic Psychological Factors in the Far East', 3 Oct. 1942, ibid No. 383; 'British Interests in the Far East', 1944 (n.d.), ibid, No. 2424.

113 E. A. Clark, *Peoples of the China Seas* (New York, 1942), 6.

114 See above, 169, and Thorne, *Allies*, 262; also C. M. Petillo, *Douglas MacArthur: the Philippine Years* (Bloomington, Indiana, 1981), 205–10, 219ff., 229ff.

115 Clapper broadcast, 31 March 1942, Clapper Papers, box 36; and see e.g. Isaacs, *Scratches On Our Minds*, 174ff.

116 Thorne, *Allies*, 172, 425.

117 See ibid, 438 and 571, and Shewmaker, op. cit., passim.

118 M. Schaller, *The U.S. Crusade in China, 1938–1945* (New York, 1979), 2.

119 W. Fairbank, *America's Cultural Experiment in China, 1942–49* (Washington, D.C., 1976), 5.

120 Fairbank memo., 4 Dec. 1942, Hornbeck Papers, box 113.

121 Thorne, *Allies*, 23.

122 Grummon memo., 13 Jan. 1942, Hornbeck Papers, box 113. For Pearl Buck's list of books and films through which to convey the essence of America to China, see *Asia*, Oct. and Nov. 1942, and the *Washington Post* of 22 Sept. 1942.

123 Buck speech of Feb. 1942, reported in *New York Herald Tribune*, 16 Feb. 1942. Cf. Minear, 'Cross-Cultural Perception and World War II', loc. cit.

124 Thorne, *Allies*, 555; and see e.g. 502–4, 536–7, 664–7.

CHAPTER SEVEN

Facing One's Friends

The conviction among Americans – officials and others – that their country was called upon to bring about fundamental change in the Far East and elsewhere became, of course, a significant element in the international relations of the war years. (They believe, reported Richard Law, Minister of State at the Foreign Office, to his Cabinet colleagues in London, 'that the United States stands for something in the world – something of which the world has need, something which the world is going to like, something, in the final analysis, which the world is going to take whether it likes it or not'.)[1] The complex series of exchanges that were carried on among Japan's enemies have already surfaced from time to time, of course, in a number of contexts: in relation to the politics of grand strategy, for example, to economic prospects and post-war security considerations, and to the future of dependent territories. Inter-Allied issues such as these have also been traced in some detail elsewhere by the present author and others. They will therefore be accorded only broad, illustrative treatment in the first part of this chapter, with special reference to the Far Eastern war, while the final part will be devoted to an examination of certain patterns of mutual images that helped shape, and in turn were partly shaped by, those political exchanges themselves.

The increasing American 'bullishness' referred to above derived in part, of course, from the extraordinary growth of U.S. resources and power during the war years. The requirements of global conflict so released the potential of the United States economy that gross national product leaped from $88.6 billion in 1939 to $198.7 billion in 1945. Output of manufactured goods increased by 300 per cent between 1940 and 1944 and of raw materials by about 60 per cent; the productive capacity of the economy as a whole expanded by around 50 per cent as the result of investment in new plant and equipment; in the agricultural sphere, productivity jumped by over 25 per cent, with a reduction of 17 per cent in the number of farm workers.[2] The American merchant fleet, which had accounted for less than 17 per cent of the world's tonnage in 1939, was to constitute 52 per cent by 1947, while the U.S. Navy had by 1944 grown to roughly three times the size of its British counterpart. (Nearly one hundred American aircraft-carriers, for example, were ranging the Pacific by the end of that year.)[3] When the Dutch Army had surrendered to the Germans in 1940, the United States had moved up to nineteenth in the rankings of the world's military powers; by 1945 she and the Soviet Union were in a class of their own.[4]

As a result of this process, and despite the war-time expansion of other economies, a growing imbalance rapidly came to exist among the Allied states that were arrayed against Japan, and manifested itself in numerous ways. In the southern Pacific, for example, the United States replaced Britain as the main economic partner of Australia during these years. Mounting American investments in the Dominion, concludes Dr Bell, were 'an index of [Australia's] growing economic dependence on the United States and the emergence of new economic relations between the two powers' – relations that were to be marked by a substantial increase in trade between them after the war.[5]* Meanwhile, within MacArthur's South West Pacific Area, Australian private soldiers were being paid £9.15 shillings a month, their American counterparts the equivalent of £17.[6] (This discrepancy – which increased as one ascended the military rankings – gave rise to considerable bitterness among the Australians, not least when they came to compete with G.I.'s for the comforts and pleasures of life away from the front, in their own country. The problem, argued the Association of Chambers of Commerce in Queensland, arose from 'a superior national economy [being] imposed upon that of Australia'.)[7] At the same time, of course, both Australia and New Zealand had become dependent on the U.S.A., rather than on Britain, for their security, a state of affairs that was reflected in the exclusion of the British Chiefs of Staff from any control over MacArthur or over operations in the U.S. Navy's South Pacific Zone, and that foreshadowed the absence of Britain from the ANZUS Pact in 1951.

Britain's own productive effort during the war was of course enormous, with national income rising by 64 per cent between 1939 and 1945.[8] But in terms of output there could be no matching the United States, the value of whose armaments manufactures had become over three times greater than that of the United Kingdom by the end of hostilities. Even earlier, by the autumn of 1943, Britain had come to depend on her ally for nearly all her transport aircraft, for example, nearly all her self-propelled artillery, heavy tank-transporters, ten ton trucks and landing-force ships, for 88 per cent of her landing craft, 68 per cent of her light bombers, and 60 per cent of her tanks.[9] Above all, in terms of the situation that was to obtain at the end of the war, Britain was having to draw upon her reserves of national wealth, such as investments in North America, in order first to survive and then to

* The average monthly value of U.S. exports to Australia in 1936–39 had been U.S. $5.583 million, and of Australian exports to the U.S. $2.09 million. Between August 1945 and August 1946, the figures were $7.321 million and $11.587 million respectively. Meanwhile, American exports to India, for example, increased during the war years from 1 to 5 per cent of the U.S. total and from 6 to 17 per cent of the Indian import total. Hess, *America Encounters India*, 158.

play a substantial part in defeating her enemies. Roughly one-quarter of that wealth would be gone by the summer of 1945. And well before this, ministers and officials in London were having to wrestle with such problems as how to restore the country's vital export trade, how to meet its indebtedness to those whose sterling balances had grown rapidly during the war (India, for example, had accumulated £1,321 million by the end of 1945, Egypt and the Sudan over £500 million), and how to obtain from the United States financial aid that was estimated by Keynes at between $1 and 2 billion, together with as much again in goods (leaving aside, that is, the question of whether Washington would demand some settlement for the $30,000 million it had provided for Britain under Lend Lease).[10]

The resulting situation in terms of Britain's position vis-à-vis the United States was epitomised by, for example, the proceedings of the second Quebec Conference of September 1944, when Churchill was reduced to asking angrily whether he should 'get on his hind legs and beg like Falla' (Roosevelt's dog) for the financial and material assistance without which Britain would not be able to play a part of any significance in the final stages of the war against Japan, once Germany had been defeated.[11] It was also reflected in the growing awareness within official circles in London that, in areas where the 'competitive' as well as the 'cooperative' nature of transatlantic relations continued to show through,* Britain dare not allow rivalry between the two countries to become unrestrained. For if this were to happen – over post-war civil aviation, for example, or the securing of oil rights – then, as Eden put it in June 1944 in regard to the second of these issues, 'we should stand to lose heavily'.[12]

Anglo-American relations between 1941 and 1945 were also affected, of course, by developments involving each of them, and particularly the United States, with the Soviet Union. The later stages of the war, as we have seen, witnessed the emergence of considerable ambivalence, to say the least, among American policy-makers regarding the likelihood of Moscow's becoming a collaborator in the creation of a new and peaceful world. Nevertheless, between the Casablanca and Yalta Conferences, especially, the degree of influence which Churchill was able to exert with Roosevelt was diminished, not simply by those changes in the balance of power between the two states noted above, but also by the President's conviction that the establishment of a close working relationship with Stalin was crucial to the winning of both the war and the peace. (As Henry Morgenthau, Secretary of the Treasury, saw it in January 1944, basing his summary on the impressions of colleagues who had attended the Cairo and Tehran Conferences, 'the

---

* See above, 38–9. Churchill's conviction, as conveyed in private to the Dominions Prime Ministers meeting in London in 1944, that the interests of Britain and the United States 'could not clash', was, if taken literally, absurd. Thorne, *Allies*, 384.

Roosevelt-Stalin axis is gaining strength and the Roosevelt-Churchill axis is losing strength in about equal ratio'. The President himself did not dissent when Morgenthau showed him the entry in question.)[13]

Even when Soviet-American relations were becoming greatly strained in the early summer of 1945, the underlying fear of Harry Hopkins, for example – a proven friend of Britain's – was that London might be seeking to 'manoeuvre' Washington into 'lining up with them as a bloc against Russia to implement England's European policy'.[14] And in part this reflected a broader aspect of American-European relations in general: one that was touched upon earlier in the context of the pre-war international scene, and that involved questions concerning the essential nature of international affairs.[15] For to men like Cordell Hull, as to John Bright and other mid-nineteenth-century British radicals, peace and wholesomeness would be established throughout the world only when that 'foul idol' known as 'the balance of power', when 'power politics' as the basis of dealings among nations, had been banished for ever.* (For Britain to recognise formally the newly-extended boundaries of the Soviet Union in 1942 would not only 'be against all the principles that we are fighting for,' observed the American Ambassador in London, John Winant, to the Australian High Commissioner, but would be superfluous, since 'in the world that was contemplated after the war strategic frontiers would not be necessary for the security of nations'.)[16]

The conviction among American officials that, in the words of an O.S.S. Research and Analysis branch survey of September 1944, 'in any foreign policy based upon the balance of power Britain [after the war] could almost certainly not rely upon the support of the United States'[17] was underlined that same autumn when Washington publicly condemned what was seen as Britain's selfish and anachronistic actions to forestall a Communist take-over in Greece. (The episode prompted Churchill to draft a bitter cable to Halifax whereby the Ambassador was to have demanded of Edward Stettinius, the amiable lightweight who had been brought in by Roosevelt to succeed Hull as Secretary of State, whether the employment of America's own vast resources to gain her ends internationally was or was not an exercise in 'power politics'.)[18] Likewise, a similarly deep-seated distrust of the French approach to foreign affairs was reinforced in July 1945, for example, when de Gaulle's refusal to withdraw his troops from the Val d'Aosta created a situation which Henry Stimson went so far as to describe in his diary as bringing the United States to 'the brink of war with France'.[19]

* To generations who have become accustomed to think of American foreign policy itself as being characterised by just such a 'power-politics' approach, it may be tempting to assume that such war-time avowals on the part of men like Hull, who were in positions of responsibility in Washington, represented at best the mere paying of lip-service to an ideal, at worst calculated hypocrisy. If so, they would be wrong.

Fundamentally, the concern of many Americans in and beyond Washington was that unless the West Europeans, as much as those states which at the time constituted the enemies of the Republic, could be brought to abandon their centuries-old pattern of international behaviour, then the sacrifices currently being made of United States blood and treasure would again, as after 1917–18, have been in vain. With great care and wariness, Roosevelt was helping to bring about within the American body-politic a consensus in favour of joining in the construction of a new world organisation that would guard the peace once Germany and Japan had been defeated. (According to one national poll, 70 per cent of the country's adults supported the idea by January 1943.)[20] There remained, however, much apprehension among those officials who regarded such a commitment on their country's part as essential, lest international developments of a 'power-politics' kind should nourish the underlying isolationist instincts of their fellow-countrymen, and thus swing the United States back towards a repetition of the behaviour it had adopted after the First World War. The President, Hull, and others were convinced that America's own long-term security and prosperity required that she continue to involve herself in international affairs, just as she must bring down the barriers to world trade. But both their private beliefs and their sensitivity to domestic politics pointed towards the conclusion splendidly summarised by Michael Howard: that the United States, 'finding its identity not so much in ethnic community or shared historical experience as in dedication to a value system', could operate 'with a clear conscience' within the international system 'only if it could remake that system in its own image'.[21]

Yet Americans were far from being alone among the Allies in believing that the creation of a 'new order' in international relations was essential. The renewal of internecine strife among Europeans so soon after the horrors of 1914–18, together with the remarkably persistent conviction that mankind not only should but could so learn and adjust as to usher in the reign of peace, had been sufficient to thrust many others towards the same conclusion. For some, that meant, in the words of the Prime Minister of New Zealand, Peter Fraser, a return to 'the principles on which the League of Nations was based', with the addition, this time round, simply of 'moral resolution among the members of such an international organisation'.[22]* Others were inclined to favour the kind of notion advanced by the All-India

* This tendency to look backwards when planning for peace was fairly widespread, embracing both a preoccupation with how to avoid another war being launched by states like Nazi Germany and a militarised Japan, and a general search for the 'lessons' of history. See e.g. E.R. May, *'Lessons' of the Past* (New York, 1973), cap. 1; D.C. Watt, 'Every War Must End: Wartime Planning for Post-War Security in Britain and America in the Wars of 1914–18 and 1939–45: the Roles of Historical Example and of Professional Historians', *Transactions of the Royal Historical Society*, 5th series, vol. 28, 1978.

Congress Committee as well: a 'world federation' that would preserve peace through disarmament and 'a world federal force';[23] or, like the French Socialist Party in 1943, to call for 'an international community that will become the united states of the world'.[24] Others again (in London, for example, officials who had to contend with Churchill's abrupt initiatives in this field, as well as with a general preoccupation with the conduct of war) sought more prosaically to devise for a new world organisation a structure that would reconcile the sovereign equality of all states with the realities of the uneven distribution of power and the non-coincidence of national interests.[25] Whatever the particular forms or preferences might be, however, there was a widespread emphasis upon the inescapable involvement of all in no less a task than the reshaping of the international order. 'The day of isolation is gone.' Curtin's repudiation in 1943 of the pre-war stance of his Australian Labour Party matched the declaration of support that was forthcoming in the same year from the Republican Party in the United States for that country's 'participation . . . in a post-war cooperative organisation . . . to prevent military aggression and to attain permanent peace with organized justice in a free world'.[26]

The urgency of such a task was of course underlined at the end of the fight against Japan by the appearance and employment of nuclear weapons. The conclusion drawn by the *Sydney Morning Herald* was widely shared: either war itself must be abolished or 'the human family' was 'doomed to perish by its own hand'.[27] Unless every nation on earth collaborated in ensuring peace, warned *Le Monde*, there would come about a catastrophe that would make the Second World War appear 'mere child's play'.[28] 'I feel shocked and ashamed,' wrote a senior British Foreign Office official privately as the news of Hiroshima came through, and as the sophisticated and the many alike asked themselves 'the awful question' posed by the *Bombay Chronicle*: 'whether mankind is ready for this epochal discovery, or whether it has arrived too soon, too fatally soon.'[29]

By the summer of 1945, it was also widely – if less generally – believed within the ranks of the Allies that this urgent need to bring about a lasting peace could not be divorced from the quest for economic and social justice. (Tojo, too, as we have seen, had been proclaiming as much on behalf of Japan.) 'Freedom from want' and 'freedom from fear', as Roosevelt had termed them, were now seen by many as interdependent. 'We have reached a stage of civilisation in which war is thoroughly repugnant to us,' wrote the Economic Adviser to the Australian High Commissioner in London,

'. . . [but] there is a new frontier which can give us all the expansion of the 19th century and more. This new frontier is to be found in human welfare . . . We should secure the agreement of all nations to place in the forefront of their economic policies two main purposes, namely, rising standards of living and high levels of employment. If we can succeed in securing real international agreement about these purposes, the effects upon world economy will be so great that we shall not need to worry about markets.'[30]

What was entailed in a programme of this kind was no less than what *Le Monde* termed 'profound social transformation'.[31] As Vice President Wallace saw it: 'the people's revolution is on the march' towards what could and must be 'the century of the common man'.[32] 'The modern world is the world of the masses,' argued the clandestine newspaper, *La France Libre*. The peace, insisted *Libération*, must reflect the wishes and interests of the people, not of politicians.[33] And Harold Laski's summary of the situation for Roosevelt has already been noted in passing in an earlier chapter: 'You have only to hear the troops discussing the Beveridge Report* ... to know that the masses are on the move.'[34]

Yet there were also those in the West to whom such visions and prescriptions were anathema. To many in America, for example, Wallace and his supporters were a menace, more interested in creating 'world-wide social revolution', as Hull saw it, than in winning the war, and prepared to risk even 'revolution in the United States' itself.[35] 'I don't believe in this brave new world,' observed Churchill privately, and the cry to which he felt himself reduced: 'fight the damned socialists', reflected a conflict of values that, even before the war had come to an end, had taken on international as well as domestic dimensions.[36] If some among Japan's opponents were convinced, with *Le Populaire*, that only socialism could abolish the spectre of war, and, with the Labour Governments of Australia and New Zealand, that full-employment policies should have pride of place when it came to establishing a new international economic order,[37] to those who were achieving a predominant position in American politics by 1944 (when Roosevelt publicly bade farewell to the New Deal, as well as dropping Wallace as Vice President)†, such goals were nothing less than 'Communistic'.[38]

Widely differing values and priorities were likewise apparent when it came to translating a general desire for a newly just and peaceful international order into specific programmes and policies in the sphere of 'high politics'. On one level, the issue involved questions concerning the future relations between particular states or groups of states: between Britain and the Dominions; between the Commonwealth and the United States; among those countries which might come together in a regional organisation for the

* See below, 290.
† See below, 296.

Far East, for example.[39] In more 'theological' terms, it raised the question, noted above in respect of American aspirations in particular, of whether, in dealings among states in general, 'power politics' could ever be transcended. And somewhere in between these two levels, it centred on the position of the 'Big Four' or 'Big Three' vis-à-vis that of smaller states in the international organisation that was to be established to secure the lasting fruits of victory: on the insistence of Australia, New Zealand and the Netherlands, among others, that (in the words of the acting New Zealand Minister to the United States) 'they could not contemplate a world run entirely by the dominant great powers' and must have a say 'in all matters where their interests and their future are concerned';[40] but also on the growing belief in Washington, and among many Americans, that if the world was to be saved, then ultimately, like the defeated foe in the Far East, it would have to be reshaped and reorganised by the country that now 'stood first among the peoples of the earth'.[41]

*

We thus come back, in terms of the Far Eastern war in particular, to the conviction cited at the end of the previous chapter, that it was now America's turn 'to bat in Asia'. As a former president of the U.S. Navy League put it in 1943 in a letter that was seen by Roosevelt himself and warmly applauded by some of the latter's senior advisers:

> 'It would be of very great post-war importance to the United States, both politically and commercially, if the war to crush Japan could be carried on, in the main, by the United States, ... rather than, so to speak, a "United Nations" undertaking ... For such a procedure would improve immeasurably the peace settlements we would be able to make in the regions of the Pacific, and our future political standing and commercial opportunities in Asia and Australasia.'[42]

The extent to which such a situation did, indeed, develop during the fight against Japan has already been indicated in terms of the severe limitations imposed upon British policy-makers and military planners by their dependence on material assistance and political approval from the other side of the Atlantic.* Whether the question concerned broad strategic choices or the future of colonial territories in Southeast Asia, the American dimension loomed large, often overwhelmingly so. On Indian constitutional issues, strong pressure from the President himself in 1942 was turned back only by Churchill's private threat to resign.[43] As was noted in chapter four, when it came to arguing about whether to strive to reopen a land-bridge to China

* See above, 106.

through northern Burma, or to direct the efforts of S.E.A.C. ('Save England's Asiatic Colonies', in American parlance) south-eastwards towards Singapore, London, like British officers on the spot, frequently found itself at a marked disadvantage.[44] Over Siam, there could be no ignoring the mounting suspicions in Washington (suspicions that did not entirely lack foundation where Churchill, personally, was concerned) that Britain had designs on the territorial integrity and independent status of that country.[45] Just as the Foreign Office and others in London felt obliged to establish a high-level inter-departmental committee on American Opinion and the British Empire, and to pursue the possibility of a joint Anglo-American declaration on dependent territories,[46] so those officials who were concerned with China in particular were having to recognise that, as one of them summarised the situation in 1943,

'Comparing [her] foreign policy ... with her attitude of ten years earlier, nothing is more striking than her dependence on America and her acceptance of American leadership in her affairs ... On our side, because we are not in a position to do otherwise, we have accepted this condition and have abdicated from the position of leadership which we have occupied in China for the past hundred years ...'[47]

In broad terms (and detailed evidence for such a conclusion will be found in the author's *Allies of a Kind*), it can be said that, whereas on the American side of the transatlantic relationship the predominant conviction was that the two states and peoples were 'miles apart in Asia', in British official circles many genuinely believed – even aside, that is, from the exigencies of the war – that in the long view the interests of the two countries were compatible in the Far East in general and in China, for example, in particular. Considerable efforts were made to get American officials and their public to appreciate that British attitudes and policies regarding that area of the globe were not simply Churchillian; and the hope also continued to be entertained that, by providing an opportunity for standing shoulder to shoulder with the United States in what most Americans considered to be their major war, the final stages of the fight against Japan would offer 'a great opportunity of getting Anglo-American relations on to a new and healthier level'.[48] Yet all such aspirations and endeavours were repeatedly overshadowed by what the Far Eastern Department of the Foreign Office described as 'a steady deterioration in Anglo-American collaboration as regards that part of the world'. Far Eastern affairs, concluded the Washington Embassy, were 'chronically difficult as an element in Anglo-American relations', and as Halifax, the Ambassador, himself observed, 'when, for reasons of domestic politics or for the promotion of some private interest or doctrine, it appears expedient to belabour the British, attacks on our conduct of affairs in the Far East can be sure not only of popular acceptance but also of approval by a great number of individuals in the armed services and in Government departments'.[49]

Meanwhile, in terms of the leverage they were able to exert vis-à-vis the United States over Far Eastern affairs, the position of the French and the Dutch was much weaker still. Where France was concerned, not all de Gaulle's proud intransigence or the achievements of General Leclerc and his men in fighting the Germans could disguise that diminution of power and status that was reflected, for example, in her absence from the Conferences at Yalta and Potsdam.* Not recognised by Britain or the United States as the Provisional Government of their country until the autumn of 1944, the Committee of National Liberation were well aware that Roosevelt in particular not only blamed France generally for having come to terms with Japan over Indochina in 1940–1, but was determined to prevent her from recovering that territory when the war was over. (Churchill, while agreeing with the Foreign Office's opposition to this aspect of American policy, shied away from tackling the President on the subject.) And if there was the consolation, not available to the Dutch, for example, of knowing that French forces and administrators – at first loyal to Vichy, but increasingly ready to deal with de Gaulle's agents – remained present in Indochina itself, Paris was virtually helpless when, in March 1945, the Japanese suddenly attacked and decimated those French units, the survivors of which managed only with great difficulty to struggle to safety in a China which was itself suspected of harbouring designs on the colony's territory.† Even the Corps Léger d'Intervention which had been prepared for action in the Far East, and which was wanted by Mountbatten for operations within S.E.A.C., was dependent for its arrival on the provision of shipping that was ultimately controlled by Washington.[50]

As for the Dutch Government in exile in London, it quickly found itself after Pearl Harbor left on the fringes of Allied decision-making, the essentially Anglo-American character of which was exemplified by the

---

* Quite apart from the disaster of 1940 and the profound divisions within her body politic, France's loss of returns on her foreign investments, for example, was probably proportionately greater than it was for the U.K. (See Milward, *War, Economy and Society*, 350.) The war-time weakness of France did not, however, prevent the State Department in Washington, as well as the Foreign Office in London, from acknowledging privately in 1944–5 that she would again occupy an important place in international affairs once Germany had been defeated. See Thorne, *Allies*, 501.

† In seeking to move to Washington on this occasion, de Gaulle warned privately that, if the French public were to realise that the United States 'was against us' over Indochina, the result could be that France would be pushed into 'the Russian orbit' after the war.

'Arcadia' Conference in Washington in December 1941–January 1942. Understandably, this situation gave rise to considerable resentment among the Dutch, not least when, for example, they found themselves being presented early in 1942 with the fait accompli of an A.B.D.A. Command that embraced their own territory and their own forces in the Far East.[51] The establishment in both London and Washington of inter-Allied Pacific War Councils did nothing to change the realities of where power and decision-making were located. The London body was rapidly shown to be super-fluous; the meetings of its counterpart in Washington were not attended by the American Chiefs of Staff, and were presided over by Roosevelt who, in his own words, 'told stories and did most of the talking', and who, as the Australian representative put it, 'always avoided critical issues'. Nor was the promise that the Foreign Minister, van Kleffens, believed he had secured from the President: that the Dutch could participate in the deliber-ations of the Combined Chiefs of Staff when the Indies were being dis-cussed, even fulfilled.[52] Thus, although they strove to protect their country's interests through direct contacts with British and American ministers and officials, the Dutch Government were unable to influence, for example, the degree of strategic priority that was accorded an invasion of their Far Eastern colony. And as the war entered its final stages, they, too, were unable (despite the good-will of the British) to have the shipping allocations that essentially had been made by the U.S. Joint Chiefs so altered that they could convey their own forces to either the fighting zone in general or close to the East Indies in particular.[53] In this situation, strong demands in the Dutch Resistance press that the Netherlands should play a major role in freeing the Indies ('Wij moeten het doen') counted for nothing.[54]

Australia, meanwhile, was directly involved in the Far Eastern war to a much greater degree than either France or the Netherlands. Her forces, having taken part in the initial fighting in Southeast Asia, became a major element in MacArthur's South West Pacific command; her territory pro-vided the vital initial base from which MacArthur launched his drive through New Guinea towards the Philippines; her Prime Minister, Curtin, formed a close relationship with the General; her economy (especially her production of foodstuffs) played an important part in providing the resources needed for the fight against Japan. Yet for Australia, too (as for New Zealand; but the expectations, and hence disappointments, of Wellington were less than those of Canberra), the international politics of the Far Eastern war proved for the most part a matter for frustration.

Following the shock occasioned by the sinking of the *Prince of Wales* and *Repulse*, the belief rapidly spread among Australians, both within and outside official circles, that the British Government was grievously under-estimating the threat posed by Japan to the safety of their country, and that, in words which Curtin accepted for public use when drafted by an adviser, Australia must now 'look to America, free of any pangs as to [her] traditional links or kinship with the United Kingdom'. Curtin, indeed, as we have seen, continued as late as June 1942 to warn that Australia 'could be lost', and Evatt assaulted both London and Washington in person in an endeavour to obtain increased supplies of aircraft and other weapons.[55] Meanwhile, like the Dutch, Canberra found itself faced with the Anglo-American creation of the A.B.D.A. Command, and although the 'Germany-first' decision over Allied grand strategy was not in fact concealed from Australian representatives as Curtin and his colleagues were later to claim,[56] subsequent decisions at the Cairo and Potsdam Conferences were indeed taken without reference to Canberra's views. Such 'test cases', as the New Zealand High Commissioner in Australia summarised how Canberra perceived the Cairo episode, not only aroused widespread indignation but played a major part in bringing about the Australian-New Zealand Conferences of January and November 1944, at which both Governments sought to establish and defend their common interests.[57]

For both Dominions, too, the Pacific War Council in Washington, in which Evatt in particular had reposed considerable expectations, proved as we have seen to be no more than a talking shop. Moreover, Australian representatives in the American capital were able to obtain only limited access to key figures in the United States administration, and when such exchanges did take place they were always dominated by the inescapable contextual consideration of the superiority of American resources. Diplomats like Eggleston, who moved from Chungking to become Minister in Washington, and military liaison officers like Lt. General Sturdee, repeatedly conveyed in their letters home a sense of frustration over what they saw as American indifference to Australian representations.[58] (Roosevelt, for his part, preferred to see Canberra's preoccupations and demands registered and discussed in London.) Even within the South West Pacific Area itself, General Blamey, though C. in C. Land Forces, found himself unable to make headway against the determination of MacArthur and his sycophantic American staff to retain tight control of the planning and conduct of operations, not to speak of the attendant publicity.[59] The readiness of Curtin and of the influential Secretary of his Defence Department, Sir Frederick Shedden, to accept MacArthur's judgements wholesale helped ensure that, in the words of Dr Horner, 'the strategy to be employed for the defence of Australia was out of the hands of that country'.[60] Thereafter, as the Allied advance towards Japan's home islands gathered momentum, Australian forces were left by MacArthur to mop up by-passed enemy units in New Guinea – to the indignation of sections of their press and public. At the same time, the say of the Australian military in matters of strategy virtually disappeared altogether. 'It seems fantastic,' wrote one senior officer to Blamey, 'that [our country] should have no real voice in any major reorganisation or new plan in [the Pacific] theatre.'[61]

Even Curtin, for all his readiness to rely upon MacArthur's perception of strategic priorities, became greatly concerned in 1944 at the extent to which the United States was threatening to dominate post-war affairs in the Far East, to the detriment, as he saw it, of the British Commonwealth and Empire.[62] Yet here, too, the attempts he now made (together with Blamey's parallel endeavours in the field of strategy)[63] to increase Commonwealth cooperation, both as regards that particular part of the world and in general, bore little fruit. From the outset of the war against Japan, Australia had been able to make scarcely any more impression on the decision-making process in London than she had on Washington's. Churchill in particular continued, as an American report rightly observed, to 'offend the suscepti-bilities of the Dominions by forgetting that the British Empire had changed since Kipling's day'.[64]* Stanley Bruce, Australia's High Commissioner in London, had on several occasions in 1942 and '43 'very nearly reached breaking point', in his own words, as he strove in vain to obtain the information and the access to Cabinet meetings that would have enabled him at least to put forward his country's view on issues that were of direct concern to her. (Churchill, he concluded, as well as reducing many of his own colleagues to mere ciphers, 'just cannot understand the new status the Dominions have acquired'.)[65] Now, at the Commonwealth Prime Ministers' gathering in London in May 1944, and aided by Canada's desire not to appear to be combining with others against the U.S.A., Churchill paid little heed to Curtin's proposals for strengthening the machinery of on-going consultation within that group of states.[66] And although London did indeed take some notice of the separate discussions held by Australia in January and November of that year with New Zealand (for all that Wellington was much less inclined than Canberra to press the British Government to meet its wishes),[67] the reaction was largely one of raised eyebrows, blended with a degree of indignation when, following the second of their Conferences, the two Dominions, as we have seen, ventured publicly to propose a scheme for post-war trusteeships that would embrace all dependent territories.[68]

Indignation had been aroused in Washington, too, by the Agreement published by Australia and New Zealand after their January discussions – an 'Anzac Monroe Doctrine', the American Minister in Canberra called it.[69] The central issue involved was that of post-war security arrangements; and the exchanges that took place in this regard between the United States on the one hand and the two Dominions on the other will serve to illustrate the inter-Allied complications that could arise as a result of the attitudes and

* And see above, 40.

assumptions that were noted in the previous chapter in the context of
Western approaches to Far Eastern affairs in general.

Initially, Australia had been willing to negotiate with the United States
arrangements whereby the latter would secure the prolonged use of certain
strategic bases, notably the island of Manus in the Admiralty group to the
north of New Guinea. Canberra's attitude had cooled considerably,
however, when it became apparent that Washington for its part was not
ready to provide a pledge of post-war cooperation within some form of
regional defence scheme, and when the scant attention paid by American
officials and senior officers to Australian views regarding the conduct of the
war against Japan seemed to bode ill for the nature of future relations in
general. (Proposals concerning Manus that were put to Australia by the
U.S.A. shortly after the end of the war were to be described by the Minister
of Defence in Canberra as 'savouring of the kind of "suggestion" that one
might expect the U.S.S.R. to make to one of its satellites'.)[70] By 1944, both
Australia and New Zealand* were looking, therefore, to ensure their own
long-term use of island bases in the South- and South-West Pacific, together
with the establishment of what the Australian Defence Committee termed 'a
scheme of Imperial defence formulated and carried out by members of the
British Commonwealth in cooperation'.[71] The Australian delegation to the
January Conference also wanted it to be made clear that neither Dominion
would agree under any circumstances to the establishment in the islands
which between them they administered 'of a condominium with the United
States as a party'.[72] And although this overtly anti-American note was
slightly muted in the ensuing Agreement, there could be no mistaking the
target of that document's statement that the construction and use of
war-time bases did not provide the grounds on which a state could thereafter
claim sovereign rights over the territory in question. Hence, anger in
Washington.†

* Although direct friction over post-war bases did not arise to this extent between New
  Zealand and the U.S.A., Wellington, too, had to face questions about American attitudes in
  this sphere. As a policy survey in 1945 summarised it: 'New Zealand is a "consumer" not a
  "producer" of security. It is the United States which will produce security in the Pacific. How
  can New Zealand ensure that she will receive military support from the United States? Do we
  regard the United States as aggressive and imperialist? If we do not, is it in New Zealand's
  interests to encourage her to take responsibility in the Pacific? What attitude should we take
  to the U.S. claim for bases?' 'New Zealand as a Pacific Country', paper (n.d.) received in the
  Prime Minister's Dpt., 3 Dec. 1945, NZ Ext, Affs. files, 56/1/1 part 2.
† The two Dominions were also forthrightly opposed to Roosevelt's wish to see France
  deprived of her Far Eastern colonies. (Thorne, *Allies*, 64, 259, 365, 469; agenda discussions
  for the January 1944 Australia-New Zealand Conference, NZ Ext. Affs. files, 153/19/4 part
  1.) New Zealand, for its part, declined to join Australia in seeking to have Britain's Solomon
  Islands territories taken over by the two of them. Nor were there to be found in Wellington
  those covetous notions regarding the Dutch East Indies that were being entertained by Evatt
  among others in Canberra. See Thorne, 'Engeland, Australië en Nederlands Indië,
  1941–1945', loc cit.

American exchanges with Australia and New Zealand can also be used to illustrate the inter-Allied dimension of the second policy area that was outlined in chapter six in terms of Western approaches to Asian affairs: that of economic interests and goals. We have seen above how, during the war years, the United States significantly increased its financial and commercial role in Australia. Indeed, Bruce in London joined the High Commissioners of the other Dominions in 1942 in expressing disquiet regarding what they saw as 'the economic imperialism of American business interests, which is quite active under the cloak of a benevolent and avuncular international-ism'.[73] (The activities within Australia of certain U.S. Army officers who were businessmen in private life served to heighten such suspicions.)[74] Both Canberra and Wellington, moreover, while waiting for the United States to remove its quotas on agricultural and dairy products, found themselves under pressure from Washington during the war in this same field of commercial policy. The removal of imperial preferences and tariff arrangements was of course a goal which Hull in particular was seeking to achieve in his dealings with London. (Roosevelt had weakened somewhat on this point when agreeing the text of the Atlantic Charter with Churchill in 1941, but Article 7 of the 1942 Mutual Aid Agreement, which governed Lend Lease, embodied the aim nonetheless.)[75] The two Pacific Dominions, also, were naturally targets for the Secretary of State's multilateralist crusade. In addition, however, they were the object of American resentment and demands arising from the most-favoured-nation tariff treatment that they had accorded various other countries, but not the United States. ('A very unfavourable impression' would be created among the American people, the New Zealand Prime Minister was informed, if this anomaly were to result in New Zealand tenders for civilian equipment being placed with another country because of the higher duties paid on such goods entering from the United States.)[76]

Canberra – unlike Wellington – did concede most-favoured-nation status to its American ally during the war. It did not, however, conclude with Washington the comprehensive trade agreement that the latter sought in a long series of negotiations between the two, nor would it agree that virtually all the raw materials and foodstuffs that Australia was exporting to the U.S.A. should be treated as reverse Lend Lease. The two countries did provide each other with considerable amounts of war-time aid,* but in their mutual dealings each had its eye on post-war economic objectives that were

---

* Estimates vary, depending partly on the rate of exchange employed (see Bell, *Unequal Allies*, 118ff.) By one calculation, U.S. aid to Australia totaled U.S. $1,570 million, that of Australia to the U.S. $1,041 million. Australia received less than 6 per cent of the U.S. Lend Lease aid supplied to the Commonwealth as a whole, but furnished about 12 per cent of the Commonwealth's reverse aid, much of it in the form of foodstuffs, above all for American troops in the South West Pacific Area.

in several respects in conflict with the other's. Australia sought to increase its
dollar holdings, to diversify its economy and to expand its secondary
industries; America to make major and lasting inroads into the Australian
market and to obtain from Canberra a pledge of support for a multilateral
international economic order. With Britain's unwillingness to undertake
binding commitments during the war over the issues surrounding Article 7
providing Curtin and his colleagues with an added reason for sidestepping
Washington's advances, Australian-American exchanges in this field 'both
reflected and accentuated the economic tension and friction between the
two powers'. As Roger Bell concludes in his survey of the subject, 'neither
country was prepared to grant trade concessions which threatened to
undermine its . . . post-war foreign economic objectives'.[77]

Nowhere did inter-Allied strains show up more clearly, however, than in
the fields of propaganda and political warfare, and in respect of those
contrasting American and European approaches to the issue of colonial
territories that were noted earlier. On the American side, there were of
course those engaged in the preparation and dissemination of such material
who were ready to acknowledge in private that their fellow-countrymen
knew 'very little about the British Empire and its colonial aspects', and that
'myth' and 'tradition' played their part in the 'strong anti-British sentiment'
that pervaded American attitudes on such matters.[78] There also tended to
be some discrimination as among the European colonial powers, with the
French record in Indochina usually receiving outright condemnation, [79] and
the Dutch being credited with laudable reforming intentions regarding the
East Indies, where the bulk of the population were expected to accept the
return of colonial rule.[80] Distinctions were made, too, in terms of political
movements among the Asian peoples themselves. In India, for example, the
Congress was identified as the crucial target for U.S. propaganda since it
'predominated in shaping public opinion', while 'the Muslims, . . . a very
strategic group', needed 'to be won away from Pakistan'. Or again, where
Burma was concerned, an O.S.S. survey in 1944 is to be found asserting that
'the dictatorial Ba Maw clique, the Thakins, and known Japanese agents
must of course be removed'.[81]

Overwhelmingly, however, the approach of American officials – those in
the State Department, the Office of War Information in Washington, and
the O.W.I. political-warfare station on the West coast, as well as O.W.I.,
O.S.S. and other personnel on the spot in India, China and within S.E.A.C.
– was based on the conviction not simply that Asian colonial peoples wished
to see the backs of their European masters, but that the presence and
policies of those European powers had been iniquitous in the first place.
Further central beliefs were that Japanese propaganda among Asian populations could be countered only if the latter's laudable desire for indepen-

dence was accorded positive acknowledgement, and that it was essential from the point of view of American interests to distance the United States from the aforesaid Europeans in Asian eyes.

The resulting blend of instincts and considerations ensured that, in India and Southeast Asia, members of William Donovan's Office of Strategic Services, in the words of the major study of that organisation, 'vied with O.W.I. representatives to see who could pour the most scorn on the undemocratic principles of their British, French and Dutch allies ...',[82] while in the United States itself, Elmer Davis and his O.W.I. officials 'made no secret', reported a British mission, 'of the fact that they wanted to see us thrown out of our Far Eastern colonies for good and all'.[83]

Confidential American analyses and papers for the guidance of political warfare sought to alert operatives in the field to the pitfalls with which the entire issue was surrounded. In broadcasts directed towards the Vietnamese, for example, it was important to 'avoid the use of the phrase "French Indochina"'; likewise, the term 'British' Malaya should not be employed when describing a territory where, as the O.S.S.'s Psychological Warfare Division saw it, America's needs for access to strategic raw materials, as well as her sympathy for the native peoples, could lead to friction between Washington and London after the war. In India (where, the O.S.S. judged, Bose – 'an able leader widely considered to be a sincere patriot' – would have 'little difficulty in persuading even the hesitant that an opportunity was at hand to drive [out] the British' if he succeeded in making a re-entry), it was vital 'not ... to identify our cause with British policies'.

Small wonder, then, that Mountbatten's attempts to integrate Allied political warfare agencies within S.E.A.C. were repeatedly thwarted, or that the Head of the Foreign Office's Far Eastern Department in London was led to conclude during the final stages of the war: 'The Americans are virtually conducting political warfare against us in the Far East and are seeking not only to belittle the efforts which we have hitherto made in that theatre of war, but also to keep us in a humiliating and subsidiary role for the future.' For his part, Roosevelt entertained equally strong views on what he saw as the intransigent and anachronistic selfishness of London's own approach to colonial issues. In private he once observed in this context: 'We will have more trouble with Great Britain after the war than we are having with Germany now.'[84]

*

If doubts such as these concerning the suitability of one another's position and policies regarding Far Eastern matters helped cloud the future, as well as sour current relations, for the Western Allies a further question regarding the war and its likely outcome in that part of the world became the subject of increasing attention during the second half of the conflict: what part could and would the Soviet Union play, both in the fight against Japan and in the shaping of the peace thereafter?

Attitudes in the West on this subject varied considerably, of course, depending in part on the way in which an individual or group viewed the Soviet Union and its professed ideology in general terms, and in part, also, on the varying overall state of relations with Moscow, alluded to earlier in this chapter.* (Interestingly, some of the perceptions involved continued to reflect the notion which we observed in the context of the inter-war years:† that the Bolshevik Revolution had entailed the re-emergence of an essentially 'Asiatic' Russian identity; and politicians and officials in the West quite often referred to Stalin in private as 'Oriental' when they found him difficult or menacing. Ironically, Japanese leaders, too, when, as we shall see below, they sought in adversity to convince themselves that they could find understanding and diplomatic assistance in Moscow, were wont to remind one another that the Soviet Union was, after all, an 'Asiatic' state.)[85]

Even so, in terms of the conflict against Japan, opinion in the West was overwhelmingly favourable to the idea of full Russian involvement. Much satisfaction and anticipation was engendered in official circles by Stalin's promise to Cordell Hull in October 1943 that he would, indeed, bring his country into the Far Eastern war once Germany had been defeated, and American military planners in particular began to think in terms of, for example, the use of bases in the Soviet Maritime Provinces for bombing the enemy's home islands. In London, too, as well as Washington, a considerable over-estimation of the strength of Japan's Kwantung Army in Manchuria led to the conclusion that Soviet military assistance in the final drive against the enemy would be invaluable, for all that such a prospect was helping to diminish the significance of the British, as well as the Chinese, contribution in American eyes.[86] Officials in the Foreign Office, like some in the State Department, also acknowledged that post-war developments in Manchuria and Korea, especially, would depend to a considerable extent on Moscow's policies in East Asia,[87] and Churchill went out of his way at both Yalta and Potsdam to emphasise to Stalin his readiness to see an increased Soviet military and naval presence in that part of the world.[88]

But, as we noted in chapter four, it was Roosevelt, of course, who at Yalta agreed to the price that Stalin was asking in return for waging war against the Japanese – and agreed it, indeed, without prior reference to the Chinese nationalists who would have to do the paying. (The shock to Mao Tse-tung and his colleagues was probably as great, if not greater.) The Chungking

* See above, 213–4.
† See above, 58.

Government was left with little option but to sign with Moscow in August 1945 an agreement which ratified the concessions which the latter had won from the President regarding ports and railways in Manchuria, together with the status of Outer Mongolia,[89] in exchange for a pledge that the Soviet Government would deal only with their Nationalist regime as the legitimate authority in China. This last treaty, moreover, was widely hailed in the Western press as entailing the abandonment by the Soviet Union of support for the Chinese Communists and as foreshadowing a stable East Asia. It was, declared the *New York Times*, 'a victory for peace as great as any scored on the battlefield', with the U.S.S.R. becoming 'a partner in America's traditional policy toward China'.[90]* Likewise, a wide range of newspapers in the West had long looked forward to a declaration of war against the Japanese by Moscow, not simply for the immediate military benefits which such a move would bring, but, as *Le Monde*, for one, argued, for the increased solidarity it would contribute to the United Nations as the victorious coalition prepared to shape the peace. 'In no way can Russia demonstrate more positively her community of interest with Britain and America,' declared the *Sydney Morning Herald* in July 1945, 'than by joining them in the overthrow of [Japan].'[91]†

Yet well before this was being written, as we have seen, a significant number of American officials had come to view the Soviet Union as a threat, rather than as a potential ally, in the Far East, and were shaping their arguments regarding the future of Korea and of European colonial territories in the region accordingly. And in the months following the Yalta Conference, the reservations which Eden and Cadogan, as members of the British delegation, had expressed there concerning the proposed deal with Stalin over his entry into the war against Japan[92] were repeated more vigorously by men like Stimson and Grew in Washington, doubly so once it became known that the atomic bomb would be ready for use against the enemy. Yet even then, discussions over whether to renege on the agreement that the late President had reached with Stalin had to come back to an acknowledgement of an inescapable fact: that, whatever the United States might do, the Soviet Union could invade Manchuria at a time of its own choosing, and once over the border could oblige the Chinese to accept its terms. As Admiral William Leahy, assistant to the President, summed up the position as both he and Truman saw it in the middle of July 1945, a Sino-Soviet agreement could be reached 'only ... through radical con-

---

* The *Bombay Chronicle* (August 13, 1945) also argued that the terms of the treaty were such that 'in the actual circumstances, there could have been nothing more satisfying for China and Asia'.

† From its fiercely anti-Soviet standpoint, the *Chicago Tribune*, too, had long been arguing (e.g., edition of August 6, 1944) that for the Russians not to be fighting Japan amounted to disgraceful backsliding on their part.

cessions by China', while Stalin for his part would 'enter the war whether or not such concessions are made and will thereafter satisfy Soviet demands regardless of what the Chinese attitude may be'.[93]

It was a situation that brought Washington face to face with one of the major limitations on its policies towards the Far East, already noted in the context of the pre-war years: the United States was not an East Asian power, whereas the Soviet Union, like China and Japan, was. And for the Japanese, too, in these last months of the war, wishful thinking ran up against the geopolitical realities obtaining at the time – realities which, in Central Europe also, were going some way at least towards vindicating the belief of Halford Mackinder, expressed long before, that control of the heart of the Eurasian land-mass, and not (as Mahan had argued) naval capacity, held the key to power in the international arena.[94] The hope entertained by certain senior figures in Tokyo as the course of the fighting moved strongly against their country, that they could 'utilise the Soviet Union to improve the situation' (that is, that they might at least prevent the U.S.S.R. from joining the ranks of their enemies, and possibly obtain Stalin's good offices for a negotiated peace with the Western powers), foundered on the inherent strength of the Soviet position in the East once the Red Army had triumphed in the West, quite apart from the pledges that Moscow had given to its partners in that other war.[95]*

The question of how to regard and approach the Soviet Union formed an important element in war-time relations between Japan and its ally, Germany.† In 1944, Tokyo returned to the suggestion that it had already placed before its Nazi friends between the autumn of 1941 and spring of 1942: that they should reach a settlement with Moscow that would put an end to the fighting on that front. And, unhesitatingly, Berlin rejected such a notion (as did Moscow itself), Ribbentrop for one returning after Stalingrad to the counter-proposal he had urged previously: that Japan herself, rather,

---

* Tokyo sought also to negotiate with Moscow over such issues as the ownership of North Sakhalin, fishing rights, and the Soviet-Manchukuo border. As the price for continuing Soviet neutrality and the employment of Moscow's good offices with the West, Japanese officials were ready to offer concessions over the Chinese Eastern Railway, South Sakhalin, the northern Kurile islands, and spheres of influence in Manchuria. Ironically, Stalin, for his part, had briefly sought the 'mediation' of Japan when faced with the shock of Germany's attack in June 1941. (Erickson, *The Road to Stalingrad*, 125.) On the extent to which he had thereafter felt able to transfer forces from the Far East to the German front once he was sure Japan was going to strike southwards, see ibid, 237–9.

† There also existed, of course, a relationship of a kind between Japan and Fascist Italy, in which the latter looked uneasily upon what in 1942 seemed as if it might become a Japanese advance towards Africa; but nevertheless, for example, supported Tokyo's suggestion (dismissed by Berlin) that in areas like the Ukraine territories conquered by the Axis might be allowed a degree of autonomous existence. Italy also, like Vichy France, agreed at Japan's request to surrender its treaty rights in China to the collaborationist Nanking regime in that country in February 1943. See e.g. Meskill, *Hitler and Japan*, 106, 122.

having failed thus far to create any form of diversion or dissuasion to check the movement of Russian forces to the German front, should now make amends by setting upon the Soviet Union from the East.[96] We have noted in an earlier chapter* how tenuous was the relationship between the two states in terms of the strategic conduct of the war (including the supply of strategic raw materials). The same was true of their political dealings with each other.†
Although they agreed, for example, in January 1942 on the 70 degrees East line of longitude as the boundary between their respective operations in the Indian Ocean area, Berlin made clear to Tokyo that it did not regard that division as setting limits to the Wehrmacht's drive eastwards on the Eurasian land-mass, nor as a demarcation that had implications of a political kind.

Indeed, just as Japan, on her side, concealed from her partner the extent of the losses she had sustained in the battles of the Coral Sea and Midway, for example, so the Germans took care not to reveal to Tokyo the extent of their ambitions vis-à-vis the Soviet Union.[97] Berlin also adopted for some time a markedly reserved attitude regarding the extent and nature of Japan's Coprosperity Sphere (or 'area', as the Germans preferred to call it), wishing to retain the ability and right to conduct its own, direct dealings with other countries in that part of the world, just as Japan for her part chose to maintain a number of diplomatic missions in Europe. And although an agreement was reached in January 1943 which defined the respective 'New Orders' of the two countries as embracing those areas then effectively under their control, it remained apparent, as it had done when Bose was in Berlin, that Germany was not prepared to commit itself where the future of India, in particular, was concerned.[98] Exchanges between the two were not entirely barren. (An understanding was reached, for example, over the matter of German business concerns in Manchukuo and China, and some cooperation was achieved regarding Vichy and Portuguese interests in the Far East.)[99] But the essentially sterile and limited nature of the relationship as a whole serves to show up the richness that is to be found within the combination of states and peoples opposing Japan, notwithstanding the tensions, disagreements and rivalries that existed there also.

*

Germany's capitulation in the early summer of 1945 evoked scorn as well as dismay in Japan. This breaking of the agreement between the two countries that neither should conclude a separate peace demonstrated, it was sugges-

---

* See above, 104.
† Relations were not helped by the distrust which the Japanese came to entertain for the German Ambassador in Tokyo until late 1942, Eugen Ott, nor by the belief in Tokyo that their own Ambassador in Berlin throughout the war, General Oshima Hiroshi, was excessively and uncritically pro-German, and out of touch with the situation in Japan itself.

ted, that the Germans were wanting in that *bushido* tradition wherein lay the greatness of the Japanese themselves. Comparisons were even drawn in this respect between Hitler's Government and that of Badoglio which had surrendered Italy twenty months earlier.[100] Policy-makers in Tokyo had in any case not identified their quintessentially Japanese regime with that of their European partners at any stage during the war.[101] The Nazis, for their part, while seeking to remove from their literature references to 'the yellow peril' and such-like that would offend their Asian allies, and while admiring the fighting qualities the latter were displaying, had not abandoned those central racial beliefs by which they were marked down as a lesser species. For Hitler, the Japanese remained 'always inferior to us on the cultural level', possessing 'no affinities' with the German people, and he continued to be somewhat ambivalent regarding their triumphs at the expense of the British Empire. (The conservative German diplomat, Ulrich von Hassell, likewise saw Japan's victories as 'deplorable from a higher European viewpoint'.)[102]

The gulf that separated the Japanese from their German friends in these respects needs to be borne in mind when we turn to look at some of the mutual images that existed during the war among Japan's enemies. We have already noted, of course, certain aspects of such inter-Allied perceptions in a number of political contexts: the incorrigible imperialist instincts and predilection for international scheming which many Americans saw as inherent in, for example, the British and French. But what of each other's societies? What of other Allied peoples within their own bodies-politic, and not simply within the international arena?

As in many other respects, obviously, it is often impossible in this connection to separate the context of the Far Eastern war from that of the Second World War as a whole. It is also impossible to do justice to the number, range and complexity of the images that were involved, and no more than a selection of themes and illustrations will be offered in what follows. The point to be repeated at the outset, however, and especially so in the light of those elements of disillusionment and dislike that will be referred to below, is that in comparision with the ties which existed between Japan and Germany, those within the Allied side were in overall terms close and rich. Indeed, the very sense of kinship that continued to exist within, say, Anglo-American or Anglo-Australian relations was itself in part accountable for the exasperation and acerbity that was manifested on occasions.

If it was the war against Germany that brought American servicemen to Britain, there to join those Dutch, French and others who were in exile from their homes on the continent of Europe, it was the Far Eastern conflict that was mainly responsible for greatly increasing contacts between Australians and New Zealanders on the one hand and Americans (and, to a lesser extent, Dutch) on the other. And during 1942 especially, when there existed both a common sense of having to face adversity and, in many quarters, relief at possessing the support of others in those circumstances, attitudes of a markedly warm and appreciative kind were widely expressed. If for many Americans, for example, the British were still endowed with at least some of the lustre they had won when they stood alone against Germany in 1940–1,* for the British themselves the arrival among them of American forces was an event that *The Times*, for one, believed, made them feel 'stronger not only physically but even more in spirit'.[103] And the same newspaper argued that 'the foundations of the future' would be 'well and truly laid' if British and Americans alike could 'seize this opportunity to sit down together round the same hearth' and learn of life in each other's country.[104] 'The attitudes of both press and politicians in England toward America,' concluded a confidential O.S.S. survey, 'have been models of friendly cooperation.'[105]

Initial enthusiasm of this kind – nowhere greater than in Australia when MacArthur arrived there from the Philippines in March 1942† – was often accompanied by special efforts to inform domestic audiences about the history and special qualities of this or that new ally. Thus the *Daily Express* in London began in July 1942 a series of features on 'Rediscovering America', followed by another entitled 'Meet the Americans', reinforcing the articles with a list of 'dos and don'ts' that readers should bear in mind when talking to these visitors.[106] Likewise, American troops proceeding abroad were usually given copies of specially-prepared surveys of the country and people awaiting them – surveys that were laudatory in nature and which, while alerting G.I.s to what they would find unfamiliar when they arrived, tended to emphasise the underlying similarities between the two

---

* This lustre had by no means entirely faded away in some American eyes, even later in the war. In August, 1943, for example, Harold Ickes, the U.S. Secretary of the Interior, emerged from a showing of a film on the Battle of Britain 'with renewed and intense admiration for the British'. (Ickes diary, August 1 1943) Or again, the journalist Raymond Clapper was reporting home in 1943 that the British people were taking 'all the inconveniences' of war 'much more in their stride' than were his fellow-Americans. (Material in Clapper Papers, box 37.) In Australia and New Zealand, meanwhile, reference was made more frequently still to the way in which, as the Wellington *Standard*, for one, saw it, 'the people of Britain have shown they can take it' (issue of February 26, 1942) – this in the context of calling for an equally unflinching stance on the part of the Dominion in question.

† 'At last,' declared the *Sydney Morning Herald* (March 19, 1942), 'we have found a man to lead all the Allied forces into battle – a tough, capable, hard-hitting fighting man, who has taken the measure of the Japanese and given them the only thorough beating they have suffered in three and a half months of war . . . The name of MacArthur has been as a shining light to the Allies. His coming surely spells the end of retreatism [sic] on the Pacific Front . . .' The New Zealand *Standard* (March 26, 1942) likewise depicted MacArthur as 'the Napoleon of Luzon'.

peoples.* And in the same fashion, Australian servicemen embarking for the United States, whilst being warned to say nothing that would add to the widespread (and 'false') American distrust of the English, were informed that they would find when they reached their destination 'one of the most hospitable people in the world, with a very soft spot for Australians. They feel,' the pamphlet added, 'that we are the same type of people as themselves, with similar outlook and ideals, and with fighting qualities remembered from the last war and proved again in this.'[107]

This notion of an essential identity of character and values between the societies concerned also formed an important element of the publicity campaigns conducted by Australia and New Zealand in the United States itself. 'We are a people very much like yourselves,' the Australian Minister to the U.S. assured a radio audience there, 'friendly, self-reliant, independent-minded, not much concerned with the old-world formalities of life.'[108]† 'Australians,' declared their Prime Minister in a message to the New York magazine *Liberty*, 'have found new kinship with their first cousins from America. It is a kinship born of grim purpose and endeavour, coupled with a ... liking of men ... who think like us, talk like us, and fight like us.'[109] And in a broadcast from Washington, the New Zealand Minister there informed his listeners that his fellow-countrymen

> 'value the same things in life as Americans cherish. New Zealand shares with America youth and freedom and a democratic outlook. In both countries, the influence of similar political traditions and a similar pioneering environment has given rise to social attitudes and to cultural values that have much in common.'[110]

---

* For example, the American Council of the I.P.R.'s pamphlet No. 7: W.L. Holland and P.E. Lilienthal, *Meet The Anzacs!*: 'The Anzac's fight is our fight. Their ideas on how to run the war are close to our own ... American soldiers in Australia are finding that the Australian way of life is fundamentally much like their own, although there are many superficial differences ... There is an engaging breeziness about the average Australian which is likely to appeal to the free and easy American ... Australia had its "New Deal" many years ago ..., although most Australians are decided individualists and believers in the advantages of private enterprise ... No one of the thirty-five United Nations is applying itself more wholeheartedly to the task of beating the Axis than New Zealand.' For an anthropologist's comments on the problems involved in such intermingling, and on her own endeavours regarding Anglo-American relations in this respect, see Margaret Mead, 'The Application of Anthropological Techniques to Cross-National Communication', in *Anthropology: A Human Science*.

† A certain distancing of Australia from Britain in such publicity directed towards Americans was sometimes less subtly achieved. The Bishop of Goulburn, for example, in a message of April 1942 sent for publication in the U.S.A., observed: 'We feel that Europe has made such a mess of things that the awe and reverence ... we felt when confronted with those trained in the great cultures of the world ... are no longer justified ... [But] we like your language, your freshness of expression, your energy and speed in action. Above all, we are rejoicing in stories about the way your men have been walking through our red tape.' Curtin Papers, correspondence, CP 156/1.

The remarkable extent to which the British authorities, too, sought to monitor American opinion and to present before it a favourable image of their own country has been detailed elsewhere by the present writer and others, as have Dutch efforts in the same direction.[111] Where Britain was concerned, the figure of Churchill, for all his forthright imperialist views, had an enormous appeal for many in the United States ('so deeply loved in this country', as the *New York Times* saw it in 1942, 'and so long since adopted as our own'),[112] just as he remained the epitome of defiance for Europeans living under German rule. The individual whose appeal went widest among the Allied peoples (and beyond), however, especially in relation to the hope of creating after the war a new international order, was Roosevelt: not only a truly great man, declared *Le Populaire* on his death, but 'a citizen of the world'; 'trusted as a friend', as *The Standard* saw it from Wellington when he was re-elected in November 1944, 'to bring into being a better world by curbing the activities of those who would stay the march of progress'; 'irreplaceable in the councils of the United Nations', in the eyes of the *Sydney Morning Herald*, and, for Churchill and well-nigh all his fellow-countrymen, 'the greatest American friend we have ever known'.[113]

Yet one has only to recall, for example, Roosevelt's own attitude towards France (and to de Gaulle and his colleagues in particular) during the war, together with the resentment and distrust that flowed in the opposite direction,[114] to be reminded that the coalition ranged against Japan was made up of states and societies that not only – and inevitably – possessed separate, and sometimes conflicting, interests, but that entertained very mixed perceptions of one another. 'We discussed America almost as an enemy,' noted one Foreign Office official privately in 1942 following a meeting held in Eden's room, while another senior figure observed in Whitehall 'an anti-American prejudice' which he attributed to 'the jealousy of the old British governing class at the "passing of power"'. Both in private and in public, American Congressmen and officials from their side accused Britain of abusing Lend Lease supplies for her own selfish political and commercial purposes. 'To hear some people talk about the British,' recorded Harry Hopkins in Washington in August 1945, 'you would think [they] were our potential enemies.'[115]

Inevitably, the relative contribution that was being made to the Allied war effort by this or that people was a subject that was approached within widely differing frameworks of reference, with equally differing opinions emerging in consequence. Asked by the Gallup Poll organisation in the summer of 1942 which of the United Nations had up till then done most towards the achievement of victory, the response of the British sample (50 per cent for the Soviet Union, 42 per cent for Britain itself, 5 per cent for China, and only 3 per cent for the U.S.A.) stood in marked contrast to that of its American counterpart (55 per cent for their own country, 32 per cent for the Soviet Union, only 9 per cent for Britain, and – especially interesting – a mere 4 per cent for China).[116] Nor did the closer contact between the two peoples, so welcomed when the G.I.s first began to arrive in Britain in 1942, always produce the hoped-for results. Mass Observation surveys conducted in 1943 suggested that the Dutch* and the Czechs were the most popular of the Allies among the British, only one-third of those questioned giving a favourable opinion of Americans, who were less well spoken of than Italians once Mussolini had fallen from power.[117] And as regards the Far Eastern war in particular, much resentment was to be occasioned in both S.E.A.C. and Britain (though this was very late in the day) by the appearance of the Warner Brothers film, *Objective Burma*, in which Errol Flynn, armoured in 'American derring-do', well-nigh single-handedly thrust the Japanese towards defeat in the jungles of Southeast Asia.[118]

Where the Far Eastern conflict was concerned, however, perhaps the most signal disappointment of those early hopes that the war would provide the setting for rediscovered kinship and mutual affection came in regard to relations between the Americans and the Australians. Behind the necessary rhetoric of solidarity, senior United States representatives in Australia itself, for example, were not finding a great deal to admire in the people of that country as they faced the test of the threat from Japan. Rather, their letters and despatches home tended to emphasise what they saw as a lack of self-reliance, balance and dignity.

> 'The average Australian,' wrote the U.S. Naval Attaché in Melbourne, 'has no conceptions of the limitations of his country . . . The standard of honesty of the people is of a low order . . . The morale of the people ebbs and flows with the war news and the proximity of operations to the Australian continent.'[119]

The American Minister in Canberra, Nelson T. Johnson (who was well-regarded by Curtin: the Prime Minister wrote of him: 'I feel I cannot exaggerate the value of [his] work in Australia. This country is deeply indebted to him'), was frequently communicating with Washington in a similar vein. Australia, as he saw it early in 1942, had 'lived like a parasite on the body of the [British] Empire', but was now seeking to 'transfer its parasitic life from the United Kingdom to the United States'. The Australian, he added, 'seems to expect us to do everything for him, fight for him, work for him', and appeared to find it 'extremely difficult . . . to see much beyond his surfing beaches'. Australian businessmen were 'selling strategic

---

* Mountbatten's Chief of Staff wrote privately: 'Of all our allies in this war, the Dutch are the most cooperative and reliable,' a Foreign Office official in London adding in the margin: 'Hear hear!' See Thorne, *Allies*, 460, 614.

goods to the United States at prices far above those which they could get in Australia, or out of the British Empire'; Australian politicians savaged one another behind their backs; politicians and people alike were incapable of acknowledging or rejoicing in America's own great achievements in the Pacific. ('The Department may be surprised to know,' wrote Johnson in June 1944, 'that the Legation has no record of even so much as a telephone call of congratulations from any official or private Australian following on the news of an American victory.')[120]

The nature and extent of war-time labour disputes in Australia, which will be indicated in a later chapter,* gave rise to particularly bitter American comment, especially when the flow of vital war materials through the docks was held up in consequence. Australian stevedores, noted one senior U.S. officer, were 'turbulent, shiftless and completely out of control of the civilian authorities'. Their behaviour, wrote Johnson to a senior official in the State Department, was 'scandalous'.[121] Australia's image was further tarnished in American eyes by the inability of its Government to send conscripted members of its armed forces (known as the Militia, as distinct from the volunteer Australian Imperial Force) out of the country, or later (when Curtin had succeeded, after fierce debate, in passing new legislation on the subject in February 1943) beyond a 'South West Pacific Zone' that encompassed only a part of MacArthur's entire South West Pacific Area. (The 'absurdity' of a situation in which 'the Australian "draftee"' could 'fight . . . in the eastern half of Java and not in the western' was ascribed in one of the more restrained and understanding American surveys of the subject to the inevitable continuation into the war years of 'the political and economic tensions of peace-time society'.)[122]

Nor did the actual companionship in arms of Australians and Americans in New Guinea† enhance, on balance, the standing of the former in the minds of senior figures in the United States itself. Although British observers on the spot were describing the Australians taking part in that campaign as 'first-class fighting men' (and the Americans as 'very poor indeed'), MacArthur's own conclusion was that they 'would not fight'. And

---

* See below, 266.

† Among other instances of inter-Allied strains arising from partnership on the field of battle was the mutual recrimination between British and Australians during and after the Japanese advance in Malaya. The Australian commander, Lt. General Gordon Bennett, was scathing about the performances of certain British and Indian units. Conversely, looting, drunkenness and desertion on the part of small numbers of Australian troops drew sharp British comments – as did the behaviour of Bennett himself, when he abandoned his men and escaped to Australia before the surrender of Singapore. (See e.g. Horner, *High Command*, 168ff., and Montgomery, *Shenton of Singapore*, 135. A copy of the subsequent Australian Court of Enquiry into Bennett's behaviour is in the Blamey Papers, for example, file 170.4.) The Australians, wrote the British Chief of Staff of the ill-fated ABDA Command in February 1942, 'are the most egotistical, conceited people imaginable'. Bond, ed., *Chief of Staff*, entry for 25 February 1942.

his view (shorn of any discrimination between the greatly differing A.I.F. and Militia units) was adopted and passed on in private to others in Washington by Roosevelt himself, seconded by the Commander of the U.S. Army Air Force, General 'Hap' Arnold, when the latter returned from a visit to the South West Pacific. The Australians, echoed Stimson in his diary, 'would not fight. As MacArthur put it, they were not good in the field, they were not good in the jungle, and they came from the slums of cities in Australia and they had no fighting spirit.' MacArthur, the President told his Cabinet in October 1942, had allowed credit to go to Australian forces in New Guinea simply in order to 'bolster their morale', whereas in reality they had been 'rescued by the Americans'. Harold Ickes, too, recorded Roosevelt as describing the Australian forces in the field as 'no better than the State militia we used to have . . ., badly trained and none too brave . . . The Japs literally chased them running down the . . . mountain . . . near Port Moresby. Then MacArthur sent in some American troops.' Australian generals, Ickes added, were apparently 'no better than State militia generals here in the past', while one U.S. Army general on the spot urged that no American troops should be placed under the control of MacArthur's land commander, Blamey, whom he described as 'a non-professional Australian drunk'.[123]

Australian views on the military prowess of some of their American partners were very similar. They 'could not be classified as attack troops', wrote Blamey himself to Curtin with reference to U.S. units engaged in the bitter fighting that took place around Buna in New Guinea. 'They are definitely not equal to the Australian Militia, and from the moment they met opposition sat down and have hardly gone a yard.'[124] The poor quality of the officers in U.S. Army units also tended to be singled out by Australian observers. Thus the Liaison Officer attached to the U.S. Army at Buna reported: 'I never heard a [G.I.] say a good word about a single officer . . . The American officers treated their men as cattle. There seemed to be no sense of responsibility for the welfare of the men.'[125]* Australian commanders also came to resent what they saw as MacArthur's attempts, encouraged by his 'Bataan-gang' American staff officers, to shift the blame for his misjudgements (and in New Guinea they were, indeed, serious) onto Australian shoulders, and to ensure that the credit for all successes was essentially his alone.[126]

Some American commanders in the area, notably General Robert Eichelberger – who himself had to take the greatest care not to appear to be

---

* Detailed surveys by the U.S. Army's own Information and Education Division showed a high percentage of soldiers responding in the affirmative to the proposition: 'Most officers put their own welfare above the welfare of enlisted men.' Stouffer et al., *The American Soldier: Adjustment During Army Life*, 227 and cap. 8.

stealing any of MacArthur's limelight – were eventually able, in cooperation with Australian colleagues, to reduce the inter-Allied friction and distrust that had come to surround the New Guinea campaign.[127]* They could not remove, however, what a report by the Australian Army's Military Intelligence Branch described as 'a general hostility towards Americans [that] is unfortunately widespread among Australian troops and is partly caused by the attitude of superiority frequently affected by U.S. soldiers themselves'. The report also attributed friction and open clashes between the two sets of servicemen inside Australia itself in part to those contrasting rates of pay that have already been illustrated and that contributed to the 'successes' of the Americans with Australian women;† in part, also, to the 'jeering' of American soldiers at Australians not in the A.I.F. that they were 'staying at home when better men were fighting their battles'; in part, again, to a 'lack of discipline, especially self-discipline, on the part of some Australian troops'. There was, it observed, 'a "dingo" element' among the latter which 'finds a natural outlet for its semi-criminal instincts in these outrages' – that is, in 'a long series of street brawls, stabbings and actual fights between small groups' of the two forces, especially in Brisbane, Melbourne and Townsville. (Of course, there were other places – Rockhampton, for example – where relations remained notably good.)[128]‡

Australians, as did Americans in reverse, tended to form judgements concerning United States society in general partly on the basis of what they perceived in their war-time visitors. (There already existed, of course, images that had been largely shaped, perhaps, by the products of Hollywood.) Gavin Long, for example, an outstanding war correspondent who subsequently became editor of the Australian *Official War History* series, saw in the Americans' 'road signs, roadside propaganda, the naming of ships, guns, vehicles' evidence of a culture that was 'richer and more colourful' than Australia's own. On the other hand, he also contrasted with the lean and fit officers of the A.I.F. their American counterparts who 'look young and plump for their ages in the 20s and 30s and then go to [seed] in the

---

* Up to the end of January 1944, American casualties in New Guinea and the adjoining islands were 8,032, those of the Australians, 10,470.

† See above, 212.

‡ There were 125,000 U.S. troops in Australia and New Guinea by the end of January 1943, together with around 2,000 shore-based members of the U.S. Navy. On the particular problems and disturbances created by the presence of black American troops in Australia, see above, 184. The Military Intelligence Report quoted here added: 'Few of our men stop to think that, when the A.I.F. was in England and the Middle East, the differences of pay and general living conditions between ourselves and the British troops were much more unfavourable to the latter than they are now to us in respect of the Americans.' Moore (*Over-Sexed, Over-Paid, and Over Here*, 277) argues that for all the inter-Allied friction, acquaintance with a people who had emerged from the American 'melting-pot' was to make 'the immigration of non-British stock' palatable to Australians after the war, as well as speeding innovation in other aspects of Australian life.

40s. Causes: too much food and drink, insufficient exercise, the pace of American life, mentally and emotionally.'[129] American troops in the field in New Guinea, he found, '*feel* their discomforts more keenly than the Australians. They lack our men's ability to rise above their conditions [and] complain about food that our men would consider exceptionally good.' Again, Long believed that something more than higher living standards was involved: American troops, he concluded, possessed in general a surprisingly low standard of education:

> 'They do not read as our men do – they just look at the pictures and the pin-up girls and the comic strips. They all say the same things and think the same things. They are very much more excitable and effusive than our men.'[130]*

In New Zealand, too, meanwhile, the early emphasis upon the fundamental similarity between the country's own society and that of the United States was beginning to give way, especially on the left, to expressions of regret that a partner 'so gifted in technique should be so backward in political theory'. As the Labour Party's newspaper, *The Standard*, put it at the beginning of 1944:

> 'While we in New Zealand have feelings of the deepest gratitude to our great ally ... for the magnificent part it is playing in the war, and particularly in the Pacific zone, and while we desire the closest relations between the United States and ourselves after the war, there are features of American commercial life which are repugnant to the vast majority of New Zealanders.'

'I cannot pretend to understand the Americans,' wrote *The Standard*'s editor on his return from a visit to the U.S.A.:

> 'I doubt whether Americans really understand themselves. They cannot be measured by any ordinary yardstick, for welded together in this nation there are dozens of nationalities, all with dissimilar characteristics and racial outlooks, the great majority ardently American, but with their opinions of the European and Pacific conflicts often coloured by their own historical backgrounds. That there is as much enthusiasm and patriotic fervour as there is is a matter for wonder, yet it exists.'[131]

Others among the Allied peoples – Aline Caro-Delvaille, for one, in a penetrating article in *Le Monde*[132] – sought to explore that extraordinary American blend of brash, evangelising confidence and nationalism on the one hand, and 'inferiority complex' on the other ('This nation,' she wrote, 'is

---

* Overall standards of education were indeed very poor in the U.S.A. at the time, 10 million American adults being illiterate when the war opened. Perrett, *Days of Sadness, Years of Triumph*, 371.

profoundly unsure of itself') that had been brought home to a much wider audience by war-time circumstances. And in Britain, for example, as in New Zealand, there were those who began to wonder if a right-wing, capitalist United States would prove a menace in terms of both domestic and international programmes for post-war reform. 'America is ... a hundred years behind us in social evolution,' wrote Eden's Private Secretary in his diary. And again:

'America is an old-fashioned country ..., fearful of political and economic change, and its bankers, businessmen and politicians side naturally with the Right and Right Centre in Europe. Yet, under the stimulus of Russia and a strong leftward wind in England, Europe is moving Leftwards. The "comfortable" capitalist regimes of pre-war are doomed. Unless it is [sic] to be communist, it must at least be Beveridge.'[133]*

The obvious irony here is that in many American eyes it was British society that was hopelessly conservative in its structure and underlying attitudes. ('The same aristocratic system that gives [the British] their fancy titles,' snarled the *Chicago Tribune* in 1942, 'gave them the brutal burocracies [sic] that alienated the people of Malaya, Burma and India.')[134] As with others' perceptions of America itself, the images involved were often simplistic or anachronistic in the extreme. That this was not always the case, however, may be seen in one, final example of the diagnoses made of the society of this or that Ally: an O.S.S. Research and Analysis survey of 'Morale in the British Armed Forces', written in the spring of 1942 following the military disasters in Singapore and the Middle East.[135]

In the Royal Navy and the R.A.F., this report concluded, morale was high. In the former, the basis for this was a 'strong community of interests' between officers who were 'highly-skilled specialists' and other ranks who were themselves 'minor specialists'; and in the R.A.F., too, 'the tie between the Pilot Officer and his [ground crew]' had created 'a democratic and unselfconscious ... relationship based on common interest in a common goal'.† In the Army, however, so the survey concluded, the attempt to build morale around 'the idea of teamwork and "playing the game"' had been 'surprisingly unsuccessful',

* I.e. a comprehensive system of social security organised by the state, as proposed in Britain by Sir William Beveridge in his Report at the end of 1942.
† That the report was not exhaustive or correct in all its findings can be seen here, for example, when one considers the socially ambiguous position of sergeant-pilots in the war-time R.A.F. On the 'caste system' among the British in India, and how it operated to the disadvantage of 'other ranks', see Stephens, *Monsoon Morning*, 27–8. For interesting reflections on 'the sense of cleavage between "us" and "them"' that could arise in the Army, see E.H. Phelps Brown, 'Morale, Military and Industrial', *Economic Journal*, March 1949. On 'social mobility' within the U.S. Army, and the higher morale overall within its air as opposed to ground units, see Stouffer et al., *The American Soldier: Adjustment During Army Life*, caps. 6 and 7, and *The American Soldier: Combat And Its Aftermath*, cap. 7.

'probably because many of the Army officers are university graduates, business and professional men with little technical training. They are leading an Army run on machines, though often they know less about mechanics than the men they command. As a result, considerable dissatisfaction has spread through the ranks, expressing itself chiefly in inter-class friction . . . which threatens the whole organisation with disunity.'*

These tensions, the report argued, owed less to the continued existence of career Army officers who were reactionary members of a privileged class than to the adoption of anachronistic attitudes by some of those who had received a commission simply as a result of war-time circumstances:

'Today, a new generation of subalterns, with the approval or by the orders of County Officers, have gone back to the polished cross-straps, swagger canes, long haircuts and Mayfair moustaches of the traditional British "military gentlemen". Superficial as these physical changes seem, they have brought to the commissioned ranks a renewed emphasis on privilege and social precedence . . . [which] is somewhat self-contradictory, since fewer of the men who make up the "officer class" are drawn from the upper strata of society than ever before . . . Inevitably, this situation has produced some officers more interested in exploiting their new-found social position than in being good leaders.'

*

This American analysis of Britain's armed forces was by no means definitive, of course. But it was shrewd, and it put its finger on some of the contradictions and tensions that war-time circumstances were creating within a British society that was, as Oliver Harvey observed, and as was to become fully apparent with the 1945 General Election, 'moving Leftwards'. Moreover, the report's concern over the qualities and values to be found within the British Army at the time matched that of a number of contemporaries among the British themselves. 'The British people . . . are getting very tired of always losing – and of losing so badly,' observed *The Economist* in February 1942. 'In the whole history of the war the British Army has not a single success to its credit . . .'[136]† Senior civilian and military figures, too,

---

* The relevance of this particular emphasis on the consequences of mechanisation to the broader issue of 'modernisation and society', raised earlier in the present work, will be apparent.

† This was an overstatement. The Italians had been driven from Ethiopia and Eritrea, for example, and in December 1940–February 1941 Wavell's forces (British, Indian, Commonwealth, Polish and French) had destroyed an Italian army six times their size in the North African desert.

were privately concluding in this pre-Alamein period that there were 'too many old men and "nice chaps"' in the fighting zones, that 'our generals are no good', or that the nation as a whole had become 'soft'. ('Are we too soft, are we too civilised?', asked Oliver Harvey in his diary after contemplating 'disquieting reports' from the Far and Middle East that 'British troops were not fighting well'.)[137] And in an informal discussion immediately following the fall of Singapore, Harold Macmillan (then Parliamentary Under Secretary at the Colonial Office) and Harold Nicolson touched on some of the issues that (unknown to them) were highlighted in the O.S.S. report to Washington:

> 'The left-wing people', noted Nicolson afterwards, 'say you must create a "revolutionary army" and that our "class army" can never fight. The right-wing say that we should go back to our old system of regimental discipline. Macmillan says that we have not the time or scope to create a revolutionary army and that we must go back to discipline. We are between two stools, he says.'[138]*

We find ourselves back, in other words, with questions of the kind that we observed in an earlier chapter being posed within domestic contexts in the years leading up to the Far Eastern war: questions that might relate to specific political or economic issues, but that, either openly or by implication, touched upon the essential qualities of the peoples concerned, and the underlying values and purposes of their societies; questions that were arising at a time when the extent and speed of change were such that 'none of the old formulae' seemed adequate when it came to shaping a response.

Now, the war itself was creating additional problems; was hastening the pace of change still more. Yet if, as in the international sphere, conflict could appear on the one hand to be bringing fresh urgency to the quest for new 'formulae', and, by shaking existing structures, to be creating a new opportunity for putting such formulae into practice, on the other it could be seen as reinforcing the argument that a society must seek strength in adversity in the order and values of its own past. We therefore turn in the following chapters to the impact of the war in domestic terms, not simply materially-speaking, but in the realm of ideas and self-perception.

---

* Macmillan nevertheless believed at the time, according to Nicolson, that 'extreme Socialism' was 'inevitable'. Nicolson himself thought that David Low, the celebrated cartoonist, 'by inventing Colonel Blimp', had 'sapped discipline' in the Army.

Notes

1 Thorne, *Allies*, 138.
2 Polenberg, *War and Society*, 139, 241 (Blum, *V Was for Victory*, 90ff., gives slightly different figures); A.S. Milward, *War, Economy and Society, 1939–1945* (London, 1977), 65, 274–5.
3 Milward, 92, 345–6.
4 G. Perrett, *Days of Sadness, Years of Triuimph: the American People, 1939–1945* (New York, 1973), 29; Spector, cap. 1.
5 R.J. Bell, *Unequal Allies* (Melbourne, 1977), 205–6.
6 Hasluck, *The Government and the People, Vol. II*, 225.
7 1944 correspondence, Australian Prime Minister's Dpt. files, A/45/1/10.
8 Milward, 89.
9 Thorne, *Allies*, 138, 278.
10 Ibid, 387.
11 See ibid, 388ff., 505–6.
12 See ibid, 280–1, 371, 391, 444, 512, 666, 700; and e.g. M.B. Stoff, *Oil, War and American Security* (New Haven, 1980). Also Watt, *Succeeding John Bull*.
13 Thorne, *Allies*, 276.
14 Ibid, 499.
15 See M. Howard, *War and the Liberal Conscience* (London, 1978), 41ff. and passim.
16 Bruce Monthly War Files, entry for 13 May 1942. And see Thorne, *Allies*, e.g. 109, 391.
17 OSS R. and A. No. 2218, 'British Security Interests in the Post-War World', 15 Sept. 1944.
18 Thorne, *Allies*, 513–15.
19 Ibid, 501.
20 See R. Divine, *Second Chance: the Triumph of Internationalism in America During World War II* (New York, 1967).
21 Howard, op. cit., 116.
22 Fraser opening speech, ANZ Conference, 17 Jan. 1944, NZ Ext. Affs. files, 153/19/4 part 1.
23 AICC Working Cttee. resolution, debates of 7–8 Aug. 1942, AICC Papers, file G–22 part 2.
24 *Le Populaire*, June 1943.
25 See e.g. P.A. Reynolds and E.J. Hughes, *The Historian As Diplomat: Charles Kingsley Webster and the United Nations, 1939–46* (London, 1977); Harvey, *The War Diaries of Oliver Harvey*, passim.
26 Curtin speech of 6 June 1943, Tonkin Papers, box 8; A.H. Vandenberg (ed.), *The Private Papers of Senator Vandenberg* (London, 1953), entry for 4 Aug. 1943, and passim; Divine, *Second Chance*, passim.
27 *Sydney Morning Herald*, 8, 9, 11 Aug. 1945.
28 *Le Monde*, 15 Aug. 1945; and e.g. 26 and 28 July, 11 Aug. 1945.
29 Harvey, op. cit., entry for 7 Aug. 1945; *Bombay Chronicle*, 8 Aug. 1945.
30 McDougall paper, 'The British Empire and the World', 4 March 1944, Bruce Monthly War Files. On McDougall and his position, see Edwards, *Prime Ministers and Diplomats*, 113–4; and cf. ibid, 169ff.
31 *Le Monde*, 28 July 1945.
32 Wallace's speech of 8 May 1942 is given in full as an appendix to J.M. Blum (ed.), *The Price of Vision: the Diary of Henry A. Wallace, 1942–1946* (Boston, 1973).
33 *La France Libre*, April 1941; *Libération*, 20 April 1943.
34 Thorne, *Allies*, 144.
35 Ibid, 142, and e.g. Blum, *V Was For Victory*, 285.
36 Moran, *Churchill*, 183, 254.
37 *Le Populaire*, e.g. 8 Aug. 1945; e.g. Evatt to Fraser, 24 Jan. 1944, NZ Ext. Affs. files, 153/19/4 part 1; also e.g. *La France Libre*, April 1941.
38 See e.g. Thorne, *Allies*, 511.
39 See ibid, passim.
40 Berendsen to Fraser, 22 Dec. 1944, NZ Ext. Affs. files, 81/1/13. And e.g. Bruce record of conversation with van Kleffens, Monthly War Files, 9 June 1944; van Kleffens to Ger-

brandy, 28 Dec. 1944, Gerbrandy Papers; Kersten, *Buitenlandse Zaken in ballingschap*, passim; A. Watt, *Australian Diplomat* (Sydney, 1972), 62ff.
41 Thorne, *Allies*, 503. Also e.g. the correspondence on this topic of Raymond Clapper, Clapper Papers, passim.
42 Thorne, *Allies*, 293.
43 Ibid, 242–5.
44 Ibid, 332ff., 409ff., 450ff.
45 Ibid, 614–21.
46 See ibid, 222–4, and above, 193.
47 Ibid, 13.
48 Ibid, 290.
49 Ibid, 400–1.
50 See ibid, 217–8, 349–50, 463–9, 621–33; and Thorne, 'The Indochina Issue Between Britain and the United States, 1942–1945', *Pacific Historical Review*, Feb. 1976.
51 Kersten, *Buitenlandse Zaken in ballingschap*, 353ff.
52 See ibid, and Thorne, *Allies*, 256, 265.
53 See ibid, 613–4. On the attempts of Dutch officials to sustain their country's interests in Allied councils, see e.g. material in the van Mook Papers, Gerbrandy's Office Papers, and the Londens archief of the records of the Ministerie van Buitenlandse Zaken. See also Thorne, 'Engeland, Australië en Nederlands Indië, 1941–1945', *Internationale Spectator* (The Hague), Aug. 1975.
54 E.g. *Trouw*, mid-July 1944; *de Bevrijding*, 12 April 1945.
55 Thorne, *Allies*, 252ff.
56 Ibid, 256, and J. Robertson, 'Australia and the "Beat Hitler First" Strategy', *Journal of Imperial and Commonwealth History*, vol. XI, No. 3, 1983.
57 Thorne, *Allies*, 364ff., 480ff., 601–2, 645ff. And e.g. NZ High Commissioner in Australia to Fraser, 21 Oct. and 5 Dec. 1943, NZ Ext. Affs. files, 63/5/3 part 1; *Sydney Morning Herald*, 31 July 1945.
58 E.g. Eggleston to Evatt, 23 Jan. 1945, Washington to Legation records, file 325, Australian Commonwealth Archives; Sturdee to Blamey, 28 May 1943, Blamey Papers, file 6.1; Bell, *Unequal Allies*, 6, 64, 139.
59 E.g. Blamey to Minister for the Army, May 1943, Blamey Papers, file 5; Horner *Crisis of Command*, 162ff., 268.
60 Horner, *High Command*, 209; also caps. 7, 9, 11, 13, and 335ff., 382ff.
61 Lt. Gen. E.K. Smart to Blamey, 6 June 1945, Blamey Papers, file 2.1; and e.g. *Sydney Morning Herald*, 1 March 1945.
62 Thorne, *Allies*, 479ff.
63 E.g. Blamey to Brooke, 29 Nov. 1943, Blamey Papers, file 2.2.
64 Thorne, *Allies*, 650.
65 Bruce, Monthly War Files, entries for e.g. 2, 28, 30 May, 28 June, 25 Sept., 4 Nov. 1942; 15 Feb., 22 April, 6 July, 19 Oct. 1943; also Thorne, *Allies*, e.g. 257–8. On Bruce's long and often significant role in London, see Edwards, *Prime Ministers and Diplomats*, 109ff., and on the wider issues surrounding Australian endeavours, ibid, passim, and Watt, *The Evolution of Australian Foreign Policy*, passim.
66 Thorne, *Allies*, 479–80.
67 E.g. communications between Fraser (Prime Minister) and others in NZ Ext. Affs. files, 81/1/13, and records of the ANZ Conference of Jan. 1944, ibid, 153/19/4 part 1.
68 Thorne, *Allies*, 482, 601.
69 See ibid, 485–6. For the Agreement in full, see T.R. Reese, *Australia, New Zealand and the United States* (London, 1969), 32ff. The observations of Dutch officials and ministers are interesting: Gerbrandy Office Papers, file 351.88(94)32.
70 Quoted in Bell, *Unequal Allies*, 160–1; and see ibid cap. 7 in general.
71 Annex to draft agenda for the Jan. 1944 ANZ Conference, NZ Ext. Affs. files, 153/19/4 part 1.
72 Ibid, record of discussions on the conference agenda.
73 Thorne, *Allies*, 140.

74 E.g. ibid, 367, 487.
75 See ibid, 92, 101–2.
76 Correspondence on NZ-US trade relations, 1942–45, NZ Ext. Affs. files, 58/9/4 part 1.
77 Bell, op. cit., 131–2. The foregoing section relies heavily on Dr Bell's work. Also, e.g., Australian Prime Minister's Dpt. records, file A/45/1/10.
78 E.g. OSS R. and A. No. 1398, 'British Colonial Policy', 28 April 1944.
79 E.g. Sharp paper, 'The French Regime in Indochina Prior to 1940', Sept. 1945, State Dpt. files, 751.51G/3–845; and see Thorne, 'The Indochina Issue Between Britain and the United States', loc. cit.
80 E.g. OSS R. and A. Nos. 2876 ('Dutch Attitudes Toward the Future of the N.E.I.', 2 Feb. 1945); 3215 (review of Logemann broadcast, 23 July 1945); 3232('Japan and Indonesia', 24 Aug. 1945).
81 Ibid, Nos. 283 ('Social Conditions, Attitudes and Propaganda in India', 14 May 1942), and 1253 ('The Problem of Law and Order in Reoccupied Burma', 14 March 1944).
82 Smith, *The Shadow Warriors*, 193.
83 Thorne, *Allies*, 404.
84 E.g. OSS R. and A. Nos. 265 ('Social Conditions, Attitudes and Propaganda in Indochina', 30 March 1942); 383 ('Basic Psychological Factors in the Far East', 3 Oct. 1942); 2424 ('British Interests in the Far East', n.d., 1944); Thorne, *Allies* 121, 163, 180, 338, 340–3, 454, 536, 591, 595.
85 See e.g. E. Barker, *Churchill and Eden at War* (London, 1978), 221; Iriye, *Power and Culture*, 171, 223.
86 See Thorne, *Allies*, 276, 297, 407, 428–9, 497, 526; Erickson, *Stalin's War With Germany: Vol. 2, The Road to Berlin*, 132, 156, 409–10.
87 See Thorne, *Allies*, 374, 424, and e.g. Langdon memo., 'Some Aspects of the Question of Korean Independence', 20 Feb. 1942, Dpt. of State files, 895.01/79; OSS R. and A. no. 2211, 'Russia, China and the Far Eastern Settlement', 5 June 1944.
88 Thorne, *Allies*, 529.
89 See ibid, 525ff., 577–8; and e.g. Far Eastern Division memo. for the Secretary of State, 'U.S. Interpretation of the Yalta Agreement'. 13 July 1945, Dpt. of State files, 761.93/7-1345.
90 *New York Times*, 28 Aug. 1945; and e.g. *Times*, 17 Aug. 1945, *Manchester Guardian*, 27 Aug. 1945. *New York Herald Tribune*, 28 Aug. 1945.
91 *Le Monde*, 7 April, 1945; *Sydney Morning Herald*, 27 July 1945. Also e.g. *Standard* (Wellington), 12 April 1945; Sydney *Daily Telegraph*, 18 July 1945.
92 See Thorne, *Allies*, 528–9.
93 Ibid, 526ff., 577–8.
94 See e.g. Kennedy, 'Mahan *versus* Mackinder', in his *Strategy and Diplomacy*.
95 See Iriye, *Power and Culture*, 168ff., 220ff., 234ff.; Butow, *Japan's Decision to Surrender*, cap. 6.
96 See Martin, *Deutschland und Japan*, 172ff.; Meskill, *Hitler and Japan*, 179ff.; Erickson, *Stalin's War With Germany, Vol. 1: The Road to Stalingrad* (London, 1975), 396; *Vol. 2: The Road to Berlin*, 43, 154–5, 162.
97 Martin, 122ff.; Meskill, 83, 108ff.
98 See Martin, 76–7, 161ff.; Meskill, 97ff., 121; Hauner, *India in Axis Strategy*, 562ff.
99 See Martin, 93; Meskill, 101ff., 107–8.
100 Meskill, 183; Martin, 220.
101 Shillony, 15–16.
102 Meskill, 114; Presseisen, 'Le Racisme et les Japonais: un dilemme Nazi', *Histoire de la Deuxième Guerre Mondiale*, July 1963; Trevor Roper, *Hitler's Table Talk*, entries for 5 and 7 Jan. 1942; *The von Hassell Diaries, 1938–1944* (London, 1948), entry for 21 Dec. 1941. Also on Hitler's continuing racist attitude towards India and the Indians, despite Bose's pleas to the contrary, see Hauner, op. cit., 29, 237ff., 357ff., 388, 435.
103 *Times*, 6 July 1942.
104 Ibid, 29 July 1942.
105 OSS R. and A. No. 315, 'English Attitudes Toward the United States Since Pearl Harbor',

1942 (n.d.).

106 *Daily Express*, e.g. 6 July, 3 Aug., 10 Sept. 1942.
107 'Australian Military Forces: notes for Service Personnel Visiting the U.S.A.', Blamey Papers, file 6.1. Cf. J. H. Moore, *Over-Sexed, Over-Paid, and Over Here* (St. Lucia, Queensland, 1981).
108 Casey interview, 9 Jan. 1942, Australian P.M.'s Dpt. Papers, A 1608.
109 Curtin message, 8 June 1942, ibid.
110 Nash broadcast, 22 March 1942, NZ Ext. Afs. files, 64/3/1 part 1A.
111 Thorne, *Allies*, passim; H.G. Nicholas (ed.), *Washington Despatches, 1941–45* (London, 1981); Kersten, *Buitenlandse Zaken in ballingschap*, passim.
112 *New York Times*, 19 June 1942.
113 *Le Populaire*, 13 April 1945; *Standard*, 16 Nov. 1944; *Sydney Morning Herald*, 9 Nov. 1944; Thorne, *Allies*, 507.
114 See e.g. M. Vioirst, *Hostile Allies: F.D.R. and Charles de Gaulle* (New York, 1975).
115 Thorne, *Allies*, 105, 145, 279, 508.
116 Ibid, 145.
117 Calder, *The People's War*, 309. Cf. Stouffer et al., *The American Soldier: Combat And Its Aftermath*, 576.
118 See I. Jarvie, 'Fanning the Flames: Anti-American Reaction to Objective Burma (1945)', in *Historical Journal of Film, Radio and Television*, vol. 1 No. 2, 1981.
119 Quoted by J. Edwards, article in *The National Times* (Sydney), 30 Jan.–4 Feb. 1978.
120 Johnson-Hornbeck correspondence, passim, Hornbeck Papers, boxes 22, 157 and 267; and see C. Thorne, 'Letters From the Minister', *Melbourne Age*, 8 and 9 Jan. 1975.
121 L.H. Brereton, *The Brereton Diaries* (New York, 1946), entry for 18–19 Jan. 1942; Steward memo., 20 Jan. 1942, Hornbeck Papers, box 22; Johnson to Hornbeck, 20 May 1943, ibid, box 262. See Moore, *Over-Sexed*, 42.
122 OSS R. and A. No. 566, 'Morale in Australia', 23 Feb. 1943; and see Hasluck, *The Government and the People, Vol. II*, 326ff.
123 For more detailed references, see C. Thorne, 'MacArthur, Australia and the British, 1942–1943', *Australian Outlook*, vol. 29, Nos. 1 and 2, April and Aug. 1975; also Stimson diary, 3 and 29 Oct. 1942; Ickes diary, 1 Nov. 1942; J. Luvaas (ed.), *Dear Miss Em* (Westport, Conn., 1972), 31; Edwards, op. cit., *National Times* (Sydney); Horner, *Crisis of Command*, 87, 147. Cf. Gavin Long diary, 13 Aug. 1943.
124 Blamey to Curtin, 4 Dec. 1942, Blamey Papers, file 12; and e.g. Gavin Long diary, 9 July 1942, 12 Jan. and 3 Oct. 1943; Long notebook No. 8, entry for 16 July 1943, Long Papers.
125 Long notebook No. 35, entry for 16 Dec. 1943.
126 E.g. Long diary, 31 Dec. 1943; Horner, *Crisis of Command*, 64, 135ff., 162ff., 227, 233, 244, 264, 268.
127 Horner, *Crisis of Command*, 264, and *High Command*, 285ff.; Luvaas, op. cit., 65.
128 'Report on Disturbances Between Australian and American Troops', 4 Dec. 1942, Blamey Papers, file 5.2; material in Australian P.M.'s Dpt. Papers, files A/45/1/10, E/45/1/10 and Z/45/2/1; Gavin Long diary, 4 June 1943; Spector, cap. 18; Moore, *Over-Sexed*, caps. 6, 8, 9, 11.
129 Long diary, 6 July 1943, 12 Aug. 1944.
130 Long notebooks, No. 19, p. 10; No. 38, p. 28; No. 40, p. 1ff. But cf. Moore, 96.
131 *Standard*, 20 Jan., 27 April, 1 June 1944, 13 Sept. 1945.
132 *Le Monde*, 9 Sept. 1945.
133 Harvey, op. cit., entries for 7 Jan., 20 Sept., 1 Dec. 1942, 14 June 1943.
134 *Chicago Tribune*, 3 Dec. 1942.
135 OSS R. and A. No. 617, 21 March 1942.
136 *Economist*, 21 Feb. 1942.
137 Thorne, *Allies*, 133; Harvey, op. cit., entry for 22 Feb. 1942.
138 Nicolson, *Harold Nicolson, Diaries and Letters, 1939–1945*, entry for 24 Feb. 1942.

CHAPTER EIGHT

Life, Death and Change

The self-criticisms being voiced by some of the British in 1942 can be related in part to an underlying conviction which, as we saw in an earlier chapter, had been proclaimed in several quarters before December 1941: that armed conflict provided a special test of a nation's qualities. Japan's very decision to launch her attack on the West had owed something to this belief. As the Imperial Navy's Chief of Staff, Admiral Nagano Osami, had expressed it in the autumn of that year, referring to the growing economic pressure being exerted by the Western powers: 'A nation which does not fight in this plight has lost its spirit and is already a doomed country.[1] Thereafter, the 'central problem' for Japan's citizens, according to one propaganda document, was whether they were 'thoroughly imbued with the spirit of the Constitution, . . . the Imperial Way, the Way of the Gods'; whether they could 'practise the national morality'.[2]

The 'test' of war could also be seen, as it was by Oliver Harvey and others in London in 1942, as revealing whether a people had become 'soft' or – an interesting term – 'too civilised'. The implication was that, in order to save or rebuild 'civilisation', one would have temporarily to forsake its precepts for more primitive modes of behaviour. Yet such behaviour was not simply viewed as a regrettable necessity. It tended to be endowed by gentle liberals and democrats, as well as by militarists and fascists, with noble and even spiritual qualities.[3]*'We've been civilised too long,' wrote the Chinese intellectual, Wen I-to, referring to his country's struggle against the Japanese,

> 'and now that we have nowhere left to go we shall have to . . . release the animal nature that has lain dormant in us for several thousand years . . . [The war] is a chance that comes once in a thousand years, to let us see whether there still exists in our blood the motive power of the ancient beasts; if not, then we had better admit that as a people we are spiritual eunuchs, and give up trying to survive in this world.'[4]

Or again, modern, total war of the kind that had erupted in the Far East in 1937 and in Europe in 1939 could be seen as posing a particular challenge to those responsible for rallying and directing a society that had itself become

* See below, 307, for a discussion of one of the wider, sociological issues that arise in this context.

involved. We find Nella Last, for example, taking time from her war-work and domestic chores to reflect in her diary in the summer of 1942, following the military disasters of Singapore and Tobruk:

'Nearly three years of war: WHY don't we get going – what stops us? Surely, by now, things could be organised better in some way. Why *should* our men be thrown against superior mechanical horrors and our equipment not be standardised for easier management and repairs? There is no flux to bind us – nothing. It is terrifying, not all this big talk of next year and the next will stop our lads dying *needlessly* . . . It is shocking.'[5]

*

We will return in the next chapter to this matter of the self-appraisals that were being made within various societies involved in the Far Eastern conflict. Before doing so, however, we need to examine further the nature of the domestic circumstances which developed during these years, a subject which will be pursued, as it was with regard to the pre-war years, on a thematic and comparative basis, notwithstanding the vast differences which obviously existed among the societies concerned,* and notwithstanding the fact that in some instances it is again impossible to distinguish entirely between the impact of the Far Eastern war in particular and that of World War Two as a whole.

We have already seen that in the period leading up to Japan's attack against the West, well-nigh all of the societies that were to be caught up in the ensuing conflict were being shaken in various ways by developments of an economic kind. The course and nature of the war itself added to this turmoil by bringing about a series of abrupt changes in the pattern of international trade. India, for example, found herself cut off from her supplies of rice in Burma and other parts of Southeast Asia; Britain and the United States from the tin and rubber they had been deriving from that same region. In some cases, the consequences of such dislocation were more severe for the primary producers concerned than for their former customers: by the end of the war, tin production in Malaya, for instance, stood at only 14 per cent of its pre-war level, in the East Indies, oil production at a mere 5 per cent; in the Philippines, the collapse of the sugar industry greatly swelled the ranks of the unemployed in those islands, while in the East Indies, likewise, the

---

* To take simply one basic measurement and illustration: the average per capita calorific intake in Bengal *before* the famine there in 1942–3 was less than one-quarter of that of a U.S. soldier. Milward, *War, Economy & Society*, 281.

sharply diminished level of tea, sugar, coffee and tobacco cultivation brought great hardship in its train.[6]

For Japan herself, perilously dependent on resources that lay beyond her control before December 1941,[7] the conquests she now achieved opened up sources of supply that were vital to her ability to continue fighting.[8] And when, subsequently, her merchant fleet went to the bottom and the flow of coal, iron-ore, oil, rubber and other materials dwindled, her entire war-economy began to seize up, her gross national product for the first half of 1945 dropping 25 per cent below the level it had reached in the previous year.[9] Bombardment from the air had also contributed to the state of near-paralysis that had overtaken Japan's economy by that final summer of the war; nor had Tokyo been able at any time since Pearl Harbor to reinforce its war-making capacity to any substantial degree through aid from its German ally.[10] Meanwhile, the devastation inflicted upon China by Japan herself from 1937 onwards had severely diminished the former's output of, for example, textiles, coal and electric power,[11] while as we have seen she had also become greatly dependent on financial and other assistance from the United States.*

Within the context of the overall amount of resources available, it was of course open to a government to decide what proportion of its country's effort and materials and wealth should be devoted to the war in a direct, military sense, and at what level civilian consumption should be maintained. Thus, while the United States, for example, came to devote approximately 40 per cent of its Gross National Product to the war effort, for both Japan and Britain the figure had reached 50 per cent by 1944, and by 1945 consumer expenditure in Japan, which had stood at 67 per cent of GNP in 1940, was down to 38 per cent.[12] Or to give another illustration in absolute terms, New Zealand, which in 1939–40 had spent for war purposes just over £7 million, was devoting almost £124 million to that end in 1944–5.[13] Choices also had to be made between various sectors of the war effort, with the Australian Government, for instance, deciding eventually to limit the size of its armed forces in order to sustain and increase that agricultural production which was so important for Britain and for Allied units in the Pacific.[14]

The demands of the conflict called into being new industries and enlarged some existing ones, the output of munitions by all parties to the World War

---

* The Nationalist Government's efforts to increase overall industrial output in the areas under its control resulted, according to some statistics, in an average annual increase of 27 per cent between 1938 and 1945. But such were the inroads made by the Japanese that in the peak year of 1943 the value of major industrial products was still only 12 per cent of the total for the whole of China immediately before war broke out in 1937. (Chi-ming Hou, 'Economic Development and Public Finance in China, 1937–1945', in Sih, *Nationalist China*, 213–17, 233.) In 1944 the Government was able to utilise under 5 per cent of the nation's GNP for its own purposes. Eastman, *Seeds of Destruction*, 41.

as a whole (about 40 per cent of it was coming from the U.S.A. by 1944) being remarkable when set against the level at which economies had been running before 1939.[15] For Australia and Canada, indeed, the war brought about 'a large and decisive shift' towards industrialization in general terms. (In Australia, the output of metals and machines, for example, increased by 120 per cent during this period, and the number of machine-tool factories from three to over one hundred.)[16] In Korea, too, the forced industrial revolution that had begun in the decade before the war* now gathered even greater pace, so that by 1943 nearly twice as many workers were employed in the colony's industries than had been the case three years before. (Significantly, this process of industrialisation was taking place in the north of the country above all, where guerrilla resistance to Japanese rule was also strongest. Both these developments were helping to provide the basis of a modern state in that area, as distinct from the traditionally more wealthy but rural south, where Japanese control, in Professor Cumings' words, had 'deeply eroded the structure of status and authority'.)[17]

Further examples of this process of sudden growth included the synthetic-rubber industry in the United States, which was brought into existence as a result of Japan's advance into Southeast Asia, and which before the end of the war had reached such a size that it looked likely to be able to meet on its own a large portion of world-wide demand for rubber thereafter. The American aluminium industry, too – again, boosted by government funds – leaped ahead in these years.[18] In both Britain and Japan, meanwhile, change in an opposite direction was taking place in the textile-manufacturing sector, where contraction was the order of the day. And in Japan's case, this development, together with an accompanying shift to metal manufacturing and engineering, and the introduction of a greater degree of technological sophistication, was to contribute significantly to the country's remarkable economic growth in the post-war era. 'The war,' writes Chalmers Johnson, 'caused a change of industrial structure almost as profound as Japan's original industrialization.'[19]†

The ways and extent to which the war fostered scientific and technological developments in general require no rehearsing here.[20] In our present context, what needs emphasising is that one result of this process was to widen the gulf that already existed between 'developed' societies and the remainder. As rapid changes in technology and production 'transformed the economic

---

* See above, 63.
† Thus, during the second half of 1942 and into 1943, and under the direction of the Ministry of Commerce and Industry's Enterprises Bureau, numerous textile mills were converted to the production of aeroplanes and aeroplane parts. Overall, the number of spindles in Japan's textile industry declined from 12,165,000 in 1937 to 2,150,000 in 1946. (Johnson, *MITI*, 164–5.) Aircraft production increased from a monthly average of 424 in 1941 and 738 in 1942 to 2,348 in 1944. Kase, *Eclipse of the Rising Sun*, 139.

arrangements under which Americans lived', as Polenberg has put it (productivity rose by about 25 per cent between 1939 and 1944, and ouput per worker-hour in industry was roughly five times that in Japan),[21] many in Southeast Asia were witnessing, rather, the destruction of their resources and livelihoods. Where Australia moved towards becoming a genuinely industrialised society, India – despite what has been described as 'a significant breakthrough in industrial production . . . in relation to the pre-war years' – still possessed too narrow a technological base (as well as being handicapped by its alien Government's handling of the economy) to fulfil the hopes and expectations of nationalist entrepreneurs, and would remain among the 'have-nots' of the world during the post-war economic revolution.[22]*

In many of the poorer societies involved in the conflict, however, as well as in the wealthier ones, the tendency during the war years was for people to move from the countryside into the towns. But whereas in the Philippines, for example, that shift was largely the result of unemployed and destitute workers from the islands' ruined sugar plantations making for Manila, or in the East Indies of peasants whose jobs on tea plantations, say, had likewise been destroyed drifting into Batavia or Surabaja, in the United States and Japan it reflected the urgent demands of war industries and the overall mobilisation of the population.† In this last respect, of course, the war was merely hastening a transfer from agricultural employment which had been in train for a long while before 1941, as we observed in chapter three. In Japan, the total loss of labour in the agricultural sector through military service had amounted to about 1.9 million people by the end of the conflict, with as many again (women as well as men) having left for jobs in industry by February 1944.[23] In the United States, the number employed in industry by June of that year was 8.3 million higher than the monthly average for 1939, and in agriculture 1.3 million lower, while during the three and a half years following Pearl Harbor, quite apart from the 12 million men who entered the country's armed forces, 15.3 million American civilians moved their homes across county lines, above all into the cities.[24]

Not every 'developed' society involved in the war followed this pattern exactly, of course. In Britain, for example, the agricultural labour force actually grew slightly during the war years,[25] and Australia's decision to

* In fact, the production of coal, pig-iron and steel ingots, for example, was in each case less in 1944 than it had been in 1940 and 1941, and, for the first two of these, less than in 1938. (Ray, *Industrialization in India*, 251.) The failure on New Delhi's part to foster industrialization did not mean that officials at various levels were not concerned with economic development and planning. See e.g. Hunt and Harrison, *The District Officer in India*, 224.

† The proportion of Japan's population living in towns moved up from 38 per cent in 1940 to 40 per cent. In 1945, however, as a result of the flight from the bombed cities and the return of people from overseas, it suddenly and temporarily dropped to below 30 per cent. Fukutake, *The Japanese Social Structure*, 99.

increase its effort in the same field has already been noted. Even so, in Britain, as in the United States, and again in marked contrast to what was happening in the rural areas of Asia, agricultural productivity rose greatly.* By 1943–4 there had taken place as a result an increase of over 40 per cent since 1938–9 in the portion of the country's annual consumption of calories that was produced domestically, with considerable advances being made in mechanisation.[26] In the United States, the yield per harvested acre of major crops rose by 13 per cent between 1940 and 1942, and by a further 13 per cent by 1945.[27] In New Zealand (where, as in Australia, agricultural output was vital to the Allied effort against Japan, especially, and where in 1943 conscription for work on the land exceeded that for service in the armed forces), the number of tractors doubled during the war years, with productivity per head of labour reaching the highest level of any of the combatant states.[28]

The war did not simply change the size and shape of economies. In various ways it frequently altered patterns of ownership and control as well. One major feature in this respect, of course, was the extension of governmental involvement in such matters as investment, direction and planning. During the second half of the war, for example, the Government of India took on the new role of regulating that country's economy,[29] while much earlier in Britain itself a plethora of new ministries and committees established Whitehall's virtually complete control in this respect – even though the underlying basis for this last development was what has been described as 'an implied contract between Government and people [whereby the latter] refused none of the sacrifices ... demanded of them for winning the war [but] in return ... expected that the Government should show imagination and seriousness in preparing for the restoration and improvement of the nation's well-being when the war had been won'.[30]

The drive for centralised control of the economy in Japan reached its peak in 1943, when, in 'a final attempt to overcome the structural disunity of the ... Government that had been imposed upon it by the Meiji Constitution', Tojo transformed the Ministry of Commerce and Industry into a Ministry of

---

* The outstanding exception to this process, among the developed states, was Australia, where the yield of many crops actually declined during the war, along with the amount of fertilizer being used per acre. (In the U.S.A., this fertilizer figure rose sharply.) 'The reserves of a richer and more complex economy were lacking,' comments Milward, 'and it was more difficult than in the United States to remedy the mistakes in the early period of the war.' (*War, Economy and Society*, 277). In Japan, too, despite attempts to compensate for the inroads being made into supplies of rice from Southeast Asia and Formosa from 1943 onwards by Allied attacks, and despite the substitution of women for men in much rural labour, crop yields fell during the final stages of the war. At the same time, however, government ordinances benefited tenant farmers and smallholders vis-à-vis landlords, foreshadowing more substantial reform in this area after the war. Milward, op. cit., 256–9, 290; Havens, *Valley of Darkness*, 98–9.

Munitions, taking its portfolio for himself, to add to the Premiership, the Army Ministry, and the post of Chief of the General Staff.[31] In Washington, meanwhile, bodies such as the War Production Board and, above all, the Office of War Mobilization (created in May 1943) sought to give coherence and direction to the great roaring machine that the country was fast becoming, while Federal agencies such as the Office of Price Administration and Selective Service also played their part in 'tying Americans more closely to their government' than ever before.[32] In France, too, the Vichy regime's attempts to develop a new technocratic order helped foster institutions that were to act as channels for governmental action in later years, and in terms of attitudes, as well, an 'acceptance of the interventionist state' was becoming more widespread.[33] The war, concludes Milward, was to leave governments in general with 'a new consciousness of their power over the domestic economy', as well as with an increased readiness to set about creating a new system at the international level to replace the 'economic anarchy of the 1930s'.[34]

Nevertheless, the degree of control established during the war by the Government in Britain was not typical among the leading states involved in the Far Eastern conflict. In both Japan and the United States, the structure of industry and the patterns of political influence and belief each contributed to the maintenance of a far more complex situation, wherein powerful groups, of which the government was only one, contended over the direction the economy was to take. This was particularly the case in Japan, where the conscription of industrial labour speeded up the existing trend towards oligopoly, as Havens terms it, many small businesses having to close, while the major manufacturing and trading combines doubled their share of the country's corporate and partnership capital.[35]

The *zaibatsu** were thus in an even stronger position than before to resist government directives whenever they so desired; at the same time their own, internecine rivalries continued (particularly between the Mitsubishi-Sumitomo coalition and Mitsui), as did 'virulent inter-agency conflict' and struggles between the Army and the Navy for the acquisition of vital resources.[36]†

---

* I.e., the great business magnates or 'financial clique', who controlled the major industrial combines and the leading financial institutions of the country.
† Japanese civilian bureaucrats nevertheless collaborated with this or that *zaibatsu* or military faction. Aware, however, in the words of an American official historian, that once the country was defeated these war-time patterns of collaboration would 'constitute a threat to their continued hegemony', they saw to it that before the Allied occupation began 'personal records were destroyed, wholesale shifts of higher officials were made, and initial steps were taken to divorce administration from some of the most obvious features of aggressive imperialism'. The Ministry of Commerce and Industry, recreated out of the Ministry of Munitions in August 1945, gave place in 1949 to a new Ministry of International Trade and

In the United States, too, the war was benefiting large firms above all. Businesses employing less than 500 workers accounted for 52 per cent of manufacturing employers in 1939, 38 per cent in 1944. Government contracts increasingly went to the big corporations. As was noted in chapter three in relation to the 1940–1 period, many of those who moved into key war-time positions in Washington were recruited from the ranks of leading business executives, and the successful transformation of the economy for war on a free-enterprise basis (corporate profits after taxes, which had been $6.4 billion in 1940, reached $10.8 billion in 1944) restored the prestige of such men and all they stood for after their years on the defensive in the 1930s. Moreover, the close contacts that were established between 1940 and 1945 between big business and the armed services were helping to lay the foundations for that post-war 'military-industrial complex' of which President Eisenhower was soon to be speaking.[37] ('The manner in which big business is being coddled and being permitted to build itself up is alarming,' noted the Secretary of the Interior, Ickes, in his diary in 1942, and he, like John J. McCloy, the Assistant Secretary of War, regarded the head of the U.S. Army's Services of Supply, Lt. General Brehon Somervell, as 'a very dangerous man', and even – like MacArthur – 'a possible man on horseback'.)[38]

The resurgence of big business and the growing involvement of the Government in the economic life of America was not matched by an increase in strength on the part of organised labour. True, union membership rose from 10.5 to 14.7 million during the war; true, also, wage agreements arrived at by collective bargaining became the norm, and prominent union figures, as already noted,* joined bodies like the National War Labor Board. But the impression of strength that was created by such developments, and by a growing bureaucratisation within major unions and their CIO–AFL coordinating organisations, was in many ways illusory. Labour leaders exercised little influence within the Washington apparatus, and were unable to stem a profound shift of mood and direction to the right, away from the kind of New Deal social-welfare reforms on which unions, among others, had set their sights.† The call for war-time unity, symbolised for most unions by a no-strike pledge,‡ pointed towards accommodation rather than confrontation with the Government and business leadership, as

Industry, which became a mainspring of Japan's ensuing economic expansion. Johnson, *MITI*, 172ff.

* See above, 84.
† See above, 83–4.
‡ The leader of the American Communist Party, Earl Browder, wrote in his *Victory and After*: 'In the United States, we have to win this war under the capitalist system. Thereafter we have to make the capitalist system work . . . , we have to help the capitalists to learn how to run their own system under war conditions.' (Quoted in Lichtenstein, *Labor's War At Home*, 145.) Cf. the roughly similar position adopted by the Indian Communist Party: above, 167.

did the fear that large-scale unemployment could return once the war was over. Where strikes did occur – and, as we shall see below, they were numerous – they were usually of a 'wildcat' variety, or were the work of dissident union leaders like John L. Lewis of the Mineworkers. As 'a flow of new recruits' joined the factory workforce, observes one student of the subject, 'women, blacks, teenagers and rural Okies, . . . to many of them the unions seemed irrelevant because of the comparatively high, steady, war-industry wages they could now command'.[39] Even in Britain, where the crucial role played by Ernest Bevin as Minister of Labour reflected a much less lop-sided partnership (in the field of working conditions for example) between Government, employers, and employees, and where union membership increased from 6.3 million in 1939 to 8.8 million in 1946, organised labour as such had comparatively little say in the direction of the economy.[40] (In Japan, of course, the labour movement had been completely eclipsed by a Government-sponsored organisation even before December 1941.)

Whatever the position of labour unions, however, the nature and extent of the war put a premium on the availability of man- and woman-power for all the main combatants. For Britain – mobilised to her full extent by the autumn of 1943, as we have already noted – the limits to her resources in this respect told increasingly thereafter, not least where the country's potential role in the Far Eastern war was concerned.[41]* The Governments of both Australia and New Zealand, with their small populations, found themselves as we have seen having to weigh the demands of agriculture and industry against the desire to maintain a prominent military contribution to the Allied cause. ('New Zealand's military record and prestige is such,' wrote her Chief of General Staff in 1945, 'that nothing less than a complete division [in the projected assault on Japan's home islands] is in accord with such prestige and dignity.')[42] The Japanese Government, for its part, was by the middle of 1944 resorting to the conscription of most school-children over ten years of age for work in the fields or factories on an almost full-time basis (by February 1945 they constituted nearly one-tenth of the civilian labour-force), as well as utilising Koreans, Chinese and prisoners of war, and lengthening the hours which people worked.[43] Within Korea itself, also, two and a half million people were mobilised for labour through youth organisations, whilst other bodies whose function was to knit together the colony with Japan 'pervaded every aspect of the daily lives' of the population.[44]

In absolute terms, Japan's armed forces numbered over 8 million by the

---

* It was calculated in 1944 that if, following the defeat of Germany, Britain were to take part in the occupation of that country, increase her exports, rebuild her cities, raise to some extent the living standards of her people, and at the same time make a significant contribution to the defeat of Japan, there would be a shortfall of 1,750,000 in the manpower available.

end of the war, Britain's over 5 million, those of the United States over 12 million. As for civilian labour forces, that of Japan was perhaps as much as 7 million more by 1945 than it had been in 1940, while over 7 million more Americans, too, entered employment between 1939 and 1944 than could have been anticipated on the basis of previous trends. War-induced expansion of similar proportions occurred in Australia and Britain, and by June 1944 55 per cent of the latter's working population were in either the armed forces or civilian war jobs, compared to 40 per cent in the U.S.A.[45] New Zealand, quite apart from its agricultural effort, enrolled about a quarter of its male population in the armed forces, as we noted earlier (205,000 out of 828,000, 135,000 of them being sent overseas); in India, besides the recruitment that took the Army from 189,000 in 1939 to 2,500,000 in 1945, some 8 million people were employed in work for the Allied armed forces, and at least another 6 million drawn into war industries and work on the railways.[46]

In all the industrialised countries involved in the war, this remarkable expansion and redeployment of jobs depended in part on a major increase in the number of women in paid employment. In the United States, for example, there were 5 million more women in this category in 1943 than had been the case two years earlier, while in Britain 80 per cent of the addition to the labour force between 1939 and 1943 consisted of women who had not previously been in paid work. Or to take a different measurement, nearly 8,000 women were serving in New Zealand's armed forces by March 1944. In Japan, meanwhile, although ('out of consideration for the family system') the Government did not go as far as its British counterpart in mobilising this section of the population, the proportion of women in the country's civilian labour force had reached 42 per cent by 1944, compared to 35 per cent before the war, with agriculture in particular being dependent on their efforts.[47]*

*

When we turn to the conditions that the peoples involved experienced during the war years, comparisons, while unavoidable, are surrounded by problems of relativity. For someone in Britain, say, the loss of several hundred calories in their daily diet might entail a certain drop in well-being and a sense of deprivation; for a Bengali, already existing on the most meagre of rations,† it could mean death. We can take individuals who entered the war from broadly similar circumstances, like the Sydney longshoreman and the Australian conscript who found himself fighting his way across the Owen Stanley range in New Guinea, and can conclude that for the

* 57.6 per cent of Japan's rural work-force were women by 1944.
† See above, 249, note.

former to go on strike because of certain 'hardships' appears absurd when set in such a context. But how does one compare the degrees of 'hardship' experienced by, say, on the one hand a well-fed American Marine enduring the slaughter on a Pacific atoll, and on the other a starving Chinese peasant, brutally dragged into service with the Army of Chiang Kai-shek but (assuming he survived) not actually committed to battle?*

Perhaps where the individual, at least, is concerned, death itself provides one measure that can be applied across the board, even though in societal terms such considerations as size of population must again be borne in mind. Over 23,000 Australians and 10,000 New Zealanders were killed in action during the war (the latter out of a population of only a little over 1,600,000). British losses in battle (though the great majority, as we have seen, were incurred in the war against Germany) amounted to over 264,000, with civilian deaths bringing the total to something like 450,000; over 320,000 Americans lost their lives – though, again, less than 20 per cent of the overall figure of one million or so who were killed or wounded resulted from the fight against Japan. Japan herself had well over 2 million of her servicemen killed, together with somewhere between 300,000 and 500,000 of her civilian population.[48] Among the Chinese, somewhere between 1 and 1.5 million troops were killed, while the total number of deaths resulting either from enemy action ('Rural Pacification Movements' and the like) or from starvation or flooding that might have been prevented but for the war has been put as high as 10 million in some estimates.[49] The liability of civilians to suffer as much, if not more, than military personnel is also underlined by the cases of India (something over 24,000 of whose men were killed in action, but where perhaps as many as one and a half million died in the Bengal famine which was partly attributable to the war), the Philippines (where over 100,000 civilians were killed during the fighting for Manila early in 1945),[50] and the Netherlands (where altogether over 200,000 non-combatants died as a result of the conflict).

In the case of the Dutch, as for the Bengalis, starvation played its part in creating these civilian losses, as the daily calorific intake which had dropped to around 1,500 by the middle of 1944 was reduced further still during the ensuing winter.[51] In China, while the direct suffering of the mass of the people at the hands of the Japanese was less after 1941 than it had been

---

* 'A large proportion of the Nationalist conscripts, often to be seen in Chinese wartime towns roped together to prevent escape, died even before reaching their assigned units. Thousands of others, deprived of basic medical care and even their rations by grafting superiors, died of neglect later.' (O. E. Clubb, *20th Century China*, New York, 1964, 233–4.) 44 per cent of those conscripted in 1943 either died or deserted before reaching their units, and over 8 million men altogether 'simply disappeared and were unaccounted for during the course of the war'. (Eastman, *Seeds of Destruction*, 146ff.) Those men, women and children conscripted in huge numbers to labour on war-construction projects also suffered greatly. Ibid, 57–8.

between 1937 and 1939, both crop and livestock production fell in the Nationalist-controlled areas after 1939,[52] and in Honan Province, following a serious failure of the spring and summer harvests in 1942, famine among the peasantry was widespread – a condition that was greatly exacerbated, reported an American observer, by the 'brutal and oppressive treatment of the farmers by their own government and army'.[53] In the small towns of Nationalist China, too, conditions were often appalling, as a British agent on the spot reported from Kwangtung Province in June 1943:

> 'The death rate from starvation is steadily rising . . . From informant's own personal observations he knows that in Toishan district the number is at least one hundred [daily] on average. In a short journey from Toishan to an outlying village, he saw eight unburied corpses. The worst feature is cannibalism. Human flesh sells at five dollars a plate. Parents leave their children at certain recognised points, where they are seized and butchered by the human-flesh vendors.'[54]

According to virtually all the Americans and British who visited the region, living conditions in the Communist-controlled area of China in the north-west were markedly better, partly due to the absence of corruption and rural banditry, as well as to the land-reform measures adopted by the regime there.[55]* In the Japanese-occupied areas of the Far East, however, especially during the second half of the war, hardship and hunger were widespread, as has been suggested in passing in earlier chapters. In Hong Kong, for example, despite the removal to China-proper of something like a million people by the Japanese during their rule over the colony, rice became increasingly scarce.[56] (We have already seen that this occurred in the Philippines, also, where the collaborationist regime unavailingly resorted to emergency powers in February 1944 in an attempt to check the crisis over food supplies.)† The removal of workers from the East Indies for forced labour elsewhere, together with the destruction of much of the existing economy that has already been noted, led to 'extreme suffering' in parts of those islands; in Korea, too, the lives of the peasantry above all were wrenched this way and that as Tokyo manipulated the territory's economic structure and labour resources for its own ends; in Malaya, as in the Indies, their control of certain sectors of trade enabled syndicates established there by Mitsubishi, Mitsui and their like to wring an increasing amount from the local populace.[57]

The war their country had launched also brought great suffering and hardship to large numbers of Japanese themselves, of course, and not only in the shape of bombardment from the air. Civilian rations, about half those

* And see below, 292–3, 311.
† See above, 159.

supplied to the military, came down to well under 2,000 calories a day in 1945, with the task of finding food for their families becoming 'a daily struggle of major proportions' for housewives in the cities, and with poor diet seemingly responsible for the diminishing size of children as well as the rise in dysentery, paratyphoid and diphtheria. Even rural families were eating nearly 19 per cent less rice by 1945 than they had in 1941, hardship in the countryside being greatly increased by the arrival of refugees – more than ten million in all – from an American bombing campaign that destroyed 24 per cent of all the country's dwellings, as well as the lives noted above.[58]

Inflation made a considerable contribution to the hardship being experienced in many parts of the Far East. It was largely thanks to this phenomenon that workers in Japan's war industries, for instance, were earning one-third less in real terms in 1944 than they had in 1939. The country's near twenty-fold increase in spending between 1937 and 1944 was financed mainly by the issue of bonds, with the average rise in real living costs exceeding 20 per cent in every one of the years between 1939 and 1945. The rapidly-growing importance of a black market – its price of rice forty-four times the official level by November 1944 – reflected the degree to which the Government lost control of the economy during the war, and to which the ordinary citizen was squeezed as the nation sought to sustain a conflict that was beyond its means.[59] Inflation was far worse in Nationalist China, however, and there, unlike Japan, it both marked and contributed to the regime's declining grip on the country in political terms. As Chungking, having taxed the peasantry to the limit and beyond, met its financial needs largely by issuing yet more notes, and as the privileged few hoarded commodities on a vast scale, the currency had plunged by the end of 1942 to about one sixty-sixth of its 1937 value, and to one two-hundred-and-twenty-eighth a year later. By 1945, the cost of goods indexed at 100 for 1937 had risen to 125,000, and, as salaries failed by a huge margin to keep pace, so the scale and extent of corruption grew as well. Those dependent on the Government for their income, concludes one survey, who were in effect 'the whole modern sector of [Nationalist] China', were 'put through an inflationary wringer' that left them 'enervated, demoralized, and eventually blaming the regime in power'.[60]

The onset of major inflation in the Philippines and the East Indies has already been noted (in the latter territory, paper money had plunged to about one-fortieth of its pre-war purchasing power by the summer of 1945).[61] In India, too, the prices of major consumer goods increased substantially during the war, helping to bring about a breakdown in the system of distribution (with hoarding by producers and merchants) which in turn made the feeding of the urban population a major problem for the

Government, and which did much to cause the 1943 famine in Bengal and diminish the standing of the British administration generally.[62]*

In contrast to these situations, inflation in both Britain and the United States was held to acceptable levels, partly by covering a substantial amount of war expenditure by taxation. Taxes met almost half the cost of the war in the U.S.A., with contributions of this kind being levied on almost all those in employment, whereas in 1939 the majority had paid no Federal taxes at all. Even so, American levels of taxation were low – few paying as much as 20 per cent – by comparison with those which obtained in Britain, where the standard rate was raised to 50 per cent in 1941, and where indirect taxes on items such as tobacco, alcohol, entertainment and luxury goods were repeatedly increased during the war years.[63] Rationing of food-stuffs and other goods was also severe in Britain, of course; but despite this, and although the average intake of calories fell slightly, people's diets appear to have constituted an advance over those of the pre-war years in medical terms, and the health of the population as a whole improved. Real earnings, too, actually rose slightly overall, partly as a result of the longer hours that were being worked.[64]

The great exception to the widespread war-time experience of hardship and suffering, however, was provided not by British but by American society. By comparison with what had been introduced in Britain and Japan in the way of rationing, for example, measures of this kind in the United States – even where petrol was concerned – amounted to little more than a gesture. Americans both at home and overseas continued to eat large quantities of food. (Various calorific figures have been given above. The rations supplied to American soldiers in the Far East amounted to 4,758, which was around 800 calories higher than even their Australian counterparts were getting; at home, the average daily consumption of calories increased by 4 per cent between 1939 and 1944.)[65] Consumer purchases of goods and services within the United States rose by 12 per cent between 1939 and 1944, with average real weekly earnings in manufacturing industry climbing from $24 to nearly $37 in the same period. Above all, of course, unlike their Dutch, French, British and Asian counterparts, those who stayed within their country's borders were, in John Morton Blum's phrase,

---

* Taking the level at August 1939 as 100, the price of rice in India had reached 172 by December 1941. In December 1943 it was 951, although it had dropped to 333 a year later. Wheat, 212 in December 1941, was 381 in December 1944, cotton manufactures 285. Of the 70 million tons of food grains grown annually in the country, only 21 million were reaching the market. Tomlinson, *The Political Economy of the Raj*, 94; Milward, *War, Economy and Society*, 280. For an eyewitness account of the Bengal famine, and of the shortcomings and evasions of the administration in New Delhi, see Stephens, *Monsoon Morning*, 169ff. and Appendices IX and X.

'fighting the war on imagination alone'.[66]*

Even so, the difficulties and hardships brought about by war are not to be measured in terms of calories or purchasing power alone. Nor, if we bring into the reckoning the effects of the conflict on family life, say, can statistical evidence be at all sufficient as a guide. For example, the near-doubling of the rate of divorce in the United States between 1940 and 1944, to the level of 27 out of every 100 couples married, would seem to constitute strong *prima facie* evidence of strain related to war-time circumstances. But how can we reach an assessment of a qualitative kind, or make a comparison with the impact of the war on family life in Japan, say, where the divorce rate remained steady at a very low level, without relating such figures to the social *mores* surrounding marriage and the family in America and Japan respectively? And similar questions of relativity occur if we turn to another aspect of stress within war-time societies: that which could arise within the families of those who were taken prisoner by the enemy.

Again, there are plenty of statistics, of course: 130,000 British, British Empire and Commonwealth military personnel captured at Singapore, for example, and 12,000 Americans on the Bataan peninsula; about 30,000 Australians all told, military and civilian, ending up in Japanese hands. But the extent to which families learned of the exact subsequent fate of such loved-ones varied, as did that fate itself. (On Bataan and in the camps of Southeast Asia generally, Allied prisoners died in their thousands – 16,000 out of 61,000 sent to work on the Burma-Siam railway, for instance – amid circumstances that have left an indelible stain on the name of the Japanese armed forces and nation.)[67]† And, again, it is scarcely possible to compare the social consequences of the war-time capture of Western or Indian or Chinese military personnel by the Japanese with those resulting from the reverse occurrence. For, whereas in the former instance the predominant reaction was likely to be one of relief that a life or lives had been preserved, to those Japanese who entered captivity, together with their families, the disgrace involved was worse than death itself, being tantamount to taking the status of a 'non-person', so that to this day it is difficult to obtain firm statistics in Japan of the number – they

---

* George Carlin, General Manager of the United Features Syndicate, wrote to Raymond Clapper in August 1942 about a woman who had been placed in a sanatorium as a mental patient and who 'wouldn't admit to herself or anyone that the war is actually going on', the point of the reference lying in the ensuing observation: 'It occurred to me that most of the population has taken the same attitude, even if they are not in sanatoria.' Clapper agreed. Clapper Papers, box 50.

† The same comment applies, of course, to the murder of thousands of Chinese civilians after the capture of Singapore, and of large numbers of Southeast Asian labourers on the Burma-Siam railway.

were, of course, remarkably few until the final six months or so of the war – who did bring themselves to lay down their arms yet go on living.[68]*

*

For all the domestic dislocation and strain brought about by the war, external conflict could engender a heightened sense of national pride and solidarity – a subject to which we will return in the next chapter. The circumstances of total war could also reduce the mental distance separating rulers from the ruled. 'Departments have not only been slow to adapt themselves to popular government,' warned a senior official of Britain's Ministry of Information in an internal memorandum of 1941. 'They have been far too inclined to think that they need only tell the public what they are doing and not why they are doing it. The intelligence of the public has been underestimated or disregarded . . . ' Conversely, Ernest Bevin believed that the experiences they had undergone between 1939 and 1945 were likely to have 'removed the inferiority complex amongst our [Labour Party] people' – a comment that, as we have seen, applied also to the attitude of various colonial peoples towards their imperial masters.[69] Nor can closely-related movements of a socio-economic or political kind – or both – among the various sections or 'classes' of a population be fully understood without reference to the international context. In Britain again, for example, war-time developments helped ensure that in 1945, in Arthur Marwick's words, 'the working class assumed a position in . . . society analogous to that assumed by the middle class after the passing of the Great Reform Act of 1832',[70] while in the United States the much more equitable distribution of a greatly enlarged national income 'flattened the pyramid of social stratification'.[71]†

* One estimate gives the total of army and navy prisoners of war as below 300 between Pearl Harbor and the end of 1943, excluding the China theatre, increasing to about 6,400 by the end of October 1944, and then to around 20,000 by the eve of surrender. (Information from Professor Ikeda Kiyoshi.) On the relevant Japanese military regulations, see above, 127, and on a particular case involving Japanese prisoners of war, below, 276. There were numerous instances where Japanese who had been captured as a result of being wounded sought to kill themselves as soon as they were in a position to do so – by tearing off their bandages, for example, or biting their tongue. (See e.g. Cruickshank, *SOE in the Far East*, 236–7.) According to Spector (*Eagle Against the Sun*, 317), in July 1944 almost two-thirds of the 12,000 Japanese civilians on Saipan also chose suicide rather than fall into American hands.

† The magnitude of the shift in the distribution of incomes in the United States can be seen in the following figures:

Percentage with incomes of:	1935–6	1945–6
Under $1,000 p.a.	43.5	8.8
$1,000 – 1,999	34.2	17.6
$2,000 – 2,999	13.1	20.3
$3,000 – 3,999	4.4	19.8
$4,000 – 4,999	1.7	12.4
Over $5,000		21.1

Perrett, *Days of Sadness, Years of Triumph* 353–4. For testimonies regarding the consequences of this change for individuals and families, see Terkel, *"The Good War"*, passim.

Two riders must immediately be added to the above observations, however. The first is that war-time developments of a socio-economic or political kind (the latter to be explored in the next chapter) did not by any means guarantee that profound and lasting change in the same direction would take place once peace had been restored. If we turn to the social structures of those countries of Western Europe that were under Nazi occupation, for example, we find that although, in Gordon Wright's words, 'the nucleus of a new elite' was gradually emerging from the various Resistance movements, its members being 'catapulted after 1944 into positions of political, economic and social prominence to which only a few of them could have aspired without the upheaval of war', yet, as the same scholar concludes, 'nowhere were they to obtain a monopoly of postwar power or status'.[72] Or if we take Japan, we find that, despite the major social and political changes brought about by defeat and MacArthur's occupation regime, a small elite at the head of large, monopolistic firms and within the bureaucracy were to continue to exercise considerable control over the country, together with those conservative Japanese politicians who succeeded in attenuating the democratic nature of many of the reforms brought in in the period immediately following surrender. And among this elite, as elsewhere in Japanese society, 'a great deal' of the traditional, 'familistic' spirit which we noted in chapter three remains, in Professor Fukutake's words, 'alive and well' in the 1980s.[73]

In Britain, despite the advance of the working class to political prominence, despite the massive victory of the Labour Party at the polls in 1945 and the major social and economic legislation that followed, 'by 1949', as Alan Bullock has put it, 'the hopes of 1945 . . . had faded', and reform 'had failed to produce the re-making of British society'.[74] In France, for all that there was taking place during the war years 'a drastic shift in public issues from the old ideological issues to economic and social ones, . . . no new political equilibrium was found'. The country's institutions were little changed and, as Stanley Hoffmann has emphasised, the Fourth Republic, as well as Vichy, 'helped to alienate the people from politics'.[75] By the autumn of 1946, Simone de Beauvoir has recalled, 'the Socialist dreams of 1944 were truly dead'. 'The 1950s confirmed and accelerated the trend towards "restoration",' comments James Wilkinson, '[and] while Europe returned to prosperity [the] fundamental goal [of the Resistance intellectuals] of "spiritual revolution" remained unfulfilled.'[76]

Further examples – the still-disadvantaged position of women in Asian and Western societies after 1945, for instance – of this failure of war-time developments to produce immediate and wholesale change will appear in what follows, as we enlarge upon the second and related qualification that must be added to the original suggestion that circumstances between 1941 and the end of the conflict often engendered a sense of national pride and led to changes which increased a society's homogeneity. For this second rider, which amounts, in fact, to an accompanying thesis of equal weight, is that war-time circumstances also tended to throw a stronger light on the existing divisions within a society, and in some cases to foster developments of a kind that were more socially divisive still.

These processes manifested themselves in a variety of ways, which Polenberg, for example, has explored in relation to the United States in particular.[77] One such phenomenon, which is not readily measurable, has been observed by several historians, who, while noting the greatly increased power of the state brought about by the exigencies of war, conclude that at the same time the experiences undergone by people during these years could 'initiate or reinforce trends towards a mood of lawlessness', and strengthen opposition to authority in general.[78] (Features of the period that may have contributed to such a development include, presumably, the disruption of family life; the heightened sense of uncertainty or desperation; the sustained focusing upon, and indeed, glorifying of, violence and destruction; and the encouragement in several contexts of 'resistance' to the *de facto*, if not always *de jure*, civil or military power.)*

Where dissent and disputes of an industrial kind were concerned, of course, a wide range of causes may have been involved even on a single occasion, and action taken in pursuit of a legitimate grievance is not to be read as denoting 'a mood of lawlessness'.† But the opposition of authority, in the shape of war-time governments and administrators, to such industrial action was clear enough. And certainly, the swollen ranks of labour on their side did not always place the requirements of national production during the conflict above all other considerations. Thus, although members of the patriotic industrial associations that had been established in Japan were less able than their counterparts in the West to reject the demands made upon them, in 1943 alone they took part in nearly 300 strikes and work stoppages, and as Dr Havens summarises more common features, 'absenteeism, moon-lighting and shoddy work were chronic, if not widespread'.[79] (Absenteeism was said to be running as high as 40 per cent in some plants, while 10 per cent of the planes delivered to the air corps were rejected as defective.) In Britain, meanwhile, 1.5 million working days were lost through strikes in 1942, and 1.8 million in the following year. About half the latter figure was accounted for by coal-miners, who also formed a substantial proportion of

---

* For historical comparisons, see e.g. C. Emsley, *British Society and the French Wars, 1793–1815* (London, 1979), and C. Hill, *The World Turned Upside Down: Radical Ideas During the English Revolution* (London, 1972).
† On the hardships and poor pay of coal-miners in Britain, for example, see Taylor, *English History, 1914–1945*, 547.

those going on strike in the United States, where the number of days lost reached 13.5 million in 1943 (involving 3 million individuals), and 9.6 million between January 1945 and the end of the war.[80] As for the situation in Australia, such was the extent and frequency of strikes and absenteeism* that in 1943 Curtin, the (Labour Party) Prime Minister, was moved to describe the second of these phenomena as 'one of [the country's] most serious war-time problems', and in the same year the threat of enlistment in the armed forces was levelled against absentee 'workers' whose particular jobs in industry had until then protected them from being conscripted. As for those whose repeated strikes were imperilling supplies of coal and preventing the loading and unloading of vital war materials in the docks, they were, declared Curtin, nothing less than traitors.[81]

One consequence, then, of the greatly increased demand for workers that the war created within industrialised societies could be the continuing expression, albeit in new forms, of those kinds of sectional attitudes and discontents that we observed in chapter three in the context of the pre-war years. Indeed, the new opportunities that were created for various groups within a society as a result of international conflict could in part serve only to bring the people concerned up against those restrictions and disadvantages which even so continued to surround their position. This tended to be the case for women and (in the United States in particular) for racial minorities.

The degree to which, during the war years, women were mobilised in industry, on the land, and in the armed forces, even, by the Western states and Japan has been illustrated earlier in this chapter.† In both Nationalist and Communist China, too, considerable emphasis was placed on the need for women to contribute to the war effort, and organisations established accordingly. In the Kuomintang's areas, nurses, cooks, stretcher-bearers and garment-makers were recruited; in Yenan, where the effort to enlist them in the fight was greater still, women, in addition to carrying out the foregoing kinds of activities, served as sentries, in intelligence gathering, and (somewhere between 200 and 500 detachments of them) as volunteers in fighting forces.[82]

To some extent, especially in the Communist areas, one consequence of these developments was a growing respect for women's capabilities on the part of Chinese men.[83] And in India, meanwhile, Gandhi's statements on

---

* In the 18 months before July 1943, the average number of working days lost per week was 10,610. There were 602 separate strikes in 1942, and 430 during the first half of 1943. During 1943, out of a potential coal output of 12,748,000 tons, 2,075,000 tons were lost through strikes and absenteeism; in the final year of the war, 2,466,000 tons were lost through strikes, and a further 1,569,000 tons through absenteeism. Hasluck, *The Government and the People, 1942–1945*, 57–60, 252–60, 388–96.

† See above, 257.

this issue were also becoming less ambiguous. Women, he wrote, who had long been 'suppressed under custom and law for which man was responsible', must become 'equal partners in the fight for swaraj'; must be accepted as the 'equals of men' with complete independence to 'shape their own destiny'.[84] There must be more places for women in higher education, argued the *Bombay Chronicle*, while Bose's *Azad Hind* stated in 1942 that 'an entire change in the life of the women of India' would be a necessary part of 'a fundamental renaissance ... in the religious [and] social life of the whole Orient'.[85] Even in the Philippines (where women were assured that their counterparts in Japan were in no way condemned to lives of subservience), the collaborationist regime emphasised the crucial role that women must play in bringing about social and political change.[86]

In India and China in particular, some Asian women themselves took advantage of the ferment of the time to renew their demands for reform, campaigning in India, for example, to bring about changes in Hindu law relating to such matters as marriage, divorce and inheritance.[87] Women like Aruna Asaf Ali also played a prominent part in the underground defiance of British rule that continued after the arrest of the Congress leadership in August 1942,[88] while outside the country Bose created a separate women's regiment of the I.N.A., named after a nationalist heroine, the Rani of Jhansi, who had died fighting the British in 1857. 'He felt that psychologically it would have a tremendous effect on Indian men,' subsequently recalled Dr Lakshmi Sahgal, who had organised both the regiment and the women's branch of the *Azad Hind* provisional government, '... and he cited the example that other countries had been using women as fighting forces ... The very fact that women were volunteering to [serve], he felt, would give the whole movement a really revolutionary aspect ... '[89]

Of course, opposition to anything approaching genuine emancipation and equality for women remained widespread and profound in all the Asian societies involved in the war. As was the case in Vichy France, also, [90] the regimes of both Nationalist China and Japan continued to be wedded to the notion that it was woman in her domestic role who was crucial for the preservation or rebuilding of an ordered and wholesome society.[91] Male prejudice – like the acceptance of their traditional role by the majority of women themselves, in the countryside, especially – was only slightly reduced here and there. 'Under the banner of patriotism,' Elisabeth Croll writes of Nationalist China, 'women came to experience new political and social activities which brought them face to face with old prohibitions.'[92] 'I wish that men ... would see women's shortcomings in the context of social reality,' expostulated the Communist intellectual, Ting Ling, in 1942. 'In the old society people could at least have said they were to be pitied, or were ill-fated, whereas today we say it's "her own doing" or "serves her right".'

Ting Ling herself was encountering in Yenan the argument that class solidarity and the achievement of political and economic reform must take precedence over the issue of women's rights, being obliged to fall silent on the subject for a long while.[93] Indian women, for their part, were still to be battling in 1951, well after their country had achieved its independence, to secure the passage of a Hindu Code Bill that was crucial to their status.

'Thousands of sensitive Hindu women,' Padmaja Naidu was to declare on that occasion, 'for the first time in their lives left the precious sanctuary of their sheltering homes [during the Quit India and similar demonstrations]. They came to the battlefield and stood beside their brothers and faced jail and lathi charges and often humiliations worse than death. If today . . . [they] are to be denied their just rights, then our hard-earned freedom is no more than a handful of dust.'[94]

Accusations of a broadly similar nature were often and justifiably to be levelled by women in other societies long after the Second World War was over. In European countries, for example, employment prospects tended to narrow and decline sharply after 1945, while both educational opportunities and wages remained inferior to those available to men.[95] In the United States, an Equal Rights Amendment would still be a divisive issue in the 1970s – and one that also brought out the lasting class differences within American society.[96] In Japan, as Dr Robins-Mowry observes, 'one hundred years after the Meiji Restoration, [women] still struggle to free themselves from deeply ingrained, restraining habits of mind, emotion and action imposed by the traditional way', and from male attitudes which in many cases go no further than a 'platitudinous acknowledgement of [women's] constitutional status . . .'[97]

Even so, if we take those Asian societies that were involved in the war, it is clear that in several of them, at least, the slow and limited process of politicisation which (as we saw in an earlier chapter) had been taking place among women in the 1920s and '30s was considerably reinforced during the years of international conflict. In China, for example, women were to constitute by 1946 between one-quarter and one-third of the members of the Communist Party, while even in the Nationalist part of the country an increasing proportion of the articles appearing in women's journals were devoted to such subjects as the decline in the peasant economy and 'the strategy and tactics for mobilising women'.[98] Even in the East Indies, where the women's movement as such 'for all practical purposes was dormant, if not dead, during the years of [Japanese] occupation', women were by 1945 poised to play an important part in the final struggle against the Dutch that was about to take place.[99]

As for the position of women within Asian societies themselves, in some places, at least, momentum had been maintained, or even increased, in the direction of, for example, the 1950 Marriage Law in China, which was to free the women of that country from having husbands imposed upon them, and to give them a genuine opportunity to divorce the husbands they already had. Even in Japan, the wholesale disruption brought about by the war had created new possibilities for long-term change in this area of national life. 'Democratization was under way through the levelling agents of destruction and need,' writes Dorothy Robins-Mowry. 'The traumatic social and physical disarray created a setting ripe for a break with the past.' The government itself had been insisting that, as a contribution to the achieving of victory against the country's enemies, women must 'cultivate self-confidence and develop your potential to meet any difficulties as a substitute for men being in the battlefield'. 'The majority of Japanese girls and women faithfully followed these instructions,' observes the same scholar. 'In doing so, ironically, they also helped prepare themselves to cope with the responsibilities and opportunities of the reforms and new rights to come after the war.'[100]

In the West, too, where women who entered war-time industries, for example, were seldom accorded economic or social equality with the men alongside them,[101] the circumstances of the time were, even so, helping to bring about significant changes of attitude on the part of a good many of those involved. Nella Last in Barrow, for one, 'could not see women settling to trivial ways [again] – women who have done worthwhile things [during the war]'.

'I feel pants [i.e., trousers as now commonly being worn by women] are more a sign of the times than I realised,' she wrote in 1943. 'A growing contempt for men in general sweeps over me ... Why this "Lords of Creation" attitude on men's part? I'm beginning to see I'm a really clever woman in my own line, and not the "odd" or "uneducated" woman that I've had dinned into me ... Why should women not be looked on as partners, as "business women"? I feel thoroughly out of time.'[102]

The similarity between this change in perception and self-perception and that being manifested by Indonesians, for example, vis-à-vis the white man* is striking. Meanwhile there were other sections of various societies whose separate identities and dissatisfaction with the existing order of things, domestically-speaking, were being reinforced as a consequence of the war. Japan's occupation of Southeast Asian territories tended to underline, rather than diminish, the plural nature of the societies involved, for example (just as in the Philippines it widened the gulf between the wealthy and, for

* See above, 161, 172.

the most part, collaborating few at one end of the social spectrum and the *Hukbalahaps* at the other, and in China's villages the gap between the larger landlords and the remainder).[103] The distinctive position in this respect of the Chinese in Malaya during these years has already been indicated – Chinese who often found Malay police being employed against them by the invader.[104]* In the East Indies, Eurasians, as well as Chinese, were subjected to especially harsh treatment by the Japanese, while friction between them and Europeans was a feature of everyday life in one of the camps set up on the islands for women internees. (In his prisoner-of-war camp there, too, Laurens van der Post discovered that the Japanese had been able to recruit many of their spies and informers from the ranks of the Eurasian captives, whom he found 'among the most bitter and resentful men of mixed blood I have ever encountered'.)[105]† In Burma, where the tensions between the Burmese themselves and the Indian population had been strongly demonstrated during the latter's wretched exodus in 1942, the readiness of many of the former to welcome or assist the Japanese stood in total contrast to the resistance that was displayed by the Karens. Both Karen and Kachin hill-tribes worked thereafter with British and American clandestine units against the Japanese, and of course were to continue their opposition to Burmese dominance long after the war was over and the British in their turn had left the country for ever.[106]

By increasing the possibility that Britain's departure from India, too, would take place much sooner than could previously have been anticipated, the war also helped exacerbate the communal issue in that country, where, as we saw in an earlier chapter, the demand for a separate Muslim state had emerged even before the onset of the Far Eastern conflict. The attempts of Bose to transcend communal differences within the Indian National Army as part of his quest for a free and united India appear to have met with a degree of success.‡ (Mohan Singh, too, as leader of the first I.N.A., was and remained thereafter fiercely opposed to any thought of partition.)[107] And in India itself, where the *Bombay Chronicle* among others saw 'the forging of . . . unity' as 'the most urgent problem',[108] Gandhi above all strove to prevent Hindu and Muslim from proceeding down separate and diverging political paths:

---

* In Fiji, also, the comparative unwillingness of the Indian community to enist in the colony's forces, together with its efforts to improve its economic situation, evoked harsh comments from among the Fijians themselves (who were on the verge of being a minority in the islands). Scarr, *Fiji*, 291ff.

† For a psychological explanation of this phenomenon, see Mannoni, *Prospero and Caliban*, 75.

‡ For example, in contrast to the segregated organisation of the Indian Army, different communites were integrated within various I.N.A. units, both Mohan Singh and Bose trying to get them to eat the same meals as one another, with the cooks being supplied in rotation by Hindus, Muslims, Sikhs, etc. Interview with Mr M. S. Bharat of Calcutta, formerly an officer in the I.N.A.

'The only real, though awful, test of our nationhood,' he urged upon Jinnah in September 1944, 'arises out of our common political sub-jugation. If you and I throw off this subjugation by our combined efforts, we shall be born a politically free nation out of our travail . . . If India was one nation before the advent of Islam, it must remain one in spite of the change of faith of a very large body of her children . . . Once the principle [that the Muslims could form a separate state] is admitted, there would be no limit to the claims for cutting up India into numerous divisions that would spell India's ruin.'[109]

But just as the leaders of the I.N.A. were far from overcoming communal tensions among their followers,* so Gandhi, for all his endeavours (for example, his advocacy of more education for children and adults alike and the adoption of Hindustani† as a common language that would increase both political awareness and a sense of unity),[110] could neither shift Jinnah from his purpose, nor weaken the support for the latter's case among the Muslims of the country. Nor could he persuade the Congress leadership to adopt those conciliatory formulae which he believed might retrieve the situation.‡

* The conclusion reached by British military intelligence in 1946 was that Bose's achievements in this direction had been superficial only, and that he himself had displayed 'partiality first to the Bengalis and then to the Hindus.' (CSDIC Monograph No. 17.) A summary of interrogations of I.N.A. deserters and prisoners in November-December 1944 had also recorded the frequent mention by those being questioned of 'strained feelings between Muslim and Hindu in the I.N.A. and I.I.L.'. (No. 5 ADV F.I.C., Monthly Digest.) Both these documents were kindly shown to the author by Colonel Hugh Toye.

† As defined by the organisation set up in 1942 to propagate this cause, Hindustani Prachar Sabha, 'Hindustani is that language which the Hindus, Muslims and all other people of villages and towns in Northern India speak, understand and use for mutual intercourse, which is written and read in both the Nagari and the Persian scripts, and the literary forms of which are recognised today as Hindi and Urdu'. Bose, too, urged the adoption of Hindustani as a common language.

‡ In 1942 there was disagreement among nationalists over whether the communal issue should or could be resolved before the winning of independence. Gandhi's position at that time was to call on Britain to 'entrust India to God or in modern parlance to anarchy. Then all parties will fight one another like dogs, or will, when real responsibility faces them, come to a reasonable agreement'. (*Collected Works, Vol. LXXVI*, 197, 213.) Thereafter, he adopted the formula proposed by C. Rajagopalachari – but rejected by the Congress leadership – whereby Pakistan would be accepted in theory, and the right of self-determination allowed in each area where Muslims were in a majority. (*Collected Works, Vol. LXXVII*, 411.) But at his talks with Gandhi in September 1944, Jinnah in any case rejected such a solution (he was insisting upon self-determination for all Muslims), along with the idea, which Gandhi had adopted, of joint agencies between an independent India and a separate Pakistan for such matters as foreign affairs and defence. (*Collected Works, Vol. LXXVIII*, 87ff.) The ensuing attempt by Wavell as Viceroy to obtain agreement on constitutional and communal issues at the Simla Conference of June-July 1945 foundered on Jinnah's insistence that his Muslim League be recognised as the sole source of Muslim nominees for the projected Viceroy's Council, and that it be given a veto over that Council's proposals, to be overriden only by a two-thirds majority. Gandhi, for his part, failed at Simla to persuade the Congress leadership to place a considerable number of non-Hindus on its own list of nominees for the Council. (*Collected Works, Vol. LXXX*, 381, 406.)

Gandhi's other efforts to bring about fundamental change within Indian society fared little better during this period, for all that he felt able to declare in 1942: 'I have visions that the end of this war will mean also the end of capital. I see coming the day of the rule of the poor.' ('It is true,' he added in 1945, 'that there are class distinctions in more or less degree in all religions . . . [But] a man should consider himself not the owner of his property but its trustee or custodian, . . ⁻ [using] it for the service of society.')[111] The caste system, and in particular what the *Bombay Chronicle* termed the 'sorrow and shame' of Untouchability, remained firmly in place.[112] Likewise in Japan, the *burakumin** continued to be discriminated against, not least in the armed forces, where they were for the most part segregated in units of the transport corps.[113]†

Meanwhile in various Western states also, the position of certain racial minorities remained that of people apart from and below the rest of the population, despite the condemnation by the Allies of racism as manifested in Nazi anti-Semitism in particular. (Indeed, anti-Semitism itself remained clearly visible in Britain, in the United States, in France, and – notwithstanding a number of courageous acts of an opposite nature – in the Netherlands.)[114] The Maoris of New Zealand, it is true (whose fine battalion in the country's Army reflected a loyalty which made nonsense of the suspicion voiced in a few white quarters, that the indigenous population might throw in their lot with the Japanese should the latter arrive on the scene),[115] were assured by their Prime Minister, Peter Fraser, that the war was helping bring about a more equitable social situation where they were concerned: that 'Pokeha and Maori are together in the canoe today, shoulder to shoulder in peace and war, in a new friendship based on democracy and sealed with the blood of the boys in the war fields'.[116] Nevertheless, complete equality and integration had yet to be achieved, while in Australia the social and economic position of the great majority of the country's 80,000 Aborigines was many times worse. (Of their condition, Paul Hasluck, later Sir Paul and Australia's Governor General, was to observe in the House of Representatives in 1950: 'When we enter into international discussions, and raise our voice . . . in defence of human rights and the protection of human welfare, our very words are mocked by the thousands of degraded and depressed people who crouch on the rubbish heap throughout this continent.')[117]

---

* See above, 75.

† On the brutal treatment accorded to Koreans in Japan's home islands during the war, see above, 130–1. Something like 60,000 Korean and over 38,000 Chinese labourers died as a result, while Korean women and young girls were despatched in large numbers to provide sexual services for Japanese troops overseas. See Hane, *Peasants, Rebels and Outcastes*, 225, 237.

The war itself did not have any drastic effect either way on these Aborigines in Australia. But in North America, as we noted in passing in an earlier chapter, it made the position of people of Japanese origin decidedly worse. In Canada, with the enthusiastic approval of the country's racist Prime Minister, Mackenzie King, over 20,000 of them were removed from the Western maritime regions lest they should collude with the external enemy.[118] In the United States, partly in response to public calls by the noted columnist, Walter Lippmann, among others, and with the endorsement of Roosevelt himself, around 110,000 were taken from the West coast and interned in camps in the centre of the country, having to dispose of much of their property at give-away prices in the process. Although there were some white Americans who were disturbed at the action being taken – Ickes, for example, thought it 'stupid and cruel' – it was clearly in line with the sentiments of the majority, among whom distrust and dislike of those interned remained high. As John Emmerson was later to summarise the situation that had been created within the United States by the Pearl Harbor attack: 'The enthusiastic exploitation of prejudice, hatred, emotion and covetousness became respectable and acceptable.'[119]

As for the Japanese-American themselves (two-thirds of those interned being U.S. citizens who had been born in that country), their reactions, like their attitudes to the Far Eastern war itself, varied considerably. For the great majority of Nisei – that is, the second-generation, born and brought up in America – identification with the United States appears to have remained complete. 'If we are ever going to prove our Americanism,' one had written in his diary when the news of Pearl Harbor came through, 'this is the time,' and he continued in internment to champion the need for 'an Americanization program [under] Caucasian leadership' for all his people.[120] Some Nisei, indeed, were permitted to enlist, and their 442nd Regimental Combat Team became the most decorated unit in the history of the U.S. Army. Yet there was also much indignation among the Nisei, not simply within the internment camps but among those, for example, who, while working for the Research and Analysis branch of the O.S.S. in Washington, found themselves treated as second-class members of that organisation.[121] Moreover, among the generation which had first emigrated from Japan – the Issei – attitudes to the war as a whole tended to be more ambivalent. Many were clearly 'feeling for Japan' even when they were not wishing to see America defeated, and the father of the Nisei diarist quoted above, for one, believed that the country of his birth was 'fighting for the equality of races'. In the event, 18,000 Japanese-Americans were deemed by the authorities to be fundamentally at odds with the United States and its cause (they included a good many Kibei – that is, Nisei who had returned to Japan for much of their education – and also some Nisei whose loyalty had been turned to hatred as a result of the treatment they had been accorded), and were placed in a separate camp at Tule Lake. Nearly half of them applied for post-war shipment back to Japan.

By far the greatest racial issue within the societies opposing Japan, however, was that arising from the position of America's black population, whose attitudes to the Far Eastern war and its surrounding colonial questions have been indicated in earlier chapters. Here again, the onset of international conflict produced a major upheaval in the lives of many of the people concerned. 700,000 black Americans left the countryside in the South, for example, to move into cities and war-production factories across the country. (Blacks constituted only 3 per cent of the defence-industries labour force in the middle of 1942, but over 8 per cent by the end of the war.)[122] Hundreds of thousands more found themselves in uniform. And for well-nigh all of them – as, indeed, for the whole of American society, even if many of its members declined to recognise it – the question which the war posed was the one asked by the (white) editor of the magazine *Asia* in April 1942: 'Are we fighting to save an American democracy which denies equality to thirteen million colored [citizens]?' Could America's blacks, in other words, achieve that 'Double V' which the overwhelming majority of them clearly desired: that is, victory over both the country's enemies without and the opponents of integration and equality within.

The answer to this last question, in short, was that they could not. Despite the support of some prominent white Americans (notably, Eleanor Roosevelt) for the blacks' cause, 'large numbers of [white] people in all regions', as a secret survey by the Office of War Information told the President, continued to take 'an illiberal attitude towards Negroes'. Roosevelt himself adopted a notably ambiguous and pusillanimous attitude towards this aspect of national life ('his politically minded staff,' comments Blum, 'were less interested in civil rights than in nullifying Southern anxieties'), despite the fears of some members of his Cabinet that the race riots which broke out in Detroit in 1943 were likely to recur in other parts of the country.[123] The majority of blacks continued to be denied the vote. In the war-industries, black men and women were subjected to discrimination on a large scale, regardless of a Presidential Executive Order to the contrary. In the armed forces, blacks were at first barred from the Navy altogether, and in the Army were segregated in units that for the most part (like those in which Japan's *burakumin* were serving) were concerned with labour and supply tasks, rather than fighting. ('The concentration . . . of Negroes in service units,' wrote Walter White of the N.A.A.C.P. to the War Department in 1944, 'has been more depressing to Negro enthusiasm for the war than almost any other single circumstance.')[124] Moreover, blacks serving in the Army – not least, those who became junior officers –

encountered vicious racist hostility from white civilians when training in the south of the United States itself, and from white American officers and troops both at home and overseas* – a hostility which on occasions encompassed the killing of blacks, among whom the white 'cracker' from the States often came to be seen as every bit as much an enemy as the German or even the Japanese. The war, subsequently concluded a black Colonel in the U.S. Army, was 'a racial nightmare' for the Negro soldier.[125]

Opinions vary as to the overall effect of the war on the position of blacks in American society. It has been argued, for example, that, by leading to the absorption of large numbers of young blacks into the armed forces, international conflict 'probably delayed concerted activism for years'. And certainly it left unresolved the black dilemma of whether to work for racial integration, along the lines advocated by White and the N.A.A.C.P., or to focus on their own, separate identity, as Garvey had urged after the 1914–18 war.[126] At the same time, however, it is clear that 'from the black perspective', in Polenberg's words (as we have seen was also the case for a good many women), 'the lowering of some barriers [during the war] made those remaining seem more intolerable'.[127] Hence, with the attitudes of some whites also hardening as a result of the arrival of blacks in their midst, either geographically or in occupational terms, racial tensions were exacerbated. 'Many of the men I have talked to,' wrote Walter White to his N.A.A.C.P. staff whilst on a tour of service units in the Far East in 1945, 'believe that their fight for democracy will begin when they reach San Francisco on their way home.'[128]

*

This heightened determination on the part of American blacks to fight for their social, economic and political rights clearly owed much to the entirely new experiences which many of them had undergone as a result of the war. It is worth recalling that during the First World War, the treatment which black American troops had received when in Britain and France had served to increase their resentment over their position within their own society, as had the entry of others into northern industries.[129] Now, similar reactions were aroused in black G.I.s when, for example, they found themselves among the (at that time) largely non-discriminating and often sympathetic British.[130] And Walter White, when describing how he had heard almost

---

* These attitudes were projected beyond the U.S.A. with the movement of American forces. In Australia, for example, Walter White found in March 1945 that the majority of the people he encountered in Sydney had met only white American soldiers, some of whom had 'spread the usual tales about negroes being illiterate, lawless, diseased, and the possessors of tails'. White to N.A.A.C.P. staff, March 23, 1945, NAACP Papers, box 583.

everywhere he went in that country in 1944 warm praise for the black soldier, added the particularly interesting reflection that

'One factor which should be mentioned is the fact that the average income of between 60 per cent and 70 per cent of the British people is £3.10 [shillings] per week, which corresponds to the average wage of many Negroes in the United States. An economic bond of sympathy appears to have been created thereby. Negro soldiers have been less prone to comment audibly in the presence of British people upon the absence of radios, automobiles, bath tubs and other mechanical devices more common in the United States than among the majority of the British people.'[131]

For others, too, as we have seen, the totally new experiences occasioned by the war could pose sharp questions regarding the existing order of things: for the young Mohan Singh as, with the victorious Japanese forces forging ahead in the Malayan jungle around him, he contemplated openly rejecting the British overlordship under which he had been born and trained;[132] or for another young officer, this time a Briton, Andrew Gilchrist, on secondment from the Foreign Office in London, as he found himself faced for the first time with the poverty and despair of Calcutta.[133] In the great majority of cases, no doubt, alien surroundings simply served to reinforce an adherence to one's own social order and values. This was evidently so among American servicemen in China, for example.* Such a process was also, clearly, the major source of strength remaining to those (disgraced, as we have seen) Japanese prisoners of war penned up in Featherston Camp in New Zealand, 48 of whom were killed and 61 wounded when, in February 1943, 'inspired by their Service traditions', as the subsequent court of enquiry put it, they carried a refusal to work as their captors required to the point of violent assault on their guards.[134]

And yet there were others who to a considerable degree, and in a totally

---

* 'The one abiding sentiment that almost all American enlisted personnel and most of the officers shared was contempt and dislike for China.' (T. H. White and A. Jacoby, *Thunder Out of China*, London, 1947, 157.) In a wider context, a leading American war correspondent wrote: 'Our men . . . are impatient with the strange peoples and customs of the countries they now inhabit. They say that if they ever get home they never want to see another foreign country.' (Ernie Pyle, quoted in Blum, *V Was for Victory*, 65. See also Spector, *Eagle Against the Sun*, cap. 18.) By way of contrast, Margaret Mead offers a glowing description of the attitudes towards the native people of the Admiralty Islands shown by the many American soldiers who passed that way. (*New Lives for Old: Cultural Transformation: Manus, 1928–1953*, New York, 1961, 151.) But, in the view of the war-time commander of those Australian 'Coast Watchers' who were reporting from behind Japanese lines in New Guinea and those islands, like the Admiralties, to the north and east, to many other members of the Australian and American forces in the region, 'natives were just "expendable", and not even human expendables'. (E. Feldt, *The Coast Watchers*, London, 1967, 220.) On relevant social-psychological investigations, see e.g. I. de S. Pool, 'Effects of Cross-National Contact on National and International Images', in Kelman, *International Behavior*.

unfamiliar setting, had to create for themselves a new social order. Such was the experience and challenge facing, for example, those Dutch, British, Australian and Eurasian women who were interned by the Japanese in the East Indies, each individual finding herself deprived of the status, as well as the material support, to which she was accustomed, each facing 'the enforced egalitarianism of total poverty', and all needing to find and accept leaders in a situation where, for men, such positions would have been indicated from the outset by the hierarchy of career.[135]

For these women internees, the circumstances brought about by the war were manifestly extraordinary. So they were too, of course, for, say, those members of the British Special Operations Executive, or the American Office of Strategic Services, or their French, Dutch and Australian colleagues, who were operating behind the Japanese lines.[136] But the point which needs to be underlined here is the extent to which, behind the statistical summaries that were presented at the beginning of this chapter, the war seized and shook the lives of vast numbers of men and women whose positions and roles were far less distinctive than those of the clandestine warriors. Consider, for example, those Chinese living in the southern province of Yunnan, who suddenly found the region being 'integrated in the cultural and economic life of the nation', with refugees flooding in from the north and east, with universities and factories being set up in their midst, and with their former backwater becoming 'a centre of intellectual, cultural and political ferment'.[137] Or let us take as another example those 17,000 men of the U.S. Army, many of them black, who found themselves removed from Harlem or Chicago or Detroit to labour in the mountains and jungles of northern Burma in order to drive that bold and futile road through to China;[138] or, as yet another, the 14,000 or so inhabitants of the Admiralty Islands, whose traditional patterns of work and family obligations were disrupted by Japanese occupation to an extent that was to foster long-term social change, especially when those early disturbances were followed by the tumultuous arrival of over a million American servicemen, bringing with them all the machinery and medicines of modern war.[139] Or, again, we should try to put ourselves, looking back, in the places of those children in Japan and Britain alike who were removed from the towns that had formed the only environment they had known to the countryside; or, less peacefully, into the minds of those Japanese peasants who were taken from their highly insular domestic environment and deposited in, say, Malaya, where (along with their often more brutal Korean colleagues) they could at least, harshly and xenophobically, relieve at the expense of other, 'lesser' species that sense of inferiority and those strong pressures from above to which they themselves had long been subjected within their own society.[140] Or, as a final example of lives dislocated *en masse*, we have the entire Japanese population, among whom in August 1945 there swirled a complex series of emotions as the announcement of their country's surrender brought 'relief at their liberation from the daily fear of death', yet also 'a bewildered sense of emptiness and loss of identity'.[141]

Of course, illustrations such as these, while helpful for indicating the nature and range of experiences that the war could bring, raise questions as well as answer them. The present chapter has sought to show how the conflict brought about or hastened, in both Asia and the West, major structural changes of economic and social kinds (as well as other shifts that were to prove less profound or long-lasting): new patterns of industry; increased urbanisation; greater governmental direction of economies and lives alike. It has tried to demonstrate the ways in which, within societies that were far apart both geographically and culturally, the war affected the composition and power of elites, and the attitudes, as well as the work and living standards, of other class or racial or sexual groups; how it introduced new horizons and expectations, as well as suffering and death. But if in these and other respects certain patterns are discernible, so, too, are numerous variations, together with the complexities that surround any attempt to explain fully the process of cause and effect in any particular case. It is easy to say, in the light of the evidence adduced above, that the war profoundly affected people's lives from America to the Admiralty Islands. Nor is it difficult to add that the impact of 'modern' ideas, as well as of modern machines, is to be discerned in almost every instance – a theme that will be pursued further in the next chapter. But the matter of variations and variables remains, nonetheless.

Here, too, the present chapter, together with the section on the pre-war situation, has sought to provide some indication, at least, of the kinds of forces that were locally involved: the degree of direct experience of the physical destructiveness of modern war; the nature of social structure and political organisation; the peculiarities of political culture and the extent of material resources. Only when such contextual considerations have been weighed – when, to revert to the dictum of Margaret Mead that was cited in the Preface of this book, cultural relativity has been applied – is it possible to arrive at an understanding of each particular case. To say as much, however, is not to invalidate the further exploration of wider, underlying processes that may have been present. Indeed, enquiries and hypotheses of this nature are obviously pertinent to the kind of question that readily arises in the comparative setting of the present chapter.* (Why, for example, was the degree of rebellion against the prevailing social order greater during the war

* On the ways in which, for example, both the First and Second World Wars fostered more extreme working-class radicalism in France than in Britain, see L. Gallie, *Social Inequality and Class Radicalism in France and Britain* (Cambridge, 1983), cap. 12 and 267–8.

among American blacks than it was among Japan's *burakumin*? Why, for all
the domestic and international outpourings of the time on the urgent need
for profound social change based on a recognition of the essential equality of
all mankind, did India's Untouchables not revolt against the position
accorded their caste, whereas India's Muslims, or at least a significant
proportion of them, became bent upon securing their own separate state?
Why were there such variations among the responses of Japanese-
Americans to internment? How far is it correct to develop the analogue
between changing self-images and expectations among on the one hand
women within a male-dominated national society, and on the other the
members of a nation subject to foreign rule? And so on.)

In this connection, certain propositions of a social-psychological nature
have already been indicated at various points in the foregoing pages, usually
in the form of footnotes to the text. And it will be sufficient here simply to
add a reminder that there exist as well other theses of a sociological kind that
may be helpful when it comes to reflecting further on, say, the general issues
surrounding the phenomenon of rebellion and consent within communities
and bodies-politic, especially as they manifested themselves during nearly
four years of total war.*

This is not to suggest, of course, that that commodity known as common-
sense (for all the questions of cultural relativity that could doubtless be
raised in that respect as well) is to be scorned when one is trying to
understand also, for example, how numerous individuals, in the face of what
in retrospect can seem appalling and potentially paralysing prospects and
circumstances, were able between December 1941 and August 1945 to
retain a sense of purpose and hope. One does not have to possess the results
of laboratory tests on the subject (perhaps they exist, even so) in order to
suspect, at least, that the mental process described by the editor of *The
Statesman* in Calcutta was widely shared: 'A curtain was drawn between one
part of one's brain and the next,' Ian Stephens recalled later. 'The theoretical part fully saw the grim implications of what was happening; but another,

---

* See e.g. the propositions advanced by Barrington Moore in his *Injustice: the Social Bases of
Obedience and Revolt*, concerning, *inter alia*, the nature and problems of 'social coordination', and the 'teaching' processes involved in the establishment of 'rough and ready
principles of social inequality' and the continuing revision of 'an implicit and sometimes
explicit social contract.' ('Human beings,' he writes, 'have a way of changing the value they
put on the items they contribute to the system of exchanges. They can teach each other that
the value of a man's contribution has something to do with the color of his skin. Then they can
teach each other that this is not the case.') Other propositions of Moore's that are relevant to
certain historical developments recorded in the present chapter include those concerning
what he sees as a continuing process of 'testing and discovery' on the part of both rulers and
ruled regarding 'the limits of obedience and disobedience'; and also the relationships that he
suggests exist between on the one hand a sense of injustice and on the other, *inter alia*, levels
of self-esteem and group solidarity, changing definitions of the inevitable and the unacceptable, and shifts, also, in the defining of friends and foes.

more instinctive part simply wouldn't, and remained separate and obstructive.'[142]

*

Whether or not it was in this fashion that people generally helped cushion themselves against the shocks that attended the Far Eastern war, the individual human experience is all too easily obscured when, as in this and preceding chapters, military, economic and social developments have to be treated for the most part in very broad terms. Manifestly, no selection of this or that moment in the lives of a few of the millions who were involved could begin to cover the range of situations and responses that arose during these years. But, simply as a complement to the evidence of a more desiccated kind that has been advanced above, let us take three examples of what, beneath the easy sweep of the statistic, 'life, death and change' could mean in the flesh.

In July 1943, Dr Robert Hardie, a British prisoner of war who was among those taken by the Japanese to Siam to help construct a railway between that country and Burma, noted down in the diary which he was secretly keeping the condition of a party of grievously ill Dutch and Indonesian servicemen, who were being discarded by their captors as now beyond further labouring, and most, if not all, of whom were about to raise the figure of those prisoners who died on the line towards its eventual total of 16,000:

'One lad, a Javanese, [was] on the point of death with tuberculosis, another dropping of dysentery, and so nearly dead that his filthy blanket was already a mass of flies and bluebottles attracted by the stink of putrefaction and death. That the sick have to reach such a desperate condition before they qualify for evacuation shows the extent of the Nipponese recognition of humanitarian principles. The whole party of just-living skeletons, collapsed and exhausted, make a ghastly picture: bearded, filthy, those who could stand staggering with match-stick legs and wasted faces, their eyes glazed with anguish and despair. No protest to the Jap authorities against this inhuman treatment of the sick, and the barbarous brutalities being inflicted by the engineers and guards on the railway workers, seems to have any effect.'[143]

Another statistic, this time one provided by the Japanese themselves, was the well-known actress, Naka Midori, who, before she became one of the hundred thousand or so who died as a result of the event, recounted what happened to her in Hiroshima on August 6, 1945:

'A sudden white light filled the room. My first reaction was that the hot-water boiler must have exploded. I immediately lost consciousness. When I came to, I was in darkness, and I gradually became aware that I was pinned beneath the ruins of the house . . . I ran my hands over my face and back: I was uninjured! Only my hands and legs were slightly scratched. I ran just as I was to the river, where everything was in flames. I jumped into the water and floated downstream. After a few hundred yards some soldiers fished me out.'

Miss Naka died of radiation sickness a little more than two weeks later, her body 'crumpled and light as a feather'.[144] Just under two years before this, Gavin Long had been recording the behaviour of some of his fellow-Australians in less dramatic, but also extremely harsh, circumstances, as they faced the enemy along the Satelberg Road in the wilds of New Guinea:

'The graves of our dead are by the roadside,' he noted. 'The mates of the dead soldier make a cross out of the wood of a packing case, then cover the cross-piece with bright tin from a food container, on which they stamp the dead man's name and number by pricking it out with the sharp point of a bayonet or knife. Sometimes the dead man's helmet is placed on the mound. Sitting by the road at Battalion HQ, I saw a soldier dash forward and drop his hat on the front shelf of a tank that was standing there. He appeared a few minutes later with a beautiful butterfly which he had killed with a drop of ether at the R[egimental] A[id] P[ost]. He cut the body off and was folding the wings carefully and wrapping the butterfly in cellophane from a cigarette packet to send home.'[145]

Notes

1 Crowley, *Modern East Asia*, 261.
2 Takeda, op. cit.
3 On the international dimensions of this topic, see Gong, op. cit.
4 Quoted in Spence, op. cit., 317. Cf. Thorstein Veblen's comments (in 1917) on what he saw as the 'incorrigibly peaceable' characteristic of the Chinese people, and its consequences. M. Lerner (ed.), *The Portable Veblen* (New York, 1947), 576–7.
5 *Nella Last's War*, entry for 25 June 1942.
6 Milward, op. cit., 355; Wertheim, *Indonesian Society in Transition*, 117ff.; Aziz, *Japan's Colonialism and Indonesia*, 189; Steinberg, *Philippine Collaboration*, 86ff.
7 See e.g. Milward, 30–35.
8 See ibid, 165–7.
9 Ibid, 317–20; Havens, *Valley of Darkness*, 175.
10 See Martin, *Deutschland und Japan*, 156ff., and Meskill, *Hitler and Japan*, 112ff., 156ff.
11 Milward, 355.
12 Ibid, 67, 85; Havens, 175.

13 'New Zealand's War Effort', NZ Ext. Affs. files, 81/1/14 part 2.
14 Hasluck, *The Government and the People, 1942–45*, 298ff., 414ff.; Thorne, *Allies*, 365, 645; Horner, *High Command*, 274ff., 373ff.
15 Milward, 59, 67, 74.
16 Ibid, 355; Bell, *Unequal Allies*, 206.
17 Cumings, *The Origins of the Korean War*, 26, 48, 383.
18 Thorne, *Allies*, 605; Milward, 69–70.
19 Milward, 85–6, 194, 233; Johnson, *MITI*, 157.
20 See e.g. Milward, cap. 6; P. Calvocoressi and G. Wint, *Total War* (London, 1972), passim.
21 Milward, 67, 230; Polenberg, *War and Society*, 242.
22 Ray, *Industrialization in India*, 251ff., 364ff.
23 Milward, 84, 232, 258; Havens, 197.
24 Milward, 233; Polenberg, *War and Society*, 138–9.
25 Milward, 233.
26 Ibid, 253–4, 275, 290.
27 Ibid, 272–3, 275; Polenberg, *War and Society*, 139.
28 Milward, 291.
29 Tomlinson, *The Political Economy of the Raj*.
30 Hancock and Gowing, *British War Economy*, 541.
31 Johnson, *MITI*, 166ff.
32 Perrett, *Days of Sadness*, 356.
33 S. Hoffmann et al., *France: Change and Tradition* (London, 1963), 42ff.
34 Milward, 130–1.
35 Havens, 92, 199.
36 Johnson, *MITI*, 171; Rice, 'Economic Mobilisation in Wartime Japan', loc. cit.; Milward, 117–22.
37 Blum, *V Was for Victory*, 105ff., 145; Polenberg, *War and Society*, 139, 219, 237.
38 Ickes diary, 14 June, 5 and 26 July 1942; and see e.g. Catton, *The War Lords of Washingon*, 37, 201. On Somervell, see Thorne, *Allies*, 288, 336, 390, 433.
39 Lichtenstein, *Labor's War At Home*, 73 and passim; also e.g. Catton, op. cit., caps. 8 and 9.
40 See Milward, 240–42.
41 Thorne, *Allies*, 278–9, 384–5, 504.
42 Puttick memo., 1 June 1945, NZ Ext. Affs. files, 86/1/6.
43 Havens, 101–3, 138.
44 Cumings, 28.
45 Milward, 217–8.
46 'New Zealand War Effort', loc. cit.; Mason, *A Matter of Honour*, 495.
47 Blum, *V Was For Victory*, 95; Milward, 219–20; 'New Zealand War Effort', loc. cit.; Havens, 107, 198.
48 Cf. Milward, 211; Havens, 202.
49 Wilson, *When Tigers Fight*, 1; A. N. Young, *China and the Helping Hand* (Cambridge, Mass., 1963), 417–8; Johnson, *Peasant Nationalism*, 60ff; Eastman, *Seeds of Destruction*, 136.
50 Petillo, 223–4.
51 W. Warmbrunn, *The Dutch Under German Occupation, 1940–1945* (Stanford, 1963), 19ff., 103; J. C. Blom, 'The Second World War and Dutch Society: Continuity and Change', in A. C. Duke and C. A. Tamse (ed.), *Britain and the Netherlands, Vol. VI* (The Hague, 1977).
52 Chi-ming Hou, loc. cit., 221.
53 J. W. Esherwick (ed.) *Lost Chance in China: the World War II Despatches of John S. Service* (New York, 1974): 'The Famine in Honan Province'; and see May, *China Scapegoat*, 87; Hinton, *Fanshen*, 35ff.; Eastman, *Seeds of Destruction*, 66ff.
54 Quoted in Ride, *BAAG*, 113–4.
55 E.g. Esherwick, op. cit., 178ff.; L. van Slyke (ed.), *The Chinese Communist Movement: A Report of the United States War Department, July 1945* (Stanford, 1968), 147; Shewmaker, op. cit., 199ff.; Thorne, *Allies*, 440.
56 Endacott and Birch, 142–3.

57 Lebra, *JGEACS*, 136ff.; Aziz, 187ff.; Cumings, e.g. 66; Purcell, *Revolution*, 67; Wertheim, 121, 269.
58 Robins-Mowry, 82ff.; Havens, 80, 93ff., 100, 124ff., 145, and caps. 9 and 10; Shillony, 103ff.; Milward, 257–8, 287.
59 Havens, 94.
60 Reischauer, Fairbank and Craig, *East Asia*, 713; Eastman, *Seeds of Destruction*, cap. 2; Thorne, *Allies*, 177, 307, 556.
61 Aziz, 191.
62 Tomlinson, 94ff.; Prasad, *The Indian Revolt of 1942*, 41.
63 Polenberg, *War and Society*, 27–9; Milward, 107; Hancock and Gowing, 326–9, 343, 501–2, 511.
64 See Milward, 238, 286; Calder, *The People's War*, passim.
65 Milward, 288.
66 Blum, *V Was For Victory*, 16, 90ff.; Polenberg, *War and Society*, 17; Milward, 63, 238.
67 See e.g. Morris, *Corregidor*; Mason, *Official History of New Zealand in the Second World War: Prisoners of War*; R. Hardie, *The Burma-Siam Railway* (London, 1983); Montgomery, *Shenton of Singapore*, cap. VIII.
68 Letters to the author, 21 Jan. and 16 Aug. 1984, by Professor Ikeda Kiyoshi, who very kindly had made numerous enquires within Japan on his behalf.
69 Quoted respectively in McLaine, op. cit., 250, and A. Marwick, 'World War II and Social Class in Great Britain', Duke and Tamse, op. cit.
70 Marwick, *Class: Image and Reality*, 229; and see e.g. Calder, passim; Addison, passim.
71 Polenberg, *One Nation Divisible*, 64–5; and see e.g. Marwick, *Class; Image and Reality*, 241ff.; A. J. P. Taylor (*English History, 1914–1945*, Oxford, 1965, 550) comments on the temporary flattening of the economic pyramid in Britain: 'Broadly speaking, the entire population settled at the standard of the skilled artisan.'
72 Wright, *The Ordeal of Total War*, 247.
73 Fukutake, 83, 145, 153.
74 Bullock, *Ernest Bevin, Foreign Secretary*, 703.
75 Hoffmann, *France: Change and Tradition*, 43, 51, 162ff.
76 S. de Beauvoir, *Force of Circumstance* (London, 1968), 179; Wilkinson, *The Intellectual Resistance*, 261.
77 Polenberg, *One Nation Divisible*, passim.
78 See e.g. Wright, *The Ordeal of Total War*, 236ff.; Perrett, 348; Steinberg, 165.
79 Havens, 45, 95–6.
80 Milward, 231, 243; Polenberg, *War and Society*, 159ff.; Lichtenstein, op. cit., 133, gives somewhat different figures to Polenberg's.
81 Curtin statements of 17 and 18 May 1943, P.M.'s Dpt. files, S/35/1/1.
82 Croll, *Feminism and Socialism in China*, caps. 6 and 7; Siu, *Women of China*, 137ff.
83 Croll, 205.
84 Gandhi, *Collected Works, Vol. LXXV*, 146ff., and e.g. *Vol. LXXVIII*, 212, 237.
85 *Bombay Chronicle*, 9 July 1942; *Azad Hind*, No. 3/4, 1942.
86 Manila *Tribune*, 14 June 1942 and e.g. 11 July 1944.
87 See Everett, *Women and Social Change in India*, cap. VII.
88 See e.g. Gandhi, *Collected Works, Vol. LXXVII*, 306.
89 Sahgal oral transcript No. 277, Nehru Library; and see e.g. Ghosh, op. cit., 156.
90 See e.g. Gordon, *Collaboration in France*, 123.
91 See in general Ch'en, *China and the West*, 380ff.; Croll, cap. 6; Robins-Mowry, *The Hidden Sun*, 80ff.
92 Croll, 180.
93 Spence, op. cit., 328–30, 334, 363; Croll, 5, 510.
94 Quoted in Everett, 179.
95 See e.g. A. Myrdal and V. Klein, *Woman's Two Roles* (London, 1968).
96 See Polenberg, *One Nation Divisible*, 268.
97 Robins-Mowry, 79, 308; and see Fukutake, 126.
98 Croll, 210; Siu, 106, 112.

99 Chipp and Green, *Asian Women in Transition*, 161 ff.
100 Robins-Mowry, 43, 82ff.; and see Havens, 97, 106ff., 198.
101 See e.g. Perrett, 343–5.
102 *Nella Last's War*, entries for 5 Dec. 1942 and 1 Aug. 1943. And see e.g. Terkel, "*The Good War*", 10.
103 See Steinberg, 127ff., and Kerkvliet, 65, 96; Eastman, *Seeds of Destruction*, 47ff. And on the war-time gulf between the Lao elite and other people in that country, see Toye, *Laos*, cap. 3.
104 See Purcell, *The Chinese in South East Asia*, 311ff., and *Memoirs of a Malayan Offical*, 349; J. M. van der Kroef, *Communism in Malaysia and Singapore* (The Hague, 1967), 17ff. Some Malays, however, did join the resistance: see Cruickshank, *SOE in the Far East*, 207.
105 Aziz, 171ff.; Warner and Sandilands, *Women Beyond the Wire*, 114; van der Post, *Night of the New Moon*, 80.
106 See e.g. Cruickshank, 69 and cap. 7; Tinker, *Burma: the Struggle for Independence*, e.g. doc. 286. Again, however, there were a few Burmese, also, who cooperated with British units behind the Japanese lines. Ibid, 168.
107 Oral transcript of recollections by Major Abid Hasan Safradi (March 1976), Netaji Bureau archives; Gill oral transcript, Nehru Library; Bose, 'Free India and Her Problems', *Azad Hind*, No. 9/10, 1942; Mohan Singh, cap. 27.
108 *Bombay Chronicle*, 22 May 1942, and passim.
109 Gandhi, *Collected Works, Vol. LXXVIII* (Delhi, 1979), 101, 122.
110 E.g. ibid, *Vol. LXXVI*, 45, 79; *Vol. LXXVIII*, 274, 277, 343.
111 Ibid, *Vol. LXXV*, 259; *Vol. LXXX*, 223 and e.g. 77. Gandhi also managed to believe in 1945: 'We are fast approaching a solution to troublesome race problems'. Ibid, 209.
112 *Bombay Chronicle*, 2 Feb. 1942, 21 Sept. 1944. And see Singhal, *History of the Indian People*.
113 Hane, 150.
114 See e.g. Calder, 192–3, 574–5; Blum, *V Was For Victory*, 172ff.; D. Farmer, *Vichy: Political Dilemma* (New York, 1955), 251ff.; M. Marrus and R. Paxton, *Vichy France and the Jews* (New York, 1981); Warmbrunn, op. cit., 83ff. and 265; Blom, op. cit.
115 NZ Army Dpt. files, series 11, file 16/11, Security Intelligence Records.
116 *Standard* (Wellington), 26 Oct. 1944.
117 S. N. Stone (ed.), *Aborigines in White Australia* (London, 1974), 191.
118 See D. R. Hughes and E. Kallen, *The Anatomy of Racism: the Canadian Dimension* (Montreal, 1974); K. Adachi, *The Enemy that Never Was* (Toronto, 1976).
119 Emmerson, *The Japanese Thread*, 149. Lippmann's article on the subject appeared in the *Washington Post* of 12 Feb. 1942; for its influence on the State Department, see DS 740.0011 PW/181. For analyses of public attitudes towards Japanese-Americans, War Relocation Authority files, boxes 140–2. On Congressional attempts to bar American citizenship to Japanese in the future, and in various states to prevent landholding by Orientals, DS 740.00115 EW (1939) 3300⅛, and 711.99/10–1244. For the disquiet of Ickes, see his diary, e.g. entry for 7 March 1942. In general, see Girdner and Loftus, op. cit., and Blum, *V Was For Victory*, 147ff.
120 Modell (ed.), *The Kikuchi Diary*, e.g. entries for 7 Dec. 1941, 8 and 24 June, 8 and 29 July 1942.
121 Smith, *The Shadow Warriors*, 380.
122 Polenberg, *One Nation Divisible*, 72–3.
123 OWI surveys of 16 March and 5 Aug. 1942, Roosevelt Papers, PSF, boxes 170 and 171; e.g. Ickes diary, 27 June 1943; Stimson diary, 24 June 1943.
124 White to War Dpt., 22 April 1944, NAACP Papers, box 577.
125 Motley, *The Invisible Soldier*, 39 and passim; Spector, 386ff.; Stouffer et al., *The American Soldier: Adjustment During Army Life*, cap. 10; Terkel, 264ff., 343ff., 366ff..
126 Cf. A. R. Buchanan, *Black Americans in World War II* (Oxford, 1977), 132–3; Myrdal, *An American Dilemma*, passim; N. A. Wynn, 'The Impact of the Second World War on the American Negro', *Journal of Contemporary History*, vol. 6 No. 2, 1971; Blum, *V Was For Victory*, 182ff.; Anderson, *A. Philip Randolph*, 242ff.; Perrett, op. cit., 310ff.

127 Polenberg, *One Nation Divisible*, 78.
128 White memo., 12 Feb. 1945, NAACP Papers, box 583.
129 Cronon, *Black Moses*, cap. 2.
130 See C. Thorne, 'Britain and the Black G.I.'s, *New Community*, Vol. III, No. 3, 1974, and Terkel, 279.
131 White, 'Observations and Recommendations on Racial Relations in the European Theater of Operations', 22 April 1944, NAACP Papers, box 577.
132 See Mohan Singh, 65.
133 Gilchrist, op. cit. 143.
134 Material on 'the Featherston mutiny', NZ Ext. Affs. files, 89/14/13 part 1; Mason, *Prisoners of War*, 358.
135 Warner and Sandilands, *Women Beyond the Wire*, 14, 105.
136 See e.g. Cruickshank, op. cit.; Smith, *O.S.S.*; Smith, *The Shadow Warriors*; N. H. Barrett, *Chinghpaw* (New York, 1962); W. Peers and D. Brelis, *Behind the Burma Road* (London, 1964); Feldt, *The Coast Watchers*; J. Sainteny, *Histoire d'Une Paix Manquée*.
137 Sih, op. cit., 334.
138 See I. Anders, *The Ledo Road* (Norman, Oklahoma, 1965), and Motley, op. cit., 117ff. Also Terkel, passim.
139 See Mead, *New Lives For Old*, passim.
140 See L. G. Daniels, 'The Evacuation of Schoolchildren in Wartime Japan', *Proceedings of the British Association for Japanese Studies*, vol. 2 (1977); Calder, *The People's War*, 40–58 and passim; Maruyama, *Thought and Behaviour in Modern Japanese Politics*, 113; Fukutake, *The Japanese Social Structure*, 65, 70.
141 Fukutake, 77.
142 Stephens, *Monsoon Morning*, 25. On the psychological effects of war-time experiences generally, see e.g. Wright, *The Ordeal of Total War*, 249ff, and Stouffer et al., *The American Soldier: Combat and Its Aftermath*, caps. 4 and 9.
143 Hardie, op. cit., entry for 12 July 1943.
144 Quoted in J. L. Henderson (ed.), *Hiroshima* (London, 1974), 45–6.
145 Gavin Long diary, 16–23 Nov. 1943.

CHAPTER NINE

Facing Oneself and the Future

We have seen in the preceding two chapters that the war was promoting considerable social change and unrest within many of the states involved, as well as prompting self-examinations whose conclusions, as will be further demonstrated below, were often critical of the performance and qualities of the nation concerned. Yet in the realms of 'high politics', it is often the degree of continuity, on the surface at least, that takes the eye – though, obviously, the nature of what was continuing varied greatly from one body-politic to another.

Not surprisingly, the explanations for this feature of the war years are to be found in part in those political characteristics of the combatant states that were examined in chapter three in relation to the period before Pearl Harbor. Thus in Japan, for example, despite the wide range of functions that he personally came to accumulate once the war had been launched, Tojo continued to lack the powers of a dictator, and still needed to retain the confidence of the various power groups that had placed him in office. If the bureaucracy had earlier helped prevent the development of anything approaching a genuinely democratic political system, now it constituted also an obstacle to the creation of the kind of regime that was installed in Berlin, and the same was true of the institution of the Throne. The bloodless fall of Tojo in July 1944, and of his successor as Prime Minister, General Koiso, in April 1945, demonstrated that in essence the pre-war system continued to function.[1] Within that system, of course, the military played a dominant role in many respects, and the state itself was essentially totalitarian in nature. (Elections to the Diet were closely supervised, and, although disquiet was occasionally voiced during proceedings, there was no opposition of any substance to the regime.* Control of the media became increasingly strict, while the 'neighbourhood associations' which we saw were formed before Pearl Harbor became the channel through which the Government directed more and more aspects of the people's daily lives.)[2] Nevertheless, underlying processes of social identification and networks of loyalty that were

---

* Not one member of Tojo's Cabinet of October 1941 had served as an elected member of the Diet, and during the war years the eclipse of political parties remained complete. Two politicians were brought into the Cabinet in April 1943, and Koiso appointed 24 members of the Diet as Parliamentary Vice-Ministers in September 1944; but these were essentially cosmetic measures, aimed at sustaining public support.

essentially independent of the regime retained their strength even amidst the circumstances of total war, as will be demonstrated further below.

To the outside world, even so, war-time Japan presented a front of well-nigh complete solidarity. And in its very different way, Britain, too, stood out in this respect. There was, it is true, a period in 1942 when, in the context of that succession of military reverses that was referred to earlier, it began to appear to some observers as if drastic changes at the top must ensue. ('We are all convinced that the P[rime] M[inister] cannot last much longer [in that office],' noted Eden's Private Secretary in his diary that February.)[3] But although on this occasion steps had to be taken, in A.J.P. Taylor's words, 'to conciliate public opinion', Churchill continued to command the support of the overwhelming majority of the British people as their war leader – never less than 78 per cent of those questioned in polls taken between July 1940 and May 1945 – while the coalition basis of the Government remained unshaken until the final summer of the war. (Even thereafter, Attlee's Labour Government, with Bevin as its Foreign Secretary, pursued a course in the field of foreign policy, at least, which, to the chagrin of its own left wing, deviated little from the line that had been followed beforehand.)[4]

In terms of their political cohesiveness, Britain and Japan stood at the opposite end of the scale to China. There, continuity between 1941 and 1945 meant the perpetuation of a fundamentally fissile condition: a condition reflected in the continued existence of the collaborationist regime in Nanking, and of warlords like Yen Hsi-shan in the north, Marshal Li Chi-shen in Kwangsi, and Lung Yun in Yunnan;[5] of a Nationalist Government in Chungking which was exiled from its urban strongholds on the east coast and subjected to the unending struggles for power among factions of the Kuomintang; which operated on the bases of nepotism and absolutism, stamped on the Federation of Chinese Democratic Parties, for all the latter's insignificance in terms of size,[6] and by February 1944 was deploying something like half a million of its best troops against the Communist areas in the north-west ('The Japanese,' pronounced Chiang Kai-shek privately, 'are a disease of the skin. The Communists are a disease of the heart'); of that Yenan Communist regime itself, no more tolerant of criticism than was Chiang Kai-shek's (intellectuals within its fold who ventured onto such ground found themselves silenced by 'rectification campaigns', as we have seen happen to Ting Ling), and already moving towards the cult of Mao Tse-tung as omniscient leader.[7]

If China thus presented an extreme case of political disunity (and those American endeavours noted in an earlier chapter, aimed at bringing reconciliation and harmony to the scene, were of course futile), there were other combatants, too, who differed considerably from Britain and Japan in this

sense. Thus continuity in both Australia and New Zealand took the form of
the perpetuation of single-party, Labour rule (even though in New Zealand
a more widely-based Government was briefly essayed),* endorsed by the
two electorates in elections of August and September 1943 respectively.[8]
('Remember,' observed Churchill to Attlee early in that year, 'that [in
Canberra] we are dealing with a Government not representative of Australia.')[9] In the United States, meanwhile, continuity meant above all, of
course, the extension as a result of the 1944 election of Roosevelt's remarkable tenure of the Presidency – this despite the fact that his opponent on that
occasion, Thomas Dewey, had succeeded in healing the major divisions
within the Republican Party. It also meant, though, that there remained no
possibility of a coalition government being formed, or of an end to fierce
political infighting (by the summer of 1942, notes Perrett, 'the notion of
[war-time] political accord had completely broken down'),[10] or the removal
of that deep suspicion, even hatred, of Roosevelt himself that was entertained by a significant portion of the American people.[11] As for France, her
experiences during the Second World War, like those of China, embraced a
major domestic conflict as well. A resolution of this struggle for control of
the country was to some extent promised by the trend which culminated in
the transformation of de Gaulle's Committee of National Liberation into a
Provisional Government in 1944. Yet even when Vichy was no more,
profound divisions remained within the body politic as a whole, and within
the ranks, too, of those who had opposed the Germans.

Whether the element of continuity took the form of apparent solidarity or
of manifest internal cleavages, however, in none of the states involved in the
Far Eastern war were old political patterns left undisturbed during these
years, even if the consequent shifts and upheavals had not always shown
themselves on the surface of national life by the time Japan surrendered.
Apart from Japan herself, it is perhaps the Netherlands that might seem to fit
this description least. We observed in chapter three how, in the
aftermath and shock of defeat and occupation, the idea had begun to be
discussed in some quarters that a complete reconstruction of the basis of

---

* The Labour Government in Wellington agreed in 1942 to form a War Administration
consisting of 7 Labour and 6 Opposition Ministers, with the Leader of the Opposition (S.G.
Holland) joining Fraser's War Cabinet, and with the life of Parliament being extended for the
duration of the war, subject to annual review. Following differences of opinion over a major
coal strike, however, 4 out of the 6 Opposition members resigned from the Government, the
War Administration itself was terminated, and in the ensuing election the Labour Party was
returned with 47.3 per cent of the votes, losing only a few seats in the process. (It had won
over 56 per cent of the vote in the previous, 1938 election, and was to win 51.5 per cent in that
of 1946.) Antagonism between the major parties continued to be fierce at times. The
Opposition, suggested *The Standard* in March 1944, were 'a band of reactionaries, ready,
like puppets, to dance to whatever tune is called by the Vested Interests which provide them
so abundantly with funds with which to fight the Labour Government'.

Dutch politics was required. And indeed, in May 1942 a group of prominent figures from various political and religious groupings met at a camp for hostages in North Brabant to consider the possibility of establishing a new, nation-wide political movement that would embrace many of the existing sectional interests – a potentially unifying process that was favoured by Queen Wilhelmina herself and that was championed by the clandestine publication, *Je Maintiendrai*. In the event, however, although a new organisation, the Nederlandse Volks Beweging, was indeed established in May 1945, it failed to translate aspiration into action or even into the creation of an actual political party, its principles proving insufficiently radical for the social democrats and too much so for the Catholics.* Certain changes did take place in Dutch politics during that year (notably, with the entry into the Government of Resistance elements, one of their number, Professor W. Schermerhorn, replacing Gerbrandy as Prime Minister in the summer). But the fundamentally pluralistic nature of the country's political culture and organisational form – the principle of many separate pillars upholding the entire structure – remained essentially unchanged.[12]

Yet the Netherlands had by no means been entirely unaffected by that wider process whereby the war in Europe had fostered political developments that in some cases were revolutionary in nature.[13] From 1943 onwards, especially, political debate, while of necessity it was conducted largely from underground, took on a new sharpness. The war and the hardship it engendered increased the political awareness of the Dutch working class in particular, while to the accompaniment of increased admiration for the Soviet Union the Communist element in the Resistance (its newspaper, *Die Waarheid*, had attained a circulation of perhaps 100,000 by the end of 1944) began to play a significant role in discussions on the country's future, contributing, for example, to a special pamphlet on the subject, *Om Nederlands Toekomst*, that was issued jointly by major sections of the underground in 1943. Overall, concludes one student of the subject, there was among the working class 'a broad radical trend . . . [which was] manifested in restiveness and rejection of the existing social and economic order'.[14]

A similar trend, but a much stronger one, was taking place in France. Even the conservatives of Vichy and the fascists who to some extent supported them were themselves looking to 'a complete reform of the social and political institutions of the nation', and Stanley Hoffmann has written of 'the continuity between Vichy and the Resistance' in terms of several aspects of social change, the two bitterly opposed sections unwittingly cooperating,

---

* The NVB continued as a movement, but the nearest it came to being translated into a political organisation was with the creation by elements of the Socialists and Liberal Democrats early in 1946 of the Partij van de Arbeid.

in effect, to 'carry [France] to the threshold of a new social order'.[15] While at one extreme the Parti Populaire Française of Jacques Doriot, for example, extolled the French socialist tradition as against the alien Marxist variety, and 'reflected a radicalizing of the formerly moderate and non-political lower-middle classes, politicized by the crises of the inter-war years and the disaster of 1940',[16] at the other the position of the Communist Party was greatly strengthened (as was also that of the Catholic Christian Democrats) by its role in the Resistance. On almost every hand, whatever the particular prescription for change might be, the belief was that the response to defeat and occupation must amount to 'a genuine social revolution' (as some perceived to be emerging from the war-time efforts of the British),[17] and the 1945 elections were to demonstrate the degree to which the pattern of politics had changed since the 1930s in consequence.*

The ways in which British society was indeed undergoing major political change beneath the surface of coalition endeavour need little rehearsing here, having been admirably explored by Paul Addison in his *The Road to 1945*. The popular reaction to the Beveridge Report on the future of the social services was but one, outstanding indication of a process that well before the end of the war had, in terms of domestic politics, divorced Churchill from the majority of those who readily looked to him as the leader of the nation in arms. Moreover, even before the massive Labour Party victory of 1945, and with the assistance of some Ministers from the Prime Minister's own, Conservative Party, legislative effect began to be given to the broad beliefs and aims that were summarised in, for example, one of the Directorate of Army Education's *British Way and Purpose* pamphlets:

'The fact is that, in spite of all the social progress in the years between the wars, there is still a great deal which cries out to be remedied in the condition of Britain. The war has eliminated some of these social evils, notably unemployment, for the time being,. . . [and] the blitzing of our cities has created an opportunity . . . for reconstructing many of our towns and cities on far more civilised and convenient lines . . . The war has [also] been . . . an excellent teacher of economics. It has shown conclusively that unemployment is not inevitable, and that the things which set the limit to what is possible in improving material conditions are not pounds, shillings and pence, but the quality and quantity of the nation's resources in manpower and materials.

* In the elections of September-October 1945, the Communists won 26 per cent of the vote, the Socialists 24 per cent. The Communist Party, with around 900,000 members, was now the strongest in the country, and its leader, Maurice Thorez, had returned from Moscow to become a Minister of State. By contrast, the Radical Socialists, who had figured so prominently in pre-war politics, achieved only 6 per cent of the vote. De Gaulle, though still a charismatic figure, did not have a widely-organised political base in the immediate post-war period, and was to resign as head of the government in January 1946.

Life will not be easy for some time after the war ... But given a clear expression of the democratic will of the people, given unmistakable battle orders to those whom we put in authority over ourselves, there is no reason why we should not ... create a much finer civilisation than anything we have ever known.'[18]

In retrospect, as was indicated in the previous chapter, one can question whether the anticipated social transformation was completed in the event. But there can be no doubting the extent to which it was hoped and expected among the British during the war years that such a transformation would take place. As one of those who was producing a stream of films for the Ministry of Information privately saw it at the time:

'Whether we like it or not we are undergoing a world social revolution here and now, and it is a revolution which must continue with increasing strength. For that is the only thing the people of Britain are fighting for. It is today the job of the documentary [film] to integrate the immediate war effort with the facts and implications of radical social and economic changes which are part and parcel of it ... Our films must be the shock-troops of propaganda.'[19]

It is not simply among the committed-left of British politics that perceptions – and, indeed, excitement – of this kind are to be found. The emphasis and the terminology employed naturally varied considerably; but Richard Law, for example, a Conservative member of the Government, was in broad terms referring to the same phenomena as the previous writer when he minuted privately in 1942 his conviction that the British people were 'experiencing a spiritual regeneration'. 'Everywhere in England,' comments A.J.P. Taylor, 'people no longer asked about a man's background, only what he was doing for the war.'[20]* And in Australia and New Zealand, also, there was a growing emphasis upon the need for that kind of post-war social change which we saw earlier† being propounded in relation to the international order as a whole. (In Australia, especially, war-time political trends were moving leftwards. In the 1943 election, referred to above, the Labour Party gained 50 per cent of the vote, where in 1940 it had won 40.2 per cent, while the main opposition Country Party declined from 30 per cent to just over 16 per cent.) When the war had been won, warned New Zealand's

---

* An interesting contrast between the British at home and those in India was later recalled by Ian Stephens, who spent most of the war in Calcutta and New Delhi but returned to the U.K. for a time. 'Britain was all efficiency, all close-knit dedication to a single cause, everyone feeling "we're in this together"; India, contrariwise, a vast variegated confusion, with no sense of unity anywhere discoverable, and the British civilians there – even more than the Service men – however enthusiastic might be their liking for Indians, feeling acutely conscious at times of being politically and racially out on a limb.' *Monsoon Morning*, viii.

† See above, 217.

Minister to the United States, 'there must be no retreat,... no return to the era when want and poverty and unemployment were accepted as inevitable'; and in place of 'economic individualism' there must be 'collective planning both to make the best of our resources and to ensure that human needs are satisfied'.[21]

A leftwards momentum was also building up during, and in no small measure as a result of, the war within the very different social context and political culture of China. Although by 1945 the Kuomintang itself had come to be dominatd by its right-wing elements, epitomised by the so-called 'CC Clique' (centred on the brothers Chen Li-fu, Minister of Education, and Chen Kuo-fu, director of Chiang Kai-shek's secretariat), the party and Government had already lost much ground to the Communists, both literally in terms of territory and people, and as regards political dynamism and attractiveness. As one, small example of the processes involved (which have already been alluded to in the context of Nationalist China's headlong inflation*), we can point to students of the Southwest Associated University in Kunming, for example, who, having been evacuated, along with that institution, from a Japanese-occupied area now found themselves 'left altogether outside the national effort', as one of them put it; but who, when they were eventually conscripted in 1944 as a result of Japan's 'Operation Ichi-go' offensive, 'sent back bitter stories of mismanagement and irrationality in China's armed forces' which helped ensure that 'the growing gulf between Kunming intellectuals and the Chungking Government widened further still'.[22] 'The political effects of Ichi-go were as devastating to the Nationalist Government as were the military effects,' writes Professor Eastman. 'For the Japanese offensive revealed as never before the corruption, ineptitude and demoralization of the central government.'[23]

At the same time, Chungking's reactionary and oppressive stance, noted above in connection with the campaign directed against the Federation of Democratic Parties, drove a growing number of educated Chinese towards the Communist alternative.[24] 'The Communists,' writes Clubb, 'had effectively exploited the Sino-Japanese War for the build-up and strengthening of their military forces and expansion of their military influence. And, during the eight years of war, they had won a potentially decisive political contest: they had identified themselves with anti-imperialism, the chief wartime drive of the people.'[25] In its opposition to corruption and its advocacy of land-reform, too, the Yenan regime's appeal to the mass of the people was far greater than that of the Kuomintang. The Generalissimo's 'mandate of heaven' was slipping from him, and what has been termed 'the first genuine social revolution in Chinese history since the establishment of the imperial order in 221 BC' was already in the making.[26] Although John

* See above, 260.

Davies, one of the American diplomats to visit Yenan, may have tended, along with most other foreign observers, to underestimate the degree to which Mao and his colleagues were guided by Marxist ideology, he was entirely correct in the conclusion that he had reached by November 1944: 'The Communists are in China to stay. And China's destiny is not Chiang's but theirs.'[27]*

In essence, a state of civil war already existed in China during the conflict with Japan. In Korea, it was in the making, and again one feature of these years was the advance of the left, among whom Kim Il Sung provides an example, to set alongside those of Mao himself and Ho Chi Minh, of those whose Communism was set within a strongly nationalistic framework. In this connection, the consequences of forced industrialisation in the north of the country were referred to in the previous chapter, together with the guerrilla resistance to the Japanese which was enhancing the Communist Party's prestige there, as was happening in France. ('For Koreans in general,' writes Bruce Cumings, 'the sacrifices of the Communists, if not the idea of Communism, made a ... far stronger appeal than any occasional bomb-throwing exercise of the Nationalists.') The dispossessed peasantry, the increasingly dislocated nature of whose existence in the years leading up to the war we noted in chapter three, were becoming increasingly politicised in a leftwards direction as they were flung into the industries of Manchuria, or Japan, or northern Korea itself. Yet at the same time other sections of society, as in the Philippines, were now all the more deeply committed to their Japanese overlords, and also to the new economic order which the latter were stamping on the country and under which they were prospering. In short, as the war increased the process of what Cumings describes as 'cataclysmic change' in the Korean peninsula, fundamental social and political issues were coming to the fore, to some extent within a setting of north-versus-south.[28]

In Indochina, too, and more particularly in Vietnam, the Far Eastern war contributed to developments which heralded civil war, as well as a new

---

* According to the Communists themselves, their party's membership stood at 1,210,000 by the end of the war, and the population of the areas they controlled at 95,500,000. An army of 80,000 in the mid-1930s had, they claimed, become one of 910,000 regulars and 2,200,000 militia. American estimates of the number of troops involved were substantially lower (and cf. J. Gittings, *The Role of the Chinese Army*, 1967, 1), but they, too, acknowledged the huge growth in Communist power and influence. A U.S. War Department survey at the end of 1943, for example, suggested that even in the regions apparently occupied by the Japanese, whose population totalled around 183 million, the Communists in fact were controlling areas containing 54 million people, and the Chungking regime areas with 16 million. (Boyle, *China and Japan at War*, 315.) Meanwhile, Japanese military reports were indicating that armed resistance from the Communists had become greater than that from the Nationalists, and that Communist troops were much less inclined to surrender. (Wilson, *When Tigers Fight*, 215.) See also Hinton, *Fanshen*, 84ff.; Johnson, *Peasant Nationalism*, cap. 3; Eastman, *Seeds of Destruction*, cap. 7.

phase of revolt against French colonial rule. In the period between Japan's entry into the country and her surrender, the Communists were able to make only a modest recovery in the south following the fierce suppression by the French of their 1940 uprising there. In north Vietnam, however, ostensibly operating, as we saw earlier,* within a multi-party confederation (the *Dong Minh Hoi*, formed in October 1942 and renewed in March 1944), they were able to strengthen considerably their underground network, and Ho Chi Minh himself re-entered the country from China in the autumn of 1944 to establish his headquarters in northern Tonkin. The sudden Japanese destruction of the French administration and military presence in March 1945 obviously created more promising circumstances still, even though those French were to return following the Japanese surrender – again, significantly, via the south of the country rather than the north – in company with British and Indian forces from Mountbatten's South East Asia Command.[29]

No such clear foreshadowings of civil war were to be found in Japan, of course, even though some prominent civilian figures, according to Prince Konoye, were fearing 'a leftish revolution more than defeat in war'.[30] A Japanese Communist Party did, indeed, exist, some of its members having found refuge in Yenan. And, more interestingly in some ways, Ozaki Hotsumi, an expert in Chinese affairs who was to be executed in 1944 for his collaboration with Moscow's master-spy in Tokyo, Richard Sorge, was developing the proposition that fundamental changes in Japanese society would have to be achieved through the construction of a 'New Order in Asia' that would be centred upon the Soviet Union, a Communist China, and 'a Japan divested of its capitalist structure'.[31] But Ozaki himself acknowledged that 'the revolutionary forces of this nation are extremely weak', and between 1941 and 1945, with 'the majority of intellectuals supporting the war or keeping silent', there remained that absence of opposition we noted earlier.[32] In social terms, the drastic break with the past was to come only with defeat and as a result of the second 'opening up' of Japan to the outside world by the Americans – 'a watershed', as Professor Fukutake sees it, 'a change in the nature of Japanese society'.[33]

Nevertheless, we have seen already how the domestic turmoil created by the war was helping to pave the way for a shift in the expectations of some Japanese women, for example. And some have viewed as at least potentially 'revolutionary' the extent to which international conflict, by accelerating the decline of village life and patriarchal authority within the family unit,† was helping to weaken traditional attitudes generally.[34] (The inadequacy of relying on kinship structures for the provision of basic welfare in an

* See above, 169.
† See above, 64–5.

industrial society made up of employees, rather than the self-employed, also had to be acknowledged to some extent by those in authority, a nation-wide contributory pension scheme for workers being established for the first time in 1942.)[35] The country's Socialist Party, which had received only 5 per cent of the vote in the election of 1936 and just under 10 per cent in 1937, was to gain 19 per cent in 1946 and 26 per cent a year later (a period which was also to witness 'the meteoric rise of labor unions, both numerically and politically'). The process and mounting costs of military defeat had begun to weaken the standing of the military in society before August 1945, and resentment against even the Emperor himself had started to emerge by that time. It was not simply a matter of expediency and time-serving when the most militantly nationalist of the large-circulation newspapers, *Mainichi*, declared immediately after the country's surrender had been announced: 'The nation should turn over a new leaf and free itself from the bonds of the past . . . [And this] great task cannot be carried out by discredited leaders and old-fashioned politicians.'[36]

In fact, the great contrast to the broad socio-political trends that were developing during the war among the West Europeans, the Chinese, the peoples of Australia and New Zealand, and many in Southeast Asia was to be found, not within Japanese society, but in that of the United States. For there, the growing prosperity which we observed earlier, together with the financial resurgence and revived standing of big business, was accompanied in the field of politics by a marked shift to the right, with a predominant outlook that was increasingly status-quo-orientated, if not backward-looking, rather than eagerly anticipating major social change. To some New Dealers like Harold Ickes, whose growing concern at the direction events were taking even before Pearl Harbor was cited in an earlier chapter, it began to seem that even a powerful 'fascist movement' might develop in the country once the war was over, and the Secretary of the Interior went so far in 1943 as to alert the British Ambassador, Halifax, to such a possibility and the need, were it to come about, for London to seek some kind of alignment with Moscow.* The country, noted Eric Sevareid on his return from overseas at the end of December 1943, was 'going rightist again', and others who had been away were similarly struck by the changing political climate.[37] Already, as a result of the mid-term elections of 1942, the Congressional alliance of Southern Democrats and Republicans which was bent upon

---

* 'I told [Halifax] that, in my opinion, our hope for the right kind of peace rested largely on Great Britain. I expressed the opinion that at the end of the war, we would be much further to the right than even the Conservatives of England. He agreed with this. I even ventured to suggest that we might be headed for an era of fascism following the war, in which event I would expect Russia and Great Britain to come to an understanding, as indeed I thought they should do'. Ickes diary, April 3, 1943; also entries for e.g. March 22, June 4, 1942, January 1, 1944.

curbing expenditure on welfare and the power of organised labour had been considerably strengthened. The dropping of Wallace from his Vice Presidential place on the Democratic ticket in 1944 merely underlined the extent to which Roosevelt himself had already begun to turn away from 'Dr New Deal', whose remedies, he declared, were no longer required. As Federal organisations and programmes devoted to social welfare, conservation and the like were killed off or reduced to a moribund condition, Archibald MacLeish (New Dealer, Librarian of Congress, and, for a time, Assistant Secretary of State) noted: 'Liberals meet in Washington these days, if they meet at all, to discuss the tragic outlook for all liberal proposals, the collapse of liberal leadership, and the inevitable defeat of all liberal aims.' The severe restrictions placed on the work of the Office of War Information (from which MacLeish himself, among others, had resigned) were, concludes the historian of that organisation, 'but one more example of the war's devastating impact on the whole liberal cause'.[38]

As the coalition of political interests that had sustained Roosevelt in the 1930s began to fall apart, American society generally, far from moving in a 'Beveridge' direction, was turning further away still. Among the clerisy, for example, much acclaim was accorded the thesis developed by Friedrich Hayek in his *The Road to Serfdom* (published in 1944) – that the displacement of liberalism by socialism 'as the doctrine held by the great majority of progressives' represented 'a sharp break ... with the whole evolution of Western civilisation', and pointed in the direction of tyranny.[39] Although at the end of 1943 there remained over 20 million people in the country who were living on poverty-level incomes, almost all attempts to introduce legislation to promote social welfare failed entirely. For the majority, the war was already bringing greater prosperity as hugely increased national wealth became more widely distributed.* Government action did assist this process through housing loans and other benefits that were granted to returning veterans. (The entire concept of higher education in America was to be radically changed as many working-class ex-G.I.s took advantage of the opportunities that were now opened up to them in that field.) But as a means to wholesale social reform Federal initiatives were generally regarded as neither necessary nor healthy in themselves. 'There was a constraining weight of long-standing habits of mind and behaviour,' concludes John Morton Blum. 'Weary of the memory of depression and of the demands of a foreign war, rather bored with politics, international or domestic, the American people accepted victory and prosperity as a sufficient achievement of the safety and security their hearts desired.'[40]

The successful quest for victory in total war greatly enhanced the standing

* See above, 263, note.

of the military, as well as big-business, within American society,* and the country's senior officers in their turn were developing a new set of inclinations and assumptions about their role in the management of the nation's affairs. ('The military attitude toward civilian control changed completely during the war,' observes Samuel Huntington. 'The plans for post-war organization of the armed services, developed by the military in 1944 and 1945, reflected a new conception of their role in government. One would hardly recognise the cowed and submissive men of the 1930s in the proud and powerful commanders of the victorious American forces, [for whom] civilian control was a relic of the past which had little place in the future.')[41] Men like General Somervell, together with the dollar-a-year 'war lords of Washington', capitalising on both the exigencies of international conflict and the strong conservative instincts within American society, helped ensure that its fear of change set the country far apart from all others on the Allied side; that, in Bruce Catton's words, 'commitment to the status quo at home, where reaction had found its voice again', soon became 'by logical extension commitment to the status quo abroad as well'; that, at the war's end and thereafter, military might and unparalleled wealth would be accompanied by an underlying fear that continues to this day.†

The indifference of the majority of Americans to the wider social impli-

---

* In France, on the other hand, the military emerged from the war not only divided by the recent Vichy/Resistance past but, in Hoffmann's words (*France: Change and Tradition*, 51), 'largely alienated from the rest of the national community'. Where the Chinese Communists were concerned, 'the years 1941–4', writes John Gittings, '. . . when [their] areas were pressed hardest by Japanese blockade and encirclement, were the army's most formative period', the emphasis being placed upon, *inter alia*, 'strict political control, the practice of economy and participation in production work, scrupulous attention to public relations, expansion of the militia, [and] democratic behaviour within the army itself . . .' *The Role of the Chinese Army*, xiii.

† Catton was to become a noted historian of (suitably) the American Civil War. His *War Lords of Washington*, courageously published (and fiercely attacked) in 1948, was based in part on his war-time observations as an official of the War Production Board, and its perspectives and judgements need to be seen in that light among others. But the book was and remains far more than a heart-felt cry of personal disillusionment, deserving to be placed alongside Julien Benda's celebrated warning to his fellow-Europeans in 1927, *La Trahison des Clercs*.

In retrospect, Catton appears to have underestimated the extent to which both the revival of 'reaction' and the conduct of 'government by public relations' were facilitated by the predilections of a sizeable proportion of the people – the electorates of 1942 and 1946, after all – in whom he reposed his faith and hopes. He also shared the delusion of many frustrated New Dealers at the time and their political heirs since, that Roosevelt's own fine intentions for the reform of American society had simply been thwarted during the war by the 'hollow men' who manoeuvred in Washington at the time, not appreciating – or perhaps unable to accept – that the President had himself wittingly betrayed the cause in question. (Lest British readers should be tempted to assume that applying the balm of political myth in this fashion is a peculiarly American characteristic, let them turn to their own recent past: for example, to the *suppressio veri* and *suggestio falsi* that were presented in the press for the collective comfort on the occasion of the death of an infinitely lesser figure than Roosevelt, Anthony Eden.) For penetrating reflections by other contempories, see Terkel, "*The Good War*", 329, 516, 573.

cations of the war (and, as we observed in earlier chapters, to its wider international significance also) did not preclude an eagerness to hear about the country's heroes at the fighting fronts, whose exploits were packaged and sold to the public in the same commercial fashion as was the war itself, in the exercise of what Catton correctly summarised as 'government by public relations'.[42] Such promptings of nationalist sentiment were frequently accompanied by an emphasis upon the successful way in which the American 'melting-pot' had created a single, great society out of people whose ethnic backgrounds were so diverse;* and indeed, the process of assimilation was being pushed forward, it seems, by the country's involvement in the war: the average number of people becoming naturalised Americans annually, which had been just over 148,000 between 1934 and 1939, rose to over 295,000 between 1940 and 1945.[43] (As Geoffrey Perrett, for one, sees it, the war was 'the supreme collective social experience in modern American history'.)[44] Where the country's black population was concerned, literature like the O.W.I.'s *Negroes and the War* and films like *The Negro Soldier* strove to depict a wholly united nation, while even those of Japanese descent who had collectively fallen under suspicion could be helped to become true Americans – as many of them, it is clear, wished:†

'I realise that one of [your] primary aims is to foster Americanization,' declared the Director of the War Relocation Authority, Dillon S. Myer, in a defensive speech to the American Legion‡ about his agency's proposal that interned Japanese Americans should be progressively released. 'That has been one of the major objectives of our program. There are many ways to define Americanism, but I have always felt that it is a quality which we absorb quite naturally while living in a thoroughly American environment . . . We have established the curriculum for our [camp] schools with particularly heavy emphasis on the history of American traditions and . . . institutions . . . But despite all our efforts, we have not succeeded . . . in duplicating the atmosphere that prevails in a normal American community.'[45]

Nationalism of a self-satisfied or heavily-assertive kind sometimes, not surprisingly, accompanied the pride taken by Americans in the massive power which their country had been able to mobilize during the war. The well-known correspondent Theodore White was later to acknowledge that when he visited units engaged in the Far Eastern conflict in 1945 '[a] sense of the American purpose as Triumph over Evil became unshakable in me, almost maniacal, as I began to flick around the map of Asia which was

* See above, 203.
† See above, 273.
‡ The American ex-servicemen's association.

opening to our conquests'.[46] 'We Americans,' proclaimed the *Saturday Evening Post*, 'can boast that we are not as other men are,' while only a shade less arrogantly Senator William Fulbright described the American way of life as 'the only way worthy of a free man'.[47] Even the suspicion that, in diplomatic terms, 'we are in the ring', as Raymond Clapper put it, 'and can't get out of it and are just being outboxed all round' (that is, by the shrewd and experienced Europeans),[48]* could be attributed to the essentially disinterested approach of the United States to international affairs – its citizens, as Roosevelt himself privately described them, 'still living in the age of innocence'.[49] And, in the same way, America's past dealings with the peoples of other lands tended to be seen in a somewhat roseate light, as when John Emmerson, for example, in his State Department memorandum of February 1942 that was cited earlier, on 'What the United States Has Done For Japan', described in the following terms Commodore Perry's insistence in 1853–4, at the point of a gun, that Japan should trade with the United States:

'Perry opened Japan. He did it with tact and forebearance. He came not as a conqueror but as a peaceful envoy to invite Japan into the society of nations . . . Japan was fortunate that her first relations were with the United States. We were not building an Empire and were not a militaristic nation. Trade with the Orient was becoming important, however, and it was natural [sic] that we should trade with Japan.'[50]†

Meanwhile, little less than a century after they had received from Perry an offer they could not refuse, the Japanese themselves, as we saw in chapter four, were frequently being reminded of their own unique and superb national qualities. Nor were enhanced national self-awareness and pride peculiar to peoples who were schooled by a xenophobic regime or who were moving to the right in political terms. For the British, for example, such attitudes and sentiments had both helped make possible, and been stimulated by, the successful defiance of Germany in 1940–1. Among the French they gave rise to the determination we noted earlier, that, in the words of the Communist *L'Humanité*, their country would 'resume her place as a great world power and stand forth in the counsels of the nations in all the grandeur bestowed on her by her suffering, her struggles and her prestige'.[51] In the event, as we have seen, the general acceptance of this high goal was not sufficient to create national unity; but the shock of defeat in 1940, and, subsequently, a growing reaction against Vichy and its works, were

---

* See above, 214–5.
† On the unilateral assertion by Westerners of the *ius commercialis* as a corollary of the natural-law doctrine of a universal international society, see Bull and Watson, *The Expansion of International Society*, 120.

nevertheless leading to what Stanley Hoffmann has described as 'a kind of rediscovery of France and the French by the French'.[52]

Such a process of national rediscovery was being urged upon the Chinese, also, by Chiang Kai-shek in his *China's Destiny*.* And if here, too, pride in a distinct and ancient culture fell far short of creating domestic political unity; if, as Professor Eastman has suggested, large numbers of peasants, even in the face of the Japanese invasion, still did not identify strongly with the cause of the nation as a whole,† even so, generally speaking, nationalist sentiments were clearly stimulated by the war, and were being channeled into a Sinified form of Marxism by Mao Tse-tung.[53]

As for those peoples caught up in the war who had yet to achieve their independence, their focusing of political ardour upon the nation was in some respects more complete than was the case in Western Europe, where the experience of war and occupation had engendered in some quarters the conviction that the nation-states of the region must be merged within some larger, supranational or at least federal entity if peace and prosperity were ever to be firmly established.[54] The surges of nationalist sentiment that were passing through the populations of dependent Asian territories – not least, through the young‡ – during the war years have been indicated in earlier chapters. The General Secretary of the Congress was not greatly exaggerating when he recorded that, when the leaders of his party were released from detention in June 1945, 'the India that greeted [them] . . . was different from the day before. There was a miraculous change in the atmosphere . . . The pent-up energy of the people broke loose . . .'[55] Nationalist fervour was indeed now beyond Britain's curbing. In the Bombay hinterland, for example, the authority of District Officers had become seriously eroded, while even in the Indian Army§ – whose volunteer soldiers had themselves been fighting for their country – nationalist sentiment was so powerful that the prospective punishment of those who had gone over to the I.N.A. was soon, in the words of a senior British officer, 'threatening to tumble down the whole edifice'. (In Burma, likewise, as a British administrator was later

* See above, 163.
† See above, 20.
‡ See above, 149. Age differences between those Chinese in the Hong Kong New Territories who joined the Communist guerrillas and those who collaborated with the Japanese were also apparent (Endacott and Birch, *Hong Kong Eclipse*, 244), while in Nationalist China the Youth Corps bitterly criticised Kuomintang leaders like H.H. Kung for their sloth and corruption. (See Eastman, *Seeds of Destruction*, cap. 4.) It is worth recalling that in France, too, just as Vichy paid special attention to the role of youth generally, so also young people played a major part in the Resistance. Hoffmann, *France: Change and Tradition*, 36, 59.
§ It is worth noting that the number of serving Indian officers in the Indian Army, which had been 1,000 in 1939, had grown to 15,740 by 1945. (Mason, *A Matter of Honour*, 511.) On the Viceroy's great concern in the autumn of 1945 over the domestic consequences of the use of Indian Army units against Indonesian nationalists, see Thorne, 'Engeland, Australië en Nederlands Indië', loc. cit.

to recall, by the late autumn of 1945 imperial authority would be in a state of 'virtual collapse'.)[56]*

Sjahrir's summary of what had been taking place in this respect in the East Indies can serve as a final reminder that between 1941 and 1945 many Asians, as well as Frenchmen, Americans, British and others in the West, came to look upon their respective nations in a new way:

> 'The old, experienced Indonesian administrators of the colonial service,' wrote Sjahrir a few years later, 'felt only contempt for the [Japanese] political ignoramuses who were placed over them. As a consequence, all layers of society came to see the past in another light. If these barbarians had been able to replace the old colonial authority, why had that authority been necessary at all? Why, instead, hadn't they handled the affairs of government themselves? Under the Japanese, the people had to endure indignities worse than any they had known before . . . [But] the national self-consciousness of the Indonesian people developed a new and powerful drive beyond anything known before in our country.'[57]

*

In many of the lands involved in the Far Eastern war, then, national self-awareness, pride and confidence were being enhanced by the peculiar circumstances of the time. And yet, as we have already seen in regard to the fear in some British quarters that a succession of military defeats might betoken an inherent 'softness' in the country and its society, doubts and self-criticism, too, were being engendered as a result of what were frequently thought of as the special 'tests' which the conflict and its consequences were setting for governments and peoples alike.

In many cases, of course, disquiet and dissatisfaction had not originated after December 1941, and it will be recalled that feelings and judgements of this kind were widely in evidence when we surveyed the period leading up to the war.† Certainly, the persistence with which some regimes and individual political leaders called, during the war years themselves, for the regeneration of their nation suggested that they found the quality of the people to have become impaired in some way over a lengthy term, and to be making a less than total and swift recovery amidst the new challenges

---

* Enhanced pride and confidence as a result of the war was not in every case linked to a demand for immediate independence. This was not so in Fiji, for example, of whose formidable fighting units in the Solomons campaign and elsewhere Lala Sukuna declared in 1944: 'Our men for the first time in the history of the Colony have had an opportunity of showing that there was something more in them than . . . muscle and brawn and fuzzy hair . . . They have [also] acquired fresh confidence and a new strength with which to face the problems of the post-war world.' Scarr, *Fiji*, 327.

† See above, 87–9.

and opportunities presented by world-wide conflict. In this connection, the prescription for national renaissance presented to his fellow-Indonesians by Soekarno in 1944 took the form of 'five rules for the conduct of life' (*Pantja Dharma*),[58] while in the Philippines Vargas and his fellow-collaborators (whose own behaviour, in the event, did much to increase corruption and cynicism) likewise issued calls for that puritan selflessness and discipline which would enable the people of the islands to cleanse themselves of the imprint left by alien 'American commercialism'.[59] Very similar, too, were the continuing endeavours of the Vichy regime to reinstate in France traditional values, disciplined toil, and the vital social units of family and village. And again this programme for renaissance (based as it was on a romanticised vision of the country's past social order, together with the belief that modern means of production could so be managed as not to impair that order's essential *mores*) entailed the ending of 'a servile imitation of foreign social developments', of 'a materialist ethic which would once more bind us in the chains of paganism'.[60]

The similarities that were noted in the context of the period before Pearl Harbor between Vichy's calls to the French and those of Chiang Kai-shek to the Chinese became if anything stronger still during the three ensuing years, as the Generalissimo strove to turn his people away from those features of the modern world that were pressing in upon China all the more as a consequence of the conflict, not least in the form of people and things American.[61] Liberalism, proclaimed Chiang in *China's Destiny*, was as alien as Communism to the nation's genius, and he made it plain that all the country's social ills, as well as the ravages inflicted upon it by war, were attributable to the foreigner. 'In the China of his dreams,' writes Payne, 'all western ideas were banished and the Chinese remained proud, undefiled, unassailably pure and devoted to Confucianism.' Yet in the event, it was those same Chinese, not least the members of his own Kuomintang, who left him bitterly disappointed.[62]

As the example of Soekarno has already indicated, such demands for national regeneration were by no means the monopoly of the right. For Mao Tse-tung and his colleagues, an 'entirely new cultural orientation', involving the cultivation of true 'proletarian consciousness' and the adoption of a disciplined, selfless life in the interests of the people and the revolution, was a *sine qua non*.[63] In France, the Resistance, like Vichy, rejected the notion of a return to unrestricted individualism, called upon the nation to rise above the corrupting selfishness of the past, and looked to the creation of a new 'moral and social order' in which personal freedom would not be exercised at the expense of 'the general interest'.[64] The trials and more direct process of purging ('*épuration*') that were

conducted against Vichyites and collaborators following the Liberation,*
like Vichy's own Riom proceedings earlier against Blum, Daladier and
Gamelin, reflected a widespread conviction that the nation had become
corrupted. And if nothing on this scale or of this depth of bitterness faced
the Dutch when they looked at themselves, they, too, as well as having
their collaborators to deal with, had questions to ask concerning the
degree of accommodation that had been displayed by the people as a
whole when the German invaders first arrived, and the decision that had
been taken then by many bureaucrats to continue functioning under the
country's new masters.[65]

It did not take occupation by the enemy, however, to bring out profound disquiet concerning the fibre of society within an established state.
Where Australia and its people were concerned, for example,† the strong
criticisms which we have seen being expressed by Americans and others
were matched by the anger – even despair, at times – of some Australians themselves. It was often those who were or had been serving abroad
who cast an especially critical eye on their fellow-countrymen at home.
'The Army [i.e., the Australian Imperial Force] thinks that it – and the
A[ir] F[orce] and Navy – is doing the hard work, while the militia and
the civilians, many of them, are "bludging",' noted Gavin Long in his
diary in August 1943; and a year earlier A.I.F. troops who had been
fetched back from the Middle East in readiness for a possible Japanese
attack on their homeland had been talking to him in a similarly scornful
vein about the 'squeals' of the public that had brought about what they
saw as an unnecessary redeployment which had meant 'letting England
down'.

'Anyone who moves about among the veteran units of the Army today,'
wrote Long publicly, 'will find evidence that soldiers are convinced that
their own people are failing to come up to the standard set by the people of
England and by the unforgettable people of Greece. Their national pride

---

* Nearly 125,000 cases were drawn up in this regard. Almost 7,000 death sentences were
pronounced, over 700 of them being carried out. In addition, there were possibly as many as
10,000 unofficial executions during and immediately after the process of Liberation. It has
been estimated that between 150,000 and 200,000 of the French were involved in collaboration movements between 1940 and 1944. See e.g. Gordon, *Collaboration in France*, and
Cotta, *La Collaboration, 1940–1944*.
† Self-criticism of a fundamental kind was far less common – and less called for, some might
think – in New Zealand. There, too, however, both industrial disputes and what some
believed to be a general failure on the part of the public to appreciate the gravity of the
country's situation (in 1942, members of the 'Awake! New Zealand!' campaign saw around
them 'defeatism' as well as complacency and selfishness) aroused strong criticism in the press.
E.g. *The Standard* (Wellington), January 29, March 12, September 24, 1942; Hon. Sec.,
'Awake! New Zealand!' campaign to Fraser, March 30, 1942, NZ External Affairs files,
84/12/2.

has been given a blow, and they are falling back more and more on regimental and personal pride.'[66]

The war was, of course, enhancing Australians' sense of their own, distinct national identity. But in January 1943, the manager of an organisation in Sydney that was engaged in surveying public opinion wrote privately to the Prime Minister to inform him of findings that appeared to corroborate what Long's A.I.F. men were saying:

'Our civilian morale is not good. Many people have not subscribed to War Loans. There is absenteeism in industry and there is apathy amongst large sections of the people towards the war effort. My staff interviews thousands of Australian people in all walks of life every year . . . [and] much of the opinion expressed is most disturbing from the point of view of morale.'[67]

Such was the level of complaint among the inhabitants of various towns in North Queensland over inconveniences occasioned by the arrival in the area of large numbers of troops, concluded a special report prepared for Curtin in the same period, that unless the authorities acknowledged the burdens he was bearing the average citizen of the region 'may well prove an easy dupe for enemy propaganda [, and a] refusal to cooperate with the Services could easily follow, together with opposition to any Government which aimed at continuing the war'.[68]

Gavin Long's belief was that, quite apart from other problems, there existed among Australians 'a sense of colonial inferiority' that could infect the country's soldiers as well as its general public.[69] The *Sydney Morning Herald* (which repeatedly expressed its dismay and sense of outrage over the 'shame and disgrace' of the strikes and absenteeism that were referred to in the previous chapter) went further. In March 1942, having posed the question, 'Is there real national unity?', it concluded:

'Plainly, as a people we have not yet found our soul . . . At no time during two and a half years of war have we truly become one people. Not even in politics have we drawn together . . . We are much too prone today to find fault with others, instead of discovering and remedying our shortcomings.'

And again in July of that year:

'Judging by the talk to be heard at every street corner, great numbers of people are seeking only their own advantage, convinced that profiteering out of the war is the fashion.'

And in May 1945, still:

'If, as Ministers have complained, Australia's contribution to the war is not appreciated abroad, this is scarcely to be wondered at in the light of the continual strikes and petty political wranglings which are hampering the national war effort and create the worst possible name for Australian sincerity among our Allies. No Australian can look around him at home today without a deep sense of shame.'[70]

As seen by another Australian newspaper, industrial strife in that country had indeed reached such a pitch by October 1944 as to create a situation of 'civil war: or very near it'.[71] And if, in the United States, meanwhile, labour disputes were somewhat less crippling and socially divisive, there, too, they were seen as cause for shame by a good many Americans themselves. 'American labor troubles are incomprehensible over here,' cabled Raymond Clapper from London in June 1943,

'and I can find no way to explain them to people who inquire. In this war there is no parallel here . . . for the course taken by [John L.] Lewis . . . People here can understand labor leaders whose men get out of hand, but not one who himself orders stoppage in basic war production industry like coalmining. Also difficult here understand Packard strike . . . For twenty thousand workmen to stop war production of motors over employment [of] three Americans of dark skin doesn't make sense abroad . . . Neither here nor in Sweden [which Clapper had also visited] is there any race problem and our troubles in that respect subject widespread interest because it is regarded as one of big minority problems in world . . . American Army officers regard labor troubles at home sourly. Feel it is not good for morale [of] American troops who in England been working night [and] day for months building airfields.'[72]

Numerous instances where the owners and managers of arms-producing industries in the U.S.A. knowingly and in pursuit of higher profits delivered defective matériel to the armed forces[73] also drew criticism from Americans, while complacency and indifference among civilians regarding the war in general, which has been alluded to already, sometimes led to clashes that involved embittered veterans who had returned home.[74] Neither in respect of these particular features of war-time America, however, nor (as we have seen) in regard to the long-standing phenomenon of racial segregation and discrimination, was the overwhelming self-satisfaction of the majority of white citizens of the United States shaken during these years. In this respect, as in its increased prosperity, its freedom from destruction at enemy hands, and its pronounced move to the right politically, America was a case apart.

In one sense, an extreme contrast to such smugness was provided by the exacting standards and related criticisms that were held up before the people of India by Gandhi. Here, again, was a leader who had proclaimed that the war both called for and would facilitate national regeneration through sacrifice. (Bose's cry: 'The blood of martyrs is the price that must be paid for liberty . . . If we would deserve freedom we must fight for it', was echoed by the Mahatma in July 1942, for example, when he went so far as to announce: 'It would be a good thing if a million [Indian] people were shot in a brave and non-violent rebellion against British rule [at a time when] the different nations are . . . avowedly . . . fighting for their liberty. Germany, Japan, Russia and China are pouring out their blood and money. What is *our* record?')[75] Yet his confidence in the nature and capacities of his fellow-Indians, as in those of mankind as a whole,* had been more than a little shaken by the summer of 1945. He had already, shortly before the outbreak of the Far Eastern war, felt obliged to denounce those members of the Congress

> 'who have no faith in khadi [i.e., the domestic manufacture of simple cotton garments], who decry untouchability in private but observe it in their homes, who, being Hindus, hate the Muslims, or who, being Muslims, hate the non-Muslims'.[76]

But it was when he emerged from confinement in the autumn of 1944 that Gandhi became greatly dismayed at what he saw as a pronounced decline in the life and spirit of Indian society, 'as though one age had succeeded another' since he had entered prison in the summer of 1942. Observing that 'we have failed to make non-violence a part of our being', he concluded that there was 'nothing left like moral public opinion' in an India where 'injustice, exploitation, and falsehood' now prevailed. It was this 'corruption' among Indians themselves, and not simply on the part of the country's alien rulers; the continuing 'sin of untouchability' and 'communal bitterness', that brought him towards the end of the year to contemplate the commencement of a new fast. 'If the fast comes,' he wrote, 'it will have nothing to do with the Government.' It was the behaviour of his own people that most grieved him now.[77]

Even in Japan itself, whose rulers' decision to launch the war had been based in no small part on a belief in the superior qualities and capacities of the nation as a whole, the test of prolonged international conflict and increasing hardship revealed weaknesses of attitude as well as of material resources. 'People certainly made a consistent show of obedience,' writes Fukutake, 'making demonstrative displays of local joy when the conscription papers arrived, for instance. But underneath, the effort selfishly to defend one's personal livelihood persisted; the conscription papers were wept over at home. So as the war situation worsened, authoritarian control had to become even more severe and the pressures of ideological exhort-

---

* In a speech of October 22, 1941, for example, Gandhi had declared: 'My faith in human nature is progressively growing. I have concluded, on the basis of my experiments, that human nature can be easily moulded.' *Collected Works, Vol. LXXV*, 45.

ation were stepped up.'[78] 'Down with family considerations!', shrilled the
Imperial Rule Assistance Association during the 1942 election campaign.
'Down with personal interests! Vote in the public and national interest!' But
'deep-rooted psychological resistance' to such demands, as Maruyama
terms it, was in its way more solidly based than even the call of national duty.
For the nation's 'primary values tended to foster sectionalism', and behind
the absenteeism and shoddy workmanship, for example, that we noted in
the previous chapter, there lay that fundamental weakness of Japan as a
modern state which was indicated in the context of the pre-war years: the
lack of organic unity among autonomous *citoyens*.[79] In this sense, it was
more than the country's armed forces that suffered defeat between 1941 and
1945.*

*

Even within the context of the country's existing political culture, the
demands of the war were creating for Japan's rulers major dilemmas
concerning the structure and nature of its society. For Tojo and the 'double
patriots' (as for the men of Vichy), it was in the countryside that the heart of
the nation lay; from the villages that there came forth 'sturdy soldiers', in
Tojo's phrase, superior to men from the towns 'in everything, not only in

* See above, 64–5. On this point, Professor Ronald Dore has raised with the author a general
question of great importance – and difficulty. He argues that 'for fighting such a war as this,
the organic unity of individuals is on the whole less effective than – to use the Durkheimian
typology – the "mechanical solidarity" of the tribe', and that it could be said that 'the best
time to fight wars is when the process of industrialization has gone far enough to produce
weapons, but not so far as to produce the individualism that breaks down the solidarity'. This
line of argument was also developed by Thorstein Veblen, notably in his *Imperial Germany
and the Industrial Revolution* (1915) and *An Inquiry Into the Nature of Peace and the Terms of
its Perpetuation* (1917), where he referred to both Imperial Japan and Imperial Germany as
having reaped the benefit of modern technology, not least in their capacity for war, 'without
being hampered with its long-term institutional consequences', each retaining 'a servile
population imbued with impeccable loyalty to its masters and with a suitably bellicose
temper'. (Lerner (ed.), *The Portable Veblen*, 547ff. and 573ff.)
   Such propositions require an acceptance of, *inter alia*, Veblen's assertion that 'modern
civilisation' and its 'machine technology' brings with it – even if, as in the states cited, the
process is delayed – 'the modern drift toward free or popular institutions'. Many contemporary social critics, however, as Barrington Moore observes, draw a connection, rather,
'between materialism, rationalism, and the drive to dominate'. (*Injustice: the Social Bases of
Obedience and Revolt*, 85.) And the Veblen/Dore propositions are also open to question in
the light of the Far Eastern war itself, for example. The Japanese Army was obviously, in
over-all terms, more ready than the British, say, to die to order and to the last man; but these
are not the only, or even necessarily the most important, qualities required on the modern
battlefield. And whilst the 'individualist' society of France cracked apart in 1940, the
'organic strength' of its British counterpart was manifested and increased, rather, by the tests
of total war, to such a degree that the country was able not only to match Japan's 'mechanical
solidarity' in the face of adversity and hardship, but to do so without sacrificing its essential
individualism and all that it represented.

physique . . . [but in their] firmer character'. It followed, therefore, that the
need to move a growing number of people out of the rural areas and into the
towns where the war-industries were located was disturbing in more than the
obvious sense. 'This is a point that truly worries me,' Tojo confessed to the
Diet in 1943:

'On the one hand I want at all costs to maintain the population of the
villages at forty per cent of the total population. I believe that the
foundation of Japan lies in giving prime importance to agriculture. On the
other hand, it is undeniable that industry is being expanded, chiefly
because of the war. It is extremely hard to reconcile these two factors . . .
A harmony must be created by degrees . . . but . . . care must be taken to
avoid making havoc of the Japanese family system. I must confess that
things are not proceeding at present in an ideal manner.'[80]

But Tokyo's dilemma went wider still, in fact. If 'the modern' in the form of
industrialization accompanied by market individualism was looked upon
askance because of its effects on Japan's rural life, the underlying, Western
associations of the entire concept, widely disliked long before the war,
became more tainted than ever once battle had been joined in December
1941. Yet it was not sufficient, for example, for those members of the clerisy
who were brought together by the literary magazine *Bungakukai* to discuss
the subject in the autumn of 1942 to declare that the solution lay in Japan's
'overcoming' modernity by moving to a higher stage of development. They
still had to agree on the bases and the nature of this new and superior species
of 'modernization', and in this they failed. 'No new formula for a Japanese-
style modernization emerged from this or any other symposium,' comments
Shillony. 'The vision of progress without Westernization remained attractive, but no one knew exactly how such a goal could be achieved.'[81] The
nation's propagandists, as noted earlier,* were obliged to fall back upon the
assertion that 'Japan is the place where Eastern and Western culture is knit
together'.[82]

The need to blend the 'two civilizations' of East and West was also
proclaimed in the West itself, as we have seen, by Pearl Buck among
others.† Yet within those Western societies that were able to remain free
from enemy occupation, the war not only swept aside what remained of the
stagnation and unemployment that had become so widespread during the
1920s and '30s; it frequently engendered a new sense of purpose and hope.
Even defeat and direct oppression could be seen as providing a new and
unique opportunity for commitment and creativity. ('We have never been
more free,' wrote Sartre, 'than under the German occupation.')[83] Western

* See above, 145.
† See above, 181–2.

societies might well be in urgent need of reform; but even that reform was widely assumed to require the development, not the abolition, of their 'modern', industrial basis, together with improved techniques of analysis and management which would represent but one more extension of that approach to the problems of man and his environment which had come to hold sway in the West since the scientific revolution of the seventeenth century. The war provided an enormous impetus to the further development of 'the modern' in the shape of science, technology, industrialisation and urbanisation. At the same time, hopes for a better future were often encouraged by accompanying developments in fields such as 'scientific budgeting' and 'operational research' (both of which emerged in Britain under siege). In both Vichy and Resistance France, for example, changing attitudes and institutions were preparing the way for the planning of the country's economy after the war. And nowhere, of course, did 'modern' techniques appear to glow with promise more than in the United States, where professional economic advisers were becoming major figures in the shaping of the country's future, where the 'social sciences' were taking wing, and where the predominant conviction and working principle within the Research and Analysis branch of the O.S.S., to take one small but significant example, was that 'thoroughly objective and neutral' study of a historical kind was not only desirable but obtainable.[84]*

Moreover, within Asia, as well, the war had fostered similar developments in some areas, and in others at least the attractiveness of 'the modern'.† In Japan, for all the emphasis upon the superiority of 'spirit' over mere machines, and upon the decadence of the materialist civilisation of the West, 'planned economic development', as we have seen, figured prominently in the programme set out at the Great East Asia Conference of 1943. Nor could there be any disguising the urgent need to develop the country's technological and scientific capacity.‡ (Where science was concerned, the emphasis was upon its applied, rather than theoretical, aspects.) The *Nippon Times* might claim that Japan was leading 'a Great East Asia scientific revolution' that owed nothing to Western achievements in that field; but even other propagandists were to be found admitting, as noted in an earlier chapter, that 'Asian civilisation' in general had been 'considerably

---

* As Bradley Smith observes with regard to this last illustration: 'This attitude grew out of the belief that the social sciences were directly analogous to the physical sciences and (as Ranke expressed it) that historians were capable of grasping the past as it really was.' *The Shadow Warriors*, 362.

† To the Council of Chiefs in Fiji, in November 1944, for example, Lala Sukuna observed: 'The old regime is finished ... [and] Fiji is now occupied by people of other races who have brought with them new ways, and these our young people are picking up ...' Scarr, *Fiji*, 358ff.

‡ The number of technical schools in Japan grew from 11 in 1935 to 413 ten years later, with a six-fold increase in students.

weakened through the absence of the scientific element', while the might of the modern resources that the West came to direct against Japan in battle was to be acknowledged with something like awe in certain quarters.[85]*

Among prominent Indian nationalists, meanwhile, Nehru's long-standing conviction† that the application of science and technology was vital to the country's future was likewise reinforced by war-time events. 'Science was born in Asia,' asserted Gobind Behari Lal to an American audience, 'and received vigorous development in its European abodes ... In the days ahead, a greater freedom can be created with a greater science – but only if East and West ... are united and work together for global liberty and light.'[86] Whether the way forward for India itself lay through the development of industrial cooperatives of the kind being established (despite the hostility of the regime) in parts of Nationalist China,[87] or via the expansion of large-scale industry, the need to modernise the economy was widely seen to be essential if rural poverty were to be abolished and independence set upon a secure foundation. In this, Bose and Nehru were at one. To the latter, Gandhi's vision of a self-sufficient rural society seemed, as he wrote privately to the Mahatma, 'completely unreal'.[88] To Bose and his colleagues, 'modern science', which was 'not foreign to the genius of India', would play a crucial part in sweeping away that 'neo-feudal economy' by means of which the British had crushed the people of the sub-continent. Total literacy, public health, 'scientific agriculture', 'foreign trade under state control': all this and more, argued those who had raised the standard of *Azad Hind*, must be established in the free India that was now within reach.[89] For all his war-time gestures of respect towards Gandhi, 'Bose', in Leonard Gordon's words, 'saw himself on the side of reason, science and modern values against the deplorable traits of superstitious, enfeebled India which Gandhi was exploiting'.[90] Mohan Singh, too, while opposed to the dictatorial nature of Bose's schemes for the transformation of India, believed, as he wrote subsequently, that the future of mankind itself required that 'the god of science should now replace the religion ... [which] should be honourably rested in some museum erected to house the Gandhian relics'.[91]

Among Chinese leaders, also, aspirations regarding the resurgence of the nation had long been closely linked with the intention to transform its economy through the introduction of modern, Western techniques (although, as was emphasised earlier, this is not to suggest that all impulsion for change was solely Western-inspired). For the founding-fathers of the country's Communist movement, writes Dr Grieder, 'Marxism [had

---

* War-time advances in medicine in the West, which were of considerable importance when it came to the fighting in the Far East, should also be borne in mind. On this topic in general, see e.g. Wright, *The Ordeal of Total War*, 91ff.
† See above, 67.

rekindled] ... the hope of harnessing the enormous power of Western technology to the task of raising China to membership in a new world order ...',[92] while for Chiang Kai-shek, too, however much he might reject what the West had to offer in the way of political and social values and beliefs, industrialisation on a huge scale was essential for the strengthening of national defence.[93]*

In Southeast Asia, the Far Eastern war, as we have seen, had created widespread disruption among economies that were based on agriculture and other primary products. As some viewed the situation, the conflict thus served to make fundamental changes in the bases of those economies appear both more practicable and more necessary than ever. The events of these years contributed, in other words, to the merging of what had sometimes been two separate streams of ideas among reformers within the dependent territories of the region: the one directed against the feudal domestic order, the other against imperial rule. Thus Marr writes of Vietnam, for example: 'By 1945, salvation from the foreigner was taken by the peasantry to include salvation from hunger, tenantry and taxes – a message of activist and reformist ambitions that fuelled the deadly struggle that ended for the French [in 1954] at Dien Bien Phu.'[94]

Yet fundamental socio-economic change might well carry currently-dependent Asian peoples along the same road as that taken by the Japanese earlier (and down which those Japanese had been driven much further by the war itself):[95] towards a completely 'modern', 'mass' society composed of anonymous individuals, essentially solitary and subject to an impersonal and all-embracing authority. Was this a price that had to be paid if the national identity and destiny were to be fulfilled; if political independence was to be maintained, as well as secured initially? Or was there, as Gellner has argued,† a reverse process in operation, so to speak, whereby the inexorable spread of modern, industrialised, 'mass' societies was prompting the creation of new 'nation-states'? In this connection, the war had clearly widened and deepened the penetration into many parts of Asia of what Gellner terms 'high' cultures, as well as disrupting subsistence agriculture and increasing

---

* Indeed, so high-flown were the Chungking regime's schemes for industrialisation that some observers emphasised how irrelevant they must seem to the majority of the population. The British teachers, Claire and William Band, who, having avoided the Japanese advance in north-east China, travelled extensively in both Communist and Nationalist regions, wrote: 'There was a marked contrast [in Chungking] to the reconstruction work going on in the Communist areas. There, every improvement, although simple and elementary, was directly related to the needs and demands of the population and was at once turned into wide-scale operation. Here, ... the [projected] industrial revolution was so revolutionary that it was above the heads of the common people. [The] industrial exhibits were fantastically remote from anything that the average Szechuan resident had ever dreamed of seeing, let alone using in everyday life.' (*Dragon Fangs*, London, 1947, 309–10.) See also Eastman, *Seeds of Destruction*, 220.

† See above, 56–7.

urbanisation.[96] Yet at the same time it had heightened ethnic and/or racial consciousness and enhanced the role of the man-at-arms (Aung San and Kim Il Sung, for example) as a symbol of the nation, as well as widening many people's horizons and raising their expectations.[97]

The war had also greatly strengthened the role of the state in general terms. Here, again, when it came to identifying the boundaries of those states that they wished to create and control for themselves, Asian nationalists for the most part were either content or obliged* to accept political, legal and administrative entities whose dimensions were essentially of Western creation.[98] And even when, as in the case of the Muslim League's now-unshakable determination to effect the partition of British India, existing territorial divisions were rejected, it remained the modern state, once more as developed in the West, that was the desired form of political and social organisation.† Professor Wang Gungwu, indeed, goes so far as to suggest that the partition of India in 1947, signifying as it did the failure of Gandhi's attempt to secure the acceptance by Muslim League and Congress alike of a radical alternative to Western political *mores*, symbolised also the inability of Asian nationalists generally 'to offer alternatives to Western political, cultural, or even spiritual values'.[99]

*

The nationalist intention that was so greatly strengthened between 1941 and 1945: to remove foreign overlordship and to take over, or even create from scratch, the entity of a state, may thus be viewed in this one sense only as being relatively straightforward, entailing as it did the acceptance as a 'given' of an existing form of institution. And if we return for a moment to the suggestion that was put forward at the conclusion of the opening section of the present work:‡ that in the years leading up to the Far Eastern conflict a widespread crisis had been developing in terms of a growing difficulty in conceptualising about both domestic and international societies, then again

* On Soekarno's original wish to create a new political unit wider than the Dutch East Indies, see above, 152.
† The case of the Chinese on Formosa/Taiwan, who had long been under Japanese rule, provides an interesting example. Although Tokyo's efforts to inculcate unconditional loyalty to the Empire through the island's educational system seem to have made little impression on the mass of the people, 'where the assimilationist message ... concentrated upon gaining acceptance of the modern changes that accompanied colonial rule, it was fairly successful among Taiwanese in all strata of society'. Moreover, it seems that 'the main stream of the Taiwanese anti-colonial movement repeatedly revealed not only a willingness to remain entirely within Japanese legal and constitutional frameworks while fighting for reform in Taiwan, but also an unquestioning acceptance of much of the economic, social, and political pillars which supported Japanese colonialism in Taiwan'. E.P. Tsurumi, 'Education and Assimilation in Taiwan Under Japanese Rule, 1895–1945', *Modern Asian Studies*, Vol. 13, No. 4, 1979; see also her essay in Myers and Peattie, *The Japanese Colonial Empire*.
‡ See above, 89–91.

(and again in this one sense only) the coming of war may be seen as having eased matters by providing immediate and overriding objectives that were straightforward enough for the majority of those, also, who were already living within their own, independent state. The goal was now to survive, and to win; the division between oneself and the enemy was clearly marked; in Britain, Japan, the Netherlands – even in the United States – a 'supreme collective social experience' was entered into; even the deeply-divided French now 'rediscovered' themselves and their country, and accepted, many of them, that their society must be reformed.

But reformed in what sense and in what direction? For, as indicated throughout the preceding chapters, the war did more than simplify immediate objectives and heighten local solidarity. At the same time it exposed the societies involved to a more searching light, made the need to pursue fundamental questions regarding values, purposes and structures appear more urgent still, and, by breaking down many existing institutions and patterns of behaviour, made the opportunity, as well as the necessity, for wholesale reform seem far greater than ever before.

With regard to the organisation of international society as a whole, it was perhaps among West Europeans in particular that the idea was being voiced that the nation-state must in some way be transcended or even superseded as the basic operating unit and focus of loyalty. But suggestions of a not entirely dissimilar kind also surrounded the notion of establishing a 'Great East Asia Coprosperity Sphere' – however marked the contrast in terms of the true natures of the respective structures that were being envisaged. And the belief that some new form of world-wide international organisation, at least, must be created was to be found in well-nigh every area involved in the current conflict. Moreover, to a good many Asians, for all that they might be seeking to establish their own state to match those of the Western powers, the world war that was taking place about them was but further proof of what Tagore and others had long been arguing:* proof that, as their spokesmen were to reiterate at the Bandung Conference of non-aligned states in 1955, 'the wisdom of the West had failed'.[100]

In this respect, and in relation to international and domestic societies alike, Gandhi's warnings against the inherently destructive and alienating attributes of modern Western civilisation retained a potentially enormous appeal among Asians, millions of whom clung instinctively to traditional

---

* See above, 30, 71. On the post-war 'rhetoric of Asia' employed by Nehru, and its rapid decline after 1955, see G. Krishna, 'India and the International Order – Retreat From Idealism', in Bull and Watson, *The Expansion of International Society*, and Hay, *Asian Ideas of East and West*, 329.

and rural ways of life.* For him, as he continued to develop the themes which we noted above in the context of the earlier part of the century,† the war, like its predecessor, 'proved the utter bankruptcy of such economic orders ... [as] Capitalism and Socialism, not excluding Marxism and Communism'. ('The experiments [in the Soviet Union] and here [in India],' he wrote, 'are as different from each other as East from West or North from South. What a difference between our spinning wheel and their machines driven by steam or electricity ... [But] the spinning wheel is a symbol of *ahimsa* [i.e., non-violence and non-cooperation], and ultimately it is *ahimsa* that will triumph.'[101] As large-scale industries, weapons of destruction and the havoc wrought by modern armies multiplied, Gandhi's call, epitomised by the 'Constructive Programme' that he issued (appropriately, in the present context) in December 1941, was for the 'decentralisation of the production and distribution of the necessities of life'; for the creation of a society based upon cooperation among villages that would each be 'a complete republic', self-sufficient in the production of clothing (*khadi*) and food; for the subordination of the city and all it represented to this new rural order. 'It cannot be denied that believers in big industry and industrialization are also friends of India,' he emphasised in September 1944, 'but the difference between them and me is like that between two poles.'[102]

As Gandhi saw it, the Second World War simply underlined what he had proclaimed in his *Hind Swaraj* over thirty years before: that it was the very potential and spiritual worth of the individual that stood to be enhanced or destroyed:

> 'In England and America,' he wrote in May 1945, 'machinery rules supreme. On the contrary, in India we have village industries, symbolizing the resurgence of human labour. In the West, a handful of persons with the aid of mechanical power rule over others ... In India, on the other hand, the great task [is to] bring out what is best in every individual ... The Western method only appears to be successful, but in truth there is nothing but failure in it. For it destroys the will to work.'[103]

Deeply saddened by 'the sharp difference of opinion that has arisen between us' in this regard, he spelled out for Nehru, in the aftermath of the dropping of the atomic bomb, his conviction that it was the future of mankind as a whole, and not of India alone, that was at stake:

---

* Not long after the war, the British scholar, G.F. Hudson, would feel obliged, indeed, to write an essay in which he sought to explain 'Why Asians Hate the West'. Hudson, *Questions of East and West* (London, 1953).
† See above, 70.

'I believe that if India, and through India the world, is to achieve real freedom, then sooner or later we shall have to go and live in the villages. Millions of people can never live in cities and palaces in comfort and peace. I have not the slightest doubt that, but for the pair, truth and non-violence, mankind is doomed. We can have the vision of that truth and non-violence only in the simplicity of the villages. That simplicity resides in the spinning wheel and what is implied by the spinning wheel. It does not frighten me at all that the world seems to be going in the opposite direction. For the matter of that, when the moth approaches its doom it whirls round faster and faster till it is burnt up ...'[104]

It is not only in the dramatic events of the 6th and 9th of August, 1945, that the relevence to war-time developments of Gandhi's vision of Western-engendered corruption becomes apparent. It can be seen, too, for example, in the almost unnoticed experiences of those three thousand or so members of the Indian Legion who remained in Europe, pledged to fight for Germany yet increasingly disorganised and wretched, after their leader, Bose, had departed for Japan. Of these thoroughly alienated men, Dr Hauner writes: 'Without spiritual guidance, many [of them] saw "Europeanisation" as a process of throwing away their religion and habits. The imitation of Europe sometimes took rather grotesque forms when some of the Indians preferred to speak broken German amongst themselves rather than Urdu, for instance ... In the broader sense, this particular Indian experience with Germany and with Europe in general could be seen as a failure of modernization in its extreme form.'[105]

Nor, as we have seen, was Gandhi alone among Asian leaders in decrying what he believed to be the corruption inherent in modern ways. For all that Chiang Kai-shek and his closest colleagues desired to develop heavy industry in China, it was essentially the traditional social order that they sought to preserve. In this respect, 'Americanised' members of the regime like T.V. Soong, who appeared bent upon Westernising China's economy and society, as did other returned students of no great political standing, were of less significance than Chen Li-fu and his kind, who sought to curb educational opportunities as being potentially subversive, and who strove to control the lives and thoughts of those who did, nevertheless, attain the status of student.[106] As Joseph Needham pointed out to the Generalissimo himself in 1945,* a 'backward-looking and timid political mentality' was fundamentally at odds with the notion of modernizing China through the application of science and technology.

More significantly, even in the West itself neither the new sense of purpose nor the gigantic leap in employment and industrial output that

* See above, 72.

accompanied the war was sufficient to banish the kind of doubts that we observed in the pre 1941 period* regarding the essential qualities of modern Western civilisation. The questions and uncertainties involved went much wider than the dogmatic concerns of, for example, those Vichy supporters for whom the peasant and the soil represented all that was best in the life of France, or of those French fascists 'who feared liberalism and Marxism as agents of modernization'.[107] Was it not possible that, as Gandhi was asserting, the war itself was but a reflection, like its predecessor of 1914–18, of some profound *malaise* that lay in the very nature of Western values and preoccupations? Could even its most hideous features, some asked, as exposed to view at Auschwitz and Buchenwald in the spring of 1945, be excluded from such a question? ('It was not self-evident,' as Michael Biddiss puts it, 'that even the special horror of the [Nazi extermination] camps could be treated entirely apart from the numerous other examples of massacre or terror which had so marked the years between 1914 and 1945.')[108]

And there were other, related fears, too. Might not the widespread unemployment of the 1920s and '30s return once the demand for soldiers and their weapons had fallen away? It was 'modern European civilisation', wrote one young (and, it must be added, a-typical) British officer serving in India, that had led to the current 'mad struggle generated by greed and fear', and which, while providing people with 'work and money' in war-time ('when everyone is reasonably happy in the pursuit of killing his fellow men'), in peace cast them back into 'unemployment, starvation and misery'.[109] Less dramatically, but following a related line of thought, Raymond Clapper in May 1942, after contemplating the mail he was receiving from the public and the wide acclaim that had greeted Wallace's speech on 'the century of the common man', wrote privately: 'People are groping for some way out of the dilemma of the modern world. The people who come along with some ideas as to how to control the machine and make it work for us are the ones who will be listened to.'[110]

Nor was Pearl Buck alone in the West in believing, as had others after the 1914–18 conflict,† that the ideas urgently needed by the inhabitants of the industrialized world were to be found in the East. And reflections of this kind were if anything to receive greater prominence once the Second World War had ended. If a Jean Monnet was then to remain convinced, as he worked to re-shape the political structure of Western Europe, that its civilisation was 'so far ahead of the rest of the world',[111] to the Dutch Marxist historian, Jan Romein, the entire development of modern European civilisation now appeared an aberration, a corrupt and destructive departure from the broad-pattern of the organic evolution of human

---

* See above, 28–9, 67–8.
† See above, 29.

societies.[112] If MacArthur could glory in the political and spiritual gifts he brought from the West in order to raise the defeated Japanese from the mire, to Sartre (and also to a significant number of the educated young in the West in the 1960s) it was not Europe and America that now, as they had done in the past, 'made history', but the long-exploited peoples of Africa and Asia who made it 'of us'.[113] Where Henry Luce and others had seen the war as inaugurating an 'American century', to some in the West, as the European retreat from empire gathered pace, it was 'the Asiatic century' that had now begun.[114]

Even during the war itself, it was not so much a heightened sense of purpose that some observers in the West discerned about them, but further manifestations of that modern, 'mass society' which they had been decrying beforehand: regimentation and anonymity; the increasing manipulation of the many by the few; a pervasive mediocrity; Ortega's 'fearful homogeneity of situations', breeding, as he saw it in 1943, 'the shell of a man . . . lack[ing] an inner self, an intimacy, inexorable and inalienable, a self that cannot be revoked'.[115] (Orwell's *Animal Farm* was published in the year the war ended, and his *Nineteen Eighty Four* was already in the making.) Science and technology, too, far from promising a better world, could more than ever be seen as casting a shadow over the existence of the entire human race. (Even before Hiroshima, Nella Last, for example, was reflecting in her diary: 'Just a *very* few people could smash civilisation in the future; it would not need marching armies.')[116] 'The creation of the [atomic] bomb', in Biddiss's words, '. . . [threw] further doubt upon any automatic concordance between the advance of the mind and the betterment of civilization. Moreover, it . . . intensified moral problems about the uses of knowledge that scientists seemed even worse equipped than philosophers and theologians to solve.'[117] Despair itself was not unknown. Another book published in 1945 was the last from the pen of that erstwhile herald of the scientific millennium, H.G. Wells: *Mind at the End of Its Tether*. 'The end of everything we call life is close at hand,' he wrote, 'and cannot be evaded.'

*

In some quarters, at least, then, the conclusion of the Second World War – a successful conclusion from the point of view of those who had rightly seen in the Nazis and their partners a threat to all that was precious in human existence – was far from removing that sense of confusion, uncertainty and fear that had surrounded the 1930s. Yet the events of the intervening years had done much, as we have seen, to prompt attempts to establish 'new categories both practically and theoretically'; to encourage 'changes of world view'.*

* See above, 89.

This is not to say, of course (to return to the suggestions that were put forward in this connection at the end of the opening section of the book), that entirely new paradigms had been widely adopted. To look at this or any other time for a 'revolution' in the realms of political and social thought akin, in its profundity and universality, to the one associated with Einstein in the field of science would be absurd. And indeed, if during the war nationalists in Asia, for example, were largely content to accept existing forms of political institution, so, also, we find when we examine the intellectual upsurge that had been taking place within the Resistance in Western Europe that there, too, as James Wilkinson has emphasised, the political and social ideas and values which lay at the heart of the movement were traditional ones: 'Freedom of expression, freedom of conscience, the defense of human dignity, all as set forth in the *Declaration of the Rights of Man and Citizen* in 1789.'[118] Or again, to turn to the international sphere, we find that that symbol of hope for a new order, the United Nations, had been endowed at its inception with a Charter which was again an expression of classic, liberal Western concepts and values (quite apart from being unable to escape from the essentially conservative qualities which are inherent in all such organisations).

Nevertheless, in many of the societies involved in the war there had taken place, to take up the phrase of Pocock's cited earlier,* 'widely disseminated changes of self-awareness'. Many more people, too, now recognised, for example, that an educated society was a priceless asset, or rejected the belief that mass unemployment had to be resignedly tolerated as an ineluctable consequence of some process that was beyond the control of man. Internationally-speaking, there had come to exist by 1945 a far greater awareness than in the 1930s of the extent and changing nature of the system; of the degree of interdependence that existed within it; of the need to think, indeed, not simply in terms of an international system but of an international society,† and to approach that society's problems on the basis of 'one world'. Many contemporaries now appreciated the dangers inherent in economic nationalism and the unwisdom of treating international commercial relations as if they were an entirely separate sphere of 'low' politics

---

* See above, 90.
† For the distinctions involved, see e.g. Hedley Bull, *The Anarchical Society: A Study of Order in World Politics* (London, 1977). In Professor Bull's words, an international society 'exists when a group of states, conscious of certain common interests and common values, form a society in the sense that they conceive themselves to be bound by a common set of rules in their relations with one another, and share in the working of common institutions'. He adds that 'the modern international system is also an international society, *at least in the sense that international society has been one of the elements permanently at work in it*'. (Emphasis added.) The point being made here is that thinking in terms of the existence and further development of such an element increased during the war. See also Bull and Watson, *The Expansion of International Society*.

among peoples. Scarcely any were now unaware of the potential consequences of total war among modern, industrialised states, while by the
time Japan surrendered there had developed in the West a much wider
acknowledgement, at least, that, in Leo Amery's words, 'very great
changes' were in the making 'in the relations of Asia to Europe'. And of
course at the same time there were those – not least in Washington, but also
in Moscow and Yenan, for example – who were so placed, internationally as
well as domestically speaking, that their own confident conceptualising,
whether or not it accorded with the 'realities' of the time as one might choose
to see them in retrospect, was itself going to help re-shape to some extent the
nature of economic, social and political environments in the post-war world.

And yet great uncertainty remained nonetheless. In part, of course, this
can be attributed to the very realisation on the part of some people that
many of their existing mental landmarks would have to be discarded; that
assumptions and expectations which in some cases had been developed over
centuries must now be replaced. Or, again, one can point to the fact that
some of those who during the war years had been prominent in emphasising
the need for changes of thought and spirit had not (of necessity, perhaps)
translated such visions into the kind of political practicalities that inevitably
confronted them and their contemporaries when the fighting eventually
ceased.[119] (Internationally speaking, for example, it was one thing to adopt
the 'one-world' perspective; another altogether to create machinery, or
revise written and unwritten 'rules of the game', to the extent required by
that world's multicultural nature.)[120] And, obviously, again, for a large
number of others – perhaps the majority – who had failed to travel even this
far towards the acceptance of radical, lasting changes in the nature of their
environment, bewilderment and fear were often the inescapable consequences of misperception or a refusal to learn and adapt.*

There is no need, however, to labour the extent to which members of the
war-time generations had been unable by 1945 to develop entirely new
perspectives within which to view their immediate past and their current
situation. (Continuing paternalist asumptions among Europeans regarding
Asian peoples provide one obvious example; a widespread failure among
the British to appreciate how drastically the international position of their
country had changed, another; or again one could point to the belief of many
Americans that the world waited to be made in their image, or to the
anachronisms surrounding Gandhi's prescriptions for the future of India and
mankind alike.) For while the underlying problem lay in part in the reluctance
of most human beings to acknowledge and mentally adapt to evidence and

---

* 'Almost nothing in the world seems able to shift the images of 40 per cent of the population in
  most countries, even within one or two decades.' Deutsch and Merritt, 'Effects of Events on
  National and International Images', in Kelman, *International Behavior*, 182–3.

demands that fail to square with assumptions of a central and long-developed kind, it was the particular nature of the circumstances that obtained in 1945 and the years that followed which made the conceptual challenge to contemporaries well-nigh overwhelming.

In this respect, the problem can be said to have lain in one of the more ironic consequences of the war: a war which had stimulated what were sometimes remarkable attempts to develop new concepts in the context of the changes and problems which had been developing in domestic and international societies alike; but a war which at the same time had itself imparted yet more momentum to the process of change itself.

The arguments and evidence put forward in the preceding chapters offer their own elaboration of the unsurprising conclusion that the war had quickened the pace of both 'social time' and 'geographical time',* and that the contrast between each of their tempi and that of 'political time' had been further diminished during these years. (It can be suggested, of course, that war had also resulted in a quickening of 'political time' itself; and certainly, many contemporaries felt that for them it had raised the pace of 'individual time' – and were not always glad when that pace slackened with the return of peace.)† Nor is there need to enlarge in any detail here on the manner and areas in which, to use James Joll's phrase, 'history has seemed to be moving too fast for our comfort' since the Second World War. We continue to struggle with the problems, as well as the possibilities, created by a 'new industrial revolution' in such fields as synthetics and electronics that owes much to what took place between 1939 and 1945. The headlong advance of science and technology as applied to armaments, again thrust on its way during those years, has made Gandhi's image of the moth circling ever more frenziedly towards its destruction the nightmare of millions. Only thirty years after Japan had surrendered, the number of member states in the United Nations had reached roughly twice the maximum figure that the best and the brightest had been able to foresee when that organisation was established. The simple, bi-polar structure of the international system, which in the 1950s and even early '60s seemed to many students of the subject likely to 'lock the world up' in its iron embrace for years to come,[121] had by the mid-1970s become only part of a pattern of far greater complexity – the mighty dollar devalued and the Bretton Woods international economic order in tatters; a 'superpower' defeated in war and the 'rules of the game' that had been drawn up anew in 1945 widely challenged once more; Islam a

* See above, 89. The reductions made during the war in the time required to travel across the Atlantic, or the Pacific, or from Europe to the Far East, provide simply one example of the ways in which mankind's geographical environment was beginning to change rapidly.

† To be clear: one is speaking here not of an increased 'rush' in an individual's life, but in the speeding up of the pace of major changes (as well as broadening of those changes) in the cycle of such a life.

resurgent force on the international scene; Japan, like West Germany, a major power despite its comparative lack of immediate military resources. (Indeed, by this time it would be possible to view the international consequences of the Far Eastern war itself in ways which would have seemed extraordinary, if not absurd, to the great majority of those witnessing the end of that conflict in 1945.)* How was power among states now to be calculated? Were states, indeed, any longer the sole international actors of importance? Should the world be viewed (as some in Asia, in essence, had been suggesting during the Far Eastern war) in terms of 'North and South' rather than East and West?[122] What now, after Hitler and Mussolini and total war, of that standard of 'civilization' that the West had held up for others to attain? What now of the concepts and 'answers' that had been developed between 1939 and '45? Once again, it had become all too easy to feel that 'the ground had been pulled from under one, with no foundations to be seen anywhere, upon which [to build]'.†

It would be quite misleading, even so, to conclude a survey of the Far Eastern war by giving the impression that at its end the mass of people in either the Western or the Asian societies involved were peering into this yet-more tumultuous future and concluding, like Wells, that 'the end of life' was near. In India, Indonesia and Indochina, for example, what many saw at hand, rather, was the opening of a bright new era for themselves and the peoples of Asia generally. ('I knew that we'd have to have our peasant groups because landlords would be coming back,' recalled a former *Hukbalahap* guerrilla in the Philippines later. 'Life was still difficult and . . . there had been so much destruction. But I think people were hopeful. I know I was. And we little people had become stronger; we were more organized.')[123] At the same time, vast numbers of Americans, not yet besieged by that hysterical fear of external threat for which their own society's war-time resistance to change had helped pave the way, believed, with the *Chicago Tribune*, that it was 'the good fortune of the world', as well as of their own country, that 'power and unquestionable intentions' now 'went together' in the Great Republic.[124]‡ Among Europeans, it is true, as

* See the Appendix to this chapter.
† Although there are those who argue that the underlying nature of international relations, for example, has not changed over the centuries. See e.g. Gilpin, *War and Change in World Politics*, cap. 6.
‡ A particularly interesting manifestation of this confidence in what American society had to offer the rest of the world was provided by Margaret Mead. She herself had cautioned her fellow-countrymen (*Anthropology: A Human Science*, 142) not to assume too readily 'that a pattern [of social development] which turned millions of diversely speaking newcomers into loyal Americans in such a short time must be a very valuable and useful one'. Yet, writing amidst the Cold-War tensions of 1953 (*New Lives For Old*, 19), she was to proclaim her conviction 'that American civilization is not simply the last flower to bloom on the outmoded tree of European history, . . . but something new and different, . . . because the men who built it have themselves incorporated the ability to change and change swiftly as the need

they contemplated the devastation of much of their continent, a sense of having been eclipsed was not uncommon. (If the headquarters of the new United Nations were to be sited in the United States, privately declared that shrewd diplomat, René Massigli, 'it is the end of Europe'.)[125] But in Britain, France and the Netherlands many were also contemplating the opportunity of creating a better society through the just and compassionate application of knowledge and understanding: Marxists and liberals alike; social democrats and paternalists; scientists and theologians (who merged in the person of Teilhard de Chardin). It was still possible, with Camus, 'to accept the reality of today, which is logical crime', to look back on 'a period which, within fifty years, uprooted, enslaved or killed seventy million human beings', and conclude, even so, that one must 'enter the lists anew' in order to 'forsake our age and its adolescent rages'.[126]

No doubt for the great majority, whose extraordinary resilience in the face of war-time uncertainty and adversity – a resilience not clothed in the big words and grand gestures required of those set above them – leaves the strongest of impressions, it was a mixture of widely differing thoughts and emotions that accompanied the ending of that particular upheaval in their lives.

'I felt,' noted Nella Last, 'as if a stone, a dead weight I'd unconsciously carried [for the past six years], had rolled off me – that my limbs felt freer, my head lighter. Then I began to think of this atomic business, wondering if its discovery was for good or ill to mankind, wondering if it was the "change" which comes on the world in each 2,000 years' cycle to speed it on its evolution. I don't feel very happy about it all.'[127]

Not as confident as *Vrij Nederland* had been on the morrow of Pearl Harbor that these were 'great times' in which to live; but not devoid of a sense of achievement, or of hope, either. Even Wells, for all his despair, could not, as a child of the Enlightenment, suppress the belief that 'a small, highly adaptable minority of the species' would survive the end of 'ordinary man'. 'The young are *life*,' wrote the dying sage, 'and there is no hope but in them.'[128] Amid turmoil and uncertainty, platitudes, too, have their place.

---

arises'. And she continued: 'As we have learned to change ourselves, so we believe that others can change also, and we believe that they will want to change, that men have only to see a better way of life to reach out for it spontaneously. Our faith includes no forebodings about the effect of destroying old customs and . . . we do not conceive of people being forcibly changed by other human beings. We conceive of them as seeing a light and following it freely.'

Appendix

As indicated in the Preface, an examination of the consequences of the Far
Eastern war after 1945 does not fall within the scope of this book. In the
present context, however, it is worth emphasising that several major
international developments which were to take place in the Far East within
only twenty or thirty years of the war's end, and which were at least in part
shaped by what had occurred during that conflict, lay well outside the
expectations of most of those who were witnessing the defeat of Japan.
There were those contemporaries, it is true, who understood by the summer
of 1945 that the position of the European powers in that part of the world
had been lastingly weakened by what had occurred since December 1941;
but few foresaw that the entire European imperial presence in Asia would
effectively have been removed within a mere decade. (If the costly attempts
of the Dutch and the French between 1945 and 1954 to prevent this coming
about appear particularly futile and myopic in retrospect, it must be added
that most British politicians were to take longer than their continental
counterparts to accept the implications of the fundamental change that had
taken place, just as they failed to recognise that the war had widened, rather
than reduced, the distance between Britain and the Dominions.)* Fewer
still anticipated, as they regarded the chaos and bitter political discord that
marked the Chinese scene in 1945, that within only four years that country
(the irrelevance of Taiwan apart) would be united under Communism and
writing *finis* to a century of enforced subordination to the foreigner. (John
Foster Dulles, no less, was writing privately in March 1945, *à propos* a
Nationalist-led China, that the country might well turn out to be not one of
the 'great nations' after all, and therefore have to be deprived of the special
great-power status which it had been accorded in the structure of the new
United Nations Organisation.)† And how many, contemplating the devastation of Japan and the latest manifestations of the unparalleled might of the

---

* See e.g. Darby, *British Defence Policy East of Suez, 1947–1968*, and Thorne, *Allies*, 686–8. In
the Netherlands, it was said that if the Indies were lost the country would become 'another
Denmark' (see H. Baudet, 'Nederland en de rang van Denemarken', in Fasseur, ed., *Geld en
geweten*). Britain's dreadful fate were she to permit Nasser to nationalise the Suez Canal,
prophesied Macmillan in 1956, would be to become 'another Netherlands'. When such fears
and images have been duly understood in the context of international power-politics, there
remains something sad, as well as amusing, about them in terms of the behaviour of the
species, *homo sapiens*.
† Thorne, *Allies*, 579.

United States, would have accepted a prediction that by the early 1970s the former would be spoken of as an 'emerging super-state' that could well be out-producing America by the end of the century,* and that the Americans themselves would have experienced defeat in war in that very area of the world where their seemingly limitless military resources now brought even a Theodore White to exult?

Of course, assessments of the international consequences of the 1941–45 war will vary in part, so close are we to the event itself, according to the particular moment between then and the present day which one chooses as the point of reckoning in terms of this or that theme.† And if one wished to speak of 'success' or 'failure', of 'gains' and 'losses' in that connection, then prior questions would have to be answered regarding not only perspective but values, criteria, and the defining of the 'national interest' of the state concerned. But one can at least suggest here that there are some among many possible readings of post-war international developments which, if they could have been shown to those who were caught up in the Far Eastern conflict itself, would have seemed not simply unlikely but downright paradoxical: which we, too, can accept as paradoxical in terms of the more obvious features of the years between Pearl Harbor and Japan's surrender, even if explanations of the apparent contradictions involved are easier with the advantage of hindsight.

We can see now how it was, for example, that a war which brought to China death and destruction on a vast scale was at the same time fostering national unification and renewal; how the advance of Communist fortunes that was entailed was to lead to a Sino-Soviet confrontation far exceeding any hostility between Moscow and the Chinese Nationalists; how a conflict which brought Britain and the Dominions closer together was in fact ensuring the end of any automatic 'Commonwealth alliance'; how Japan, though defeated, had succeeded in hastening the end of Western empires in Asia, and how this brutal shortening of their years of imperial decline, while shocking and painful at the time, could come to be seen as having been to the benefit of the European states concerned; how Japan herself, so manifestly brought low, was turned away thereby from the course of costly and futile military aggrandisement, and enabled (her industrial structure reformed

---

* See H. Kahn, *The Emerging Japanese Superstate* (New York, 1970), and, for perspective on this and other analyses, E. Wilkinson, *Japan Versus Europe: A History of Misunderstanding* (London, 1983).

† It is said of one Chinese historian that, asked not many years ago what he thought had been the consequences of the French Revolution, he replied that it was too early to say. To impatient Western minds, many of them no doubt eagerly awaiting the opportunities that the bicentennial anniversary of 1789 will bring for pronouncing authoritatively on that very subject, such an approach is likely to appear a trifle excessive. Nevertheless, many would accept that judgements regading the consequences of the 1941–5 war, arrived at a mere forty years after the event, could only be of an interim nature.

and her value to Washington enhanced by what the war had helped bring about in China and in Soviet-American relations) to achieve wealth and influence far greater and more lasting than any she could have secured by the sword;* how the United States, in 1941 brought at last to China's side as Luce *père* and his like had so earnestly wished, was helping thereafter to ensure that its relationship with the new, 'awakening' China would soon be one of bitter hostility; how the United States, indeed, brought by the war to believe that its moment had come 'to bat in Asia', to shape (for the benefit of others and not only of itself) the destinies of what people like Stimson and MacArthur had long seen as 'our part of the world', to prevent any further threats to its security and prosperity arising from that quarter, and to distribute and protect there the blessing of 'the American way of life' for peoples who must seek only that – how the United States, so manifestly 'the winner' of the Far Eastern war in 1945, could by the 1970s be seen as having been in certain senses the greatest of its long-term 'losers'. But that, as they say, is another story.

Notes

1 See Shillony, 43ff., 76–7, 87; Johnson, *MITI*, 31ff.; Havens, 203.
2 Shillony, 28, 44; Havens, 60ff.; Ienaga, 97ff.
3 Harvey, op. cit., entry for 27 Feb. 1942; see also ibid, entries for 12 and 14 Feb. 1942; Taylor, *English History*, 544; Addison, 206–10; Thorne, *Allies*, 133, 144.
4 Thorne, *Allies*, 93; and see Bullock, *Ernest Bevin, Foreign Secretary*.
5 See e.g. L. Eastman, 'Regional Politics and the Central Government: Yunnan and Chungking', in Sih, op. cit.
6 See e.g. L.N. Shyu, 'China's "Wartime Parliament": the People's Political Council, 1938–1945', in ibid; and Eastman, *Seeds of Destruction*, passim.
7 See e.g. Boyle, *China and Japan at War*, 310ff.; R. Payne, *Chiang Kai-shek* (New York, 1969), 255ff.; Spence, op. cit., 320, 327ff.; Clubb, op. cit., 238.; Schram, *Mao Tse-tung*, 233.
8 See e.g. Hasluck, *The Government and the People, 1942–45*, 366–8.
9 Quoted in Horner, *High Command*, 175.
10 Perrett 247.
11 See e.g. Polenberg, *War and Society*, 185; Catton, op. cit., 16.
12 See L. de Jong, 'Les Pays-Bas Dans la Seconde Guerre Mondiale', *Histoire de la Deuxième Guerre Mondiale*, April 1963; J. Bank, *Opkomst en ondergang van de Nederlandse Volks Beweging* (Deventer, 1978); Warmbrunn, *The Dutch Under German Occupation*, 185ff.; Blom, 'The Second World War and Dutch Society', loc. cit.; W. Banning, *Hendaagse Sociale Bewegingen* (Arnhem, 1954); issues of *Je Maintiendrai*, passim.
13 See Wright, *The Ordeal of Total War*, 147ff., 234ff.
14 Blom, op. cit., 238–9.
15 Hoffmann, *France: Change and Tradition*, 58–9.
16 Gordon, *Collaboration in France*, 147. And see e.g. Farmer, 216.

* On the continuing debate as to whether or not Japan is 'Western' rather than 'Eastern' and on whether she has succeeded since the war in creating by peaceful means the essence of a 'Great East Asia Coprosperity Sphere', see e.g. Miwa, 'Japan in Asia, Past and Present', loc. cit. For the continuing and related debate about the essential nature of 'Western civilisation' and relations between East and West, cf. e.g. Needham, *Within the Four Seas: The Dialogue of East and West*, and J. Ellul, *Trahison de l'Occident* (Paris, 1975).

17 *Le Populaire*, 1 Oct. and 5 Nov. 1944; and e.g. *L'Humanité*, 23 Jan. 1945; *Le Monde*, 28 July 1945; Michel and Guetzévitch, op. cit., passim; H. Michel, *Les Courants de Pensée de la Résistance* (Paris, 1962); Wilkinson, *The Intellectual Resistance*, e.g. 267, and passim.
18 'Citizens of Britain', BWP No. 1, Nov. 1942, *The British Way and Purpose* (consolidated edition, Nos. 1–18, London, 1944).
19 Basil Wright, quoted in Short, *Film and Radio Propaganda in World War Two*, 63.
20 Thorne, *Allies*, 150; Taylor, 508 and e.g. 455.
21 Nash broadcast, 22 March 1942, loc. cit.
22 Israel, in Sih, op. cit., 139, 143.
23 Ibid, 343.
24 Ibid, 303.
25 Clubb, 254; and see e.g. Payne, 257; Johnson, *Peasant Nationalism*, 44 and passim.
26 Crowley, *Modern East Asia*, 281.
27 Thorne, *Allies*, 434ff., 567ff.
28 Cumings, xxiff., 30ff., 48ff., 402. For an analysis which emphasises, however, the gulf between Kim Il Sung and the old Communist leadership in Korea, see D.S. Suh, *The Korean Communist Movement, 1918–1948* (Princeton, 1967), esp. cap. 9.
29 See e.g. Lancaster, 112ff.; Chen, *Vietnam and China*, cap. 2.
30 Iriye, *Power and Culture*, 176.
31 See Hashikawa, 'Japanese Perspectives on Asia', in Iriye (ed.), *Chinese and Japanese*, 350–1; Ienaga, *Japan's Last War*, 218–20.
32 Shillony, 119ff.
33 Fukutake, 4, 141ff.
34 Havens, 197, 202–5.
35 Fukutake, 107, 197.
36 Quoted in Shillony, 108–9. And see Ienaga, 221–3, and Reischauer, *The Japanese*, 276ff.; R. Scalapino, *The Japanese Communist Movement, 1920–1966* (Berkeley, 1967); A. Cole, G. Totten and C. Uyehara, *Socialist Parties in Postwar Japan* (New Haven, 1966).
37 Sevareid notes, 22 Dec. 1943, Sevareid Papers, box D3. And e.g. Clapper to Howard, 24 June 1942, Clapper Papers, box 50.
38 Winkler, 71 and passim; also Polenberg, *War and Society*, 73ff., 91ff., 189ff.
39 F.A. Hayeck, *The Road to Serfdom* (London, 1944), e.g. 10, 18–20; and see Perrett, op. cit., 287ff.
40 Blum, *V Was For Victory*, 6, 13, 105ff., 234ff., 283ff., 332; Perrett, 325ff. For examples of the educational revolution effected by the G.I. Bill, see Terkel, 57–8, 145.
41 S.P. Huntington, *The Soldier and the State* (New York, 1957), 335–6.
42 See Blum, *V Was For Victory*, 27ff., 38–9, 53ff.; Winkler, 64 and passim; Catton, 80, 141, 169, 258.
43 Polenberg, *One Nation Divisible*, 57.
44 Perrett, 433.
45 Dillon speech, Indianapolis, 16 Nov. 1943, WRA files, box 282.
46 White, *In Search of History*, 223. And see Thorne, *Allies*, e.g. 138, and Winkler, 154.
47 Quoted in Perrett, 418.
48 Clapper to Thurston, 14 Oct. 1943, Clapper Papers, box 51; and e.g. 'CBI Master Narrative', p. 281, Stilwell Papers, box 1.
49 Roosevelt to Lamont, 29 March 1945, Lamont Papers, file 127/26.
50 Emmerson memo., 5 Feb. 1942, St. Dpt. files, 740.0011 PW/2037⅛.
51 *L'Humanité*, 23 Aug. 1944. Also e.g. ibid, 23 Jan. 1945; *Libération*, 11 Jan. 1944; *L'Université Libre*, July 1944; *Aurore*, Oct. 1943; *Le Monde*, 2 Jan. 1945.
52 Hoffmann, *France, Change and Tradition*, 58.
53 See Schram, *Mao Tse-tung*, 220ff.
54 See e.g. Wright, op. cit., 266.
55 Report on Wartime Relations With Britain, AICC files, G–22 part 2.
56 S. Epstein, 'District Officers in Decline: the Erosion of British Authority in the Bombay Countryside, 1919 to 1947', *Modern Asian Studies*, vol. 16, No. 3, 1982; Ghosh, 228ff.;

Toye, 170ff.; Mohan Singh, 368; Donnison narrative in Tinker, *Burma: the Struggle for Independence*, 1005.
57 Sjahrir, 248. And see e.g. Wertheim, 78–9, 306–7; van der Kroef, *The Communist Party of Indonesia*, 26.
58 See Dahm, 283; Aziz, 235.
59 E.g. Manila *Tribune*, 1 March, 19 May, 25 Nov. 1942; Steinberg, 75–7, 165–6.
60 *Le Temps*, 23 Feb. 1941; *L'Action* (Hanoi), 2 Sept. 1944; and see e.g. Hoffmann, op. cit., 36ff.; Farmer, op. cit., passim; Gordon, op. cit., 44; Paxton, op. cit., passim.
61 See e.g. Thorne, *Allies*, 729.
62 Payne, *Chiang Kai-shek*, 250; Jaffe (ed.), *China's Destiny*, passim; Reischauer, Fairbank and Craig, op. cit., 713; Eastman, *Seeds of Destruction*, cap. 9.
63 See e.g. Levenson, *Confucian China and its Modern State, Vol. I*, cap. X; Ch'en, *China and the West*, 452; Crowley, *Modern East Asia*, 280ff.
64 *Combat*, 25 Sept. 1943; and e.g. *Cahiers du Témoignage Chrétien*, May and July 1943; *L'Aurore*, Oct. 1943; *L'Humanité*, 1 Jan. 1944.
65 See e.g. Warmbrunn, 11 ff., 34ff., 83ff., 131–2, 267ff.
66 Long diary, 27 July 1942 and 14 Aug. 1943; *Sydney Morning Herald*, 26 Aug. 1942.
67 Lacey to Curtin, 14 Jan. 1943, Prime Minister's Dpt. files, U/57/1/1.
68 'Civilian Morale in North Queensland', 1 Feb. 1943: report by Prof. R.D. Wright and Dr. I. Hogbin, ibid, BA/29/1/2.
69 Long diary, 7 July 1942.
70 *Sydney Morning Herald*, 7 March and 15 July 1942; 17 May 1945; also e.g. 17 and 21 Jan., 9, 14, 15 April, 16 and 21 Dec. 1942; 2 Jan., 30 and 31 March, 6, 8 and 16 April 1943; 7 and 27 Jan. 1944. Also e.g. Sydney *Daily Telegraph*, 28 Oct. 1944.
71 Sydney *Daily Telegraph*, 30 Oct. 1944.
72 Clapper cable, June 1943, Clapper Papers, box 37.
73 See Perrett, 302.
74 See ibid, 339, and in general e.g. Blum, *V Was For Victory*, 89.
75 *Azad Hind*, No. 3/4, 1943; Gandhi, quoted in Hutchins, *India's Revolution*, 195.
76 Speech of Oct. 1941, *Collected Works*, Vol. LXXV, 9.
77 Speech of 1 Sept. 1944, ibid, *Vol. LXXVIII*, 62ff.; conversation with Mridula Sarabhai, 26 Oct. 1944, ibid, 232; note of 14 Nov. 1944, ibid, 301.
78 Fukutake, 73.
79 Maruyama, 147–8; and e.g. Havens, 150–1.
80 Quoted in Maruyama, 47, 49. On the tendency of smaller village communities in Fiji to disintegrate in this period, see Scarr, op. cit., e.g. 332ff., 363.
81 Shillony, 140.
82 Takeda, *The Great East Asia War*, loc. cit.
83 J-P. Sartre, 'The Republic of Silence', quoted in S. Hawes and R. White (ed.), *Resistance in Europe, 1939–45* (London, 1976), 132; and see Wilkinson, op. cit., 33ff.
84 See e.g. Wright, op. cit., 51, 80, 87; Milward, cap. 6; R.V. Jones, *Most Secret War* (London, 1978); Perrett, 110–12, 431; Hoffmann, *France*, 39ff., 54, 152ff.
85 Shillony, 134ff.; K. Miwa, 'Japanese Images of War with the United States', in A. Iriye (ed.), *Mutual Images: Essays on American-Japanese Relations* (Cambridge, Mass., 1975); Kase, *Eclipse of the Rising Sun*, 9; Miwa, 'Japan in Asia, Past and Present', loc. cit.
86 Lal, 'India's Science Movement', *Asia and the Americas*, Jan. 1943.
87 E.g. Anup Singh to Nehru, 2 April 1942, Nehru Papers, Corresp., vol. 13; *Bombay Chronicle*, 26 May 1942.
88 Quoted in Hutchins, 292.
89 E.g. Banerji, 'International Importance of India's Independence', *Azad Hind*, Jan. 1943; Sengupta, 'Economic Causes of the Famine in India', ibid, No. 2, 1944; Bose, 'Free India and its Problems', ibid, No. 9/10, 1942.
90 Gordon, in S.K. Bose (ed.), *Nataji and India's Freedom* (Calcutta, 1975), 13.
91 Mohan Singh, 280. For a recent commentary, see S. Ghose, 'Science and Anti-Science: the Cow Not So Sacred', *The Statesman*, (Calcutta) 28 Nov. 1979.
92 Grieder, 'Communism, Nationalism and Democracy', in Crowley, *Modern East Asia*, 220.

93 See e.g. Reischauer, Fairbank and Craig, op. cit., 713; Ch'en, op. cit., 173ff.; Thorne, *Allies*, 313, 425, 565, 707.
94 Marr, *Vietnamese Anti-Colonialism*, 276–7.
95 Fukutake, 115ff.
96 See Gellner, *Nations and Nationalism*, e.g. 18, 39ff., 111.
97 See e.g. Smith, *The Ethnic Revival*, 74ff.; Anderson, *Imagined Communities*, 17ff.
98 See e.g. Wang Gungwu, 'Nationalism in Asia', in Kamenka, *Nationalism*, 92.
99 Ibid, 93–4.
100 See e.g. R. Wright, *The Colour Curtain* (London, 1956); R. Payne, *The Revolt of Asia* (London, 1948); Hay, *Asian Ideas of East and West*.
101 Gandhi, forward to Bharatan Kumarappa's *Capitalism, Socialism, or Villagism* (1945), *Collected Works, Vol. LXXXI*, 275; Gandhi to Narandas Gandhi, 20 May 1944, ibid, *Vol. LXXVII*, 277.
102 Gandhi, e.g. 'Constructive Programme', 13 December. 1941, ibid, *Vol. LXXV*, 146ff.; 'Village Swaraj', 18 July 1942, ibid, *Vol. LXXVI*, 308; speech to Congressmen, 29 June 1944, ibid, *Vol. LXXVII*, 341; on the 'Constructive Programme', 28 July 1944, ibid, 429; discussion with D. Ramaswami, Aug. 1944, ibid, *Vol. LXXVIII*, 6ff., 45, 68ff., 161ff.; speech of 1 Sept. 1944, ibid, 62ff.; discussions with Sec. of All India Spinners' Association, 10 Oct. 1944, ibid, 171ff.; forward to *The Cow in India* (1945), ibid, *Vol. LXXX*, 149; interview with Ramachandra Rao, 19 June 1945, ibid, 352.
103 'How to Improve Village Industries', 21 May 1945, ibid, *Vol. LXXX*, 152.
104 Gandhi to Nehru, 5 Oct. 1945, ibid, *Vol. LXXXI*, 319.
105 Hauner, *India in Axis Strategy*, 589.
106 See e.g. Payne, *Chiang Kai-shek*, 3–5, 258; Eastman, *Seeds of Destruction*, 217–8 and cap. 5; Thorne, *Allies*, 426. For the remarkable retrospective views of Chen Li-fu himself, cited in a collection of essays, many of which are essentially apologia for the Nationalist regime, see Sih, op. cit., 120.
107 Gordon, *Collaboration*, 20, 44; Farmer, *Vichy*, passim.
108 Biddiss, *The Age of the Masses*, 200.
109 See C. Thorne, 'The British Cause and Indian Nationalism: An Officer's Rejection of Empire', *Journal of Imperial and Commonwealth History*, vol. X, No. 3, 1982. Cf. on 19th century European fascination for Indian religion and philosophy, Singhal, op. cit., cap. 20.
110 Clapper to Landon, 29 May 1942, Clapper Papers, box 50.
111 J. Monnet, *Mémoires* (Paris, 1976), 572.
112 J. Romein, *Aera van Europa: de Europese Geschiedenis als Afwijking van het Algemeen Menselijk Patroon* (Leiden, 1954).
113 Preface to F. Fanon, *The Wretched of the Earth* (trans. C. Farrington, London, 1965).
114 E.g. Payne, *The Revolt of Asia*, 300.
115 See Giner, *Mass Society*, 75ff. and passim.
116 *Nella Last's War*, entry for 5 Aug. 1945.
117 Biddiss, 274; and see Nisbet, *History of the Idea of Progress*, 317ff., and Gong, 87ff.
118 Wilkinson, *The Intellectual Resistance*, 45.
119 See e.g. ibid, 55.
120 See Bozeman, *The Future of Law in a Multicultural World*, and Gong, 242ff.
121 See above, cap. 2, ref. 163.
122 For a broad survey of some major post-war international developments of this kind, see e.g. the special, anniversary issue of *International Affairs*, Nov. 1970.
123 Kerkvliet, 109.
124 *Chicago Tribune*, 8 Dec. 1944.
125 Reynolds and Hughes, *The Historian As Diplomat*, 77.
126 A. Camus, *The Rebel* (trans. A. Bower, London, 1962), 11, 270; and see e.g. Wilkinson, 263ff.
127 *Nella Last's War*, entry for 11 Aug. 1945.
128 H.G. Wells, *Mind at the End of Its Tether* (London, 1945), 28, 30, 34.

Sources

A *Unpublished Material*
1. Official documents.
  (a) *International*
     International Military Tribunal for the Far East. (Imperial War Museum, London.)
  (b) *Australia*
     Advisory War Council.
     Department of Defence.
     Department of External Affairs.
     Prime Minister's Department.
     War Cabinet.
     Washington Legation. (All Commonwealth Archives, Canberra.)
  (c) *Great Britain*
     Burma Office. (India Office Library, London.)
     India Office. (India Office Library.)
     Colonial Office. (Public Record Office, London; and all the following.)
     Dominions Office
     Prime Minister's Office.
     Cabinet conclusions and memoranda.
     Cabinet Committees and documents: on India; Indian finance; Indian food grains;
       Malaya and Borneo; Armistice and Post-War; Defence (Operations).
     Far Eastern Committee and Far Eastern (Ministerial) Committee.
     Pacific War Council. (London.)
     Cabinet Office documents on arrangements in event of war with Japan.
     Hankey, official files.
     Chiefs of Staff Committee.
     Chiefs of Staff: inter-Allied conferences.
     Joint Planning Sub-Committee.
     Combined Chiefs of Staff, and Combined Staff Planners.
     Foreign Office departments: Economic; Reconstruction; Economic and
      Reconstruction; Far Eastern; French; General; North American.
  (d) *Netherlands*
     Colonial Ministry. (Ministerie van Binnenlandse Zaken, The Hague.)
     Council of Ministers. (Algemeen Rijksarchief, The Hague; also the following.)
     Gerbrandy Office Papers
     Ministry of Foreign Affairs: Londens archief: Political Reports, Chungking and
      Washington; French files; IPR files; Washington Embassy files; van Kleffens and
      Bylandt files.
     Ministry of Warfare.
  (e) *New Zealand*
     Army Department. (National Archives, Wellington; also the following.)
     Cabinet: war decisions and minutes.
     Department of External Affairs.
  (f) *United States*
     China Theater, Wedemeyer files. (Federal Archives, Suitland, Maryland.)
     South East Asia Command, War Diary. (Suitland.)
     U.S. Navy: Double Zero; Leahy; China; Naval Group China; War Plans Division;
      General Board Studies; New Caledonia report. (Operational Archives, Naval
      Dockyard, Washington D.C.)

Office of Territories. (National Archives, Washington D.C.; also the following.)
Office of High Commissioner, Philippines.
Office of Strategic Services.
War Relocation Authority.
Joint Chiefs of Staff.
State-War-Navy Coordinating Committee and Sub-Committees.
U.S. Army: Operational Plans Division.
Department of State: decimal files; Notter Files; Pasvolsky files; Matthews-Hickerson files; Secretary's Staff Committee.

2. Private Papers. (Titles, etc., as in 1941–45.)
   (a) *Australia*
   Blamey, General Sir Thomas (Australian War Memorial Library, Canberra.)
   Bruce, Stanley (Australian Commonwealth Archives.)
   Curtin, John (Commonwealth Archives.)
   Eggleston, Sir Frederick (Australian National Library, Canberra.)
   Evatt, H. V. (Flinders University, Adelaide.)
   Latham, Sir John (Australian National Library.)
   Long, Gavin (Australian War Memorial Library.)
   Officer, Keith (Australian National Library.)
   Page, Sir Earle (Australian National Library.)
   Watt, Alan (Australian National Library.)
   (b) *China*
   Wunsz King (Hoover Institute.)
   (c) *Great Britain*
   Alexander, A. V. (Churchill College, Cambridge.)
   Attlee, C. R. (Churchill College, and New College, Oxford.)
   Beaverbrook, Lord (House of Lords Record Office.)
   Bevin, Ernest (Churchill College.)
   Brooke-Popham, Air Chief Marshal Sir Robert (King's College, London.)
   Chatfield, Admiral of the Fleet Lord (National Maritime Museum, Greenwich.)
   Cherwell, Lord (Nuffield College, Oxford.)
   China Association (China Association, London.)
   Clark Kerr, Sir Archibald (Public Record Office.)
   Cripps, Sir Stafford (Nuffield College.)
   Crozier, W. P. (Manchester University Library.)
   Cunningham, Admiral of the Fleet Sir Andrew (British Museum.)
   Dalton, Hugh (London School of Economics.)
   Dorman-Smith, Sir Reginald (India Office Library.)
   Grigg, Sir P. J. (Churchill College.)
   Halifax, Lord (Public Record Office; and Churchill College.)
   Hankey, Lord, (Churchill College.)
   Ismay, General Sir Hastings (King's College, London.)
   Linlithgow, Lord (India Office Library.)
   Martin, Kingsley (University of Sussex.)
   Maze, Sir Frederick (School of Oriental and African Studies, London.)
   Needham, Dr Joseph (Cambridge University.)
   Royal Institute of International Affairs (Chatham House, London.)
   Somerville, Admiral of the Fleet Sir James (Churchill College.)
   Wilkinson, Lt. Col. G. W. (Churchill College.)
   Woolf, Leonard (University of Sussex.)
   (d) *India*
   All India Congress Committee (Nehru Memorial Library, New Delhi.)
   Bose, Subhas Chandra (Netaji Bureau, Calcutta.)
   Menon, K. P. K. (Nehru Memorial Library.)
   Nehru, Jawaharlal (Nehru Memorial Library.)
   Oral history transcripts, various (Nehru Memorial Library.)

(e) *Netherlands*
  Gerbrandy, P. S. (Algemeen Rijksarchief, The Hague.)
  van Mook, Dr H. J. (Algemeen Rijksarchief.)
(f) *New Zealand*
  Fraser, Peter (National Archives, Wellington.)
(g) *United States*
  Alsop, Joseph (Library of Congress, Washington D.C.)
  Arnold, General of the Army H. H. (Library of Congress.)
  Ballantine, Joseph W. (Hoover Institute, Stanford.)
  Barrett, Col. David D. (Hoover Institute.)
  Baruch, Bernard (Princeton University.)
  Chennault, Maj. Gen. Claire L. (Hoover Institute.)
  Clapper, Raymond (Library of Congress.)
  Connally, Tom (Library of Congress.)
  Dulles, John Foster (Princeton University.)
  Forrestal, J. V. (Princeton University.)
  Frankfurter, Felix (Library of Congress.)
  Gardiner, W. H. (Houghton Library, Harvard University.)
  Goodfellow, Col. Preston (Hoover Institute.)
  Grew, Joseph C. (Houghton Library.)
  Hamilton, Maxwell M. (Hoover Institute.)
  Hopkins, Harry (Roosevelt Memorial Library, Hyde Park, N.Y.)
  Hornbeck, Stanley K (Hoover Institute.)
  Hrdlicka, Ales (Smithsonian Institution.)
  Hull, Cordell (Library of Congress.)
  Ickes, Harold (Library of Congress.)
  Institute of Pacific Relations (Columbia University.)
  Johnson, Nelson T. (Library of Congress.)
  King, Fleet Admiral Ernest J. (U.S. Navy Operational Archives, Washington
    D.C.)
  Knox, Frank (Library of Congress.)
  Lamont, Thomas W. (Baker Library, Harvard Business School.)
  Leahy, Fleet Admiral Wiliam D. (Library of Congress.)
  Long, Breckenridge (Library of Congress.)
  MacArthur, General of the Army Douglas (MacArthur Library, Norfolk,
    Virginia.)
  Morgenthau, Henry Jr. (Roosevelt Library.)
  National Association for the Advancement of Colored Peoples (Library of
    Congress.)
  Phillips, William (Houghton Library.)
  Roosevelt, Franklin D. (Roosevelt Library.)
  Rosenman, Samuel I. (Roosevelt Library.)
  Sayre, Francis B. (Library of Congress.)
  Sevareid, Eric (Library of Congress.)
  Stilwell, General Joseph W. (Hoover Institute.)
  Stimson, Henry L. (Sterling Memorial Library, Yale University.)
  Taussig, Charles W. (Roosevelt Library.)
  Truman, Harry S. (Truman Memorial Library, Independence, Missouri.)
  United China Relief Inc. (Princeton University.)
  Wallace, Henry A. (Roosevelt Library.)
  White, Harry Dexter (Princeton University.)

B *Published Official Documents*
  1. *Germany*
    Documents on German Foreign Policy, 1918–1945, Series D: Vols. VIII–XIII (London,
      1956–64).

2. *Great Britain*
Documents on British Foreign Policy, 1919–1939, Second Series: Vol. XIII (London, 1973); *Third Series, Vols. VIII and IX* (London, 1955).
Hansard, House of Commons Debates, 5th Series, vols. 374–411 (London, 1942–45).
Mansergh, N. (ed.), *The Transfer of Power, 1942–7: Vol. 1, The Cripps Mission* (London, 1970).
Mountbatten, Lord, *Report to the Combined Chiefs of Staff* (London, 1951).
Nicholas, H. G. (ed.), *Washington Despatches, 1941–45: Weekly Political Reports from the British Embassy* (London, 1981).
Tinker, H. (ed.), *Burma: the Struggle for Independence, 1944–48: Vol. 1* (London, 1983).
3. *Japan*
Ike, N. (ed.), *Japan's Decision For War* (Stanford, 1967).
4. *Netherlands*
A. F. Manning and A. E. Kersten (ed.), *Documenten Betreffende de Buitenlandse Politiek van Nederland, 1919–1945, periode C, 1940–1945, Vols. 1–3* (The Hague, 1976–1980).
van der Wal, S. L. (ed.), *Bescheiden Betreffende de Nederlands-Indonesische Betrekkingen, 1945–1950, Vol. 1* (The Hague, 1971).
5. *New Zealand*
Documents Relating to New Zealand's Participation in the Second World War, Vols. I–III (Wellington, 1949–63).
6. *United States*
Congressional Record, June, 1948; Chennault Testimony (Washington, 1948).
Esherwick, J. W. (ed.), *Lost Chance in China: the World War Two Despatches of John S. Service* (New York, 1974).
Foreign Relations of the United States (all published Washington): *Japan, 1931–1941, Vol. II* (1943); *U.S. Relations With China* (1949); *1941, Vol. IV* (1956); *Conferences at Washington and Casablanca* (1968); *1942, Vol. I* (1960); *1942, China* (1956); *Conferences at Washington and Quebec, 1943* (1970); *1943, China* (1957); *1943, vols. III and IV* (1963–4); *Conferences at Cairo and Tehran, 1943* (1961); *Conference at Quebec, 1944* (1972); *1944, Vols. III, V, VI* (1965–67); *Conferences at Malta and Yalta, 1945* (1955); *1945, Vols. I, VI, VII* (1967–69); *Conference at Berlin, Vols. I and II* (1960).
Notter, H. A. (ed.), *Post-war Foreign Policy Preparation* (Washington, 1949).
van Slyke, L. (ed.), *The Chinese Communist Movement: A Report of the U.S. War Department* (Stanford, 1968).
7. *International*
Kimball, W. F. (ed.), *Churchill and Roosevelt: The Complete Correspondence* (3 vols., Princeton, 1984). These volumes appeared too late for specific references to be included in the present work.

C *Newspapers and Journals*
1. *Australia* (National Library, Canberra)
Daily Telegraph (Sydney); *Sydney Morning Herald*.
2. *France and French Indochina* (Bibliothèque Nationale, Paris)
J'accuse; *L'Action* (Hanoi); *L'Action Française*; *L'Aurore*; *Cahiers du Témoignage Chrétien*; *Combat*; *Défense de la France*; *Destin*; *La France Libre* (London); *L'Humanité*; *L'Indépendence Tonkinoise* (Hanoi); *Les Lettres Française*; *Libération*; *Le Monde*; *Le Nouveau Laos* (Vientiane); *Le Nouvelliste de l'Indochine* (Saigon); *Les Petits Ailes de France*; *Le Populaire*; *La République* (Hanoi); *Résistance*; *Le Temps*; *L'Union* (Hanoi and Saigon); *L'Université Libre*; *Vérité*; *La Vérité Française*.
3. *Great Britain* (British Museum Newspaper Library, Colindale, and Chatham House Press Library)
Daily Express; *Daily Herald*; *Daily Telegraph*; *Economist*; *International Affairs*; *Manchester Guardian*; *Times*.

4. *India*
   Azad Hind (Berlin; Netaji Bureau, Calcutta); *Bombay Chronicle* (Nehru Memorial
   Library, New Delhi); *Forward Bloc* (Calcutta; Netaji Bureau).
5. *Japan*
   Syonan Shimbun (Singapore; Netaji Bureau).
6. *Netherlands* (All save as indicated Rijksinstituut voor Oorlogsdocumentatie,
   Amsterdam)
   De Bevrijding; *Je Maintiendrai*; *Het Parool*; *Trouw*; *Vrij Nederland*; *Vrij Nederland*
   (London; National Library, The Hague); *De Vrije Katheder*; *Die Waarheid*.
7. *New Zealand* (General Assembly Library, Wellington)
   The Dominion; *The Standard*.
8. *Philippines*
   The Tribune (Manila; Gaimusho archives, Tokyo).
9. *United States* (Library of Congress, and Chatham House Press Library, except as
   otherwise indicated)
   Asia/Asia and the Americas (Columbia University Library); *Chicago Tribune*; *Christian
   Science Monitor*; *New York Herald Tribune*; *New York Times*; *San Francisco
   Examiner*; *Washington Post*.

D *Film* (Imperial War Museum, London)
   1. *Canada*
      'Fortress Japan'; 'Mask of Nippon'.
   2. *Great Britain*
      'China'; 'Common Cause'; 'Pacific Thrust'; 'This was Japan'; 'War in the Pacific'.
   3. *Japan*
      'La Jeunesse Feminine Nippone'; Newsreels, various; 'Nippons Wilder Adler'; 'La Vie
      Industrielle du Japon'; 'Der Weg Nach Hawaii'.
   4. *United States*
      'Japanese Relocation' (or 'America Moves Her Japs'); 'Know Your Enemy: Japan';
      'The Stilwell Road'; 'Why We Fight' ('Prelude to War'; 'Battle of China'; 'War Comes
      to America').

E *Other Contemporary Material*
   Benda, H. J., et al. (ed.) *Japanese Military Administration in Indonesia: Selected
      Documents* (New Haven, 1965).
   Berger, G. M. (ed.), *Kenkenroku: A Diplomatic Record of the Sino-Japanese War, 1894–95*
      (Tokyo, 1982).
   Berle, B., and Jacobs, T. (ed.), *Navigating the Rapids: From the Papers of Adolph Berle*
      (New York, 1973).
   Blum, J. M. (ed.), *From the Morgenthau Diaries: Years of War, 1941–45* (Boston, 1967)
      The Price of Vision: The Diary of Henry A. Wallace, 1942–1946 (Boston, 1973).
   Blyden, E. W., *Christianity, Islam, and the Negro Race* (1887; Edinburgh, 1967).
   Bond, B. (ed.), *Chief of Staff: the Diaries of Lt. Gen. Sir Henry Pownall, Vol. II* (London,
      1974).
   Bose, S. C. *Correspondence, 1924–1932* (Calcutta, 1967).
      Crossroads (Bombay, 1962).
      Testament (Delhi, 1946).
      Through Congress Eyes (Allahabad, 1937).
   Brereton, L. H., *The Brereton Diaries* (New York, 1946).
   Broad, R. and Fleming, S. (ed.) *Nella Last's War: A Mother's Diary, 1939–1945* (London,
      1981).
   Brown, C., *Suez to Singapore* (New York, 1942).
   Bryant, A., *The Turn of the Tide, 1939–1943* (London, 1957).
      Triumph in the West, 1943–1946 (London, 1959).
   Campbell, T. and Herring, G. (ed.), *The Diaries of Edward R. Stettinius Jr. 1943–1946*
      (New York, 1975).

Cantril, H. and Strunk, M., *Public Opinion, 1935–1946* (Princeton, 1951).
Chapman, J. W. (ed.), *The Price of Admiralty: the War Diary of the German Naval Attaché in Japan, 1939–1943, Vol. 1* (Ripe, Sussex, 1982).
China Association, *Annual Reports: 1941–42; 1942–3; 1943–4; 1944–5; 1945–6* (London, 1942–46).
Crouter, N., *Forbidden Diary* (New York, 1980).
D'Encausse, H. C. and Schram, S., *Le Marxisme et L'Asie, 1853–1964* (Paris, 1965).
Dilks, D. (ed.), *The Diaries of Sir Alexander Cadogan* (London, 1971).
Directorate of Army Education, *The British Way and Purpose, Nos. 1–18* (London, 1944).
Gallup Poll archives, London.
Gandhi, M. K., *Collected Works, Vols. X* (Delhi, 1963); *LXXV* (1979); *LXXVI* (1979); *LXXVII* (1979); *LXXVIII* (1979); *LXXIX* (1980); *LXXX* (1980); *LXXXI* (1980).
Garvey, A. J. (ed.), *Philosophy and Opinions of Marcus Garvey* (New York, 1967).
Gide, A., *Journals, 1889–1949* (London, 1967).
Guénon, R., *East and West* (trs. W. Massey, London, 1941).
Hailey, Lord, *The Future of Colonial Peoples* (London, 1943).
Hancock, W. K., *Argument of Empire* (London, 1943).
Hardie, R., *The Burma-Siam Railway* (London, 1983).
Harvey, J. (ed.), *The Diplomatic Diaries of Oliver Harvey, 1937–1940* (London, 1970).
The War Diaries of Oliver Harvey, 1941–1945 (London, 1978).
Henderson, J. C. (ed.), *Hiroshima* (London, 1974).
Hitler, A., *Table Talk* (intr. H. R. Trevor-Roper, London, 1953).
Hornbeck, S. K., *The United States in the Far East* (Boston, 1942).
Hyndman, H. M., *The Awakening of Asia* (London, 1919).
Ickes, H. L., *The Secret Diary of Harold L. Ickes, Vol. III* (London, 1955).
Institute of Pacific Relations (American Council of):
  I.P.R. in Wartime (New York, 1944).
  Window on the Pacific (New York, 1947).
  Asia's Captive Colonies (by P. Lilienthal and J. Oakie, New York, 1944).
  Meet the Anzacs! (by W. Holland and P. Lilienthal, New York, 1944).
  Pacific Islands in War and Peace (by M. Keesing, New York, 1944).
  Korea for the Koreans (by A. Grajelanzer, New York, 1943).
  Philippine Emergency (by C. Porter, New York, 1941).
  What Are We Doing With Japan? (by A. W. Johnstone, New York, 1946).
  Spotlight on the Far East (by J. M. Bernstein et al., St. Louis, 1945).
  Our Far Eastern Record (by W. Lockward, New York, 1940).
  America's Stake in the Far East (by M. Farley, New York, 1941).
  The ABC's of Modern Japan (by W. Morris, New York, 1946).
  America's Role in China (by E. Hawkins, New York, 1947).
  Changing China (by G. Taylor and M. Steward, St. Louis, 1942).
  Modern Japan (by W. Chamberlain, St. Louis, 1942).
  Twentieth Century India (by K. Mitchell and K. Goshal, St. Louis, 1944).
  Peoples of the China Seas (by E. Clark, St. Louis, 1942).
Israel, F. L. (ed.), *The War Diaries of Breckenridge Long* (Lincoln, Nebraska, 1966).
Jaffe, P. (ed.), *Chiang Kai-shek: China's Destiny and Chinese Economic Theory* (New York, 1947).
Japanese oral testimonies and documents: collection held by Imperial War Museum, London.
Joshi, P. C., *For the Final Bid for Power! Freedom Programme of Indian Communists* (Bombay, 1946).
Kersten, A. E. (ed.), *het Dagboek van dr. G.H.C. Hart* (The Hague, 1976).
Krishnan, N. K. (ed.), *National Unity for the Defence of the Motherland* (Bombay, 1943).
Lattimore, O., *Solution in Asia* (London, 1945).
Lebra, J. C. (ed.), *Japan's Greater East Asia Co-Prosperity Sphere in World War II: Selected Readings and Documents* (Kuala Lumpur, 1975).

Lenin, V. I., 'Better Fewer, But Better', *Collected Works, Vol. 33* (Moscow, 1965).
Leutze, J. (ed.), *London Observer: The Journal of General Raymond E. Lee* (London, 1972).
Lippmann, W., *United States War Aims* (London, 1944).
Malraux, A., *La Tentation de l'Occident* (Lausanne, 1962).
  Les Conquérants (Paris, 1927).
  La Condition Humaine (Paris, 1933).
Masaryk, T.G., *The New Europe: The Slav Viewpoint* (Washington D.C., 1918).
Massis, H., *Défense de l'Occident* (Paris, 1927).
Michel, H., and Mirkine-Guetzévitch, B. (ed.), *Les idées politiques et sociales de la Résistance* (Paris, 1954).
Millis, W. (ed.), *The Forrestal Diaries* (London, 1952).
Modell, J. (ed.), *The Kikuchi Diary: Chronicle From An American Concentration Camp* (Urbana, Illinois, 1973).
Montagu, A., *Man's Most Dangerous Myth: the Fallacy of Race* (5th edn., New York, 1974).
Moon, P. (ed.), *Wavell: The Viceroy's Journal* (London, 1973).
Morgenthau, H. Jr., *Diary, China, Vols. I and II* (Washington D.C., 1965).
Morrison, I., *Malayan Postscript* (London, 1942).
Mumford, L., *Technics and Civilization* (London, 1946).
Nehru, J., *Toward Freedom* (New York, 1942).
Nicolson, N. (ed.), *Harold Nicolson: The War Years, 1939–1945: Diaries and Letters* (London, 1967).
Park, R.E., *Race and Culture* (New York, 1950).
Pearson, C., *National Life and Character* (London, 1894).
Perham, M., *Colonial Sequence, 1930–1949* (London, 1967).
Ranadive, B.T., *Working Class and National Defence: Report to First Congress of the Communist Party of India, 1943* (Bombay, 1943).
Rolland, R., *Inde Journal, 1915–1943* (Paris, 1960).
Roosevelt, E. (ed.), *FDR: His Personal Letters, 1928–1945, Vol. II* (New York, 1950).
Scarr, D. (ed.), *Fiji: The Three-Legged Stool: The Selected Writings of Ratu Sir Lala Sukuna* (London, 1984).
Schram, S. (ed.), *The Political Thought of Mao Tse-tung* (London, 1969).
Schurmann, H. and Schell, O. (ed.), *Republican China* (London, 1968).
Seeley, J.R., *The Expansion of England* (London, 1883).
Sitsen, H. W., *Industrial Development of the Netherlands Indies* (New York, 1944).
Sjahrir, S., *Out of Exile* (New York, 1949).
Snow, E., *Red Star Over China* (London, 1937).
Spengler, O., *Decline of the West: Form and Actuality* (trans. C. Atkinson, London, 1926).
Stone, I. F., *The Truman Era* (New York, 1973).
Tagore, R., *Nationalism* (London, 1917).
Takeda, Lt. Col. Koji, *The Great East Asia War and Ideological Warfare* (1943; summary and translated extracts, Japanese Translation Series, No. 242, Far Eastern Bureau, British Ministry of Information, New Delhi, 1944: NZ External Affairs files, 84/6/1 part 3).
Tojo, Gen. Hideki, address to Greater East Asia Conference, Tokyo, November 1943 (translation in Gaimusho archives, Tokyo).
Toynbee, A.J., *Survey of International Affairs, 1931* (Oxford, 1932).
Vandenberg, A. (ed.), *The Private Papers of Senator Arthur Vandenberg* (London, 1953).
van der Poel, J. (ed.), *Selections from the Smuts Papers, Vol. VI* (Cambridge, 1973).
van Namen, A.H. (ed.), *Het Ondergroondse Vrij Nederland* (Baarn, 1970).
Wallace, H., *Our Job in the Pacific* (New York, 1944).
Weber, M., *The Protestant Ethic and the Spirit of Capitalism* (trans. T. Parsons, New York, 1958).
Wells, H.G., *Mind At The End Of Its Tether* (London, 1945).
White, T.H. (ed.), *The Stilwell Papers* (New York, 1948).

F *Interviews and Correspondence with Contemporaries*
  Dr Anak Agung Gde Agung, Prince of Bali
  Eric Battersbee, A.D.C. to the Governor of Burma.
  Sir Isaiah Berlin, British Embassy, Washington.
  Dr Hank Bethe, Dutch Resistance.
  M.S. Bharat, Indian National Army.
  Dr Dorothy Borg, Institute of Pacific Relations.
  Sir Ronald Campbell, Minister of the British Embassy, Washington.
  Sir Olaf Caroe, Secretary of the External Affairs Department, Government of India.
  Sir Ashley Clark, Head of the Far Eastern Department, British Foreign Office.
  Lord Coleraine, as Richard Law, M.P., Minister of State at the British Foreign Office.
  John Paton Davies, American Foreign Service Officer in China.
  Mr den Hollander, Attaché to Netherlands Senior Naval Officer in Melbourne.
  Major General R.H. Dewing, Commander of U.K. Army and Air Force Liaison Staff in
    Australia.
  Sir Reginald Dorman-Smith, Governor of Burma.
  Professor J.K. Fairbank, U.S. Cultural Relations programme in China.
  W.D. Forsyth, Head of Postwar Planning Section, Australian Ministry of External Affairs.
  Sir Berkeley Gage, British Embassy, Chungking.
  Lord Gladwyn, Head of the Economic and Reconstruction Department of the British
    Foreign Office.
  Leo Handley-Derry, British Military Mission to China.
  W. Averell Harriman, special representative of President Roosevelt in London, and U.S.
    Ambassador in Moscow.
  Sir William Hayter, British Embassy, Washington.
  Konrad Hsu, British intelligence, with special reference to the Far East.
  Professor Ikeda Kiyoshi, Imperial Japanese Navy.
  George Kennan, Counsellor, U.S. Embassy in London; Minister-Counsellor, U.S.
    Embassy in Moscow.
  Sir John Keswick, British Special Operations Executive in China; Counsellor of Embassy in
    Chungking.
  J. G. Kist, Secretary to the Government of the Netherlands Indies in Australia.
  Professor Owen Lattimore, Personal Adviser to Chiang-Kai-shek; Director, Pacific
    Operations for U.S. Office of War Information; member of Wallace mission to China.
  Dr Philip Mason, Secretary of the Chiefs of Staff Committee, India; Head of Conference
    Section. S.E.A.C.
  René Massigli, Commissioner for Foreign Affairs, French Committee of Liberation;
    Ambassador in London.
  H. Freeman Matthews, Chief of the Division of European Affairs, U.S. Department of
    State.
  Marinus Meijer, internee in the Netherlands East Indies.
  Sir Robert Menzies, Prime Minister of Australia, subsequently Leader of the Opposition.
  Earl Mountbatten of Burma, Supreme Allied Commander, S.E.A.C.
  Dr Joseph Needham, British Scientific and Cultural Mission in China.
  Dame Margery Perham, involved in the training of British colonial administrators.
  A.D.C. Peterson, Deputy Director of Psychological Warfare, S.E.A.C.
  General Sir Sydney Rowell, Commander of Australian forces in New Guinea.
  John S. Service, American Foreign Service Officer in China.
  Sir Horace Seymour (with Lady Seymour), British Ambassador to China.
  Dr T. Dale Stewart, colleague of Dr Hrdlicka, Division of Physical Anthropology,
    Smithsonian Institution.
  Colonel Hugh Toye, British Army investigator of I.N.A.
  Dr J.E. van Hoogstraten, Chairman of the Netherlands Indies Commission in Australia.
  Dr E.N. van Kleffens, Netherlands Minister for Foreign Affairs.
  Dr J. H. van Roijen, Permanent Head of the Netherlands Foreign Ministry; subsequently
    escaped to London.

Sir John Wheeler-Bennett, British Political Warfare Mission in U.S.A.
Sir Alan Watt, Counsellor of the Australian Legation in Washington.

G *Memoirs*

Acheson, D., *Present At the Creation* (London, 1970).
Adamson, I., *The Forgotten Men* (London, 1965).
Allen, G.C., *Appointment in Japan* (London, 1983).
Amery, J., *Approach March* (London, 1973).
Amery, L.S., *My Political Life, Vol. III* (London, 1955).
Arnold, H.H,. *Global Mission* (London, 1951).
Arnold, R., *A Very Quiet War* (London, 1962).
Attlee, C.R., *As It Happened* (London, 1954).
Avon, Lord, *Memoirs: the Reckoning* (London, 1965).
Ba Maw, *Breakthrough in Burma* (New Haven, 1968).
Band, C. and W., *Dragon Fangs* (London, 1947).
Barrett, D.D., *The Dixie Mission* (Berkeley, 1976).
Barrett, N.H., *Chinghpaw* (New York, 1962).
Baruch, B., *The Public Years* (London, 1961).
Bertram, J., *The Shadow of a War* (London, 1947).
Bohlen, C.E., *Witness to History* (London, 1973).
Butler, R.A., *The Art of the Possible* (London, 1971).
Byrnes, J.F., *Speaking Frankly* (London, 1948).
Casey, Lord, *Personal Experience* (London, 1962).
Chandos, Lord, *Memoirs* (London, 1962).
Chapman, F.S., *The Jungle is Neutral* (London, 1949).
Chennault, C.L. *Way of a Fighter* (New York, 1949).
Churchill, W.S., *The Second World War, Vols. I–VI* (London, 1948–54).
Craigie, R., *Behind the Japanese Mask* (London, 1946).
Cunningham, Lord, *A Sailor's Odyssey* (London, 1951).
Dalton, H., *Memoirs, 1931–1945: the Fateful Years* (London, 1957).
Davies, J.P., *Dragon By The Tail* (New York, 1972).
Deane, J.R., *The Strange Alliance* (London, 1947).
de Beauvoir, S., *The Prime of Life* (London, 1962).
  Force of Circumstance (London, 1965).
de Gaulle, C., *War Memoirs: Unity, 1942–1944* (London, 1960).
  War Memoirs: Salvation, 1944–1946 (London, 1960).
Dixon, P. (ed.), *Double Diploma: the Life of Sir Pierson Dixon* (London, 1968).
Duclos, J., *Mémoires: Dans la Bataille Clandestine* (Parts 1 and 2; Paris, 1970).
Eichelberger, R.L., *Our Jungle Road to Tokyo* (New York, 1950).
Eldridge, F., *Wrath in Burma* (New York, 1946).
Emmerson, J.K. *The Japanese Thread* (New York, 1978).
Evatt, H.V., *Australia in World Affairs* (Sydney, 1946).
Feis, H., *Seen From E.A.* (New York, 1947).
Field, H., *'M' Project for F.D.R.: Studies in Migration and Settlement* (Ann Arbor, 1962).
Freedman, M. (ed.), *Roosevelt and Frankfurter* (London, 1967).
Fujiwara, I., *F. Kikan* (trans. Y. Akashi; Hong Kong, 1983).
Gilchrist, A., *Bangkok Top Secret* (London, 1970).
Gladwyn, Lord, *Memoirs* (London, 1972).
Gore-Booth, P., *With Great Truth and Respect* (London, 1974).
Grew, J.C., *Ten Years in Japan* (London, 1945).
  Turbulent Era, Vol. 2 (London, 1953).
Guillain, R., *La Guerre au Japon* (Paris, 1979).
Harriman, W.A. and Able, E., *Special Envoy to Churchill and Stalin, 1941–1946* (London, 1976).
Hassett, W.D., *Off the Record with F.D.R.* (New Brunswick, N.J., 1958).
Hayter, W., *A Double Life* (London, 1974).

Hull, C., *Memoirs, Vol. II* (London, 1948).
Hunt, R. and Harrison, J. (ed.), *The District Officer in India, 1930–1947* (London, 1980).
Ismay, Lord, *Memoirs* (London, 1960).
James R.R., *Chindit* (London, 1980).
Kase, T., *Eclipse of the Rising Sun* (London, 1951).
Kemp, P., *Alms for Oblivion* (London, 1961).
Kennan, G., *Memoirs, 1925–1950* (London, 1968).
Kennedy, J., *The Business of War* (London, 1957).
Kennedy, M.D., *The Estrangement of Great Britain and Japan* (Manchester, 1969).
King, E.J. and Whitehill, W., *Fleet Admiral King* (London, 1953).
Lapwood, R. and N., *Through the Chinese Revolution* (London, 1954).
Leahy, W.D., *I Was There* (London, 1950).
Lindsay, M., *The Unknown War: North China, 1937–1945* (London, 1975).
Luuvaas, J. (ed.), *Dear Miss Em.* (Westport, Conn., 1972).
MacArthur, C., *Reminiscences* (London, 1964).
Macmillan, H., *The Blast of War, 1939–1945* (London, 1967).
Mason, P.M *A Shaft of Sunlight* (London, 1978).
Masters, J., *The Road Past Mandalay* (London, 1961).
Mehta, V., *Daddyji. Mamaji* (London, 1984).
Menzies, R.G., *Afternoon Light* (London, 1967).
Miles, M.E., *A Different Kind of War* (New York, 1967).
Mohan Singh, *Soldier's Contribution to Indian Independence* (New Delhi, 1975).
Monnet, J., *Mémoires* (Paris, 1976).
Moran, Lord, *Winston Churchill: The Struggle For Survival, 1940–1965* (London, 1966).
Motley, M.P. (ed.), *The Invisible Soldier: the Experience of the Black Soldier in World War II* (Detroit, 1975).
Needham, J., *Chinese Science* (London, 1945).
   Science Outpost (London, 1948).
Peers, W. and Brelis, D., *Behind the Burma Road* (London, 1964).
Peterson, M., *Both Sides of the Curtain* (London, 1950).
Phillips, W., *Ventures in Diplomacy* (London, 1955).
Purcell, V., *The Memoirs of a Malayan Official* (London, 1965).
Roosevelt, E., *As He Saw It* (New York, 1946).
Rosenman, *Working With Roosevelt* (London, 1952).
Sabattier, G., *Le Destin de l'Indochine* (Paris, 1952).
Sainteny, J., *History d'une Paix Manquée* (Paris, 1953).
Sansom, K., *Sir George Sansom and Japan: A Memoir* (Tallahassee, Florida, 1972).
Service, J.S., *The Amerasia Papers* (Berkeley, 1971).
Shigemitsu, M., *Japan and Her Destiny* (London, 1958).
Slim, W., *Defeat Into Victory* (London, 1960).
Smedley, A., *Battle Hymn of China* (London, 1943).
Snow, E., *Journey to the Beginning* (London, 1959).
Stein, G., *The Challenge of Red China* (London, 1945).
Stephens, I., *Monsoon Morning* (London, 1966).
Stettinius, E.R., *Roosevelt and the Russians* (London, 1950).
Stimson, H.L. and Bundy, M., *On Active Service In Peace And War* (New York, 1948).
Strang, Lord, *At Home And Abroad* (London, 1956).
Sweet-Escott, B., *Baker Street Irregular* (London, 1965).
Taylor, E., *Richer By Asia* (London, 1948).
   Awakening From History (London, 1971).
Tedder, Lord, *With Prejudice* (London, 1966).
Terkel, S. (ed.), *"The Good War". An Oral History of World War Two* (New York, 1984).
Thakin Nu, *Burma Under the Japanese* (London, 1954).
Thompson, R.W. (ed.), *Churchill and Morton* (London, 1976).
Tsuji, M., *Singapore: the Japanese Version* (London, 1972).
Truman, H.S. *Year of Decisions, 1945* (London, 1955).

van der Post, L., *The Night of the New Moon* (London, 1970).
van Mook, H.J. *Indonesië, Nederland en de Wereld* (Amsterdam, 1949).
    The Status of Democracy in Southeast Asia (New York, 1950).
Watt, A., *Australian Diplomat* (Sydney, 1972).
Wavrin, A. de, *Souvenirs, Vol. I* (Monte Carlo, 1947).
Wedermeyer, A.C., *Wedemeyer Reports* (New York, 1958).
Welles, S., *A Time For Decision* (London, 1944).
Wheeler-Bennett, J. (ed.), *Action This Day: Working With Churchill* (London, 1968).
    Special Relationships (London, 1975).
White, T.H., *In Search of History* (New York, 1978).
White T.H. and Jacoby, A., *Thunder Out Of China* (London, 1947).
Wiart, C. de, *Happy Odyssey* (London, 1950).
Williams, F., *A Prime Minister Remembers* (London, 1961).
Winant, J.G., *A Letter From Grosvenor Square* (London, 1947).

H *Secondary Works; Books*
Adachi, K., *The Enemy That Never Was* (Toronto, 1976).
Addison, P., *The Road to 1945* (London, 1975).
Adler, S., *The Isolationist Impulse* (New York, 1960).
Agawa, H., *The Reluctant Admiral: Yamamoto and the Imperial Navy* (trans. J. Bester, Tokyo, 1979).
Albertini, R. von, *European Colonial Rule, 1880–1940: the Impact of the West on India, Southeast Asia and Africa* (trans. J. Williamson, Westport, Conn., 1982).
Allen, G.C. and Donnithorne, A.G., *Western Enterprise in Far Eastern Economic Development* (London, 1962).
Allen, H.C., *Great Britain and the United States* (London, 1954).
Allen, L., *The End of the War in Asia* (London, 1976).
    Singapore, 1941–1942 (London, 1977).
Almond, G.A., *The American People and Foreign Policy* (New York, 1965).
Ambrose, S., *Rise to Globalism: American Foreign Policy, 1938–1980* (London, 1980).
Anders, L., *The Ledo Road* (Norman, Oklahoma, 1965).
Anderson, B., *Imagined Communities: Reflections on the Origins and Spread of Nationalism* (London, 1983).
Anderson, I.H., *The Standard-Vacuum Oil Company and United States East Asian Policy, 1933–1941* (Princeton, 1975).
Anderson, J., *A Philip Randolph* (New York, 1973).
Anglo, M., *Service Newspapers of the Second World War* (London, 1977).
Aron, R., *Peace and War: A Theory of International Relations* (London, 1966).
    The Imperial Republic (London, 1975).
Aziz, M-A., *Japan's Colonialism in Indonesia* (The Hague, 1955).
Ballhatchet, K., *Race, Sex and Class Under the Raj* (London, 1980).
Bank, J., *Opkomst en ondergang van de Nederlandse Volks Beweging* (Deventer, 1978).
Banning, W., *Hendaagse Sociale Bewegingen* (Arnham, 1954).
Banton, M., *The Idea of Race* (London, 1977).
Barker, E., *Churchill and Eden at War* (London, 1978).
Barnard, E., *Wendell Willkie: Fighter For Freedom* (Marquette, Michigan, 1980).
Barnett, C., *The Collapse of British Power* (London, 1972).
Bauzon, L.E., *Philippine Agrarian Reform, 1880–1965: the Revolution That Never Was* (Singapore, 1975).
Beitzell, R., *The Uneasy Alliance: America, Britain and Russia, 1941–1943* (New York, 1972).
Bell, D., *The Cultural Contradictions of Capitalism* (New York, 1976).
Bell, R.J., *Unequal Allies* (Melbourne, 1977).
Bellanger, C., *Presse Clandestine, 1940–1944* (Paris, 1966).
Beloff, M., *Imperial Sunset, Vol. 1* (London, 1969).

Benda, H.J. *The Crescent and the Rising Sun: Indonesian Islam Under the Japanese Occupation, 1942–1945* (The Hague, 1958).
Benedict, R., *Patterns of Culture* (London, 1968).
   The Chrysanthemum and the Sword (London, 1967).
Berlin, I., *Mr Churchill in 1940* (London, 1950).
Betts, R.F., *Uncertain Dimensions: European Overseas Empires in the Twentieth Century* (forthcoming).
Biddiss, M.D., *The Age of the Masses* (London, 1977).
Birkenhead, Lord, *The Prof. in Two Worlds* (London, 1961).
   Halifax (London, 1965).
Bishop, J., *F.D.R.'s Last Year* (New York, 1974).
Blum, J.M., *V Was For Victory: Politics and American Culture During World War II* (New York, 1976).
Boardman, R., *Britain and the People's Republic of China, 1949–1974* (London, 1976).
Bond, B., *British Military Policy Between the Two World Wars* (Oxford, 1980).
   War and Society in Europe, 1870–1970 (London, 1984).
Borg, D., *The United States and the Far Eastern Crisis of 1933–1938* (Cambridge, Mass., 1964).
   Historians and American Far Eastern Policy (New York, 1966).
Borg, D., and Okamoto, S. (ed.), *Pearl Harbor As History* (New York, 1973).
Borg, D. and Heinrichs, W. (ed.), *Uncertain Years: Chinese-American Relations, 1947–1950* (New York, 1980).
Bose, M., *The Lost Hero* (London, 1982).
Bose, S. K. (ed.), *Netaji and India's Freedom* (Calcutta, 1975).
Bowle, J., *The Imperial Achievement: The Rise and Transformation of the British Empire* (London, 1974).
Boyle, A., *Poor, Dear Brendan* (London, 1974).
Boyle, J. H., *China and Japan At War, 1937–1945* (Stanford, 1972).
Bozeman, A. B., *Politics and Culture in International History* (Princeton, 1960).
   The Future of Law in a Multicultural World (Princeton, 1971).
Braudel, F., *On History* (trans. S. Matthews, London, 1980).
Brecher, M., *The Foreign Policy System of Israel* (London, 1972).
Breuilly, J., *Nationalism and the State* (Manchester, 1982).
Buchanan, A. R., *Black Americans in World War II* (Oxford, 1977).
Buckley, R., *Occupation Diplomacy: Britain, the United States and Japan, 1945–1952* (Cambridge, 1982).
Buhite, R. D., *Patrick Hurley and American Foreign Policy* (Ithica, N.Y., 1973).
Bull, H., *The Anarchical Society: A Study of Order in World Politics* (London, 1977).
Bull, H. and Watson, A. (ed.), *The Expansion of International Society* (London, 1984).
Bullen, R. J. et al. (ed.), *Ideas Into Politics: Aspects of European History, 1880–1950* (London, 1984).
Bullock, A., *The Life and Times of Ernest Bevin, Vol. II* (London, 1967).
   Ernest Bevin, Foreign Secretary (London, 1983).
Burke, P. (ed.), *New Cambridge Modern History, Vol. XIII* (Cambridge, 1979).
Burns, J. M., *Roosevelt: The Soldier of Freedom, 1940–1945* (London, 1971).
Butcher, J. G., *The British In Malaya* (Kuala Lumpur, 1979).
Butler, J. R. M., *Grand Strategy, Vol. II* (London, 1957).
   Grand Strategy Vol. III pt. II (London, 1964).
Butow, R. J., *Japan's Decision to Surrender* (Stanford, 1954).
   Tojo and the Coming of War (Princeton, 1961).
   John Doe Associates: Backdoor Diplomacy for Peace, 1941 (Stanford, 1974).
Calder, A., *The People's War, Britain, 1939–45* (London, 1969).
Caillois, R., *Bellone, ou la pente de la guerre* (Brussels, 1963).
Calvocoressi, P., *Top Secret Ultra* (London, 1980).
Calvocoressi, P. and Wint, G., *Total War* (London, 1972).
Carlton, D., *Anthony Eden* (London, 1981).

Carr, R., *Spain, 1808–1939* (Oxford, 1966).
Castles, F. G., *Pressure Groups and Political Culture* (London, 1967).
Catton, B., *The War Lords of Washington* (New York, 1948).
Charlesworth, J. C., *Contemporary Political Analysis* (New York, 1968).
Ch'en, J., *China and the West* (London, 1979).
Chen, K. C., *Vietnam and China, 1938–1954* (Princeton, 1969).
Chipp, S. and Green, J. (ed.), *Asian Women in Transition* (Pennsylvania, 1980).
Clarke, I. F., *Voices Prophesying War, 1763–1984* (Oxford, 1966).
    The Pattern of Expectation (London, 1979).
Clemens, D., *Yalta* (New York, 1970).
Clubb, O. E., *20th Century China* (New York, 1964).
Cohen, P. A., *Discovering History in China: American Historical Writing on the Recent Chinese Past* (New York, 1984).
Cohen, W. I., *America's Response to China* (New York, 1971).
    The Chinese Connection (New York, 1978).
    (ed.), *New Frontiers in American-East Asian Relations* (New York, 1983).
Cole, A., Totten, G. and Uyehara, C., *Socialist Parties in Postwar Japan* (New Haven, 1966).
Collis, M., *First And Last In Burma* (London, 1956).
Connell, J., *Wavell, Scholar and Soldier* (London, 1964).
Cook, C., *The Life of Richard Stafford Cripps* (London, 1957).
Cosgrave, P., *Churchill At War, Vol. 1* (London, 1974).
Costello, J., *The Pacific War, 1941–1945* (London, 1981).
Cotta, M., *La Collaboration, 1940–1945* (Paris, 1964).
Coupland, R., *Indian Politics, 1936–1942* (Oxford, 1944).
Craig, A.and Shively, D. (ed.), *Personality in Japanese History* (Berkeley, 1970).
Croll, E., *Feminism and Socialism in China* (London, 1978).
Cronon, E. D., *Black Moses: Marcus Garvey and the Universal Negro Improvement Association* (Madison, Wisconsin, 1969).
Crossman, R. H. (ed.), *The God That Failed* (New York, 1954).
Crowley, J. B., *Japan's Quest For Autonomy* (Princeton, 1966).
    (ed.) *Modern East Asia: Essays in Interpretation* (New York, 1970).
Cruickshank, C., *SOE in the Far East* (Oxford, 1983).
Cruickshank, J., *Variations on Catastrophe: Some French Responses to the Great War* (Oxford, 1982).
Cumings, B., *The Origins of the Korean War: Liberation and the Emergence of Separate Regimes, 1945–1947* (Princeton, 1981).
Dahm, B., *Sukarno and the Struggle for Indonesian Independence* (Ithica, N.Y., 1969).
Dallek, R., *Franklin D. Roosevelt and American Foreign Policy, 1932–1945* (New York, 1979).
    The American Style of Foreign Policy (New York, 1983).
Darby, P., *British Defence Policy East of Suez, 1947–1968* (London, 1974).
Dawson, R., *The Chinese Experience* (London, 1978).
    The Chinese Chameleon (London, 1967).
De Conde, A. (ed.), *Isolation and Security* (Durham, N. Carolina, 1957).
de Kadt, J., *De Indonesische Tragedie: Het Treurspel der Gemiste Kansen* (Amsterdam, 1949).
DePorte, A. W., *Europe Between the Superpowers* (New Haven, 1979).
Devilliers, P., *Histoire du Viêt-Nam, 1940–1952* (Paris, 1952).
Divine, R., *Second Chance: the Triumph of Internationalism in America During World War II* (New York, 1967).
    Roosevelt and World War II (Baltimore, 1969).
Donnison, F. S., *British Military Administration in the Far East, 1943–46* (London, 1956).
Drachman, E. R., *United States Policy Toward Vietnam, 1940–1945* (Rutherford, N.J., 1970)
Drinnon, R., *Facing West: the Metaphysics of Indian-Hating and Empire Building* (New York, 1980).

Duiker, W. J., *The Rise of Nationalism in Vietnam, 1900–1941* (Ithica, N.Y., 1976).
Duke, A. C. and Tamse, C. A. (ed.), *Britain and the Netherlands, Vol. VI: War and Society* (The Hague, 1977).
Dunn, F. S., *Peacemaking and the Settlement with Japan* (Princeton, 1963).
Dunn, J., *Timor: A People Betrayed* (Milton, Queensland, 1983).
Duroselle, J. B., *La Politique Extérieure de la France, 1914 à 1945* (Paris, 1965).
La Décadence, 1932–1939 (Paris, 1979).
Eastman, L. E., *The Abortive Revolution: China Under Nationalist Rule, 1927–1937* (Cambridge, Mass., 1974).
Seeds of Destruction: Nationalist China in War and Revolution, 1937–1949 (Stanford, 1984).
Edwards, C., *Bruce of Melbourne* (London, 1965).
Edwards, P. G., *Prime Ministers and Diplomats: the Making of Australian Foreign Policy, 1901–1949* (Melbourne, 1983).
Ehrman, J., *Grand Strategy, Vol. V* (London, 1956).
Grand Strategy, Vol. VI (London, 1956).
Elias, N., *The Civilizing Process, Vol. 2: State Formation and Civilization* (trans. E. Jephcott, Oxford, 1982).
Ellul, J., *Trahison de l'Occident* (Paris, 1975).
Elsbree, W. H., *Japan's Role in Southeast Asian Nationalist Movements, 1940–1945* (Cambridge, Mass., 1953).
Endacott, G. and Birch, A., *Hong Kong Eclipse* (Hong Kong, 1978).
Endicott, S. C., *Dipolomacy and Enterprise: British China Policy, 1933–37* (Manchester, 1975).
Erickson, J., *The Soviet High Command* (London, 1962).
Stalin's War With Germany, Vols. 1 and 2 (London, 1975–83).
Everett, J. M., *Women and Social Change in India* (New Delhi, 1981).
Fairbank, J. K., *The United States and China* (Cambridge, Mass., 1971).
China Perceived (New York, 1974).
Fairbank, W., *America's Cultural Experiment in China, 1942–1949* (Washington, D.C., 1976).
Farmer, P., *Vichy: Political Dilemma* (New York, 1955).
Fasseur, C. (ed.), *Geld en geweten* (The Hague, 1980).
Feis, H., *The Road to Pearl Harbor* (Princeton, 1971).
Churchill, Roosevelt and Stalin (Princeton, 1967).
Between War and Peace (Princeton, 1960).
The China Tangle (Princeton, 1972).
Japan Subdued (Princeton, 1961).
Feldt, E., *The Coast Watchers* (London, 1946).
Fieldhouse, D. K., *The Colonial Empires: a Comparative Survey from the Eighteenth Century* (London, 1982).
Fifield, R. H., *Southeast Asia in United States Policy* (New York, 1963).
Fishel, W. R., *The End of Extraterritoriality in China* (Berkeley, 1952).
Fisher, A. G. B., *The Clash of Progress and Security* (London, 1935).
Economic Progress and Social Security (London, 1946).
Fitzgerald, C.P., *The Chinese View of Their Place in the World* (London, 1964).
The Birth of Communist China (London, 1964).
Foot, M., *Aneurin Bevan, 1897–1945* (London, 1975).
Fox, J. P., *Germany and the Far Eastern Crisis, 1931–1938* (Oxford, 1982).
Friedel, F., *Franklin D. Roosevelt: the Apprenticeship* (Boston, 1952); *The Ordeal* (1954); *The Triumph* (1956); *Launching the New Deal* (1973).
Friend, T., *Between Two Empires* (New Haven, 1965).
Fukutake, T., *The Japanese Social Structure: its Evolution in the Modern Century* (trans. R. P. Dore, Tokyo, 1982).
Fussell, P., *The Great War in Modern Memory* (London, 1975).
Gaddis, J. L., *The United States and the Origins of the Cold War, 1941–1947* (New York, 1972).

Gallie, D., *Social Inequality and Class Radicalism in France and Britain* (Cambridge, 1983).
Gardner, L. C., *Economic Aspects of New Deal Diplomacy* (Boston, 1971).
  Architects of Illusion (Chicago, 1972).
  A Covenant With Power (New York, 1984).
Gardner, R. N., *Sterling Dollar Diplomacy* (Oxford, 1956).
Gellner, E., *Nations and Nationalism* (Oxford, 1983).
Ghosh, K. K., *The Indian National Army* (Meerut, 1969).
Gibbs, N., *Grand Strategy, Vol. I* (London, 1976).
Gilbert, M., *Winston S. Churchill, Vols. V and VI* (London, 1976, '83).
Gilpin, R., *War and Change in World Politics* (Cambridge, 1981).
Giner, S., *Mass Society* (London, 1976).
Girdner, A. and Loftus, A., *The Great Betrayal: the Evacuation of the Japanese-Americans During World War II* (Toronto, 1969).
Gittings, J., *China and the World, 1922–1972* (London, 1974).
  The Role of the Chinese Army (London, 1967).
Gong, G. W., *The Standard of 'Civilization' in International Society* (Oxford, 1984).
Goodman, G. K. (ed.), *Imperial Japan and Asia: A Reassessment* (New York, 1967).
  An Experiment in Wartime Intercultural Relations: Philippine Students in Japan, 1943–1945 (Ithica, N.Y., 1962).
Goodspeed, S. S., *The Nature and Function of International Organization* (New York, 1967).
Gopal, S., *Jawaharlal Nehru* (London, 1975).
Gordon, B. M., *Collaboration in France in the Second World War* (Ithica, N.Y., 1980).
Gowing, M., *Britain and Atomic Energy, 1939–1945* (London, 1964).
Grattan, C. H., *The United States and the Southwest Pacific* (Cambridge, Mass., 1961).
Greenfield, K. R., *Command Decisions* (London, 1960).
Grimal, H., *La Decolonisation, 1919–1963* (Paris, 1965).
Gull, E. M., *British Economic Interests in the Far East* (London, 1943).
Gupta, P. S., *Imperialism and the British Labour Movement, 1914–1964* (London, 1975).
Gwyer, J. M., *Grand Strategy, Vol. III, pt. 1* (London, 1964).
Haggie, P., *Britannia At Bay: the Defence of the British Empire Against Japan, 1931–1941* (Oxford, 1981).
Hall, W. H., *North American Supply* (London, 1955).
Hammer, E., *The Struggle for Indochina* (Stanford, 1954).
Hancock, W., *Smuts, The Fields of Force, 1919–1950* (Cambridge, 1968).
Hancock, W. and Gowing, M., *British War Economy* (London, 1949).
Hane, M., *Peasants, Rebels and Outcastes: the Underside of Modern Japan* (New York, 1982).
Harrod, R. F., *The Life of John Maynard Keynes* (London, 1951).
Hasluck, P., *The Government and the People, 1939–41* (Canberra, 1952).
  The Government and the People, 1942–45 (Canberra, 1972).
Hathaway, R. M., *Ambiguous Partnership: Britain and America, 1944–1947* (New York, 1981).
Hauner, M., *India in Axis Strategy: Germany, Japan and Indian Nationalists in the Second World War* (Stuttgart, 1981).
Havens, T. R., *Valley of Darkness: the Japanese People and World War Two* (New York, 1978).
Hawes, S. and White, R., *Resistance in Europe, 1939–1945* (London, 1975).
Hay, D., *Europe: the Emergence of an Idea* (Edinburgh, 1968).
Hay, S. N., *Asian Ideas of East and West* (Cambridge, Mass., 1970).
Hayashida, T., *Netaji Subhas Chandra Bose: His Great Struggle and Martyrdom* (Bombay, 1970).
Haslehurst, C., *Menzies Observed* (Sydney, 1979).
Headrick D. R., *Tools of Empire: Technology and European Imperialism in the Nineteenth Century* (New York, 1981).

Heinrichs, W. H., *American Ambassador* (Boston, 1965).

Hess, G. R., *America Encounters India, 1941–1947* (Baltimore, 1971).

Hetherington, J., *Blamey* (Melbourne, 1954).

Hilvert, J., *Blue-Pencil Warriors: Censorship and Propaganda in World War Two* (St. Lucia, Queensland, 1984).

Hinsley, F. H., et al., *British Intelligence in the Second World War, Vols. I–III* (London, 1979–84).

Hinton, W., *Fashen: A Documentary of Revolution in a Chinese Village* (New York, 1968).

Hodgart, A., *The Economics of European Imperialism* (London, 1977).

Hoffmann, S., *Gulliver's Troubles* (New York, 1968).

Hoffmann, S. et al., *France: Change and Tradition* (London, 1963).

Hofstadter, R., *The American Political Tradition* (New York, 1967).
   The Paranoid Style in American Politics (New York, 1964).
   Anti-Intellectualism in American Life (New York, 1963).

Holland, R. F., *Britain and the Commonwealth Alliance, 1918–1939* (London, 1981).

Holland, W. L. (ed.), *Asian Nationalism and the West* (New York, 1953).

Horner, D. M., *High Command: Australia and Allied Strategy, 1939–1945* (Sydney, 1982).
   Crisis of Command: Australian Generalship and the Japanese Threat, 1941–1943 (Canberra, 1978).

Horrowitz, D., *From Yalta to Vietnam* (London, 1967).

Howard, M., *Grand Strategy, Vol. IV* (London, 1972).
   The Continental Commitment (London, 1972).
   The Mediterranean Strategy in World War Two (London, 1968).
   War and the Liberal Conscience (London, 1978).

Hudson, G. F., *The Far East in World Politics* (London, 1939).
   Questions of East and West (London, 1953).

Hughes, D. and Kallen, E., *The Anatomy of Racism: the Canadian Dimension* (Montreal, 1974).

Hunt, M., *Frontier Defense and the Open Door* (New Haven, 1973).

Huntington, S. P., *The Soldier and the State* (Cambridge, Mass., 1957).

Hutchins, F. G., *India's Revolution: Gandhi and the Quit India Movement* (Cambridge, Mass., 1973).

Hyde, H.M., *The Quiet Canadian* (London, 1962).

Ienaga, S., *Japan's Last War* (Oxford, 1979).

Iriye, A., *Pacific Estrangement* (Cambridge, Mass., 1972).
   Across the Pacific (New York, 1967).
   After Imperialism (Cambridge, Mass., 1965).
   Power and Culture: the Japanese-American War (Cambridge, Mass., 1981).
   The Cold War In Asia (Englewood Cliffs, N.J., 1974).
   (ed.) *Mutual Images: Essays in American-Japanese Relations* (Cambridge, Mass., 1975).
   (ed.) *The Chinese and the Japanese* (Princeton, 1980).

Isaacs, H.R., *Scratches On Our Minds* (New York, 1963).
   No Peace for Asia (Cambridge, Mass., 1967).

Ishii, O., *Cotton-Textile Diplomacy: Japan, Great Britain and the United States, 1930–1936* (Ann Arbor, Michigan, 1977).

Iyer, R. (ed.), *The Glass Curtain Between Asia and Europe* (London, 1965).

James, R.R., *Churchill, A Study in Failure, 1900–1939* (London, 1970).

Jansen, M.B., *The Japanese and Sun Yat-sen* (Cambridge, Mass., 1954).
   (ed.) *Changing Japanese Attitudes Toward Modernisation* (Princeton, 1965).

Jeffreys-Jones, R. (ed.), *Eagle and Empire: American Opposition to European Imperialism, 1914–1982* (Aix-en-Provence, 1983).

Jervis, R., *Perception and Misperception in International Politics* (Princeton, 1976).

Jog, N.G., *In Freedom's Quest* (New Delhi, 1969).

Johnson, C., *MITI and the Japanese Miracle* (Stanford, 1982).
  Peasant Nationalism and Communist Power: the Emergence of Revolutionary China, 1937–1945 (Stanford, 1963).
Johnson, S.K., *American Attitudes Toward Japan, 1941–1945* (Washington D.C., 1975).
Joll, J., *The Second International, 1889–1914* (London, 1975).
  Europe Since 1870: An International History (London, 1973).
Kahn, E.J., *The China Hands* (New York, 1975).
Kamenka, E. (ed.), *Nationalism: the Nature and Evolution of an Idea* (London, 1976).
Kedourie, E., *Nationalism* (London, 1960).
Kelman, H., *International Behavior* (New York, 1966).
Kennan, G., *American Diplomacy, 1900–1950* (New York, 1951).
Kerkvliet, B.J., *The Huk Rebellion: a Study of Peasant Revolt in the Philippines* (Berkeley, 1977).
Kersten, A.E., *Buitenlandse Zaken in ballingschap* (Alphen, 1981).
Kiernon, V.G., *The Lords of Human Kind* (London, 1969).
  European Empires, From Conquest to Collapse, 1815–1960 (London, 1982).
Kimball, W., *The Most Unsordid Act* (Baltimore, 1969).
  (ed.) *Franlin D. Roosevelt and the World Crisis, 1937–1945* (Lexington, Mass., 1973).
Kinross, Lord, *Atatürk: The Rebirth of a Nation* (London, 1964).
Kirby, S.W., *The War Against Japan, Vols. I–V* (London, 1957–69).
  Singapore: The Chain of Disaster (London, 1971).
Knapp, W., *A History of War and Peace, 1939–1965* (London, 1967).
Knightly, P., *The First Casualty* (New York, 1975).
Koen, R.Y., *The China Lobby in American Politics* (New York, 1974).
Kohn, H., *The Idea of Nationalism* (New York, 1946).
Kolko, G., *The Politics of War* (London, 1968).
Kubek, A., *How the Far East Was Lost* (Chicago, 1953).
Kuhn, T.S., *The Structure of Scientific Revolutions* (Chicago, 1970).
Lancaster, D., *The Emancipation of French Indochina* (London, 1961).
Langer, W., *Our Vichy Gamble* (New York, 1947).
Lash, J.P., *Roosevelt and Churchill, 1939–1941* (London, 1977).
Latham, A.J., *The International Economy and the Underdeveloped World, 1865–1914* (London, 1978).
Lebra, J.C., *Japanese-Trained Armies in Southeast Asia* (Hong Kong, 1977).
  Jungle Alliance: Japan and the Indian National Army (Singapore, 1971).
Lee, B.A., *Britain and the Sino-Japanese War, 1937–1939* (Stanford, 1973).
Lee, J.M. and Petter, M., *The Colonial Office, War and Development Policy* (London, 1982).
Leed, E.J., *No Man's Land: Combat and Identity in World War One* (Cambridge, 1979).
M. Lerner (ed.), *The Portable Veblen* (New York, 1948).
Leurdijk, J.H. (ed.), *The Foreign Policy of the Netherlands* (Alphen, 1978).
Leutze, J.R., *Bargaining For Supremacy: Anglo-American Naval Collaboration, 1937–1941* (Chapel Hill, 1977).
Levenson, J.R., *Confucian China and Its Modern State: Vols. I–III* (London, 1958–65).
Levi, W., *American-Australian Relations* (Minneapolis, 1947).
Lewin, R., *Churchill As Warlord* (London, 1973).
  Slim: The Standbearer (London, 1976).
  The Other Ultra: Codes, Ciphers and the Defeat of Japan (London, 1982).
Lichtenstein, N., *Labor's War At Home: the C.I.O. in World War Two* (Cambridge, 1982).
Lichteim, G., *Imperialism* (London, 1971).
Lindsay, O., *The Lasting Honour: the Fall of Hong Kong, 1941* (London, 1978).
  At the Going Down of the Sun (London, 1981).
Lingeman, R., *Don't You Know There's A War On?* (New York, 1970).
Liska, G., *Imperial America* (Baltimore, 1967).
  Nations in Alliance (Baltimore, 1962).
Lissington, M.P., *New Zealand and the United States, 1840–1944* (Wellington, 1972).

Lohbeck, D., *Patrick J. Hurley* (Chicago, 1956).
Louis, W.R., *British Strategy in the Far East, 1919–1939* (Oxford, 1971).
  Imperialism At Bay (Oxford, 1977).
Lovell, J.P., *Foreign Policy in Perspective* (New York, 1970).
Lowe, P., *Great Britain and Japan, 1911–1915* (London, 1969).
  Great Britain and the Origins of the Pacific War (Oxford, 1977).
  Britain in the Far East (London, 1981).
Manchester, W., *American Caesar: Douglas MacArthur, 1880–1964* (London, 1979).
Mannoni, O., *Prospero and Caliban: the Psychology of Colonization* (trans. P. Powesland; New York, 1964).
Mansergh, N., *The Commonwealth Experience* (London, 1969).
Manvell, R., *Films and the Second World War* (London, 1974).
Marder, A.J. *Old Friends, New Enemies: the Royal Navy and the Imperial Japanese Navy* (Oxford, 1981).
Marr, D., *Vietnamese Anti-Colonialism, 1885–1925* (Berkeley, 1971).
Marrus, M. and Paxton, R., *Vichy France and the Jews* (New York, 1981).
Marshall, D.B., *The French Colonial Myth and Constitution-Making in the Fourth Republic* (New Haven, 1973).
Martin, B., *Deutschland und Japan im Zweiten Weltkrieg* (Göttingen, 1969).
Maruyama, M., *Thought and Behaviour in Modern Japanese Politics* (London, 1963).
Marwick, A., *Britain in the Century of Total War* (London, 1968).
  Class: Image and Reality in Britain, France and the U.S.A. Since 1930 (London, 1980).
Mason, P., *Prospero's Magic* (London, 1962).
  A Matter of Honour (London, 1974).
  Patterns of Dominance (London, 1971).
Mason, W.W., *Prisoners of War* (Wellington, N.Z., 1954).
Mastny, V., *Russia's Road to the Cold War* (New York, 1979).
Matloff, M. and Snell, E., *Strategic Planning for Coalition Warfare, 1941–1942* (Washington, D.C., 1953).
Matloff, M., *Strategic Planning for Coalition Warfare, 1943–1944* (Washington, 1959).
Maung Maung (ed.), *Aung San of Burma* (The Hague, 1962).
May, E.R., *Imperial Democracy: the Emergence of America as a Great Power* (New York, 1961).
  'Lessons' of the Past (London, 1975).
May, E.R. and Thomson, J. (ed.), *American-East Asian Relations* (Cambridge, Mass., 1972).
May, G., *China Scapegoat: the Diplomatic Ordeal of John Carter Vincent* (Washington, D.C., 1979).
McLaine, I., *Ministry of Morale: Home Front Morale and the Ministry of Information in World War II* (London, 1979).
Mead, M., *Anthropology: a Human Science* (Princeton, 1964).
  New Lives For Old: Cultural Transformation: Manus, 1928–1953 (New York, 1961).
  Ruth Benedict (New York, 1974).
  (ed.), *Cultural Patterns and Technical Change* (New York, 1955).
Meo, L.D., *Japan's Radio War on Australia, 1941–1945* (Melbourne, 1968).
Merrill, J.M., *A Sailor's Admiral* (New York, 1976).
Meskill, J.M. *Hitler and Japan: the Hollow Alliance* (New York, 1966).
Michel, H., *Les Courants de Pensée de la Résistance* (Paris, 1962).
Milward, A.S., *War, Economy and Society, 1939–1945* (London, 1977).
Minear, R.H., *Victor's Justice* (Princeton, 1971).
Montgomery, B., *Shenton of Singapore: Governor and Prisoner of War* (London, 1984).
Moore, B., *Injustice: the Social Bases of Obedience and Revolt* (London, 1978).
Moore, J. H., *Over-Sexed, Over-Paid, and Over Here: Americans in Australia, 1941–1945* (St. Lucia, Queensland, 1981).
Morison, E.E., *Turmoil and Tradition* (Boston, 1960).
Morison, S.E., *Two-Ocean War* (Boston, 1963).

Morley, J.W. (ed.), *Dilemmas of Growth in Pre-War Japan* (Princeton, 1972).
    Deterrent Diplomacy: Japan, Germany and the U.S.S.R., 1935–1940 (New York, 1977).
    The Fateful Choice: Japan's Advance Into Southeast Asia, 1939–1941 (New York, 1980).
    The China Quagmire: Japan's Expansion on the Asian Continent, 1933–1941 (New York, 1983).
Morris, E., *Corregidor: the Nightmare in the Philippines* (London, 1982).
Morton, L., *Strategy and Command: the First Two Years* (Washington, D.C., 1962).
Mueller, J.E., *War, Presidents and Public Opinion* (New York, 1973).
Murphey, R., *The Outsiders: the Western Experience in India and China* (Ann Arbor, Michigan, 1977).
Myers, R. and Peattie, M. (ed.), *The Japanese Colonial Empire, 1895–1945* (Princeton, 1984).
Myrdal, A. and Klein, V., *Woman's Two Roles* (London, 1968).
Myrdal, G., *An American Dilemma, Vol. II* (New York, 1944).
Nagai, Y. and Iriye, A. (ed.), *The Origins of the Cold War in Asia* (Tokyo, 1977).
Needham, J., *Within the Four Seas* (London, 1969).
Nef, J.U., *War and Human Progress* (London, 1950).
Nedipath, J., *The Singapore Base and the Defence of Britain's Eastern Empire, 1919–1941* (Oxford, 1981).
Neumann, W.L., *America Encounters Japan* (Baltimore, 1963).
Nicholas, H.G., *The United States and Britain* (Chicago, 1975).
Nisbet, R., *History of the Idea of Progress* (New York, 1980).
Nish, I., *The Anglo-Japanese Alliance* (London, 1966).
    Alliance in Decline (London, 1972).
    Japanese Foreign Policy, 1869–1941 (London, 1977).
    (ed.) *Indonesian Experience: the Role of Japan and Britain, 1943–1948* (London, 1979).
    (ed.) *Anglo-Japanese Alienation, 1919–1952* (Cambridge, 1982).
Offner, A., *American Appeasement* (Cambridge, Mass., 1969).
Ogata, S.N., *Defiance in Manchuria* (Berkeley, 1964).
Ogburn, W.F., *On Culture and Social Change* (Chicago, 1964).
Osgood, R.E., *Ideals and Self-Interest in America's Foreign Policy* (Chicago, 1953).
    Alliances and American Foreign Policy (Baltimore, 1971).
Pandey, B.N., *The Break-Up of British India* (London, 1969).
Panikkar, K.M., *Asia and Western Dominance* (London, 1953).
Paxton, R.O., *Vichy France: Old Guard and New Order, 1940–1944* (New York, 1972).
Payne, R., *The Revolt of Asia* (London, 1948).
    Chiang Kai-shek (New York, 1969).
Peden, G.C., *British Rearmament and the Treasury, 1932–1939* (Edinburgh, 1979).
Pelling, H., *Winston Churchill* (London, 1974).
Pelz, S.E., *Race to Pearl Harbor* (Cambridge, Mass., 1974).
Perrett, G., *Days of Sadness, Years of Triumph: the American People, 1939–1945* (New York, 1973).
Petillo, C.M. *Douglas MacArthur: the Philippine Years* (Bloomington, Indiana, 1981).
Pocock, J.G., *Politics, Language and Time* (London, 1972).
Pogue, F.C., *George C. Marshall: Ordeal and Hope, 1939–1942* (New York, 1966).
    George C. Marshall: Organizer of Victory, 1943–1945 (New York, 1973).
Polenberg, R., *War and Society: the United States, 1941–1945* (Philadelphia, 1972).
    One Nation Divisible: Class, Race and Ethnicity in the United States Since 1938 (New York, 1980).
Potter, D.M. *The People of Plenty* (Chicago, 1968).
Potter, E.B., *Nimitz* (Annapolis, Maryland, 1976).
Prange, G.W., *At Dawn We Slept* (London, 1982).
Prasad, A., *The Indian Revolt of 1942* (Delhi, 1958).
Presseisen, E.L., *Germany and Japan: A Study in Totalitarian Diplomacy, 1933–1941* (The Hague, 1958).
Purcell, V., *The Revolution in Southeast Asia* (London, 1962).

The Chinese in Southeast Asia (Oxford, 1965).

Range, W., *Franklin D. Roosevelt's World Order* (Athens, Georgia, 1959).

Rappaport, A., *The Navy League of the United States* (Detroit, 1962).

Ray, R.K., *Industrialisation in India: Growth and Conflict in the Private Corporate Sector, 1914–1947* (New Delhi, 1979).

Reardon-Anderson, J., *Yenan and the Great Powers: the Origins of Chinese Communist Foreign Policy, 1944–1946* (New York, 1980).

Reese, T.R., *Australia, New Zealand and the United States* (London, 1969).

Reischauer, E.O., *The Japanese* (Cambridge, Mass., 1978).

Reischauer, E., Fairbank, J. and Craig, A., *East Asia: the Modern Transformation* (London, 1965).

Reynolds, D., *The Creation of the Anglo-American Alliance, 1937–1941* (London, 1981).

Reynolds, P. and Hughes, E., *The Historian as Diplomat: Charles Kingsley Webster and the United Nations, 1939–46* (London, 1977).

Rhodes, A., *Propaganda: The Art of Persuasion: World War II* (London, 1976).

Richard, D.E., *United States Naval Administration of the Trust Territory of the Pacific Islands* (Washington, D.C., 1957).

Ride, E., *B.A.A.G.: Hong Kong Resistance, 1942–1945* (Hong Kong, 1981).

Robins-Mowry, D., *The Hidden Sun: Women of Modern Japan* (Boulder, Colorado, 1983).

Roff, W.R., *The Origins of Malay Nationalism* (New Haven, 1967).

Rolph, C.H., *Kingsley* (London, 1973).

Romanus, C. and Sunderland, R., *Stilwell's Mission to China* (Washington, D.C., 1953).
Stilwell's Command Problems (Washington, 1956).
Time Runs Out in C.B.I. (Washington, 1959).

Romein, J., *Aera van Europa: de Europese Geschiedenis als Afwijking van het Algemeen Menselijk Patroon* (Leiden, 1954).

Ronan, C.A., *The Shorter Science and Civilisation in China, Vol. 1* (Cambridge, 1978).

Rose, S., *Britain and Southeast Asia* (London, 1962).

Roskill, S.W., *The War At Sea, Vols. I–III* (London, 1954–61).
Hankey, Man of Secrets, Vols. II–III (London, 1972–74).
Naval Policy Between the Wars, Vols. I–II (London, 1968–76).
Churchill and the Admirals (London, 1977).

Said, E.W., *Orientalism* (London, 1978).

Sainteny, J., *Histoire d'Une Paix Manquée* (Paris, 1953).

Scalapino, R.A., *Democracy and the Party Movement in Pre-War Japan* (Berkeley, 1962).
The Japanese Communist Movement, 1920–1966 (Berkeley, 1967).

Schaller, M., *The U.S. Crusade in China, 1938–1945* (New York, 1979).

Schelling, T.C., *Arms and Influence* (New Haven, 1966).

Schlesinger, A.M., *The Imperial Presidency* (London, 1974).

Schmultzer, E.J., *Dutch Colonial Policy and the Search for Identity in Indonesia, 1920–1931* (Leiden, 1977).

Schram, S., *Mao Tse-tung* (London, 1967).

Shai, A., *Origins of the War in the East* (London, 1976).
Britain and China, 1941–1947 (London, 1984).

Sherwin, M., *A World Destroyed: the Atomic Bomb and the Grand Alliance* (New York, 1977).

Sherwood, R.G., *Roosevelt and Hopkins* (New York, 1948).

Shewmaker, K.E., *Americans and Chinese Communists, 1927–1945* (Ithica, N.Y., 1971).

Shillony, B.A., *Politics and Culture in Wartime Japan* (Oxford, 1981).

Short, K.R. (ed.), *Film and Radio Progaganda in World War II* (Knoxville, Tenn., 1983).

Sih, P.K. (ed.), *Nationalist China During the Sino-Japanese War, 1937–1945* (Hicksville, N.Y., 1977).

Singhal, D. P., *A History of the Indian People* (London, 1983).

Siu, B., *Women of China: Imperialism and Women's Resistance, 1900–1949* (London, 1982).

Smith, A.D., *The Ethnic Revival in the Modern World* (Cambridge, 1981).

Smith, B.F., *The Shadow Warriors: O.S.S. and the Origins of the C.I.A.* (London, 1983).

Smith, G., *American Diplomacy During the Second World War* (New York, 1965).
Smith, R.B., *Vietnam and the West* (Ithica, N.Y., 1971).
   An International History of the Vietnam War, Vol. 1 (London, 1984).
Smith, R.H., *O.S.S.* (Berkeley, 1972).
Sorokin, P.A., *Social and Cultural Dynamics, Vol. 3: Fluctuation of Social Relationships, War and Revolution* (New York, 1937).
Spector, R.H., *Eagle Against the Sun* (New York, 1984).
Spence, J.D., *The Gate of Heavenly Peace: the Chinese and Their Revolution 1895–1980* (London, 1982).
Steele, A.T., *The American People and China* (New York, 1966).
Steinberg, D.J., *Philippine Collaboration in World War II* (Ann Arbor, Michigan, 1967).
Stevenson, W., *A Man Called Intrepid* (New York, 1976).
Stoff, M. B., *Oil, War and American Security* (New Haven, 1980).
Stone, S. N. (ed.), *Aborigines in White Australia* (London, 1974).
Storry, G. R., *A History of Modern Japan* (London, 1962).
   The Double Patriots (London, 1957).
   Japan and the Decline of the West in Asia (London, 1979).
Stouffer, S. A., et al., *The American Soldier: Adjustment During Army Life* (Princeton, 1949).
   The American Soldier: Combat and Its Aftermath (Princeton, 1949).
Suh, D-S., *The Korean Communist Movement, 1918–1948* (Princeton, 1967).
Sykes, C., *Orde Wingate* (London, 1959).
Tang, P. S., *Russian and Soviet Policy in Manchuria and Outer Mongolia, 1911–1931* (Durham, N.C., 1959).
Tang Tsou, *America's Failure in China, 1941–50* (Chicago, 1962).
Tate, D. J., *The Making of Modern South-East Asia, Vol. Two* (Kuala Lumpur, 1979).
Taylor, A. J. P., *English History, 1914–1945* (Oxford, 1965).
   Beaverbrook (London, 1972).
Taylor, A. J. P. et al., *Churchill, Four Faces and the Man* (London, 1969).
Taylor, L., *A Trial of Generals: Homma, Yamashita, MacArthur* (South Bend, Indiana, 1981).
Thomas, J. N., *The Institute of Pacific Relations* (Seattle, 1974).
Thorne, C., *The Limits of Foreign Policy* (London, 1972).
   Allies of a Kind (London, 1978).
   Racial Aspects of the Far Eastern War of 1941–1945 (London, 1982).
Thornton, A. P., *The Imperial Idea And Its Enemies* (London, 1966).
Tinker, H., *Race, Conflict and the International Order* (London, 1977).
Tint, H., *The Decline of French Patriotism, 1870–1940* (London, 1964).
Tokayer, M. and Swartz, M., *The Fugu Plan* (London, 1979).
Tomlinson, B. R., *The Political Economy of the Raj, 1914–1947* (London, 1979).
Toye, H., *The Springing Tiger: a Study of a Revolution* (London, 1959).
   Laos: Buffer State or Battleground (London, 1971).
Treadgold, D. W., *The West in Russia and China: Vol. 1, Russia, 1472–1917* (Cambridge, 1973).
   Vol. II, China, 1582–1949 (Cambridge, 1973).
Trotter, A., *Britain and East Asia, 1933–1937* (Cambridge, 1975).
Tuchman, B., *Sand Against the Wind: Stilwell and the American Experience of China, 1911–1945* (London, 1971).
Tugwell, R., *In Search of Roosevelt* (Cambridge, Mass., 1972).
van der Kroef, J., *The Dialectic of Colonial Indonesian History* (Amsterdam, 1963).
   The Communist Party of Indonesia (Vancouver, 1965).
   Communism in Malaya and Singapore (The Hague, 1967).
Varg, P., *Missionaries, Chinese and Diplomats* (Princeton, 1958).
   The Making of a Myth: the United States and China, 1897–1912 (East Lansing, Michigan, 1968).
Viorst, M., *Hostile Allies: F.D.R. and Charles de Gaulle* (New York, 1975).

Warmbrunn, W., *The Dutch Under German Occupation, 1940–1945* (Stanford, 1963).
Warner, L. and Sandilands, J., *Women Behind the Wire* (London, 1982).
Watt, A., *The Evolution of Australian Foreign Policy* (Cambridge, 1967).
Watt, D.C., *Succeeding John Bull: America in Britain's Place, 1900–1975* (Cambridge, 1984).
Weber, E., *Action Française* (Stanford, 1962).
Weinberg, A. K., *Manifest Destiny* (Baltimore, 1935).
Wertheim, W.F., *Indonesian Society in Transition* (The Hague, 1964).
Weston, R. F., *Racism in U.S. Imperialism* (Columbia, S.C., 1972).
Wheeler, G. E., *Prelude to Pearl Harbor* (Columbia, Missouri, 1963).
Wheeler-Bennett, J., *King George VI* (London, 1958).
   John Anderson, Viscount Waverley (London, 1962).
Wilkinson, E., *Japan versus Europe: A History of Misunderstanding* (London, 1983).
Williams, W. A., *The Roots of the Modern American Empire* (New York, 1969).
   From Colony to Empire (New York, 1972).
Williamson, J. D., *The Intellectual Resistance in Europe* (Cambridge, Mass., 1981).
Wilson, D., *When Tigers Fight: the Story of the Sino-Japanese War, 1937–1945* (London, 1982).
Winkler, A.M., *The Politics of Propaganda: the Office of War Information, 1942–1945* (New Haven, 1978).
Wint, G., *The British in Asia* (New York, 1954).
Winterbotham, F. W., *The Ultra Secret* (London, 1974).
Wiseman, H. V., *Political Systems: Some Sociological Approaches* (London, 1966).
Wohl, R., *The Generation of 1914* (London, 1980).
Wohlstetter, R., *Pearl Harbor: Warning and Decision* (Stanford, 1962).
Wolf, E. R., *Europe and the People Without History* (Berkeley, 1982).
Wolfers, A., *Discord and Collaboration* (Baltimore, 1965).
Woodward, L., *British Foreign Policy in the Second World War, Vols. I–V* (London, 1970–76).
Wright, G., *The Ordeal of Total War, 1939–1945* (New York, 1968).
Wright, Q., *A Study of War* (Chicago, 1942).
Wright, R., *The Colour Curtain* (London, 1956).
Yergin, D., *Shattered Peace: the Origins of the Cold War and the National Security State* (London, 1978).
Young, A. N., *China and the Helping Hand, 1937–1945* (Cambridge, Mass., 1963).

I *Articles*

Allen, L., 'Japanese Literature in the Second World War', *Proceedings of the British Association for Japanese Studies*, Vol. 2, 1977.
Beasley, W. G., 'Japan and the West in the Mid-Nineteenth Century', *Proceedings of the British Academy*, Vol. LX, 1980.
Chan Lau Kit-Ching, 'The Hong Kong Question During the Pacific War', *Journal of Imperial and Commonwealth History*, Vol. 2, No. 1, 1973.
Dallek, R., 'Franklin Roosevelt As World Leader', *American Historical Review*, Vol. 76, No. 5, 1971.
Daniels, G., 'Japanese Broadcasting in the Pacific War', *Proceedings of the British Association for Japanese Studies*, Vol. 6, Part 1, 1981.
   'The Evacuation of Schoolchildren in Wartime Japan', ibid, Vol. 2, 1977.
De Jong, L., 'Les Pays-Bas Dans La Seconde Guerre Mondiale', *Histoire de la Deuxième Guerre Mondiale*, April, 1963.
Dulles, F. and Ridinger, G., 'The Anti-Colonial Policies of Franklin D. Roosevelt', *Political Science Quarterly*, March 1955.
Edwards, J., 'The War Behind the War', *National Times* (Sydney), Jan. 30 – Feb. 4, 1978.
Epstein, S., 'District Officers in Decline: the Erosion of British Authority in the Bombay Countryside, 1919 to 1947', *Modern Asian Studies*, Vol. 16, No. 3, 1982.

Fasseur, C., 'Nederland en het Indonesische nationalisme. De balans nog eens opgemaakt', in *Bijdragen en Mededingen betreffende de Geschiedenis der Nederlanden*, Vol. 99, 1984.
'Een Wissel op de Toekomst: de Rede van Koningen Wilhelmina van 6/7 December 1942', in van Arooij, F. (ed.), *Between People and Statistics: Essays on Modern Indonesian History* (The Hague, 1979).
Homan, G., 'The United States and the Indonesian Question, 1941–1946', *Tijdschrift voor Geschiedenis*, No. 93, 1980.
Hosoya, C., 'George Sansom: Diplomat and Historian', *Hitotsubashi Journal of Law and Politics*, Vol. 8, 1979.
International Affairs, 1970: fiftieth anniversay issue.
Ion, A. H., 'The formation of the *Nippon Kirisutokyodan*, 1941', *Proceedings of the British Association for Japanese Studies*, Vo. 5, Part 1, 1980.
Jarvie, I., 'Fanning the Flames: Anti-American Reactions to "Objective Burma" (1945)', *Historical Journal of Film, Radio and Television*, Vol. 1, No. 2, 1981.
Joll, J., 'The Ideal and the Real: Changing Concepts of the International System, 1815–1982', *International Affairs*, Spring 1982.
Kimball, W., 'Churchill and Roosevelt: the Personal Equation', *Prologue*, Fall 1974.
Lawry, J., 'A Catch on the Boundary: Australia and Free French Movement in 1940', *Journal of Pacific History*, Vol. 10, 1975.
Lafeber, W., 'Roosevelt, Churchill and Indochina, 1942–1945', *American Historical Review*, LXXX, 1975.
Lewis, B., 'The Question of Orientalism', *New York Review of Books*, 24 June 1982.
Lowe, P., 'The Soviet Union in Britain's Far Eastern Policy, 1941', *International Studies* (London School of Economics), 1981.
Manning, A. F., 'The Position of the Dutch Government in London Up to 1942', *Journal of Contemporary History*, Vol. 13, 1978.
Minear, R. H., 'Cross-Cultural Perception and World War II: American Japanists and Their Images of Japan', *International Studies Quarterly*, Dec. 1980.
Miwa, K., 'Japan on the Periphery of Both East and West', Institute of International Relations research papers, No. A–34, Sophia University, Tokyo, 1979.
'Japan in Asia, Past and Present', Institute of International Relations research papers, No. A–42, Sophia University, 1981.
'Japanese Policies and Concepts for a Regional Order in Asia, 1938–1940', Institute of International Relations research papers, No. A–46, Sophia University, 1983.
Morton, L., 'War Plan Orange: Evolution of a Strategy', *World Politics*, Jan. 1959.
Peterson, A., 'Britain and Siam: the Latest Phase', *Pacific Affairs*, Dec. 1946.
Phelps, Brown, E. H., 'Morale, Military and Industrial', *Economic Review*, March 1949.
Presseisen, E. L., 'Le Racisme et les Japonais: un Dilemme Nazi', *Histoire de la Deuxième Guerre Mondiale*, July 1963.
Rice, R., 'Economic Mobilisation in Wartime Japan', *Journal of Asian Studies*, August, 1979.
Robertson, J., 'Australia and the "Beat Hitler First" Strategy, 1941–42', *Journal of Imperial and Commonwealth History*, May 1983.
Salaff, S., 'The Diary and the Cenotaph: Racial and Atomic Fever in the Canadian Record', *Bulletin of Concerned Asian Scholars*, Vol. 10, No. 2, 1978.
Shai, A., 'Le conflit anglo-japonais de Tientsin, 1939', *Revue d'Histoire Moderne et Contemporaine*, April-June 1975.
Shillony, B-A., 'Japanese Intellectuals During the Pacific War', *Proceedings of the British Association for Japanese Studies*, Vol. 2, 1977.
Stephan, J., 'The Tanaka Memorial (1927): Authentic or Spurious?', *Modern Asian Studies*, XII, No. 4, 1973.
Tarling, N., ' "A Vital British Interest": Britain, Japan and the Security of the Netherlands Indies During the Inter-War Period', *Journal of Southeast Asian Studies*, September 1978.
'Lord Mountbatten and the Return of Civil Government to Burma', *Journal of Imperial and Commonwealth History*, January 1983.

Thorne, C., 'Viscount Cecil, The Government and the Far Eastern Crisis of 1931', *Historical Journal*, Vol. 14, No. 4, 1971.

'Britain and the Black G.I.s: Racial Issues and Anglo-American Relations in 1942', *New Community*, Vol. III, No. 3, 1974.

'Australia and the Americans: Letters from the Minister', *The Age* (Melbourne), 8 and 9 Jan. 1975.

'Evatt, Curtin and the United States', *The Age* (Melbourne), 30 June and 1 July, 1974.

'MacArthur, Australia and the British', *Australian Outlook*, April and August, 1975.

'Engeland, Australië en Nederlands Indië, 1941–1945', *Internationale Spectator* (The Hague), Aug. 1975.

'The Indochina Issue Between Britain and the United States, 1942–1945', *Pacific Historical Review*, Feb. 1976.

'Chatham House, Whitehall and Far Eastern issues, 1941–1945', *International Affairs*, Jan. 1978.

'The British Cause and Indian Nationalism in 1940: an Officer's Rejection of Empire', *Journal of Imperial and Commonwealth History*, Vol. X, No. 3, 1982.

Tinker, H., 'A Forgotten Long March: the Indian Exodus from Burma, 1941', *Journal of Southeast Asian Studies*, March 1975.

Tsurumi, E. P., 'Education and Assimilation in Taiwan Under Japanese Rule, 1895–1945', *Modern Asian Studies*, Vol. 13, No. 4, 1979.

Venkataramani, M. and Shrivastava, B., 'The United States and the Cripps Mission', *India Quarterly*, Vol. XIX, No. 3.

Vromans, A. G., 'Les Indes Néerlandaises, 1929–1945', *Histoire de la Deuxième Guerre Mondiale*, April 1963.

Watt, D. C., 'Every War Must End: Wartime Planning for Post-War Security in Britain and America in the Wars of 1914–18 and 1939–45: the Roles of Historical Example and of Professional Historians', *Transactions of the Royal Historical Society*, 5th Series, Vol. 28, 1978.

'American Anti-Colonial Policies and the End of European Colonial Empires', in A. N. den Hollander (ed.), *Contagious Conflict* (Leiden, 1973).

Williams, J. E., 'The Joint Declaration on the Colonies', *British Journal of International Studies*, vol. 2, 1976.

Wynn, N. A., 'The Impact of the Second World War on the American Negro', *Journal of Contemporary History*, vol. 6, No. 2, 1971.

J   *Unpublished Papers*

Addis, J., 'The Philippines Under Japanese Occupation: the Hukbalahap Movement' (St. Antony's College, Oxford, seminar paper, 1982).

George, M. L., 'Australian Attitudes and Policies Towards the Netherlands East Indies and Indonesian Independence, 1942–49' (Ph.D. thesis, A.N.U., Canberra, 1973).

Index